D1116341

High-Speed VLSI Interconnections

WILEY SERIES IN MICROWAVE AND OPTICAL ENGINEERING

KAI CHANG, Editor
Texas A & M University

High-Speed VLSI Interconnections:
Modeling, Analysis, and Simulation

ASHOK K. GOEL
Department of Electrical Engineering
Michigan Technological University

A WILEY-INTERSCIENCE PUBLICATION
JOHN WILEY & SONS, INC.
NEW YORK / CHICHESTER / BRISBANE / TORONTO / SINGAPORE

This text is printed on acid-free paper.

Copyright © 1994 by John Wiley & Sons, Inc.

All rights reserved. Published simultaneously in Canada.

Reproduction or translation of any part of this work beyond
that permitted by Section 107 or 108 of the 1976 United
States Copyright Act without the permission of the copyright
owner is unlawful. Requests for permission or further
information should be addressed to the Permissions Department,
John Wiley & Sons, Inc., 605 Third Avenue, New York, NY
10158-0012.

Library of Congress Cataloging in Publication Data:

Goel, Ashok K., 1953–
    High speed VLSI interconnections: modeling, analysis, and
simulation / Ashok K. Goel
        p.   cm.—(Wiley series in microwave and optical engineering)
    Includes index.
    ISBN 0-471-57122-9
    1. Very high speed integrated circuits—Mathematical models.
2. Very high speed integrated circuits—Defects—Mathematical
models. I. Title. II. Series.
TK7874.7.G63   1994
621.39'5—dc20   93-45326

Printed in the United States of America

10 9 8 7 6 5 4 3 2

To

My parents Kamal and D. N. Goel
My wife Sangita
and
My son Sumeet and daughter Rachna

Foreword

It would be hard to find a topic with greater potential for improving productivity and developing exciting new applications than high-speed VLSI interconnections. Ashok Goel's book provides comprehensive coverage of this essential topic and is destined to become the seminal work in this field. Goel provides a tutorial perspective, suitable for both relative newcomers and established VLSI designers in his initial chapter. Subsequently, he covers the major topics of parasitic capacitance and inductance, propagation delay, and crosstalk analysis in detail through complete mathematical and physical analysis. For classroom use, he provides numerous, class-tested exercises. For researchers, he provides complete references from the international literature with dozens of citations per chapter.

A high point of this book is its extensive treatment of electromigration-induced failure analysis. As circuits are scaled down, electomigration becomes an increasingly likely reason for circuit failure. Goel tackles this problem by reviewing major factors that induce electromigration and by analyzing the major models of it. His coverage includes the most comprehensive mathematical analysis of electromigration ever aggregated into a book chapter. He includes coverage of CAD tools for predicting reliability and parameters of circuits as well as describing and providing source code for the program EMVIC that he and his students have developed to study the dependence of electromigration-induced mean time to failure on component parameters.

The final chapter looks at three promising interconnection technologies for future high-speed integrated circuits: active interconnections driven by various mechanisms, optical interconnections, and superconducting interconnections. The advantages and challenges of each promising interconnection technology are presented, compared, and contrasted.

In writing this book, Goel has drawn on not only the global literature but his own extensive research in this field. He has been the principal investigator on eight research projects on this topic, funded by the National Science

Foundation, the U.S. Air Force Office of Scientific Research, and the U.S. Army Research Office. In this book he shares his encyclopedic knowledge with such a clear writing style that all readers who are interested in VLSI can benefit.

MARTHA SLOAN

Michigan Technological University

Preface

Continuous advances in very large scale integrated circuit (VLSIC) technology have resulted in more complex chips having millions of interconnections that integrate the components on a microprocessor, gate array, or high-speed computer chip. In recent years, customer demands for higher speeds and smaller chips have led to the use of interconnections in multilevel and multilayer configurations. The term *multilevel* is used to describe interconnections that are separated by a dielectric or an insulator, whereas the term *multilayer* refers to different metals tiered together in one level of the interconnections. On-chip and chip-to-chip interconnections play the most significant role in determining the size, power consumption, and clock frequency of a digital system. In particular, parasitic effects, such as capacitances, inductances, crosstalk, and propagation delays associated with the interconnections in high-density environments on a chip or wafer, have become the major factors in the evolution of very high speed integrated circuit (VHSIC) technology.

This book focuses on the various issues associated with VLSI interconnections used for high-speed applications. These include parasitic capacitances and inductances, propagation delays, crosstalk, and electromigration-induced failure. This book has been written as a textbook for a graduate-level course and as a reference book for a practicing professional who wants to gain a better understanding of the several factors associated with modeling, analyzing, and simulating high-density high-speed interconnections. The reader is expected to have a basic understanding of electromagnetic wave propagation.

The chapters in this book are designed such that they can be read independently of one another, while, at the same time, being part of one coherent unit. To maintain independence among the chapters, some material has been intentionally repeated. Several appropriate exercises are provided at the end of each chapter which are designed to be challenging as well as helping the student gain further insight into the contents of the chapter.

Brief descriptions of the contents of the six chapters contained in this book are as follows.

Chapter 1 — Preliminary Concepts and More

In this chapter some of the basic techniques used in this book are presented, and some advanced concepts regarding wave propagation in an interconnection are discussed. Various types of interconnections employed in VLSI applications are discussed. The method of images used to find the Green's function matrix in Chapter 2 is presented, and the method of moments used to determine interconnection capacitances is discussed. The even- and odd-mode capacitances for two and three coupled conductors are discussed, and transmission line equations are derived. Miller's theorem used to uncouple the coupled interconnections and coupled electrodes in a MESFET in Chapter 3 is presented. An efficient numerical inverse Laplace transformation technique is described. A resistive interconnection has been modeled as a ladder network and the various modes that can exist in a microstrip interconnection are described. A quasi-TEM analysis of the slow-wave mode propagation in the interconnections is presented, and lossy waveguide interconnections are modeled as transmission lines. The definitions of various measures of propagation delays including the delay time and rise time are given.

Chapter 2 — Parasitic Capacitances and Inductances

In this chapter various numerical techniques used to determine the interconnection capacitances and inductances on a high-density VLSI chip are discussed, and the dependence of the parasitic elements on the various interconnection parameters is discussed. Approximate formulas for calculating the parasitic capacitances for a few interconnection structures are presented. An algorithm to obtain the interconnection capacitances by the Green's function method, where the Green's function is calculated by using the method of images, is presented. The Green's function is also calculated by using the Fourier integral approach, and a numerical technique to determine the capacitances for a multilevel interconnection structure in the $Si–SiO_2$ composite is presented. An improved network analog method to determine the parasitic capacitances and inductances associated with high-density multilevel interconnections on GaAs-based integrated circuits is presented. A comparison of the interconnection capacitances and inductances on oxide-passivated silicon, sapphire, and semi-insulating gallium-arsenide substrates is given. The electrode parasitic capacitances in a GaAs MESFET are also calculated by using the Green's function method. Source codes of a few computer programs to compute the parasitic capacitances and inductances are given in the appendices.

Chapter 3 — Propagation Delays

In this chapter several numerical algorithms to calculate propagation delays in single and multilevel parallel and crossing interconnections are presented, and the dependence of the interconnection delays on the various interconnection parameters is discussed. An analysis of interconnection delays on very high-speed VLSI chips using a metal–insulator–semiconductor microstrip line model is presented. A computer-efficient model based on the transmission line analysis of high-density single-level interconnections on GaAs-based integrated circuits is presented. The signal propagation in single-, bi-, and trilevel high-density interconnections on GaAs-based integrated circuits is studied, and a computer-efficient model of propagation delays in bilevel parallel and crossing interconnections on GaAs-based integrated circuits is presented. A SPICE model for lossless parallel interconnections modeled as multiple coupled microstrips is presented, and this model is extended to include lossy parallel and crossing interconnections. High-frequency effects, such as conductor loss, dielectric loss, skin effect, and frequency-dependent effective dielectric constant, are studied for a microstrip interconnection. For the sake of completeness, algorithms to determine transverse propagation delays in GaAs MESFETs and GaAs/AlGaAs MODFETs are also derived. A simplified model of the interconnection delays in multilayer integrated circuits is presented. The source codes of a few computer programs used to determine the propagation delays are included in the appendices.

Chapter 4 — Crosstalk Analysis

In this chapter the mathematical algorithms to study the crosstalk effects in single and multilevel parallel and crossing interconnections are discussed, and the dependence of the crosstalk signals on the various interconnection parameters is studied. Crosstalk among the neighboring interconnections is calculated by using a lumped-capacitance approximation. Crosstalk in very high-speed VLSICs is analyzed by using a coupled multiconductor metal–insulator–semiconductor microstrip line model for the interconnections. Single-level interconnections are investigated by the frequency domain modal analysis, and a transmission line model of the crosstalk effects in single-, bi-, and trilevel high-density interconnections on GaAs-based integrated circuits is presented. This is followed by an analysis of the crossing bilevel interconnections on GaAs-based integrated circuits. The crosstalk effects in multiconductor buses in high-speed GaAs logic circuits are analyzed. The source codes of a few computer programs used to analyze the crosstalk effects are included in the appendices.

Chapter 5 — Electromigration-Induced Failure Analysis

In this chapter the degradation of the reliability of an interconnection due to electromigration is discussed. First, several factors related to electromigration in VLSI interconnections are reviewed. The basic problems that cause electromigration are outlined, the mechanisms and dependence of electromigration on several factors are discussed, testing and monitoring techniques and guidelines are presented, and the methods of reducing electromigration in VLSI interconnections are briefly discussed. The various models of integrated circuit reliability, including the series model of failure mechanisms in VLSI interconnections, are presented. A model of electromigration due to repetitive pulsed currents is developed. The series model has been used to analyze electromigration-induced failure in several VLSI interconnection components. The several computer programs available for studying electromigration in VLSI interconnections are discussed briefly. The source code of a computer program used to analyze electromigration-induced failure effects in interconnection components is included in an appendix.

Chapter 6 — Future Interconnection Technologies

In this chapter the three interconnection technologies that seem promising for future integrated circuits are discussed. First, active interconnections driven by several mechanisms are analyzed. The advantages, issues, and challenges associated with optical interconnections are discussed. The propagation characteristics and a comparison of superconducting interconnections with normal metal interconnections are presented. The source codes of computer programs used to determine the propagation delays in an active interconnection driven by several mechanisms are provided in the appendices.

It should be noted that the various computer models presented in this book may not have yet been validated by experimental measurements and therefore should be used in computer-aided design programs keeping it in mind. Furthermore, the various computer programs provided in the appendices were written for different computer systems and may need modifications to be suitable for the user's system.

I would like to thank several individuals for their help and encouragement during the preparation of this book. I am grateful to Professor Kai Chang of Texas A & M University and editor of *Microwave and Optical Technology Letters* for asking me to write this book. I am also thankful to Professor Martha Sloan of Michigan Technological University for writing the Foreword to this book. I would also like to thank my graduate students Yiren R. Huang, P. Joy Prabhakaran, Manish K. Mathur, Wei Xu, and Matthew M. Leipnitz for their assistance in developing the various computer programs and obtaining the simulation results presented at several instances in this book. I am also thankful to the Institute of Electrical and Electronics Engineers (United States of America) and the Institution of Electrical Engineers (United Kingdom) for their permission to use copyrighted material from over 23 papers published in the IEEE Transactions, IEE Proceedings, and their other publications. I also owe special thanks to my wife Sangita for her constant love and support. Finally, I express my deep appreciation to my son Sumeet and daughter Rachna for their patience and understanding during the preparation of this book.

The information presented in this book is believed to be accurate, and great care has been taken to ensure its accuracy. However, no responsibility is assumed by the author for its use and for any infringement of patents or other rights of third parties that may result from its use. Furthermore, no license is granted by implication or otherwise under any patent, patent rights, or other rights.

Readers are welcome to suggest any corrections or improvements of any part of this book, and these will be seriously considered for future editions. It would be most appreciated if these are communicated to me in writing.

A. K. G.

Houghton, Michigan

Contents

High-Speed VLSI Interconnections

CHAPTER ONE

Preliminary Concepts and More

In this chapter some of the basic concepts and techniques used in this book are presented and some advanced concepts regarding wave propagation in interconnections are discussed. First, the various types of interconnections employed in very large scale integrated (VLSI) applications are discussed in Section 1.1. The method of images used to find the Green's function matrix in Chapter 2 is presented in Section 1.2. Then in Section 1.3 the method of moments used to determine the various interconnection capacitances in Chapter 2 is discussed. Even- and odd-mode capacitances for two and three coupled conductors are discussed in Section 1.4. In Section 1.5 transmission line equations are derived and coupled transmission lines are discussed. Then Miller's theorem which is used to uncouple the coupled interconnections and coupled electrodes in a metal semiconductor field effect transistor (MESFET) in Chapter 3, is presented in Section 1.6. In Section 1.7 a computer-efficient numerical inverse Laplace transformation technique is described. In Section 1.8 a resistive interconnection has been modeled as a ladder network. The various modes that can exist in a microstrip interconnection are described in Section 1.9. A quasi transverse electromagnetic (TEM) analysis of slow-wave mode propagation in the interconnection is presented in Section 1.10, and in Section 1.11 lossy waveguide interconnections have been modeled as transmission lines. The definitions of various measures of propagation delays used in the literature including the delay time and rise time are presented in Section 1.12.

1.1 INTERCONNECTIONS FOR VLSI APPLICATIONS

Continuous advances in integrated circuit (IC) technology have resulted in smaller device dimensions, larger chip sizes, and increased complexity. There is an increasing demand for circuits with higher speeds and higher component densities. In recent years, the growth of GaAs on a silicon (Si) substrate has met with a great deal of interest because of its potential applications in new hybrid technologies [1.1–1.11]. GaAs-on-Si unites the high speed and optoelectronic capability of GaAs circuits with the low material cost and superior mechanical properties of the Si substrate. The heat sinking of such devices is better because the thermal conductivity of Si is three times more than that of GaAs. This technology is expanding rapidly from material research to device and circuit development. Functional GaAs static random access memories (SRAMs) of up to 1K in complexity have been demonstrated on the Si substrate. Light emitting diode (LED) modulation rates up to 27 Mbit/s have been demonstrated on monolithically integrated GaAs/AlGaAs LEDs and Si metal-oxide-semiconductor field effect transistors (MOSFETs) [1.12–1.15]. So far, the various IC technologies have employed metallic interconnections, and there is a possibility of using optical interconnections in the near future. Currently, the possibility of using superconducting interconnections is also being explored.

1.1.1 Metallic Interconnections

VLSI chips require millions of closely spaced interconnection lines that integrate the components on a chip. As VLSI technology advanced to meet the needs of customers, it became necessary to use multilayer interconnections in two or more levels to achieve higher packing densities, shorter transit delays, and smaller chips. In this book the term *level* will be used to describe conductors that are separated by an insulator, and the term *layer* will be used to describe different conductors tiered together in one level of interconnection as shown in Figure 1.1.1. In most cases, because of its low resistivity and silicon compatibility as shown in Table 1.1.1 [1.16], aluminum has been used to form the metal interconnections. However, as the device dimensions are decreased, the current density increases, resulting in decreased reliability due to electromigration and hillock formation causing electrical shorts between successive levels of Al [1.17–1.20]. Tungsten has also been used for interconnections [1.21–1.23], and sometimes Al/Cu is used to solve problems characteristic of pure Al [1.24], although this choice has not been without problems [1.25, 1.26]. There have been several studies [1.27–1.34] aimed at reducing electromigration. All these studies have used layers of two or more metals in the same level of the interconnection. Some of the multilayer structures studied so far include Al/Ti/Cu [1.28], Al/Ta/Al [1.30], Al/Ni [1.31], Al/Cr [1.32], Al/Mg [1.33], and Al/Ti/Si [1.34]. Coevaporation of Al–Cu–Ti, Al–Cu–Co, and Al–Co has also been shown to decrease electromigration [1.27]. There have been many studies on the problem of hillock formation as well [1.16, 1.35–1.44]. One method of reducing these hillocks on silicon-based circuits has been to deposit a film of WSi [1.36] or MoSi between Al and the silicon substrate. A complete elimination of hillocks is

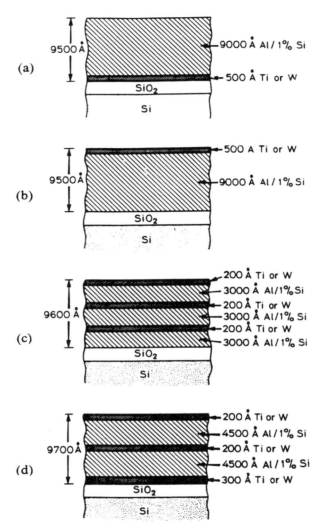

FIGURE 1.1.1 Schematic diagrams of layered interconnection structures using (*a*) Ti layer to match the aluminum and silicon expansion coefficients; (*b*) Ti or W layer on top of aluminum to constrain hillocks; (*c*) and (*d*) multiple layers of Ti or W alternated with aluminum [1.16]. (© 1985 IEEE)

TABLE 1.1.1   Resistivity and Expansion Coefficients [1.16] (© 1985 IEEE)

Material	Resistivity ($\mu\Omega \cdot$ cm)	Thermal Expansion Coefficient ($^\circ C^{-1}$)	Melting Point ($^\circ$ C)
Pure aluminum (bulk)	2.65	$25.0 \cdot 10^{-6}$	660° C
Sputtered Al and Al/Si	2.9–3.4	$25.0 \cdot 10^{-6}$	660° C
Sputtered Al/2% Cu/1% Si	3.9	$25.0 \cdot 10^{-6}$	660° C
LPCVD aluminum	3.4	$25.0 \cdot 10^{-6}$	660° C
Pure tungsten (bulk)	5.65	$4.5 \cdot 10^{-6}$	3410° C
CVD tungsten	7–15	$4.5 \cdot 10^{-6}$	3410° C
Evaporated/sputtered tungsten	14–20	$4.5 \cdot 10^{-6}$	3410° C
Ti (bulk)	42.0	$8.5 \cdot 10^{-6}$	1660° C
$TiAl_3$ (bulk)	17–22	—	1340° C
$CuAl_2$ (bulk—θ phase)	5–6	—	591° C
WAl_{12}	—	—	647° C
Si	—	$3.3 \cdot 10^{-6}$	—
SiO_2	—	$0.5 \cdot 10^{-6}$	—

reported in studies where the VLSI interconnections were fabricated by layering alternatively Al and a refractory metal (Ti or W) [1.16, 1.42–1.44].

1.1.2   Optical Interconnections

As an alternative to electrical interconnections, optical interconnections have emerged in recent years which offer fast, reliable, and noise-free data transmission [1.45–1.49]. So far, they have been used for computer-to-computer communications and for processor-to-processor interconnections. At this time, however, their applicability at lower levels of the packaging hierarchy, such as for module-to-module connections at the board level, for chip-to-chip connections at the module level, and for gate-to-gate connections at the chip level, is still under investigation. The principal advantages of optical interconnections over electrical connections are higher bandwidth, lower dispersion, and lower attenuation. Some of the problems with the optical interconnections currently under investigation include size incompatibility with the integrated circuits, high power consumption, and tight alignment requirements.

1.1.3   Superconducting Interconnections

In recent years, the advent of high-critical-temperature superconductors has opened up the possibility of realizing high-density and very fast interconnections on silicon as well as GaAs-based high-performance integrated circuits. The major advantages of superconducting interconnections over normal metal interconnections can be summarized as follows: (1) Signal propagation time on a superconducting interconnection will be much smaller as compared to that on a normal metal interconnection; (2) the packing density of the integrated circuit can be increased without incurring the high losses associated with high-density normal metal interconnections; and (3) there is virtually no signal dispersion on the superconducting interconnections for frequencies up to several tens of gigahertz.

1.2   METHOD OF IMAGES

The method of images can be used to find the potential due to a given electric charge in the presence of conducting planes and dielectric surfaces. To illustrate this method, let us consider a line charge ρ lying in a medium of dielectric constant ε_1 at a distance d above a second medium of dielectric constant ε_2, as shown in Figure 1.2.1. At the interface of the two media, the following two boundary conditions must be satisfied:

1. The normal component of the electric flux density D_n must be the same on the two sides of the interface.
2. The tangential component of the electric field E_t must also be the same across the interface.

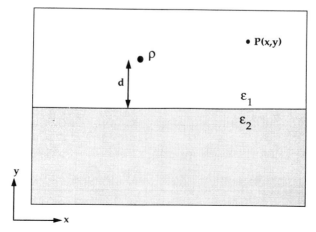

FIGURE 1.2.1   Line charge ρ lying in a medium of dielectric constant ε_1 at a distance d above a second medium of dielectric constant ε_2.

Using the coordinate system of Figure 1.2.1, this means that, at $y = 0$,

$$D_{n1} = D_{n2} \quad \text{or} \quad \varepsilon_1 E_{y1} = \varepsilon_2 E_{y2} \tag{1.2.1}$$

and

$$E_{x1} = E_{x2} \tag{1.2.2}$$

The potential V due to an infinite line charge ρ in a medium of dielectric constant ε at a distance r is given by

$$V = \frac{-\rho}{4\pi\varepsilon} \ln(r^2) \tag{1.2.3}$$

When a second dielectric is present, the real charge ρ produces image charges across the dielectric interface. If the observation point P is above the interface, that is, on the same side as the real line charge (see Figure 1.2.2a), an image charge ρ_1 will be at a distance d below the interface. With the real line charge at $x = 0$ and $y = d$, the distance between the real charge and the observation point is given by

$$r = \sqrt{x^2 + (y - d)^2}$$

and with the image charge at $x = 0$ and $y = -d$, the distance between the image charge and the observation point is given by

$$r_i = \sqrt{x^2 + (y + d)^2}$$

Using Equation 1.2.3, the potential at all points above the interface, that is, for $y \geq 0$, will be

$$V_1 = \frac{-1}{4\pi\varepsilon_1} \left[\rho \ln(r^2) + \rho_1 \ln(r_i^2) \right]$$

Now, because

$$E_{x1} = -\frac{\partial V_1}{\partial x}$$

therefore, for $y \geq 0$,

$$E_{x1} = \frac{1}{4\pi\varepsilon_1} \frac{\partial}{\partial x} \left[\rho \ln\left(x^2 + (y - d)^2\right) + \rho_1 \ln\left(x^2 + (y + d)^2\right) \right]$$

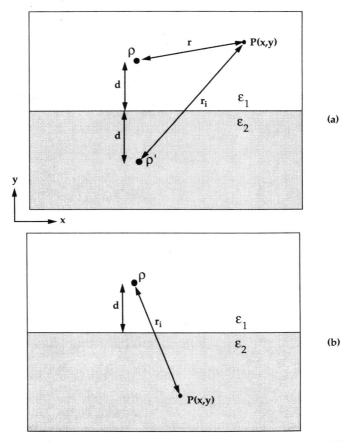

FIGURE 1.2.2 (*a*) Observation point *P* on the same side as the real line charge; (*b*) observation point *P* below the dielectric interface.

or

$$E_{x1} = \frac{1}{4\pi\varepsilon_1}\left[\rho\frac{2x}{x^2 + (y - d)^2} + \rho_1\frac{2x}{x^2 + (y + d)^2}\right] \qquad (1.2.4)$$

Similarly,

$$E_{y1} = -\frac{\partial V_1}{\partial y}$$

Therefore, for $y \geq 0$,

$$E_{y1} = \frac{1}{4\pi\varepsilon_1} \frac{\partial}{\partial y} \left[\rho \ln\left(x^2 + (y - d)^2\right) + \rho_1 \ln\left(x^2 + (y + d)^2\right) \right]$$

or

$$E_{y1} = \frac{1}{4\pi\varepsilon_1} \left[\rho \frac{2(y - d)}{x^2 + (y - d)^2} + \rho_1 \frac{2(y + d)}{x^2 + (y + d)^2} \right] \qquad (1.2.5)$$

If the observation point P lies below the dielectric interface, that is, in the medium with dielectric constant ε_2 (see Figure 1.2.2b), then the real line charge ρ must be modified to take care of the effect of the dielectric interface. This modified charge, say ρ_2, can be found in terms of ρ as follows. The distance between the observation point and the charge ρ is again given by

$$r = \sqrt{x^2 + (y - d)^2}$$

The potential V_2 below the interface is then given by

$$V_2 = \frac{-1}{4\pi\varepsilon_2} \left[\rho_2 \ln(r^2) \right]$$

Now, because

$$E_{x2} = -\frac{\partial V_2}{\partial x}$$

therefore, for $y \leq 0$,

$$E_{x2} = \frac{1}{4\pi\varepsilon_2} \frac{\partial}{\partial x} \left[\rho_2 \ln\left(x^2 + (y - d)^2\right) \right]$$

or

$$E_{x2} = \frac{1}{4\pi\varepsilon_2} \left[\rho_2 \frac{2x}{x^2 + (y - d)^2} \right] \qquad (1.2.6)$$

Similarly,

$$E_{y2} = -\frac{\partial V_2}{\partial y}$$

Therefore, for $y \leq 0$,

$$E_{y2} = \frac{1}{4\pi\varepsilon_2} \frac{\partial}{\partial y} \Big[\rho_2 \ln\big(x^2 + (y - d)^2\big) \Big]$$

or

$$E_{y2} = \frac{1}{4\pi\varepsilon_2} \left[\rho_2 \frac{2(y - d)}{x^2 + (y - d)^2} \right] \qquad (1.2.7)$$

Applying the continuity condition (1.2.2) to Equations 1.2.4 and 1.2.6, we get

$$\frac{1}{4\pi\varepsilon_1} [\rho + \rho_1] \left[\frac{2x}{x^2 + d^2} \right] = \frac{\rho_2}{4\pi\varepsilon_2} \left[\frac{2x}{x^2 + d^2} \right]$$

From this it follows that

$$\frac{\rho + \rho_1}{\varepsilon_1} = \frac{\rho_2}{\varepsilon_2} \qquad (1.2.8)$$

Applying the continuity condition (1.2.1) to Equations 1.2.5 and 1.2.6, we find that

$$\frac{\varepsilon_1}{4\pi\varepsilon_1} (-\rho + \rho_1) \left[\frac{2d}{x^2 + d^2} \right] = \frac{\varepsilon_2 \rho_2}{4\pi\varepsilon_2} \left[\frac{-2d}{x^2 + d^2} \right]$$

from which it follows that

$$-\rho + \rho_1 = -\rho_2 \qquad (1.2.9)$$

Combining Equations 1.2.8 and 1.2.9, we get

$$\frac{\rho + \rho_1}{\varepsilon_1} = \frac{\rho - \rho_1}{\varepsilon_2}$$

from which the image charges ρ_1 and ρ_2 can be found in terms of the real charge ρ and the dielectric constants ε_1 and ε_2 to be

$$\rho_1 = \rho \left(\frac{\varepsilon_1 - \varepsilon_2}{\varepsilon_1 + \varepsilon_2} \right) \qquad (1.2.10)$$

and

$$\rho_2 = \rho \left(\frac{2\varepsilon_2}{\varepsilon_1 + \varepsilon_2} \right) \qquad (1.2.11)$$

To find the image of a charge in a grounded conducting plane, it is well known that the image charge has the same magnitude as the real charge but an opposite sign and that it lies as much distance below the ground plane as the real charge is above it.

1.3 METHOD OF MOMENTS

The method of moments is a basic mathematical technique for reducing functional equations to matrix equations [1.50]. Consider the inhomogeneous equation

$$L(f) = g \qquad (1.3.1)$$

where L is a linear operator, f is a field or response (the unknown function to be determined), and g is a source or excitation (a known function). We assume that the problem is deterministic; that is, there is only one solution function f associated with a given excitation g.

Let us expand the function f in a series of basis functions $f_1, f_2, f_3, \ldots, f_n$ in the domain of L as

$$f = \sum_n \alpha_n f_n \qquad (1.3.2)$$

where α_n are constants. The functions f_n are called expansion functions or basis functions. For exact solutions, Equation 1.3.2 is usually an infinite summation and the functions f_n form a complete set of basis functions. For approximate solutions, Equation 1.3.2 is usually a finite summation. Substituting Equation 1.3.2 into Equation 1.3.1 and using the linearity of the operator L, we have

$$\sum_n \alpha_n L(f_n) = g \qquad (1.3.3)$$

Now, defining a set of weighting functions or testing functions $w_1, w_2, w_3, \ldots$ in the range of L and taking the inner product with each w_m, the result is

$$\sum_n \alpha_n \langle w_m, Lf_n \rangle = \langle w_m, g \rangle \qquad m = 1, 2, 3, \ldots$$

This set of equations can be written in matrix form as

$$[l_{mn}][\alpha_n] = [g_m]$$

where

$$[l_{mn}] = [\langle w_m, Lf_n \rangle]$$

and $[\alpha_n]$ and $[g_m]$ are column vectors. If the matrix $[l_{mn}]$ is nonsingular, then the matrix $[l_{mn}]^{-1}$ exists. The constants α_n are then given by

$$[\alpha_n] = [l_{mn}]^{-1}[g_m]$$

and the solution function f is given by Equation 1.3.2 as

$$f = \sum_n \alpha_n f_n = [l_{mn}]^{-1}[g_m][f_n]$$

This solution may be exact or approximate depending on the choice of the functions f_n and the weighting functions w_n. The particular choice $w_n = f_n$ is known as the Galerkin method. If the matrix $[l_{mn}]$ is of infinite order, it can be solved only in special cases, for example, if it is diagonal. If the sets f_n and w_n are finite, then the matrix $[l_{mn}]$ is of finite order and can be inverted by known methods such as the Gauss–Jordan reduction method.

In most problems of practical interest, the integration involved in evaluating $l_{mn} = \langle w_m, Lf_n \rangle$ is usually difficult to perform. A simple way to obtain approximate solutions is to require that Equation 1.3.3 be satisfied at certain discrete points in the region of interest. This process is called a point-matching method. In terms of the method of moments, it is equivalent to using Dirac delta functions as the weighting functions. Another approximation useful for practical problems involves dividing the region of interest into several small subsections and requiring that the basis functions f_n are constant over the areas of the subsections. This procedure, called the method of subsections, often simplifies the evaluation of the matrix $[l_{mn}]$. Sometimes, it is more convenient to use the method of subsections in conjunction with the point-matching method.

One of the most important tasks in any particular problem is the proper choice of the functions f_n and w_n. The functions f_n should be linearly independent and chosen so that some superposition (1.3.3) can approximate the function f reasonably accurately. The functions w_n should also be linearly independent and chosen so that the products $\langle w_n, g \rangle$ depend on the relative independent properties of g. Some additional considerations in choosing the functions f_n and w_n include the accuracy of the solution desired, the ease of evaluation of the matrix elements, the size of the matrix that can be inverted, and the realization of a well-conditioned matrix.

1.4 EVEN- AND ODD-MODE CAPACITANCES

In this section the even- and odd-mode capacitances associated with systems of two or three coupled conductors are discussed.

1.4.1 Two Coupled Conductors

Two coupled conductors of different dimensions lying in the same plane at a distance d above the ground plane are shown in Figure 1.4.1. We are interested in finding the self-capacitances and mutual (or coupling) capacitance for this system. In other words, we want to find the capacitances between each conductor and the ground (denoted by C_{11} and C_{22}) and the capacitance between the two conductors (denoted by C_{12}). To simplify the analysis, the problem can be split into even and odd modes. In the even mode each conductor is assumed to be at 1-V potential with the same sign for each conductor. In the odd mode the first conductor is assumed to be at a positive 1-V potential, whereas the second conductor is kept at a negative 1-V potential. First, we will determine the even- and odd-mode capacitances for each conductor separately.

In the even mode shown in Figure 1.4.2, there are no electric field lines at the center between the two conductors. Therefore, this plane can be treated as a magnetic wall which represents an open circuit to any mutual capacitance between the two conductors. Therefore, we can say that

$$C_1^{(e)} = C_{11} \tag{1.4.1}$$

and

$$C_2^{(e)} = C_{22} \tag{1.4.2}$$

where $C_1^{(e)}$ is the even-mode capacitance for the first conductor and $C_2^{(e)}$ is the even-mode capacitance for the second conductor.

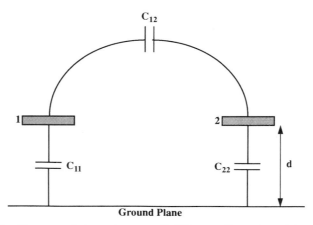

FIGURE 1.4.1 Two coupled conductors of different dimensions lying in the same plane at a distance d above the ground plane.

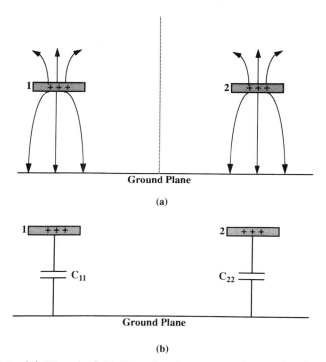

FIGURE 1.4.2 (*a*) Electric field lines for the two conductors in the even mode; (*b*) equivalent circuit for the two conductors in the even mode.

In the odd mode shown in Figure 1.4.3, the plane of symmetry between the two conductors can be treated as a grounded electric wall. This represents a short circuit to the mutual capacitance C_{12}. Therefore, in this case

$$C_1^{(o)} = C_{11} + 2C_{12} \qquad (1.4.3)$$

and

$$C_2^{(o)} = C_{22} + 2C_{12} \qquad (1.4.4)$$

where $C_1^{(o)}$ and $C_2^{(o)}$ are the odd-mode capacitances for the first and second conductor, respectively. The mutual capacitance C_{12} can be expressed in terms of $C_1^{(o)}$ and $C_1^{(e)}$ by using Equations 1.4.1 and 1.4.3 as

$$C_{12} = \frac{\left[C_1^{(o)} - C_1^{(e)} \right]}{2}$$

whereas the self-capacitances are given by Equations 1.4.1 and 1.4.2.

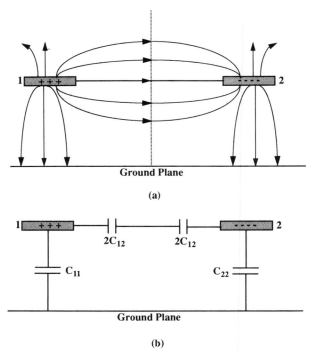

FIGURE 1.4.3 (*a*) Electric field lines for the two conductors in the odd mode; (*b*) equivalent circuit for the two conductors in the odd mode.

1.4.2   Three Coupled Conductors

As in the case of two conductors, the three-conductor case can also be treated by splitting it into even and odd modes. In the even mode each conductor is again assumed to be at a positive 1-V potential. In the odd mode one conductor is kept at a positive 1-V potential while the other two conductors are assumed to be at negative 1-V potentials. This means that when finding the odd-mode charge on the first conductor, for example, the potentials on the second and third conductors are of the opposite sign to that on the first conductor. Figure 1.4.4 shows the self-capacitances and mutual capacitances for the three conductors. These capacitances can be found in terms of the even- and odd-mode capacitances of the three conductors. In the even mode

$$C_1^{(e)} = C_{11}$$
$$C_2^{(e)} = C_{22} \qquad\qquad (1.4.5)$$
$$C_3^{(e)} = C_{33}$$

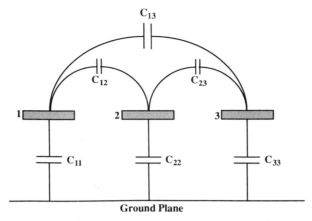

FIGURE 1.4.4 Self-capacitances and mutual capacitance for the three conductors.

In the odd mode

$$C_1^{(o)} = C_{11} + 2C_{12} + 2C_{13}$$
$$C_2^{(o)} = C_{22} + 2C_{12} + 2C_{23} \qquad (1.4.6)$$
$$C_3^{(o)} = C_{33} + 2C_{13} + 2C_{23}$$

Solving these equations, we can find that the mutual capacitances will be given by

$$C_{12} = \frac{\left[-C_1^{(e)} - C_2^{(e)} + C_3^{(e)} + C_1^{(o)} + C_2^{(o)} - C_3^{(o)}\right]}{4}$$

$$C_{13} = \frac{\left[-C_1^{(e)} + C_2^{(e)} - C_3^{(e)} + C_1^{(o)} - C_2^{(o)} + C_3^{(o)}\right]}{4} \qquad (1.4.7)$$

$$C_{23} = \frac{\left[C_1^{(e)} - C_2^{(e)} - C_3^{(e)} - C_1^{(o)} + C_2^{(o)} + C_3^{(o)}\right]}{4}$$

The self-capacitances are given by Equations 1.4.5.

1.5 TRANSMISSION LINE EQUATIONS

A transmission line can be treated as a repeated array of small resistors, inductors, and capacitors. In fact, transmission line theory can be developed in terms of alternating current (AC) circuit analysis but the equations become extremely complicated for all but the simple cases [1.51]. It is more convenient to treat such lines in terms of differential equations that lead naturally

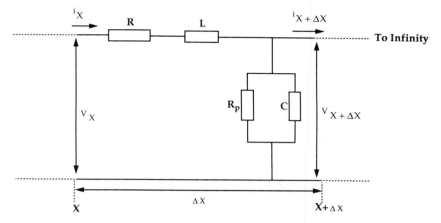

FIGURE 1.5.1 Equivalent circuit for a uniform transmission line.

to a wave equation which is of fundamental importance to electromagnetic theory in general.

We can develop the differential equations for a uniform transmission line by a simple circuit analysis of its equivalent circuit shown in Figure 1.5.1, consisting of several incremental lengths, and then taking the limit as the length of the increment approaches 0. The voltage and current at some general points x and $(x + \Delta x)$ along the line are shown in Figure 1.5.1. The parameters R, L, G, and C are the resistance, inductance, conductance, and capacitance values per unit length of the line, respectively. As Δx is changed these values remain the same. We assume that the voltage and current are sinusoidal and that at any point x along the line, the time variation of the voltage is given by

$$v_x = V_0 e^{j\omega t}$$

Now, if we apply Kirchhoff's voltage law around the first incremental loop in Figure 1.5.1, we obtain

$$v_x = i_x R \, \Delta x + i_x (j\omega L) \, \Delta x + v_{x+\Delta x}$$

or

$$v_{x+\Delta x} - v_x = -i_x(R + j\omega L) \, \Delta x \qquad (1.5.1)$$

In the preceding equations R and L have been multiplied by Δx to get the actual values of the resistance and inductance for an incremental section of length Δx. Now the total current i_x into the first incremental section at x minus the total current $i_{x+\Delta x}$ into the next section at $x + \Delta x$ must be equal to the total current through the shunt capacitance C and the parallel resistance R_p, that is,

$$i_x - i_{x+\Delta x} = \frac{v_x}{R_p/\Delta x} + \frac{v_x}{1/(j\omega C \Delta x)}$$

or, setting $1/R_p = G$, the conductance per unit length, we get

$$i_{x+\Delta x} - i_x = -v_x(G + j\omega C)\,\Delta x \qquad (1.5.2)$$

In Equation 1.5.1 the left-hand side represents the incremental voltage drop along the line denoted by Δv_x. Dividing both sides of Equation 1.5.1, we get

$$\frac{\Delta v_x}{\Delta x} = -i_x(R + j\omega L)$$

Similarly, Equation 1.5.2 can be expressed as

$$\frac{\Delta i_x}{\Delta x} = -v_x(G + j\omega C)$$

Now, if Δx is made very very small, then the incremental voltage or current change per incremental distance becomes the corresponding derivative. Thus, we get the two fundamental differential equations for a uniform transmission line

$$\frac{dv_x}{dx} = -(R + j\omega L)i_x \qquad (1.5.3)$$

$$\frac{di_x}{dx} = -(G + j\omega C)v_x \qquad (1.5.4)$$

where all line parameters are per unit distance. These equations can be solved if they can be written in terms of one unknown (v_x or i_x). An equation in terms of v_x can be written by first taking the derivative of Equation 1.5.3 with respect to x to yield

$$\frac{d^2 v_x}{dx^2} = -(R + j\omega L)\frac{di_x}{dx} \qquad (1.5.5)$$

and then substituting Equation 1.5.4 into Equation 1.5.5 to get

$$\frac{d^2 v_x}{dx^2} = (R + j\omega L)(G + j\omega C)v_x = \gamma^2 v_x \qquad (1.5.6)$$

where

$$\gamma^2 = (R + j\omega L)(G + j\omega C) \tag{1.5.7}$$

Similarly, an equation in terms of i_x can be obtained by first differentiating Equation 1.5.4 and then substituting Equation 1.5.3 to yield

$$\frac{d^2 i_x}{dx^2} = (R + j\omega L)(G + j\omega C) i_x = \gamma^2 i_x \tag{1.5.8}$$

Equations 1.5.6 and 1.5.8 are the fundamental relationships governing wave propagation along a uniform transmission line.

The symbol γ, as defined by Equation 1.5.7, is known as the propagation constant; that is,

$$\gamma = \sqrt{(R + j\omega L)(G + j\omega C)}$$

In general, γ is a complex number. The real part of γ gives the reduction in voltage or current along the line. This quantity, when expressed per unit length of the line, is referred to as the attenuation constant α given by

$$\alpha = \text{Re}\sqrt{(R + j\omega L)(G + j\omega C)}$$

For a transmission line with no losses, $\alpha = 0$; that is, a line with no losses has no attenuation. The imaginary part of γ, when expressed per unit length of the line, is known as the phase constant β given by

$$\beta = \text{Im}\sqrt{(R + j\omega L)(G + j\omega C)}$$

For a lossless line where $R = G = 0$, the phase constant becomes

$$\beta = \omega\sqrt{LC}$$

with dimensions of radians per meter in RMKS units. The phase shift per unit length along the line is a measure of the velocity of propagation of a wave along the line; that is,

$$v = \frac{\omega}{\beta} = \frac{1}{\sqrt{LC}}$$

1.6 MILLER'S THEOREM

Miller's theorem is an important theorem that can be used to uncouple nodes in electric circuits. Consider a circuit configuration with N distinct nodes $1, 2, 3, \ldots, N$ as shown in Figure 1.6.1a. The node voltages can be denoted

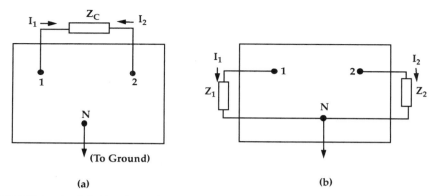

FIGURE 1.6.1   (a) Circuit configuration with N distinct nodes; (b) circuit configuration equivalent to that shown in (a).

by $V_1, V_2, V_3, \ldots, V_N$, where V_N is 0 because N is the reference node. Nodes 1 and 2 are connected by an impedance Z_c. We assume that the ratio V_2/V_1 is known or can be determined by some means. Let us denote this ratio by K which, in general, can be a complex number.

It can be demonstrated that the configuration shown in Figure 1.6.1a is equivalent to that shown in Figure 1.6.1b provided Z_1 and Z_2 have certain specific values. These values of Z_1 and Z_2 can be found by equating the currents leaving nodes 1 and 2 in the two configurations. The current I_1 leaving node 1 through the impedance Z_c in Figure 1.6.1a is given by

$$ I_1 = \frac{V_1 - V_2}{Z_c} = V_1 \frac{1 - K}{Z_c} = \frac{V_1}{Z_c/(1 - K)} $$

whereas the current leaving node 1 through the impedance Z_1 in Figure 1.6.1b is given by V_1/Z_1. Therefore, we conclude that

$$ Z_1 = \frac{Z_c}{1 - K} $$

In a similar manner, the current I_2 leaving node 2 through the impedance Z_c in Figure 1.6.1a is given by

$$ I_2 = \frac{V_2 - V_1}{Z_c} = V_2 \frac{1 - 1/K}{Z_c} = \frac{V_2}{Z_c/(1 - 1/K)} $$

whereas the current leaving node 2 in Figure 1.6.1b is V_2/Z_2. Therefore, the value of the impedance Z_2 should be

$$Z_2 = \frac{Z_c}{1 - 1/K} = Z_c \frac{K}{K - 1}$$

Because Figures 1.6.1a and b have identical nodal equations, these represent electrically identical configurations. However, we note that Miller's theorem will be useful only if the value of the ratio K can be determined by some independent means.

1.7   INVERSE LAPLACE TRANSFORMATION

In several cases it is more convenient to solve the equations in the frequency domain, that is, the s domain, and then obtain the time domain solution by an inverse Laplace transformation of the s-domain solution. Various techniques for numerical inverse Laplace transformation are available in the literature. The technique presented in this section is simple yet efficient and can be easily incorporated into computer programs. It uses the Padé approximation and does not require the computation of poles and residues [1.52, 1.53].

The inverse Laplace transform of $V(s)$ is given by

$$v(t) = \frac{1}{2\pi jt} \int_{(c-j\infty)}^{(c+j\infty)} V(s) e^{st} \, ds \tag{1.7.1}$$

The variable t can be removed from e^{st} by the transformation

$$z = st \tag{1.7.2}$$

and then using the approximation for e^z. Substituting Equation 1.7.2 into Equation 1.7.1, we obtain

$$v(t) = \frac{1}{2\pi jt} \int_{(c'-j\infty)}^{(c'+j\infty)} V(s) e^z \, dz \tag{1.7.3}$$

According to the Padé approximation, the function e^z can be approximated by a rational function

$$R_{N,M}(z) = \frac{P_N(z)}{Q_M(z)} \tag{1.7.4}$$

where $P_N(z)$ and $Q_M(z)$ are polynomials of order N and M, respectively.

Inserting Equation 1.7.4 into Equation 1.7.3, we obtain

$$\hat{v}(t) = \frac{1}{2\pi j} \int_{(c'-j\infty)}^{(c'+j\infty)} V\left(\frac{z}{t}\right) R_{NM}(z) \, dz \qquad (1.7.5)$$

where $\hat{v}(t)$ is the approximation for $v(t)$. The integral (1.7.5) can be evaluated by using residue calculus and by choosing the path of integration along the infinite arc either to the left or to the right. To ensure that the path along the infinite arc does not contribute to the integral, M and N are chosen such that the function

$$F(z) = V(z/t) R_{N,M}(z) \qquad (1.7.6)$$

has at least two more poles than zeros. This gives

$$\int_C F(z) \, dz = \pm 2\pi j \sum (\text{residue at poles inside the closed path}) \quad (1.7.7)$$

where the positive sign is used when the path C is closed in the left half plane and the negative sign is used when C is closed in the right half plane. For $N < M$ we have

$$R_{N,M}(z) = \sum_{i=1}^{M} \frac{K_i}{z - z_i} \qquad (1.7.8)$$

where z_i are the poles of $R_{N,M}(z)$ and K_i are the corresponding residues. Closing the path of integration around the poles of $R_{N,M}(z)$ in the right half plane, we get the basic inversion formula

$$\hat{v}(t) = -\frac{1}{t} \sum_{i=1}^{M} K_i V\left(\frac{z_i}{t}\right) \qquad (1.7.9)$$

When M is even we can write

$$\hat{v}(t) = -\frac{1}{t} \sum_{i=1}^{M'} \text{Re}\left[K_i' V\left(\frac{z_i}{t}\right) \right] \qquad (1.7.10)$$

where $M' = M/2$ and $K_i' = 2K_i$. When M is odd $M' = (M + 1)/2$ and $K_i' = K_i$ for the residue corresponding to the real poles. The poles z_i and residues K_i' have been calculated with high precision and are used in the programs in this book.

To summarize, for a given function $V(s)$ in the s domain, the response $v(t)$ at any time t can be obtained by the following steps:

1. Select appropriate values of N and M and take values of z_i and K'_i from the computed tables [1.52, 1.53].
2. Divide each z_i by t and substitute z_i/t for each s in $V(s)$.
3. Multiply each $V(z_i/t)$ by the corresponding K'_i and add the products.
4. Retain only the real part of the result in step 3 and divide by $-t$.

Note that, because of division by t, the value of $v(t)$ at $t = 0$ cannot be calculated by the procedure discussed previously. However, this value can either be obtained by using the initial value theorem or an approximate value can be found by selecting a very small initial value of t. The technique described previously is suitable for the calculation of the system response to a nonperiodic excitation such as a step or an impulse.

1.8   A RESISTIVE INTERCONNECTION AS A LADDER NETWORK

It is well known that interconnections made of high-resistivity materials such as polycrystalline silicon (poly-Si) result in much higher signal delays than low-resistivity metallic interconnections. However, in the past, poly-Si was a principal material for second-level interconnections. In order to analyze high-speed signal propagation in resistive interconnections, it is important to understand their transmission characteristics. In this section it will be shown that resistive interconnections can be modeled as ladder RC networks under open-circuit, short-circuit as well as capacitive loading conditions [1.54, 1.55].

1.8.1   Open-Circuit Interconnection

From transmission line theory [1.56], the open-circuit voltage transfer function of a resistive transmission line is given by

$$\frac{V_2}{V_1} = \frac{1}{\cosh(\sqrt{sRC})} \tag{1.8.1}$$

where R is the total line resistance and C is the total line capacitance including the capacitance due to the fringing fields as described by Ruehli and Brennan [1.57]. Using infinite partial fraction expansions [1.58], Equation 1.8.1 can be written as

$$\frac{V_2}{V_1} = \frac{1}{\cosh(\sqrt{sRC})} = \frac{4}{\pi} \sum_{k=1}^{\infty} \left[(-1)^{k+1} \frac{2k-1}{(2k-1)^2 + sRC(4/\pi^2)} \right] \tag{1.8.2}$$

If $v_1(t)$ is a Dirac pulse, then the voltage $v_2(t)$ can be easily found by finding the inverse Laplace transforms of the terms on the right-hand side of Equation 1.8.2. If $v_1(t)$ is a unit step voltage, then $V_1 = V_0/s$ (with $V_0 = 1$) and $v_2(t)$ can be obtained after a simple integration to be

$$v_2(t) = L^{-1}\left[\frac{1/s}{\cosh(\sqrt{s}RC)}\right]$$

$$= \sum_{k=1}^{\infty} (-1)^{k+1}\frac{4}{\pi(2k-1)}\left(1 - \exp\left[-\frac{(2k-1)^2\pi^2 t}{4RC}\right]\right)$$

or

$$v_2(t) = \frac{4}{\pi}\left(1 - \frac{1}{3} + \frac{1}{5} - \frac{1}{7} + \cdots\right)$$

$$- \frac{4}{\pi}\left(\exp\left(-\frac{\pi^2 t}{4RC}\right) - \frac{1}{3}\exp\left(-\frac{9\pi^2 t}{4RC}\right) + \cdots\right)$$

$$= 1 - 1.273\exp\left(-\frac{\pi^2 t}{4RC}\right) + 0.424\exp\left(-\frac{9\pi^2 t}{4RC}\right)$$

$$- 0.254\exp\left(-\frac{25\pi^2 t}{4RC}\right) + \cdots \tag{1.8.3}$$

It should been noted that expression (1.8.3) differs from the corresponding approximate expression in reference [1.54]

$$v_{\text{out}}(t) = 1 - 1.172\exp\left(-\frac{\pi^2 t}{4RC}\right)$$

$$+ 0.195\exp\left(-\frac{9\pi^2 t}{4RC}\right) - 0.023\exp\left(-\frac{25\pi^2 t}{4RC}\right) \tag{1.8.4}$$

which was obtained by a finite partial fraction expansion of an infinite expansion of Equation 1.8.1. It can be seen that the terms of the second and higher orders in Equation 1.8.4, which are particularly important at low values of time, are far from correct.

A T network and the corresponding n-stage ladder network for an interconnection line are shown in Figures 1.8.1a and b, respectively. In Figure 1.8.1b, $r_i = R/(n+1)$ and $c_i = C/n$. Now we need to determine the number of ladder stages required to generate the output voltage based on the transmission line model given by Equation 1.8.3. Assuming unit step input, a comparison of the plots of the output voltage versus time for an open-circuit

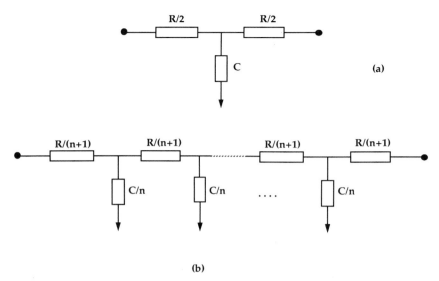

FIGURE 1.8.1 Representation of an interconnection line as (*a*) *T* network and (*b*) *n*-stage ladder network [1.54]. (© 1983 IEEE)

interconnection obtained by using Equation 1.8.3, those obtained by a numerical simulation of the *T* network, and those obtained by numerical simulations of the ladder network with a different number of stages is shown in Figure 1.8.2. For the sake of comparison, the output voltage plot obtained by using the approximate expression (1.8.4) is also included in Figure 1.8.2. It can be seen that the plot obtained by using Equation 1.8.3 almost coincides with that obtained for the ladder network with five stages. In fact, there is negligible difference between the results for the 5-stage and 10-stage ladder networks.

For an interconnection line loaded with a capacitance C_L, the voltage transfer function can be easily obtained in the *s* domain, but its analytical inverse Laplace transformation is not possible. Therefore, lumped-circuit approximations have to be used. It can be shown that, for a wide range of C_L/C values, a five-stage ladder network yields sufficient accuracy. Thus, the conclusion for an open-circuit interconnection also holds for a capacitively loaded interconnection.

1.8.2 Short-Circuit Interconnection

For a short-circuit *RC* transmission line, the output current for a step input voltage V_0/s is given by

$$I = CV_0 \frac{1}{(\sqrt{sRC})\sinh(\sqrt{sRC})} \tag{1.8.5}$$

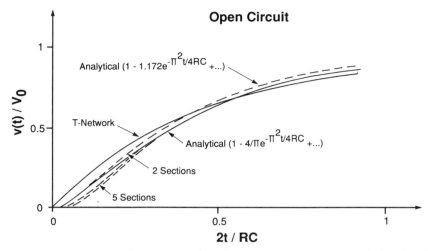

FIGURE 1.8.2   Output voltage versus time for an open resistive transmission line for a unit step input voltage [1.55]. (© 1983 IEEE)

Using infinite partial fraction expansion [1.58], Equation 1.8.5 can be written as

$$I = CV_0 \left[\frac{1}{sRC} + \frac{2}{RC} \sum_{k=1}^{\infty} (-1)^k \frac{1}{s + \left(\dfrac{\pi^2 k^2}{RC} \right)} \right] \qquad (1.8.6)$$

The output current in the time domain can then be easily obtained by finding the inverse Laplace transforms of the terms on the right-hand side of Equation 1.8.6 to be

$$i(t) = \frac{V_0}{R} \left[1 - 2\exp\left(-\frac{\pi^2 t}{RC} \right) + 2\exp\left(-\frac{\pi^2 4t}{RC} \right) - 2\exp\left(-\frac{\pi^2 9t}{RC} \right) + \cdots \right]$$
$$(1.8.7)$$

Assuming unit step input, a comparison of the plots of the output current versus time for a short-circuit interconnection obtained by using Equation 1.8.7, those obtained by a numerical simulation of the T network, and those obtained by numerical simulations of the ladder network with a different number of stages is shown in Figure 1.8.3. It can be seen that, for a short-circuit interconnection, at least 10 stages are required in the ladder network to obtain a good agreement with the analytical solution.

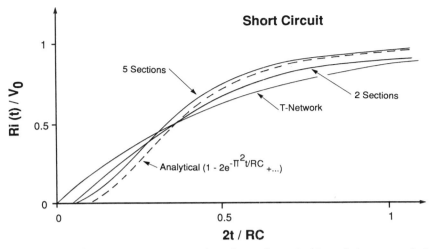

FIGURE 1.8.3   Output current versus time for a short-circuit resistive transmission line for a unit step input voltage [1.55]. (© 1983 IEEE)

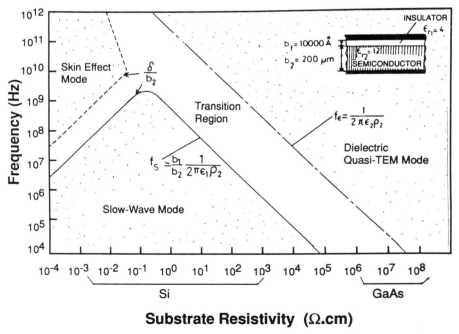

FIGURE 1.9.1   Resistivity–frequency mode chart of the MIS microstrip line [3.11]. (© 1984 IEEE)

1.9   PROPAGATION MODES IN A MICROSTRIP INTERCONNECTION

It can be seen from the resistivity–frequency mode chart of the metal–insulator–semiconductor (MIS) microstrip line shown in Figure 1.9.1, where δ is the skin depth and ρ is the semiconductor resistivity, that the propagation mode in the microstrip depends on the substrate resistivity and the frequency of operation. Figure 1.9.1 shows that (1) when the substrate resistivity is low (less than approximately 10^{-3} $\Omega \cdot$ cm), the substrate acts like an imperfect metal wall having a large skin effect resulting in the skin effect mode; (2) when the substrate resistivity is high (greater than approximately 10^4 $\Omega \cdot$ cm), the substrate acts like an insulator and the dielectric quasi-TEM mode propagates; and (3) for an MIS waveguide, the slow-wave mode propagates when the substrate is semiconducting and the frequency is low. The slow-wave mode results because, in the low frequency limit (note that this frequency limit extends into the gigahertz range at certain substrate resistivities), the electric field lines do not penetrate into the semiconductor, whereas the magnetic field lines can fully penetrate into it causing spatially separated storage of electric and magnetic energies.

1.10   SLOW-WAVE MODE PROPAGATION

In this section a quasi-TEM analysis of slow-wave mode propagation in micron-size coplanar MIS transmission lines on heavily doped semiconductors [1.59] is presented. The analysis includes metal losses as well as semiconductor losses. The quantities derived from the quasi-TEM analysis are compared with those measured experimentally for a system of four micron-size copolar MIS transmission lines fabricated on N^+ silicon.

1.10.1   Quasi-TEM Analysis

The geometry of the microstructure MIS transmission lines used in this analysis is shown in Figure 1.10.1. For the experimental results presented in the following discussion, these structures consist of coplanar aluminum strips (fabricated by evaporating Al on SiO_2) separated from an antimony-doped N^+ silicon substrate, with a doping density $N_d \sim 3 \times 10^{18}$ cm^{-3} and an electrical conductivity of 80 $(\Omega \cdot$ cm$)^{-1}$, by a thin SiO_2 layer. For the four transmission lines used in the experimental results, the wafer thickness d is 530 μm, the length l is 2500 μm, and the metal thickness t is 1 μm. The values of the other dimensions shown in Figure 1.10.1 and the capacitance scaling factor used later in this analysis for each of the four lines are listed in Table 1.10.1. Because of the low impedance of the N^+ semiconductor, most of the electrical energy is confined to the insulating layer immediately below the center conductor. However, because the semiconductor is a nonmagnetic

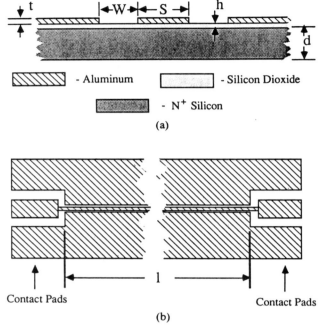

FIGURE 1.10.1 (a) Cross-sectional view and (b) plan view of micron-size coplanar MIS transmission lines [1.59]. (© 1986 IEEE)

material, the magnetic field freely penetrates the N^+ substrate. This separation of the electric and magnetic energies results in slow-wave mode propagation.

For quasi-TEM propagation of the slow-wave mode of the coplanar microstructure MIS transmission line, equivalent circuit of the line used in this analysis is shown in Figure 1.10.2. The inductance per unit length L is

TABLE 1.10.1 Dimensions S, W, and h and Capacitance Scaling Factor K of the Experimental Lines [1.59] (© 1986 IEEE)

Line	S	W	h	K
1	4.2	6.0	0.53	1.3
2	4.2	14.0	0.53	1.3
3	8.7	9.5	0.28	1.1
4	4.7	13.5	0.28	1.2

All dimensions are in micrometers.

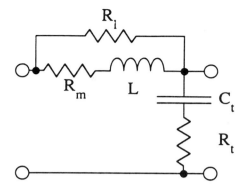

FIGURE 1.10.2 Slow-wave mode equivalent circuit of a micron-size coplanar MIS transmission line used in quasi-TEM analysis [1.59]. (© 1986 IEEE)

given by

$$L = \frac{1}{c^2 C_{air}} \qquad (1.10.1)$$

where c is the phase velocity in a vacuum and C_{air} is the capacitance per unit length of an equivalent air-filled transmission line. C_{air} can be determined by conformal mapping [1.60] leading to the following expression for L:

$$L = \frac{1}{4c^2 \varepsilon_0 F} \qquad (1.10.2)$$

where ε_0 is the permittivity of free space and F is a geometrical factor given approximately by [1.60]

$$F = \frac{\ln\left[\dfrac{2(1 + \sqrt{k})}{1 - \sqrt{k}}\right]}{\pi} \qquad 0.707 \le k \le 1$$

and

$$F = \frac{\pi}{\ln\left[\dfrac{2(1 + \sqrt{k'})}{1 - \sqrt{k'}}\right]} \qquad 0 \le k \le 0.707 \qquad (1.10.3)$$

with

$$k = \frac{S}{S + 2W} \qquad (1.10.4)$$

and

$$k' = \sqrt{1 - k^2} \tag{1.10.5}$$

In Figure 1.10.2 the resistance R_m in series with L represents the correction due to metal conductive losses. Its value in ohms per unit length is approximately equal to the effective resistance of the center conductor given by

$$R_m = \frac{1}{\sigma_m t S} \quad \text{for } t \le \delta_m \tag{1.10.6}$$

and

$$R_m = \frac{1}{\sigma_m \delta_m S} \quad \text{for } t \ge \delta_m$$

where σ_m and δ_m are the conductivity and skin depth of aluminum, respectively. The ground plane contribution to R_m can be ignored because the current densities in it are much smaller than those in the center conductor.

The resistance R_L is inserted in the equivalent circuit of Figure 1.10.2 to account for the loss caused by the longitudinal current flowing in the N^+ semiconductor parallel to the current in the center conductor. Because the longitudinal semiconductor current flows in addition to the longitudinal current in the metal, a parallel connection has been used. The value of R_L is given by

$$R_L = \frac{1}{\sigma_S \delta_S S} \tag{1.10.7}$$

where σ_S and δ_S are the conductivity and skin depth of the N^+ semiconductor, respectively. Equation 1.10.7 is based on the assumption that the longitudinal electric field under the center conductor decays exponentially in the vertical direction with decay constant δ_S.

To account for the energy storage and loss associated with the transverse electric field and current, the transverse capacitance C_t and transverse resistance R_t have been included in Figure 1.10.2. The transverse capacitance per unit length is given approximately by

$$C_t = \frac{\varepsilon_i \varepsilon_0 S K}{h} \tag{1.10.8}$$

where ε_i is the dielectric constant of SiO_2 and K is a geometrical factor listed in Table 1.10.1 and introduced here to account for the capacitance associated with the fringing fields. Equation 1.10.8 is based on the assumption that most of the electric energy is stored in the dielectric layer under the center conductor. The value of the transverse resistance is given approximately by

$$R_t = \frac{1}{2\sigma_S F} \tag{1.10.9}$$

where F is the geometric factor given by Equation 1.10.3. In this analysis we have ignored the finite transverse capacitance through the air because its susceptance is very small compared with that of C_t and R_t in series.

Now, for a transmission line consisting of the circuit elements of Figure 1.10.2, the complex propagation constant γ and the complex characteristic impedance Z_0 are given by

$$\gamma = \alpha + j\beta = \sqrt{ZY} \tag{1.10.10}$$

$$Z_0 = Z_0' + jZ_0'' = \sqrt{\frac{Z}{Y}} \tag{1.10.11}$$

where

$$Z = \frac{1}{\dfrac{1}{R_L} + \dfrac{1}{R_m + j\omega L}} \tag{1.10.12}$$

$$Y = \frac{1}{R_t + \dfrac{1}{j\omega C_t}} \tag{1.10.13}$$

and the quality factor Q and the slowing factor λ_0/λ_g are given by

$$Q = \frac{\beta}{2\alpha} \tag{1.10.14}$$

$$\frac{\lambda_0}{\lambda_g} = \frac{\beta}{\omega\sqrt{\mu_0\varepsilon_0}} \tag{1.10.15}$$

The quasi-TEM mode analysis presented previously is valid only at frequencies which satisfy both $f \ll f_1$ and $f \ll f_2$ where

$$f_1 = \frac{1}{\pi\sigma_S\mu_0(W + S/2)^2} \tag{1.10.16}$$

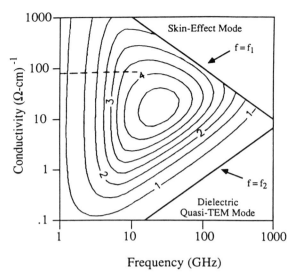

FIGURE 1.10.3 Contours of constant Q for transmission line 2. Dashed line corresponds to the experimental parameters [1.59]. (© 1986 IEEE)

and

$$f_2 = \frac{\sigma_S}{2\pi\varepsilon_0\varepsilon_S} \qquad (1.10.17)$$

The contours of constant Q for transmission line 2 are shown in Figure 1.10.3. This figure shows that, at frequencies satisfying $f \ll f_1$ and $f \ll f_2$, the mode of propagation is the slow-wave mode because, in this region, the magnetic field freely penetrates the substrate whereas the electric field does not. When $f_2 < f < f_1$ both transverse electric and magnetic fields freely penetrate the semiconductor substrate and the mode of propagation is the dielectric quasi-TEM mode. On the other hand, when $f_1 < f < f_2$ neither field penetrates the substrate and the mode of propagation is the skin effect mode. Using worst-case parameters for the four transmission lines studied in this section, we can determine that $f_1 = 120$ GHz and $f_2 = 12,000$ GHz. Therefore, all four lines satisfy the criteria for slow-wave mode propagation and for validity of the quasi-TEM analysis.

1.10.2 Comparison with Experimental Results

The experimental results presented in the following discussion are obtained by measuring the S parameters over the frequency range 1.0 to 12.4 GHz [1.59]. The attenuations of the four lines versus frequency are shown in Figures 1.10.4a–d. The solid lines represent theoretical values obtained from the quasi-TEM analysis presented previously. The real (Z_0') and imaginary (Z_0'') parts of the characteristic impedance as functions of frequency for the four lines are shown in Figures 1.10.5a–d. It can be seen that the characteristic impedances of all four lines are nearly real, of the order of 50 Ω, and almost independent of frequency. The dependences of the slowing factors (λ_0/λ_g) on frequency for the four lines are shown in Figures 1.10.6a–d, which also display the quality factor Q versus frequency. It can be seen that each of the four quality factors increases with frequency reaching values in the range 3.6 to 4.3 at 12.4 GHz.

1.10.2.1 *Discussion of Results* It is obvious that there is excellent agreement between theory and experiments over the full frequency range from 1.0 to 12.4 GHz for all four transmission lines. It can be concluded from this close agreement that the slow-wave mode propagating on these micron-size

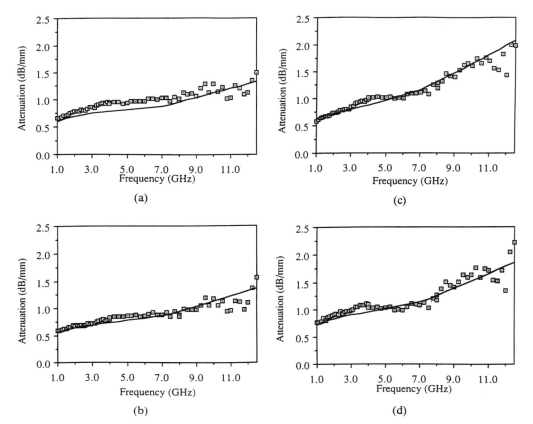

FIGURE 1.10.4 Dependence of attenuation on frequency for (a) line 1, (b) line 2, (c) line 3, and (d) line 4. Solid lines represent theoretical values obtained from quasi-TEM analysis. Symbols represent experimental values [1.59]. (© 1986 IEEE)

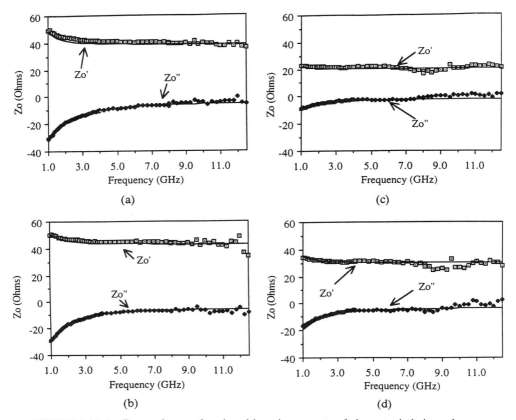

FIGURE 1.10.5 Dependence of real and imaginary parts of characteristic impedance on frequency for (a) line 1, (b) line 2, (c) line 3, and (d) line 4. Solid lines represent theoretical values obtained from quasi-TEM analysis. Symbols represent experimental values [1.59]. (© 1986 IEEE)

MIS transmission lines is, in fact, a quasi-TEM mode and can therefore be analyzed by elementary techniques.

In this analysis we have included three loss mechanisms, namely the metal loss, the longitudinal semiconductor loss, and the transverse semiconductor loss. It can be shown that the relative contribution of each loss mechanism in the preceding model can be approximately (within 1 percent) calculated by keeping the corresponding resistance in the circuit of Figure 1.10.2 while setting the other two resistances to 0 each. The results for transmission line 2 are shown in Figure 1.10.7. It can be seen that the metal loss contribution is dominant at frequencies below 25 GHz and decreases with increasing frequency, although, even at 100 GHz, it accounts for nearly 20 percent of the total loss. It can also be noted that both the transverse and the longitudinal

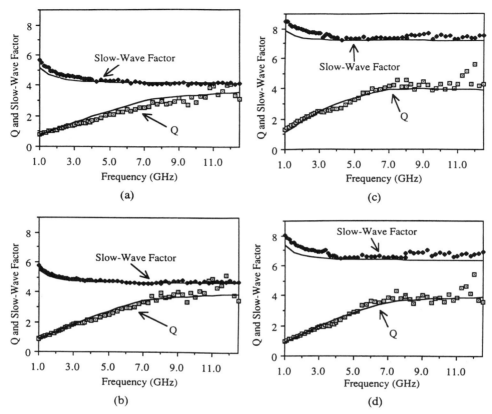

FIGURE 1.10.6 Dependence of quality and slow-wave factors on frequency for (*a*) line 1, (*b*) line 2, (*c*) line 3, and (*d*) line 4. Solid lines represent theoretical values obtained from quasi-TEM analysis. Symbols represent experimental values [1.59]. (© 1986 IEEE)

semiconductor losses increase with frequency, although the transverse loss component is very small.

1.11   TRANSMISSION LINE MODELS OF LOSSY WAVEGUIDE INTERCONNECTIONS

In its crudest form, at very low frequencies, the behavior of an interconnection line is determined by the line capacitance, the driving source impedance, and the load impedance. As the frequency increases, the interconnection can be satisfactorily modeled as a distributed *RC* transmission line. As the frequency increases further, the line inductance becomes important and the

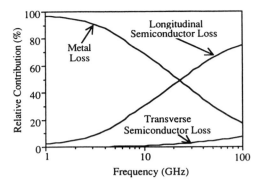

FIGURE 1.10.7   Relative contributions of the three loss mechanisms for transmission line 2 [1.59]. (© 1986 IEEE)

interconnection can be modeled as an RLC transmission line. Furthermore, as is well known, a transmission line is characterized by a series impedance $R + j\omega L$ and a shunt admittance $G + j\omega C$, where R, L, G, and C are the resistance, inductance, conductance, and capacitance per unit length and ω is the frequency in radians per second.

In general, an interconnection line behaves as a waveguide which, in turn, is analyzed by solving Maxwell's equations for the electric and magnetic fields. However, for the sake of continuity with the RC and RLC transmission line models of an interconnection, it is desirable to derive a transmission line model of a waveguide. It is interesting to note that waveguides and transmission lines are analogous in that waveguides propagate waves of electric and magnetic fields whereas transmission lines propagate waves of voltage and current. Furthermore, if the z direction is the direction of propagation, then the transverse electric field in the waveguide and the voltage wave in the corresponding transmission line have the same z dependence. In addition, the z dependences of the transverse magnetic field in the waveguide and the current wave in the corresponding transmission line are the same. In this section the R, L, G, and C parameters are found for a transmission line that models a lossy waveguide characterized by a complex propagation constant and a complex average power flow [1.61]. First, these are derived for the simplified case of a lossy waveguide with only one propagating wave with no reflections, and then the analysis is carried out starting from Maxwell's equations for the general case of a lossy waveguide in an inhomogeneous medium. Equivalent circuits for the driver and load are also derived.

1.11.1   Lossy Waveguide with Single Propagating Wave

To derive the parameters of the equivalent transmission line in this case, we assume that, either from measurements or by solving Maxwell's equations, two waveguide parameters, that is, the complex propagation constant γ and the complex average power P traveling down the waveguide, are known. For the propagation constant, we can write

$$\gamma = \alpha + j\beta \qquad (1.11.1)$$

where α is the attenuation constant and β is the phase constant. The average power P can be expressed in terms of Poynting's vector as

$$P = \frac{1}{2} \int dx \int (E \times H^*)_z \, dy \qquad (1.11.2)$$

where the superscript * denotes the complex conjugate. Assuming propagation of a single wave traveling in the z direction, the electric field is given by the real part of

$$E(x, y, z, t) = E(x, y)e^{-\gamma z + j\omega t} \qquad (1.11.3)$$

For the corresponding transmission line, the propagation constant γ is given by

$$\gamma^2 = (R + j\omega L)(G + j\omega C) \qquad (1.11.4)$$

and, for the case of a single propagating wave with no reflections and a single mode of propagation, the complex average power $P(z)$ is given in terms of the voltage $V(z)$ and current $I(z)$ by the expression

$$P(z) = \frac{1}{2} V(z) I(z)^* = \frac{1}{2} |I(z)|^2 Z_0 = \frac{1}{2} \frac{|V(z)|^2}{Z_0^*} \qquad (1.11.5)$$

where Z_0 is the complex characteristic impedance. We require that the propagation constant γ for the waveguide and the average power P traveling down the waveguide are the same as these quantities for the corresponding transmission line.

Writing P and Z_0 in terms of their real and imaginary parts as

$$P = P_r + jP_i \qquad (1.11.6)$$

$$Z_0 = Z_{0r} + jZ_{0i} \qquad (1.11.7)$$

we can define a power quotient Q at any position along the line as

$$Q \equiv \frac{P_i}{P_r} = \frac{Z_{0i}}{Z_{0r}} \qquad (1.11.8)$$

It should be noted that Q is independent of position z because both the real and imaginary parts of P attenuate at the same rate $[\exp(-2\alpha z)]$.

From the transmission line equations, the characteristic impedance Z_0 is given by

$$Z_0^2 = \frac{(R + j\omega L)}{(G + j\omega C)} \tag{1.11.9}$$

Using Equation 1.11.4, we can write for Z_0:

$$Z_0 = \left[\frac{R + j\omega L}{\gamma}\right] = \frac{R + j\omega L}{\alpha + j\beta} \tag{1.11.10}$$

Using Equation 1.11.10 in Equation 1.11.8, we can write for Q:

$$Q = \frac{\alpha\omega L - \beta R}{\alpha R + \beta\omega L} \tag{1.11.11}$$

Using Equations 1.11.4 and 1.11.9, Z_0 can also be expressed as

$$Z_0 = \frac{\gamma}{G + j\omega C} = \frac{\alpha + j\beta}{G + j\omega C} \tag{1.11.12}$$

Using Equation 1.11.12 in Equation 1.11.8, we can write for Q:

$$Q = \frac{\beta G - \alpha\omega C}{\beta\omega C + \alpha G} \tag{1.11.13}$$

From Equations 1.11.11 and 1.11.13, we can derive the following equations:

$$\frac{\omega L}{R} = \frac{\alpha Q + \beta}{\alpha - \beta Q} \tag{1.11.14}$$

$$\frac{\omega C}{G} = -\frac{\alpha Q - \beta}{\alpha + \beta Q} \tag{1.11.15}$$

$$GR = \frac{\alpha^2 - \beta^2 Q^2}{1 + Q^2} \tag{1.11.16}$$

$$\omega^2 LC = -\frac{\alpha^2 Q^2 - \beta^2}{1 + Q^2} \tag{1.11.17}$$

Equations 1.11.14 to 1.11.17 can be used to find the values of R, L, G, and C for the equivalent transmission line in terms of the known values of γ and Q for the waveguide. It should be noted that γ and Q depend on the mode of propagation in the waveguide and hence the parameters R, L, G, and C will be different for each mode of propagation. In addition, note that Equation 1.11.17 is not independent; it follows from multiplying Equations 1.11.14, 1.11.15, and 1.11.16. Therefore, Equations 1.11.14 to 1.11.17 can be used to determine three of the four parameters and the fourth parameter is arbitrary and can be chosen to obtain agreement with a particular low-frequency equivalent circuit. It can also be chosen to simplify the equivalent transmission line or the equivalent circuit of any driver or termination.

It is interesting to note that, for a three-parameter transmission line, the power quotient Q depends on the propagation constant γ only. For example, if $R = 0$ or if $L = 0$, then Equation 1.11.11 yields for Q:

$$Q = \frac{\alpha}{\beta} \quad \text{for } R = 0 \tag{1.11.18}$$

$$Q = -\frac{\beta}{\alpha} \quad \text{for } L = 0 \tag{1.11.19}$$

and, if $G = 0$ or if $C = 0$, then Equation 1.11.13 yields for Q:

$$Q = -\frac{\alpha}{\beta} \quad \text{for } G = 0 \tag{1.11.20}$$

$$Q = \frac{\beta}{\alpha} \quad \text{for } C = 0 \tag{1.11.21}$$

Conversely, it can be stated that if the power quotient of a waveguide is given approximately by the ratio $\pm(\alpha/\beta)$ or its inverse, then it can be modeled approximately by a three-parameter transmission line.

1.11.2 Equivalent Circuits for Waveguide Drivers and Loads

Now, we need to find the transmission line load impedance and the Thevenin voltage-source (or Norton current-source) equivalent circuit for the waveguide driver in terms of the known waveguide parameters. To accomplish these objectives, we note that the z dependences of both the transverse electric field in the waveguide and the voltage in the equivalent transmission line are given by the function

$$V(z) = Ae^{-\gamma z} + Be^{\gamma z} \tag{1.11.22}$$

where A and B are the forward and reflected wave amplitudes determined by the driver and the load. Similarly, the z dependences of both the transverse magnetic field in the waveguide and the current in the equivalent transmission line are given by the function

$$I(z) = \frac{1}{Z_0}[Ae^{-\gamma z} - Be^{\gamma z}] \qquad (1.11.23)$$

Now, the reflection coefficient Γ_L looking toward the load is the quantity characteristic of the waveguide termination and is defined as

$$\Gamma_L = \frac{B}{A} \qquad (1.11.24)$$

The load impedance Z_L for the equivalent transmission line can now be determined by requiring that it results in the same Γ_L as exists in the waveguide. Therefore, if l is the length of the transmission line, then Equations 1.11.22 and 1.11.23 yield at $z = l$:

$$Z_L \equiv \frac{V(l)}{I(l)} = Z_0\left[\frac{1 + \Gamma_L e^{2\gamma l}}{1 - \Gamma_L e^{2\gamma l}}\right] \qquad (1.11.25)$$

Because both Γ_L and γ are fixed by the wave behavior in the waveguide and Z_0 is determined by conditions (1.11.14) to (1.11.17) and because of the requirement of agreement with a low-frequency circuit, the load Z_L can be determined from Equation 1.11.25.

For the waveguide driver, the Thevenin voltage-source equivalent circuit (input voltage V_{in} and impedance Z_{in}) for the corresponding transmission line can be determined by requiring that the equivalent circuit result in the correct complex input power (P_{in}) and the correct reflection coefficient from the driver (Γ_D). The input power is given by

$$P_{in} = \frac{1}{2}V_{in}I(0)^* = \frac{1}{2}V_{in}\left[\frac{V_{in}}{Z_{in} + Z_i}\right]^* \qquad (1.11.26)$$

where Z_i is the line input impedance which can be determined from Equations 1.11.22 and 1.11.23 to be

$$Z_i \equiv \frac{V(0)}{I(0)} = Z_0\left(\frac{1 + \Gamma_L}{1 - \Gamma_L}\right) \qquad (1.11.27)$$

The impedance Z_{in} is given by

$$Z_{in} = Z_0\left(\frac{1 + \Gamma_D}{1 - \Gamma_D}\right) \qquad (1.11.28)$$

Then, using Equations 1.11.27 and 1.11.28, Equation 1.11.26 becomes

$$P_{in} = \frac{1}{4}|V_{in}|^2 \frac{1}{Z_0^*}\left[\frac{(1-\Gamma_D)(1-\Gamma_L)}{1-\Gamma_D\Gamma_L}\right]^* \qquad (1.11.29)$$

Knowing the power input to the waveguide and the two reflection coefficients Γ_D and Γ_L, $|V_{in}|$ can be determined. The reflection coefficients can be determined from standing wave measurements in the waveguide or by calculations in certain special cases.

1.11.3   Lossy Waveguide in an Inhomogeneous Medium

In this subsection the transmission line parameters R, L, G, and C for a transmission line equivalent to a lossy waveguide in an inhomogeneous medium are derived from Maxwell's equations. In this case the material parameters of the waveguide medium are taken as complex and dependent on the transverse position. In other words, if the z direction is the direction of propagation, then the dielectric permittivity ε and magnetic permeability μ are given by

$$\varepsilon = \varepsilon_0\kappa(x,y) + \frac{\sigma(x,y)}{j\omega} \qquad (1.11.30)$$

$$\mu = \mu_1(x,y) + j\mu_2(x,y) \qquad (1.11.31)$$

where κ is the dielectric constant and σ is the conductivity of the medium. The electric and magnetic fields at any angular frequency ω are also considered to be complex and are given by

$$E(x,y,z) = E_t(x,y)V(z) + \eta E_l(x,y)I(z) \qquad (1.11.32)$$

$$H(x,y,z) = H_t(x,y)I(z) + \frac{1}{\eta}H_l(x,y)V(z) \qquad (1.11.33)$$

where the subscript t denotes the transverse vector with x and y components, the subscript l denotes a longitudinal component in the z direction, and η is the intrinsic impedance of empty space given by

$$\eta = \sqrt{\frac{\mu_0}{\varepsilon_0}} \approx 376.7\ \Omega \qquad (1.11.34)$$

It should be noted that the electric and magnetic fields given by Equations 1.11.32 and 1.11.33 represent one mode of propagation only; the general solution of Maxwell's equations will be given by summations over all propagation modes.

1.11.3.1 Separation of Longitudinal and Transverse Components Assuming a single traveling wave, we will now derive a few basic equations by substituting Equations 1.11.32 and 1.11.33 into Maxwell's equations and separating the longitudinal and transverse components. Substituting (1.11.32) and (1.11.33) into the Maxwell equation

$$\nabla \times E = -j\omega\mu H \qquad (1.11.35)$$

we get

$$V(z)\nabla \times E_t(x, y) + \frac{d}{dz}V(z)\hat{k} \times E_t(x, y) + I(z)\eta\nabla \times E_l(x, y)$$

$$= -j\omega\mu \left[I(z)H_t(x, y) + V(z)\frac{1}{\eta}H_l(x, y) \right] \qquad (1.11.36)$$

where $\hat{k}$ is a unit vector in the z direction. Taking the z components of Equation 1.11.36, we get

$$V(z)\left[\nabla \times E_t(x, y) + \frac{j\omega\mu}{\eta}H_l(x, y) \right] = 0 \qquad (1.11.37)$$

Because $V(z)$ is nonzero, we get

$$\nabla \times E_t(x, y) + \frac{j\omega\mu}{\eta}H_l(x, y) = 0 \qquad (1.11.38)$$

Now, taking the transverse components of Equation 1.11.36, we get

$$\eta\nabla \times E_l(x, y) + j\omega\mu H_t(x, y) = -\hat{k} \times E_t(x, y)\left[\frac{1}{I(z)} \frac{d}{dz}V(z) \right] \qquad (1.11.39)$$

Because the left-hand side of Equation 1.11.39 is independent of z, it follows that

$$\left[\frac{1}{I(z)} \frac{d}{dz}V(z) \right] = \text{constant} = c_1 \qquad (1.11.40)$$

Substituting (1.11.32) and (1.11.33) into the Maxwell equation

$$\nabla \times H = j\omega\varepsilon E \qquad (1.11.41)$$

and following the preceding steps, we get from the z components:

$$I(z)\left[\nabla \times H_t(x, y) - j\omega\varepsilon\eta E_l\right] = 0 \qquad (1.11.42)$$

and, because $I(z)$ is nonzero, we get

$$\nabla \times H_t - j\omega\varepsilon\eta E_l = 0 \qquad (1.11.43)$$

Taking the transverse components, we get

$$\frac{1}{\eta}\nabla \times H_l(x, y) - j\omega\varepsilon E_t(x, y) = -\hat{k} \times H_t(x, y)\left[\frac{1}{V(z)}\frac{d}{dz}I(z)\right] \qquad (1.11.44)$$

Because the left-hand side of Equation 1.11.44 is independent of z, it follows that

$$\left[\frac{1}{V(z)}\frac{d}{dz}I(z)\right] = \text{constant} = c_2 \qquad (1.11.45)$$

Equations 1.11.40 and 1.11.45 can be written in the form of transmission line equations by choosing the arbitrary constants c_1 and c_2 as

$$c_1 = -\gamma Z_0 \qquad (1.11.46)$$

$$c_2 = -\frac{\gamma}{Z_0} \qquad (1.11.47)$$

Substituting (1.11.32) and (1.11.33) into the Maxwell equation

$$\nabla \cdot \left[\varepsilon(x, y)E(x, y, z)\right] = 0 \qquad (1.11.48)$$

we get

$$V(z)\nabla \cdot \left[\varepsilon(x, y)E_t(x, y)\right] + \frac{d}{dz}I(z)\varepsilon(x, y)\eta\hat{k} \cdot E_l(x, y) = 0 \quad (1.11.49)$$

Using Equations 1.11.45 and 1.11.47 in Equation 1.11.49, we get

$$V(z)\left[\nabla \cdot \left[\varepsilon(x, y)E_t(x, y)\right] - \frac{\gamma}{Z_0}\left(\varepsilon(x, y)\eta\hat{k} \cdot E_l(x, y)\right)\right] = 0 \quad (1.11.50)$$

and, because $V(z)$ is nonzero, we get

$$\nabla \cdot [\varepsilon E_t] - \frac{\gamma}{Z_0}\left(\varepsilon \eta \hat{k} \cdot E_l\right) = 0 \qquad (1.11.51)$$

Substituting (1.11.32) and (1.11.33) into the Maxwell equation

$$\nabla \cdot [\mu(x,y)H(x,y,z)] = 0 \qquad (1.11.52)$$

we get

$$I(z)\nabla \cdot [\mu(x,y)H_t(x,y)] + \frac{1}{\eta}\mu(x,y)\hat{k} \cdot H_l(x,y)\frac{d}{dz}V(z) = 0$$

$$(1.11.53)$$

which, when combined with Equations 1.11.40 and 1.11.46, leads to

$$I(z)\left[\nabla \cdot [\mu(x,y)H_t(x,y)] - \gamma Z_0 \frac{1}{\eta}\mu(x,y)\hat{k} \cdot H_l(x,y)\right] = 0 \quad (1.11.54)$$

and, because $I(z)$ is nonzero, we get

$$\nabla \cdot [\mu H_t] - \gamma Z_0 \frac{1}{\eta}\mu \hat{k} \cdot H_l = 0 \qquad (1.11.55)$$

Using Equations 1.11.46 and 1.11.47 in Equation 1.11.39, we get

$$\gamma Z_0 \hat{k} \times E_t - j\omega\mu H_t - \eta\nabla \times E_l = 0 \qquad (1.11.56)$$

and using Equations 1.11.46 and 1.11.47 in Equation 1.11.44, we get

$$\frac{\gamma}{Z_0}\hat{k} \times H_t + j\omega\varepsilon E_t - \frac{1}{\eta}\nabla \times H_l = 0 \qquad (1.11.57)$$

In addition, using Equations 1.11.46 and 1.11.47 in Equations 1.11.40 and 1.11.45, we get the transmission line equations

$$\frac{d}{dz}V(z) = -\gamma Z_0 I(z) \qquad (1.11.58)$$

$$\frac{d}{dz}I(z) = -\frac{\gamma}{Z_0}V(z) \qquad (1.11.59)$$

whose general solutions are known to be given by

$$V(z) = Ae^{-\gamma z} + Be^{\gamma z} \qquad (1.11.60)$$

$$I(z) = \frac{1}{Z_0}[Ae^{-\gamma z} - Be^{\gamma z}] \qquad (1.11.61)$$

where A and B are the complex amplitudes of the forward and reverse traveling waves whose values can be determined by the characteristics of the driver and load of the line.

Eigenvalue Equation for γ   Divide Equation 1.11.38 by μ and take the *curl* of the resulting equation. Next, divide Equation 1.11.51 by ε and take the gradient of the resulting equation. Then, subtracting the second equation from the first, we get

$$\mu\nabla \times \left[\frac{1}{\mu}(\nabla \times E_t)\right] - \nabla\left[\frac{1}{\varepsilon}\nabla \cdot (\varepsilon E_t)\right]$$

$$= j\omega\mu\left[-\frac{\gamma}{Z_0}\hat{k} \times H_t - j\omega\varepsilon E_t\right] - \frac{\gamma}{Z_0}\eta\nabla(\hat{k} \cdot E_t) \quad (1.11.62)$$

Now, taking the cross product of Equation 1.11.56 with $\hat{k}$, we get

$$j\omega\mu(\hat{k} \times H_t) = -\gamma Z_0 E_t - \eta\nabla(\hat{k} \cdot E_t) \qquad (1.11.63)$$

Substituting from Equation 1.11.63 into Equation 1.11.62, we get the eigenvalue equation for γ:

$$\mu\nabla \times \left[\frac{1}{\mu}(\nabla \times E_t)\right] - \left[\nabla\left(\frac{1}{\varepsilon}\nabla \cdot (\varepsilon E_t)\right) + (\gamma^2 + \omega^2\varepsilon\mu)E_t\right] = 0 \quad (1.11.64)$$

The eigenvalues of Equation 1.11.64 can be discrete, continuous, or a combination of both depending on the functions ε and μ.

1.11.3.2   *Power*   Using Poynting's vector, the average power at position z in the waveguide is given by

$$P(z) = \frac{1}{2}\int dx \int dy\, [E_{tx}H_{ty}^* - E_{ty}H_{tx}^*]V(z)I(z)^* \quad (1.11.65)$$

Because we require that the equivalent transmission line carrying the same average power as the waveguide, we get

$$P(z) = \tfrac{1}{2}V(z)I(z)^* \qquad (1.11.66)$$

Combining Equations 1.11.65 and 1.11.66, we get the condition

$$\int dx \int dy \left[E_{tx} H_{ty}^* - E_{ty} H_{tx}^* \right] = 1 \qquad (1.11.67)$$

Using Equations 1.11.62 and 1.11.51, we can eliminate H_t and condition (1.11.67) can be expressed in terms of E_t alone as

$$\int dx \int dy\, E_t \cdot \left[\frac{Z_0}{j\omega\gamma} \left(\nabla \times \left(\frac{1}{\mu} \nabla \times E_t \right) - \omega^2 \varepsilon E_t \right) \right]^* = 1 \quad (1.11.68)$$

Integrating Equation 1.11.68 by parts and assuming that the fields vanish at the waveguide boundaries (or at ∞), we get

$$\int dx \int dy \left[\frac{1}{\mu} (\nabla \times E_t) \cdot (\nabla \times E_t)^* - \omega^2 \varepsilon |E_t|^2 \right] = \frac{j\omega\gamma}{Z_0} \quad (1.11.69)$$

If we now eliminate E_t in Equation 1.11.67, the condition can be expressed in terms of H_t alone as

$$\int dx \int dy \left[\frac{1}{\varepsilon} (\nabla \times H_t) \cdot (\nabla \times H_t)^* - \omega^2 \mu |H_t|^2 \right] = j\omega\gamma Z_0 \quad (1.11.70)$$

Conditions (1.11.69) and (1.11.70) normalize the transverse fields to ensure that both the waveguide power and the transmission line power are given by Equation 1.11.66.

1.11.3.3 Expressions for R, L, G, and C
Using the customary expressions defining γ and Z_0, that is,

$$\gamma^2 = (R + j\omega L)(G + j\omega C) \qquad (1.11.4)$$

and

$$Z_0^2 = \frac{R + j\omega L}{G + j\omega C} \qquad (1.11.9)$$

we can write

$$G + j\omega C = \frac{\gamma}{Z_0} \qquad (1.11.71)$$

$$R + j\omega L = \gamma Z_0 \qquad (1.11.72)$$

Using Equation 1.11.71 and the normalization condition (1.11.69), we can find the following expressions for G and C:

$$G = \int dx \int dy \left[\sigma |E_t|^2 - \frac{\omega \mu_2 |H_l|^2}{\eta^2} \right] \tag{1.11.73}$$

$$C = \int dx \int dy \left[\kappa \varepsilon_0 |E_t|^2 - \frac{\mu_1 |H_l|^2}{\eta^2} \right] \tag{1.11.74}$$

Similarly, using Equation 1.11.72 and the normalization condition (1.11.70), we can find the following expressions for R and L:

$$R = \int dx \int dy \left[\sigma \eta^2 |E_l|^2 - \omega \mu_2 |H_t|^2 \right] \tag{1.11.75}$$

$$L = \int dx \int dy \left[\mu_1 |H_t|^2 - \kappa \varepsilon_0 \eta^2 |E_l|^2 \right] \tag{1.11.76}$$

For the case of a homogeneous medium, the corresponding expressions can be found by replacing the transverse and longitudinal field quantities with the field components in Equations 1.11.32 and 1.11.33, yielding

$$G = \frac{1}{|V(z)|^2} \int dx \int dy \left[\sigma |E_n(x,y,z)|^2 - \omega \mu_2 |H_z(x,y,z)|^2 \right] \tag{1.11.77}$$

$$C = \frac{1}{|V(z)|^2} \int dx \int dy \left[\kappa \varepsilon_0 |E_n(x,y,z)|^2 - \mu_1 |H_z(x,y,z)|^2 \right] \tag{1.11.78}$$

$$R = \frac{1}{|I(z)|^2} \int dx \int dy \left[\sigma |E_z(x,y,z)|^2 - \omega \mu_2 |H_n(x,y,z)|^2 \right] \tag{1.11.79}$$

$$L = \frac{1}{|I(z)|^2} \int dx \int dy \left[\mu_1 |H_n(x,y,z)|^2 - \kappa \varepsilon_0 |E_z(x,y,z)|^2 \right] \tag{1.11.80}$$

where the subscript n denotes the component of the field normal to the direction of propagation. After some manipulation, it can be proved that expressions (1.11.73) to (1.11.76) result in the same values of the ratios in Equations 1.11.14 and 1.11.15.

1.12 PROPAGATION DELAYS

In the literature three measures of propagation delays in an electric circuit are defined [1.62] as follows:

Delay time: The time required by the output signal (current or voltage) to reach 50 percent of its steady-state value.

Rise time: The time required by the output signal (current or voltage) to rise from 10 to 90 percent of its steady-state value.

Propagation time: The time required by the output signal (current or voltage) to reach 90 percent of its steady-state value.

EXERCISES

E1.1   In the circuit shown in Figure E1.1.1 using an ideal voltage amplifier of gain 0.5, determine the input resistance R_{in}.

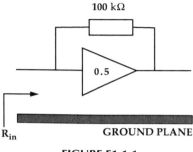

100 kΩ

0.5

R_{in} **GROUND PLANE**

FIGURE E1.1.1

E1.2   In the circuit shown in Figure E1.2.1 using an ideal voltage amplifier of gain -10, determine the input capacitance C_{in}.

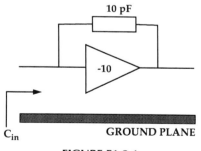

10 pF

-10

C_{in} **GROUND PLANE**

FIGURE E1.2.1

E1.3   Following the steps in Section 1.4, write expressions for the even- and odd-mode capacitances for a system of four coupled conductors and find the self-capacitances and mutual capacitances for the four conductors. Comment on the accuracy of your results.

E1.4   Following the steps in Section 1.4, write expressions for the even- and odd-mode capacitances for a system of five coupled conductors and

find the self-capacitances, and mutual capacitances for the five conductors. Comment on the accuracy of your results.

E1.5 Suggest situations where it will be preferable to model an interconnection as a lumped circuit, as a transmission line, or as a waveguide.

E1.6 Equation 1.10.29 can be used to determine the magnitude of V_{in} only
and not its phase. Comment on the relative significance of the phase
of V_{in}.

E1.7 Based on the discussion in Section 1.10, show that $V(z)$ and $I(z)$ can
be expressed as the weighted averages of the transverse electric and
magnetic fields over the cross section of the waveguide. In particular,
prove that

$$V(z) = \int dx \int dy\, E(x, y, z) \cdot \left[\frac{Z_0}{j\omega\gamma} \left(\nabla \times \left(\frac{1}{\mu} \nabla \times E_t \right) - \omega^2 \varepsilon E_t \right) \right]^*$$

and

$$I(z) = \int dx \int dy\, H(x, y, z) \cdot \left[\frac{1}{j\omega\gamma Z_0} \left(\nabla \times \left(\frac{1}{\varepsilon} \nabla \times H_t \right) - \omega^2 \mu H_t \right) \right]^*$$

E1.8 Prove that expressions (1.10.73) to (1.10.76) for R, L, G, and C result
in the same values of the ratios in Equations 1.10.14 and 1.10.15.

CHAPTER TWO

Parasitic Capacitances and Inductances

An electrical interconnection is characterized by three parameters: series resistance, capacitance, and inductance. Series resistance can be an important parameter and can be rather easily determined by the material and dimensions of the interconnection. Parasitic capacitances and inductances associated with the interconnections in the high-density environment of an integrated circuit have become the primary factors in the evolution of very high speed integrated circuit technology. An accurate model of these capacitances must include the contribution of the fringing fields as well as the shielding effects due to the presence of neighboring conductors.

In the literature several numerical techniques have been presented that can be used to characterize the interconnection lines, although with limited applications. For example, the Schwarz–Christoffel conformal mapping technique [2.1] can be used to obtain exact results in terms of elliptic integrals for a symmetrical two-strip conductor; for systems with more than two strips or for asymmetrical two-strip conductors, the method becomes very cumbersome and significant results cannot be obtained. The technique employing Galerkin's method [2.2] in the spectral domain uses a Fourier series which becomes quite complicated for mixed or inhomogeneous dielectric multiconductor structures. The Green's function integral equation technique [2.3] is suitable for conductors of rectangular or annular shapes but becomes extremely difficult for irregular geometric shapes. The finite element method [2.4] and the finite difference method [2.5] involve determination of the charge distributions on the conductor surfaces and can be applied to several conductor geometries. The network analog method, evolved from the finite difference representation of partial differential equations [2.6], has been used for finite substrates in two dimensions [2.7], open substrates in three dimensions [2.8, 2.9] as well as for lossy, anisotropic, and layered structures

[2.10–2.14]. In the past, capacitance models have been developed for integrated circuit metallization wires [2.15–2.17] and the system of equations for infinite printed conductors has been solved [2.18–2.20]. Work on systems of conductors with finite dimensions has also been reported. [2.21–2.27].

In this chapter approximate formulas for calculating the parasitic capacitances for a few interconnection structures are presented in Section 2.1. In Section 2.2 an algorithm to obtain the interconnection capacitances by the Green's function method, which employs the method of moments in conjunction with a Green's function appropriate for the geometry of the interconnections, is presented. The Green's function is calculated by using the method of multiple images. In Section 2.3 the Green's function is calculated using the Fourier integral approach and a numerical technique to determine the capacitances for a multilevel interconnection structure in the Si–SiO$_2$ composite is presented. In Section 2.4 an improved network analog method to determine the parasitic capacitances and inductances associated with high-density multilevel interconnections on GaAs-based integrated circuits is presented. A few simplified formulas for calculating the interconnection capacitances and inductances on oxide-passivated silicon, sapphire, and semi-insulating gallium-arsenide substrates are given in Section 2.5. Finally, in Section 2.6 the electrode parasitic capacitances in a GaAs MESFET have been calculated using the Green's function method.

2.1 APPROXIMATE FORMULAS FOR CAPACITANCES

In order to accurately determine the interconnection capacitances on VLSI circuits, two- and three-dimensional effects must be taken into account. This requires rigorous numerical analysis which can be too time consuming when used in computer-aided design (CAD) programs. Therefore, approximate formulas to estimate the interconnection capacitances are sometimes desirable. In this section such empirical formulas suggested by Sakurai and Tamaru [2.23] for a few interconnection structures are presented.

2.1.1 Single Line on a Ground Plane

A schematic diagram of a single interconnection line placed on bulk silicon (considered as the ground plane) is shown in Figure 2.1.1a. The capacitance C_1 per unit length in terms of the various dimensions shown in Figure 2.1.1a can be estimated from the approximate formula

$$C_1 = \varepsilon_{ox}\left[1.15\left(\frac{W}{H}\right) + 2.80\left(\frac{T}{H}\right)^{0.222}\right] \qquad (2.1.1)$$

where ε_{ox} is the dielectric constant of the insulator such as SiO$_2$ for which

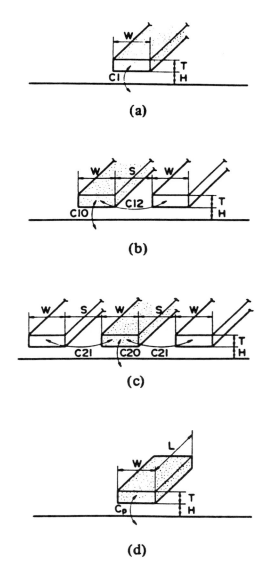

FIGURE 2.1.1 Schematic diagram of (*a*) single line on a conducting ground plane; (*b*) two lines on a ground plane; (*c*) three lines on a ground plane; and (*d*) single plate of finite dimensions on a ground plane [2.23]. (© 1983 IEEE)

$\epsilon_{ox} = 3.9 \times 8.855 \times 10^{-14}$ F/cm. The relative error of formula (2.1.1) is within 6 percent for $0.3 < (W/H) < 30$ and $0.3 < (T/H) < 30$.

2.1.2   Two Lines on a Ground Plane

A schematic diagram of two interconnection lines placed on bulk silicon (considered as the ground plane) is shown in Figure 2.1.1b. In this case the total capacitance C_2 of one line per unit length includes the ground capacitance C_{10} and the coupling capacitance C_{12} between the lines; that is, $C_2 = C_{10} + C_{12}$. In terms of the various dimensions shown in Figure 2.1.1b, C_2 can be estimated from the approximate formula

$$C_2 = C_1 + \varepsilon_{ox}\left[0.03\left(\frac{W}{H}\right) + 0.83\left(\frac{T}{H}\right) - 0.07\left(\frac{T}{H}\right)^{0.222}\right]\left(\frac{S}{H}\right)^{-1.34} \quad (2.1.2)$$

The relative error of formula (2.1.2) is less than 10 percent for $0.3 < (W/H) < 10$, $0.3 < (T/H) < 10$, and $0.5 < (S/H) < 10$. It should be noted that formula (2.1.2) tends to the single-line formula (2.1.1) as the line separation S approaches ∞.

2.1.3   Three Lines on a Ground Plane

A schematic diagram of three interconnection lines placed on bulk silicon (considered as the ground plane) is shown in Figure 2.1.1c. In this case the total capacitance of one line includes the ground capacitance C_{20} and the coupling capacitance C_{21} between the lines. For example, the total capacitance C_3 of the middle line per unit length is equal to $C_{20} + 2C_{21}$. In terms of the various dimensions shown in Figure 2.1.1c, C_3 can be estimated from the approximate formula

$$C_3 = C_1 + 2\varepsilon_{ox}\left[0.03\left(\frac{W}{H}\right) + 0.83\left(\frac{T}{H}\right) - 0.07\left(\frac{T}{H}\right)^{0.222}\right]\left(\frac{S}{H}\right)^{-1.34} \quad (2.1.3)$$

The relative error of formula (2.1.3) is less than 10 percent for $0.3 < (W/H) < 10$, $0.3 < (T/H) < 10$, and $0.5 < (S/H) < 10$. It should be noted that formula (2.1.3) tends to the single-line formula (2.1.1) as the line separation S approaches ∞.

2.1.4   Single Plate with Finite Dimensions on a Ground Plane

A schematic diagram of a single plate with finite dimensions placed on bulk silicon (considered as the ground plane) is shown in Figure 2.1.1d. In this case the capacitance C_p between the plate and the ground includes the three-dimensional effects. In terms of the various dimension parameters shown in Figure 2.1.1d, C_p can be estimated from the approximate formula

$$C_p = \varepsilon_{ox}\left[1.15\left(\frac{\text{plate area}}{H}\right) + 1.40\left(\frac{T}{H}\right)^{0.222}(\text{plate circumference})\right.$$

$$\left. + 4.12H\left(\frac{T}{H}\right)^{0.728}\right] \quad (2.1.4)$$

Compared to the data published by Ruehli and Brennan [2.17], the relative error of formula (2.1.4) is within 10 percent for $0 < (W/L) < 1$, $0.5 < (W/H) < 40$, and $0.4 < (T/H) < 10$. It should be noted that formula (2.1.4) tends to formula (2.1.1) as the plate length approaches ∞.

2.2 GREEN'S FUNCTION METHOD: USING THE METHOD OF IMAGES

In this section the parasitic capacitances for a system of closely spaced conducting interconnection lines printed on the GaAs substrate which in turn is placed on a conducting ground plane are determined by using the method of moments [2.28] in conjunction with a Green's function appropriate for the geometry of the interconnections. The Green's function is obtained by using the method of multiple images [2.3, 2.29]. It is assumed that the interconnections are of negligible thickness.

2.2.1 Green's Function Matrix for Interconnections Printed on the Substrate

The Green's function is a solution of a partial differential equation for a unit charge and with specified boundary conditions. To find the Green's function, the first step is to determine the potential due to the source charge everywhere in the region of interest. In this subsection the problem will be solved in two dimensions and then it will be extended to the three-dimensional case in the next subsection.

Consider the case of charged interconnections printed on a dielectric substrate which in turn is placed on a conducting ground plane as shown in Figure 2.2.1. Obviously, there is more than one interface and we need to consider the formation of image charges about the dielectric interface and about the ground plane by a process known as multiple imaging. Each image of the real charge also images across all other interfaces. For example, the real charge ρ will form an image across the dielectric interface as $[\rho(\varepsilon_1 - \varepsilon_2)/(\varepsilon_1 + \varepsilon_2)]$. This image will then form another image about the bottom ground plane as $[(-\rho)(\varepsilon_1 - \varepsilon_2)/(\varepsilon_1 + \varepsilon_2)]$. This new image will in turn image back across the dielectric interface with its magnitude changed by a

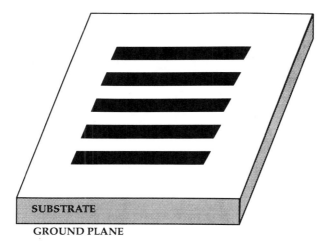

FIGURE 2.2.1   Schematic diagram of a few interconnections printed on top of the substrate which in turn is placed on a conducting ground plane.

factor of $[(\varepsilon_2 - \varepsilon_1)/(\varepsilon_1 + \varepsilon_2)]$ and so on. In addition, the real charge will image about the bottom ground plane as $-\rho$. This image charge itself will image back across the dielectric interface modified by a factor of $[(\varepsilon_2 - \varepsilon_1)/(\varepsilon_1 + \varepsilon_2)]$. This process will continue until ∞, producing an infinite number of image charges.

For the two-dimensional case of a line charge ρ lying in a medium of dielectric constant ε_0 above a medium of dielectric constant ε with a conducting ground plane under it, the magnitudes and locations of a number of images are shown in Figure 2.2.2. First, the real charge reflects across the dielectric interface. Then both the real charge and this first image reflect across the ground plane, changing in sign. These two new images then reflect back across the dielectric interface, changing by a factor of k where

$$k = \frac{\varepsilon - \varepsilon_0}{\varepsilon + \varepsilon_0}$$

and the process continues until ∞.

Now, the potential at any field point (x_i, y_i) due to a line charge ρ at the location (x_j, y_j) can be determined. In general, if r is the distance from the source charge to the field point, then

$$V(x_i, y_i) = -\frac{\rho}{4\pi\varepsilon_0} \ln(r^2)$$

However, the distance between the source charge and the field point will be different for each image; that is, the potential due to the nth image is given by

$$V_n(x_i, y_i) = -\frac{\rho}{4\pi\varepsilon_0}\ln(r_n^2)$$

and the total potential at the field point is given by

$$V(x_i, y_i) = \sum_{n=1}^{\infty} V_n$$

Therefore, it follows from Figure 2.2.2 that, for $y_i \geq T$ and $y_j \geq T$,

$$
\begin{aligned}
V(x_i, y_i) = \frac{\rho}{4\pi\varepsilon_0}\Big\{ &-\ln\big[(x_i - x_j)^2 + (y_i - y_j)^2\big] \\
&+ k\ln\big[(x_i - x_j)^2 + (y_i - y_j - 2T)^2\big] \\
&- k^2\ln\big[(x_i - x_j)^2 + (y_i - y_j - 4T)^2\big] + \cdots \\
&+ k\ln\big[(x_i - x_j)^2 + (y_i + y_j - 2T)^2\big] \\
&- k^2\ln\big[(x_i - x_j)^2 + (y_i + y_j - 4T)^2\big] \\
&+ k^3\ln\big[(x_i - x_j)^2 + (y_i + y_j - 6T)^2\big] + \cdots \\
&- k\ln\big[(x_i - x_j)^2 + (y_i - y_j + 2T)^2\big] \\
&+ k^2\ln\big[(x_i - x_j)^2 + (y_i - y_j + 4T)^2\big] \\
&- k^3\ln\big[(x_i - x_j)^2 + (y_i - y_j + 6T)^2\big] + \cdots \\
&- \ln\big[(x_i - x_j)^2 + (y_i + y_j)^2\big] \\
&- k\ln\big[(x_i - x_j)^2 + (y_i + y_j + 2T)^2\big] \\
&+ k^2\ln\big[(x_i - x_j)^2 + (y_i + y_j + 4T)^2\big] + \cdots \Big\} \quad (2.2.1)
\end{aligned}
$$

The Green's function $G(x_i, y_i; x_j, y_j)$ for the real charge at (x_j, y_j) and the field point at (x_i, y_i) can now be determined from Equation 2.2.1 by setting

- $-k\rho\,(x, 2T + y)$

- $k^2\rho\,(x, 4T - y)$

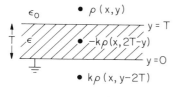

- $\rho\,(x, y)$

- $-k\rho(x, 2T - y)$

- $k\rho\,(x, y - 2T)$

- $-\rho\,(x, -y)$

- $-k^2\rho\,(x, y - 4T)$

- $k\rho\,(x, -2T - y)$

FIGURE 2.2.2 Magnitudes and locations of the images formed when a line charge ρ lies in a medium of dielectric constant ε_0 above a medium of dielectric constant ε with a conducting ground plane under it.

$\rho = 1$. Therefore,

$$G(x_i, y_i; x_j, y_j)$$

$$= \frac{1}{4\pi\varepsilon_0} \sum_{n=1}^{\infty} \left\{ (-1)^n k^{n-1} \ln\left[(x_i - x_j)^2 + (y_i - y_j - 2(n-1)T)^2\right] \right.$$

$$+ (-1)^{n+1} k^n \ln\left[(x_i - x_j)^2 + (y_i + y_j - 2nT)^2\right]$$

$$- (-1)^{n+1} k^n \ln\left[(x_i - x_j)^2 + (y_i - y_j + 2nT)^2\right]$$

$$\left. - (-1)^n k^{n-1} \ln\left[(x_i - x_j)^2 + (y_i + y_j + 2(n-1)T)^2\right] \right\} \quad (2.2.2)$$

If all the interconnections are printed in the same plane on the substrate, then $y_i = y_j = T$. Equation 2.2.2 then becomes

$$G(x_i, T; x_j, T) = \frac{1}{4\pi\varepsilon_0} \sum_{n=1}^{\infty} \left\{ (-1)^n k^{n-1} \ln\left[(x_i - x_j)^2 + (2(n-1)T)^2\right] \right.$$

$$+ (-1)^{n+1} k^n \ln\left[(x_i - x_j)^2 + (2(n-1)T)^2\right]$$

$$- (-1)^{n+1} k^n \ln\left[(x_i - x_j)^2 + (2nT)^2\right]$$

$$\left. - (-1)^n k^{n-1} \ln\left[(x_i - x_j)^2 + (2nT)^2\right] \right\}$$

or

$$G(x_i, T; x_j, T) = \frac{1}{4\pi\varepsilon_0} \sum_{n=1}^{\infty} \{((-1)^n k^{n-1} + (-1)^{n+1} k^n)$$
$$\times \ln[(x_i - x_j)^2 + (2(n-1)T)^2]$$
$$- ((-1)^{n+1} k^n + (-1)^n k^{n-1})$$
$$\times \ln[(x_i - x_j)^2 + (2nT)^2]\}$$

or

$$G(x_i, T; x_j, T) = \left(-\frac{1}{4\pi\varepsilon_0}\right) \sum_{n=1}^{\infty} (1-k)((-1)^{n+1} k^{n-1})$$
$$\times \{\ln[(x_i - x_j)^2 + (2(n-1)T)^2]$$
$$- \ln[(x_i - x_j)^2 + (2nT)^2]\}$$

Because

$$1 - k = 1 - \frac{\varepsilon - \varepsilon_0}{\varepsilon + \varepsilon_0} = \frac{2\varepsilon_0}{\varepsilon + \varepsilon_0}$$

therefore,

$$G(x_i, T; x_j, T) = \frac{1}{2\pi(\varepsilon + \varepsilon_0)} \sum_{n=1}^{\infty} ((-1)^{n+1} k^{n-1})$$
$$\times \{\ln[(x_i - x_j)^2 + (2nT)^2]$$
$$- \ln[(x_i - x_j)^2 + (2(n-1)T)^2]\}$$

We can rewrite this expression for the two-dimensional Green's function element as

$$G(x_i, T; x_j, T) = \sum_{n=1}^{\infty} A_n[g_{ijn1} - g_{ijn2}] \qquad (2.2.3)$$

where

$$A_n = \frac{1}{2\pi(\varepsilon + \varepsilon_0)} [(-1)^{n+1} k^{n-1}]$$

g_{ijn1} is the free-space Green's function for the nth image at a distance of $y_j - y_i = 2nT$ from the field point and g_{ijn2} is the free-space Green's function for the nth image at a distance of $y_j - y_i = 2(n-1)T$ from the field point.

Now, we can extend Equation 2.2.3 to the case when the charge is limited to a finite length and a finite width. First, we need to find the expression for the free-space potential due to a charge in three dimensions. Consider a conductor on the surface of a dielectric which is divided into a large number of rectangular subsections. Consider a subsection of length Δx_j, width Δy_j, and area Δs_j located at the source point (x_j, y_j, z_j). For this rectangular subsection in free space (i.e, without the dielectric present), the potential at a field point (x_i, y_i, z_i) can be determined by integration over the surface of the subsection; that is, for a unit charge density,

$$V(x_i, y_i, z_i) = \frac{1}{4\pi\varepsilon_0} \int_{x_1}^{x_2} \int_{y_1}^{y_2} \frac{1}{\left[(x_i - x_j)^2 + (y_i - y_j)^2 + (z_i - z_j)^2\right]^{1/2}} \, dx \, dy$$

where

$$x_1 = x_j - \frac{\Delta x_j}{2}$$

$$y_1 = y_j - \frac{\Delta y_j}{2}$$

$$x_2 = x_j + \frac{\Delta x_j}{2}$$

$$y_2 = y_j + \frac{\Delta y_j}{2}$$

After the integration is performed, we get

$$\begin{aligned}
V(x_i, y_i, z_i) = \frac{1}{4\pi\varepsilon_0} \Bigg\{ &(x_j - x_i) \ln\left[\frac{(c + A_1)(d + B_1)}{(d + C_1)(c + D_1)}\right] \\
&+ \left(\frac{\Delta x_j}{2}\right) \ln\left[\frac{(d + B_1)(d + C_1)}{(c + D_1)(c + A_1)}\right] \\
&+ (y_j - y_i) \ln\left[\frac{(a + A_1)(b + B_1)}{(b + D_1)(a + C_1)}\right] \\
&+ \left(\frac{\Delta y_j}{2}\right) \ln\left[\frac{(b + B_1)(b + D_1)}{(a + C_1)(a + A_1)}\right] \\
&- h\left[\arctan\left(\frac{ac}{hA_1}\right) + \arctan\left(\frac{bd}{hB_1}\right)\right] \\
&+ h\left[\arctan\left(\frac{ad}{hC_1}\right) + \arctan\left(\frac{bc}{hD_1}\right)\right]\Bigg\} \quad (2.2.4)
\end{aligned}$$

where

$$h = z_j - z_i$$

$$a = x_j - x_i - \frac{\Delta x_j}{2}$$

$$b = x_j - x_i + \frac{\Delta x_j}{2}$$

$$c = y_j - y_i - \frac{\Delta y_j}{2}$$

$$d = y_j - y_i + \frac{\Delta y_j}{2}$$

$$A_1 = \sqrt{a^2 + c^2 + h^2}$$

$$B_1 = \sqrt{b^2 + d^2 + h^2}$$

$$C_1 = \sqrt{a^2 + d^2 + h^2}$$

$$D_1 = \sqrt{b^2 + c^2 + h^2}$$

Now, extension of Equation 2.2.3 to three dimensions is accomplished by multiplying this equation by $-4\pi\varepsilon_0$, by replacing the term g_{ijn1} by the free-space Green's function for the nth image at a distance of $h = z_j - z_i = 2nT$ from the field point, and by replacing the term g_{ijn2} by the free-space Green's function for the nth image at a distance of $h = z_j - z_i = 2(n - 1)T$ from the field point. The new expressions for g_{ijn1} and g_{ijn2} will become

$$
\begin{aligned}
g_{ijn1} = \frac{1}{4\pi\varepsilon_0} &\left\{ (x_j - x_i) \ln\left[\frac{(c + A_2)(d + B_2)}{(d + C_2)(c + D_2)}\right] \right. \\
&+ \left(\frac{\Delta x_j}{2}\right) \ln\left[\frac{(d + B_2)(d + C_2)}{(c + D_2)(c + A_2)}\right] \\
&+ (y_j - y_i) \ln\left[\frac{(a + A_2)(b + B_2)}{(b + D_2)(a + C_2)}\right] \\
&+ \left(\frac{\Delta y_j}{2}\right) \ln\left[\frac{(b + B_2)(b + D_2)}{(a + C_2)(a + A_2)}\right] \\
&- 2nT\left[\arctan\left(\frac{ac}{2nTA_2}\right) + \arctan\left(\frac{bd}{2nTB_2}\right)\right] \\
&+ \left. 2nT\left[\arctan\left(\frac{ad}{2nTC_2}\right) + \arctan\left(\frac{bc}{2nTD_2}\right)\right]\right\} \quad (2.2.5)
\end{aligned}
$$

where

$$A_2 = \sqrt{a^2 + c^2 + (2nT)^2}$$

$$B_2 = \sqrt{b^2 + d^2 + (2nT)^2}$$

$$C_2 = \sqrt{a^2 + d^2 + (2nT)^2}$$

$$D_2 = \sqrt{b^2 + c^2 + (2nT)^2}$$

and

$$
\begin{aligned}
g_{ijn2} = \frac{1}{4\pi\varepsilon_0} \Bigg\{ &(x_j - x_i)\ln\left[\frac{(c + A_3)(d + B_3)}{(d + C_3)(c + D_3)}\right] \\
&+ \left(\frac{\Delta x_j}{2}\right)\ln\left[\frac{(d + B_3)(d + C_3)}{(c + D_3)(c + A_3)}\right] \\
&+ (y_j - y_i)\ln\left[\frac{(a + A_3)(b + B_3)}{(b + D_3)(a + C_3)}\right] \\
&+ \left(\frac{\Delta y_j}{2}\right)\ln\left[\frac{(b + B_3)(b + D_3)}{(a + C_3)(a + A_3)}\right] \\
&- 2(n-1)T\left[\arctan\left(\frac{ac}{2(n-1)TA_3}\right)\right. \\
&\qquad\qquad \left. + \arctan\left(\frac{bd}{2(n-1)TB_3}\right)\right] \\
&+ 2(n-1)T\left[\arctan\left(\frac{ad}{2(n-1)TC_3}\right)\right. \\
&\qquad\qquad \left. + \arctan\left(\frac{bc}{2(n-1)TD_3}\right)\right] \Bigg\}
\end{aligned}
\qquad (2.2.6)
$$

where

$$A_3 = \sqrt{a^2 + c^2 + (2(n-1)T)^2}$$

$$B_3 = \sqrt{b^2 + d^2 + (2(n-1)T)^2}$$

$$C_3 = \sqrt{a^2 + d^2 + (2(n-1)T)^2}$$

$$D_3 = \sqrt{b^2 + c^2 + (2(n-1)T)^2}$$

Substituting for g_{ijn1} and g_{ijn2} from Equations 2.2.5 and 2.2.6 into Equation 2.2.3, multiplying by the factor $-4\pi\varepsilon_0$, and after simplifying, we get for the Green's function element in three dimensions

$$G_{ij} = G(x_i, T; x_j, T)$$

$$= \frac{1}{2\pi(\varepsilon + \varepsilon_0)} \sum_{n=1}^{\infty} (-1)^{n+1} k^{n-1}(T_1 + T_2 + T_3 + T_4 - T_5 + T_6 + T_7 - T_8)$$

$$(2.2.7)$$

where

$$T_1 = (x_j - x_i) \ln\left[\frac{(c + A_3)(d + B_3)(d + C_2)(c + D_2)}{(d + C_3)(c + D_3)(c + A_2)(d + B_2)}\right]$$

$$T_2 = \left(\frac{\Delta x_j}{2}\right) \ln\left[\frac{(d + B_3)(d + C_3)(c + D_2)(c + A_2)}{(c + D_3)(c + A_3)(d + B_2)(d + C_2)}\right]$$

$$T_3 = (y_j - y_i) \ln\left[\frac{(a + A_3)(b + B_3)(b + D_2)(a + C_2)}{(b + D_3)(a + C_3)(a + A_2)(b + B_2)}\right]$$

$$T_4 = \left(\frac{\Delta y_j}{2}\right) \ln\left[\frac{(b + B_3)(b + D_3)(a + C_2)(a + A_2)}{(a + C_3)(a + A_3)(b + B_2)(b + D_2)}\right]$$

$$T_5 = 2(n - 1)T\left[\arctan\left(\frac{ac}{2(n - 1)TA_3}\right) + \arctan\left(\frac{bd}{2(n - 1)TB_3}\right)\right]$$

$$T_6 = 2(n - 1)T\left[\arctan\left(\frac{ad}{2(n - 1)TC_3}\right) + \arctan\left(\frac{bc}{2(n - 1)TD_3}\right)\right]$$

$$T_7 = 2nT\left[\arctan\left(\frac{ac}{2nTA_2}\right) + \arctan\left(\frac{bd}{2nTB_2}\right)\right]$$

$$T_8 = 2nT\left[\arctan\left(\frac{ad}{2nTC_2}\right) + \arctan\left(\frac{bc}{2nTD_2}\right)\right]$$

and T is the substrate thickness.

2.2.2   Green's Function Matrix for Interconnections Embedded in the Substrate

If all the interconnections are embedded in the substrate, then their heights above the bottom ground plane denoted by H will be less than the thickness of the substrate denoted by T. First, as in the previous subsection, the Green's function for a line charge ρ in two dimensions will be found by using

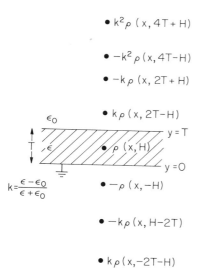

- $k^2\rho\ (x, 4T + H)$

- $-k^2\rho\ (x, 4T-H)$
- $-k\rho\ (x, 2T + H)$

- $k\rho\ (x, 2T-H)$

ϵ_0

$y = T$

$\rho\ (x, H)$

$y = 0$

$k = \dfrac{\epsilon - \epsilon_0}{\epsilon + \epsilon_0}$

- $-\rho\ (x, -H)$

- $-k\rho\ (x, H-2T)$

- $k\rho\ (x, -2T-H)$

- $k^2\rho\ (x, H-4T)$

FIGURE 2.2.3   Magnitudes and locations of the images formed when a line charge ρ is embedded in a medium of dielectric constant ε with a conducting ground plane under it and surrounded by another medium of dielectric constant ε_0.

the method of images and then, the expression for the Green's function will be extended to the three-dimensional case. The results can be checked for accuracy by reducing them to the case when the interconnections are printed on the substrate by setting $H = T$ and ensuring that the resulting expression for the Green's function agrees with Equation 2.2.7.

Let us first find the magnitudes and locations of the image charges when a real line charge ρ is placed at a height H ($H < T$) above the bottom ground plane. The real charge will first reflect up across the dielectric interface and give rise to an image charge equal to $k\rho$. This first image and the real charge will then both reflect across the ground plane, changing in sign. These two new images will then reflect back across the dielectric interface and so on. The process will continue to ∞ giving rise to the images shown in Figure 2.2.3. To find the potential at a point (x_i, y_i) inside the dielectric, we need to find the sum of all the potentials at this point due to the real charge and all its image charges; that is,

$$V(x_i, y_i) = \sum_{n=1}^{\infty} V_n = \left(-\frac{\rho}{4\pi\varepsilon_0}\right)\ln\left(r_n^2\right)$$

where

$$\varepsilon = \varepsilon_0\varepsilon_r$$

It follows from Figure 2.2.3 that, for $y_i \leq T$ and $y_j \leq T$,

$$
\begin{aligned}
V(x_i, y_i) = \frac{\rho}{4\pi\varepsilon} \Big(&-\ln\left[(x_i - x_j)^2 + (y_i - H)^2\right] \\
&+ k \ln\left[(x_i - x_j)^2 + (y_i - H - 2T)^2\right] \\
&- k^2 \ln\left[(x_i - x_j)^2 + (y_i - H - 4T)^2\right] + \cdots \\
&- k \ln\left[(x_i - x_j)^2 + (y_i + H - 2T)^2\right] \\
&+ k^2 \ln\left[(x_i - x_j)^2 + (y_i - H - 4T)^2\right] \\
&- k^3 \ln\left[(x_i - x_j)^2 + (y_i + H - 6T)^2\right] + \cdots \\
&+ \ln\left[(x_i - x_j)^2 + (y_i + H)^2\right] \\
&- k \ln\left[(x_i - x_j)^2 + (y_i + H + 2T)^2\right] \\
&+ k^2 \ln\left[(x_i - x_j)^2 + (y_i + H - 4T)^2\right] + \cdots \\
&+ k \ln\left[(x_i - x_j)^2 + (y_i - H + 2T)^2\right] \\
&- k^2 \ln\left[(x_i - x_j)^2 + (y_i - H + 4T)^2\right] \\
&+ k^3 \ln\left[(x_i - x_j)^2 + (y_i - H + 6T)^2\right] + \cdots \Big) \quad (2.2.8)
\end{aligned}
$$

The Green's function $G(x_i, y_i; x_j, y_j)$ for the real charge at (x_j, y_j) and the field point at (x_i, y_i) can now be determined from Equation 2.2.8 by setting $\rho = 1$. Therefore,

$$
\begin{aligned}
G(x_i, &y_i; x_j, y_j) \\
= \frac{1}{4\pi\varepsilon} \sum_{n=1}^{\infty} \Big\{ &-(-1)^{n+1} k^{n-1} \ln\left[(x_i - x_j)^2 + (y_i - H - 2(n-1)T)^2\right] \\
&+ (-1)^n k^n \ln\left[(x_i - x_j)^2 + (y_i + H - 2nT)^2\right] \\
&- (-1)^n k^n \ln\left[(x_i - x_j)^2 + (y_i - H + 2nT)^2\right] \\
&- (-1)^{n+1} k^{n-1} \\
&\times \ln\left[(x_i - x_j)^2 + (y_i + H + 2(n-1)T)^2\right] \Big\} \quad (2.2.9)
\end{aligned}
$$

If all the interconnections are in the same plane on the substrate, then $y_i = y_j = H$. Equation 2.2.9 then becomes

$$G(x_i, H; x_j, H)$$

$$= \frac{1}{4\pi\varepsilon} \sum_{n=1}^{\infty} \left\{ (-1)^n k^n \ln\left[(x_i - x_j)^2 + (2H - 2nT)^2 \right] \right.$$

$$- (-1)^n k^n \ln\left[(x_i - x_j)^2 + (2nT)^2 \right]$$

$$+ (-1)^{n+1} k^{n-1} \ln\left[(x_i - x_j)^2 + \{2H + 2(n-1)T\}^2 \right]$$

$$\left. - (-1)^{n+1} k^{n-1} \ln\left[(x_i - x_j)^2 + \{2(n-1)T\}^2 \right] \right\}$$

We can rewrite this expression for the two-dimensional Green's function element as

$$G(x_i, H; x_j, H) = \sum_{n=1}^{\infty} \left[A_n(g_{ijn1} - g_{ijn2}) + B_n(g_{ijn3} - g_{ijn4}) \right] \quad (2.2.10)$$

where

$$A_n = (-1)^n k^n$$

and

$$B_n = (-1)^{n+1} k^{n-1}$$

g_{ijn1} is the free-space Green's function for the nth image at a distance of $y_j - y_i = 2H - 2nT$ from the field point, g_{ijn2} is the free-space Green's function for the nth image at a distance of $y_j - y_i = 2nT$ from the field point, g_{ijn3} is the free-space Green's function for the nth image at a distance of $y_j - y_i = 2H + 2(n-1)T$ from the field point, and g_{ijn4} is the free-space Green's function for the nth image at a distance of $y_j - y_i = 2(n-1)T$ from the field point.

Now, extension of Equation 2.2.10 to three dimensions is accomplished by replacing the term g_{ijn1} by the free-space Green's function for the nth image at a distance of $h = z_j - z_i = 2H - 2nT$ from the field point, by replacing the term g_{ijn2} by the free-space Green's function for the nth image at a distance of $h = z_j - z_i = 2nT$ from the field point, by replacing the term g_{ijn3} by the free-space Green's function for the nth image at a distance of $h = z_j - z_i = 2H - 2(n-1)T$ from the field point, and by replacing the term g_{ijn4} by the free-space Green's function for the nth image at a distance of $h = z_j - z_i = -2(n-1)T$ from the field point. The new expressions for g_{ijn1}, g_{ijn2}, g_{ijn3}, and g_{ijn4} will become

$$
\begin{aligned}
g_{ijn1} = \frac{1}{4\pi\varepsilon} \Bigg\{ & (x_j - x_i) \ln\left[\frac{(c + A_4)(d + B_4)}{(d + C_4)(c + D_4)} \right] \\
& + \left(\frac{\Delta x_j}{2}\right) \ln\left[\frac{(d + B_4)(d + C_4)}{(c + D_4)(c + A_4)} \right] \\
& + (y_j - y_i) \ln\left[\frac{(a + A_4)(b + B_4)}{(b + D_4)(a + C_4)} \right] \\
& + \left(\frac{\Delta y_j}{2}\right) \ln\left[\frac{(b + B_4)(b + D_4)}{(a + C_4)(a + A_4)} \right] \\
& - (2H - 2nT)\left[\arctan\left(\frac{ac}{(2H - 2nT)A_4} \right) \right. \\
& \qquad\qquad\qquad\quad \left. + \arctan\left(\frac{bd}{(2H - 2nT)B_4} \right) \right] \\
& + (2H - 2nT)\left[\arctan\left(\frac{ad}{(2H - 2nT)C_4} \right) \right. \\
& \qquad\qquad\qquad\quad \left. \left. + \arctan\left(\frac{bc}{(2H - 2nT)D_4} \right) \right] \right\}
\end{aligned}
\qquad (2.2.11)
$$

where

$$
A_4 = \sqrt{a^2 + c^2 + (2H - 2nT)^2}
$$

$$
B_4 = \sqrt{b^2 + d^2 + (2H - 2nT)^2}
$$

$$
C_4 = \sqrt{a^2 + d^2 + (2H - 2nT)^2}
$$

$$
D_4 = \sqrt{b^2 + c^2 + (2H - 2nT)^2}
$$

$$g_{ijn2} = \frac{1}{4\pi\varepsilon} \left\{ (x_j - x_i) \ln\left[\frac{(c + A_5)(d + B_5)}{(d + C_5)(c + D_5)}\right] \right.$$

$$+ \left(\frac{\Delta x_j}{2}\right) \ln\left[\frac{(d + B_5)(d + C_5)}{(c + D_5)(c + A_5)}\right]$$

$$+ (y_j - y_i) \ln\left[\frac{(a + A_5)(b + B_5)}{(b + D_5)(a + C_5)}\right]$$

$$+ \left(\frac{\Delta y_j}{2}\right) \ln\left[\frac{(b + B_5)(b + D_5)}{(a + C_5)(a + A_5)}\right]$$

$$- 2nT\left[\arctan\left(\frac{ac}{2nTA_5}\right) + \arctan\left(\frac{bd}{2nTB_5}\right)\right]$$

$$\left. + 2nT\left[\arctan\left(\frac{ad}{2nTC_5}\right) + \arctan\left(\frac{bc}{2nTD_5}\right)\right]\right\} \quad (2.2.12)$$

where

$$A_5 = \sqrt{a^2 + c^2 + (2nT)^2}$$

$$B_5 = \sqrt{b^2 + d^2 + (2nT)^2}$$

$$C_5 = \sqrt{a^2 + d^2 + (2nT)^2}$$

$$D_5 = \sqrt{b^2 + c^2 + (2nT)^2}$$

$$g_{ijn3} = \frac{1}{4\pi\varepsilon} \left\{ (x_j - x_i) \ln\left[\frac{(c + A_6)(d + B_6)}{(d + C_6)(c + D_6)}\right] \right.$$

$$+ \left(\frac{\Delta x_j}{2}\right) \ln\left[\frac{(d + B_6)(d + C_6)}{(c + D_6)(c + A_6)}\right]$$

$$+ (y_j - y_i) \ln\left[\frac{(a + A_6)(b + B_6)}{(b + D_6)(a + C_6)}\right]$$

$$+ \left(\frac{\Delta y_j}{2}\right) \ln\left[\frac{(b + B_6)(b + D_6)}{(a + C_6)(a + A_6)}\right]$$

$$- (2H + 2(n - 1)T)\left[\arctan\left(\frac{ac}{(2H + 2(n - 1)T)A_6}\right)\right.$$

$$\left. + \arctan\left(\frac{bd}{(2H + 2(n - 1)T)B_6}\right)\right]$$

$$+ (2H + 2(n-1)T)$$

$$\times \left[\arctan\left(\frac{ad}{(2H + 2(n-1)T)C_6} \right) \right.$$

$$\left. + \arctan\left(\frac{bc}{(2H + 2(n-1)T)D_6} \right) \right] \Bigg\}$$

$$(2.2.13)$$

where

$$A_6 = \sqrt{a^2 + c^2 + (2H + 2(n-1)T)^2}$$

$$B_6 = \sqrt{b^2 + d^2 + (2H + 2(n-1)T)^2}$$

$$C_6 = \sqrt{a^2 + d^2 + (2H + 2(n-1)T)^2}$$

$$D_6 = \sqrt{b^2 + c^2 + (2H + 2(n-1)T)^2}$$

and

$$g_{ijn4} = \frac{1}{4\pi\varepsilon} \left\{ (x_j - x_i) \ln\left[\frac{(c + A_7)(d + B_7)}{(d + C_7)(c + D_7)} \right] \right.$$

$$+ \left(\frac{\Delta x_j}{2} \right) \ln\left[\frac{(d + B_7)(d + C_7)}{(c + D_7)(c + A_7)} \right]$$

$$+ (y_j - y_i) \ln\left[\frac{(a + A_7)(b + B_7)}{(b + D_7)(a + C_7)} \right]$$

$$+ \left(\frac{\Delta y_j}{2} \right) \ln\left[\frac{(b + B_7)(b + D_7)}{(a + C_7)(a + A_7)} \right]$$

$$- 2(n-1)T \left[\arctan\left(\frac{ac}{2(n-1)TA_7} \right) \right.$$

$$\left. + \arctan\left(\frac{bd}{2(n-1)TB_7} \right) \right]$$

$$+ 2(n-1)T \left[\arctan\left(\frac{ad}{2(n-1)TC_7} \right) \right.$$

$$\left. + \arctan\left(\frac{bc}{2(n-1)TD_7} \right) \right] \Bigg\} \quad (2.2.14)$$

where

$$A_7 = \sqrt{a^2 + c^2 + (2(n-1)T)^2}$$

$$B_7 = \sqrt{b^2 + d^2 + (2(n-1)T)^2}$$

$$C_7 = \sqrt{a^2 + d^2 + (2(n-1)T)^2}$$

$$D_7 = \sqrt{b^2 + c^2 + (2(n-1)T)^2}$$

Substituting for g_{ijn1}, g_{ijn2}, g_{ijn3}, and g_{ijn4} from Equations 2.2.11 to 2.2.14 into Equation 2.2.10 and after simplifying, we get for the Green's function element in three dimensions

$$G_{ij} = G(x_i, H; x_j, H)$$

$$= \frac{1}{4\pi\varepsilon} \sum_{n=1}^{\infty} \left([-1]^{n-1} k^n [T_9 + T_{10} + T_{11} + T_{12} - T_{13} + T_{14} + T_{15} - T_{16}] \right.$$

$$+ [-1]^n k^{n-1} [T_{17} + T_{18} + T_{19} + T_{20}$$

$$\left. - T_{21} + T_{22} + T_{23} - T_{24}] \right)$$

where

$$T_9 = (x_j - x_i) \ln\left[\frac{(c + A_4)(d + B_4)(d + C_5)(c + D_5)}{(d + C_4)(c + D_4)(c + A_5)(d + B_5)} \right]$$

$$T_{10} = \left(\frac{\Delta x_j}{2} \right) \ln\left[\frac{(d + B_4)(d + C_4)(c + D_5)(c + A_5)}{(c + D_4)(c + A_4)(d + B_5)(d + C_5)} \right]$$

$$T_{11} = (y_j - y_i) \ln\left[\frac{(a + A_4)(b + B_4)(b + D_5)(a + C_5)}{(b + D_4)(a + C_4)(a + A_5)(b + B_5)} \right]$$

$$T_{12} = \left(\frac{\Delta y_j}{2} \right) \ln\left[\frac{(b + B_4)(b + D_4)(a + C_5)(a + A_5)}{(a + C_4)(a + A_4)(b + B_5)(b + D_5)} \right]$$

$$T_{13} = (2H - 2nT)\left[\arctan\left(\frac{ac}{(2H - 2nT)A_4} \right) + \arctan\left(\frac{bd}{(2H - 2nT)B_4} \right) \right]$$

$$T_{14} = (2H - 2nT)\left[\arctan\left(\frac{ad}{(2H - 2nT)C_4} \right) + \arctan\left(\frac{bc}{(2H - 2nT)D_4} \right) \right]$$

$$T_{15} = 2nT\left[\arctan\left(\frac{ac}{2nTA_5} \right) + \arctan\left(\frac{bd}{2nTB_5} \right) \right]$$

$$T_{16} = 2nT \left[\arctan\left(\frac{ad}{2nTC_5} \right) + \arctan\left(\frac{bc}{2nTD_5} \right) \right]$$

$$T_{17} = (x_j - x_i) \ln \left[\frac{(c + A_6)(d + B_6)(d + C_7)(c + D_7)}{(d + C_6)(c + D_6)(c + A_7)(d + B_7)} \right]$$

$$T_{18} = \left(\frac{\Delta x_j}{2} \right) \ln \left[\frac{(d + B_6)(d + C_6)(c + D_7)(c + A_7)}{(c + D_6)(c + A_6)(d + B_7)(d + C_7)} \right]$$

$$T_{19} = (y_j - y_i) \ln \left[\frac{(a + A_6)(b + B_6)(b + D_7)(a + C_7)}{(b + D_6)(a + C_6)(a + A_7)(b + B_7)} \right]$$

$$T_{20} = \left(\frac{\Delta y_j}{2} \right) \ln \left[\frac{(b + B_6)(b + D_6)(a + C_7)(a + A_7)}{(a + C_6)(a + A_6)(b + B_7)(b + D_7)} \right]$$

$$T_{21} = (2H + 2(n - 1)T) \left[\arctan\left(\frac{ac}{(2H + 2(n - 1)T)A_6} \right) \right.$$
$$\left. + \arctan\left(\frac{bd}{(2H + 2(n - 1)T)B_6} \right) \right]$$

$$T_{22} = (2H + 2(n - 1)T) \left[\arctan\left(\frac{ad}{(2H + 2(n - 1)T)C_6} \right) \right.$$
$$\left. + \arctan\left(\frac{bc}{(2H + 2(n - 1)T)D_6} \right) \right]$$

$$T_{23} = 2(n - 1)T \left[\arctan\left(\frac{ac}{2(n - 1)TA_7} \right) \right.$$
$$\left. + \arctan\left(\frac{bd}{2(n - 1)TB_7} \right) \right]$$

$$T_{24} = 2(n - 1)T \left[\arctan\left(\frac{ad}{2(n - 1)TC_7} \right) \right.$$
$$\left. + \arctan\left(\frac{bc}{2(n - 1)TD_7} \right) \right]$$

2.2.3 Application of the Method of Moments

The following algorithm is suitable for a system of four interconnection lines and can be easily modified for a different number of lines. For a system of four conducting lines, the known potential V_i on the ith ($i = 1, 2, 3, 4$) conductor is related to the unknown surface charge density σ_j on each conductor by the following system of integral equations:

$$V_i = \sum_{j=1}^{4} \int_{S_j} G(x_i, y_i; x_j, y_j; z) \sigma_j(x_j, y_j) \, dx_j \, dy_j$$

where G is the Green's function and S_j is the area of the jth conductor. If the conductors are divided into a total of N subsections with areas ds_j, then the potential V_i of the ith subsection is given by

$$V_i = \sum_{j=1}^{4} \sigma_j G_{ij}$$

where σ_j is now the unknown surface charge density of the jth subsection and G_{ij} is the element of the Green's function pertinent to the problem. If the subsections are made small enough so that the charge density can be assumed constant over the area of each subsection, then the method of moments can be used to convert this equation into its matrix form

$$[V] = [\sigma_j][G]$$

Then, by matrix inversion, the unknown σ_j can be determined from

$$[\sigma_j] = [G]^{-1}[V]$$

where $[\sigma_j]$ and $[V]$ are two N-dimensional column matrices and $[G]$ is the N-dimensional square matrix. Then the total charge on the jth conductor is given by

$$Q_j = \sum_{j=1}^{N_j} \sigma_j \, ds_j \qquad j = 1, 2, 3, 4$$

where N_j is the number of subsections on the jth conductor.

2.2.4   Even- and Odd-Mode Capacitances

For the system of four interconnection lines, an even–odd-mode excitation can first be used to calculate the even- and odd-mode capacitances of each line separately. For even-mode excitation, each line is assumed to be at $+1$-V potential with respect to the conducting ground plane. For odd-mode excitation, one line is kept at $+1$ V, whereas the other three lines are kept at -1-V potential. This means that when finding the odd-mode charge on the first line, the potential on the first line is kept at $+1$ V whereas the potentials on each of the second, third, and fourth lines are kept at -1 V, and so on.

First, the four lines are divided into N_1, N_2, N_3, and N_4 subsections. Thus, the total number of subsections becomes

$$N = N_1 + N_2 + N_3 + N_4$$

Then the voltage excitation for the even mode of each interconnection line is an N-row unit column matrix, that is,

$$[V]_{even} = \begin{bmatrix} 1 \\ \cdots \\ \cdots \\ 1 \\ 1 \\ \cdots \\ \cdots \\ 1 \\ 1 \\ \cdots \\ \cdots \\ 1 \\ 1 \\ \cdots \\ \cdots \\ 1 \end{bmatrix}$$

whereas the odd-mode excitation for the first line is represented by the matrix

$$[V] = _{odd,\,1} = \begin{bmatrix} 1 \\ \cdots \\ \cdots \\ 1 \\ -1 \\ \cdots \\ \cdots \\ -1 \\ -1 \\ \cdots \\ \cdots \\ -1 \\ -1 \\ \cdots \\ \cdots \\ -1 \end{bmatrix}$$

and similarly for $[V]_{odd,\,2}$, $[V]_{odd,\,3}$, and $[V]_{odd,\,4}$.

If the inverse of the Green's function matrix is denoted by $[R]$, then we can define the following 16 quantities by summing the ijth elements in the 16 submatrices of the matrix $[R]$:

$$R_1 = \sum_{i=1}^{N_1} \sum_{j=1}^{N_1} R_{ij}$$

$$R_2 = \sum_{i=1}^{N_1} \sum_{j=N_1+1}^{N_1+N_2} R_{ij}$$

$$R_3 = \sum_{i=1}^{N_1} \sum_{j=N_1+N_2+1}^{N_1+N_2+N_3} R_{ij}$$

$$R_4 = \sum_{i=1}^{N_1} \sum_{j=N_1+N_2+N_3+1}^{N} R_{ij}$$

$$R_5 = \sum_{i=N_1+1}^{N_1+N_2} \sum_{j=1}^{N_1} R_{ij}$$

$$R_6 = \sum_{i=N_1+1}^{N_1+N_2} \sum_{j=N_1+1}^{N_1+N_2} R_{ij}$$

$$R_7 = \sum_{i=N_1+1}^{N_1+N_2} \sum_{j=N_1+N_2+1}^{N_1+N_2+N_3} R_{ij}$$

$$R_8 = \sum_{i=N_1+1}^{N_1+N_2} \sum_{j=N_1+N_2+N_3+1}^{N} R_{ij}$$

$$R_9 = \sum_{i=N_1+N_2+1}^{N_1+N_2+N_3} \sum_{j=1}^{N_1} R_{ij}$$

$$R_{10} = \sum_{i=N_1+N_2+1}^{N_1+N_2+N_3} \sum_{j=N_1+1}^{N_1+N_2} R_{ij}$$

$$R_{11} = \sum_{i=N_1+N_2+1}^{N_1+N_2+N_3} \sum_{j=N_1+N_2+1}^{N_1+N_2+N_3} R_{ij}$$

$$R_{12} = \sum_{i=N_1+N_2+1}^{N_1+N_2+N_3} \sum_{j=N_1+N_2+N_3+1}^{N} R_{ij}$$

$$R_{13} = \sum_{i=N-N_4+1}^{N} \sum_{j=1}^{N_1} R_{ij}$$

$$R_{14} = \sum_{i=N-N_4+1}^{N} \sum_{j=N_1+1}^{N_1+N_2} R_{ij}$$

$$R_{15} = \sum_{i=N-N_4+1}^{N} \sum_{j=N_1+N_2+1}^{N_1+N_2+N_3} R_{ij}$$

$$R_{16} = \sum_{i=N-N_4+1}^{N} \sum_{j=N-N_4+1}^{N} R_{ij}$$

The even- and odd-mode capacitances for each of the four lines are determined from the relationships

$$C_j^{(e,o)} = \frac{Q_j^{(e,o)}}{V_j^{(e,o)}} \qquad j = 1,2,3,4$$

Now, because

$$[\sigma] = [G]^{-1}[V]$$

the even- and odd-mode capacitances for the four lines can be expressed as

$$C_1^e = (R_1 + R_2 + R_3 + R_4)\,\Delta s_1$$

$$C_2^e = (R_5 + R_6 + R_7 + R_8)\,\Delta s_2$$

$$C_3^e = (R_9 + R_{10} + R_{11} + R_{12})\,\Delta s_3$$

$$C_4^e = (R_{13} + R_{14} + R_{15} + R_{16})\,\Delta s_4$$

$$C_1^o = (R_1 - R_2 - R_3 - R_4)\,\Delta s_1$$

$$C_2^o = (R_6 - R_5 - R_7 - R_8)\,\Delta s_2$$

$$C_3^o = (R_{11} - R_9 - R_{10} - R_{12})\,\Delta s_3$$

$$C_4^o = (R_{16} - R_{13} - R_{14} - R_{15})\,\Delta s_4$$

2.2.5   Ground and Coupling Capacitances

Finally, the ground and coupling interconnection capacitances can be obtained by solving the following set of equations:

$$
\begin{aligned}
C_1^e &= C_{11} \\
C_2^e &= C_{22} \\
C_3^e &= C_{33} \\
C_4^e &= C_{44} \\
C_1^o &= C_{11} + 2C_{12} + 2C_{13} + 2C_{14} \\
C_2^o &= C_{22} + 2C_{12} + 2C_{23} + 2C_{24} \\
C_3^o &= C_{33} + 2C_{13} + 2C_{23} + 2C_{34} \\
C_4^o &= C_{44} + 2C_{14} + 2C_{24} + 2C_{34}
\end{aligned}
\tag{2.2.15}
$$

Because the number of unknowns is greater than the number of equations, Equations 2.2.15 cannot be solved exactly. In this case, one can use the method of unconstrained multivariable optimization to solve the equations approximately.

2.2.6   The Program IPCSGV

The source code of the program IPCSGV, developed to determine the interconnection parasitic capacitances on GaAs-based VLSI circuits, is presented in Appendix 2.1. It is based on the various calculation steps presented previously and is written in FORTRAN. The program can be modified to include more interconnections, although the relative precision of the results will be affected. One can utilize the method of unconstrained multivariable optimization to solve Equations 2.2.15 for an interconnection configuration consisting of four interconnections, three of the top plane and one embedded in the substrate shown in Figure 2.2.4.

2.2.7   Parametric Dependence of Interconnection Capacitances

The program IPCSGV can be used to study the dependences of the ground and coupling interconnection capacitances on the various interconnection parameters shown in Figure 2.2.4. In the following results one of the parameters is varied in a specific range while the others are kept fixed at their selected typical values. These typical values are chosen to be the following: interconnection lengths, 100 μm each; widths, 1 μm each; separations, 2 μm; interlevel distance, 2 μm; and thickness of the GaAs substrate, 200 μm.

The dependences of the ground and coupling capacitances on the lengths of the bilevel interconnections are shown in Figures 2.2.5 and 2.2.6, respec-

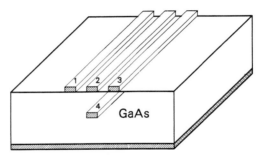

FIGURE 2.2.4 Schematic diagram of the four interconnections in the bilevel configuration used in program IPCSGV.

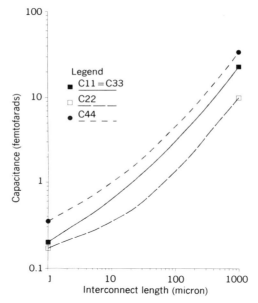

FIGURE 2.2.5 Dependence of the ground capacitances for the four bilevel interconnections on the interconnection lengths.

tively. Figure 2.2.5 shows that C_{22} is always less than C_{11} and C_{33}. This is due to larger shielding of the electric field lines that constitute the capacitance C_{22} by those that constitute the capacitances C_{12} and C_{23}. This figure also shows that, for interconnection lengths above about 10 μm, the ground capacitances vary almost linearly with length. Departure from linearity for smaller lengths is due to a more dominant role played by the fringing fields

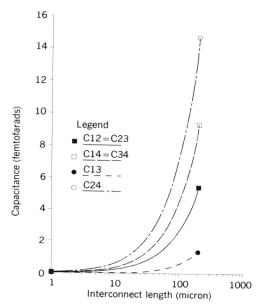

FIGURE 2.2.6   Dependence of the coupling capacitances for the four bilevel interconnections on the interconnection lengths.

for smaller interconnection dimensions. The dependences of the ground and coupling capacitances on the widths of the interconnection lines are shown in Figures 2.2.7 and 2.2.8, respectively. As functions of the interconnection separation, the ground and coupling capacitances are shown in Figures 2.2.9 and 2.2.10, respectively. The dependences of the ground and coupling capacitances on the interlevel separation of the interconnection lines are shown in Figures 2.2.11 and 2.2.12, respectively. As functions of the thickness of the GaAs substrate, the ground and coupling capacitances are shown in Figures 2.2.13 and 2.2.14, respectively. Figures 2.2.15 and 2.2.16 show the effects of changing the relative angle of the fourth line in the bilevel configuration on the various ground and coupling capacitances. Figure 2.2.16 shows that C_{14}, C_{24}, and C_{34} decrease sharply, whereas C_{12}, C_{23}, and C_{13} increase when the angle is increased.

2.3   GREEN'S FUNCTION METHOD: FOURIER INTEGRAL APPROACH

The parasitic capacitances for a system of multilevel conducting interconnections can also be determined by the Green's function method obtained by the

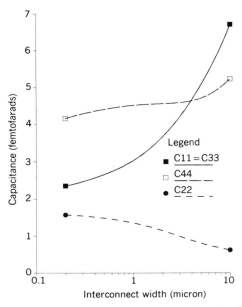

FIGURE 2.2.7 Dependence of the ground capacitances for the four bilevel interconnections on the interconnection widths.

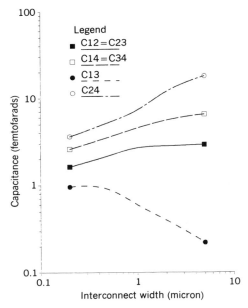

FIGURE 2.2.8 Dependence of the coupling capacitances for the four bilevel interconnections on the interconnection widths.

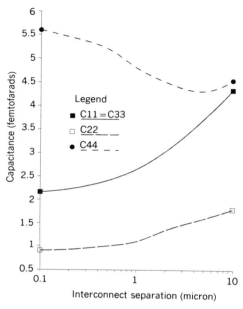

FIGURE 2.2.9   Dependence of the ground capacitances for the four bilevel interconnections on the interconnection separations.

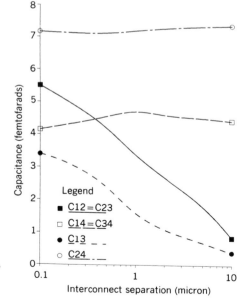

FIGURE 2.2.10   Dependence of the coupling capacitances for the four bilevel interconnections on the interconnection separations.

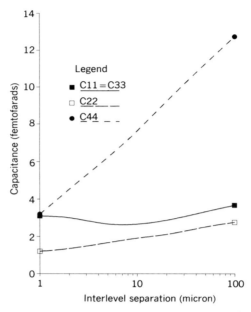

FIGURE 2.2.11 Dependence of the ground capacitances for the four bilevel interconnections on the interlevel separation.

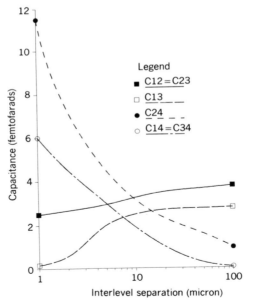

FIGURE 2.2.12 Dependence of the coupling capacitances for the four bilevel interconnections on the interlevel separation.

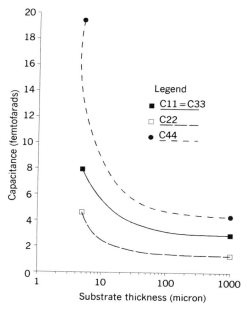

FIGURE 2.2.13 Dependence of the ground capacitances for the four bilevel inter-connections on the substrate thickness.

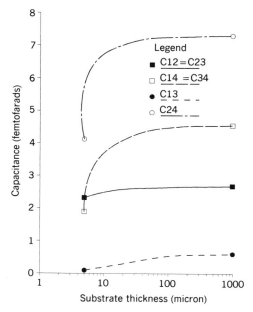

FIGURE 2.2.14 Dependence of the coupling capacitances for the four bilevel inter-connections on the substrate thickness.

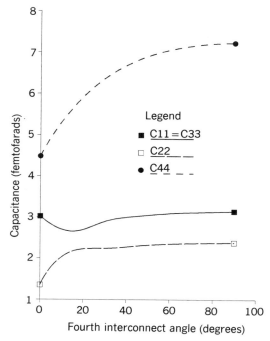

FIGURE 2.2.15   Dependence of the ground capacitances for the four bilevel interconnections on the relative angle of the fourth interconnection.

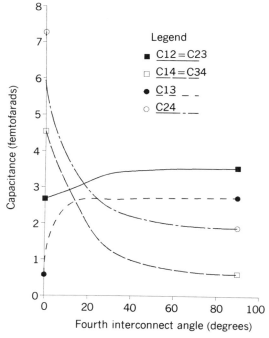

FIGURE 2.2.16   Dependence of the coupling capacitances for the four bilevel interconnections on the relative angle of the fourth interconnection.

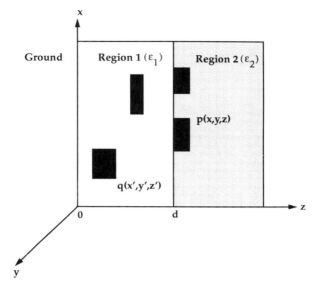

FIGURE 2.3.1 Representation of three multilevel interconnections in the Si–SiO$_2$ composite [2.24]. (© 1987 IEEE)

Fourier integral approach and by using a piecewise linear approximation for the charge density distributions [2.24] on the conducting interconnections. This method reduces the order of integration and the number of equations needed, thereby reducing the computation time and the memory required. In this section the Green's function for the Si–SiO$_2$ system is derived using the Fourier integral approach, and the integral equations are solved for a multilevel interconnection structure using a piecewise linear approximation for the charge density distributions [2.24].

2.3.1 Green's Function for Multilevel Interconnections

A representation of three multilevel conducting interconnections in the Si–SiO$_2$ composite is shown in Figure 2.3.1. The solution of the Laplace equation governing the potentials on the conductors can be written as

$$\Phi(p) = \int_{\text{all charge}} G(p,q)\sigma(q)\,dq \qquad (2.3.1)$$

where $\sigma(q)$ is the charge density at point $q(x', y', z')$ in Figure 2.3.1 and $G(p,q)$ is the appropriate Green's function describing the potential induced at point $p(x, y, z)$ by a unit point charge at point $q(x', y', z')$. For a system of N conductors, the potential on the jth conductor is given by

$$\Phi_j(p) = \sum_{i=1}^{N} \int_{S_i} G(p,q)\sigma_i(q)\,ds_i(q) \qquad j = 1, 2, \ldots, N \quad (2.3.2)$$

where $\sigma_i(q)$ denotes the charge density on the surface S_i of the ith conductor.

The Green's function $G(p, q)$ can be expressed as a Fourier integral [2.30] as

$$G(p,q) = \frac{1}{4\pi\varepsilon_1} \int_0^\infty J_0(m\rho)e^{-m|z_1|}\,dm \qquad (2.3.3)$$

where ε_1 is the dielectric constant of SiO_2, J_0 is the Bessel function of the first kind and zero order, m is the variable of integration, $z_1 = z - z'$, and

$$\rho = \sqrt{(x - x')^2 + (y - y')^2}$$

The Green's function in region 1 $(0 < z \le d)$ shown in Figure 2.3.1 can now be written as

$$G_1(p,q) = \frac{1}{4\pi\varepsilon_1} \int_0^\infty J_0(m\rho)\left[e^{-m|z_1|} + \Theta_1(m)e^{mz_1} + \Theta_2(m)e^{-mz_1}\right]dm$$

$$(2.3.4)$$

and the Green's function in region 2 $(d \le z < \infty)$ is given by

$$G_2(p,q) = \frac{1}{4\pi\varepsilon_1} \int_0^\infty J_0(m\rho)\left[\Psi_1(m)e^{-mz_1} + \Psi_2(m)e^{mz_1}\right]dm \quad (2.3.5)$$

where the unknown functions Θ_1, Θ_2, Ψ_1, and Ψ_2 are determined by using the following boundary conditions:

$$
\begin{aligned}
G_1(p,q) &= G_2(p,q) & \text{at } z = d \\
\varepsilon_1 \frac{\partial}{\partial z_1}(G_1) &= \varepsilon_2 \frac{\partial G_2}{\partial z_1} & \text{at } z = d \\
G_1(p,q) &= 0 & \text{at } z = 0 \\
G_2(p,q) &= 0 & \text{at } z = \infty
\end{aligned}
\qquad (2.3.6)
$$

to be given by

$$\begin{bmatrix} \Theta_1 \\ \Theta_2 \\ \Psi_1 \\ \Psi_2 \end{bmatrix} = \begin{bmatrix} \beta K(\alpha e^{2mz'} - 1) \\ (\beta K - 1)e^{-2mz'} - \beta K\alpha \\ \beta\gamma(\alpha - e^{-2mz'}) \\ 0 \end{bmatrix} \qquad (2.3.7)$$

with

$$K = \frac{\varepsilon_1 - \varepsilon_2}{\varepsilon_1 + \varepsilon_2}$$

$$\alpha = e^{-m[(|d-z'|)-(d-z')]}$$

$$\beta = \frac{1}{K + e^{2md}}$$

$$\gamma = (1 + K)e^{2md}$$

Substituting Equation 2.3.7 into Equations 2.3.4 and 2.3.5 and solving the resulting integrals, we can find that the Green's function for the case when the points p and q are both in region 1 is given by

$$G_{11}(p,q) = \left(\frac{1}{4\pi\varepsilon_1}\right)\left(\frac{1}{\sqrt{z_1^2 + \rho^2}} - \frac{1}{\sqrt{(2z' + z_1)^2 + \rho^2}} + \sum_{n=0}^{\infty}(-1)^n K^{n+1}\right.$$

$$\times \left[\frac{1}{\sqrt{[2(n+1)d - (2z' + z_1)]^2 + \rho^2}}\right.$$

$$- \frac{1}{\sqrt{[2(n+1)d + z_1]^2 + \rho^2}}$$

$$+ \frac{1}{\sqrt{[2(n+1)d + (2z' + z_1)]^2 + \rho^2}}$$

$$\left.\left.- \frac{1}{\sqrt{[2(n+1)d - z_1]^2 + \rho^2}}\right]\right) \qquad (2.3.8)$$

the Green's functions for the cases when the points p and q are located in different regions are given by

$$
G_{12}(p,q) = \left(\frac{1}{4\pi\varepsilon_1}\right)\left(\frac{1}{\sqrt{z_1^2 + \rho^2}} - \frac{1}{\sqrt{(2z' + z_1)^2 + \rho^2}} + \sum_{n=0}^{\infty}(-1)^n K^{n+1}\right.
$$

$$
\times\left[\frac{1}{\sqrt{(2nd - z_1)^2 + \rho^2}} - \frac{1}{\sqrt{(2nd + 2z' + z_1)^2 + \rho^2}}\right.
$$

$$
\left.\left. + \frac{1}{\sqrt{[2(n+1)d + 2z' + z_1]^2 + \rho^2}} - \frac{1}{\sqrt{[2(n+1)d - z_1]^2 + \rho^2}}\right]\right)
$$

$$(2.3.9)$$

$$
G_{21}(p,q) = \left(\frac{1+K}{4\pi\varepsilon_1}\right)\left(\sum_{n=0}^{\infty}(-1)^n K^n\right.
$$

$$
\times\left[\frac{1}{\sqrt{(2nd + z_1)^2 + \rho^2}}\right.
$$

$$
\left.\left. - \frac{1}{\sqrt{(2nd + 2z' + z_1)^2 + \rho^2}}\right]\right) \qquad (2.3.10)
$$

and the Green's function for the case when the points p and q are both in region 2 is given by

$$
G_{22}(p,q) = \left(\frac{1+K}{4\pi\varepsilon_1}\right)\left(\sum_{n=0}^{\infty}(-1)^n K^n\right.
$$

$$
\times\left[\frac{1}{\sqrt{[2(n-1)d + 2z' + z_1]^2 + \rho^2}}\right.
$$

$$
\left.\left. - \frac{1}{\sqrt{(2nd + 2z' + z_1)^2 + \rho^2}}\right]\right) \qquad (2.3.11)
$$

2.3.2 Multiconductor Interconnection Capacitances

For the three-conductor problem shown in Figure 2.3.2a, the total charges Q_i $(i = 1, 2, 3)$ on the three conductors are given in terms of the ground and coupling capacitances shown in Figure 2.3.2b and in terms of the potentials

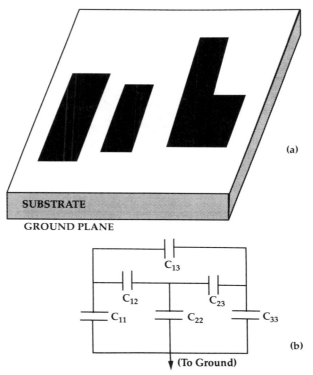

FIGURE 2.3.2 (*a*) Three finite interconnection metallization lines; (*b*) equivalent circuit showing ground and coupling capacitances [2.24]. (© 1987 IEEE)

Φ_j ($j = 1, 2, 3$) of the three conductors by the equations

$$Q_1 = C_{11}\Phi_1 + C_{12}(\Phi_1 - \Phi_2) + C_{13}(\Phi_1 - \Phi_3)$$
$$Q_2 = C_{21}(\Phi_2 - \Phi_1) + C_{22}\Phi_2 + C_{23}(\Phi_2 - \Phi_3) \qquad (2.3.12)$$
$$Q_3 = C_{31}(\Phi_3 - \Phi_1) + C_{32}(\Phi_3 - \Phi_2) + C_{33}\Phi_3$$

For a system of N conductors, Equations 2.3.12 can be written as

$$Q_i = C_{ii}\Phi_i + \sum_{j=0}^{N} C_{ij}(\Phi_i - \Phi_j) \qquad i = 1, 2, \ldots, N \qquad (2.3.13)$$

which can be rewritten in terms of the short-circuit capacitances C_{sij} as

$$Q_i = \sum_{j=1}^{N} C_{sij}\Phi_j \qquad i = 1, 2, \ldots, N \qquad (2.3.14)$$

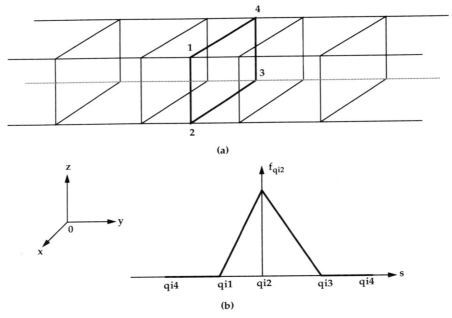

FIGURE 2.3.3 (*a*) Division of a conductor into discrete elements; (*b*) shape of the piecewise linear charge function on each element [2.24]. (© 1987 IEEE)

Comparing Equations 2.3.13 and 2.3.14, the ground and coupling interconnection capacitances can be obtained from the short-circuit capacitances by using the relationships

$$C_{ii} = \sum_{j=1}^{N} C_{sij} \qquad i = 1, 2, \ldots, N \qquad (2.3.15)$$

$$C_{ij} = -C_{sij} \qquad i \neq j \qquad (2.3.16)$$

which in turn require determination of the charge on each conductor for known values of the potentials Φ_j.

2.3.3 Piecewise Linear Charge Distribution Function

For a system of N conductors, each conductor is divided into a number of discrete elements as shown in Figure 2.3.3*a* and, on each of these elements, the charge density is approximately expressed by a linear combination of four piecewise linear functions. Thus, the charge density $\sigma_i(q)$ on the ith element is given by

$$\sigma_i(q) = \sum_{l=1}^{4} \alpha_{il} f_{il}(q) \tag{2.3.17}$$

where $f_{il}(q)$ is the lth of the four charge shape functions used to describe the charge distribution on the ith element and a_{il} are the unknown coefficients which need to be determined. If the ith conductor is divided into N_i elements, then the total charge on this conductor is given by

$$Q_i = \sum_{j=1}^{N_i} \int_{m\text{th element}} \sigma_m(q)\, ds_m(q) \tag{2.3.18}$$

where

$$m = j + \sum_{k=2}^{i} N_{k-1}$$

For a single conductor having a rectangular cross section, the charge shape function is shown in Figure 2.3.3b and is given by

$$\begin{aligned}
f_{qi2} &= A(s - a_i) \quad &&\text{for } qi2 \le s < qi3 \\
f_{qi2} &= B(s - b_i) \quad &&\text{for } qi1 < s \le qi2 \\
f_{qi2} &= 0 \quad &&\text{for } qi4 \le s \le qi1 \text{ or } qi3 \le s \le qi4
\end{aligned} \tag{2.3.19}$$

where

$$A = -\frac{2}{w_i(w_i + t_i)}$$

$$B = -\frac{2}{t_i(w_i + t_i)}$$

$$a_i = s_{ix0} + w_i$$

$$b_i = s_{iz0} + t_i$$

2.3.4   Calculation of Interconnection Capacitances

Now, in order to determine the interconnection capacitances, we need to find the $4N$ unknown coefficients $(\alpha_{11}, \ldots, \alpha_{14}, \alpha_{21}, \ldots, \alpha_{N4})$. Substituting for charge density from Equation 2.3.17 into Equation 2.3.2, we get

$$\Phi_j(p) = \sum_{i=1}^{N} \sum_{l=1}^{4} \alpha_{il} F_{il}(p) \qquad j = 1, 2, \ldots, N \tag{2.3.20}$$

where

$$F_{il}(p) = \int_{i\text{th element}} G(p,q) f_{il}(q) \, ds_i(q) \qquad (2.3.21)$$

Now, following the Ritz–Rayleigh method [2.31], both sides of Equation 2.3.20 are projected onto the space spanned by the original charge shape functions. Using the following equations for the jth element:

$$\big(\Phi_j(p), f_{il}(p)\big) = 0 \quad \text{when } i \neq j$$

and

$$\big(\Phi_j(p), f_{il}(p)\big) = \Phi_j \quad \text{when } i = j$$

we get from Equation 2.3.20:

$$\sum_{i=1}^{N} \sum_{l=1}^{4} \alpha_{il} P_{ijl} = \big(\Phi_j(p), f_{jl}(p)\big) \qquad j = 1, 2, \ldots, N \qquad (2.3.22)$$

where

$$P_{ijl} = \int_{i\text{th element}} \int_{j\text{th element}} G(p,q) f_{jl}(p) f_{il}(q) \, ds_j(p) \, ds_i(q) \quad (2.3.23)$$

Equation 2.3.22 can be written in matrix form as

$$[P][A] = [F][\Phi] \qquad (2.3.24)$$

where $A = (\alpha_{11}, \ldots, \alpha_{14}, \alpha_{21}, \ldots, \alpha_{N4})^T$ is the vector of $4N$ unknown coefficients, P is the $4N \times 4N$ matrix of the evaluated double integrals, $\Phi = (\Phi_1, \Phi_2, \ldots, \Phi_N)^T$ is the vector of N known potentials of the N conductors, and F is a $4N \times N$ incidence matrix of elements and conductors. Using any standard technique, Equation 2.3.24 can be solved for the unknown coefficients. Then the charge densities can be obtained by using Equation 2.3.17 and the charges on each conductor can be found from Equation 2.3.18. Finally, the short-circuit capacitances required for the determination of the interconnection capacitances can be obtained by using Equations 2.3.14 and 2.3.18 or can be found directly by using

$$C_s = [F]^T [P]^{-1} [F] \qquad (2.3.25)$$

2.4   NETWORK ANALOG METHOD

In this section the parasitic capacitances and inductances associated with single-, bi-, and trilevel interconnections on GaAs-based integrated circuits are determined by a network analog method [2.25]. The developed algorithm is suitable for open substrates and finite interconnection dimensions in single or multiple levels. Furthermore, the algorithm allows greater flexibility in the choice of spatial domains, thereby reducing the number of nodes and hence the computer processing time. In principle, the method allows for any number of lines in the interconnection configurations. However, the amount of computation time as well as the memory size required for solving the problem will increase with an increase in the number of interconnection lines. The method involves division of the interconnection lines and the underlying substrate into subregions, representation of each subregion by an appropriate network analog, diagonalization of the network analog system and calculation of the parasitic capacitances for the diagonalized system using a recursive scheme, and, finally, determination of the parasitic capacitances for the system of interconnection lines.

2.4.1   Representation of Subregions by Network Analogs

For a semi-insulating and nonmagnetic GaAs substrate, Maxell's equations in the quasistatic case (i.e., $\partial \mathbf{B}/\partial t = 0$) reduce to

$$\nabla \times \mathbf{E} = 0 \tag{2.4.1}$$

and

$$\nabla \times \mathbf{H} = \sigma \mathbf{E} + \varepsilon \frac{\partial \mathbf{E}}{\partial t} \tag{2.4.2}$$

Defining a potential V such that

$$\mathbf{E} = -\nabla V$$

and using the identity

$$\nabla \cdot \nabla \times \mathbf{H} = 0$$

we obtain from Equation 2.4.2:

$$\nabla^2 \left(\sigma + \varepsilon \frac{\partial}{\partial t} \right) V = 0 \tag{2.4.3}$$

In three-dimensional rectangular coordinates, the finite difference form of

Equation 2.4.3 can be written as

$$\left(\sigma + \epsilon_x \frac{\partial}{\partial t}\right) \frac{(V(x + \Delta x) - V(x - \Delta x))}{(\Delta x)^2}$$

$$+ \left(\sigma + \epsilon_y \frac{\partial}{\partial t}\right) \frac{(V(y + \Delta y) - V(y - \Delta y))}{(\Delta y)^2}$$

$$+ \left(\sigma + \epsilon_z \frac{\partial}{\partial t}\right) \frac{(V(z + \Delta z) - V(z - \Delta z))}{(\Delta z)^2} = 0 \qquad (2.4.4)$$

where ϵ_x, ϵ_y, and ϵ_z are the permittivities along the x, y, and z directions, respectively. Multiplying each term of Equation 2.4.4 by $2(\Delta x)(\Delta y)(\Delta z)$, it becomes

$$2(\Delta y)(\Delta z)\left(\sigma + \epsilon_x \frac{\partial}{\partial t}\right) \frac{(V(x + \Delta x) - V(x - \Delta x))}{\Delta x}$$

$$+ 2(\Delta x)(\Delta z)\left(\sigma + \epsilon_y \frac{\partial}{\partial t}\right) \frac{(V(y + \Delta y) - V(y - \Delta y))}{\Delta y}$$

$$+ 2(\Delta x)(\Delta y)\left(\sigma + \epsilon_z \frac{\partial}{\partial t}\right) \frac{(V(z + \Delta z) - V(z - \Delta z))}{\Delta z} = 0 \quad (2.4.5)$$

Equation 2.4.5 implies that the entire region consisting of the lower substrate (GaAs) placed on a conducting ground plane, metallic lines, and the upper open substrate can be divided into subregions, each of dimensions Δx, Δy, and Δz, consisting of circuit elements whose values depend on the conductivity σ and the permittivity ε.

2.4.2 Diagonalized System for Single-Level Interconnections

A schematic diagram of the three single-level interconnections printed on the GaAs substrate is shown in Figure 2.4.1a. In this case the total admittance matrix G for the nodes in the plane of the interconnection lines is given by

$$G = G_u + G_l \qquad (2.4.6)$$

where G_u and G_l are the admittance matrices for the upper and lower substrates, respectively. The matrix G can be determined by first obtaining the impedance matrix Z_k for the kth layer ($k = 1, 2, \ldots, L_l$) using a recurrence formula

$$Z_k = z_{k-1} + \left[G_{k-1} + [Z_{k-1}]^{-1}\right]^{-1} \qquad (2.4.7)$$

where G_k, the admittance matrix for the network analog of the kth layer, is given by

$$G_k = \begin{bmatrix} G_k^{(1)} & [G_k^{(2)}]^T \\ G_k^{(2)} & G_k^{(1)} \end{bmatrix}$$

where

$$G_k^{(1)} = \begin{bmatrix} 2(a+b) & -a & 0 & \cdots & 0 \\ -a & 2(a+b) & -a & \cdots & 0 \\ 0 & -a & 2(a+b) & \cdots & 0 \\ \cdots & \cdots & \cdots & \cdots & \cdots \\ 0 & 0 & 0 & \cdots & 2(a+b) \end{bmatrix}$$ (2.4.8)

$$G_k^{(2)} = \begin{bmatrix} -b & 0 & 0 & \cdots & -a \\ 0 & -b & 0 & \cdots & 0 \\ 0 & 0 & -b & \cdots & 0 \\ \cdots & \cdots & \cdots & \cdots & \cdots \\ 0 & 0 & 0 & \cdots & -b \end{bmatrix}$$

and the values of a and b are determined by the dimensions, conductivity, and permittivity of the subsections on the kth layer as given by

$$a = \frac{1}{2}(j\omega\varepsilon_r\varepsilon_0 + \sigma)\left[\frac{(\Delta y)(\Delta z_k)}{\Delta x} + \frac{(\Delta y)(\Delta z_{k+1})}{\Delta x}\right]$$

$$b = \frac{1}{2}(j\omega\varepsilon_r\varepsilon_0 + \sigma)\left[\frac{(\Delta x)(\Delta z_k)}{\Delta y} + \frac{(\Delta x)(\Delta z_{k+1})}{\Delta y}\right]$$ (2.4.9)

z_k in Equation 2.4.7 is the impedance of each element on the kth layer and is given by

$$z_k = \frac{\Delta z_k}{(j\omega\varepsilon_r\varepsilon_0 + \sigma)(\Delta x)(\Delta y)}$$ (2.4.10)

Then, for the lower substrate,

$$G_l = [Z_{L_l}]^{-1} + G_{L_l}$$ (2.4.11)

Similarly, for the upper substrate,

$$G_u = [Z_{L_u}]^{-1} + G_{L_u}$$

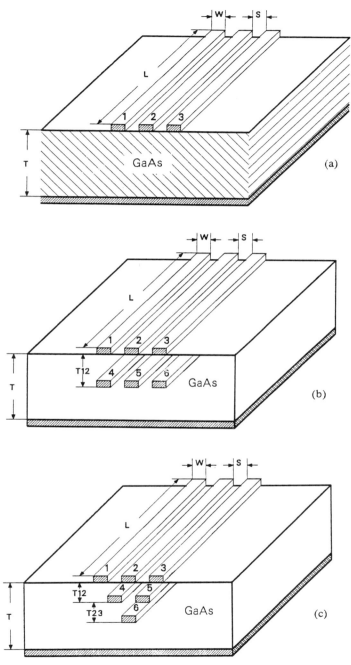

FIGURE 2.4.1   Schematic diagrams of (*a*) three single-level, (*b*) six bilevel, and (*c*) six trilevel interconnections printed on or embedded in the GaAs substrate.

In the past, the network analog method was restricted to the case $\Delta x = \Delta y$. However, greater flexibility can be introduced if Δx is not necessarily equal to Δy. Furthermore, computer processing time can be lowered if Δz is increased as the distance of the layer from the interconnections increases. With these modifications the admittance matrix G_k has a special band form as shown in Equation 2.4.8 and can be diagonalized. If $N(i, j)$ denotes the node number corresponding to the ith row ($i = 1, 2, \ldots, N_x$) and the jth column ($j = 1, 2, \ldots, N_y$), then the eigenvalue corresponding to this node is given by

$$\lambda[N(i, j)] = 2a\left[1 - \cos\left(\frac{i\pi}{N_x + 1}\right)\right] + 2b\left[1 - \cos\left(\frac{j\pi}{N_y + 1}\right)\right] \quad (2.4.12)$$

and an element of the corresponding orthonormal eigenvector matrix E is given by

$$E[N(m, n), N(i, j)] = \frac{2}{\sqrt{N_x + 1}\sqrt{N_y + 1}} \sin\left(\frac{im\pi}{N_x + 1}\right) \sin\left(\frac{jn\pi}{N_y + 1}\right)$$

$$(2.4.13)$$

where N_x and N_y are the number of subdivisions along the x and y directions, respectively. It can be proved that the eigenvector E in Equation 2.4.13 is orthonormal; that is, $E^T = E^{-1}$. The diagonalized admittance matrix can now be written as

$$G_k^D = \text{diag}\left(\lambda_1, \lambda_2, \ldots, \lambda_{N_x \cdot N_y}\right)$$

and is related to the matrix G_k by

$$G_k = EG_k^D E^T$$

Similarly, the diagonalized impedance matrix Z_k^D is related to the matrix Z_k by

$$Z_k = EZ_k^D E^T$$

and the recurrence formula for the diagonalized system becomes

$$Z_k^D = z_{k-1}I + \left[G_{k-1}^D - \left[Z_{k-1}^D\right]^{-1}\right]^{-1} \quad k = 1, 2, \ldots, L_{u,l} \quad (2.4.14)$$

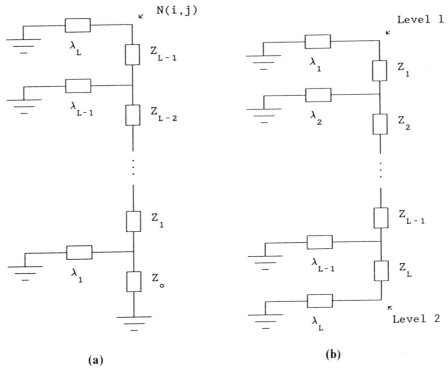

(a)   **(b)**

FIGURE 2.4.2 (*a*) Representation of a node on the single-level interconnections in the diagonalized system; (*b*) representation of a node between any two levels of multilevel interconnections in the diagonalized system.

and then, for the upper and lower substrates,

$$G_{u,l}^{D} = \left[Z_{u,l}^{D} \right]^{-1} \tag{2.4.15}$$

The representation of the node $N(i, j)$ due to the lower substrate in the diagonalized system is shown in Figure 2.4.2*a*. The corresponding representation due to the upper substrate can be obtained on the same lines. First, the matrices G_u^D and G_l^D are obtained and then the total impedance matrix Z is obtained by

$$Z = E \left[G_u^D + G_l^D \right]^{-1} E^T \tag{2.4.16}$$

2.4.3   Diagonalized System for Multilevel Interconnections

Schematic diagrams of the interconnections in bi- and trilevel configurations are shown in Figures 2.4.1*b* and *c*, respectively. In this case the network analogs for the upper open substrate and for the substrate between the lowest interconnection level and the bottom ground plane can be reduced by the technique used for single-level interconnections. However, the substrate between the successive levels needs to be considered. The diagonalized system for a node in the x–y plane on a layer between any two levels can be shown as in Figure 2.4.2b. The values of the elements $z_1, z_2, \ldots, z_L$ and $\lambda_1, \lambda_2, \ldots, \lambda_L$ are determined by the dielectric permittivity, the conductance, and the dimensions of the subsections at the node. In order to reduce computation time, the substrate between the two successive interconnection levels can be divided into two symmetric halves and then the reduced network for the upper half can be combined with the equivalent network for the lower half.

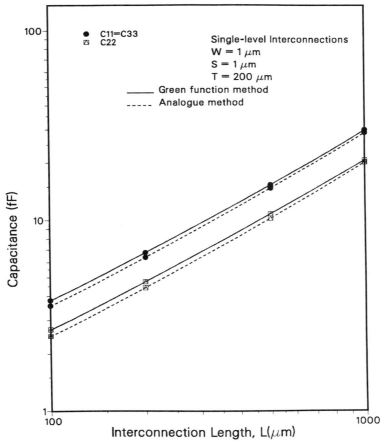

FIGURE 2.4.3 Dependences of the ground capacitances for the interconnections shown in Figure 2.4.1a on the interconnection lengths as determined by the Green's function and network analog methods.

2.4.4   Interconnection Capacitances and Inductances

It can be shown that only nodes located on interconnection lines determine the interconnection characteristics. For multilevel interconnections the total impedance matrix contains submatrices that connect nodes on the interconnection lines on all levels. For example, for three interconnection lines in any configuration, the impedance matrix is given by

$$[Z] = \begin{bmatrix} [Z_{i11}] & [Z_{i12}] & [Z_{i13}] \\ [Z_{i21}] & [Z_{i22}] & [Z_{i23}] \\ [Z_{i31}] & [Z_{i32}] & [Z_{i33}] \end{bmatrix}$$

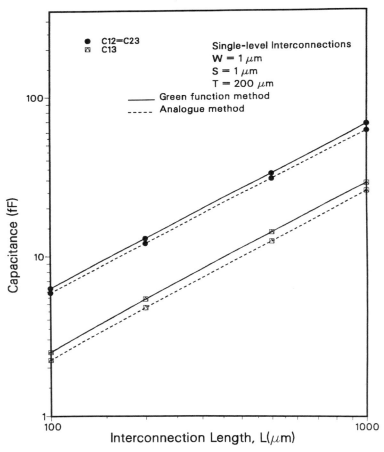

FIGURE 2.4.4   Dependences of the coupling capacitances for the interconnections shown in Figure 2.4.1a on the interconnection lengths as determined by the Green's function and network analog methods.

where the matrix $[Z_{i12}]$ represents coupling between the nodes on the first and the second interconnections and so on. The ground and coupling capacitances associated with the multilevel interconnections can then be determined as follows.

Let

$$[Y] = [Z]^{-1} = \begin{bmatrix} [Y_{i11}] & [Y_{i12}] & [Y_{i13}] \\ [Y_{i21}] & [Y_{i22}] & [Y_{i23}] \\ [Y_{i31}] & [Y_{i32}] & [Y_{i33}] \end{bmatrix}$$

Furthermore, let Y_{ixy}^s denote the sum of the elements of the submatrix $[Y_{ixy}]$;

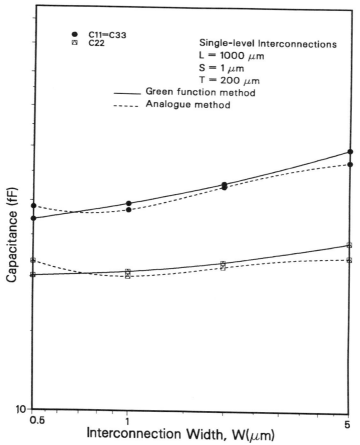

FIGURE 2.4.5 Dependences of the ground capacitances for the interconnections shown in Figure 2.4.1*a* on the interconnection widths as determined by the Green's function and network analog methods.

that is,

$$Y_{ixy}^s = \sum_{m=1}^{M} \sum_{n=1}^{N} Y_{ixy}(m, n)$$

Then the ground interconnection capacitances are given by

$$C_{xx} = Y_{ixx}^s + \sum_{x \neq y} Y_{ixy}^s$$

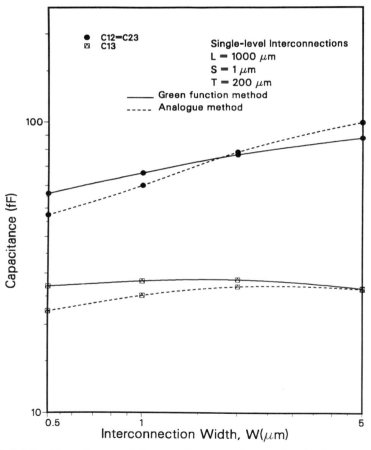

FIGURE 2.4.6 Dependences of the coupling capacitances for the interconnections shown in Figure 2.4.1*a* on the interconnection widths as determined by the Greeris function and network analog methods.

and the coupling interconnection capacitances are given by

$$C_{xy} = -Y^s_{ixy} \qquad x \neq y \tag{2.4.17}$$

The inductance matrix can be computed from the capacitance matrix for the corresponding two-dimensional interconnection configuration (consisting of infinite-length interconnections) in free space by matrix inversion. The telegraphist equations for the lossless case in free space are

$$\frac{\partial V}{\partial x} = -L\frac{\partial I}{\partial t}$$

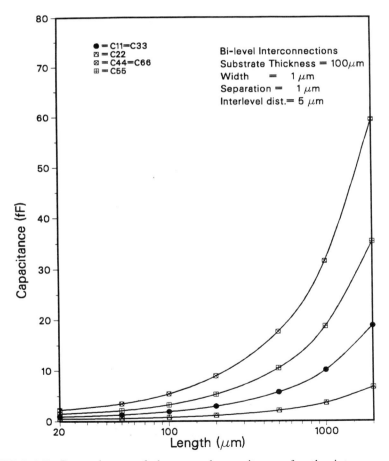

FIGURE 2.4.7 Dependences of the ground capacitances for the interconnections shown in Figure 2.4.1*b* on the interconnection lengths.

and

$$\frac{\partial I}{\partial x} = -C_0 \frac{\partial V}{\partial t}$$

or

$$\frac{\partial^2 V}{\partial x^2} = LC_0 \frac{\partial^2 V}{\partial t^2}$$

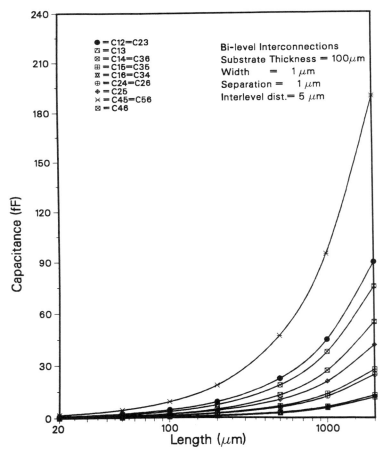

FIGURE 2.4.8   Dependences of the coupling capacitances for the interconnections shown in Figure 2.4.1*b* on the interconnection lengths.

Now, in free space, the wave should travel with the speed of light; that is,

$$\frac{\partial^2 V}{\partial x^2} = \frac{1}{v^2} \frac{\partial^2 V}{\partial t^2}$$

Therefore,

$$LC_0 = \frac{1}{v^2} = \mu_0 \varepsilon_0$$

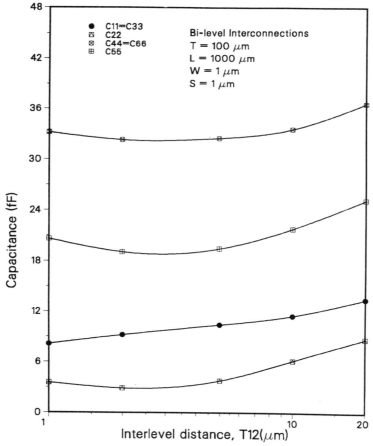

FIGURE 2.4.9 Dependences of the ground capacitances for the interconnections shown in Figure 2.4.1b on the interlevel distance T_{12}.

or in matrix form

$$[L] = \mu_0 \varepsilon_0 [C_0]^{-1} \tag{2.4.18}$$

In Equation 2.4.18, μ_0 and ε_0 are the permeability and permittivity for free space and $[C_0]$ is the capacitance matrix for the two-dimensional interconnection configuration in free space.

2.4.5 The Program ICIMPGV

A listing of the computer program ICIMPGV, which can be used to compute the parasitic capacitances and inductances for multilevel parallel intercon-

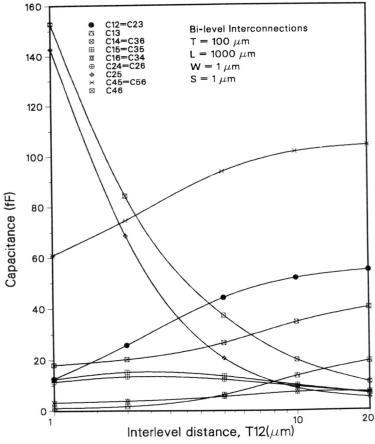

FIGURE 2.4.10 Dependences of the coupling capacitances for the interconnections shown in Figure 2.4.1b on the interlevel distance T_{12}.

nections on GaAs-based high-density integrated circuits and which is based on the numerical technique given previously, is presented in Appendix 2.2. In the following two subsections the program ICIMPGV has been used to study the dependences of the interconnection capacitances and inductances on the various interconnection parameters.

2.4.6   Parametric Dependence of Interconnection Capacitances

First, for single-level interconnections, the capacitance results are compared to those obtained using the Green's function method and an excellent agreement can be seen. For example, as a function of the interconnection

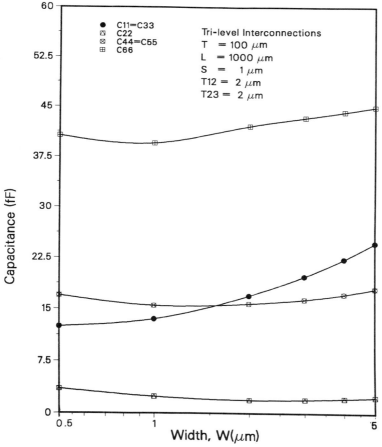

FIGURE 2.4.11   Dependences of the ground capacitances for the interconnections shown in Figure 2.4.1c on the interconnection widths.

length, the dependences of the ground and coupling capacitances determined by using the two methods are shown in Figures 2.4.3 (p. 97) and 2.4.4 (p. 98), respectively, and the same comparisons as functions of the interconnection width are shown in Figures 2.4.5 (p. 99) and 2.4.6 (p. 100), respectively. For a system of more than four interconnections, the results obtained using the Green's function method can only be approximate at best. Therefore, the results for the bilevel and trilevel configurations presented in the following discussion are obtained by the network analog method only.

For the bilevel interconnections shown in Figure 2.4.1*b*, the dependences of the various ground and coupling capacitances on the lengths of the interconnection lines in the range 20 to 2000 μm, keeping the other parameters at their fixed chosen values, are shown in Figures 2.4.7 (p. 101) and 2.4.8

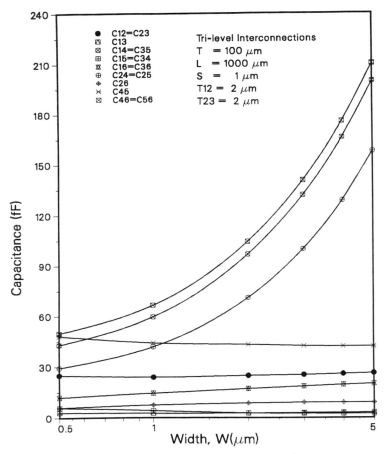

FIGURE 2.4.12 Dependences of the coupling capacitances for the interconnections shown in Figure 2.4.1*c* on the interconnection widths.

(p. 102), respectively. As functions of the interlevel distance in the range 1 to 20 μm, the ground and coupling capacitances for the same bilevel configuration are shown in Figures 2.4.9 (p. 103) and 2.4.10 (p. 104), respectively.

For the trilevel interconnections shown in Figure 2.4.1c, the dependences of the ground and coupling capacitances on the widths of the interconnection lines in the range 0.5 to 5 μm are shown in Figures 2.4.11 (p. 105) and 2.4.12 (p. 106), respectively. The values of the fixed parameters are also shown in the figures. As functions of the interconnection separation in the range 0.5 to 10 μm, the ground and coupling capacitances for the trilevel interconnections are shown in Figures 2.4.13 (p. 107) and 2.4.14 (p. 108), respectively. Figures 2.4.15 (p. 109) and 2.4.16 (p. 110) show the variations of the various ground and coupling capacitances for the trilevel configuration on the interlevel distance T_{23} in the range 2 to 50 μm.

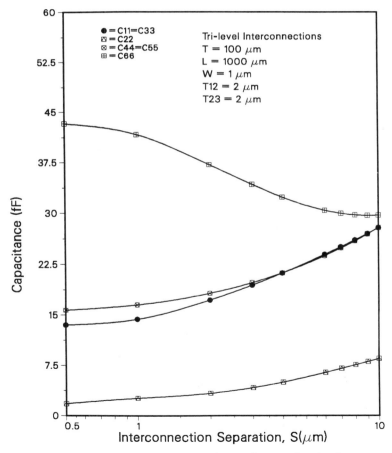

FIGURE 2.4.13 Dependences of the ground capacitances for the interconnections shown in Figure 2.4.1c on the interconnection separations.

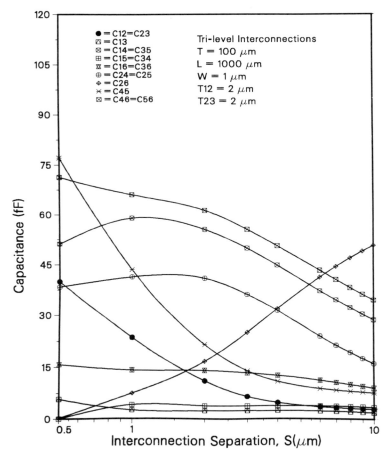

FIGURE 2.4.14   Dependences of the coupling capacitances for the interconnections shown in Figure 2.4.1c on the interconnection separations.

2.4.7   Parametric Dependence of Interconnection Inductances

While modeling the interconnections for very high speed signal propagations, the inductances coupling the various interconnection lines should also be considered. The program ICIMPGV can be used to study the dependences of the various coupling inductances for the single-, bi-, and trilevel interconnection configurations shown in Figure 2.4.1 on the various interconnection parameters. For example, for the three single-level interconnections, Figure 2.4.17 (p. 111) shows the dependences of the coupling inductances in nanohenrys per centimeter on the interconnection widths in the range 0.5 to 5 μm, whereas Figure 2.4.18 (p. 112) shows those on the interconnection separations in the range 0.5 to 10 μm. For the bilevel configuration, the

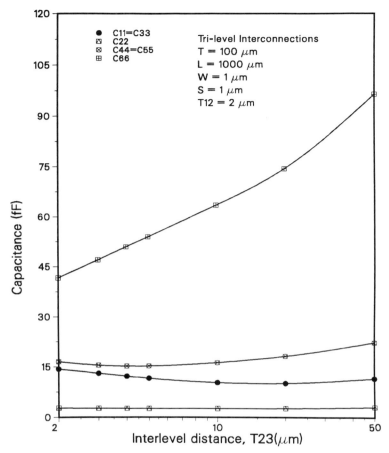

FIGURE 2.4.15 Dependences of the ground capacitances for the interconnections shown in Figure 2.4.1c on the interlevel distance T_{23}.

dependences of the various coupling inductances on the interconnection widths are shown in Figure 2.4.19 (p. 113), whereas those on the interconnection separations are shown in Figure 2.4.20 (p. 114). For the bilevel configuration, the dependences of the various coupling inductances on the thickness of the GaAs substrate in the range 3 to 200 μm are shown in Figure 2.4.21 (p. 115), whereas those on the interlevel distance T_{12} in the range 1 to 50 μm are shown in Figure 2.4.22 (p. 116). For the trilevel interconnections, the various coupling inductances as functions of the interconnection widths in the range 0.5 to 4 μm are shown in Figure 2.4.23 (p. 117), those as functions of the interconnection separations in the range 0.5 to 5 μm are shown in Figure 2.4.24 (p. 118), and those as functions of the interlevel distance T_{23} are shown in Figure 2.4.25 (p. 119).

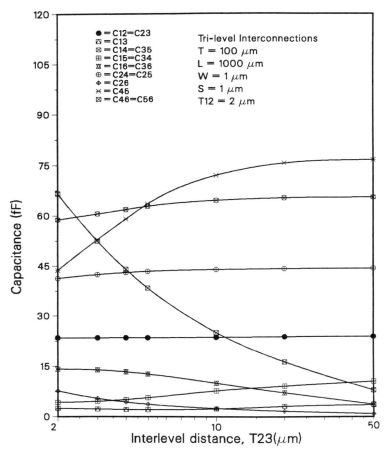

FIGURE 2.4.16 Dependences of the coupling capacitances for the interconnections shown in Figure 2.4.1c on the interlevel distance T_{23}.

2.5   SIMPLIFIED FORMULAS FOR INTERCONNECTION CAPACITANCES AND INDUCTANCES ON SILICON, SAPPHIRE, AND GALLIUM-ARSENIDE SUBSTRATES

In recent years, insulating substrates such as sapphire and Cr-doped semi-insulating gallium arsenide have emerged as alternatives to silicon. This is partially because of the argument that interconnections fabricated on these substrates offer considerably lower capacitances than those fabricated on silicon. In this section simplified formulas for finding the line as well as coupling capacitances and inductances for interconnections fabricated on

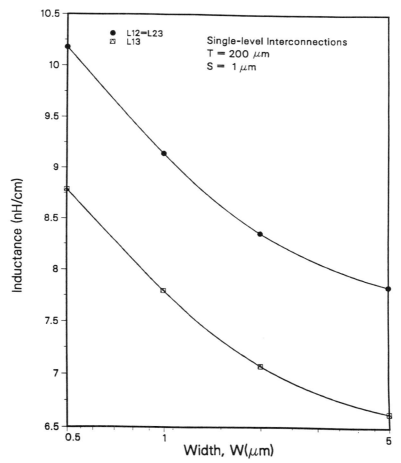

FIGURE 2.4.17 Dependences of the coupling inductances (in nH/cm) for the interconnections shown in Figure 2.4.1*a* on the interconnection widths.

oxide-passivated silicon, sapphire, and semi-insulating gallium-arsenide substrates are presented [2.26].

2.5.1 Line Capacitances and Inductances

The cross section of an interconnection fabricated on an insulating substrate is shown in Figure 2.5.1*a* (p. 120). It is defined by its width w, the height of the substrate h, and the relative dielectric constant of the material of the substrate ε_r. It is assumed that the thickness of the interconnection line is negligibly small. Under these conditions the approximate values of the line

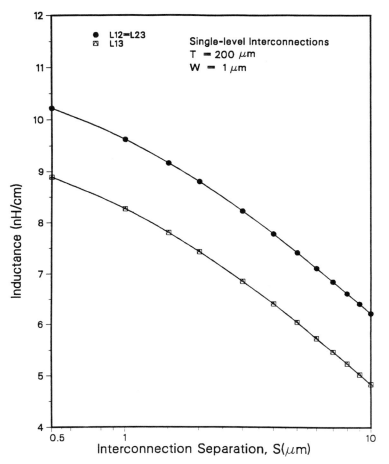

FIGURE 2.4.18 Dependences of the coupling inductances (in nH/cm) for the interconnections shown in Figure 2.4.1a on the interconnection separations.

capacitance and inductance of the interconnection can be determined by using the formulas [2.26]

$$C = \frac{2\pi\varepsilon_0\varepsilon_{\text{eff}}}{\ln\left[\dfrac{8h}{w} + \dfrac{w}{4h}\right]} \qquad w \le h$$

$$L = \frac{\mu_0}{2\pi}\ln\left[\frac{8h}{w} + \frac{w}{4h}\right]$$

(2.5.1)

where ε_{eff} is the effective dielectric constant of the substrate material given

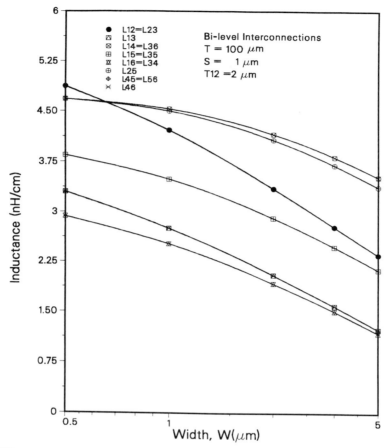

FIGURE 2.4.19 Dependences of the coupling inductances (in nH/cm) for the interconnections shown in Figure 2.4.1*b* on the interconnection widths.

by

$$\varepsilon_{\text{eff}} = \frac{\varepsilon_r + 1}{2} + \frac{\varepsilon_r - 1}{2}\left[1 + 10\frac{h}{w}\right]^{-0.5}$$

The cross section of an interconnection fabricated on an oxide-passivated silicon substrate is shown in Figure 2.5.1*b*. In this figure t_{ox} is the oxide thickness and t_{Si} is the thickness of the silicon substrate. For frequencies below 1000 MHz, the approximate values of the line capacitance and inductance of the interconnection on an oxide-passivated silicon substrate can be

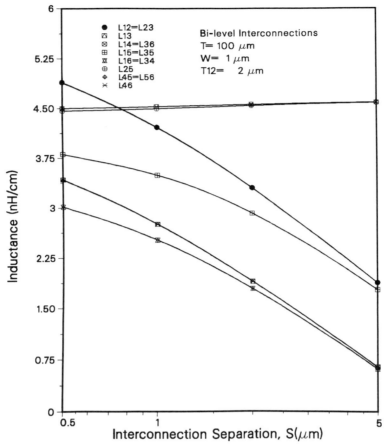

FIGURE 2.4.20 Dependences of the coupling inductances (in nH/cm) for the interconnections shown in Figure 2.4.1*b* on the interconnection separations.

determined by using the formulas

$$C = \frac{2\pi\varepsilon_0\varepsilon_{\text{eff}}}{\ln\left[\dfrac{8h}{w} + \dfrac{w}{4h}\right]} \qquad w \leq t_{\text{ox}}$$

$$C = \varepsilon_0\varepsilon_r\left[\frac{w}{t_{\text{ox}}} + 2.42 - 0.44\frac{t_{\text{ox}}}{w} + \left(1 - \frac{t_{\text{ox}}}{w}\right)^6\right] \qquad w \geq t_{\text{ox}} \qquad (2.5.2)$$

$$L = \frac{\mu_0}{2\pi}\ln\left[\frac{8h}{w} + \frac{w}{4h}\right] \qquad h = t_{\text{ox}} + t_{\text{Si}}$$

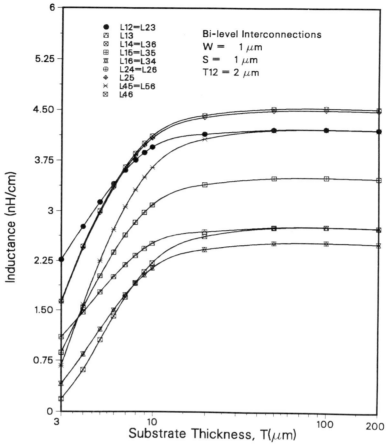

FIGURE 2.4.21 Dependences of the coupling inductances (in nH/cm) for the interconnections shown in Figure 2.4.1*b* on the substrate thickness.

2.5.2   Coupling Capacitances and Inductances

The Maxwellian capacitance matrix for an array of n conductors referring to a common ground plane has the following general form:

$$
\begin{bmatrix}
C_{11} & C_{12} & \cdots & C_{1n} \\
C_{21} & C_{22} & \cdots & C_{2n} \\
\cdots\cdots & \cdots\cdots & \cdots\cdots & \cdots\cdots \\
C_{n1} & C_{n2} & \cdots & C_{nn}
\end{bmatrix}
$$

The diagonal element C_{ii} is the self-capacitance of conductor i and is a measure of the capacitance of a single conductor when all other conductors are grounded. The diagonal element C_{ij} is the coefficient of induction and is a measure of the negative of the mutual capacitance between conductor i

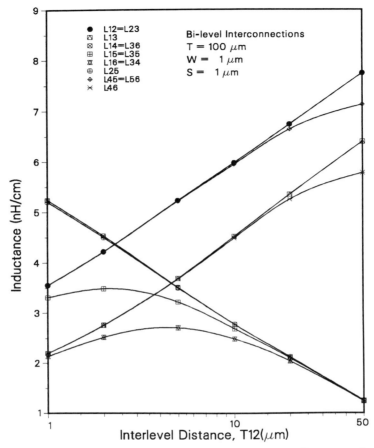

FIGURE 2.4.22 Dependences of the coupling inductances (in nH/cm) for the interconnections shown in Figure 2.4.1*b* on the interlevel distance T_{12}.

and conductor j. The Maxwellian capacitance matrices for a system of five conductors with equal line widths equal to 1 μm each and equal separations equal to 1 μm each fabricated on oxide-passivated silicon, sapphire, and semiinsulating gallium arsenide [2.26] are as follows:

Substrate: 1-μm SiO$_2$ on Si:

$$
C_{ij} = \begin{bmatrix}
0.776 & -0.043 & -0.004 & -0.002 & 0 \\
-0.044 & 0.760 & -0.004 & -0.004 & -0.001 \\
-0.004 & -0.045 & 0.759 & -0.004 & -0.004 \\
-0.001 & -0.004 & -0.004 & 0.760 & -0.044 \\
0 & -0.002 & -0.004 & -0.044 & 0.766
\end{bmatrix} \text{pF/cm}
$$

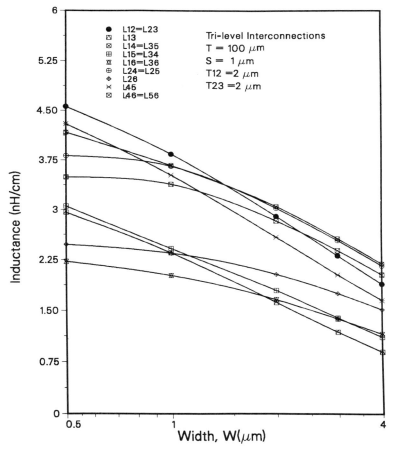

FIGURE 2.4.23 Dependences of the coupling inductances (in nH/cm) for the interconnections shown in Figure 2.4.1c on the interconnection widths.

Substrate: Sapphire:

$$
C_{ij} = \begin{bmatrix}
0.908 & -0.411 & -0.132 & -0.078 & -0.080 \\
-0.441 & 1.120 & -0.386 & -0.106 & -0.078 \\
-0.132 & -0.386 & 1.132 & -0.386 & -0.132 \\
-0.078 & -0.106 & -0.386 & 1.120 & -0.441 \\
-0.080 & -0.078 & -0.132 & -0.444 & 0.908
\end{bmatrix} \text{pF/cm}
$$

Substrate: GaAs:

$$
C_{ij} = \begin{bmatrix}
1.066 & -0.520 & -0.154 & -0.092 & -0.094 \\
-0.520 & 1.315 & -0.454 & -0.124 & -0.091 \\
-0.155 & -0.454 & 1.329 & -0.454 & -0.155 \\
-0.091 & -0.124 & -0.454 & 1.315 & -0.520 \\
-0.094 & -0.092 & -0.155 & -0.520 & 1.066
\end{bmatrix} \text{pF/cm}
$$

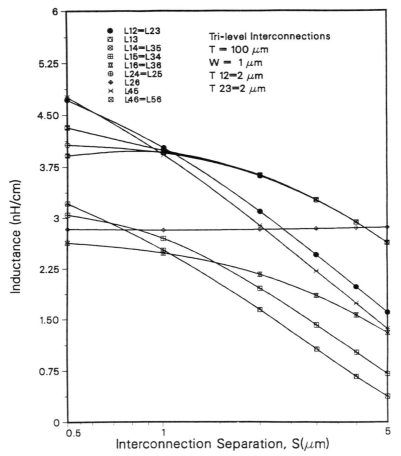

FIGURE 2.4.24   Dependences of the coupling inductances (in nH/cm) for the interconnections shown in Figure 2.4.1c on the interconnection separations.

For a nonmagnetic and lossless substrate, the inductance matrix for the system of conductors can be derived from the Maxwellian capacitance matrix for the same system of conductors in free space, that is, for $\varepsilon_r = 1$. If $v_0 = 1/\sqrt{LC}$ is the speed of light in free space, then the inductance matrix is given by

$$\left[L_{ij}\right] = \frac{1}{v_0^2}\left[C_{ij}\right]^{-1}$$

The inductance matrix for a system of five conductors with equal line widths

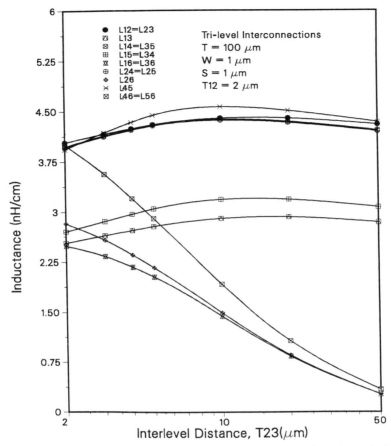

FIGURE 2.4.25 Dependences of the coupling inductances (in nH/cm) for the interconnections shown in Figure 2.4.1c on the interlevel distance T_{23}.

equal to 1 μm each and equal separations equal to 1 μm each fabricated on either of oxide-passivated silicon, sapphire, or gallium-arsenide substrates is

$$
L_{ij} = \begin{bmatrix}
15.126 & 10.597 & 9.235 & 8.429 & 7.859 \\
10.597 & 15.086 & 10.579 & 9.227 & 8.429 \\
9.235 & 10.579 & 15.080 & 10.579 & 9.235 \\
8.429 & 9.227 & 10.579 & 15.086 & 10.597 \\
7.859 & 8.429 & 9.235 & 10.597 & 15.115
\end{bmatrix} \text{nH/cm}
$$

Note that the inductance matrix given previously is valid for all frequencies

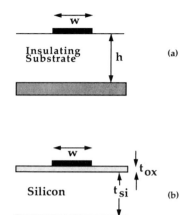

FIGURE 2.5.1 Schematic diagram of the cross section of a typical interconnection on an (a) insulating substrate and (b) oxide-passivated silicon substrate [2.26]. (© 1982 IEEE)

on insulating substrates but only below 1000 MHz on silicon substrates. From an examination of the capacitance and inductance matrices, it can be seen that the magnetic couplings have a longer range than the electrical couplings. For example, the mutual inductance between line 1 and line 5 is only 30 percent less than that between line 1 and line 2, whereas the mutual capacitance has decreased by almost a factor of 5.

2.6 ELECTRODE CAPACITANCES IN A GaAs MESFET

In this section the electrode parasitic capacitances in a GaAs MESFET [2.27], which are used in the model of transverse propagation delays in a GaAs MESFET in Chapter 3, are determined. Consider the schematic diagram of a recessed-gate MESFET as shown in Figure 2.6.1. For a self-aligned MESFET, the source, gate, and drain electrodes will be printed in the same plane on the GaAs substrate. The Green's function elements for a recessed-gate MESFET can be determined by following the steps outlined in Section 1.1 and those for a self-aligned MESFET can then be obtained by setting the depth of recession of the gate electrode denoted by DR equal to 0.

2.6.1 Ground and Coupling Capacitances

The electrode capacitances in a MESFET can be found by first reducing Equations 2.2.15 for the even- and odd-mode capacitances for a system of three electrodes, resulting in

$$C_s^e = C_s$$

$$C_g^e = C_g$$

$$C_d^e = C_d$$

$$C_s^o = C_s + 2C_{sg} + 2C_{sd}$$

$$C_g^o = C_g + 2C_{sg} + 2C_{gd}$$

$$C_d^o = C_d + 2C_{sd} + 2C_{gd}$$

and then solving these equations exactly, resulting in the following expressions for the ground and coupling electrode parasitic capacitances in a MESFET:

$$C_s = C_s^e$$

$$C_g = C_g^e$$

$$C_d = C_d^e$$

$$C_{sg} = \frac{C_d^e - C_s^e - C_g^e + C_s^o + C_g^o - C_d^o}{4}$$

$$C_{sd} = \frac{C_g^e - C_s^e - C_d^e + C_s^o + C_d^o - C_g^o}{4}$$

$$C_{gd} = \frac{C_s^e - C_g^e - C_d^e + C_g^o + C_d^o - C_s^o}{4}$$

2.6.2   The Program EPCSGM

The source code of a computer program called Electrode Parasitic Capacitances in a Single-Gate GaAs MESFET (EPCSGM), which incorporates the steps outlined previously, is presented in Appendix 2.3. For a given set of MESFET dimensions, the program computes the locations and dimensions of the rectangular subsections on the three electrodes, calculates the elements of the Green's function matrix, inverts the matrix, evaluates the even- and odd-mode capacitances for each electrode separately, and finally determines the ground and coupling electrode parasitic capacitances in the MESFET in femtofarads. The inversion of the Green's function matrix can be achieved by using the standard subroutine called MINV.

2.6.2.1   *Locations and Dimensions of Subsections*   The Cartesian coordinate system used to specify the locations of the subsections is shown in Figure 2.6.2. Along the x direction, the source, gate, and drain electrodes are

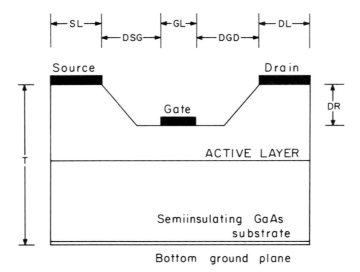

FIGURE 2.6.1   Schematic diagram of a GaAs MESFET with a deep-recessed gate. DR is the depth of recession of the gate; DR = 0 corresponds to the MESFET with a self-aligned gate.

divided into N_{1x}, N_{2x}, and N_{3x} sections, respectively, whereas, along the y direction, all three electrodes are divided into N_y sections. Then the number of sections on the three electrodes are given by

Source: $$N_1 = N_{1x} \times N_{1y}$$

Gate: $$N_2 = N_{2x} \times N_y$$

Drain: $$N_3 = N_{3x} \times N_y$$

and the total number of subsections becomes

$$N = N_1 + N_2 + N_3$$

If the source length is denoted by SL, the gate length by GL, the drain length by DL, the source–gate separation by DSG, the gate–drain separation by DGD, and the width of the MESFET by W, then the length of the subsection along the x direction on the three electrodes will be given by

Source: $$\Delta x_1 = \frac{SL}{N_{1x}}$$

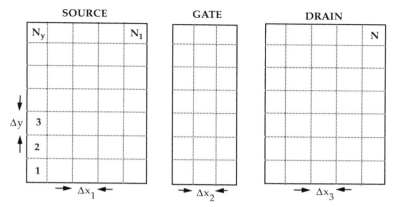

FIGURE 2.6.2 Coordinate system used for determining the locations and dimensions of the rectangular subsections.

Gate:
$$\Delta x_2 = \frac{GL}{N_{2x}}$$

Drain:
$$\Delta x_3 = \frac{DL}{N_{3x}}$$

and the width of each subsection along the y direction on each electrode is given by

$$\Delta y = \frac{W}{N_y}$$

If i denotes the number of a subsection $(i = 1, 2, 3, \ldots, N)$, then the x coordinates of the midpoints of the subsections on the three electrodes can be found by the following scheme:

Source:
$$x_i = \frac{\Delta x_1}{2} \quad \text{for } i = 1 \text{ to } N_y$$

$$x_i = 3 \frac{\Delta x_1}{2} \quad \text{for } i = N_y + 1 \text{ to } N_y$$

and so on, until, for $i = N_1 - N_y + 1$ to N_1,

$$x_i = \left(N_{1x} - \tfrac{1}{2} \right) \Delta x_1$$

Gate: $x_i = \text{SL} + DSG + \dfrac{\Delta x_2}{2}$ for $i = N_1 + 1$ to $N_1 + N_y$

$$x_i = \text{SL} + DSG + 3\dfrac{\Delta x_2}{2}$$

and so on, until, for $i = N_1 + N_2 - N_y + 1$ to $N_1 + N_2$,

$$x_i = \text{SL} + DSG + \left(N_{2x} - \tfrac{1}{2}\right)\Delta x_2$$

Drain: $x_i = \text{SL} + DSG + GL + DGD + \dfrac{\Delta x_3}{2}$

for $i = N_1 + N_2 + 1$ to $N_1 + N_2 + N_y$

$$x_i = \text{SL} + DSG + GL + DGD + 3\dfrac{\Delta x_3}{2}$$

for $i = N_1 + N_2 + N_y + 1$ to $N_1 + N_2 + 2N_y$

and so on, until, for $i = N - N_y + 1$ to N,

$$x_i = \text{SL} + DSG + GL + DGD + \left(N_{3x} - \tfrac{1}{2}\right)\Delta x_3$$

The y coordinates of the midpoints of the subsections can be determined by the following scheme:

$$y_i = \dfrac{\Delta y}{2}   \text{for } i = 1, N_y + 1, 2N_y + 1, \ldots, N - N_y + 1$$

$$y_i = 3\dfrac{\Delta y}{2}   \text{for } i = 2, N_y + 2, 2N_y + 2, \ldots, N - N_y + 2$$

and so on, until, for $i = N_y, 2N_y, 3N_y, \ldots, N$,

$$y_i = \left(N_y - \tfrac{1}{2}\right)\Delta y$$

The z coordinates of the midpoints of the subsections can be determined by the following scheme:

Self-aligned MESFET:
    $z_i = T$ for $i = 1, 2, 3, \ldots, N$

Deep-recessed-gate MESFET:
    $z_i = T$ for $i = 1, 2, 3, \ldots, N_1$ and for $i = N_1 + N_2 + 1, \ldots, N$

whereas for the subsections on the gate electrode, that is, for $i = N_1 + 1, \ldots, N_1 + N_2$,

$$z_i = T - DR$$

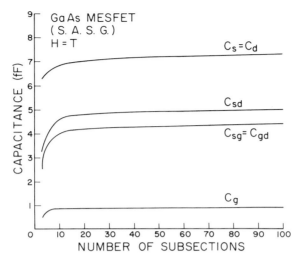

FIGURE 2.6.3   Dependence of electrode parasitic capacitances for a GaAs MESFET with typical dimensions on the number of rectangular subsections.

2.6.2.2 Computer Processing Time   The computer processing unit (cpu) time needed for running the program EPCSGM for a given set of MESFET dimensions increases approximately as the square of the total number of subsections. In principle, to justify the assumption of constant charge density over the surface of the subsection, its dimensions should be as small as possible and therefore the number of subsections should be as large as possible. However, the dependence of the values of the various electrode parasitic capacitances on the number of subsections used in the program is shown in Figure 2.6.3. It shows that, for typical MESFET dimensions, the capacitances increase as the number of subsections is increased but after a particular value of N, the increase is negligibly small or, in other words, the capacitances converge to their true values. Therefore, one way to reduce the cpu time will be to determine the capacitance values using a small number of subsections and then to use an appropriate extrapolation scheme to determine the true values. For example, in the present case, it can be verified that capacitance values within 10 percent of their true values can be obtained by first using only six to eight subsections in EPCSGM and then multiplying the self-capacitances (C_s, C_g, and C_d) by 1.1 and the coupling capacitances (C_{sg}, C_{gd}, and C_{sd}) by 1.2. It is possible to develop other extrapolation schemes to reduce the cpu time.

2.6.3   Dependence on MESFET Dimensions

The program EPCSGM can be used to study the dependence of the electrode parasitic capacitances in a GaAs MESFET on the various MESFET

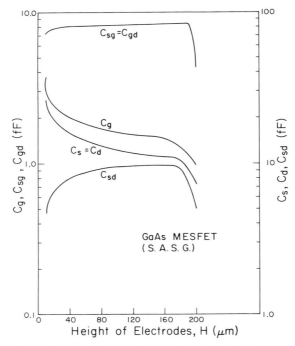

FIGURE 2.6.4 Electrode parasitic capacitances in a self-aligned GaAs MESFET as a function of the height of the electrodes above the bottom ground plane.

dimensions. For the following results, one of the dimensions is varied in a specific range while the other dimensions are set at some fixed typical values which are chosen to be the following: SL = DL = 10 μm, GL = 0.5 μm, DSG = DGD = 2 μm, T = 200 μm, and the device width W = 100 μm.

The dependence of the electrode parasitic capacitances in a self-aligned GaAs MESFET on the height of the electrodes above the bottom ground plane in the range 10 to 200 μm is shown in Figure 2.6.4. It shows that all the electrode capacitances, particularly C_{sg} and C_{gd}, decrease sharply when the electrodes are printed on the substrate as compared to when they are embedded in the substrate. Therefore, the following results were obtained for the case when the electrodes are printed on top of the substrate. Figure 2.6.5 shows the dependence of the electrode capacitances on the source and drain lengths (keeping SL = DL) in the range 0.1 to 50 μm. It shows that C_g decreases as SL and DL are increased. This is because of the increased shielding of the electric field lines between the gate electrode and the ground by the field lines between the source and the gate and by those between the drain and the gate electrodes. Such a shielding also explains the rapid increase in C_g when the source–gate and gate–drain separations (keeping DSG = DGD) are increased as shown in Figure 2.6.6. This figure also shows

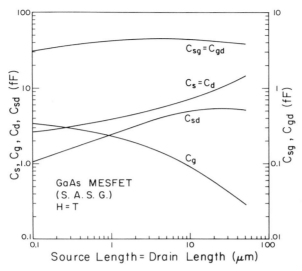

FIGURE 2.6.5   Electrode parasitic capacitances in a self-aligned GaAs MESFET as a function of the source and drain lengths (keeping SL = DL).

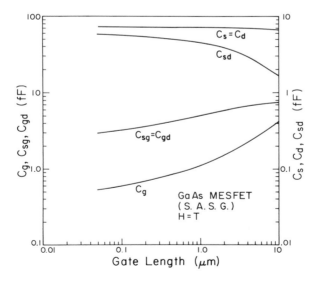

FIGURE 2.6.6   Electrode parasitic capacitances in a self-aligned GaAs MESFET as a function of the source–gate and gate–drain separations (keeping $DSG = DGD$).

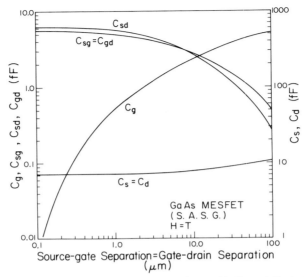

FIGURE 2.6.7 Electrode parasitic capacitances in a self-aligned GaAs MESFET as a function of the gate length.

the significant decrease in C_{sg}, C_{gd}, and C_{sd} when DSG and DGD are increased. The dependence of the electrode capacitances on the gate length in the range 0.05 to 10 μm is shown in Figure 2.6.7. Figure 2.6.8 shows the dependence of the electrode capacitances on the substrate thickness in the range 2 to 500 μm. It suggests that all the self-capacitances increase, whereas the mutual capacitances decrease when the substrate thickness is decreased. As a function of the width of the MESFET, the variation of the various capacitances is shown in Figure 2.6.9. This figure shows that as the device width is increased, all the capacitances increase almost linearly. Variations from near linear behavior for small device widths are due to the increased contribution of the fringing fields. For a GaAs MESFET with a deep recessed gate, Figure 2.6.10 shows the variation of the electrode capacitances as the depth of recession of the gate is increased in the range 0 to 10 μm. In the preceding results the possible shielding of the electric field lines between the electrodes and the bottom ground plane by the active layer (see Figure 2.6.2) in the conducting state has not been considered. Such a shielding, if present, will increase C_s, C_g, and C_d and decrease C_{sg}, C_{gd}, and C_{sd}.

2.6.4 Comparison with Internal MESFET Capacitances

The equivalent-circuit diagram for a GaAs MESFET with the source electrode grounded, including the electrode parasitic capacitances [denoted by the superscript (e)], is shown in Figure 2.6.11. $C_{sg}^{(i)}$, $C_{gd}^{(i)}$, and $C_{dc}^{(i)}$ represent

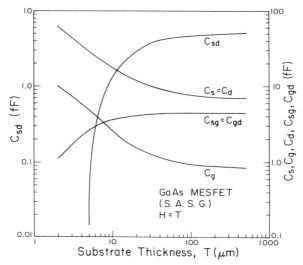

FIGURE 2.6.8 Electrode parasitic capacitances in a self-aligned GaAs MESFET as a function of the substrate thickness.

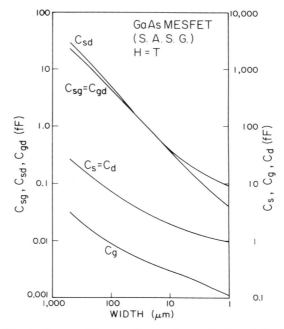

FIGURE 2.6.9 Electrode parasitic capacitances in a self-aligned GaAs MESFET as a function of the width of the MESFET.

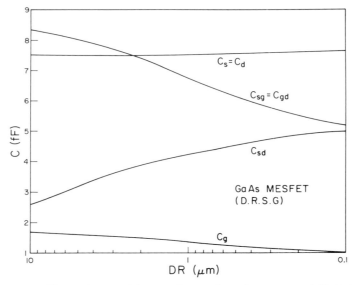

FIGURE 2.6.10   Electrode parasitic capacitances in a deep-recessed GaAs MESFET as a function of the depth of recession of the gate electrode.

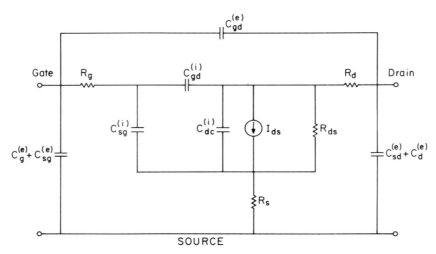

FIGURE 2.6.11   Equivalent-circuit diagram for a GaAs MESFET including the electrode parasitic capacitances.

TABLE 2.6.1 Comparison of Internal Capacitances and Electrode Parasitic Capacitances in GaAs MESFETs

Reference	MESFET Dimensions	Internal Capacitances[a]	Electrode Parasitic Capacitances
[2.32]	$GL = 1 \; \mu m$	$C_{gs}^{(i)} = 620 \; fF$	$C_{gs}^{(e)} = 26 \; fF$
		$C_{gd}^{(i)} = 14 \; fF$	$C_{gd}^{(e)} = 26 \; fF$
	$W = 500 \; \mu m$	$C_{dc}^{(i)} = 20 \; fF$	$C_{sd}^{(e)} = 25 \; fF$
			$C_{d}^{(e)} = 26 \; fF$
			$C_{g}^{(e)} = 4 \; fF$
[2.33][b]	$GL = 1.5 \; \mu m$	$C_{gs}^{(i)} = 675 \; fF$	$C_{gs}^{(e)} = 34 \; fF$
			$C_{gd}^{(e)} = 34 \; fF$
	$W = 600 \; \mu m$	$C_{gd}^{(i)} = 20 \; fF$	$C_{sd}^{(e)} = 30 \; fF$
			$C_{d}^{(e)} = 31 \; fF$
			$C_{g}^{(e)} = 6 \; fF$

[a] Internal capacitances are at $V_{gs} = 0$ and $V_{ds} = 5$ V.
[b] Internal capacitances are measured values for high-pinchoff-voltage devices.

the internal capacitances in the MESFET. $C_{dc}^{(i)}$ stands for the capacitance of the dipole layer; the other symbols are self-explanatory. A comparison of the internal capacitances and the electrode parasitic capacitances for two GaAs MESFETs [2.27] is shown in Table 2.6.1. Electrode parasitic capacitances are determined by using the given values of GL and W, whereas the other dimensions are set equal to their typical values. Table 2.6.1 shows that although $C_{gs}^{(i)}$ is more than 20 times $C_{gs}^{(e)}$, the other electrode capacitances are comparable or even greater in magnitude than the internal capacitances $C_{gd}^{(i)}$ and $C_{dc}^{(i)}$.

EXERCISES

E2.1 Consider a charge placed in air above a dielectric material of permittivity ε_1 which is deposited on another material of permittivity ε_2 which in turn is placed on a bottom ground plane.

(*a*) Draw a diagram showing the image charges for this system.

(*b*) Determine an expression for the Green's function matrix element G_{ij} for this system.

E2.2 Consider a charge embedded in a dielectric material of permittivity ε_1 which is deposited on another material of permittivity ε_2 which in turn is placed on a bottom ground plane.

(*a*) Draw a diagram showing the image charges for this system.

(*b*) Find the Green's function matrix element G_{ij} for this system.

E2.3   Modify the program IPCSGV given in Appendix 2.1 to include one more interconnection exactly below the fourth interconnection. Comment on the relative accuracy of the results obtained with the modified program.

E2.4   Develop another extrapolation scheme to determine the parasitic capacitance values in a MESFET with considerable saving of cpu time. Comment on the cpu time saved as well as on the relative precision of your proposed scheme.

E2.5   Develop a qualitative explanation of the sharp reductions in the coupling electrode capacitances in a MESFET when the substrate thickness is decreased below a certain value.

E2.6   Use Equations 2.5.1 and 2.5.2 to calculate the line capacitances of an interconnection on 250-μm-thick silicon (assume 1-μm SiO_2 thickness), sapphire, and GaAs for line widths in the range 1 to 100 μm. Plot your values and make comments on the relative lowering of capacitance on an insulating substrate as the interconnection width increases.

E2.7   Using Equations 2.5.1 and 2.5.2, calculate and plot the line inductances of an interconnection on 250-μm-thick silicon (assume 1-μm SiO_2 thickness), sapphire, and GaAs for line widths in the range 1 to 100 μm.

E2.8   Review the various numerical techniques presented in this chapter and comment on their computer efficiency.

E2.9   List and discuss the desirable characteristics of a numerical model that make it more suitable for inclusion in a CAD tool. Review the various techniques presented in this chapter from the point of view of their suitability for inclusion in a CAD tool.

APPENDIX 2.1

IPCSGV
Parasitic Capacitances for Single-Level Interconnections on GaAs-Based VLSI Using the Green's Function Method

```
    INTEGER N1X,N2X,N3X,NY,N1,N2,N3,N,I,J,EN,CNT,CR
    REAL A1,B1,C1,D1,A2,B2,C2,D2,E2,F2,G2,I2,J2,K2,
   $     L2,M2,O2,P2,Q2,S2,G(6,6),GIJ,GIJ1,R1,R2,
   $     R3,R4,R5,R6,R7,R8,R9,C1E,C2E,C3E,C1O,
   $     C2O,C3O,C11,C22,C33,C12,C13,C23,DS1,DS2,
   $     DS3,IW,T1,T2,T3,T4,T5,T6,T7,T8,T9,T10,T11,
   $     T12,T13,T14,T15,T16,X(6),Y(6),Z(6),DX(6),
   $     DY,IL,T,K1,S12,S23,L(10),M(10)
```

```
      OPEN (5, FILE = 'IPCD1')
      OPEN (6, FILE = 'IPCR', STATUS = 'NEW')
      WRITE (6,132)
 132  FORMAT (' INTERCONNECTION PARASITIC
     $          CAPACITANCES',/
     $           'Single-Level Interconnections')
      WRITE (*,132)
C*****READ INTERCONNECTION DIMENSIONS IN MICRONS
 10   READ (5,131) IW,IL,S12,S23,T
 131  FORMAT (5F6.1)
      WRITE (6,133) IW,IL,S12,S23,T
 133  FORMAT ( //, ' Interconnection WIDTH    =
     $              ',F8.1,' microns',/
     $             ' Interconnection LENGTH   =
     $              ',F8.1, ' microns',/
     $             ' Separation S12           =
     $              ',F8.1, ' microns',/
     $             ' Separation S23           =
     $              ',F8.1, ' microns',/
     $             ' GaAs Substrate Thickness=
     $              ',F8.1, ' microns')
      WRITE (*,133) IW,IL,S12,S23,T
      GIJ = 0.0
      I = 1
      J = 1
      EN = 1
      K1 = 0.859155
      N1X = 1
      N2X = 1
      N3X = 1
      NY = 2
      N1 = N1X*NY
      N2 = N2X*NY
      N3 = N3X*NY
      N = N1 + N2 + N3
      DY = IL / NY
      DO 151 J = 1,N1,1
      DX(J) = IW / NIX
 151  CONTINUE
      DO 152 J = N1 + 1,N1 + N2,1
      DX(J) = IW / N2X
 152  CONTINUE
      DO 153 J = N1 + N2 + 1,N,1
      DX(J) = IW / N3X
```

```
 153   CONTINUE
       DS1 = DX(N1)*DY
       DS2 = DX(N1 + N2)*DY
       DS3 = DX(N)*DY
C*****X- COORDINATES OF SUBSECTIONS
       CNT = 0.0
       DO 5500  CR = 1,N1X,1
       DO 5900  I = CNT + 1,CNT + NY,1
       X(I) = (2*CR- 1)*((DX(N1)) / 2)
 5900  CONTINUE
       CNT = I
 5500  CONTINUE
       CNT = N1
       DO 6500  CR = 1,N2X,1
       DO 6900  I = CNT + 1,CNT + NY,1
       X(I) = (IW + S12) + (2*CR- 1)*((DX(N1 + N2)) / 2)
 6900  CONTINUE
       CNT = I
 6500  CONTINUE
       CNT = N1 + N2
       DO 7500  CR = 1,N3X,1
       DO 7900  I = CNT + 1,CNT + NY,1
       X(I) = (IW + S12 + IW + S23) + (2*CR- 1)*((DX(N)) / 2)
 7900  CONTINUE
       CNT = I
 7500  CONTINUE
C*****Y- COORDINATES OF SUBSECTIONS
       DO 8000  CR = 1,NY,1
       DO 8500  I = CR,N,NY
       Y(I) = (2*CR- 1)*(DY / 2)
 8500  CONTINUE
 8000  CONTINUE
C*****Z- COORDINATES OF SUBSECTIONS
       DO 9000  I = 1,N,1
       Z(I) = T
 9000  CONTINUE
C*****ELEMENTS OF THE GREEN'S FUNCTION MATRIX
       DO 300  I = 1,N,1
       DO 310  J = 1,N,1
       A1 = X(J) - X(I) - ((DX(J)) / 2)
       B1 = X(J) - X(I) + ((DX(J)) / 2)
       C1 = Y(J) - Y(I) - (DY / 2)
       D1 = Y(J) - Y(I) + (DY / 2)
       GIJ1 = 0.0
       EN = 1
```

```
320   A2 = SQRT(A1**2 + C1**2 + ((2*T- 2*EN*T)**2))
      B2 = SQRT(B1**2 + D1**2 + ((2*T- 2*EN*T)**2))
      C2 = SQRT(A1**2 + D1**2 + ((2*T- 2*EN*T)**2))
      D2 = SQRT(B1**2 + C1**2 + ((2*T- 2*EN*T)**2))
      E2 = SQRT(A1**2 + C1**2 + ((2*EN*T)**2))
      F2 = SQRT(B1**2 + D1**2 + ((2*EN*T)**2))
      G2 = SQRT(A1**2 + D1**2 + ((2*EN*T)**2))
      I2 = SQRT(B1**2 + C1**2 + ((2*EN*T)**2))
      J2 = SQRT(A1**2 + C1**2 + ((2*T + (2*EN- 2)*T)**2))
      K2 = SQRT(B1**2 + D1**2 + ((2*T + (2*EN- 2)*T)**2))
      L2 = SQRT(A1**2 + D1**2 + ((2*T + (2*EN- 2)*T)**2))
      M2 = SQRT(B1**2 + C1**2 + ((2*T + (2*EN- 2)*T)**2))
      S2 = SQRT(A1**2 + C1**2 + ((2*EN- 2)*T)**2)
      O2 = SQRT(B1**2 + D1**2 + ((2*EN- 2)*T)**2)
      P2 = SQRT(A1**2 + D1**2 + ((2*EN- 2)*T)**2)
      Q2 = SQRT(B1**2 + C1**2 + ((2*EN- 2)*T)**2)
      T1 = (X(J)- X(I))*(LOG(C1 + A2) + LOG(D1 + B2) + LOG(D1
     $    +G2) + LOG(C1 + I2)- LOG(D1 + C2)- LOG(C1 + D2)-
     $    LOG(C1 + E2)- LOG(D1 + F2))
      T2 = ((DX(J)) / 2)*(LOG(D1 + B2) + LOG(D1 + C2) + LOG(C1
     $    +E2) + LOG(C1 + I2)- LOG(C1 + D2)- LOG(C1 + A2)
     $    -LOG(D1 + G2)- LOG(D1 + F2))
      T3 = (Y(J)- Y(I))*(LOG(A1 + A2) + LOG(B1 + B2) + LOG(B1
     $    +I2) + LOG(A1 + G2)- LOG(B1 + D2)- LOG(A1 + C2)- LOG
     $    (A1 + E2)- LOG(B1 + F2))
      T4 = (DY / 2)*(LOG(B1 + B2) + LOG(B1 + D2) + LOG(A1 + E2)
     $    +LOG(A1 + G2)- LOG(A1 + C2)- LOG(A1 + A2)- LOG(B1 +
     $    I2)- LOG(B1 + F2))
      IF (EN .EQ. 1) THEN
      T5 = 0.0
      T6 = 0.0
      ELSE
      T5 = (2*T- 2*EN*T)*(ATAN(A1*C1 / ((2*T- 2*EN*T)*A2))
     $    +ATAN(B1*D1 / ((2*T- 2*EN*T)*B2)))
      T6 = (2*T- 2*EN*T)*(ATAN(A1*D1 / ((2*T- 2*EN*T)*C2))
     $    +ATAN(B1*C1 / ((2*T- 2*EN*T)*D2)))
      END IF
      T7 = (2*EN*T)*(ATAN(A1*C1 / (2*EN*T*E2)) + ATAN(B1
     $    *D1 / 2*EN*T*F2)))
      T8 = (2*EN*T)*(ATAN(A1*D1 / (2*EN*T*G2)) + ATAN(B1
     $    *C1 / (2*EN*T*I2)))
      T9 = (X(J)- X(I))*(LOG(D1 + K2) + LOG(C1 + J2) + LOG(D1
     $    +P2) + LOG(C1 + Q2)- LOG(D1 + L2)- LOG(C1 + M2)- LOG
     $    (C1 + S2)- LOG(D1 + O2))
```

```
 T10 = ((DX(J))/2)*(LOG(D1+K2)+LOG(D1+L2)+LOG
$      (C1+S2)+LOG(C1+Q2)-LOG(C1+M2)-LOG(C1+
$      J2)-LOG(D1+O2)-LOG(D1+P2))
 T11 = (Y(J)-Y(I))*(LOG(A1+J2)+LOG(B1+K2)+LOG(A1
$      +P2)+LOG(B1+Q2)-LOG(B1+M2)-LOG(B1+O2)-
$      LOG(A1+L2)-LOG(A1+S2))
 T12 = (DY/2)*(LOG(B1+K2)+LOG(B1+M2)+LOG(A1+
$      P2)+LOG(A1+S2)-LOG(A1+L2)-LOG(A1+J2)-
$      LOG(B1+O2)-LOG(B1+Q2))
 T13 = (2*T+(2*EN-2)*T)*(ATAN(A1*C1/((2*T+(2*EN-
$      2)*T)*J2))+ATAN(B1*D1/((2*T+(2*EN-2)*T)
$      *K2)))
 T14 = (2*T+(2*EN-2)*T)*(ATAN(A1*D1/((2*T+(2*EN-
$      2)*T)*L2))+ATAN(B1*C1/((2*T+(2*EN-2)
$      *T)*M2)))
 T15 = 0.0
 T16 = 0.0
 IF (EN .GT. 1) THEN
 T15 = ((2*EN-2)*T)*(ATAN(A1*C1/((2*EN-2)*T*S2))
$      +ATAN(B1*D1/((2*EN-2)*T*O2)))
 T16 = ((2*EN-2)*T)*(ATAN(A1*D1/((2*EN-2)*T*P2))
$      +ATAN(B1*C1/((2*EN-2)*T*Q2)))
 END IF
 GIJ = 00.68*(((((-1)**(EN-1)*(K1**EN))*(T1+T2+T3
$      +T4-T5+T6+T7-T8)+(((-1)**EN)*(K1**(EN-
$      1)))*(T9+T10+T11+T12-T13+T14+T15-T16)))
 GIJ1 = GIJ1+GIJ
 IF (ABS(GIJ).GT.(0.0001)) THEN
 EN = EN+1
 GO TO 320
 ELSE
 G(I,J) = GIJ1
 END IF
310  CONTINUE
300  CONTINUE
     CALL MINV(G,N,D,L,M)
     R1 = 0.0
     R2 = 0.0
     R3 = 0.0
     R4 = 0.0
     R5 = 0.0
     R6 = 0.0
     R7 = 0.0
     R8 = 0.0
```

```
      R9 = 0.0
      DO 1000 I = 1,N1,1
      DO 1001 J = 1,N1,1
      R1 = R1 + G(I,J)
 1001 CONTINUE
      DO 1002 J = N1 + 1,N1 + N2,1
      R2 = R2 + G(I,J)
 1002 CONTINUE
      DO 1003 J = N1 + N2 + 1,N,1
      R3 = R3 + G(I,J)
 1003 CONTINUE
 1000 CONTINUE
      DO 1300 I = N1 + 1,N1 + N2,1
      DO 1301 J = 1,N1,1
      R4 = R4 + G(I,J)
 1301 CONTINUE
      DO 1302 J = N1 + 1,N1 + N2,1
      R5 = R5 + G(I,J)
 1302 CONTINUE
      DO 1303 J = N1 + N2 + 1,N,1
      R6 = R6 + G(I,J)
 1303 CONTINUE
 1300 CONTINUE
      DO 1600 I = N1 + N2 + 1,N,1
      DO 1601 J = 1,N1,1
      R7 = R7 + G(I,J)
 1601 CONTINUE
      DO 1602 J = N1 + 1,N1 + N2,1
      R8 = R8 + G(I,J)
 1602 CONTINUE
      DO 1603 J = N1 + N2 + 1,N,1
      R9 = R9 + G(I,J)
 1603 CONTINUE
 1600 CONTINUE
      C1E = (R1 + R2 + R3)*DS1
      C2E = (R4 + R5 + R6)*DS2
      C3E = (R7 + R8 + R9)*DS3
      C1O = (R1- R2- R3)*DS1
      C2O = (R5- R4- R6)*DS2
      C3O = (R9- R7- R8)*DS3
C*****INTERCONNECTION CAPACITANCES
      C11 = C1E*1.1
      C22 = C2E*1.1
      C33 = C3E*1.1
```

```
      C12 = (C3E- C2E- C1E + C1O + C2O- C3O) *0.3
      C13 = (C2E- C1E- C3E + C1O + C3O- C2O) *0.3
      C23 = (C1E- C2E- C3E- C1O + C2O + C3O) *0.3
      WRITE (6,134)
 134  FORMAT ( // '****** INTERCONNECTION CAPACITANCES
     $                 IN fF ******'/ )
      WRITE (*,134)
      WRITE (*,1800) C11,C22,C33,C12,C13,C23
1800  FORMAT ( 'C11 = 'F9.3,/, ' C22 = 'F9.3,/, ' C33 =
     $         'F9.3,/, ' C12 = 'F9.3,/, ' C13 = 'F9.3,/,
     $         ' C23 = 'F9.3)
      WRITE (6,1800) C11,C22,C33,C12,C13,C23
      GO TO 10
      STOP
      END
C
      SUBROUTINE MINV(A,N,D,L,M)
      IMPLICIT REAL (A- H,O- Z)
      DIMENSION L(1),M(1),A(1)
      D = 1.0
      NK = -N
      DO 80 K = 1,N
      N = NK + N
      L(K) = K
      M(K) = K
      KK = NK + K
      BIGA = A(KK)
      DO 20 J = K,N
      IZ = N*(J- 1)
      DO 20 I = K,N
      IJ = IZ + 1
 10   IF (ABS(BIGA)- ABS(A(IJ))) 15,20,20
 15   BIGA = A(IJ)
      L(K) = I
      M(K) = J
 20   CONTINUE
      J = L(K)
      IF (J- K) 35,35,25
 25   KI = K- N
      DO 30 I = 1,N
      KI = KI + N
      HOLD = -A(KI)
      JI = KI- K + J
      A(KI) = A(JI)
 30   A(JI) = HOLD
```

```
35    I = M(K)
      IF (I- K) 45,45,38
38    JP = N*(I- 1)
      DO 40 J = 1,N
      JK = NK + J
      JI = JP + J
      HOLD = -A(JK)
      A(JK) = A(JI)
40    A(JI) = HOLD
45    IF (BIGA) 48,46,48
46    D = 0.0
      RETURN
48    DO 55 I = 1,N
      IF (I- K) 50,55,50
50    IK = NK + I
      A(IK) = A(IK) / (- BIGA)
55    CONTINUE
      DO 65 I = 1,N
      IK = NK + I
      HOLD = A(IK)
      IJ = I- N
      DO 65 J = 1,N
      IJ = IJ + N
      IF (I- K) 60,65,60
60    IF (J- K) 62,65,62
62    KJ = IJ- I + K
      A(IJ) = HOLD*A(KJ) + A(IJ)
65    CONTINUE
      KJ = K- N
      DO 75 J = 1,N
      KJ = KJ + N
      IF (J- K) 70,75,70
70    A(KJ) = A(KJ) / BIGA
75    CONTINUE
      D = D*BIGA
      A(KK) = 1.0 / BIGA
80    CONTINUE
      K = N
100   K = K- 1
      IF (K) 150,150,105
105   I = L(K)
      IF (I- K) 120,120,108
108   JQ = N*(K- 1)
      JR = N*(I- 1)
      DO 110 J = 1,N
```

```
        JK = JQ + J
        HOLD = A(JK)
        JI = JR + J
        A(JK) = -A(JI)
110     A(JI) = HOLD
120     J = M(K)
        IF (J-K) 100,100,125
125     KI = K- N
        DO 130 I = 1,N
        KI = KI + N
        HOLD = A(KI)
        JI = KI- K + J
        A(KI) = -A(JI)
130     A(JI) = HOLD
        GO TO 100
150     RETURN
        END
```

APPENDIX 2.2

ICIMPGV
Parasitic Capacitances and Inductances for Multilevel Parallel Interconnections on GaAs-Based VLSI Using the Network Analog Method

```
DIRECTORY OF VARIABLES USED:
(ALL DIMENSION VALUES ARE IN MICROMETERS)
     CE:    THE DIELECTRIC CONSTANT
     NX:    THE NUMBER OF COLUMNS TO BE TAKEN
     NY:    THE NUMBER OF ROWS TO BE TAKEN
     CEL:   SUBSTRATE PERMEABILITY EPSILON
     DELTX: VALUE FOR THE INTERVAL DELT IN X DIRECTION
     DELTY: VALUE FOR THE INTERVAL DELT IN Y DIRECTION
     DELTZ: VALUE FOR THE INTERVAL DELT IN Z DIRECTION
     CWX:   WIDTH OF SUBSTRATE IN X DIRECTION
     CWY:   WIDTH OF SUBSTRATE IN Y DIRECTION
     CLU:   THICKNESS OF UPPER SUBSTRATE
     NL:    NUMBER OF LEVELS OF INTERCONNECTIONS
     IS(I): NUMBER OF MICROSTRIPS IN LEVEL (I)
     KS:    NUMBER OF MICROSTRIPS
     CM(I): INTERLEVEL DISTANCE BETWEEN LEVEL I AND
            I- 1.
     CM(1): SUBSTRATE THICKNESS
     CLL:   SUBSTRATE THICKNESS
     WSX:   WIDTH OF MICROSTRIP
```

```
      WSY:    LENGTH OF MICROSTRIP
      SS:     SPACE OF MICROSTRIP
C*****INPUT DATA FROM THE DATA FILE
        IMPLICIT REAL*4 (A- F,R- Z)
        IMPLICIT INTEGER(I- N)
        COMMON /A / NXT,NYT / B / RPI / C / DELTXT,DELTYT
        DIMENSION IS(3),CM(3)
        DIMENSION A(500,50,6)
        OPEN(1,FILE = 'VLDTA',STATUS = 'NEW')
        OPEN(2,FILE = 'VLITA',STATUS = 'OLD')
        OPEN(3,FILE = 'VLPTA',STATUS = 'NEW')
        C = 1.0
        RPI = ASIN(C)*2.0
        WRITE(1,38)
   38   FORMAT(1X, 'THE DIMENSIONS ARE IN MICROMETERS',/ )
        CALL REDRE(CEL)
        CALL REDIN(NL)
        DO 4 I = 1,NL
        CALL REDRE(CM(I))
        CALL REDIN(IS(I))
   4    CONTINUE
        CALL REDRE(WSX)
        CALL REDRE(WSY)
        CALL REDRE(SS)
        WRITE(*,5)
   5    FORMAT(1X, '(1) THICKNESS (2) WIDTH
       $           (3) SEPARATION (4) LENGTH',/ )
        CALL REDIN(IC)
        IF(IC.NE.1) GOTO 500
WRITE(*,6)
   6    FORMAT(1X, 'NUMBER OF LEVEL THAT THICKNESS IS
       $           CHANGED',/ )
        CALL REDIN(IT)
  500   CALL REDRE(XX)
        WRITE(3,*)XX
        IF(IC.EQ.1)THEN
        CM(IT) = XX
        END IF
        IF(IC.EQ.2) THEN
        WSX = XX
        END IF
        IF(IC.EQ.3) THEN
        SS = XX
        END IF
        IF(IC.EQ.4) THEN
```

```
      WSY = XX
      END IF
      IF(XX .EQ. 9999) GOTO 600
C*****CHOOSE DELTX, DELTY, SUBSTRATE WIDTH AND LENGTH
      KS = 0
      DO 70 I = 1,NL
 70   KS = KS + IS(I)
      CL = CM(1)
      DELTX = MIN(SS,WSX)
      DELTX = DELTX / 2.0
      DELTY = WSY / 2
      CWX = 4*CL + 3*KS*(SS + WSX)
      CWY = 6*WSY + 4*CL
      NX = INT(CWX / DELTX + 0.5)
      IF(NX.LE.500) GOTO 20
      WRITE(1,30)
 30   FORMAT(1X, 'THE X- DIMENSION OF SUBSTRATE IS TOO
     $            LARGE!')
      NX = 500
 20   NY = INT(CWY / DELTY + 0.5)
      IF(NY.LE.50) GOTO 40
      WRITE(1,50)
 50   FORMAT(1X, 'THE Y- DIMENSION OF SUBSTRATE IS TOO
     $            LARGE!')
      NY = 50
 40   NSS = INT(SS / DELTX + 0.5)
      NWS = INT(WSX / DELTX + 0.5)
      NLS = INT(WSY / DELTY + 0.5)
C*****DETERMINE INDEX FOR REPEATING COMPUTATION
C     (TO REDUCE SAME COMPUTATIONS)
      ICR = -1
      IF(DELTX.NE.DELTXT) GOTO 100
      IF(DELTY.NE.DELTYT) GOTO 100
      IF(NX.NE.NXT) GOTO 100
      IF(NY.NE.NYT) GOTO 100
      ICR = IT
100   WRITE(1,*)DELTX,DELTY,NX,NY
      WRITE(1,*)NWS,NLS,NSS
      DELTXT = DELTX
      DELTYT = DELTY
      NXT = NX
      NYT = NY
      CALL VLSI(CEL,NL,CM,IS,NWS,NLS,NSS)
      GOTO 500
```

```
 600   CLOSE(UNIT = 1)
       CLOSE(UNIT = 2)
       CLOSE(UNIT = 3)
       END
C*****MAIN SUBROUTINE TO COMPUTE THE INDUCTANCES
       SUBROUTINE VLSI(CEL,NL,CM,IS,NWS,NLS,NSS)
       IMPLICIT REAL*4 (A- F)
       IMPLICIT REAL*4 (R- Z)
       IMPLICIT INTEGER(I- N)
       COMMON /A / NX,NY / B / RPI / C / DELTX,DELTY
       DIMENSION CM(3),IS(3)
       DIMENSION A(500,50,6)
       DIMENSION R(30,2,30,2,6)
       DIMENSION NS(1000,3),NT(3)
       CEU1 = 1.0
       CLU = NX*DELTX / 4.0
       CLL = CM(1)
C      IF(ICR.EQ.0) GOTO 30
       IF(NL.EQ.1) GOTO 10
       DO 20 I = 2,NL
  20   CLL = CLL- CM(I)
  10   CALL DIGIMO(1,CLU,CEU1,A)
       CALL DIGIMS(NL,CLL,CEL,A)
       IF(NL.EQ.1) GOTO 45
       DO 40 I = 2,NL
       CALL DIGIMM(I,CM,CEL,A)
  40   CONTINUE
  45   CALL TOTIMP(NL,A)
  30   DO 50 I = 1,NL
  50   CALL NODE(I,IS,NWS,NSS,NS,NT)
C*****COMPUTE IMPEDANCE MATRIX OF THE NODES ON STRIPS
       DO 60 I = 1,NL
  60   CALL TRANS(I,A,NS,NT,NLS,R)
       IF(NL.EQ.1) GOTO 80
       DO 70 I = 1,NL- 1
       DO 70 J = I + 1,NL
       CALL TRANM(I,J,A,NS,NT,NLS,R)
  70   CONTINUE
  80   CALL COND(NL,NT,IS,NLS,R)
       RETURN
       END
C*****FIND THE NODES OF THE MICROSTRIPS ON THE
C      SUBSTRATE
       SUBROUTINE NODE(II,IS,NWS,NSS,NS,NT)
```

```
       COMMON  /A / NX,NY / B / RPI / C / DELTX,DELTY
       DIMENSION NS(1000,3),NT(3),IS(3)
       KS = IS(II)
       NI = NX / 2.0- (KS*NWS + (KS- 1)*NSS) / 2
       NMID = NI + 1
       I = 0
       K = 1
 10    J = 1
 20    I = I + 1
       NS(I,II) = NMID
       J = J + 1
       NMID = NMID + 1
       IF(J.LE.NWS) GOTO 20
       K = K + 1
       NMID = NMID + NSS
       IF(K.LE.KS) GOTO 10
       NT(II) = I
       RETURN
       END
C*****TRANSFORMATION BACK FROM MUTUAL DIAGONALIZED
C      SYSTEM
       SUBROUTINE TRANM(II,KK,A,NS,NT,NLS,R)
       IMPLICIT REAL*4 (C- F,S- Z)
       IMPLICIT INTEGER(I- N)
       DIMENSION A(500,50,6)
       DIMENSION R(30,2,30,2,6)
       DIMENSION NS(1000,3),NT(3),NO(4,4)
       COMMON  /A / NX,NY / B / RPI / C / DELTX,DELTY
       CALL ORDER(4,NO)
       JJ = NO(II,KK)
       N1 = NT(II)
       N2 = NT(KK)
       DO 14 I1 = 1,N1
       DO 14 J1 = 1,N2
       DO 14 K1 = 1,NLS
       DO 14 L1 = 1,NLS
       R(I1,K1,J1,L1,JJ) = 0
 14    CONTINUE
       DO 20 I1 = 1,N1
       DO 20 J1 = 1,N2
       DO 20 K1 = 1,NLS
       DO 20 L1 = 1,NLS
       IF(R(I1,K1,J1,L1,JJ).NE.0) GOTO 20
       K = K1 + (NY / 2.0- NLS / 2.0)
```

```
      L = L1 + ( NY / 2.0 - NLS / 2.0 )
      I = NS ( I1 , II )
      J = NS ( J1 , KK )
      C = 0.0
      DO 30 MX = 1 , NX
      DO 30 MY = 1 , NY
      C1 = I*MX*RPI / ( NX + 1.0 )
      CL = SIN ( C1 )
      C1 = K*MY*RPI / ( NY + 1.0 )
      CL = SIN ( C1 ) *CL
      C1 = J*MX*RPI / ( NX + 1.0 )
      CR = SIN ( C1 )
      C1 = L*MY*RPI / ( NY + 1.0 )
      CR = SIN ( C1 ) *CR
      C = 4.0*CL*CR / ( NX + 1.0 ) / ( NY + 1.0 ) *A ( MX , MY , JJ ) + C
30    CONTINUE
      C = C / 8.85433E- 3
C     WRITE ( * , * ) I1 , K1 , J1 , L1 , C
C     WRITE ( * , * ) I , J , K , L
      R ( I1 , K1 , J1 , L1 , JJ ) = C
      R ( N1- I1 + 1 , K1 , N2- J1 + 1 , L1 , JJ ) = C
      R ( I1 , NLS- K1 + 1 , J1 , NLS- L1 + 1 , JJ ) = C
      R ( N1- I1 + 1 , NLS- K1 + 1 , N2- J1 + 1 , NLS- L1 + 1 , JJ ) = C
20    CONTINUE
      RETURN
      END
C*****TRANSFORMATION BACK FROM DIAGONALIZED SYSTEM
      SUBROUTINE TRANS ( II , A , NS , NT , NLS , R )
      IMPLICIT REAL*4 ( A )
      IMPLICIT REAL*4 ( C- F , S- Z )
      IMPLICIT INTEGER ( I- N )
      COMMON / A / NX , NY / B / RPI / C / DELTX , DELTY
      DIMENSION A ( 500 , 50 , 6 )
      DIMENSION R ( 30 , 2 , 30 , 2 , 6 )
      DIMENSION NS ( 1000 , 3 ) , NT ( 3 ) , NO ( 4 , 4 )
      CALL ORDER ( 4 , NO )
      JJ = NO ( II , II )
      N = NT ( II )
      C1 = 2.0000
      CST = SQRT ( C1 )
      DO 14 I1 = 1 , N
      DO 14 J1 = 1 , N
      DO 14 K1 = 1 , NLS
      DO 14 L1 = 1 , NLS
```

```
      R(I1,K1,J1,L1,JJ) = 0.0000
 14   CONTINUE
      DO 20 I1 = 1,N
      DO 20 J1 = I1,N
      DO 20 K1 = 1,NLS
      DO 20 L1 = 1,NLS
      IF(R(I1,K1,J1,L1,JJ).NE.0) GOTO 20
      K = K1 + (NY / 2.0- NLS / 2.0)
      L = L1 + (NY / 2.0- NLS / 2.0)
      I = NS(I1,II)
      J = NS(J1,II)
      C = 0.0
      DO 30 MX = 1,NX
      DO 30 MY = 1,NY
      C1 = I*MX*RPI / (NX + 1.0)
      CL = SIN(C1)
      C1 = K*MY*RPI / (NY + 1.0)
      CL = SIN(C1)*CL
      C1 = J*MX*RPI / (NX + 1.0)
      CR = SIN(C1)
      C1 = L*MY*RPI / (NY + 1.0)
      CR = SIN(C1)*CR
      C = 4.0*CL*CR / (NX + 1) / (NY + 1)*A(MX,MY,JJ) + C
 30   CONTINUE
      C = C / 8.85433E- 3
      R(I1,K1,J1,L1,JJ) = C
      R(J1,L1,I1,K1,JJ) = C
      R(N- I1 + 1,K1,N- J1 + 1,L1,JJ) = C
      R(N- J1 + 1,L1,N- I1 + 1,K1,JJ) = C
      R(I1,NLS- K1 + 1,J1,NLS- L1 + 1,JJ) = C
      R(J1,NLS- L1 + 1,I1,NLS- K1 + 1,JJ) = C
      R(N- I1 + 1,NLS- K1 + 1,N- J1 + 1,NLS- L1 + 1,JJ) = C
      R(N- J1 + 1,NLS- L1 + 1,N- I1 + 1,NLS- K1 + 1,JJ) = C
 20   CONTINUE
      RETURN
      END
C*****SUBROUTINE TO COMPUTE THE CAPACITANCES
      SUBROUTINE COND(NL,NT,IS,NLS,R)
      IMPLICIT REAL*4 (A- F)
      IMPLICIT REAL*4 (T- Z)
      COMMON /A / NX,NY / B / RPI / C / DELTX,DELTY
      DIMENSION R(30,2,30,2,6),T(150,150),Y(150,150)
      DIMENSION NT(3),IS(3)
      DO 10 I = 1,NL
      DO 10 J = I,NL
```

```
 10       CALL RT(I,J,NT,T,R,NLS)
          MN = 0
          DO 20 I = 1,NL
 20       MN = NT(I)*NLS + MN
C         CALL WRM(MN,T,'RESI')
          CALL CHOL(MN,T,Y)
C         CALL WRM(MN,T,'CAPC')
          DO 30 I = 1,NL
          DO 30 J = I,NL
 30       CALL TR(I,J,NT,T,R,NLS)
          CALL CAP(NL,NT,IS,R,NLS)
          RETURN
          END
C*****CHANGE THE R MATRIX TO BE T,R(*,*,*,*) TO T(*,*)
          SUBROUTINE RT(II,JJ,NT,T,R,NLS)
          IMPLICIT REAL*4 (A-F)
          IMPLICIT REAL*4 (T-Z)
          DIMENSION R(30,2,30,2,6),T(150,150)
          DIMENSION NT(3),NO(4,4)
          CALL ORDER(4,NO)
          KK = NO(II,JJ)
          IA = 0
          DO 10 I = 1,II- 1
 10       IA = IA + NT(I)*NLS
          JA = 0
          DO 30 J = 1,JJ- 1
 30       JA = JA + NT(J)*NLS
          N1 = NT(II)
          N2 = NT(JJ)
          DO 20 K = 1,NLS
          DO 20 L = 1,NLS
          DO 20 I = 1,N1
          DO 20 J = 1,N2
          I1 = I + N1*(K- 1) + IA
          J1 = J + N2*(L- 1) + JA
          T(I1,J1) = R(I,K,J,L,KK)
          T(J1,I1) = R(I,K,J,L,KK)
 20       CONTINUE
          RETURN
          END
C*****CHANGE THE T MATRIX TO BE R,T(*,*) TO R(*,*,*,*)
          SUBROUTINE TR(II,JJ,NT,T,R,NLS)
          IMPLICIT REAL*4 (A-F)
          IMPLICIT REAL*4 (T-Z)
          DIMENSION R(30,2,30,2,6),T(150,150)
```

```
       DIMENSION NT(3),NO(4,4)
       CALL ORDER(4,NO)
       KK = NO(II,JJ)
       IA = 0
       DO 10 I = 1,II- 1
 10    IA = IA + NT(I)*NLS
       JA = 0
       DO 30 J = 1,JJ- 1
 30    JA = JA + NT(J)*NLS
       N1 = NT(II)
       N2 = NT(JJ)
       DO 120 K = 1,NLS
       DO 120 L = 1,NLS
       DO 120 I = 1,N1
       DO 120 J = 1,N2
       I1 = I + N1*(K- 1) + IA
       J1 = J + N2*(L- 1) + JA
       R(I,K,J,L,KK) = T(I1,J1)
 120   CONTINUE
       RETURN
       END
C*****COMPUTING GROUNDING AND MUTUAL CAPACITANCES
       SUBROUTINE CAP(NL,NT,IS,R,NLS)
       IMPLICIT REAL*4 (R- Z)
       COMMON /A / NX,NY / B / RPI / C / DELTX,DELTY
       REAL*4 CL
       DIMENSION R(30,2,30,2,6),C(30,30,6),CL(10,10)
       DIMENSION B(30,30),NT(3),IS(3)
       CT = 0
       DO 10 I = 1,NL
       DO 10 J = I,NL
 10    CALL RC(NT,I,J,R,C,NLS)
       DO 20 I = 1,NL
       DO 20 J = I,NL
 20    CALL CB(I,J,NT,IS,C,B)
       KS = 0
       DO 25 I = 1,NL
 25    KS = IS(I) + KS
       DO 40 I = 1,KS
       DO 40 J = 1,KS
       CL(I,J) = B(I,J)
C      WRITE(1,*)I,J,CL(I,J)
 40    CONTINUE
       XL = NLS*DELTY
       CALL IND(KS,CL,XL)
```

```
70     FORMAT(1X,2I4,2F12.7)
       RETURN
       END
C*****FIND THE INDUCTANCE MATRIX
       SUBROUTINE IND(N,A,XL)
       DIMENSION A(10,10),B(10,10)
       REAL*4 A,B,C
       DO 5 I=1,N
       DO 6 J=1,N
6      B(I,J)=0.0
       B(I,I)=1.0
5      CONTINUE
       DO 10 I=1,N
       DO 20 J=1,N
       IF(I.EQ.J) GOTO 20
       C=A(J,I)/A(I,I)
C      WRITE(*,*)J,I,A(J,I)
       DO 30 K=1,N
C      IF(K.EQ.I) GOTO 30
       A(J,K)=A(J,K)-C*A(I,K)
       B(J,K)=B(J,K)-C*B(I,K)
       WRITE(*,*)J,K,B(J,K)
30     CONTINUE
20     CONTINUE
10     CONTINUE
       DO 40 I=1,N
       DO 40 L=1,N
       B(I,L)=B(I,L)/A(I,I)
40     CONTINUE
       DO 50 I=1,N
       DO 50 L=1,N
       A(I,L)=B(I,L)
50     CONTINUE
       DO 60 I=1,N
       DO 60 J=1,N
       WRITE(1,70)I,J,A(I,J)/2.997925/2.997925*XL
       WRITE(3,*)I,J,A(I,J)/2.997925/2.997925*XL
60     CONTINUE
70     FORMAT(1X,'THE INDUCTANCE ',I2,I2,'= ',F12.7,
       $            'NH / MICROMETER')
       RETURN
       END
C*****ADD THE CAPACITANCE MATRIX IN X DIRECTION
       SUBROUTINE CB(II,JJ,NT,IS,C,B)
       IMPLICIT REAL*4 (A-F)
```

```
      IMPLICIT REAL*4 (R-Z)
      DIMENSION C(30,30,6),NO(4,4)
      DIMENSION B(30,30),NT(3),IS(3)
      IA = 0
      JA = 0
      DO 10 I = 1,II-1
 10   IA = IA + IS(I)
      DO 20 J = 1,JJ-1
 20   JA = JA + IS(J)
      N1 = NT(II)
      N2 = NT(JJ)
      KS1 = IS(II)
      KS2 = IS(JJ)
      CALL ORDER(4,NO)
      KK = NO(II,JJ)
      DO 120 I = 1,KS1
      DO 120 J = 1,KS2
      X = 0.0
      DO 110 K = (I-1)*N1 / KS1 + 1,I*N1 / KS1
      DO 110 L = (J-1)*N2 / KS2 + 1,J*N2 / KS2
      X = X + C(K,L,KK)
 110  CONTINUE
      B(I + IA,J + JA) = X
      B(J + JA,I + IA) = X
 120  CONTINUE
      RETURN
      END
C*****ADD THE CAPACITANCE MATRIX IN Y DIRECTION
      SUBROUTINE RC(NT,II,JJ,R,C,NLS)
      IMPLICIT REAL*4 (A-F)
      IMPLICIT REAL*4 (R-Z)
      DIMENSION R(30,2,30,2,6),C(30,30,6),NO(4,4),
     $          NT(3)
      CALL ORDER(4,NO)
      KK = NO(II,JJ)
      N1 = NT(II)
      N2 = NT(JJ)
      DO 190 I = 1,N1
      DO 190 J = 1,N2
      X = 0.0
      DO 180 K = 1,NLS
      DO 180 L = 1,NLS
      X = X + R(I,K,J,L,KK)
 180  CONTINUE
      C(I,J,KK) = X
```

```
 190    CONTINUE
        RETURN
        END
C*****FIND THE R MATRIX FROM C MATRIX,R = INV(C)
        SUBROUTINE TOTIMP(NL,A)
        COMMON /A / NX,NY / B / RPI / C / DELTX,DELTY
        DIMENSION A(500,50,6),B(4,4)
        DIMENSION NO(4,4)
        REAL*4 B
        CALL ORDER(4,NO)
        DO 10 I = 1,NX
        DO 10 J = 1,NY
        DO 20 K = 1,NL
        DO 20 L = K,NL
        B(K,L) = A(I,J,NO(K,L))
        B(L,K) = B(K,L)
  20    CONTINUE
        CALL LU(NL,B)
        DO 30 K = 1,NL
        DO 30 L = K,NL
        A(I,J,NO(K,L)) = B(K,L)
  30    CONTINUE
  10    CONTINUE
        RETURN
        END
C*****SUBROUTINE FOR G OF FINITE SUBSTRATE
        SUBROUTINE DIGIMS(II,CW,CE,A)
        IMPLICIT REAL*4 (A- F,R- Z)
        COMMON /A / NX,NY / B / RPI / C / DELTX,DELTY
        DIMENSION A(500,50,6),NO(4,4)
        CALL ORDER(4,NO)
        JJ = NO(II,II)
        CALL DIGIMP(JJ,CW,CE,A)
        RETURN
        END
C*****SUBROUTINE FOR G OF INFINITE SUBSTRATE
        SUBROUTINE DIGIMO(II,CW,CE,A)
        IMPLICIT REAL*4 (A- F,R- Z)
        COMMON /A / NX,NY / B / RPI / C / DELTX,DELTY
        DIMENSION A(500,50,6),NO(4,4),D(200)
        CL = NY*DELTY*0.2 + CW*2
        CALL ORDER(4,NO)
        JJ = NO(II,II)
        IF(CW.LE.0.0) GOTO 200
        CX = CE*DELTY / DELTX
```

```
      CY = CE*DELTX / DELTY
      CZ = CE*DELTX*DELTY
      CZ = 1 / CZ
      CALL ZDIV(D,CL,N,DELTX)
      DO 10 I = 1,NX
      C1 = I*RPI / (NX + 1)
      AM = COS(C1)
      AM = (1- AM)*CX
      DO 10 J = 1,NY
      C1 = J*RPI / (NY + 1)
      AN = COS(C1)
      AN = (1- AN)*CY
      AMDA = AM + AN
      C = 0.0
      DO 40 K = 1,N
      DELTZ = D(K)
      C = C + AMDA*DELTZ
      C = 1 / C + CZ*DELTZ
      C = 1 / C = AMDA*DELTZ
40    CONTINUE
120   A(I,J,II) = C
10    CONTINUE
200   RETURN
      END
C*****SUBROUTINE FOR G OF DIAGONALIZED SYSTEM
      SUBROUTINE DIGIMP(II,CW,CE,A)
      IMPLICIT REAL*4 (A- F,R- Z)
      COMMON /A / NX,NY / B / RPI / C / DELTX,DELTY
      DIMENSION A(500,50,6),D(200)
      IF(CW.LE.0.0) GOTO 200
      CX = CE*DELTY / DELTX
      CY = CE*DELTX / DELTY
      CZ = CE*DELTX*DELTY
      CZ = 1 / CZ
      CALL ZDIV(D,CW,N,DELTX)
      DO 10 I = 1,NX
      C1 = I*RPI / (NX + 1)
      AM = COS(C1)
      AM = (1- AM)*CX
      DO 10 J = 1,NY
      C1 = J*RPI / (NY + 1)
      AN = COS(C1)
      AN = (1- AN)*CY
      AMDA = AM + AN
      C = 1E9
```

```
      DO 40 K = 1,N
      DELTZ = D(K)
      C = C + AMDA*DELTZ
      C = 1 / C + CZ*DELTZ
      C = 1 / C + AMDA*DELTZ
40    CONTINUE
120   A(I,J,II) = C + A(I,J,II)
10    CONTINUE
200   RETURN
      END
C*****CHOOSING VALUES FOR DELTZ
      SUBROUTINE ZDIV(D,CW,N,DELTX)
      DIMENSION D(200)
      N = 0
      CL = CW
80    DELTZ = CL / 8.0
90    IF(DELTZ.LE.CL / 4.0) GOTO 100
      DELTZ = DELTZ / 2.0
      GOTO 90
100   N = N + 1
      D(N) = DELTZ
      CL = CL- DELTZ
      IF(CL.GT.DELTX*5) GOTO 90
      DELTZ = CL / 6.0
      DO 200 I = 1,6
      N = N + 1
      D(N) = DELTZ
200   CONTINUE
      RETURN
      END
C*****G OF DIAGONALIZED SYSTEM OF LAYER BETWEEN LEVEL
C     I&II
      SUBROUTINE DIGIMM(II,CM,CE,A)
      IMPLICIT REAL*4 (A- F,R- Z)
      COMMON /A/ NX,NY / B / RPI / C / DELTX,DELTY
      DIMENSION A(500,50,6),DZ(200)
      DIMENSION CM(3),NO(4,4)
      CW = CM(II)
      CALL ORDER(4,NO)
      JJ = NO(II- 1,II)
      CX = CE*DELTY / DELTX
      CY = CE*DELTX / DELTY
      CZ = CE*DELTX*DELTY
      RZ = 1 / CZ
      CLI = CW / 2
```

```
      CALL ZDIV(DZ,CLI,N,DELTX)
      DO 10 I = 1,NX
      C1 = I*RPI / (NX + 1)
      AM = COS(C1)
      AM = (1- AM)*CX
      DO 10 J = 1,NY
      C1 = J*RPI / (CY + 1)
      AN = COS(C1)
      AN = (1- AN)*CY
      AMDA = AM + AN
      CA = 0
      RB = 0
      CC = 0
      IF(AMDA.EQ.0) CC = 1E- 9
C*****Y- DELTA TRANSFORMATION(BC,CR) TO (CA,CB,CC)
      DO 100 K = 1,N
      DELTZ = DZ(K)
      CYM = CC + AMDA*DELTZ
      RYM = 1 / CYM
      RZM = RZ*DELTZ
      RXM = RB
      XX = RXM*RYM + RYM*RZM + RZM*RXM
      CAM = RZM / XX
      CBM = RYM / XX
      CCM = RXM / XX
      CA = CAM + CA
      RB = 1 / CBM
      CC = CCM + AMDA*DELTZ
  100 CONTINUE
C*****SIMPLIFY BY SYMMETRY OF TWO HALVES OF MIDDLE
C     LAYER
      RYM = RB
      RZM = 0.5*CA
      RXM = RB
      XX = RXM*RYM + RYM*RZM + RZM*RXM
      CAM = RYM / XX
      CBM = RZM / XX
      CCM = RXM / XX
      CA = CAM + CC
      CB = CBM
      CC = CCM + CC
      A(I,J,NO(II- 1,II- 1)) = CC + A(I,J,NO(II- 1,II- 1)) +
     $                          CB
      A(I,J,NO(II,II)) = CA + A(I,J,NO(II,II)) + CB
      A(I,J,NO(II- 1,II)) = -CB
```

```
 10     CONTINUE
        RETURN
        END
C*****TO GET THE ORDER OF THE MATRIX
        SUBROUTINE ORDER(II,NO)
        DIMENSION NO(4,4)
        JJ = 0
        DO 10 J = 1,II
        DO 10 I = 1,J
        JJ = JJ + 1
        NO(I,J) = JJ
 10     CONTINUE
        RETURN
        END
C*****SUBROUTINE FOR WRITING THE MATRIX
        SUBROUTINE WRM(N,G,CH)
        DIMENSION G(150,150)
        REAL*4 G
        CHARACTER*4 CH
        WRITE(1,100)CH
100     FORMAT(1X, 'THE MATRIX ',A4, ' IS AS FOLLOWS',/ )
        DO 10 I = 1,N
        L = L + 1
        IF(L.LE.6) GOTO 40
C       WRITE(*,50)I
 50     FORMAT(1X, 'ROW ',I2)
        L = 1
 40     WRITE(1,*)(G(I,J),J = 1,N)
 10     CONTINUE
        WRITE(1,30)
 30     FORMAT(1X, '     ',/ )
        RETURN
        END
C*****CHOLESKY'S METHOD FOR LINEAR EQUATIONS A = INV(A)
        SUBROUTINE CHOL(N,A,B)
        DIMENSION A(150,150),B(150,150)
        REAL*4 A,B,C
C       A = BBT
        DO 10 I = 1,N
        DO 20 J = I,N
        C = A(J,I)
        IF(I.EQ.1) GOTO 32
        DO 30 M = 1,I- 1
 30     C = C- B(I,M)*B(J,M)
 32     IF(J.GT.I) GOTO 35
```

```
         B(I,I) = SQRT(C)
         GOTO 20
  35     B(J,I) = C / B(I,I)
  20     CONTINUE
  10     CONTINUE
C        B = BINV
         DO 110 I = 1,N
         IF(I.EQ.1) GOTO 120
         DO 120 J = 1,I- 1
         C = 0.0
         DO 130 K = J,I- 1
 130     C = C- B(K,J)*B(I,K)
         B(I,J) = C / B(I,I)
 120     CONTINUE
         B(I,I) = 1 / B(I,I)
 110     CONTINUE
C        A = BTB
         DO 210 I = 1,N
         DO 210 J = I,N
         L = MAX0(I,J)
         C = 0.0
         DO 220 K = L,N
 220     C = C + B(K,I)*B(K,J)
         A(I,J) = C
         A(J,I) = C
 210     CONTINUE
         RETURN
         END
C*****LU FACTORIZATION FOR INVERSE MATRIX A = INV(A)
         SUBROUTINE LU(N,A)
         DIMENSION A(4,4),B(4,4)
         REAL*4 A,B,C
         DO 5 I = 1,N
         DO 6 J = 1,N
  6      B(I,J) = 0.0
         B(I,I) = 1.0
  5      CONTINUE
         DO 10 I = 1,N
         DO 20 J = 1,N
         IF(I.EQ.J) GOTO 20
         C = A(J,I) / A(I,I)
         DO 30 K = 1,N
C        IF(K.EQ.I) GOTO 30
         A(J,K) = A(J,K)- C*A(I,K)
         B(J,K) = B(J,K)- C*B(I,K)
```

```
30      CONTINUE
20      CONTINUE
10      CONTINUE
        DO 40 I = 1,N
        DO 40 L = 1,N
        B(I,L) = B(I,L) / A(I,I)
40      CONTINUE
        DO 50 I = 1,N
        DO 50 L = 1,N
        A(I,L) = B(I,L)
50      CONTINUE
        RETURN
        END
C*****READ A REAL NUMBER
        SUBROUTINE REDRE(X)
        REAL*4 X
        CHARACTER*20 CH
        READ(2,*)CH
        READ(2,*)X
        WRITE(*,10)CH,X
        WRITE(1,10)CH,X
10      FORMAT(1X,A20, '= ',F12.5)
        RETURN
        END
C*****READ AN INTEGER
        SUBROUTINE REDIN(K)
        CHARACTER*20 CH
        READ(2,*)CH
        READ(2,*)K
        WRITE(*,10)CH,K
        WRITE(1,10)CH,K
10      FORMAT(1X,A20, '= ',I4)
        RETURN
        END
```

APPENDIX 2.3

EPCSGM
Electrode Parasitic Capacitances in a Single-Gate GaAs MESFET

```
        INTEGER N1X,N2X,N3X,NY,N1,N2,N3,N,I,J,EN,CNT,CR
        REAL A1,B1,C1,D1,A2,B2,C2,D2,E2,F2,G2,I2,J2,K2,
$          L2,M2,O2,P2,Q2,S2,G(6,6),GIJ,GIJ1,R1,R2,R3,
$          R4,R5,R6,R7,R8,R9,C1E,C2E,C3E,C1O,C2O,C3O,
```

```
      $      C11,C22,C33,C12,C13,C23,DS1,DS2,DS3,T1,T2,
      $      T3,T4,T5,T6,T7,T8,T9,T10,T11,T12,T13,T14,
      $      T15,T16,X(6),Y(6),Z(6),DX(6),DY,SL,GL,DL,W,
      $      T,H,K1,DSG,DGD,DR,L(10),M(10)
       OPEN (5, FILE = 'EPCD')
       OPEN (6, FILE = 'EPCR', STATUS = 'NEW')
       WRITE (6,132)
 132   FORMAT( 'ELECTRODE PARASITIC CAPACITANCES IN GaAs
      $          MESFET',// )
       WRITE (*,132)
C*****READ MESFET DIMENSIONS IN MICRONS
 10    READ (5,131) SL,DSG,GL,DGD,DL,W,T,H,DR
 131   FORMAT (9(F6.2,1X))
       WRITE (6,133)SL,DSG,GL,DGD,DL,W,T,H,DR
 133   FORMAT ( 'MESFET DIMENSIONS IN MICRONS:',//
      $          ' Source Length          =
      $          ',F8.2, ' microns',/
      $          ' Source-Gate Distance   =
      $          ',F8.2, ' microns',/
      $          ' Gate Length            =
      $          ',F8.2, ' microns',/
      $          ' Gate-Drain Distance    =
      $          ',F8.2, ' microns',/
      $          ' Drain Length           =
      $          ',F8.2, ' microns',/
      $          ' Width of the MESFET    =
      $          ',F8.2, ' microns',/
      $          ' Substrate Thickness    =
      $          ',F8.2, ' microns',/
      $          ' Height of Source/Drain=
      $          ',F8.2, ' microns',/
      $          ' Depth of Gate          =
      $          ',F8.2, ' microns')
       WRITE (*,133)SL,DSG,GL,DGD,DL,W,T,H,DR
       GIJ = 0.0
       I = 1
       J = 1
       EN = 1
       K1 = 0.859155
       N1X = 1
       N2X = 1
       N3X = 1
       NY = 2
       N1 = N1X*NY
       N2 = N2X*NY
```

```
       N3 = N3X*NY
       N = N1 + N2 + N3
       DY = W / NY
       DO 151 J = 1,N1,1
       DX(J) = SL / N1X
 151   CONTINUE
       DO 152 J = N1 + 1,N1 + N2,1
       DX(J) = GL / N2X
 152   CONTINUE
       DO 153 J = N1 + N2 + 1,N,1
       DX(J) = DL / N3X
 153   CONTINUE
       DS1 = DX(N1)*DY
       DS2 = DX(N1 + N2)*DY
       DS3 = DX(N)*DY
C*****X-, Y-, AND Z-COORDINATES OF SUBSECTIONS
       CNT = 0.0
       DO 5500 CR = 1,N1X,1
       DO 5900 I = CNT + 1,CTN + NY,1
       X(I) = (2*CR- 1)*((DX(N1)) / 2)
 5900  CONTINUE
       CNT = I
 5500  CONTINUE
       CNT = N1
       DO 6500 CR = 1,N2X,1
       DO 6900 I = CNT + 1,CNT + NY,1
       X(I) = (SL + DSG) + (2*CR- 1)*((DX(N1 + N2)) / 2)
 6900  CONTINUE
       CNT = I
 6500  CONTINUE
       CNT = N1 + N2
       DO 7500 CR = 1,N3X,1
       DO 7900 I = CNT + 1,CNT + NY,1
       X(I) = (SL + DSG + GL + DGD) + (2*CR- 1)*((DX(N)) / 2)
 7900  CONTINUE
       CNT = I
 7500  CONTINUE
       DO 8000 CR = 1,NY,1
       DO 8500 I = CR,N,NY
       Y(I) = (2*CR- 1)*(DY / 2)
 8500  CONTINUE
 8000  CONTINUE
       DO 9000 I = 1,N,1
       Z(I) = T
 9000  CONTINUE
```

```
      DO 9100 I = N1 + 1,N1 + N2,1
      Z(I) = T- DR
 9100 CONTINUE
C*****ELEMENTS OF THE GREEN'S FUNCTION MATRIX
      DO 300 I = 1,N,1
      DO 310 J = 1,N,1
      A1 = X(J) - X(I) - ((DX(J)) / 2)
      B1 = X(J) - X(I) + ((DX(J)) / 2)
      C1 = Y(J) - Y(I) - (DY / 2)
      D1 = Y(J) - Y(I) + (DY / 2)
      GIJ1 = 0.0
      EN = 1
  320 A2 = SQRT(A1**2 + C1**2 + ((2*H- 2*EN*T)**2))
      B2 = SQRT(B1**2 + D1**2 + ((2*H- 2*EN*T)**2))
      C2 = SQRT(A1**2 + D1**2 + ((2*H- 2*EN*T)**2))
      D2 = SQRT(B1**2 + C1**2 + ((2*H- 2*EN*T)**2))
      E2 = SQRT(A1**2 + C1**2 + ((2*EN*T)**2))
      F2 = SQRT(B1**2 + D1**2 + ((2*EN*T)**2))
      G2 = SQRT(A1**2 + D1**2 + ((2*EN*T)**2))
      I2 = SQRT(B1**2 + C1**2 + ((2*EN*T)**2))
      J2 = SQRT(A1**2 + C1**2 + ((2*H + (2*EN- 2)*T)**2))
      K2 = SQRT(B1**2 + D1**2 + ((2*H + (2*EN- 2)*T)**2))
      L2 = SQRT(A1**2 + D1**2 + ((2*H + (2*EN- 2)*T)**2))
      M2 = SQRT(B1**2 + C1**2 + ((2*H + (2*EN- 2)*T)**2))
      S2 = SQRT(A1**2 + C1**2 + ((2*EN- 2)*T)**2)
      O2 = SQRT(B1**2 + D1**2 + ((2*EN- 2)*T)**2)
      P2 = SQRT(A1**2 + D1**2 + ((2*EN- 2)*T)**2)
      Q2 = SQRT(B1**2 + C1**2 + ((2*EN- 2)*T)**2)
      T1 = (X(J) - X(I)) * (LOG(C1 + A2) + LOG(D1 + B2) + LOG(D1
     $     +G2) + LOG(C1 + I2) - LOG(D1 + C2) - LOG(C1 + D2) -
     $     LOG(C1 + E2) - LOG(D1 + F2))
      T2 = ((DX(J)) / 2) * (LOG(D1 + B2) + LOG(D1 + C2) + LOG(C1
     $     +E2) + LOG(C1 + I2) - LOG(C1 + D2) - LOG(C1 + A2) - LOG
     $     (D1 + G2) - LOG(D1 + F2))
      T3 = (Y(J) - Y(I)) * (LOG(A1 + A2) + LOG(B1 + B2) + LOG(B1
     $     +I2) + LOG(A1 + G2) - LOG(B1 + D2) - LOG(A1 + C2) -
     $     LOG(A1 + E2) - LOG(B1 + F2))
      T4 = (DY / 2) * (LOG(B1 + B2) + LOG(B1 + D2) + LOG(A1 + E2)
     $     +LOG(A1 + G2) - LOG(A1 + C2) - LOG(A1 + A2) - LOG(B1
     $     +I2) - LOG(B1 + F2))
      IF ((EN .EQ. 1) .AND. (T .EQ. H)) THEN
      T5 = 0.0
      T6 = 0.0
      ELSE
      T5 = (2*H- 2*EN*T) * (ATAN(A1*C1 / ((2*H- 2*EN*T)*A2)))
```

```
$      +ATAN(B1*D1 / ((2*H- 2*EN*T)*B2)))
 T6 = (2*H- 2*EN*T)*(ATAN(A1*D1 / ((2*H- 2*EN*T)*C2))
$      +ATAN(B1*C1 / ((2*H- 2*EN*T)*D2)))
 END IF
 T7 = (2*EN*T)*(ATAN(A1*C1 / (2*EN*T*E2)) + ATAN(B1*
$      D1 / (2*EN*T*F2)))
 T8 = (2*EN*T)*(ATAN(A1*D1 / (2*EN*T*G2)) + ATAN(B1*
$      C1 / (2*EN*T*I2)))
 T9 = (X(J)- X(I))*(LOG(D1 + K2) + LOG(C1 + J2) + LOG(D1
$      +P2) + LOG(C1 + Q2)- LOG(D1 + L2)- LOG(C1 + M2)-
$      LOG(C1 + S2)- LOG(D1 + O2))
 T10 = ((DX(J)) / 2)*(LOG(D1 + K2) + LOG(D1 + L2) + LOG
$      (C1 + S2) + LOG(C1 + Q2)- LOG(C1 + M2)- LOG(C1 +
$      J2)- LOG(D1 + O2)- LOG(D1 + P2))
 T11 = (Y(J)- Y(I))*(LOG(A1 + J2) + LOG(B1 + K2) + LOG(A1
$      +P2) + LOG(B1 + Q2)- LOG(B1 + M2)- LOG(B1 + O2)-
$      LOG(A1 + L2)- LOG(A1 + S2))
 T12 = (DY / 2)*(LOG(B1 + K2) + LOG(B1 + M2) + LOG(A1 +
$      P2) + LOG(A1 + S2)- LOG(A1 + L2)- LOG(A1 + J2)-
$      LOG(B1 + O2)- LOG(B1 + Q2))
 T13 = (2*H + (2*EN- 2)*T)*(ATAN(A1*C1 / ((2*H + (2*EN-
$      2)*T)*J2)) + ATAN(B1*D1 / ((2*H + (2*EN- 2)*T)*
$      K2)))
 T14 = (2*H + (2*EN- 2)*T)*(ATAN(A1*D1 / ((2*H + (2*EN-
$      2)*T)*L2)) + ATAN(B1*C1 / ((2*H + (2*EN- 2)*T)
$      *M2)))
 T15 = 0.0
 T16 = 0.0
 IF (EN .GT. 1) THEN
 T15 = ((2*EN- 2)*T)*(ATAN(A1*C1 / ((2*EN- 2)*T*S2))
$      +ATAN(B1*D1 / ((2*EN- 2)*T*O2)))
 T16 = ((2*EN- 2)*T)*(ATAN(A1*D1 / ((2*EN- 2)*T*P2))
$      +ATAN(B1*C1 / ((2*EN- 2)*T*Q2)))
 END IF
 GIJ = 00.68*(((((-1)**(EN- 1)*(K1**EN))*(T1 + T2 + T3
$      +T4- T5 + T6 + T7- T8) + (((-1)**EN)*(K1**(EN-
$      1)))*(T9 + T10 + T11 + T12- T13 + T14 + T15- T16)))
 GIJ1 = GIJ1 + GIJ
 IF (ABS(GIJ).GT.(0.0001)) THEN
 EN = EN + 1
 GO TO 320
 ELSE
 G(I,J) = GIJ1
 END IF
310  CONTINUE
```

```
 300  CONTINUE
      CALL MINV(G,N,D,L,M)
C*****EVEN- AND ODD-MODE CAPACITANCES
      R1 = 0.0
      R2 = 0.0
      R3 = 0.0
      R4 = 0.0
      R5 = 0.0
      R6 = 0.0
      R7 = 0.0
      R8 = 0.0
      R9 = 0.0
      DO 1000 I = 1,N1,1
      DO 1001 J = 1,N1,1
      R1 = R1 + G(I,J)
 1001 CONTINUE
      DO 1002 J = N1 + 1,N1 + N2,1
      R2 = R2 + G(I,J)
 1002 CONTINUE
      DO 1003 J = N1 + N2 + 1,N,1
      R3 = R3 + G(I,J)
 1003 CONTINUE
 1000 CONTINUE
      DO 1300 I = N1 + 1,N1 + N2,1
      DO 1301 J = 1,N1,1
      R4 = R4 + G(I,J)
 1301 CONTINUE
      DO 1302 J = N1 + 1,N1 + N2,1
      DO 1302 J = N1 + 1,N1 + N2,1
      R5 = R5 + G(I,J)
 1302 CONTINUE
      DO 1303 J = N1 + N2 + 1,N,1
      R6 = R6 + G(I,J)
 1303 CONTINUE
 1300 CONTINUE
      DO 1600 I = N1 + N2 + 1,N,1
      DO 1601 = 1,N1,1
      R7 = R7 + G(I,J)
 1601 CONTINUE
      DO 1602 J = N1 + 1,N1 + N2,1
      R8 = R8 + G(I,J)
 1602 CONTINUE
      DO 1603 J = N1 + N2 + 1,N,1
      R9 = R9 + G(I,J)
 1603 CONTINUE
```

```
1600 CONTINUE
     C1E = (R1 + R2 + R3)*DS1
     C2E = (R4 + R5 + R6)*DS2
     C3E = (R7 + R8 + R9)*DS3
     C1O = (R1- R2- R3)*DS1
     C2O = (R5- R4- R6)*DS2
     C3O = (R9- R7- R8)*DS3
C*****ELECTRODE CAPACITANCES IN THE MESFET
     C11 = C1E*1.1
     C22 = C2E*1.1
     C33 = C3E*1.1
     C12 = (C3E- C2E- C1E + C1O + C2O- C3O)*0.3
     C13 = (C2E- C1E- C3E + C1O + C3O- C2O)*0.3
     C23 = (C1E- C2E- C3E- C1O + C2O + C3O)*0.3
     WRITE (6,134)
134  FORMAT ( / 'ELECTRODE CAPACITANCES IN
     $           FEMTOFARADS:'/ )
     WRITE (*,134)
     WRITE (*,1800) C11,C22,C33,C12,C13,C23
1800 FORMAT ( ' Cs = 'F9.3,/, ' Cg = 'F9.3,/, ' Cd =
     $          'F9.3,/,
     $          ' Csg = 'F9.3,/, ' Csd = 'F9.3,/, ' Cgd =
     $          'F9.3)
     WRITE (6,1800) C11,C22,C33,C12,C13,C23
     WRITE (*,1810)
1810 FORMAT(/, '-----------------------------',/ )
     WRITE (6,1810)
     GO TO 10
     STOP
     END

     SUBROUTINE MINV
     (Same as in Appendix 2.1)
```

CHAPTER 3

Propagation Delays

Among some of the recent advancements in VLSI technology, high-speed silicon and GaAs technologies have been developed rapidly, and propagation delay times of less than 10 ps per gate have been achieved [3.1, 3.2]. In the near future, high electron mobility transistors (HEMTs) and modulation-doped field effect transistors (MODFETs) are expected to have switching speeds of less than 5 ps and ballistic electron speeds of less than 1 ps [3.3]. For very large scale integrated circuits, the propagation delays and the crosstalk noise associated with signal transmissions on the interconnections have become the primary factors in limiting circuit speed and chip density. In most cases interconnection delays on an IC chip account for more than 50 percent of the total delays. A comprehensive understanding of the dependence of interconnection delays on the various interconnection parameters is urgently needed for optimum chip design.

In the literature many numerical techniques used to model the time domain pulse propagation in the interconnection lines on high-speed digital circuits, including multilevel interconnections, are available [3.4–3.17]. The method of characteristics, modified to include frequency-dependent losses, has been employed in references [3.4] to [3.6]. The well-known transmission line theory has been used to analyze interconnections in references [3.16] and [3.17]. The use of congruent modeling techniques, whereby researchers have attempted to model interconnections in terms of lumped- and distributed-circuit elements available in computer-aided design programs such as SPICE, is demonstrated in references [3.9] and [3.13]. Specialized techniques to compute the time domain pulse responses of interconnection structures terminated in linear and nonlinear networks from their frequency domain analysis are reported in references [3.12] and [3.15]. In most cases interconnections have been modeled as single lossy lines or multiple coupled lossless microstrip lines. High-frequency effects, such as conductor loss, dielectric loss, skin effect, and frequency-dependent effective dielectric constant, have been studied for a microstrip interconnection in reference [3.18].

164

In this chapter an analysis of interconnection delays on very high speed VLSI chips using a metal–insulator–semiconductor microstrip line model is presented in Section 3.1. In Section 3.2 a computer-efficient model based on a transmission line analysis of propagation delays in high-density single-level interconnections on GaAs-based very high speed integrated circuits is presented. In Section 3.3 a computer-efficient algorithm for studying signal propagation in single-, bi- and trilevel high-density interconnections on GaAs-based integrated circuits is presented. In Section 3.4 a computer-efficient model of propagation delays in bilevel parallel and crossing interconnections on GaAs-based very high speed integrated circuits is presented. A SPICE model for lossless parallel interconnections modeled as multiple coupled microstrips is presented in Section 3.5, and, in Section 3.6, this model is extended to lossy parallel and crossing interconnections. High-frequency effects, such as conductor loss, dielectric loss, skin effect, and frequency-dependent effective dielectric constant, have been studied for a microstrip interconnection in Section 3.7. For the sake of completion, a model for calculating transverse propagation delays in GaAs MESFETs is developed in Section 3.8, and, in Section 3.9, the GaAs MESFET model is extended to study transverse propagation delays in a GaAs/AlGaAs MODFET. Finally, a simplified model of interconnection delays in multilayer integrated circuits is presented in Section 3.10.

3.1 METAL – INSULATOR – SEMICONDUCTOR MICROSTRIP LINE MODEL OF AN INTERCONNECTION

In this section interconnection delays on a very high speed integrated circuit chip are investigated using a metal–insulator–semiconductor (MIS) microstrip line model for the interconnection [3.11].

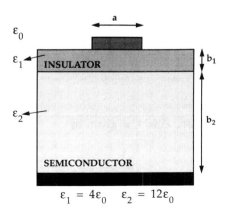

$\varepsilon_1 = 4\varepsilon_0 \quad \varepsilon_2 = 12\varepsilon_0$

FIGURE 3.1.1 MIS microstrip line model for an interconnection [3.11]. (© 1984 IEEE)

parameter h of the Schwarz–Christoffel transformation is given by

$$h = \left| E' - K'k^2 sn^2\left(\frac{\pi W^2}{2b} \right) \right|$$

where sn is Jacobi's elliptic function and K' and E' are complete elliptic integrals of the first and second kinds with modulus k, respectively. Note that $Z_s(\omega)$ is frequency dependent because of the skin effect in the semiconductor.

For a given interconnection geometry, the transient waveforms can be calculated by the following steps: (1) calculation of the equivalent-circuit parameters; (2) calculation of characteristic impedance and propagation constants based on the equivalent circuit shown in Figure 3.1.2; and (3) calculation of the transient waveforms under arbitrary excitation and termination conditions by the inverse Laplace transformation. The last step involving the inverse Laplace transformation can be carried out using the standard trigonometric function expansion method.

3.1.2 Simulation Results

3.1.2.1 Semi-Infinite Interconnections   For an interconnection of semi-infinite length (which is equivalent to the line of finite length terminated with a hypothetical matched load), the dependences of the propagation delay time (time to 50 percent rise) and rise time (time from 10 to 90 percent rise) of the

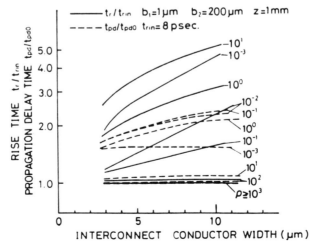

FIGURE 3.1.4 Dependences of the delay time and rise time on the interconnection width for a semi-infinite interconnection. The rise time of the input pulse is assumed to be 8 ps [3.11]. (© 1984 IEEE)

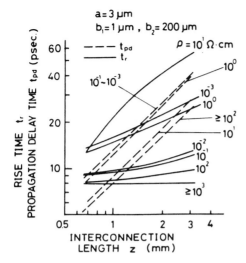

FIGURE 3.1.5 Dependences of the delay time and rise time on the distance z from the signal source for a semi-infinite interconnection. The rise time of the input pulse is assumed to be 8 ps [3.11]. (© 1984 IEEE)

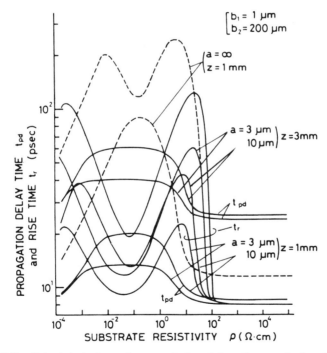

FIGURE 3.1.6 Calculated dependences of the delay time and rise time on the substrate resistivity for a semi-infinite interconnection. The rise time of the input pulse is assumed to be 8 ps [3.11]. (© 1984 IEEE)

step response on the width of the interconnection are shown in Figure 3.1.4. Figure 3.1.5 shows these dependences on the distance z from the signal source. For a semi-infinite interconnection, the dependences of the delay and rise times on the substrate resistivity in the range 10^{-4} to 10^5 $\Omega \cdot$ cm are shown in Figure 3.1.6. The responses are calculated at positions with distances of $z = 1$ mm and $z = 3$ mm from the signal source. The results of Figure 3.1.6 can be explained in terms of three fundamental modes, that is, the skin effect mode, the slow-wave mode, and the dielectric quasi-TEM mode, as follows: (1) The increase of the delay time in the midresistivity range is due to the slow-wave mode; and (2) the rise time peaks on both sides of the delay time peak are due to mode transitions from the slow-wave mode either to the dielectric quasi-TEM mode or to the skin effect mode.

3.1.2.2 Interconnections Between Logic Gates For an interconnection connecting two logic gates as shown in Figure 3.1.7*a*, an equivalent model is shown in Figure 3.1.7*b*, where R_s is the output resistance of the driving gate and corresponds to the resistance of the input signal source, whereas C_L is the input capacitance of the driven gate and corresponds to the load capacitance of the interconnection line. In gates consisting of FET-type devices such as MESFETs, MOSFETs, and HEMTs, R_s is approximately

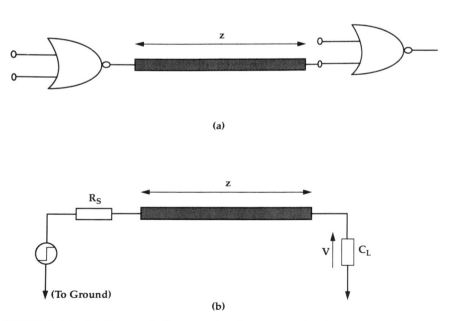

(a)

(b)

FIGURE 3.1.7 (*a*) Schematic diagram of an interconnection between two logic gates and (*b*) its equivalent model [3.11]. (© 1984 IEEE)

TABLE 3.1.1   Transconductance g_m and R_s of Various FET Devices (gate length, 1 μm; gate width, 10 μm) [3.11] (© 1984 IEEE)

Device	g_m (mS)	R_s (Ω)
GaAs MESFET	1.4	710
Si MOSFET	0.8	1250
HEMT (77K)	2.9	350

equal to the inverse of the transconductance g_m. To determine C_L, the following rule of thumb can be used: A standard 1-μm-gate GaAs MESFET has approximately an input gate capacitance of 1 fF per 1-μm gate width. The transconductance g_m and the output resistance R_s of various FET devices, each with a gate length of 1 μm and a gate width of 10 μm, are given in Table 3.1.1.

The calculated voltage waveforms for an interconnection with a width of 3 μm and a length of 3 mm for two source resistances of 1 kΩ and 100 Ω and for various substrate resistivity values are given in Figures 3.1.8a and b, respectively. For the sake of comparison, the waveforms based on the lumped-capacitance approximation for $\rho = \infty$ and $\rho = 0$ are also included in Figures 3.1.8a and b. It can be concluded that the lumped-capacitance approximation yields reasonably good results when the source resistance is high and the response is slow. However, if the source resistance is low and the response is fast, then the results based on the lumped-capacitance approximation become rather inadequate.

The dependences of the calculated delay times and rise times on the signal source resistance for several substrate resistivity values are shown in Figures 3.1.9 and 3.1.10, respectively. For the sake of comparison, the values based on the lumped-capacitance approximation for $\rho = \infty$ and $\rho = 0$ are also included in Figures 3.1.9 and 3.1.10. It can be seen that the lumped-capacitance approximation yields reasonably good results when the delay time is nearly over 200 ps. The results in Figures 3.1.9 and 3.1.10 also indicate that semi-insulating substrates offer a significant advantage over semiconducting substrates in both delay and rise times.

3.2   TRANSMISSION LINE ANALYSIS OF SINGLE-LEVEL INTERCONNECTIONS

In this section a computer-efficient algorithm for calculating propagation delays in high-density single-level interconnections on GaAs-based very high speed integrated circuits is presented. The interconnection has been modeled as a distributed-element equivalent circuit, and the effect of capacitive

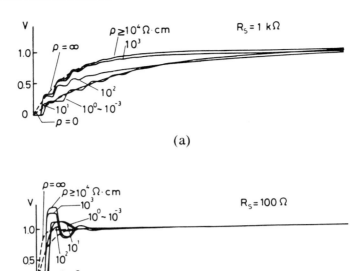

(a)

(b)

FIGURE 3.1.8 Calculated step response waveforms for (*a*) $R_s = 1$ kΩ and (*b*) $R_s = 100$ Ω. Dimension parameters are: $a = 3$ μm, $z = 3$ mm, $b_1 = 1$ μm, and $b_2 = 200$ μm. Results based on the lumped-capacitance approximation are shown by the dashed curves [3.11]. (© 1984 IEEE)

coupling with neighboring interconnections have been included. The technique presented in the model can be applied to lossy as well as lossless lines and can be easily extended to include coupling with any number of neighboring lines. The interconnection capacitances can be determined by the method of moments in conjunction with a Green's function appropriate for the geometry of the interconnections [3.19]. As mentioned earlier, the capacitances thus determined include the fringing fields as well as the shielding effects due to the presence of neighboring conductors. The model has been used to determine the dependences of the delay times and the rise times (defined as the time taken by the output voltages to rise from 0 to 50 percent and from 10 to 90 percent of their steady-state values, respectively [3.20]) on the interconnection dimensions and other parameters.

3.2.1 The Model

An interconnection, modeled as a transmission line driven by a unit step voltage source and terminated by a load Z_L, is shown in Figure 3.2.1. All the

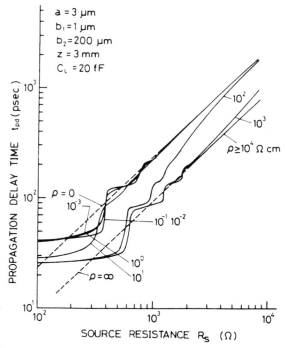

FIGURE 3.1.9 Dependence of the calculated delay times on the signal source resistance for several substrate resistivity values. Results based on the lumped-capacitance approximation are shown by the dashed curves [3.11]. (© 1984 IEEE)

elements shown in the figure are per unit length of the interconnection. Capacitive couplings of the line with its first and second neighbors are also shown in the figure. The series resistance and inductance elements for the neighboring interconnections will not affect the propagation characteristics along the interconnection in question; therefore, these are not included in the model. The various symbols used in the equivalent circuit of Figure 3.2.1 are defined as follows:

R = resistance of the interconnection line

L = inductance of the interconnection line

C_i = self-capacitance (i.e., the capacitance between the conductor and the ground plane) of the interconnection line

C_{il1} = mutual capacitance between the interconnection and its first neighbor on the left

C_{ir1} = mutual capacitance between the interconnection and its first neighbor on the right

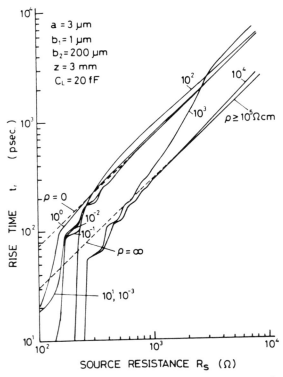

FIGURE 3.1.10 Dependence of the calculated rise times on the signal source resistance for several substrate resistivity values. Results based on the lumped-capacitance approximation are shown by the dashed curves [3.11]. (© 1984 IEEE)

C_{il2} = mutual capacitance between the interconnection and its second neighbor on the left

C_{ir2} = mutual capacitance between the interconnection and its second neighbor on the right

C_{l1} = self-capacitance of the first neighbor on the left of the interconnection

C_{l2} = self-capacitance of the second neighbor on the left of the interconnection

C_{r1} = self-capacitance of the first neighbor on the right of the interconnection

C_{r2} = self-capacitance of the second neighbor on the right of the interconnection

As far as propagation along the interconnection is concerned, the effect of its

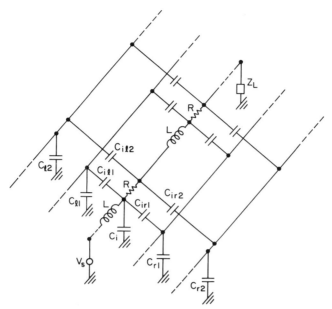

FIGURE 3.2.1   Interconnection modeled as a transmission line driven by a unit step voltage source and terminated by a load Z_L. Coupling of the interconnection with its nearest two neighbors on each side is also shown.

coupling with its first right neighbor is to connect an impedance Z_1 in parallel with the capacitance C_i, where

$$Z_1 = \frac{C_{ir1} + C_{r1}}{sC_{r1}C_{ir1}} \qquad (3.2.1)$$

Similarly, the contributions of coupling of the interconnection with its second right neighbor, first left neighbor, and second left neighbor are to connect impedances Z_2, Z_3, and Z_4, respectively, in parallel with C_i, where

$$Z_2 = \frac{C_{ir2} + C_{r2}}{sC_{r2}C_{ir2}} \qquad (3.2.2)$$

$$Z_3 = \frac{C_{il1} + C_{l1}}{sC_{l1}C_{il1}} \qquad (3.2.3)$$

and

$$Z_4 = \frac{C_{il2} + C_{l2}}{sC_{l2}C_{il2}} \qquad (3.2.4)$$

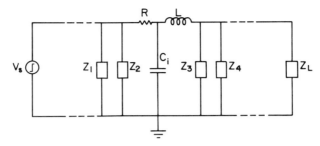

FIGURE 3.2.2   One section of the uncoupled interconnection line equivalent to each section of the coupled lines of Figure 3.2.1.

Therefore, the equivalent circuit of Figure 3.2.1 can be reduced to that shown in Figure 3.2.2. Figure 3.2.2 shows one section of the equivalent circuit only and can be used to determine the propagation constant for the interconnection line as follows. The propagation constant γ is defined by the relationship

$$\gamma = \sqrt{\frac{Z_s}{Z_p}} \tag{3.2.5}$$

where the series impedance per unit length Z_s is given by

$$Z_s = R + sL \tag{3.2.6}$$

and the parallel impedance per unit length Z_p is the impedance of the parallel combination of C_i, Z_1, Z_2, Z_3, and Z_4; that is,

$$\frac{1}{Z_p} = \frac{1}{Z_1} + \frac{1}{Z_2} + \frac{1}{Z_3} + \frac{1}{Z_4} + sC_i$$
$$= (Y_1 + Y_2 + Y_3 + Y_4 + C_i)s \tag{3.2.7}$$

where

$$Y_1 = \frac{C_{r1}C_{ir1}}{C_{ir1} + C_{r1}} \tag{3.2.8}$$

$$Y_2 = \frac{C_{r2}C_{ir2}}{C_{ir2} + C_{r2}} \tag{3.2.9}$$

$$Y_3 = \frac{C_{l1}C_{il1}}{C_{il1} + C_{l1}} \tag{3.2.10}$$

$$Y_4 = \frac{C_{l2}C_{il2}}{C_{il2} + C_{l2}} \tag{3.2.11}$$

The propagation constant will then be given by

$$\gamma = \sqrt{(R + sL)s\left\{\sum_{i=1}^{4} Y_i + C_i\right\}}$$

(3.2.12)

and the characteristic impedance will be given by

$$Z_0 = \sqrt{\frac{R + sL}{s\left(C_i + \sum_{i=1}^{4} Y_i\right)}}$$

(3.2.13)

In the Laplace transform domain, the voltage and current distributions along an interconnection satisfy the following transmission line equations:

$$\frac{d^2V}{dz^2} = \gamma^2 V$$

(3.2.14)

and

$$\frac{d^2I}{dz^2} = \gamma^2 I$$

(3.2.15)

The most general solutions for the voltage and current along the interconnection length (denoted by the coordinate z) are given by

$$v_z = Ae^{-\gamma z} + Be^{-\gamma z}$$

(3.2.16)

$$i_z = \frac{Ae^{-\gamma z} - Be^{-\gamma z}}{Z_0}$$

(3.2.17)

where the constants A and B can be determined by employing the known boundary conditions. If the interconnection is driven at the end $z = 0$ by a source of voltage V_s having an internal impedance R_s, then at this end

$$v_z = V_s - iR_s$$

(3.2.18)

Furthermore, if the interconnection is terminated by a load Z_L at $z = l$, then at this end

$$\frac{v_z}{i_z} = Z_L$$

(3.2.19)

Substituting conditions (3.2.18) and (3.2.19) into Equations 3.2.16 and 3.2.17, the values of A and B are given by

$$A = \frac{V_s Z_0}{R_s + Z_0 - \left(\dfrac{Z_L - Z_0}{Z_L + Z_0}\right)(R_s - Z_0)e^{-2\gamma l}} \tag{3.2.20}$$

$$B = A\left(\frac{Z_L - Z_0}{Z_L + Z_0}\right)e^{-2\gamma l} \tag{3.2.21}$$

In order to determine the propagation delays (i.e., the delay time and the rise time) for an interconnection, one needs to know how the voltage at the load varies as a function of time in response to a unit step voltage applied at $z = 0$. In s space, a unit step voltage source is represented by

$$V_s = \frac{1}{s} \tag{3.2.22}$$

The voltage at the load end ($z = 1$) is given by Equation 3.2.16 to be

$$V(s) = Ae^{-\gamma l} + Be^{-\gamma l} \tag{3.2.23}$$

where the propagation constant γ in s space is given by Equations 3.2.5 to 3.2.12 and the constants A and B are given by Equations 3.2.20 and 3.2.21, respectively.

The time domain response of the output voltage can be obtained by an inverse Laplace transformation of $V(s)$. Because of the presence of branch points associated with the propagation constant γ, an inverse transformation can be obtained by using the concept of Bromwich integrals; that is,

$$v(t) = \frac{1}{2\pi j}\int_{\text{Br}} V(s)e^{st}\,ds \tag{3.2.24}$$

Using Simpson's rule, it can be rewritten as

$$v(t) \sim \frac{1}{2\pi j}\sum_{n=-N}^{N} V(s)e^{st}\,\Delta s \tag{3.2.25}$$

Writing the complex frequency in terms of its real and imaginary parts as

$$s = \sigma + j\omega \tag{3.2.26}$$

we have

$$\Delta s = j\,\Delta\omega \tag{3.2.27}$$

and

$$s = \sigma + jn\,\Delta\omega \qquad (3.2.28)$$

Therefore,

$$v(t) \sim \frac{1}{2\pi} \sum_{n=-N}^{N} V(\sigma + jn\,\Delta\omega)e^{(\sigma + jn\,\Delta\omega)t}\,\Delta\omega \qquad (3.2.29)$$

In principle, any positive s and $\Delta\omega$ that will cause two consecutive terms in the summation in Equation 3.2.29 to be sufficiently close to each other can be used. However, these should be carefully chosen to optimize the speed of convergence. The best values for s and $\Delta\omega$ depend on the time t (in seconds) and can be found to be $s = 0.5t$ and $\Delta\omega = 0.05/t$. The best choice for N also depends on t, ranging from 500 to 1000 for small t and large t, respectively.

3.2.2   The Program PDSIGV

A listing of the computer program called Propagation Delays in Single-Level Interconnections on GaAs-based VLSI (PDSIGV), which incorporates the steps given previously, is presented in Appendix 3.1. For a given set of interconnection dimensions, that is, the interconnection lengths, the interconnection widths, the interconnection separations, the resistivity of the interconnection material, the load capacitance, and the resistance of the unit step voltage source, the program computes the characteristic impedance and the propagation constant for the interconnection, performs the summation in Equation 3.2.29, and finally calculates the normalized voltage at the load as a function of time in any desired time range. The output voltage is normalized

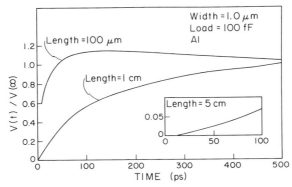

FIGURE 3.2.3   Normalized output voltages for interconnection lengths of 100 μm and 1 cm. The insert shows the output voltage for an interconnection length of 5 cm.

in the sense that it is the ratio of the voltage at the load at a given time t to its value at time $t = \infty$. The resistance and inductance of the interconnection line are kept as $R = 2 \times \rho \times 10^4$ Ω/m and $L = 10^{-6}$ H/m, where ρ is the resistivity of the interconnection material. The value of R is for 0.5 μm thickness of the interconnection. The values of the self-capacitances and mutual capacitances for the system of interconnections are determined by using the model developed earlier [3.19]. The overshoot and ringing observed in the following curves are due to a finite number of terms included in the approximation expressed by Equation 3.2.29 used to find $v(t)$.

3.2.3   Dependence on Interconnection Parameters

The program PDSIGV can be used to study the dependences of the delay time and the rise time on the interconnection dimensions, namely the length and width of the interconnection and the resistivity of the interconnection material. All the results are obtained for a load capacitance of 100 fF and with the resistance of the unit step voltage source set equal to 700 Ω. This corresponds to the interconnection line being driven by a typical GaAs MESFET with a gate width equal to 10 μm. Figure 3.2.3 shows the normalized output voltages for interconnection lengths of 100 μm and 1 cm. The insert in this figure shows that for "long" interconnections, no output voltage is expected to be observed for some time. Figure 3.2.4 shows the dependence of the delay time on the interconnection length, whereas the dependence of the rise time on the interconnection length is shown in Figure 3.2.5. These figures indicate that for interconnection lengths above 100 μm the delay time and rise time increase significantly, whereas they are almost constant below about 100 μm. As a function of the interconnection width, the delay time and the rise time are shown in the Figures 3.2.6 and 3.2.7, respectively. Figure 3.2.8 shows the normalized output voltages for interconnection widths of 1.0 and 0.1 μm. Figures 3.2.6 and 3.2.7 indicate that the propagation delays decrease when the interconnection width is increased from 0.1 to about

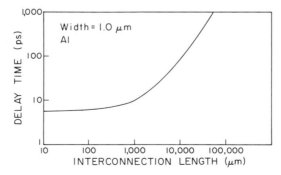

FIGURE 3.2.4   Dependence of the delay time on the interconnection length.

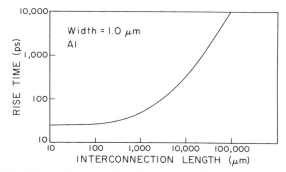

FIGURE 3.2.5   Dependence of the rise time on the interconnection length.

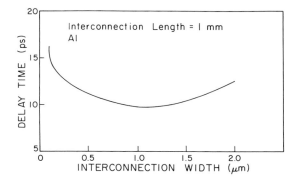

FIGURE 3.2.6   Dependence of the delay time on the interconnection width.

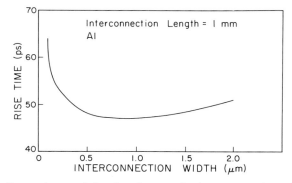

FIGURE 3.2.7   Dependence of the rise time on the interconnection width.

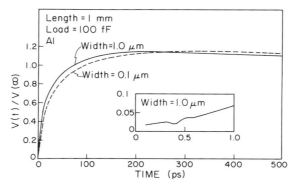

FIGURE 3.2.8 Normalized output voltages for interconnection widths of 1.0 and 0.1 μm. The insert shows the output voltage for an interconnection width of 1.0 μm for times less than 1.0 ps.

1 μm. For interconnection widths above about 1 μm, both the delay time and the rise time increase somewhat. The initial decrease in the transit times below about 1 μm is due to the decreasing line resistance, whereas the increase observed above about 1 μm is due to the increasing interconnection capacitances. Figure 3.2.9 shows the normalized output voltages when the interconnection metal is aluminum, WSi_2, or polysilicon. These correspond to the interconnection metal resistivities of 3, 30, and 500 $\mu\Omega \cdot$ cm respectively. Figure 3.2.9 shows that, as the resistivity is increased, the time for the output voltage to reach its steady-state value increases as well. The resulting increases in the delay time and the rise time are shown in Figure 3.2.10. Figure 3.2.11 shows the normalized output voltages for the load capacitances of 10 fF and 1 pF. The effect of including the coupling of the interconnection with the neighboring lines in the present model is shown in Figure 3.2.12. As

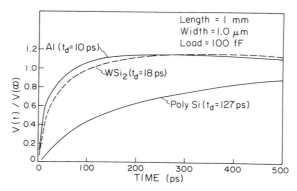

FIGURE 3.2.9 Normalized output voltages for the interconnection metals of Al, WSi_2, and polysilicon.

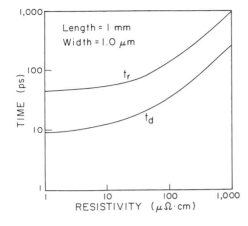

FIGURE 3.2.10 Dependences of the delay time and the rise time on the interconnection metal resistivity.

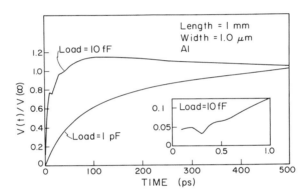

FIGURE 3.2.11   Normalized output voltages for load capacitances of 10 fF and 1 pF.

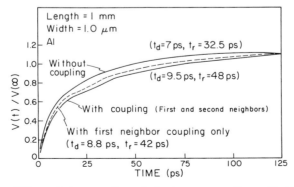

FIGURE 3.2.12   Effect of the coupling of the interconnection with its neighbors on the output voltage.

shown in Figure 3.2.12, it takes longer for the output voltage to reach its steady-state value when the coupling is present, as expected.

3.3   TRANSMISSION LINE ANALYSIS OF PARALLEL MULTILEVEL INTERCONNECTIONS

In this section a transmission line analysis of signal propagation in multilevel interconnections, including single-, bi-, and trilevel high-density interconnections, on GaAs-based integrated circuits is presented. The model has been utilized to study the dependences of the load voltages and the delay times on the interconnection parameters such as their lengths, widths, separations, interlevel distances, driving transistor resistance, and load capacitance.

3.3.1   The Model

As shown in Figure 3.3.1, the interconnection line can be modeled as a transmission line driven by a unit step voltage source having resistance R_s, loaded by the capacitance C_L and coupled to the neighboring interconnection lines by the mutual capacitances and inductances (not shown in the figure). The resistance R_s is determined by the dimensions of the driving transistor and the capacitance C_L is determined by the parasitic capacitances of the transistor loading the interconnection line. For interconnection lines printed on or embedded in a semi-insulating GaAs substrate, quasi-TEM is the dominant mode of wave propagation, and the transmission line equations are given by

$$\frac{\partial}{\partial x}V(x,t) = -\left[R + L\frac{\partial}{\partial t}\right]I(x,t) \tag{3.3.1}$$

$$\frac{\partial}{\partial x}I(x,t) = -\left[G + C\frac{\partial}{\partial t}\right]V(x,t) \tag{3.3.2}$$

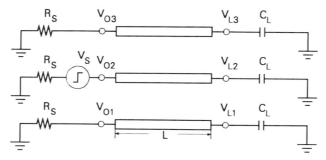

FIGURE 3.3.1   Interconnection driven by a unit step voltage source V_s of resistance R_s and terminated by the load capacitance C_L. The terminal endings on the neighboring interconnections are also shown. Interconnection capacitances as well as the capacitive and inductive couplings between the interconnections are not shown in the figure.

where L and C are the inductance and capacitance matrices per unit length of the interconnections, R is determined by the resistance per unit length of the interconnections, and G is the conductance matrix determined by the conductivity of the substrate. For a semi-insulating GaAs substrate, G can be neglected. The matrices L and C can be determined by the network analog method developed earlier [2.25]. In the s domain, Equations 3.3.1 and 3.3.2 can be written as

$$\frac{d}{dx}V(x,s) = -[R + sL]I(x,s) \tag{3.3.3}$$

$$\frac{d}{dx}I(x,s) = -[G + sC]V(x,s) \tag{3.3.4}$$

Defining

$$Z = R + sL$$

and

$$Y = G + sC$$

Equations 3.3.3 and 3.3.4 can be solved in the s domain, yielding

$$V(x,s) = e^{-\sqrt{ZY}(x)}V_i(s) + e^{-\sqrt{ZY}(L-x)}V_r(s) \tag{3.3.5}$$

$$I(x,s) = \sqrt{\frac{Y}{Z}}\left[e^{-\sqrt{ZY}(x)}V_i(s) - e^{-\sqrt{ZY}(L-x)}V_r(s)\right] \tag{3.3.6}$$

In Equations 3.3.5 and 3.3.6, L is the total length of the transmission line, $V_i(s)$ is the voltage vector of the incident wave at $x = 0$, and $V_r(s)$ is the voltage vector of the reflected wave at $x = L$. At the end points, $x = 0$ and $x = L$, Equations 3.3.5 and 3.3.6 yield

$$V(0,s) = V_i(s) + e^{-\sqrt{ZY}L}V_r(s) \tag{3.3.7}$$

$$I(0,s) = \sqrt{\frac{Y}{Z}}\left[V_i(s) - e^{-\sqrt{ZY}L}V_r(s)\right] \tag{3.3.8}$$

$$V(L,s) = e^{-\sqrt{ZY}L}V_i(s) + V_r(s) \tag{3.3.9}$$

$$I(L,s) = \sqrt{\frac{Y}{Z}}\left[e^{-\sqrt{ZY}L}V_i(s) - V_r(s)\right] \tag{3.3.10}$$

Incorporating the boundary conditions determined by the lumped-circuit elements connected to the interconnection line, that is,

$$V(0, s) = V_s(s) - R_s I(0, s) \tag{3.3.11}$$

and

$$V(L, s) = \frac{1}{sC_L} I(L, s) \tag{3.3.12}$$

we have

$$V_i(s) + e^{(-\sqrt{ZY})L} V_r(s) = (-R_s)\sqrt{\frac{Y}{Z}} \left[V_i(s) - e^{-\sqrt{ZY}L} V_r(s) \right] + V_s(s) \tag{3.3.13}$$

and

$$e^{-\sqrt{ZY}L} V_i(s) + V_r(s) = -\left(\frac{1}{sC_L} \right)\sqrt{\frac{Y}{Z}} \left[e^{-\sqrt{ZY}L} V_i(s) - V_r(s) \right] \tag{3.3.14}$$

which can be solved to yield, for $V_i(s)$ and $V_r(s)$,

$$V_r(s) = V_s(s) \left\{ -\left[1 + R_s \sqrt{\frac{Y}{Z}} \right] \left[e^{\sqrt{ZY}L} \right] \left[1 - \frac{1}{sC_L} \sqrt{\frac{Y}{Z}} \right]^{-1} \left[1 + \frac{1}{sC_L} \sqrt{\frac{Y}{Z}} \right] \right.$$

$$\left. + \left[1 - R_s \sqrt{\frac{Y}{Z}} \right] \left[\frac{1}{e^{\sqrt{ZY}L}} \right] \right\}^{-1} \tag{3.3.15}$$

$$V_i(s) = -\left[e^{-\sqrt{ZY}L} - \frac{1}{sC_L} \sqrt{\frac{Y}{Z}} e^{-\sqrt{ZY}L} \right]^{-1} \left[1 + \frac{1}{sC_L} e^{-\sqrt{ZY}L} \right] V_r(s) \tag{3.3.16}$$

The values for $V_i(s)$ and $V_r(s)$ can be substituted into Equations 3.3.7 to 3.3.10 to obtain expressions for the current and voltage at $x = 0$ and $x = L$ in the s domain. The load voltage is the element of $V(L, s)$ that corresponds to the line on which the voltage source is applied.

In principle, the time domain response can be obtained by the inverse Laplace transformation or by the Fourier transformation. However, the Fourier transformation results in errors due to a finite number of terms included in the summation. Therefore, the inverse Laplace transformation technique is preferred. If $F(s)$ denotes the Laplace transform of $f(t)$, then

$$F(s) = \int_0^\infty f(t) e^{-st} \, dt \qquad (3.3.17)$$

It can be shown [3.21] that, for t on the interval $(0, 2T)$,

$$f(t) = h(t) - E(t) \qquad (3.3.18)$$

where $h(t)$ is given by

$$h(t) = \frac{1}{T} \left\{ \frac{F(a)}{2} + \sum_{k=1}^\infty \left(\mathrm{Re}\left[F\left(a + \frac{k\pi t}{T}\right) \cos\left(\frac{k\pi t}{T}\right)\right] \right.\right.$$
$$\left.\left. - \mathrm{Im}\left[F\left(a + \frac{k\pi t}{T}\right) \sin\left(\frac{k\pi t}{T}\right)\right] \right) \right\} \qquad (3.3.19)$$

and the error $E(t)$ is bounded by

$$E(t) \le M \left[\frac{e^{at}}{e^{2T(a-\alpha)} - 1} \right] \qquad (3.3.20)$$

where $1/T$ is the frequency step, M is a constant, and α is related to $f(t)$ such that $f(t)$ is an exponential of order a (i.e., $|f(t)| \le Ce^{\alpha t}$). When $2T(a - \alpha)$ is large enough and we want our precision to be ε, then a can be chosen to be [3.21]

$$a = \alpha - \frac{\ln(\varepsilon)}{2T} \qquad (3.3.21)$$

Choosing a suitable value of T for the desired accuracy depends on the time range of interest (e.g., 0 to t_{max}) and the computation time. When t is much smaller than $2T$, the approximation of $f(t)$ by Equation 3.3.18 converges very slowly because the frequency step determined by $1/T$ is too small and we need to include many terms for the summation to converge. On the other hand, if t is too close to $2T$, then the error due to the term $E(t)$ in Equation 3.3.18 becomes large as can be seen from Equation 3.3.20. A good choice for T lies in the range $(0.8t_{max}, 1.2t_{max})$.

Numerical computations show that if we apply the inverse Laplace transformation directly, then the summation converges very slowly for small values of t. This is because the frequency step determined by $1/T$ is too small for small t. To solve this problem, we can divide the time range $[0, t_{max}]$ into several time ranges $[0, p^k t_{max}], (p^k t_{max}, p^{k-1} t_{max}], \ldots, (p t_{max}, t_{max}]$ and choose a different value of T for each time range such that T is not too large and the summation in Equation 3.3.19 converges faster. The value of p can be determined by a compromise between the desired accuracy and the computation time and in our case is 0.8.

The summation in Equation 3.3.19 usually converges very slowly; it takes more than 5000 terms to achieve an accuracy of four significant digits. To

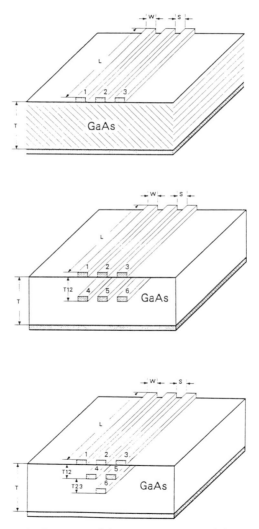

FIGURE 3.3.2   Schematic diagram of (a) three single-level, (b) six bilevel, and (c) six trilevel interconnection configurations.

overcome this problem, we can use the Wynn algorithm [3.21, 3.22] to accelerate the summation. The algorithm can be described as follows:

For a summation series S_m defined as

$$S_m = \sum_{n=1}^{m} a_n \qquad m = 1, 2, 3, \ldots \tag{3.3.22}$$

we define a two-dimensional array as

$$\varepsilon_{p+1}^{(m)} = \varepsilon_{p-1}^{(m)} + \frac{1}{\varepsilon_p^{(m)} - \varepsilon_p^{(m-1)}} \qquad p = 1, 2, 3, \ldots \tag{3.3.23}$$

with

$$\varepsilon_0^{(m)} = 0 \tag{3.3.24}$$

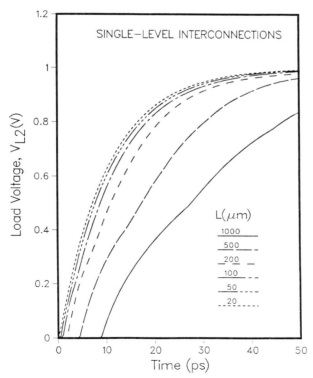

FIGURE 3.3.3 Load voltage waveforms in the range 0 to 50 ps for several interconnection lengths in the single-level configuration.

and

$$\varepsilon_1^{(m)} = S_m \qquad (3.3.25)$$

In principle, $\varepsilon_3^{(m)}, \varepsilon_5^{(m)}, \varepsilon_7^{(m)}, \varepsilon_9^{(m)}, \ldots$ will be better approximations for the summation S_m in Equation 3.3.22. From numerical experiments it can be found that $\varepsilon_9^{(m)}$ is the best choice for the present problem because higher-order transformations result in rounding errors.

3.3.2 Numerical Simulation Results

A listing of the computer program DCMPVI, based on the inverse Laplace transformation technique using the Wynn algorithm and the improved time range selection described previously and written in FORTRAN, is presented in Appendix 4.1. The program has been used to study the dependences of the load voltage and the delay time for the interconnections in the configurations shown in Figures 3.3.2*a*, *b*, and *c*. One of the parameters is varied in a

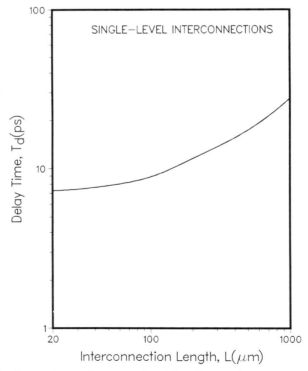

FIGURE 3.3.4 Dependence of propagation delay time on the interconnection lengths in the single-level configuration.

specific range, whereas the others are kept fixed at their typical values. Typical values of the various parameters are as follows: interconnection lengths (L), 1000 μm; interconnection widths (W), 1 μm; interconnection separations (S), 1 μm; interconnection metal resistivity (ρ), 3 $\mu\Omega \cdot$ cm; interlevel distances $(T_{12}$ and $T_{23})$, 2 μm; thickness of the GaAs substrate (T), 200 μm; driving transistor output resistance or source resistance (R_s), 100 Ω; and loading transistor input capacitance or load capacitance (C_L), 100 fF. The thickness of each of the interconnection lines is kept equal to $0.5W$. In the following discussion the single-level interconnection configuration shown in Figure 3.3.2a is assumed unless otherwise specified, and the source is applied to one end of the second interconnection on the first level. Furthermore, as in the literature [3.20], the delay time is defined as the time taken by the output voltage to reach 50 percent of its steady-state value.

Variations of the load voltages with time in the range 0 to 50 ps for several interconnection length values are shown in Figure 3.3.3, whereas Figure 3.3.4 shows the dependence of the delay time on the interconnection lengths in the

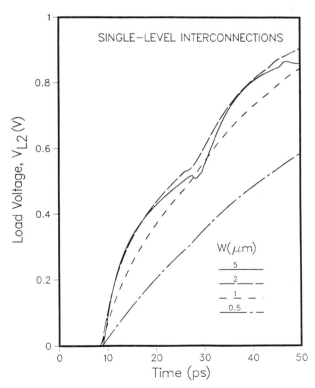

FIGURE 3.3.5 Load voltage waveforms in the range 0 to 50 ps for several interconnection widths in the single-level configuration.

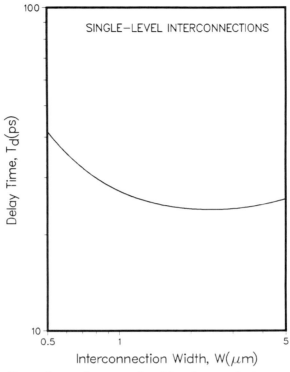

FIGURE 3.3.6   Dependence of propagation delay time on the interconnection widths in the single-level configuration.

range 20 to 1000 μm. Figure 3.3.4 shows that the delay time increases almost linearly for interconnection lengths above about 100 μm. For lengths below about 100 μm, the delay is caused mainly by the RC delay of the source resistance and the load capacitance. For several interconnection width values, load voltage waveforms in the time range 0 to 50 ps are shown in Figure 3.3.5, and the dependence of the delay time on the interconnection widths in the range 0.5 to 5 μm is shown in Figure 3.3.6. Figure 3.3.6 shows that the delay time becomes a minimum when the interconnection widths are about 2μm each. The increase in delay time for widths below about 2 μm is due to the increasing line resistance caused by the decreasing cross-sectional area, whereas the increase in delay time for widths above about 2 μm is due to the increasing ground and coupling capacitances of the interconnection lines. For four different interconnection separation values, load voltage waveforms in the range 0 to 50 ps are shown in Figure 3.3.7, and the dependence of the delay time on the interconnection separations in the range 0.5 to 5 μm is shown in Figure 3.3.8. Figure 3.3.8 shows that the delay time decreases as the separations are increased. This is because the coupling capacitances decrease as the distances between the neighboring interconnection lines are increased.

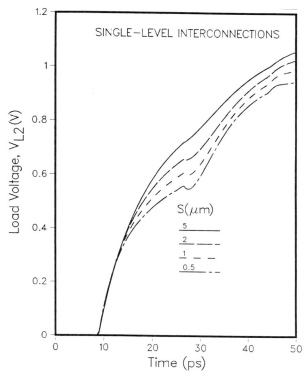

FIGURE 3.3.7   Load voltage waveforms in the range 0 to 50 ps for several interconnection separations in the single-level configuration.

Load voltage waveforms in the time range 0 to 500 ps for several interconnection metal resistivity values are shown in Figure 3.3.9, and the dependence of the delay time on the resistivities in the range 0.1 to 1000 $\mu\Omega \cdot$ cm is shown in Figure 3.3.10 (p. 196). This figure   shows that for resistivities above about 10 $\mu\Omega \cdot$ cm, the delay time increases significantly. It should be noted that, besides aluminum, WSi_2 and poly-Si, which have resistivities of about 30 and 500 $\mu\Omega \cdot$ cm, respectively, have also been used as interconnection metals. For several source resistance values, load voltage waveforms in the time range 0 to 200 ps are shown in Figure 3.3.11 (p.197). On a realistic IC chip, the source resistance corresponds to the output resistance of the transistor driving the interconnection. For a 100-μm-wide GaAs MESFET with a gate length of 1μm, this resistance is approximately 700 Ω. Dependence of the delay time on the source resistance in the range 0.1 to 1000 Ω is shown in Figure 3.3.12 (p. 198). This figure shows that for source resistance above about 10 Ω, the delay time increases considerably. Figure 3.3.13 (p. 199) shows load voltage waveforms in the range 0 to 200 ps for several

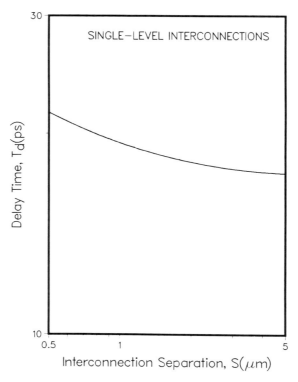

FIGURE 3.3.8   Dependence of propagation delay time on the interconnection separation in the single-level configuration.

load capacitance values. In practice, load capacitance refers to the input capacitance of the loading transistor. For a typical GaAs MESFET of 1 μm gate length and 100 μm width, this is approximately 100 fF. Dependence of the delay time on the load capacitance in the range 1 to 1000 fF is shown in Figure 3.3.14 (p. 200). This figure shows that for load capacitances above about 10 fF, the delay time increases significantly.

Load voltage waveforms for different numbers of interconnection lines in a single-level configuration are shown in Figure 3.3.15 (p. 201). Three interconnections correspond to one neighbor on each side of the driven line, whereas five interconnections correspond to two neighboring lines on each side of the driven line. This figure shows that the effect of the second neighbors on the delay time is much smaller than that of the first neighbors. For the bilevel interconnections shown in Figure 3.3.2b, the load voltage waveforms in the range 0 to 200 ps, resulting from the application of the driving source to different interconnection lines, are shown in Figure 3.3.16 (p. 202). This figure shows that the signal delays are longer for the intercon-

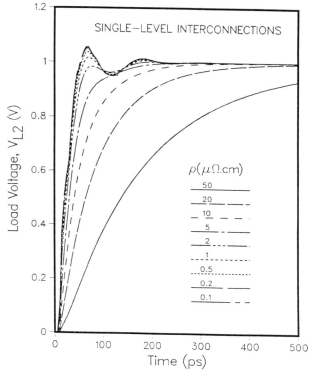

FIGURE 3.3.9   Load voltage waveforms in the range 0 to 500 ps for several interconnection resistivities in the single-level configuration.

nection lines embedded in the substrate compared to those printed on the substrate. Similar conclusions can be drawn from Figure 3.3.17 (p. 203), which shows load voltage waveforms when the source is applied to different interconnection lines in the trilevel configuration shown in Figure 3.3.2c.

3.4   ANALYSIS OF CROSSING INTERCONNECTIONS

A schematic layout of the bilevel crossing interconnections and the substrate is shown in Figure 3.4.1 (p. 204). As shown in the previous section, the interconnection lines that run parallel to each other can be studied by using transmission line equations. However, when the interconnections cross each other, the transmission line approximation is no longer valid. This is because, in this case, the coupling of the lines is no longer uniform along the entire length of the interconnection but is rather localized to the crossing areas. In

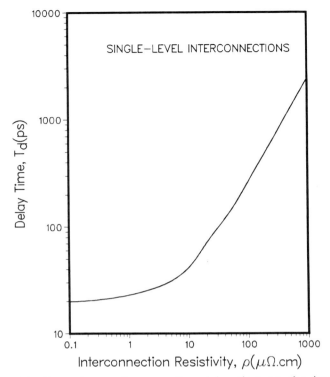

FIGURE 3.3.10 Dependence of propagation delay time on the interconnection resistivity in the single-level configuration.

this section the effect of several crossing lines embedded in the substrate on the propagation delay in the main (driven) line printed on the top plane will first be studied using a simplified model. Only the capacitive couplings will be considered in this analysis. Then the modifications required in order to develop a more complete model of the crossing interconnections having several parallel interconnections on the top plane and including the capacitive as well as the inductive couplings between the interconnections will be discussed.

3.4.1 Simplified Analysis of Crossing Interconnections

A schematic diagram of the crossing interconnections analyzed in this section is shown in Figure 3.4.2 (p. 205). A driving source is applied only on the main line on the top plane, and the crossing lines in the second plane are not energized. One way of analyzing this interconnection configuration is to divide it into three sections: the transmission line section, the crossing

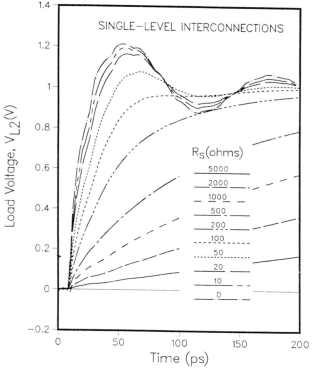

FIGURE 3.3.11   Load voltage waveforms in the range 0 to 200 ps for several source resistances in the single-level configuration.

section, and the load section. The equivalent circuit used for the interconnections is shown in Figure 3.4.3 (p. 205). The various elements used in Figure 3.4.3 and the algorithm are defined as follows:

V_s = voltage source

R_s = source resistance

L_B = self-inductance of the portion of the driven line between two consecutive crossing lines

R_B = resistance of the portion of the driven line between two consecutive crossing lines

C_c = coupling capacitance between the main line and a crossing line

R_{cl} = line resistance of a crossing line on the left side of the main line

R_{cr} = line resistance of a crossing line on the right side of the main line

L_{cl} = self-inductance of a crossing line on the left side of the main line

L_{cr} = self-inductance of a crossing line on the right side of the main line

C_L = load capacitance

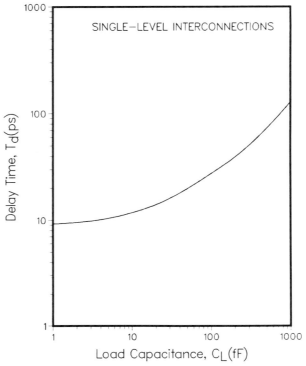

FIGURE 3.3.14 Dependence of propagation delay time on the load capacitance in the single-level configuration.

substrate. For semi-insulating substrates (e.g., GaAs), G can be considered negligibly small. In the complex frequency (s) domain, Equations 3.4.1 and 3.4.2 can be written as

$$\frac{\partial}{\partial x}V(x,s) = -[R + sL]I(x,s) \qquad (3.4.3)$$

$$\frac{\partial}{\partial x}I(x,s) = -[G + sC]V(x,s) \qquad (3.4.4)$$

Defining

$$Z = R + sL \qquad (3.4.5)$$

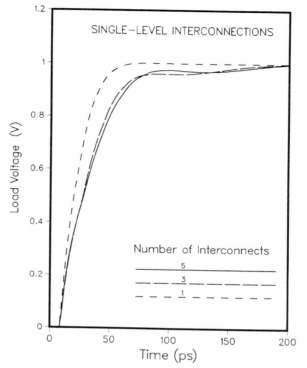

FIGURE 3.3.15   Load voltage waveforms in the range 0 to 200 ps for different number of interconnections in the single-level configuration.

and

$$Y = G + sC \tag{3.4.6}$$

the transmission line equations can be solved for V and I, yielding

$$V(x, s) = e^{-\sqrt{ZY}x}V_i(s) + e^{-\sqrt{ZY}(l-x)}V_r(s) \tag{3.4.7}$$

$$I(x, s) = \sqrt{\frac{Y}{Z}}\left[e^{-\sqrt{ZY}x}V_i(s) - e^{-\sqrt{ZY}(l-x)}V_r(s)\right] \tag{3.4.8}$$

where l is the total length of the transmission line, $V_i(s)$ is the Laplace

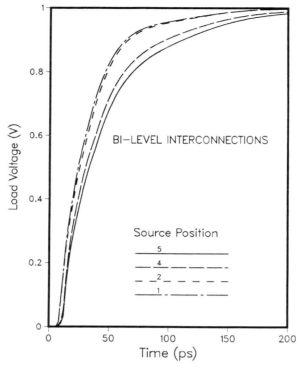

FIGURE 3.3.16 Load voltage waveforms in the range 0 to 200 ps for the driving source applied to different interconnections in the bilevel configuration.

transform of the incident voltage waveform, and $V_r(s)$ is the Laplace transform of the reflected wave at $x = l$. At the boundary points, that is, $x = 0$ and $x = l$, we get

$$V(0, s) = V_i(s) + e^{-\sqrt{ZY}l}V_r(s) \qquad (3.4.9)$$

$$I(0, s) = \sqrt{\frac{Y}{Z}}\left[V_i(s) - e^{-\sqrt{ZY}l}V_r(s)\right] \qquad (3.4.10)$$

$$V(l, s) = e^{-\sqrt{ZY}l}V_i(s) + V_r(s) \qquad (3.4.11)$$

$$I(l, s) = \sqrt{\frac{Y}{Z}}\left[e^{-\sqrt{ZY}l}V_i(s) - V_r(s)\right] \qquad (3.4.12)$$

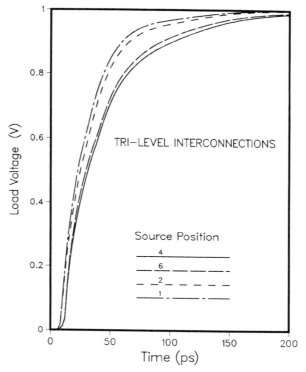

FIGURE 3.3.17 Load voltage waveforms in the range 0 to 200 ps for the driving source applied to different interconnections in the trilevel configuration.

The boundary conditions at the source and the load ends are:

$$V(0, s) = V_s(s) - R_s I(0, s) \qquad (3.4.13)$$

$$V(l, s) = Z_{TX} I(l, s) \qquad (3.4.14)$$

where Z_{TX} is the equivalent load on the transmission line.

$$V_s(s) = \frac{1}{s} \qquad (3.4.15)$$

for an input unit step voltage source. For an input periodic (pulse train) voltage waveform of period T,

$$V_s(s) = \frac{(1 - e^{-sT})}{s} \qquad (3.4.16)$$

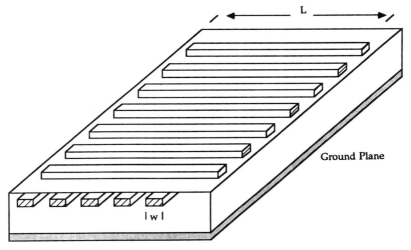

FIGURE 3.4.1   Schematic diagram of the layout of the bilevel crossing interconnections and the substrate.

Equations 3.4.9 to 3.4.14 can be solved to yield, for $V_i(s)$ and $V_r(s)$,

$$V_r(s) = \frac{V_s(s)e^{-\sqrt{ZY}l}\left[1 - Z_{TX}\sqrt{\dfrac{Y}{Z}}\right]}{\left[1 - R_s\sqrt{\dfrac{Y}{Z}}\right]\left[1 - Z_{TX}\sqrt{\dfrac{Y}{Z}}\right]e^{-2\sqrt{ZY}l} - \left[1 + R_s\sqrt{\dfrac{Y}{Z}}\right]\left[1 + Z_{TX}\sqrt{\dfrac{Y}{Z}}\right]}$$

(3.4.17)

$$V_i(s) = -\frac{1 + Z_{TX}e^{-\sqrt{ZY}l}}{\left[1 - Z_{TX}\sqrt{\dfrac{Y}{Z}}\right]e^{-\sqrt{ZY}l}}V_r(s)$$

(3.4.18)

Using the expressions for $V_i(s)$ and $V_r(s)$ from Equations 3.4.17 and 3.4.18, we can get the expressions for voltage and current in the s domain at the end of the transmission line section, that is, at $x = l$, from Equations 3.4.11 and 3.4.12. The current $I(l, s)$ is indeed the input current for the next section, that is, the crossing section.

3.4.1.2 Crossing Section   This is the section where the driven line on the top plane and the second level interconnections embedded in the substrate

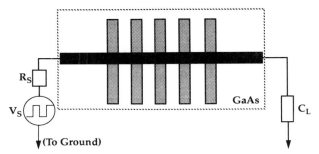

FIGURE 3.4.2 Schematic diagram of the bilevel crossing interconnections analyzed in this section. (Terminal endings on crossing interconnections are not shown.)

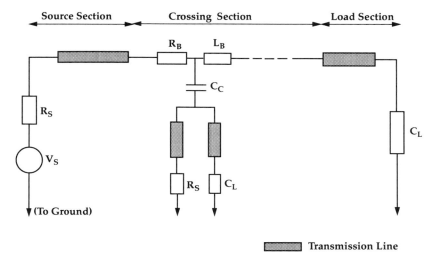

FIGURE 3.4.3 Equivalent circuit of the bilevel crossing interconnections, including capacitive couplings. Inductive couplings are not included.

cross each other. This section is driven by the output of the transmission line section and the output of this section drives the next section, that is, the load section. The driven line is coupled to the crossing lines by the coupling capacitances which depend on the crossing area (which in turn depends on the line widths and the crossing angle), the interlevel separation, and the substrate's dielectric constant. It is assumed that all the interconnection lines are of the same width, thickness, and material. The algorithm can be easily modified for different situations.

The schematic diagram of one part of a typical crossing section depicting ith crossing line coupled to main line is shown in Figure 3.4.5. Its impedance,

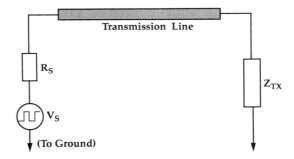

FIGURE 3.4.4   Schematic diagram of the source section.

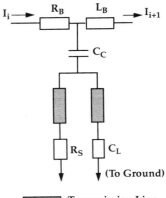

FIGURE 3.4.5   Schematic diagram of the crossing section involving the ith crossing line.

Z_x as seen by the current flowing in the driven line, is given by

$$Z_x = \frac{1}{sC_c} + (R_{cl} + sL_{cl} + R_s) \left\| \left(R_{cr} + sL_{cr} + \frac{1}{sC_L} \right) \right. \qquad (3.4.19)$$

If I_{TX} denotes the current flowing from the transmission line section into the crossing section, then the currents I_i flowing in the driven line after "seeing" the ith crossing line are given by

$$I_1 = I_{TX} \frac{Z_x}{Z_x + Z_{p1}}$$

$$I_2 = I_1 \frac{Z_x}{Z_x + Z_{p2}}$$

and so on, until

$$I_n = I_{n-1} \frac{Z_x}{Z_x + Z_L'} \qquad (3.4.20)$$

where Z_L' is the total impedance of the load section. I_n represents the current flowing into the load section. The partial loads Z_{pi} used in the preceding equations are given by

$$Z_{p1} = Z_{p2} \| Z_x + Z_B$$

where

$$Z_B = R_B + sL_B$$
$$Z_{p2} = Z_{p3} \| Z_x + Z_B$$

and so on, until

$$Z_{p(n-2)} = Z_{p(n-1)} \| Z_x + Z_B$$
$$Z_{p(n-1)} = Z_{pn} \| Z_x + Z_B$$

and the total impedance of the load section (same as Z_{pn}) is given by

$$Z_L' = R_r + sL_B + \frac{1}{sC_r} \left\| \left(sL_r + \frac{1}{sC_L} \right) \right. \qquad (3.4.21)$$

The load impedance Z_{TX} seen by the source-side transmission line is given by

$$Z_{TX} = Z_{p1} \| Z_x + R_B$$

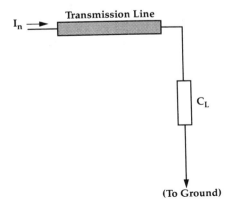

Transmission Line

I_n

C_L

(To Ground)

FIGURE 3.4.6 Schematic diagram of the load section.

3.4.1.3 Load Section The load section refers to the portion of the driven line after the crossing section and includes the load C_L driven by the line. Its schematic representation is shown in Figure 3.4.6. This section can also be modeled as a transmission line driven by a source voltage V'_s given by

$$V'_s(s) = [I_n - I_{n-1}] \times Z_x \qquad (3.4.22)$$

where n is the number of crossing lines. Proceeding as for the source section transmission line, it can be easily shown that the voltage across the load will now be given by

$$V_L(s) = \sqrt{\frac{Y}{Z}} \left[e^{-\sqrt{ZY} l'} V'_i(s) - V'_r(s) \right] \times \frac{1}{sC_L} \qquad (3.4.23)$$

where l' is the length of the load section transmission line,

$$V'_r(s) = \frac{V'_s(s) e^{-\sqrt{ZY} l'} \left[1 - \frac{1}{sC_L} \sqrt{\frac{Y}{Z}} \right]}{\left[1 - \frac{1}{sC_L} \sqrt{\frac{Y}{Z}} \right] e^{-2\sqrt{ZY} l'} - \left[1 + \frac{1}{sC_L} \sqrt{\frac{Y}{Z}} \right]} \qquad (3.4.24)$$

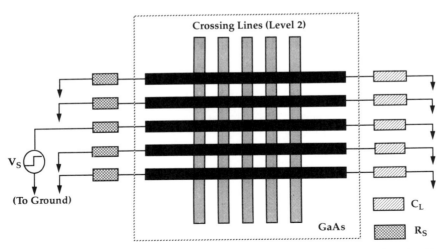

FIGURE 3.4.7 Layout of the bilevel crossing interconnections, including the line endings for the first-level interconnections. Each of the crossing lines is also terminated by the source resistance (R_s) on one side and the load capacitance (C_L) on the other side (not shown in the figure).

and

$$V_i'(s) = -\frac{1 + \dfrac{1}{sC_L}e^{-\sqrt{ZY}l'}}{\left[1 - \dfrac{1}{sC_L}\sqrt{\dfrac{Y}{Z}}\right]e^{-\sqrt{ZY}l'}}V_r'(s) \qquad (3.4.25)$$

The load voltage in the time domain can then be obtained by an inverse Laplace transformation of the expression in Equation 3.4.23.

3.4.2 Comprehensive Analysis of Crossing Interconnections

In this subsection we will note the modifications required to extend the analysis presented in the previous subsection by adding two neighboring interconnections on each side of the driven line on the top plane. The resulting layout of the interconnection lines, including the driving step source, source resistances, and capacitive loads, is shown in Figure 3.4.7. In addition, in this analysis the inductive couplings among the interconnections on the top plane and those between the two levels will also be included. Once again, the transmission line model cannot be applied to the whole problem and therefore, as was done in Section 3.4.1, we can divide it into three sections: the source section, the crossing section, and the load section shown in Figures 3.4.8, 3.4.9, and 3.4.10, respectively.

The source section along with its source and its load is shown in Figure 3.4.8. where V_s is the driving source voltage and R_s is the source resistance. The load of this section includes the effects of the crossing section, the load section, and the load capacitance on the interconnection line. As shown earlier, the effects of the two neighboring parallel interconnection lines on each side of the driven line can be simulated by additional capacitances

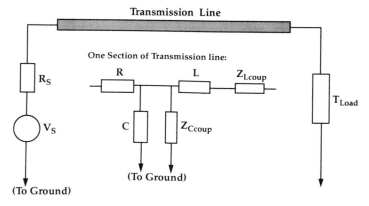

FIGURE 3.4.8 Schematic diagram of the source section.

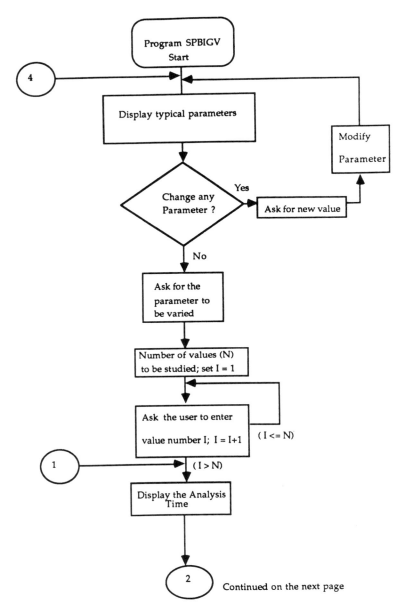

FIGURE 3.4.11 Flowchart of the program SPBIGV.

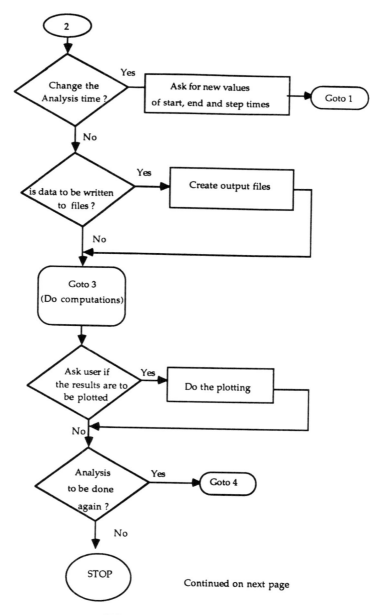

FIGURE 3.4.11   (*Continued*)

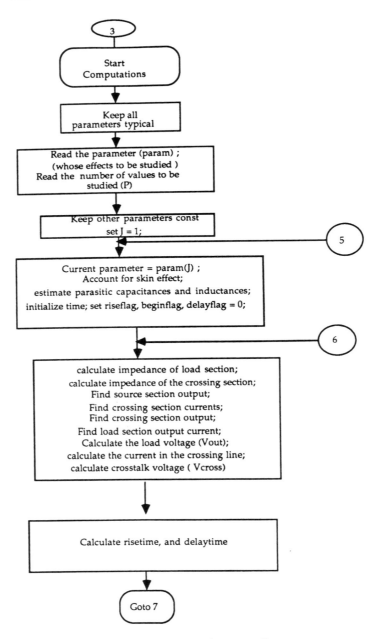

FIGURE 3.4.11 (*Continued*)

approximation [1.52] to carry out the inverse Laplace transformation. The program assumes that the lengths of the source section and the load section are equal and all interconnections are made of the same material and are of the same dimensions. The program also assumes that the separations between the neighboring parallel lines on the top level as well as on the second level are the same and that the crossing interconnection lines are perpendicular to those on the first level. The flowchart of SPBIGV is shown in Figure 3.4.11.

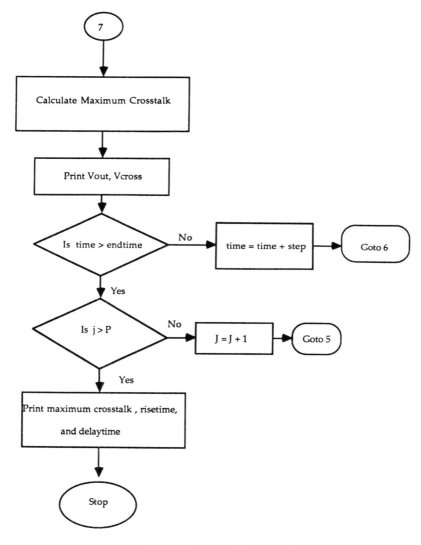

FIGURE 3.4.11 (*Continued*)

3.4.4 Simulation Results Using SPBIGV

In the following results obtained by using SPBIGV, one of the parameters is varied in a specific range, whereas the other parameters are kept fixed at their typical values which are as follows: interconnection lengths, 100 μm each; interconnection widths, 1.0 μm each; interconnection thicknesses, 0.5 μm each; interconnection separations, 1.0 μm each; interconnection material resistivity, 3.0 $\mu\Omega \cdot$ cm for aluminum; interlevel distance, 2.0 μm; substrate thickness, 200.0 μm; driving source resistance, 100 Ω; and load capacitance, 100 fF. In addition, the number of crossing lines is 16.

Load voltage waveforms for several interconnection length values in the time range 0 to 150 ps are shown in Figure 3.4.12. This figure shows that longer lines take a longer time to transmit energy from the input source to the output load, as expected. The dependences of the delay time and the rise time as functions of the interconnection lengths in the range 50 to 5000 μm are shown in Figure 3.4.13. For two interconnection width values, load

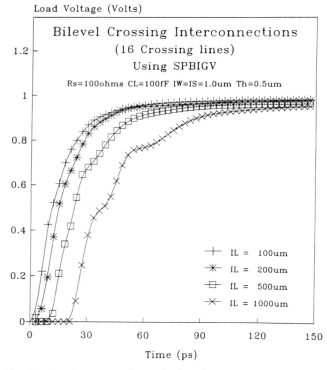

FIGURE 3.4.12 Load voltage waveforms in the time range 0 to 150 ps for several interconnection length values.

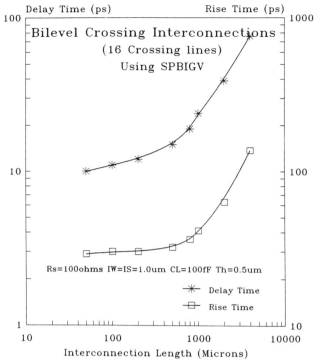

FIGURE 3.4.13 Dependences of the delay time and the rise time on the interconnection lengths.

voltage waveforms in the time range 0 to 150 ps are shown in Figure 3.4.14. Figure 3.4.15 (p. 219) shows the dependences of the delay time and the rise time as functions of the interconnection widths in the range 0.1 to 4 μm. These figures suggest that propagation delays are minimum when the interconnection widths are nearly 1 μm each. This can be understood qualitatively by considering the two opposing effects of increasing the interconnection widths on the propagation delays, that is, decreasing interconnection resistance and increasing interconnection capacitance. For two interconnection thickness values, while keeping the other parameters fixed, load voltage waveforms in the time range 0 to 100 ps are shown in Figure 3.4.16 (p. 220), whereas Figure 3.4.17 (p. 221) shows the dependences of the delay time and the rise time on the interconnection thicknesses in the range 0.1 to 10 μm. For two interconnection separation values, while keeping the other parameters fixed, load voltage waveforms in the time range 0 to 150 ps are shown in Figure 3.4.18 (p. 222), whereas Figure 3.4.19 (p. 223) shows the dependences of the delay time and the rise time on the interconnection separations in the range 1 to 6 μm.

Load Voltage (Volts)

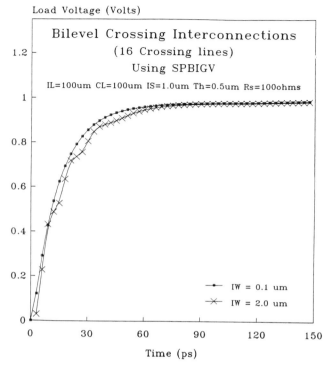

FIGURE 3.4.14   Load voltage waveforms in the time range 0 to 150 ps for two interconnection width values.

For several interconnection material resistivity values, load voltage waveforms in the time range 0 to 150 ps are shown in Figure 3.4.20 (p. 224), whereas the dependences of the delay time and the rise time on the resistivities in the range 1 to 500 $\mu\Omega \cdot$ cm are shown in Figure 3.4.21 (p. 225). For several driving source resistance values, load voltage waveforms in the time range 0 to 150 ps are shown in Figure 3.4.22 (p. 226), whereas the dependences of the delay time and the rise time on the source resistance in the range 10 to 1000 Ω are shown in Figure 3.4.23 (p. 227). Load voltage waveforms for several load capacitance values in the time range 0 to 150 ps are shown in Figure 3.4.24 (p. 228), whereas the dependences of the delay time and the rise time on the load capacitance in the range 10 to 2000 fF are shown in Figure 3.4.25 (p. 229). As expected, propagation delays in the driving interconnection increase with an increase in its material resistivity, load capacitance, or source resistance and vice versa.

Figure 3.4.26 (p. 230) shows the dependences of the delay time and the rise time on the thickness of the GaAs substrate in the range 10 to 500 μm.

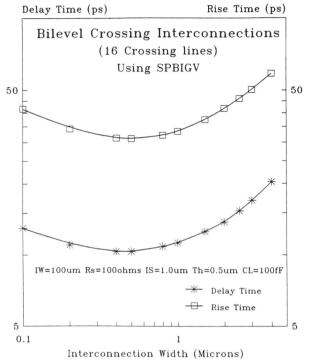

FIGURE 3.4.15 Dependences of the delay time and the rise time on the interconnection widths.

For several interlevel distance values, that is, the distance between the top level containing the driven interconnection and the second level containing the crossing interconnections, load voltage waveforms in the time range 0 to 150 ps are shown in Figure 3.4.27 (p. 231), whereas the dependences of the delay time and the rise time on the interlevel distance in the range 0.1 to 10 μm are shown in Figure 3.4.28 (p. 232). As expected, the effect of crossing lines on propagation delays in the driven line decreases as the distance between the two levels increases. The relative effects of coupling of the driven interconnection with its two neighbors on each side on the top plane and with the crossing lines in the second level are shown by the load voltage waveforms plotted in Figure 3.4.29 (p. 233). For several values of the number of crossing lines, load avoltage waveforms in the time range 0 to 150 ps are shown in Figure 3.4.30 (p. 234), whereas the dependences of the delay time and the rise time on the number of crossing lines in the range 1 to 80 are shown in Figure 3.4.31 (p. 235). This figure suggests that the larger the number of crossing lines, the greater will be their effect on propagation delays in the driven interconnection, as expected.

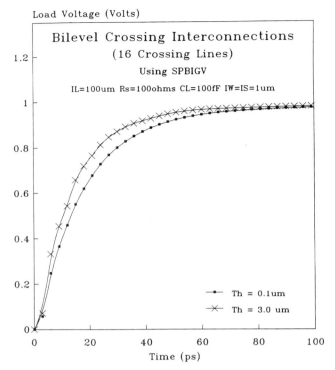

FIGURE 3.4.16 Load voltage waveforms in the time range 0 to 100 ps for two interconnection thickness values.

3.5 PARALLEL INTERCONNECTIONS MODELED AS MULTIPLE COUPLED MICROSTRIPS

In the literature multiple coupled distributed parameter systems including coupled transmission lines have been analyzed in detail. For example, normal mode propagation constants, impedances, and eigenvectors for coupled n-line structures are derived in matrix form [3.23–3.30], and these properties are available in explicit closed form for two-, three-, and four-line systems [3.30–3.33]. Coupled-line equations can also be used to model the propagation characteristics of interconnections in high-speed digital circuits. Such a model [3.13] is presented in this section.

3.5.1 The Model

A schematic diagram of a general multiple coupled-line structure is shown in Figure 3.5.1 (p. 235). The voltages and currents on a lossless n-line system

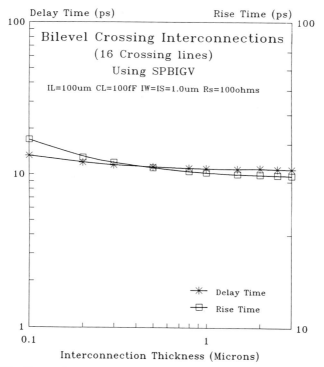

FIGURE 3.4.17 Dependences of the delay time and the rise time on the interconnection thicknesses.

are described by the following transmission line equations:

$$\frac{\partial \mathbf{v}}{\partial z} = -[L]\frac{\partial \mathbf{i}}{\partial t} \qquad (3.5.1a)$$

$$\frac{\partial \mathbf{i}}{\partial z} = -[C]\frac{\partial \mathbf{v}}{\partial t} \qquad (3.5.1b)$$

where the vectors

$$\mathbf{v} = [v_1, v_2, \ldots, v_n]^T$$

and

$$\mathbf{i} = [i_1, i_2, \ldots, i_n]^T$$

represent voltages and currents in the time domain along n lines of the

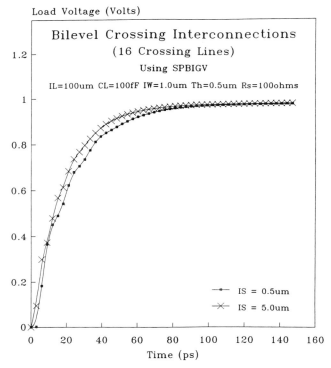

FIGURE 3.4.18 Load voltage waveforms in the time range to 0 to 150 ps for two interconnection separation values.

coupled structure, the superscript T denotes the transpose, and the matrices $[L]$ and $[C]$ are the inductance and capacitance matrices per unit length of the lines. As is well known $[L]$ is a positive-definite matrix, whereas $[C]$ is a hyperdominant matrix.

Now, we can consider Equations 3.5.1a and 3.5.1b in the frequency domain. If **V** and **I** are the voltage and current vectors in the frequency domain, then, for $e^{j(\omega t - \beta z)}$ variation in the time domain, these equations can be easily decoupled to result in the following eigenvalue equations for voltages and currents in the frequency domain:

$$[[L][C] - \lambda[U]]\mathbf{V} = [0] \qquad (3.5.2a)$$

$$[[C][L] - \lambda[U]]\mathbf{I} = [0] \qquad (3.5.2b)$$

where $\lambda = \beta^2/\omega^2$, $[U]$ is the unit matrix, and $[0]$ is the null vector. The

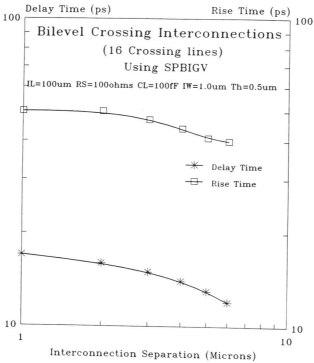

FIGURE 3.4.19   Dependences of the delay time and the rise time on the interconnection separations.

preceding equations can be rewritten as

$$[C]\mathbf{V} = \lambda[L]^{-1}\mathbf{V} \tag{3.5.3a}$$

$$[L]\mathbf{I} = \lambda[C]^{-1}\mathbf{I} \tag{3.5.3b}$$

In most cases the dielectric substrates used in interconnection structures are nonmagnetic; that is, their magnetic properties are the same as those of free space. For these cases, if $[L_0]$ and $[C_0]$ are the inductance and capacitance matrices for the interconnection structure with the dielectric removed, then the inductance matrix for the interconnection structure with the dielectric is given by

$$[L] = [L_0] = \mu_0\varepsilon_0[C_0]^{-1} \tag{3.5.4}$$

Using Equation 3.5.4, Equations 3.5.3a and 3.5.3b can be written in terms of the capacitance matrices only.

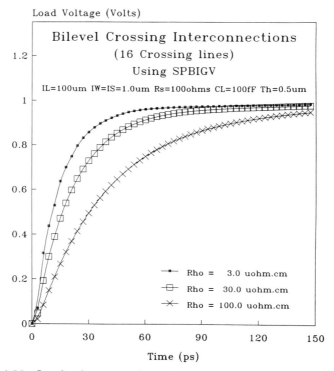

FIGURE 3.4.20   Load voltage waveforms in the time range 0 to 150 ps for several interconnection material resistivity values.

If $[M_V]$ and $[M_I]$ denote the voltage and current eigenvector matrices, then, using the orthogonality requirement, we have

$$[M_I] = \left[[M_V]^T \right]^{-1} \tag{3.5.5}$$

Furthermore, writing

$$\mathbf{v} = [M_V]\mathbf{e} \tag{3.5.6a}$$

and

$$\mathbf{i} = [M_I]\mathbf{j} \tag{3.5.6b}$$

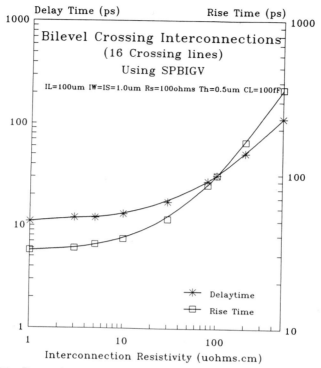

FIGURE 3.4.21 Dependences of the delay time and the rise time on the interconnection material resistivities.

we have

$$
\begin{bmatrix} \mathbf{v} \\ \mathbf{j} \end{bmatrix} = \begin{bmatrix} [M_V] & 0 \\ 0 & [M_V]^T \end{bmatrix} \begin{bmatrix} \mathbf{e} \\ \mathbf{i} \end{bmatrix} \tag{3.5.7}
$$

Substituting Equations 3.5.6a and 3.5.6b, Equations 3.5.1a and 3.5.1b can be rewritten as

$$
\frac{\partial \mathbf{e}}{\partial z} = -\mathrm{diag}[L_k]\frac{\partial \mathbf{j}}{\partial t} \tag{3.5.8a}
$$

$$
\frac{\partial \mathbf{j}}{\partial z} = -\mathrm{diag}[C_k]\frac{\partial \mathbf{e}}{\partial t} \tag{3.5.8b}
$$

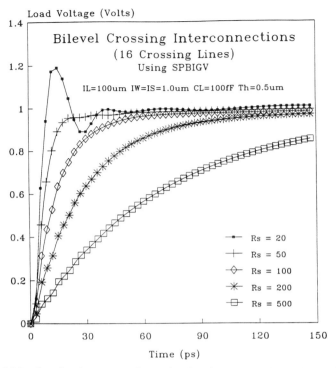

FIGURE 3.4.22 Load voltage waveforms in the time range 0 to 150 ps for several source resistance values.

where diag[L_k] and diag[C_k] are the diagonal matrices with elements given by

$$L_k = [M_V]^{-1}[L][[M_V]^T]^{-1} = \frac{1}{u_k^2 C_k} \qquad (3.5.9a)$$

$$C_k = [M_V]^T[C][M_V] \qquad (3.5.9b)$$

where u_k is the phase velocity of the kth mode. The characteristic impedance of the kth mode is given by

$$Z_k = \left[\frac{L_k}{C_k}\right]^{1/2} \qquad (3.5.10)$$

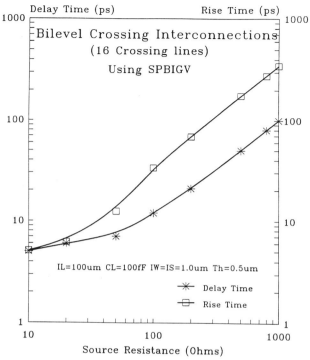

FIGURE 3.4.23 Dependences of the delay time and the rise time on the source resistance.

For a general n-line system, Equations 3.5.6 to 3.5.8 lead to the equivalent-circuit model shown in Figure 3.5.2. In other words, the model shown in Figure 3.5.2 is a circuit that is the solution of the coupled transmission line equations (Equations 3.5.1a and 3.5.1b).

3.5.2 Simulation Results

Because all the model elements shown in Figure 3.5.2 (p. 236) are available in the CAD program called SPICE, the simulation results given in the following discussion can be obtained by using SPICE [3.13].

For an asymmetric coupled two-line system (also called a four-port), the SPICE model, its model parameters, and its step response are shown in Figures 3.5.3a–e (pp. 237–239). The step response for characteristic non-mode converting terminations $Z_1 = 48.6 \ \Omega$ and $Z_2 = 73.4 \ \Omega$ are shown in Figures 3.5.3c and d, and, for the sake of comparison, the step response of the same structure terminated in 50-Ω resistances is also included in Figures 3.5.3e and f. Figure 3.5.3 shows that mismatch in normal-mode phase

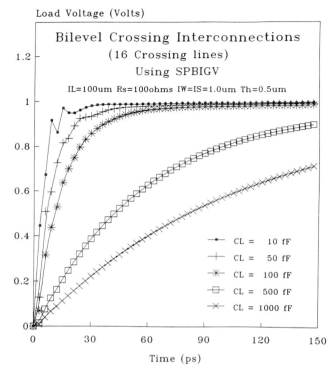

FIGURE 3.4.24 Load voltage waveforms in the time range 0 to 150 ps for several load capacitance values.

velocities results in a finite pulse at the isolated port for both the nonmode terminations and the 50-Ω terminations.

In order to illustrate the application of the model to nonlinear terminations, it has been applied to a three-line system terminated in logic gates shown in Figure 3.5.4a (pp. 240–241). When the input signal is applied to the gate on the outside lines, the step response results at all other ports are shown in Figures 3.5.4b–d. The effects of interactions among the gates and the interconnections are apparent in the results. The rise time and the gate propagation delays correspond to subnanosecond performance.

3.6 MODELING OF LOSSY PARALLEL AND CROSSING INTERCONNECTIONS AS COUPLED LUMPED DISTRIBUTED SYSTEMS

In this section a model of parallel and crossing interconnections in terms of coupled lumped distributed lossy networks [3.14] is presented. This method is an extension of that presented in Section 3.5 for lossless parallel interconnections.

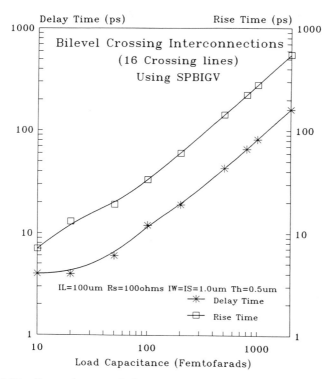

FIGURE 3.4.25   Dependences of the delay time and the rise time on the load capacitance.

3.6.1   The Model

A schematic diagram of the interconnections analyzed in this section is shown in Figure 3.6.1 (p. 242). The interconnection lines at the same or different levels that are parallel to each other are modeled as lossy parallel coupled transmission lines. The coupling between the crossing interconnections in adjacent levels is assumed to be in the immediate vicinity of the crossover and has been modeled as a lumped element. Therefore, the crossing interconnections have been modeled as lumped distributed circuits.

In terms of normal propagation modes, the voltages and currents in an n-line system are described by the following transmission line equations:

$$\frac{\partial \mathbf{v}}{\partial z} = -[R]\mathbf{i} - [L]\frac{\partial \mathbf{i}}{\partial t} \tag{3.6.1}$$

$$\frac{\partial \mathbf{i}}{\partial z} = -[G]\mathbf{v} - [C]\frac{\partial \mathbf{v}}{\partial t} \tag{3.6.2}$$

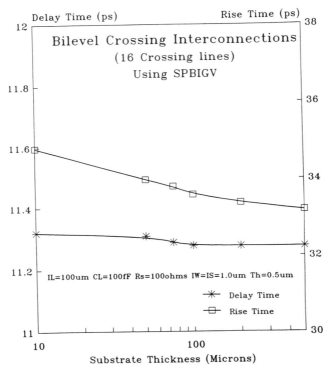

FIGURE 3.4.26 Dependences of the delay time and the rise time on the substrate thickness.

where the vectors

$$\mathbf{v} = \left[v_1, v_2, \ldots, v_n \right]^T$$

and

$$\mathbf{i} = \left[i_1, i_2, \ldots, i_n \right]^T$$

represent voltages and currents in the time domain along n lines of the coupled structure, the superscript T denotes the transpose, and the matrices $[R]$, $[L]$, $[G]$, and $[C]$ are the series resistance, series inductance, shunt conductance, and shunt capacitance matrices per unit length of the lines, respectively.

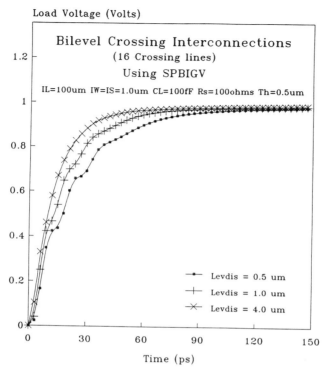

FIGURE 3.4.27 Load voltage waveforms in the time range 0 to 150 ps for several interlevel distance values.

Now, we can consider Equations 3.6.1 and 3.6.2 in the frequency domain. If **V** and **I** are the voltage and current vectors in the frequency domain, then, for $e^{j\omega t - \gamma z}$ variation in the time domain, these equations can be easily decoupled to result in the following eigenvalue equations for voltages and currents in the frequency domain:

$$[[Z_S][Y_{SH}] - \lambda[U]]\mathbf{V} = [0] \qquad (3.6.3)$$

$$[[Y_{SH}][Z_S] - \lambda[U]]\mathbf{I} = [0] \qquad (3.6.4)$$

where $[Z_S] = [R] + j\omega[L]$, $[Y_{SH}] = [G] + j\omega[C]$, $\lambda = -\gamma^2$, $[U]$ is the unit matrix, and $[0]$ is the null vector. Equations 3.6.3 and 3.6.4 represent the generalized matrix eigenvalue and eigenvector problem. If $[M_v]$ denotes the complex eigenvector matrix associated with the characteristic matrix $[Z_S][Y_{SH}]$, then, following the same procedure as in Section 3.5, it can be

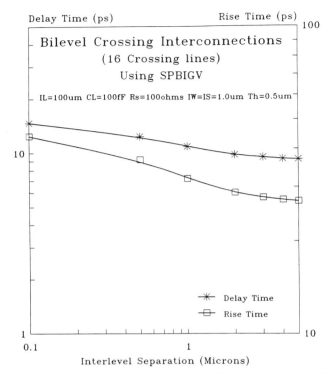

FIGURE 3.4.28 Dependences of the delay time and the rise time on the interlevel separation.

shown that the voltage eigenvector **e** and the current eigenvector **j** are solutions of the following set of decoupled equations:

$$\frac{d\mathbf{e}}{dz} = -\operatorname{diag}[\gamma_k/y_k]\mathbf{j} \tag{3.6.5}$$

$$\frac{d\mathbf{j}}{dz} = -\operatorname{diag}[\gamma_k y_k]\mathbf{e} \tag{3.6.6}$$

where γ_k is the propagation constant of the kth mode equal to the square root of the kth eigenvalue of $[Z_S][Y_{SH}]$, y_k is the characteristic admittance of the kth mode equal to the corresponding element of the diagonal matrix $[Y_k]$ given by

$$[Y_k] = [M_v]^{-1}[Y_{SH}][M_v] \tag{3.6.7}$$

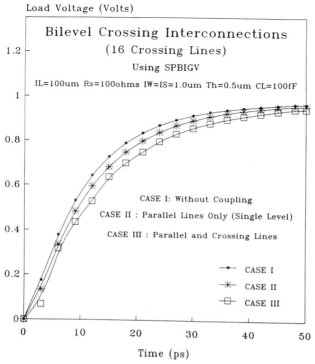

FIGURE 3.4.29 Effects of the coupling of the driven interconnection with its parallel and crossing neighbors on its load voltage waveform.

and

$$\begin{bmatrix} \mathbf{V} \\ \mathbf{I} \end{bmatrix} \begin{bmatrix} [M_v] & [0] \\ [0] & [[M_v]^T]^{-1} \end{bmatrix} \begin{bmatrix} \mathbf{e} \\ \mathbf{j} \end{bmatrix} \qquad (3.6.8)$$

For a system of n lossy parallel interconnection lines, the preceding equations lead to the $2n$-port circuit model shown in Figure 3.6.2 (p. 243) which consists of lossy uncoupled lines with a modal decoupling network at the input end and a complementary coupling network at the output end. The values of the linear real or complex dependent sources in the network are given by the elements of the voltage eigenvector matrix $[M_v]$. The model presented in Figure 3.6.2 differs from that presented in Section 3.5 for lossless lines in that, in the present case, the uncoupled lines are lossy, having complex impedances and propagation constants, and that the dependent

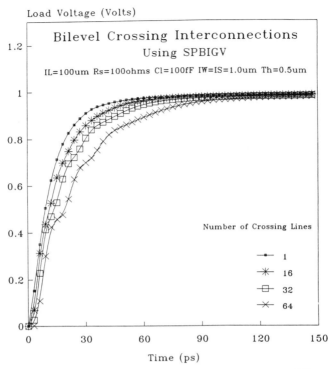

FIGURE 3.4.30 Load voltage waveforms in the time range 0 to 150 ps for several values of the number of crossing lines.

sources are generally not in phase with the independent variables. It should be noted that, given the frequency-dependent behaviors of the impedances and propagation constants of these lossy lines, they can be represented as two-ports consisting of lossless lines and lumped elements as shown in Figure 3.6.3 (p. 244) for skin effect losses. The time domain response of the interconnection lines can be calculated directly by using the model for linear as well as nonlinear terminations.

3.6.2 Simulation Results

The simulation results presented in the following discussion are obtained by modeling the multiple coupled lumped distributed parameter networks representing the interconnections terminated in passive or active elements on the computer-aided design program SPICE [3.14]. The parasitic elements for the interconnections have been calculated by the network analog method

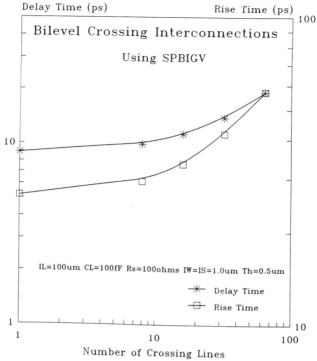

FIGURE 3.4.31 Dependences of the delay time and the rise time on the number of crossing interconnection lines.

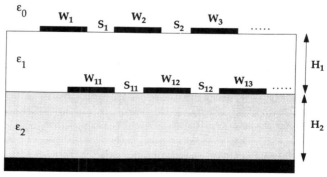

FIGURE 3.5.1 Cross-sectional view of a multiple coupled-line structure [3.13]. (© 1985 IEEE)

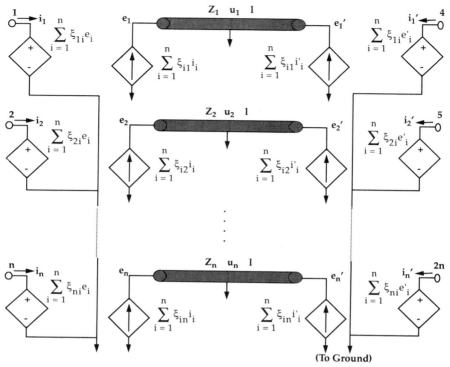

FIGURE 3.5.2 Equivalent-circuit model for the multiple coupled lines [3.13]. (© 1985 IEEE)

applied to the three-dimensional interconnection structures in layered lossy media, including the frequency-dependent coupling between the crossing lines.

The step response for a pair of crossing lines in the SiO_2 medium is shown in Figure 3.6.4 (p. 244). The schematic of the interconnections is shown in the inset. The line widths and the separation are 10 μm each, the length is 3 mm, and the terminations are 100 Ω each.

For a two-level interconnection structure consisting of four lines in the Si–SiO_2 system, the SPICE results for the step response are shown in Figure 3.6.5 (pp. 245–246). The geometry of the interconnection structure and its schematic diagram are shown in Figures 3.6.5a and b, respectively, with $W = H_1 = H_2 = 2D = S/2 = 5\ \mu$m, $H_3 = 250\ \mu$m, $l = 10$ mm, and $Z = 100$ Ω. The SPICE model parameters for this case can be obtained from Figure 3.6.2 with $N = 4$ as follows:

Normal mode line 1: impedance $Z_1 = 11.23$ Ω; delay $T_d = 54.24$ ps.
Normal mode line 2: impedance $Z_2 = 55.16$ Ω; delay $T_d = 59.98$ ps.

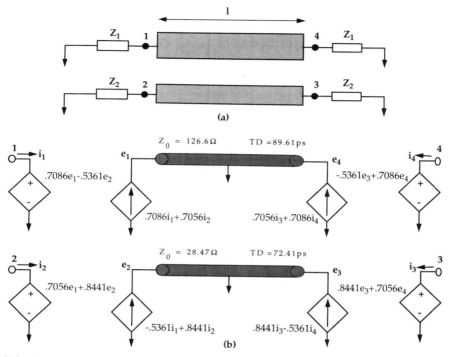

FIGURE 3.5.3 Step response of the asymmetric coupled microstrip four-port: (*a*) schematic diagram of the coupled lines; (*b*) equivalent SPICE model for $W_1/H = 2W_2/H = 0.46$, $S/H = 0.038$, and $\varepsilon_r = 9.8$; (*c*) and (*d*) step response for characteristic nonmode converting terminations $Z_1 = 46.8$ Ω and $Z_2 = 73.4$ Ω; (*e*) and (*f*) step response for 50-Ω terminations [3.13]. (© 1985 IEEE)

Normal mode line 3: impedance $Z_3 = 49.79$ Ω; delay $T_d = 75.69$ ps.
Normal mode line 4: impedance $Z_4 = 179.7$ Ω; delay $T_d = 68.79$ ps.

The dependent sources in the SPICE subcircuit, denoted by ξ_{jk} in Figure 3.6.2, are given by the elements of the following voltage eigenvector matrix:

$$[M_v] = \begin{bmatrix} 2.0 & 1.01726 & 1.02429 & 0.050117 \\ -1.86303 & 1.09345 & 0.99017 & -0.077621 \\ 0.54591 & 0.16732 & 1.40569 & 0.415290 \\ -0.43182 & 0.22045 & 1.39422 & -0.424816 \end{bmatrix}$$

The SPICE results for the step response of coupled crossing lines at adjacent levels in the SiO_2 medium, including the effects of distributed as well as lumped couplings, are shown in Figure 3.6.6 (p. 247). For these

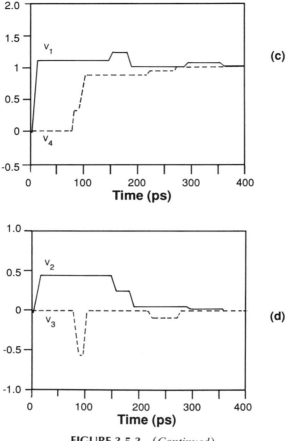

FIGURE 3.5.3 (*Continued*)

results, the line lengths are 3 mm, the separation is 10 μm, the layer thickness is 7 μm, and the terminations are 100 Ω each.

Figure 3.6.7 (p. 249) shows the schematic, the SPICE model, and the step response of a pair of coupled interconnections on the semi-insulating GaAs substrate, including skin effect losses. The losses are modeled in terms of the *RL* circuits (see Figure 3.6.3) represented by the impedances Z_1 and Z_2 in the inset of Figure 3.6.7. Other parameters are as follows: $W = S = 10$ μm, $T = 2$ μm, $H_1 = 2$ μm, $H_2 = 100$ μm, $l = 2$ mm; the terminating impedances are 100 Ω each.

The results for a general lossy layered structure consisting of three interconnection lines on a GaAs system, including frequency-dependent skin effect losses and dielectric losses, are shown in Figure 3.6.8 (p. 250). The

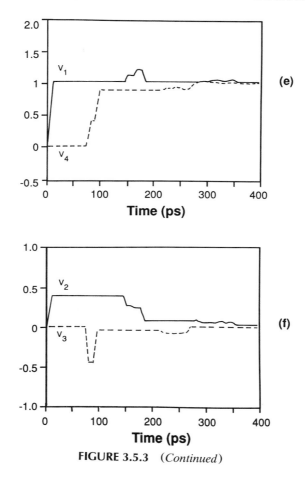

FIGURE 3.5.3 (*Continued*)

interconnection structure cross section and its schematic diagram are shown in the insets. The input signal is a 100-ps pulse with $Z_1 = 0$; all other Z's are 100 Ω each.

3.7 VERY HIGH FREQUENCY LOSSES
IN A MICROSTRIP INTERCONNECTION

For very high speed VLSI circuits, several phenomena, such as reflections at discontinuities, substrate losses, conductor losses, geometric dispersion, and inductive effects, become important and should be included in the interconnection delay models. The interconnection line is dispersive because the propagation factor of the corresponding transmission line varies nonlinearly

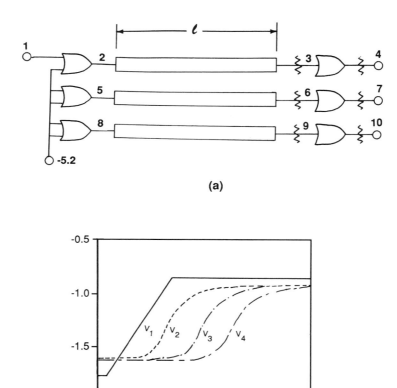

FIGURE 3.5.4 Step response of a three-line structure terminated in ECL-OR gates on the alumina substrate and with $W/H = S/H = 1$. The termination symbols denote 50 Ω consisting of two resistors in parallel—81 Ω to ground and 130 Ω to -5.2 V [3.13]. (© 1985 IEEE)

with the width of the line. This is further caused by the geometric dispersion in the microstrip line reflected in the frequency dependence of the effective dielectric constant, by the finite conductivity of the silicon substrate, and by the frequency dependence (due to the skin effect) of the resistance of the metal conductor.

In this section a model of pulse propagation in an isolated microstrip interconnection on an Si substrate, including several high-frequency effects [3.34], is presented. Quasi-TEM mode propagation is assumed, and the analysis is valid for frequencies up to the lowest frequency at which non-TEM

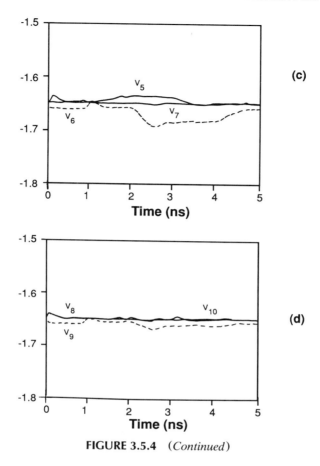

FIGURE 3.5.4 (*Continued*)

modes can propagate in the microstrip interconnection. This limit corresponds to the cutoff frequency for the surface wave mode [3.35] which is
inversely related to the substrate thickness and is 50 GHz for a silicon wafer
of 450 μm thickness.

3.7.1   The Model

A schematic diagram of the microstrip interconnection on the Si substrate is
shown in Figure 3.7.1 (p. 251). We assume that the dielectric constant ε_r of
the substrate is real and constant which is valid in silicon for frequencies up
to 10^{13} Hz. Furthermore, we include the effect of the insulator (the oxide
layer) by treating it as an open circuit at zero frequency and as a short circuit

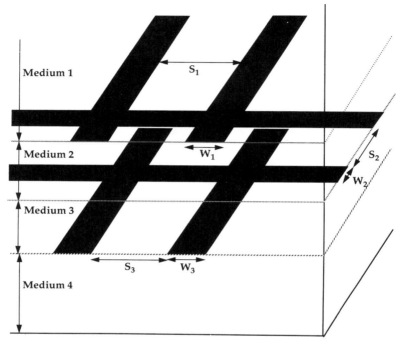

FIGURE 3.6.1 Schematic diagram of the parallel and crossing interconnections modeled in this section [3.14]. (© 1987 IEEE)

at all other frequencies. This assumption is valid because, even at 100 MHz, the impedance introduced by the capacitance of the oxide layer is negligible as long as its thickness t_0 is much smaller than the substrate thickness h. As stated previously, we also assume quasi-TEM mode propagation which is justified at the substrate resistivities and frequencies used in this section. This can be further justified by finding the ratio of the longitudinal and tangential electric fields of the mode and verifying that this ratio is much smaller than 1. Using the parallel-plate model, this ratio is given by

$$\frac{|E_z|}{|E_x|} = \frac{2\varepsilon_r\varepsilon_0}{\sigma\delta\mu_0} \qquad t \gg \delta \qquad (3.7.1a)$$

$$\frac{|E_z|}{|E_x|} = \frac{\varepsilon_r\varepsilon_0}{\sigma t\mu_0} \qquad t \ll \delta \qquad (3.7.1b)$$

where t is the conductor thickness, σ is the conductivity of the conductor,

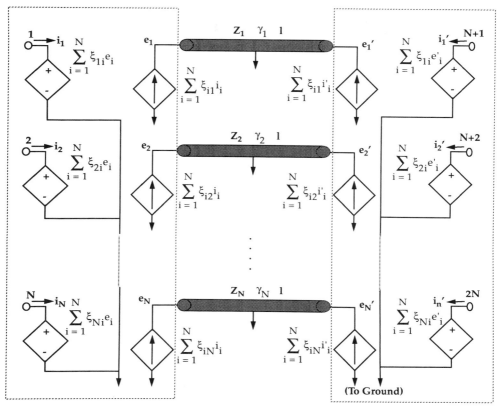

FIGURE 3.6.2 $2n$-port circuit model representing the n parallel lossy coupled interconnections [3.14]. (© 1987 IEEE)

and δ is the skin depth in the conductor. For the results presented in this section, this ratio is much smaller than 1. In fact, it is the largest ($= 0.1$) for a 0.5-μm-thick poly-Si line (resistivity $= 500$ $\mu\Omega \cdot$ cm) for frequencies below 10^{12} Hz.

For a given voltage waveform $v(0, t)$ at one end of the microstrip, we need to find the voltage waveform $v(z, t)$ at any point z along the microstrip line. This can be accomplished by carrying out the Fourier decomposition of $v(0, t)$, multiplying the various terms by the corresponding propagation factors, and then performing the inverse Fourier transformation; that is,

$$v(z, t) = F^{-1}\left[F\{v(0, t)\} \times e^{-(\alpha + j\beta)z}\right] \qquad (3.7.2)$$

where α is the attenuation constant, β is the propagation constant, F

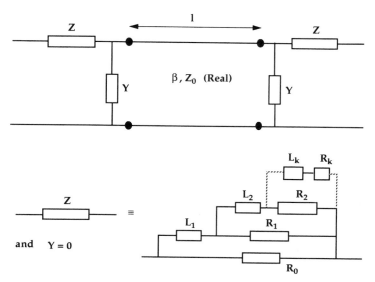

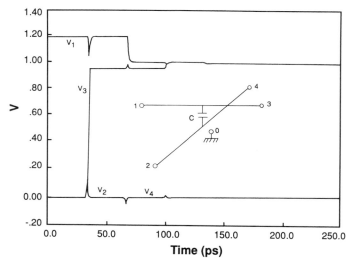

FIGURE 3.6.3 Model for a single lossy uncoupled line with frequency-dependent skin effect losses [3.14]. (© 1987 IEEE)

FIGURE 3.6.4 Step response for a pair of crossing lines in the SiO_2 medium. The schematic of the interconnections is shown in the inset. The line widths and the separation are 10 μm each, the length is 3 mm, and the terminations are 100 Ω each [3.14]. (© 1987 IEEE)

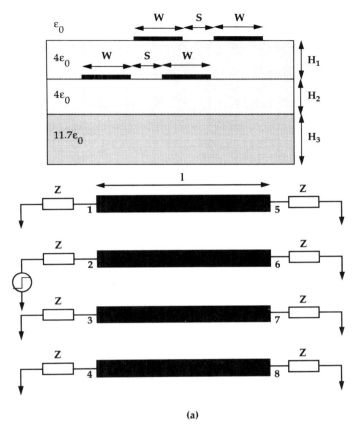

(a)

FIGURE 3.6.5 SPICE results for the step response for a two-level interconnection structure consisting of four lines in the $Si-SiO_2$ system. The geometry of the interconnection structure and its schematic diagram are shown in (a) with $W = H_1 = H_2 = 2D = S/2 = 5 \ \mu m$, $H_3 = 250 \ \mu m$, $l = 10$ mm, and $Z = 100 \ \Omega$ [3.14]. (© 1987 IEEE)

denotes the Fourier transformation, and F^{-1} represents the inverse Fourier transformation.

Using the symbols shown in Figure 3.7.1, the effective dielectric constant ε_{eff} and the characteristic impedance Z_0 at zero frequency have been calculated by Schneider [3.36] to be

$$\varepsilon_{\text{eff}} = 0.5 \left[(\varepsilon_r + 1) + \frac{\varepsilon_r - 1}{\sqrt{1 + 10\dfrac{h}{w}}} \right] \qquad (3.7.3)$$

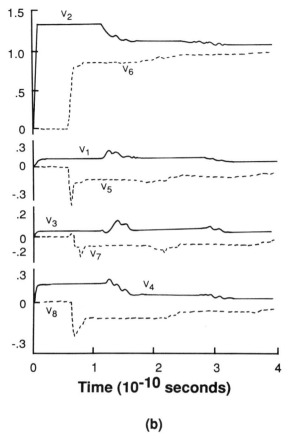

(b)

FIGURE 3.6.5   (*Continued*)

$$Z_0 = \frac{60}{\sqrt{\varepsilon_{\text{eff}}}} \times \ln\left[\frac{8h}{w} + \frac{w}{4h}\right] \qquad w < h$$

$$Z_0 = \frac{120\pi}{\left[\left\{\frac{w}{h} + 2.42 - \frac{0.44h}{w} + \left(1 - \frac{h}{w}\right)^6\right\}\sqrt{\varepsilon_{\text{eff}}}\right]} \qquad w > h \qquad (3.7.4)$$

The maximum relative error in expressions (3.7.3) and (3.7.4) is less than 2 percent; however, corrections [3.37] are required for $(t/h) > 0.005$. The expression for ε_{eff} at high frequencies has been derived by Yamashita et al.

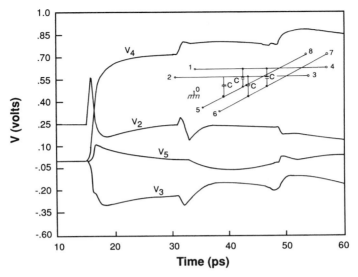

FIGURE 3.6.6 SPICE results for the step response of coupled crossing lines at adjacent levels in the SiO_2 medium. The line lengths are 3 mm, the separation is 10 μm, the layer thickness is 7 μm, and the terminations are 100 Ω each [3.14]. (© 1987 IEEE)

[3.38] and is given by

$$\sqrt{\varepsilon_{\text{eff}}(f)} = \sqrt{\varepsilon_{\text{eff}}(0)} + \frac{\sqrt{\varepsilon_r} - \sqrt{\varepsilon_{\text{eff}}(0)}}{1 + 4F^{-1.5}} \qquad (3.7.5)$$

where

$$F \equiv \frac{4fh}{c} \sqrt{\varepsilon_r - 1} \left[0.5 + \left\{ 1 + 2\log\left(1 + \frac{w}{h}\right) \right\}^2 \right]$$

f is the frequency and c is the speed of light in a vacuum. The error in expression (3.7.5) is less than 1 percent.

For a lossless material the propagation constant β_0 is given by

$$\beta_0 = \frac{2\pi f \sqrt{\varepsilon_{\text{eff}}}}{c} \qquad (3.7.6)$$

However, for a conductor of finite resistivity and a substrate material of finite conductivity, the attenuation should be considered. At low frequencies where the current distribution in the conductor can be considered uniform, the conductor loss factor α_c is given in nepers by

$$\alpha_c = \frac{\rho_c}{2wtZ_0} \tag{3.7.7}$$

where ρ_c is the resistivity of the metal. However, at high frequencies where the current distribution is not uniform due to the skin effect, the conductor loss is given by [3.39]:

$$\alpha_c = \left[\frac{R_s}{2\pi Z_0 h}\right]\left[1 - \left(\frac{w'}{4h}\right)^2\right]\left[1 + \frac{h}{w'} + \frac{h\left\{\ln\left(\frac{4\pi w}{t}\right) + \frac{t}{w}\right\}}{\pi w'}\right] \qquad \frac{w}{h} < \frac{1}{2\pi}$$

$$\alpha_c = \left[\frac{R_s}{2\pi Z_0 h}\right]\left[1 - \left(\frac{w'}{4h}\right)^2\right]\left[1 + \frac{h}{w'} + \frac{h\left\{\ln\left(\frac{4h}{t}\right) - \frac{t}{h}\right\}}{\pi w'}\right] \qquad \frac{1}{2\pi} < \frac{w}{h} < 2$$

$$\alpha_c = \frac{R_s/(Z_0 h)}{\left[\frac{w'}{h} + \frac{2}{\pi}\ln\left\{2\pi e\left(0.94 + \frac{w'}{2h}\right)\right\}\right]^2}\left[\frac{w'}{h} + \frac{\frac{w'}{\pi h}}{0.94 + \frac{w'}{2h}}\right]$$

$$\times \left[1 + \frac{h}{w'} + \frac{h\left\{\ln\left(\frac{2h}{t}\right) - \frac{t}{h}\right\}}{\pi w'}\right] \qquad \frac{w}{h} > 2 \tag{3.7.8}$$

where μ is the permeability of the metal, $R_s \equiv \sqrt{(\pi f \mu \rho_c)}$, and

$$w' = w + \frac{t}{\pi}\left[1 + \ln\left(\frac{4\pi w}{t}\right)\right] \qquad \frac{w}{h} < \frac{1}{2\pi}$$

$$w' = w + \frac{t}{\pi}\left[1 + \ln\left(\frac{2h}{t}\right)\right] \qquad \frac{w}{h} > \frac{1}{2\pi}$$

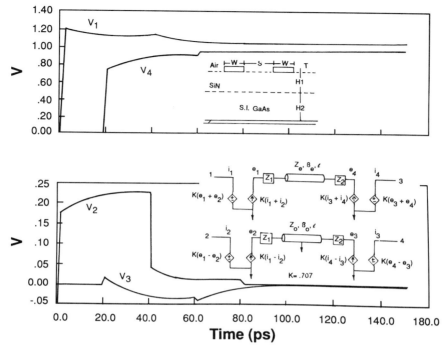

FIGURE 3.6.7 Schematic diagram, SPICE model, and step response of a pair of coupled interconnections on a semi-insulating GaAs substrate including skin effect losses. Parameters are: $W = S = 10$ μm, $T = 2$ μm, $H_1 = 2$ μm, $H_2 = 100$ μm, $l = 2$ mm, and the terminating impedances are 100 Ω each [3.14]. (© 1987 IEEE)

The dielectric loss α_d caused by the nonzero conductivity of the substrate has been derived by Welch and Pratt [3.40] and is given by

$$\alpha_d = \frac{60\pi\sigma_s(\varepsilon_{\text{eff}} - 1)}{(\varepsilon_r - 1)\sqrt{\varepsilon_{\text{eff}}}} \tag{3.7.9}$$

where σ_s is the conductivity of the substrate. For a 50-Ω, 0.5-μm-thick aluminum microstrip line on a 450-μm-thick Si wafer of resistivity 100 $\Omega \cdot$ cm, the dependences of the conductor loss, dielectric loss, and line loss on the frequency in the range 10^8 to 10^{13} Hz are shown in Figure 3.7.2 (p. 251).

A circuit diagram and circuit equations for the transmission line model of the microstrip interconnection are given in Figure 3.7.3 (p. 252), where L and C denote the inductance and capacitance per unit length for the lossless line and R_c and R_d denote the resistances per unit length introduced by the conductor resistance and the substrate conductance. The circuit equations

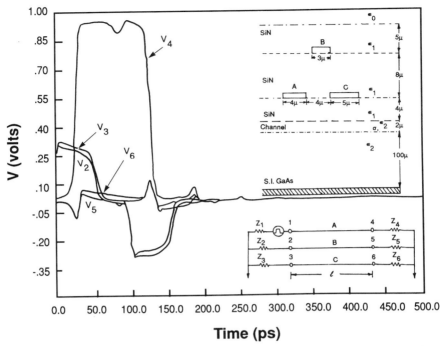

FIGURE 3.6.8 Step response for a general lossy layered structure consisting of three interconnection lines on a GaAs system, including the frequency-dependent skin effect losses and the dielectric losses. The interconnection structure cross section and its schematic diagram are shown in the insets. The input signal is a 100-ps pulse with $Z_1 = 0$ and all other Z's are 100 Ω each [3.14]. (© 1987 IEEE)

can be solved to yield the following expressions for the general attenuation constant α and propagation constant β:

$$\alpha = \sqrt{\frac{-f_1 + \sqrt{f_2}}{2}} \qquad (3.7.10a)$$

$$\beta = \sqrt{\frac{f_1 + \sqrt{f_2}}{2}} \qquad (3.7.10b)$$

where

$$f_1 = \omega^2 LC - \frac{R_c}{R_d}$$

$$f_2 = \left[\omega^2 LC + \left(\frac{R_c}{Z_0}\right)^2\right]\left[\omega^2 LC + \left(\frac{Z_0}{R_d}\right)^2\right] \qquad (3.7.11)$$

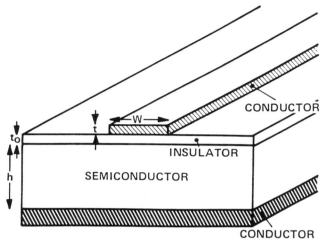

FIGURE 3.7.1 Schematic diagram of a microstrip interconnection line on a silicon substrate [3.34].

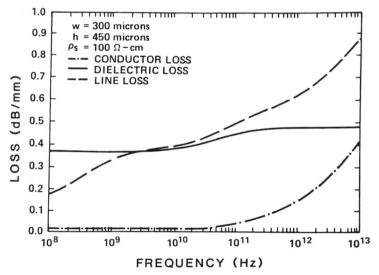

FIGURE 3.7.2 Dependences of the conductor loss, the dielectric loss, and the line loss on frequency [3.34].

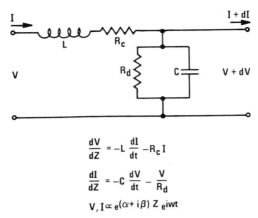

$$\frac{dV}{dZ} = -L\frac{dI}{dt} - R_c I$$

$$\frac{dI}{dZ} = -C\frac{dV}{dt} - \frac{V}{R_d}$$

$$V, I \propto e^{(\alpha + i\beta)Z} e^{iwt}$$

FIGURE 3.7.3   Circuit diagram and circuit equations for the transmission line model of the microstrip interconnection [3.34].

with $Z_0 = (L/C)^{0.5}$. For low-loss conditions the circuit model of Figure 3.7.3 yields

$$\alpha_c = \frac{R_c}{2Z_0}$$

$$\alpha_d = \frac{Z_0}{2R_d} \qquad (3.7.12)$$

$$\beta_0 = \omega\sqrt{LC}$$

Equations 3.7.11 and 3.7.12 can be combined to rewrite f_1 and f_2 in terms of β_0, α_c, and α_d as

$$f_1 = \beta_0^2 - 4\alpha_c\alpha_d$$
$$f_2 = (\beta_0^2 + 4\alpha_c^2)(\beta_0^2 + 4\alpha_d^2) \qquad (3.7.13)$$

Then Equations 3.7.6 and 3.7.9 can be combined with Equations 3.7.10 and 3.7.13 to obtain α and β for all loss conditions. If α_c and α_d are small compared to β_0, as will be the case under low-loss conditions, then α and β are given by

$$\alpha = \alpha_c + \alpha_d$$

$$\beta = \sqrt{(\alpha_c - \alpha_d)^2 + \beta_0^2} \qquad (3.7.14)$$

3.7.2   Simulation Results

The simulation results are obtained for two input high-speed logic waveforms consisting of square-wave and exponential pulses. The input square-wave

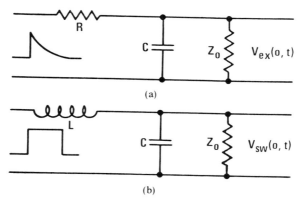

FIGURE 3.7.4 Circuits used to produce the (*a*) exponential and (*b*) square-wave input pulses for the simulation results presented in this section [3.34].

pulses are of 50 ps duration with 12-ps rise and fall times. The input exponential pulses are of the form

$$v(t) = e^{-(t/\tau_1)}[1 - e^{(-t/\tau_2)}]$$

Input pulses $v_{sw}(0, t)$ and $v_{ex}(0, t)$ with finite rise and fall times can be produced by applying ideal square-wave and exponential pulses to the circuits shown in Figure 3.7.4. By choosing the circuit parameters in Figure 3.7.4, a variety of pulses can be obtained. The Fourier transforms of the input

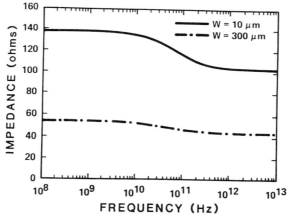

FIGURE 3.7.5 Characteristic impedance versus frequency for two microstrip interconnections of widths 10 and 300 μm [3.34].

square-wave pulses are given by

$$V_{sw}(0, f) = \left[\frac{1 - e^{-(j\omega\tau_1)}}{j\omega} \right] \left[\frac{1}{1 + j\omega\tau_2 - \dfrac{\omega^2}{\omega_1^2}} \right]$$

where

$$\omega_1^2 = \frac{1}{LC}$$

and

$$\tau_2 = \frac{L}{Z_0}$$

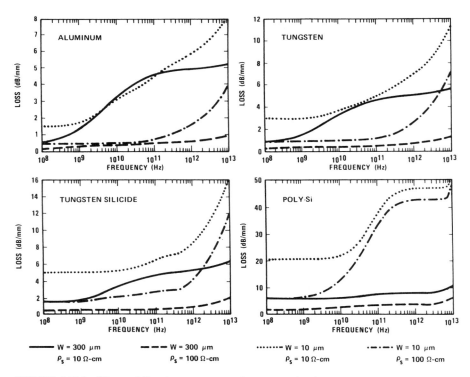

FIGURE 3.7.6 Plots of line loss α versus frequency for interconnection materials of Al ($\rho = 2.7 \ \mu\Omega \cdot cm$), W ($\rho = 10 \ \mu\Omega \cdot cm$), WSi$_2$ ($\rho = 30 \ \mu\Omega \cdot cm$), and poly-Si ($\rho = 500 \ \mu\Omega \cdot cm$) on a 450-$\mu$m-thick Si wafer [3.34].

The Fourier transforms of the input exponential pulses are given by

$$V_{ex}(0, f) = \left[\frac{1}{j\omega + \dfrac{1}{\tau_1}} \right] \left[\frac{1}{1 + j\omega\tau_2 + \dfrac{\tau_2}{\tau_1}} \right]$$

where

$$\tau_1 = Z_0 C$$

and

$$\tau_2 = RC$$

As stated earlier, the voltage response $v(z, t)$ at a distance z along the microstrip line is obtained by multiplying the Fourier transform of the input

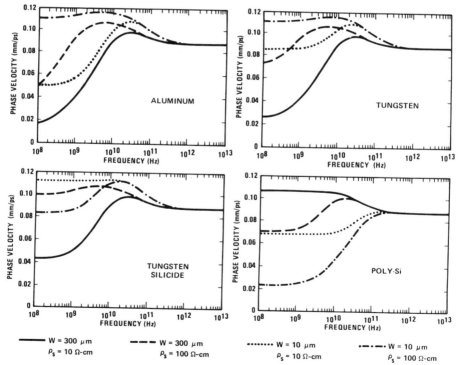

FIGURE 3.7.7 Plots of phase velocity versus frequency for interconnection materials of Al ($\rho = 2.7 \ \mu\Omega \cdot$ cm), W ($\rho = 10 \ \mu\Omega \cdot$ cm), WSi$_2$ ($\rho = 30 \ \mu\Omega \cdot$ cm), and poly-Si ($\rho = 500 \ \mu\Omega \cdot$ cm) on a 450-μm-thick Si wafer [3.34].

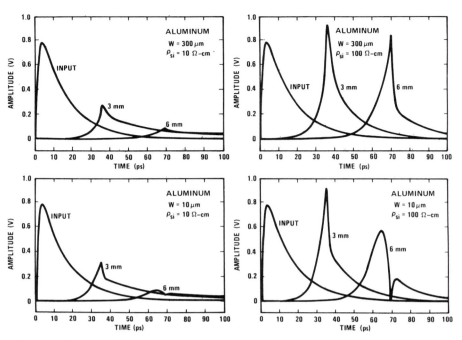

FIGURE 3.7.8 Plots of time domain exponential pulses after 0, 3, and 6 mm of propagation on Al microstrip lines on a 450-μm-thick Si wafer [3.34].

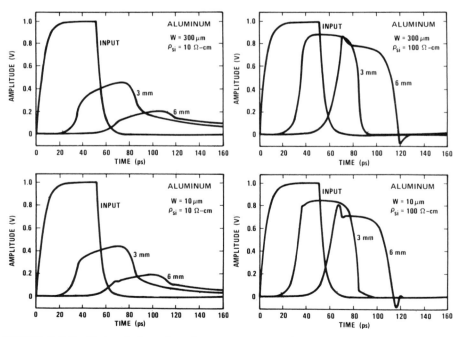

FIGURE 3.7.9 Plots of time domain square-wave pulses after 0, 3, and 6 mm of propagation on Al microstrip lines on a 450-μm-thick Si wafer [3.34].

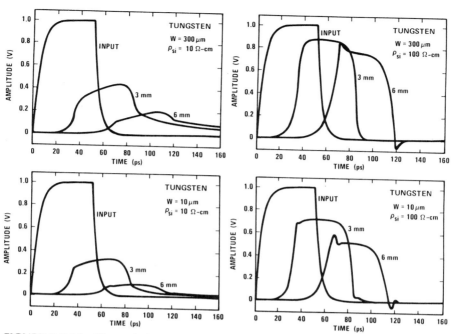

FIGURE 3.7.10 Plots of time domain square-wave pulses after 0, 3, and 6 mm of propagation on W microstrip lines on a 450-μm-thick Si wafer [3.34].

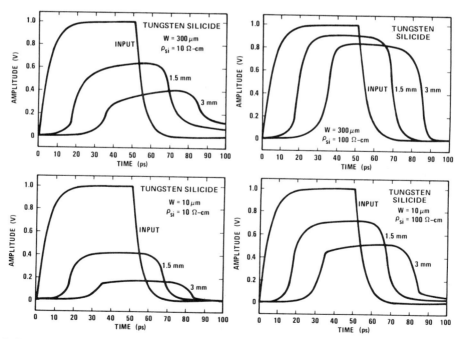

FIGURE 3.7.11 Plots of time domain square-wave pulses after 0, 1.5, and 3 mm of propagation on WSi_2 microstrip lines on a 45-μm-thick Si wafer [3.34].

waveform (at $z = 0$) by the propagation factor $\exp[(\alpha + j\beta)z]$ and then taking the inverse Fourier transform.

The dependences of the characteristic impedance on frequency for two microstrips of widths 10 and 300 μm on a Si wafer of thickness 450 μm are shown in Figure 3.7.5 (p. 253). This figure shows that the region of geometric dispersion extends from 10 to 300 GHz and that this effect is more pronounced for the narrow line width of 10 μm. Figure 3.7.6 (p. 254) shows the line losses versus frequency for microstrip lines made of aluminum, tungsten, WSi$_2$, and poly-Si of widths 10 and 300 μm on two substrates with resistivities of 10 and 100 $\Omega \cdot$ cm. The dependences of the phase velocity on frequency for the same set of parameters as in Figure 3.7.6 are shown in Figure 3.7.7 (p. 255).

For an exponential input pulse (with $\tau_1 = 15$ ps and $\tau_2 = 1$ ps) and a square-wave input pulse (with $\tau_1 = 50$ ps, $\tau_2 = 5$ ps, and $\omega_1 = 10^{12}$ Hz), the time domain waveforms for aluminum interconnections of widths 10 and 300 μm on two substrates with resistivities of 10 and 100 $\Omega \cdot$ cm at $z = 3$ and 6 mm are shown in Figures 3.7.8 (p. 256) and 3.7.9 (p. 256). It should be noted that, for a substrate resistivity of 10 $\Omega \cdot$ cm, the signal is severely attenuated by 6 mm, whereas, for a substrate resistivity of 100 $\Omega \cdot$ cm, it is not affected as much. Thus, it can be concluded that high-resistivity sub-

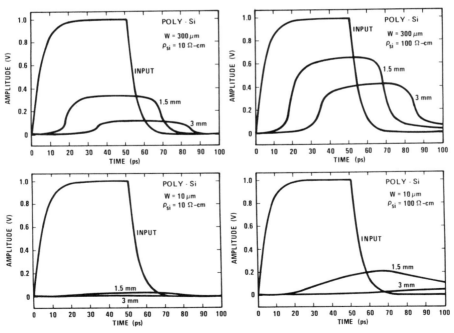

FIGURE 3.7.12   Plots of time domain square-wave pulses after 0, 1.5, and 3 mm of propagation on poly-Si microstrip lines on a 450-μm-thick Si wafer [3.34].

strates are more appropriate when designing microstrip interconnections for high-frequency integrated circuits.

For interconnection materials of tungsten, WSi_2, and poly-Si and for square-wave input pulses, the time domain waveforms at a few locations on the microstrip interconnection on two substrates with resistivities of 10 and 100 $\Omega \cdot$ cm are shown in Figures 3.7.10 to 3.7.12 (pp. 257–258). It should be noted that the conductor loss becomes increasingly significant as we proceed from aluminum to tungsten to WSi_2, but the changes are not dramatic. Figure 3.7.12 shows that, for poly-Si lines, the loss becomes very large for very high speed pulses, although significant improvement is achieved by choosing higher-resistivity substrates as is the case with other lines as well.

3.8   TRANSVERSE DELAYS IN A GaAs MESFET

The total propagation delay in a MESFET consists of two parts. First, the time taken by the electrons to move from the source to the drain electrode, usually called the *longitudinal* delay, can be approximately calculated by dividing the channel length by the average velocity of the electrons in the channel. This is typically of the order of 3 to 5 ps. The second part, usually called the *transverse* delay, arises because, at high frequencies, the signal applied to one end of the gate takes a finite time in traveling along the width of the gate. In other words, the depletion layer along the entire width under the gate electrode is not formed instantaneously. Studies [3.41–3.44] have shown that, at frequencies above 10 GHz, one must include the effects of wave propagation along the gate width. A recent study by LaRue et al. [3.45] has shown very clearly that at frequencies above 18 GHz, standing waves exist along the gate width in a GaAs MESFET. This means that, at frequencies above 10 GHz, a lumped-element equivalent circuit for a MESFET will not be adequate to explain the MESFET performance completely, and the MESFET should be modeled as a distributed-element equivalent circuit. In the past, equivalent circuits for GaAs MESFETs valid for microwave frequencies but including only the intrinsic elements in the MESFET have been developed [3.45–3.47]. In this section a model for calculating transverse propagation delays in GaAs MESFETs is developed. First, a distributed-element equivalent circuit for a GaAs MESFET is presented. Then a technique to obtain transverse delays in the MESFET is developed. The model is then used to find the dependences of the delay and rise times on the MESFET dimensions and other parameters.

3.8.1   Distributed-Element Equivalent Circuit for a GaAs MESFET

A GaAs MESFET modeled as two lossy transmission lines coupled to each other by the gate–drain distributed capacitances is shown in Figure 3.8.1. The gate line is fed by an input signal in the form of a unit step voltage on one end and its other end is open circuited. All the elements shown in Figure 3.8.1 are per unit length along the width of the device (denoted by the coordinate z). The circuit includes the intrinsic as well as the extrinsic elements in the MESFET. The various symbols used in Figure 3.8.1 are defined as follows:

R_g = gate metallization resistance
R_d = drain metallization resistance
L_g = inductance of the gate line
L_d = inductance of the drain line
C_{gs} = intrinsic capacitance between the gate and source electrodes (due to the presence of the depletion layer under the gate)

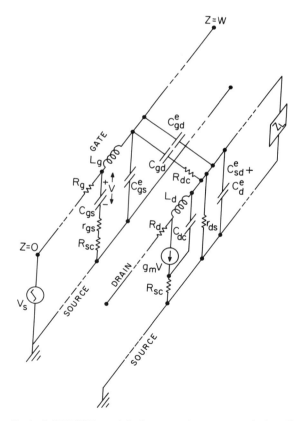

FIGURE 3.8.1   GaAs MESFET modeled as two lossy transmission lines coupled to each other by the distributed capacitances C_{gd} and C_{gd}^e. All the elements shown in the figure are per unit length along the width of the device (denoted by the coordinate z).

C_{gd} = intrinsic capacitance between the gate and drain electrodes

C_{dc} = capacitance due to the presence of the dipole layer in the channel of the MESFET

R_{sc} = contact resistance of the source electrode

R_{dc} = contact resistance of the drain electrode

r_{gs} = channel resistance between the gate and source electrodes

r_{ds} = channel resistance between the source and drain electrodes

g_m = transconductance of the MESFET

C_{gs}^e = electrode parasitic capacitance between the source and gate electrodes

C_{gd}^e = electrode parasitic capacitance between the gate and drain electrodes

C_{sd}^e = electrode parasitic capacitance between the source and drain electrodes

C_d^e = self-capacitance of the drain electrode

V = voltage across the capacitance C

V_s = unit step voltage source

Z_L = load applied to the drain line

3.8.2 Numerical Determination of Transverse Propagation Delays

An input signal in the form of a unit step voltage is applied to the gate line as shown in Figure 3.8.1. This signal propagates along the gate line, suffering distortion in its waveform. Due to the presence of the coupling capacitances C_{gd} and C_{gd}^e and the transconductance g_m, a distributed current wave is induced in the drain line. Because, in a typical MESFET, the gate metal resistance is much higher than the drain metal resistance, the induced wave in the drain line propagates at a much higher speed than does the signal in the gate line. In other words, as far as the determination of propagation delays in the MESFET is concerned, the propagation of the input signal in the gate line decides the speed at which the current at the load end of the drain line reaches its steady-state value. Therefore, in the following analysis, the small resistance and inductance associated with the drain line (L_d and R_d) are neglected.

In the complex frequency space (the s space), the voltage and current distributions along the gate line satisfy the following transmission line equations:

$$\frac{d^2 V_g}{dz^2} = \gamma^2 V_g \tag{3.8.1}$$

$$\frac{d^2 I_g}{dz^2} = \gamma^2 I_g \tag{3.8.2}$$

where γ is the propagation constant. Most general solutions of the preceding differential equations are given by

$$V_g(z) = A \cosh(\gamma z) + B \sinh(\gamma z) \qquad (3.8.3)$$

and

$$I_g(z) = \frac{A \sinh(\gamma z) - B \cosh(\gamma z)}{Z_0} \qquad (3.8.4)$$

where Z_0 is the characteristic impedance of the line and the constants A and B can be determined by using the known boundary conditions. In s space a unit step is represented by $(1/s)$. Therefore, using the boundary condition at $z = 0$, that is,

$$V_g(0) = \frac{1}{s} \qquad (3.8.5)$$

Equation 3.8.3 yields

$$A = \frac{1}{s} \qquad (3.8.6)$$

and, using the boundary condition at $z = W$, that is,

$$I_g(W) = 0 \qquad (3.8.7)$$

because this end is open circuited, Equation 3.8.4 yields

$$B = \frac{\sinh(\gamma W)}{s \cosh(\gamma W)} \qquad (3.8.8)$$

Substituting for A and B in Equation 3.8.3, the voltage along the gate line is given by

$$V_g(z) = \frac{\cosh[\gamma(W - z)]}{s \cosh(\gamma W)} \qquad (3.8.9)$$

The gate line was uncoupled from the drain line by using Miller's theorem [3.48]. A section of the gate and drain lines coupled by the impedance Z_c is shown in Figure 3.8.2. An equivalent circuit used to obtain Z_c is also shown in Figure 3.8.2. The ratio between the voltages at nodes 2 and 1, that is,

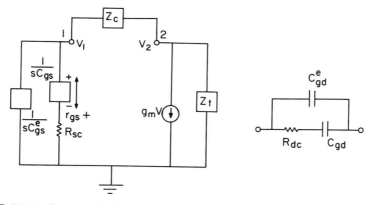

FIGURE 3.8.2 Section of the gate and drain lines coupled by the impedance Z_c; equivalent circuit used to obtain the coupling impedance Z_c is also shown.

V_2/V_1, can be found by equating the total current leaving node 2 to 0. This yields

$$\frac{V_2 - V_1}{Z_c} + \frac{V_2}{Z_t} + g_m V = 0 \tag{3.8.10}$$

where V is the voltage across the capacitance C_{gs} and an equivalent circuit used to obtain the impedance Z_t is shown in the Figure 3.8.3. The voltages V_1 and V are related by the expression

$$V = \frac{\dfrac{V_1}{sC_{gs}}}{r_{gs} + R_{sc} + \dfrac{1}{sC_{gs}}} = kV_1 \quad (\text{say}) \tag{3.8.11}$$

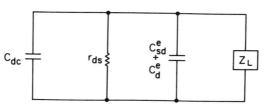

FIGURE 3.8.3 Equivalent circuit used to obtain the impedance Z_t.

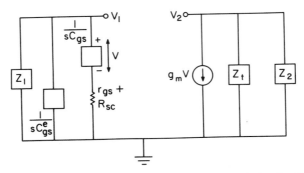

FIGURE 3.8.4 Uncoupled circuit equivalent to the coupled circuit of Figure 3.8.2.

Then Equation 3.8.10 becomes

$$V_2\left(\frac{1}{Z_c} + \frac{1}{Z_t}\right) = \frac{V_1}{Z_c} - kg_m V_1 \tag{3.8.12}$$

or

$$K = \frac{V_2}{V_1} = \frac{(1 - kg_m Z_c)Z_t}{Z_t + Z_c} \tag{3.8.13}$$

Now, according to Miller's theorem, the circuit of Figure 3.8.2 is equivalent to the uncoupled circuit of Figure 3.8.4, provided the impedances Z_1 and Z_2 are given by

$$Z_1 = \frac{Z_c}{1 - K}$$

and

$$Z_2 = \frac{Z_c}{1 - (1/K)}$$

Substituting for K from Equation 3.8.13, Z_1 and Z_2 are given by

$$Z_1 = \frac{Z_t + Z_c}{1 + kg_m W Z_t} \tag{3.8.14}$$

$$Z_2 = \frac{Z_c(1 - kg_m W Z_c)Z_t}{(1 - kg_m W Z_c)Z_t - (Z_t + Z_c)} \tag{3.8.15}$$

where W is the width of the MESFET. It has been inserted because g_m has been defined as the transconductance of the MESFET per unit length of the gate line. The series impedance per unit length of the gate line is now given by

$$Z_s = R_g + sL_g \tag{3.8.16}$$

whereas the parallel impedance per unit length of the gate line, Z_p, is equal to the impedance of the parallel combination of Z_1 and C_{gs}^e and the series combination of C_{gs}, r_{gs}, and R_{sc} (see Figure 3.8.4). The propagation constant γ can then be obtained by using Equation 3.2.5.

A measure of the intrinsic speed of the MESFET is given by its short-circuit output current. Current induced in one section of the drain line is given by $-g_m V$, where V, the voltage across the capacitance C_{gs}, is given by Equation 3.8.11. Voltage at any point on the gate line V_g is given by Equation 3.8.3. Therefore, the current induced in one section becomes

$$dI(s) = \frac{-g_m \cosh[\gamma(W - z)]\, dz}{s \cosh(\gamma W)[1 + sC_{gs}(r_{gs} + R_{sc})]} \tag{3.8.17}$$

where dz is the length of the section. The total current induced in the drain line will then be given by

$$I(s) = \frac{-g_m}{s \cosh(\gamma W)[1 + sC_{gs}(r_{gs} + R_{sc})]} \int_0^W \cosh(\gamma(W - z))\, dz \tag{3.8.18}$$

After the integration is performed, the expression for $I(s)$ becomes

$$I(s) = \frac{-g_m \tanh(\gamma W)}{\gamma s[1 + sC_{gs}(r_{gs} + R_{sc})]} \tag{3.8.19}$$

The time domain response of the output current can be obtained by an inverse Laplace transformation of $I(s)$. Because of the presence of branch points associated with the propagation constant γ, the inverse transformation can be obtained by using the Bromwich integrals; that is,

$$i(t) = \frac{1}{2\pi j} \int_{Br} I(s) e^{st}\, ds \tag{3.8.20}$$

Using Simpson's rule,

$$i(t) \sim \frac{1}{2\pi j} \sum_{n=-N}^{N} I(s) e^{st} \Delta s \tag{3.8.21}$$

Following the same steps as in Section 3.2, Equation 3.8.21 becomes

$$i(t) \sim \frac{1}{2\pi} \sum_{n=-N}^{N} I(\sigma + jn\,\Delta\omega)e^{(\sigma+jn\,\Delta\omega)t}\,\Delta\omega \qquad (3.8.22)$$

Again, any positive σ and $\Delta\omega$ that will cause two consecutive terms in the summation in Equation 3.8.22 to be sufficiently close to each other can be used. However, these should be carefully chosen to optimize the speed of convergence. The choice of N depends on the speed of convergence as well, but it should be chosen to be sufficiently large.

3.8.3   The Program TPDGM

A listing of the program called Transverse Propagation Delays in a GaAs MESFET (TPDGM), which incorporates the steps of the preceding section, is presented in Appendix 3.2. For given values of the gate length, the MESFET width, and the electrode material resistivity, the program calculates the propagation constant, performs the summation in Equation 3.8.22, and determines the normalized drain current as a function of time in any desired time range. The output response is normalized in the sense that it is the ratio of the output current at a given time t to its value at time $t = \infty$. The program uses the following values for the equivalent-circuit elements: $C_{gs} = 1.5 \times 10^{-9}$ F/m, $C_{gd} = 4.5 \times 10^{-11}$ F/m, $L_g = 10^{-6}$ H/m, $R_g = 2 \times \rho \times 10^4$ Ω/m, $r_{gs} = 3.3 \times 10^{-3}$ $\Omega \cdot$ m, $r_{ds} = 0.2$ $\Omega \cdot$ m, $R_{sc} = 10^{-3}$ $\Omega \cdot$ m, $R_{dc} = 10^{-3}$ $\Omega \cdot$ m, $g_m = 100$ S/m, and $C_{dc} = 4.0 \times 10^{-11}$ F/m, where ρ is the electrode material resistivity. All values are per unit length (per meter) of the width of the MESFET. These values represent a typical GaAs MESFET with a 1-μm gate length, 0.5-μm-thick gate metal, and 10^{23}/m^3 channel doping density. The program takes care of the fact that the values of C_{gs}, C_{gd}, L_g, and R_g depend on the value of the gate length currently being used. The values of the electrode parasitic capacitances [3.49] are determined by using the subroutine EPCSSGM, which is obtained from the program EPCSGM developed earlier (Appendix 2.3).

3.8.4   Dependence of Transverse Delays on MESFET Parameters

The program TPDGM has been used to study the dependences of the delay time and the rise time on the MESFET dimensions, namely the gate length and the device width, and the resistivity of the gate metal. The overshoot and ringing observed in the following curves are due to a finite number of terms included in the approximation expressed by Equation 3.8.22 used to find $i(t)$.

Figure 3.8.5 shows the normalized short-circuit output currents for gate lengths of 0.2 and 5 μm. For these results the width of the MESFET is fixed at 100 μm and the gate metal is taken to be aluminum with $\rho = 3$ $\mu\Omega \cdot$ cm.

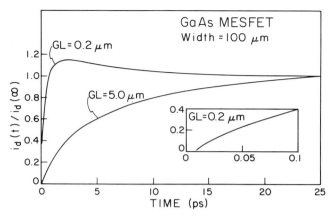

FIGURE 3.8.5 Normalized short-circuit drain currents in a typical GaAs MESFET for gate lengths of 0.2 and 5.0 μm. The insert shows the drain current for a gate length of 0.2 μm for times less than 0.1 ps.

Figure 3.8.6 shows the dependence of the delay time on the gate length, whereas the dependence of the rise time on the gate length is shown in the Figure 3.8.7. These two figures show that, for gate lengths above 0.5 μm, the delay time and the rise time increase significantly. This increase in the propagation delays is due to the increase in the capacitances C_{gs} and C_{gd} when the gate length is increased. As a function of the width of the MESFET, the delay time and the rise time are shown in Figures 3.8.8 and 3.8.9, respectively. Figure 3.8.10 shows the normalized short-circuit output currents for gate widths of 50 and 500 μm. For these results the gate metal is

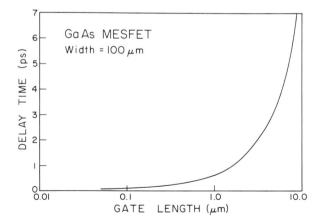

FIGURE 3.8.6 Dependence of the delay time on the gate length in a typical GaAs MESFET.

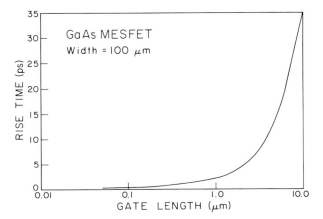

FIGURE 3.8.7   Dependence of the rise time on the gate length in a typical GaAs MESFET.

again aluminum, and the gate length is fixed at 0.5 μm. Figures 3.8.8 and 3.8.9 indicate that the propagation delays increase significantly for device widths greater than 100 μm. Once again, this is due to the increase in the capacitances C_{gs} and C_{gd} as the width is increased. For widths less than 100 μm, the propagation times are almost constant as the width is increased. Figure 3.8.11 shows the normalized short-circuit drain currents for gate metal resistivities of 5 and 200 $\mu\Omega \cdot$ cm. For these results the gate length is fixed at 0.5 μm, whereas the width of the MESFET is kept at 100 μm. Figure 3.8.11

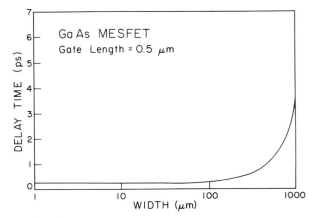

FIGURE 3.8.8   Delay time in a typical GaAs MESFET as a function of the width of the MESFET.

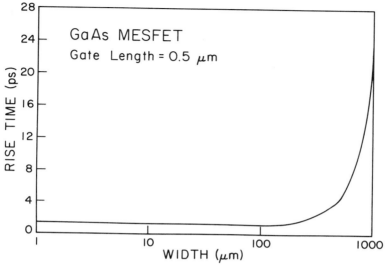

FIGURE 3.8.9   Rise time in a typical GaAs MESFET as a function of the width of the MESFET.

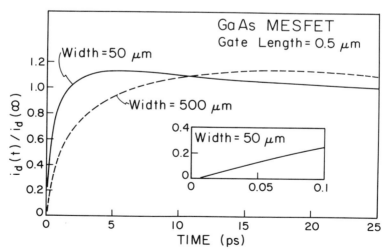

FIGURE 3.8.10   Normalized short-circuit drain currents in a typical GaAs MESFET for gate widths of 50 and 500 μm. The insert shows the drain current for a gate width of 50 μm for times less than 0.1 ps.

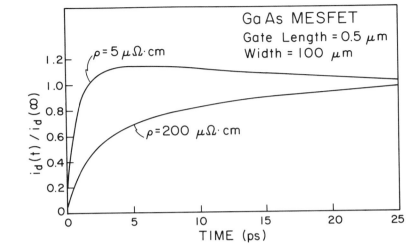

FIGURE 3.8.11 Normalized short-circuit drain currents in a typical GaAs MESFET for gate metal resistivities of 5 and 200 $\mu\Omega \cdot$ cm.

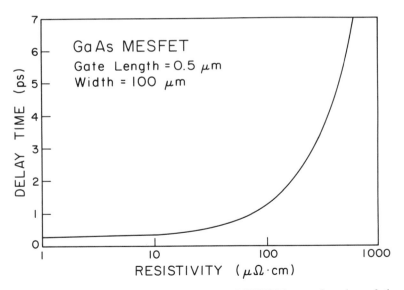

FIGURE 3.8.12 Delay time in a typical GaAs MESFET as a function of the gate metal resistivity.

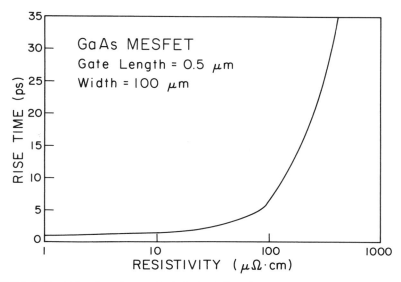

FIGURE 3.8.13   Rise time in a typical GaAs MESFET as a function of the gate metal resistivity.

shows that the drain current rises more slowly toward its steady-state value when the resistivity is increased. The dependences of the delay time and the rise time on the gate metal resistivity are shown in Figures 3.8.12 and 3.8.13, respectively.

3.9   TRANSVERSE DELAYS IN A GaAs/AlGaAs MODFET

A schematic diagram of the GaAs/AlGaAs MODFET modeled in this section is shown in Figure 3.9.1. As in a MESFET, when a signal is applied to the gate electrode in the MODFET, the depletion layer under the gate is not formed instantaneously, resulting in additional propagation delays in the MODFET. In other words, the signal applied to one end of the gate takes a finite time to travel across the width of the gate. This kind of propagation delay is usually called *transverse* delay. Studies [3.50] have shown that at frequencies above 10 GHz, the transverse propagation delay has to be taken into consideration. This is because, at frequencies above 10 GHz, standing waves exist along the gate width in a GaAs MESFET [3.45] and the same will be true for a GaAs/AlGaAs MODFET. In this section the transverse propagation delays in a MODFET have been studied. A three-dimensional model has been set up to model the two lossy gate and drain lines coupled to each other via the gate–drain capacitances. Intrinsic parameters as well as extrinsic parameters are taken into account in this model. Then a technique to obtain the transverse delays in the MODFET

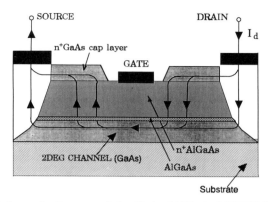

FIGURE 3.9.1 Schematic diagram of the GaAs/AlGaAs MODFET modeled in this section.

is developed. Finally, the dependences of these delays on the various MODFET parameters, such as the gate length, the device width, and the gate metal resistivity, have been studied.

3.9.1 Distributed-Element Equivalent Circuit for a GaAs / AlGaAs MODFET

A schematic diagram of a GaAs/AlGaAs MODFET is shown in Figure 3.9.1, and the MODFET modeled as two lossy transmission lines coupled to each other by the gate–drain distributed capacitances is shown in Figure 3.9.2. The gate line is fed by an input signal in the form of a unit step voltage on one end and its other end is open circuited. All elements shown in Figure 3.9.2 are per unit length along the width of the device (denoted by the coordinate z). The various symbols used in Figure 3.9.2 and the following analysis are defined as follows:

ε = semiconductor permittivity

μ_0 = low-field carrier mobility

V_1 = effective voltage along the gate width

W = channel width or gate width

L_g = gate length

G_o = output conductance

R_{ss} = source resistance

R_{gg} = gate series resistance

R_{dd} = drain series resistance

C_0 = gate charging capacitance per unit area

d_0 = distance between the two-dimensional electron gas and the gate electrode

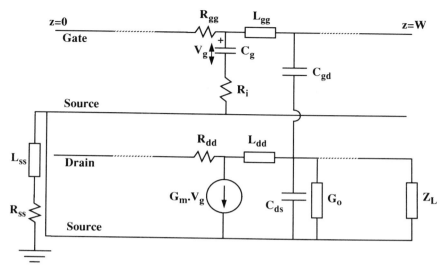

FIGURE 3.9.2 GaAs/AlGaAs MODFET modeled as two lossy transmission lines coupled to each other by the distributed capacitance C_{gd}. All the elements shown in the figure are per unit length along the width of the device (denoted by the coordinate z).

ν_{sat} = saturation velocity of electrons in the channel

C_{gd} = gate–drain feedback capacitance

C_{ds} = drain–source output capacitance

G_m = transconductance

L_{gg} = inductance of the gate line

L_{dd} = inductance of the drain line

Z_L = load impedance

V_s = unit step voltage

C_g = effective capacitance of the depletion layer under the gate

R_i = effective intrinsic resistance between the gate and the source

Other symbols used in the analysis are defined as they appear.

3.9.2   Numerical Determination of Transverse Propagation Delays

In this subsection a method for the determination of transverse propagation delays in a GaAs/AlGaAs MODFET is presented. An input signal in the form of a unit step voltage is applied to the gate line as shown in Figure 3.9.2. This signal propagates along the gate line, suffering distortion in its waveform. Due to the presence of the coupling capacitances C_{gd} and the transconductance G_m, a distributed current wave is induced in the drain line. Because, in a typical MODFET, the gate metal resistance is much higher than the drain metal resistance, the induced wave in the drain line propagates at a much higher speed than does the signal in the gate line. In other words, as far as the determination of propagation delays in the MODFET is concerned, the propagation of the input signal in the gate line decides the speed at which the current at the load end of the drain line reaches its steady-state value. Therefore, in the following analysis, the small resistance and inductance associated with the drain line (R_{dd} and L_{dd}) are neglected.

As in the case of a MESFET, in the complex frequency space (the s space), the voltage and current distributions along the gate line satisfy the following transmission line equations:

$$\frac{d^2V}{dz^2} = \gamma^2 V \tag{3.9.1}$$

$$\frac{d^2I}{dz^2} = \gamma^2 I \tag{3.9.2}$$

where γ is the propagation constant. Once again, the most general solutions of the preceding differential equations are given by

$$V(z) = A \cosh(\gamma z) + B \sinh(\gamma z) \tag{3.9.3}$$

and

$$I(z) = \frac{A \sinh(\gamma z) - B \cosh(\gamma z)}{Z_0} \tag{3.9.4}$$

where Z_0 is the characteristic impedance of the gate line and the constants A and B can be determined by using the known boundary conditions. Using the boundary condition at $z = 0$, that is,

$$V(0) = \frac{1}{s}$$

we get, from Equation 3.9.3,

$$A = \frac{1}{s}$$

and, using the boundary condition at $z = W$, that is, $I(W) = 0$ (because this end is open circuited), we get, from Equation 3.9.4,

$$B = \frac{\tanh(\gamma W)}{s}$$

Substituting for A and B in Equation 3.9.3 and after simplifying, we get the following expression for the voltage along the gate line:

$$V(z) = \frac{\cosh(\gamma(W - z))}{s \cosh(\gamma W)} \tag{3.9.5}$$

The propagation constant for a transmission line is given by

$$\gamma = \sqrt{\frac{Z_s}{Z_p}} \tag{3.9.6}$$

where Z_s is the series impedance per unit length along the line and Z_p is the parallel impedance per unit length along the line. However, in order to use Equation 3.9.6, the line should not be coupled with any other line. Therefore, the first step is to decompose the conductance G_3 shown in Figure 3.9.3 into

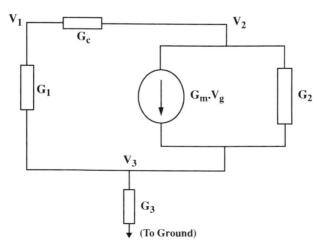

FIGURE 3.9.3   Section of the gate and drain lines coupled by the admittance G_c.

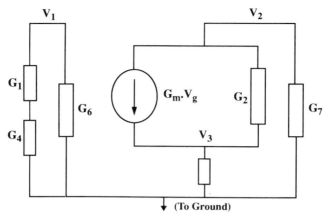

FIGURE 3.9.4   Uncoupled circuit equivalent to the coupled circuit of Figure 3.9.3.

the conductances G_4 and G_5 shown in Figure 3.9.4. G_4 and G_5 can be found by using the following equations:

$$G_3 = G_4 + G_5 \tag{3.9.7}$$

$$(V_1 - V_3)G_1 = G_4V_3 \tag{3.9.8}$$

$$G_mV_g + (V_2 - V_3)G_2 = V_3G_5 \tag{3.9.9}$$

$$(V_1 - V_3)G_1 + G_mV_g + (V_2 - V_3)G_2 = V_3G_3 \tag{3.9.10}$$

$$(V_1 - V_2)G_c = V_3G_5 \tag{3.9.11}$$

where V_g is the voltage across the capacitance C_g shown in Figure 3.9.2, given by

$$V_g = D(s)(V_1 - V_2) \tag{3.9.12}$$

where

$$D(s) = \frac{1}{1 + sR_iC_g} \tag{3.9.13}$$

Combining Equations 3.9.7 to 3.9.13, we find the following expressions for G_5

and G_4:

$$G_5 = \frac{\dfrac{G_m DG_3}{G_1} + \dfrac{G_2 G_3}{G_1}}{\dfrac{G_m D}{G_1} + \dfrac{G_2}{G_c} + \dfrac{G_2}{G_1} + 1} \qquad (3.9.14)$$

and

$$G_4 = G_3 - G_5$$

In order to use Equation 3.9.6, the next step is to uncouple the gate line from the drain line. This can be accomplished by using Miller's theorem [3.51]. The uncoupled circuit equivalent to the coupled circuit of Figure 3.9.3 is shown in Figure 3.9.4, where the admittances G_6 and G_7 are given by the following equations:

$$\begin{aligned} G_6 &= G_c(1 - K) \\ G_7 &= G_c\left[1 - \frac{1}{K}\right] \end{aligned} \qquad (3.9.15)$$

where

$$K = \frac{V_2}{V_1} = 1 - \frac{G_1 G_5}{G_c(G_1 + G_3 - G_5)}$$

The series impedance per unit length of the gate line is now given by

$$Z_s = R_{gg} + s L_{gg} \qquad (3.9.16)$$

whereas the parallel impedance per unit length of the gate line, Z_p, is equal to the parallel combination of G_6 and the series combination of G_1 and G_4 (see Figure 3.9.4). The propagation constant γ can then be obtained by using Equation 3.9.6.

An indication of the intrinsic speed of the MODFET can be obtained from its short-circuit drain current. Current induced in one section of the drain is given by $-V_3 G_5$, where V_3 is defined in Figure 3.9.4. Again, combining Equations 3.9.7 to 3.9.13, V_3 can be expressed in terms of the various admittances and V_1. Then, using V_1 from Equation 3.9.5, the current induced in one section of the drain line becomes

$$dI(s) = \frac{-G_1 G_5}{G_1 + G_3 - G_5} \frac{1}{\cosh(\gamma W)} \frac{\cosh[\gamma(W - z)]}{s}$$

where dz is the length of the section. The total current induced in the drain line will then be given by

$$I(s) = \frac{-G_1 G_5}{\cosh(\gamma W) s (G_1 + G_3 - G_5)} \int_0^W \cosh[\gamma(W - z)] \, dz$$

After the integration is performed, the expression for $I(s)$ becomes

$$I(s) = \frac{-G_1 G_5}{G_1 + G_3 - G_5} \frac{\tanh(\gamma W)}{\gamma s} \tag{3.9.17}$$

The output drain current $i(t)$ in the time domain can then be obtained by an inverse Laplace transformation of $I(s)$.

3.9.3   Determination of MODFET Parameters

Instead of using the various parameter values published in the literature, the following physical equations can be used to determine the values of the MODFET parameters depicted in Figure 3.9.1. The transconductance G_m is given by

$$G_m = \beta_1 V_c (1 - \gamma_1) \frac{\exp\left(\dfrac{-j\omega k_0 \tau_0}{a}\right)}{1 + \dfrac{j\omega \tau_0}{a}} \tag{3.9.18}$$

where

$$\beta_1 = \frac{W C_0 \mu_0}{L_g}$$

$$V_c = \frac{L_g \nu_{sat}}{\mu_0}$$

$$\gamma_1 = \frac{1}{\sqrt{1 + \dfrac{2V_1}{V_c}}}$$

$$\tau_0 = \frac{2\gamma_1 L_g}{3\nu_{sat}(1 - \gamma_1)}$$

$$k_0 = 0.61$$

$$a = 39$$

and ω is the imaginary value of s in the s plane. The capacitance C_g can be calculated by using the equation:

$$C_g = C_{g1} + C_{g2} \tag{3.9.19}$$

where

$$C_{g1} = \tfrac{2}{3}\gamma_1 C_0 W L_g$$

and

$$C_{g2} = (1 - \gamma_1)W(L_g + \Delta L_g)C_0$$

where ΔL_g is the additional effective gate length because the depletion layer under the gate electrode extends beyond the actual gate length. The resistance R_i is given by

$$R_i = \frac{R_{i1}}{\left[1 + \dfrac{C_{g2}}{C_{g1}}\right]^2} \tag{3.9.20}$$

where

$$R_{i1} = \frac{1}{5\beta_1 V_c(1 - \gamma_1)}$$

The capacitances C_{gd} and C_{ds} can be calculated by using the following expressions [3.52]:

$$C_{gd} = W\varepsilon \tag{3.9.21}$$

and

$$C_{ds} = W\varepsilon \frac{K(m)}{2K(n)} \tag{3.9.22}$$

where

$$n = \frac{L_g}{L_g + \Delta L_g}$$

and

$$m^2 + n^2 = 1$$

and K is the complete elliptic integral of the first kind. The source resistance R_{ss} can be determined by using the model proposed by Feuer [3.53] according to which

$$R_{ss} = \frac{r_{s1} r_{s2} L}{r_{s1} + r_{s2}}$$

$$+ \frac{\alpha_2 + \beta_2 \cosh(K_1 L) + \gamma_2 K_1 \sinh(K_1 L)}{(r_{s1} + r_{s2})^2 \cosh(K_1 L) + (r_{s1} + r_{s2}) K_1 (R_{c1} + R_{c2}) \sinh(K_1 L)}$$

where

$$\alpha_2 = 2r_{s2}(r_{s1} R_{c2} - r_{s2} R_{c1})$$

$$\beta_2 = 2r_{s2}^2 R_{c1} + (r_{s1}^2 + r_{s2}^2) R_{c2}$$

$$\gamma_2 = (r_{s1} + r_{s2}) R_{c1} R_{c2} + r_s^2 \rho_{12}$$

and

$$K_1 = \sqrt{\frac{r_{s1} + r_{s2}}{\rho_{12}}}$$

3.9.4 Dependence of Transverse Delays on MODFET Parameters

The simulation results presented in the following discussion are calculated by using a program called Transverse Propagation Delays in a GaAs/AlGaAs MODFET (TPDGAM), which incorporates the steps of the preceding sections. A listing of the user-friendly program TPDGAM written in FORTRAN is given in Appendix 3.3. For given values of the gate length, the MODFET width, and gate electrode material resistivity, the program calculates the propagation constant and determines the normalized drain current as a function of time in any desired time range. The output response is normalized in the sense that it is the ratio of the output current at a given time t to its value at time $t = \infty$. The values of the model parameters ρ_{12}, R_{c1}, R_{c2}, r_{s1}, and r_{s2} used in the TPDGAM are the same as those extracted by Feuer from measurements of the resistances of gated and ungated MODFET structures of various lengths [3.53]. These are: $\rho_{12} = 1.5 \times 10^{-5}$ $\Omega \cdot cm^2$, $R_{c1} = 0.255$ $\Omega \cdot mm$, $R_{c2} = 1.2$ $\Omega \cdot mm$, $r_{s1} = 216$ Ω, and $r_{s2} = 1164$ Ω. The program also uses the following values of the other equivalent-circuit elements: $R_{gg} = 2.0 \times \rho \times 10^4$ Ω/m, $L_{gg} = 10^{-6}$ H/m, and $G_o = 0.1G_m$, where ρ is the gate electrode material resistivity. All values are per unit length (per meter) of the width of the MODFET.

The program TPDGAM has been used to study the dependences of the delay times and the rise time on the GaAs/AlGaAs MODFET dimensions, namely the gate length and the device width, and the resistivity of the gate

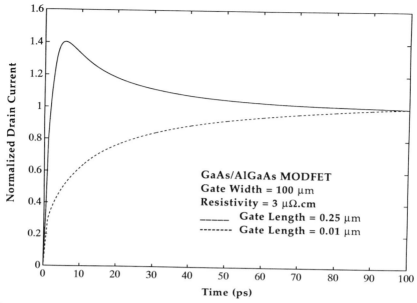

FIGURE 3.9.5 Normalized short-circuit drain currents in a GaAs/AlGaAs MODFET for gate lengths of 0.25 and 0.01 μm in the time range 0 to 100 ps.

metal. The overshoot and ringing observed in the curves are due to the finite step size used to find $i(t)$ in Equation 3.9.17.

Figure 3.9.5 shows the normalized short-circuited output drain currents for gate lengths of 0.25 and 0.01 μm. For these results the width of the MODFET is fixed at 1000 μm, and the gate metal is taken to be aluminum with $\rho = 3\ \mu\Omega \cdot$ cm. Figure 3.9.6 shows the dependence of the rise time on the gate length. This figure shows that, for gate lengths less than approximately 0.4 μm, the rise time decreases, whereas the gate length increases. On the other hand, for gate lengths greater than about 0.4 μm, the rise time increases, whereas the gate length increases. The increase in the propagation delay is due to the increase in the capacitances C_{gs} and C_{gd} when the gate length is increased. On the contrary, the decrease in the propagation delay is due to the decrease of the gate resistance R_{gg} when the gate length increases. In other words, the gate resistance dominates the propagation delay when the gate length is less than approximately 0.4 μm, whereas the capacitances dominate the delay instead when the gate length is greater than about 0.4 μm.

Figure 3.9.7 shows the normalized short-circuit drain currents for gate widths of 100 and 500 μm, and, as a function of the width of the MODFET, the rise time is shown in Figure 3.9.8. For these results the gate metal is again aluminum, and the gate length is fixed at 0.1 μm. Figure 3.9.8 indicates

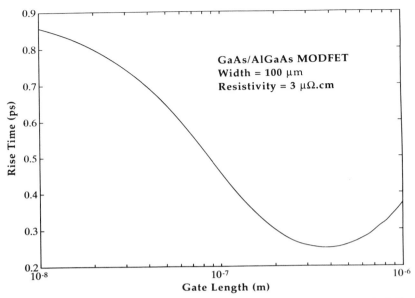

FIGURE 3.9.6 Dependence of the rise time on the gate length in a typical GaAs/AlGaAs MODFET in the range 0.01 to 1 μm.

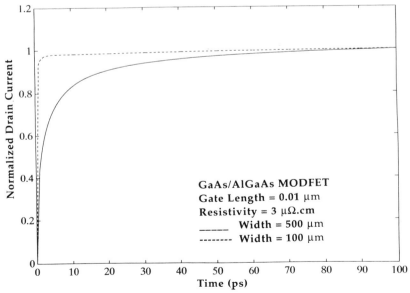

FIGURE 3.9.7 Normalized short-circuit drain currents in a GaAs/AlGaAs MODFET for widths of 100 and 500 μm in the time range 0 to 100 ps.

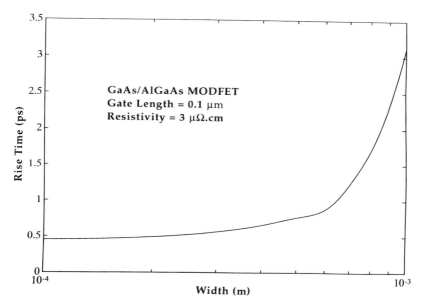

FIGURE 3.9.8   Rise time in a typical GaAs/AlGaAs MODFET as a function of the width of the MODFET in the range 100 to 1000 μm.

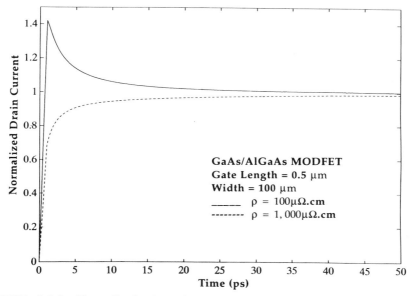

FIGURE 3.9.9   Normalized short-circuit drain currents in a GaAs/AlGaAs MODFET for gate metal resistivities of 100 and 1000 $\mu\Omega \cdot$ cm in the time range 0 to 50 ps.

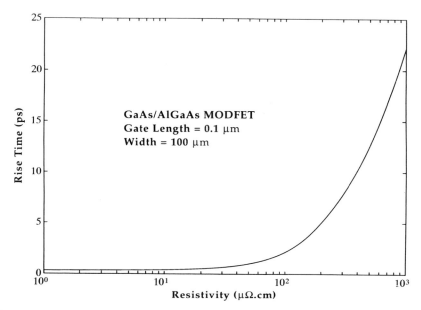

FIGURE 3.9.10 Rise time in a typical GaAs/AlGaAs MODFET as a function of the gate metal resistivity in the range 1 to 1000 $\mu\Omega \cdot$ cm.

that the propagation delay increases as the device width increases. This is due to the increase in the capacitances C_{gs} and C_{gd} as the width is increased. Figure 3.9.9 shows the normalized short-circuit drain currents for gate metal resistivities of 100 and 1000 $\mu\Omega \cdot$ cm. For these results the gate length is fixed at 0.5 μm, whereas the width of the MESFET is kept at 100 μm. Figure 3.9.9 shows that, as the resistivity is increased, the drain curent rises more

TABLE 3.9.1 Comparison of Propagation Delays in MESFETs and MODFETs

FET Parametres	GaAs MESFET		GaAs/AlGaAs MODFET	
	Delay Time (ps)	Rise Time (ps)	Delay Time (ps)	Rise Time (ps)

Gate length = 1.0 μm
  Width = 100 μm
  $\rho = 3\,\mu\Omega \cdot$ cm
	0.55	2.25	0.25	0.37

Gate length = 0.5 μm
  Width = 100 μm
  $\rho = 3\,\mu\Omega \cdot$ cm
	0.25	1.00	0.16	0.26

Gate length = 0.5 μm
  Width = 100 μm
  $\rho = 100\,\mu\Omega \cdot$ cm
	1.20	6.6	0.35	0.56

slowly toward its steady-state value. The dependence of the rise time on the gate metal resistivity is shown in Figure 3.9.10.

A comparison of the delay times and rise times in a few GaAs MESFETs and GaAs/AlGaAs MODFETs with nearly the same common FET parameters is shown in Table 3.9.1. The table also shows that the propagation delays in a MODFET will be much smaller than in a MESFET with the same common technology parameters, as expected.

3.10 INTERCONNECTION DELAYS IN MULTILAYER INTEGRATED CIRCUITS

Recently, there has been interest in extending the concept of multilevel interconnections to three-dimensional integrated circuits with active devices such as transistors, gates, cells, and so forth on several planes. The potential for fabricating integrated circuit chips with multiple planes of almost independent circuits [3.54–3.59] has been demonstrated by researchers using silicon-on-insulator techniques [3.60]; this technology is called multilayer circuit (MLC) technology.

In this section a simplified model of interconnection delays in multilayer integrated circuits [3.61] is presented. The interconnection delay in an MLC chip is normalized to that in an equivalent single-plane chip. This is followed by a study of the dependences of these interconnection delays on several parameters of the MLC chip, such as the number of devices on the chip, the number of circuit planes, the interconnection complexity, and the characteristics of the interconnection material.

3.10.1 The Simplified Model

For this analysis a multilayer circuit is defined as one consisting of independent circuits on more than one plane; that is, an MLC chip looks like a stack of two or more independent chips with vertical interconnections between them. In other words, the placement of transistors and interconnections on each plane does not depend on the fabrication and other characteristics of the other planes. An example of a four-layer MLC is shown in Figure 3.10.1. Generally, aluminum is considered to be a suitable interconnection material for the top plane of an MLC chip, whereas, for the other planes, the interconnection material is chosen from refractory metals, silicides, and polysilicon.

In this analysis several simplifying assumptions are made. First, it is assumed that each plane of the MLC chip uses the same basic technology and that it is the same as that of the single-plane chip used for normalization. Next, it is assumed that the various devices are evenly divided among all planes of the MLC chip; that is, if n is the number of devices and p is the number of planes, then the number of devices on each plane is equal to n/p.

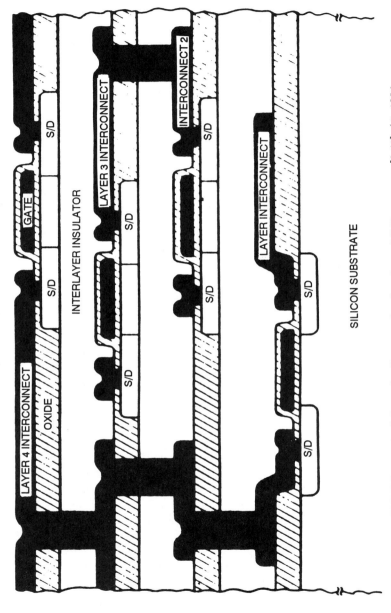

FIGURE 3.10.1 Schematic diagram of a four-layer MLC structure [3.61]. (© 1986 IEEE)

It is further assumed that there exists an interconnection complexity factor m which represents the degree to which the interconnection complexity influences the circuit area and that m is the same for each plane. If k represents a technology-dependent normalization constant, then the chip area A is modeled as

$$A = k\left(\frac{n}{p}\right)^{m} \qquad (3.10.1)$$

Therefore, when $m = 1$, the total area required for constructing the MLC chip will be the same as that of the corresponding single-plane chip, and, when $m > 1$, it will be less than that for the single-plane chip because of the reduction in the fractional area required for the interconnections.

A simple model for the interconnection delay τ can be constructed in terms of the RC time constant associated with the interconnection line. For an interconnection of length L and width W, τ can be written as

$$\tau = RC = \rho_p\left(\frac{L}{W}\right)(cLW) = \rho_p cL^2 \qquad (3.10.2)$$

where ρ_p is the thin-film resistivity of the interconnection material and c is its capacitance per unit area. The fringing fields as well as the coupling capacitances with the neighboring conductors have been neglected. Obviously, the maximum interconnection delay is associated with the longest interconnection line and an estimate of the maximum interconnection length L_p on any one plane of the MLC chip of area A is given by [3.62]

$$L_p = \frac{\sqrt{A}}{2} \qquad (3.10.3)$$

Assuming that all planes of the MLC chip are equal in area, each plane can have interconnections of maximum length given by Equation 3.10.3. If f is the number of planes that have interconnection lines to be driven by the same device, then the effective total length of the interconnection is given by L_{tot}, where

$$L_{\text{tot}} = fL_p \qquad 1 \leq f \leq p \qquad (3.10.4)$$

Combining Equations 3.10.1 to 3.10.4, an estimate of the maximum interconnection delay for the MLC chip is given by

$$\tau_p = \rho_p cL_{\text{tot}}^2 = \rho_p cf^2 L_p^2 = \frac{1}{4}\rho_p cf^2 A = \frac{1}{4}\rho_p cf^2 k\left(\frac{n}{p}\right)^{m} \qquad (3.10.5)$$

TABLE 3.10.1   Thin-Film Resistivities of Interconnection Materials [3.61]
(© 1986 IEEE)

Material	Thin-Film Resistivity $(\mu\Omega \cdot cm)$	r
Aluminum	2	1.0
Refractory metals	5–10	2.5–5
Silicides	15–100	7.5–50
Polysilicon	1000	500

On the other hand, the time constant for the corresponding single-plane chip ($p = 1$) is given by

$$\tau_1 = \frac{1}{4}\rho_1 ck(n)^{m_1} \tag{3.10.6}$$

where ρ_1 and m_1 are the thin-film resistivity of the interconnection material and the interconnection complexity factor for the single-plane chip. Then, assuming that the capacitance per unit area c is the same for single-plane and MLC chips, the ratio R_r of the maximum interconnection delay on the MLC chip to that on the single-plane chip becomes

$$R_r = \frac{\tau_p}{\tau_1} = \frac{f^2(n/p)^m \rho_p}{(n)^{m_1}\rho_1} = rf^2(p)^{-m}(n)^{m-m_1} \tag{3.10.7}$$

where $r = \rho_p/\rho_1$. Assuming that the single-plane chip uses aluminum interconnections, the thin-film resistivities [3.63] and the corresponding r values for aluminum, refractory metals, silicides, and polysilicon are listed in Table 3.10.1.

3.10.2   Simulation Results and Discussion

The dependences of the normalized interconnection delays on the interconnection complexity factor for several values of the number of circuit planes, keeping $r = 1$ and $f = 1$, are shown in Figure 3.10.2. The normalized interconnection delays as functions of the circuit size for several values of the interconnection complexity factor, keeping $r = 3$, $f = 1$, $m_1 = 1.2$, and $p = 4$, are shown in Figure 3.10.3. Based on the discussion of MLCs, presented in

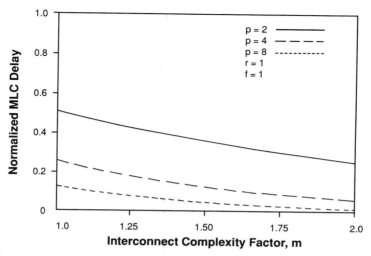

FIGURE 3.10.2 Dependences of the normalized interconnection delays on the interconnection complexity factor for several values of the number of circuit planes. Fixed parameters: $r = 1$ and $f = 1$ [3.61]. (© 1986 IEEE)

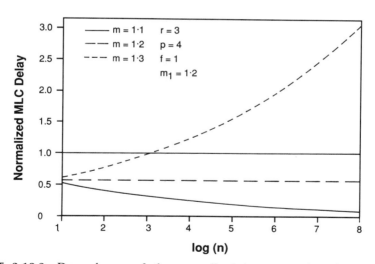

FIGURE 3.10.3 Dependences of the normalized interconnection delays on the circuit size for several values of the interconnection complexity factor. Fixed parameters: $r = 3$, $f = 1$, $m_1 = 1.2$, and $p = 4$ [3.61]. (© 1986 IEEE)

this section and from the results presented in Figures 3.10.2 and 3.10.3, the following comments can be made:

1. Partitioning of the integrated circuit into virtually independent subcircuits fabricated on separate planes reduces the lengths of the interconnection lines on any one plane, thereby reducing the interconnection delays.

2. When the availability of the third dimension in an MLC permits the reduction of the interconnection complexity factor m compared to m_1 for a single-plane chip, the area per plane is reduced by a factor of $p^{-m}n^{m-m1}$ with a proportional reduction in the normalized interconnection delay R_r.

3. An important factor in maximizing the speed of an MLC is partitioning the original integrated circuit such that a device on a given plane drives a maximum-length interconnection on one plane only. This will minimize f and hence R_r because $R_r \propto f^2$.

4. The assumptions made in the preceding analysis can be considered extrapolations of the best-case MLC technology. If these assumptions are modified to account for more realistic MLCs, the resulting interconnection delay will increase.

EXERCISES

E3.1 In this chapter interconnections are modeled using various numerical techniques. Comment on the computer efficiency of these techniques.

E3.2 List and discuss the desirable characteristics of a numerical model that make it more suitable for inclusion in a CAD tool. Review the various techniques presented in this chapter from the point of view of their suitability for inclusion in a CAD tool.

E3.3 Using the modifications suggested in Section 3.4.2, develop an algorithm for comprehensive analysis of the crossing interconnections shown in Figure 3.4.7.

E3.4 Combining the propagation delay models for interconnections and transistors, develop a model for propagation delays in the various logic gates.

E3.5 Referring to Section 3.7, comment on the relative significance of high-frequency losses in an aluminum interconnection on GaAs in the following frequency ranges: (*a*) below 10 MHz; (*b*) 10 MHz to 1 GHz; (*c*) 1 to 10 GHz; (*d*) 10 to 100 GHz; and (*e*) above 100 GHz.

APPENDIX 3.1

PDSIGV
Propagation Delays in Single-Level Interconnections on GaAs-Based VLSI

```
      REAL IW, IL, SIGMA, DW, T, S1, S2, LI, RI, RS,
     $     T1, V, CI, CL1, CL2, CR1, CR2, CIL1, CIR1,
     $     CIL2, CIR2, NF, TERM1, RO, IL1, C, C1, IW1
      INTEGER N, M, P, M1, P1, P2
      COMPLEX S, G, VS, VT, TERM, S3, Y1, Y2, Y3, Y4,
     $        ZL, Z0, A, B
      OPEN (5, FILE = `IPDD1')
      OPEN (6, FILE = `IPDR1', STATUS = `NEW')
      WRITE (6, 160)
 160  FORMAT ( ` PROPAGATION DELAYS IN PARALLEL
     $        INTERCONNECTIONS.'/, ` RESULTS FOR
     $        LOSSY LINES'//
     $        `LOAD:C'/ `SOURCE RESISTANCE = RS'/
     $        ` COUPLING INCLUDED: FIRST AND SECOND
     $        NEIGHBORS'// )
      WRITE (*, 160)
C*****INPUT (IW AND IL ARE IN MICROMETERS; RO IS IN
C     MICROOHM.CM)
 10   READ (5, 100, END = 999) M1, P1, P2
 100  FORMAT (3(I6))
C*****TYPICAL VALUES FOR INTERCONNECTIONS WITH IL = 1 M,
C     THICKNESS = 0.5 MICROMETER)
      C1 = 100.0
      IW = 1.0
      IL = 100.0
      RO = 3.0
      LI = IW * (10.0 ** (-6))
      RI = R0*2.0 * (10.0 ** 4) / IW
      RS = 700.0
C*****CALCULATING V(T) AFTER INCLUDING THE NEIGHBOR
C     COUPLINGS:
      CALL SCIC(IW, C11, C22, C33, C12, C13, C23)
      WRITE (6, 164)
 164  FORMAT ( / , ` SCIC USED ')
      WRITE (6, 166) C11, C22, C33, C12, C13, C23
 166  FORMAT (6F9.3)
      CI = C22*(10.0 ** (-12))
      CIR1 = C23*(10.0 ** (-12))
      CIR2 = C13*(10.0 ** (-12))
```

```
      CIL1 = C12*(10.0 ** (-12))
      CIL2 = C13*(10.0 ** (-12))
      CR1 = C22*(10.0 ** (-12))
      CR2 = C22*(10.0 ** (-12))
      CL1 = C22*(10.0 ** (-12))
      CL2 = C22*(10.0 ** (-12))
      C = C1*(10.0 ** (-15))
      IL1 = IL*(10.0 ** (-6))
      IW1 = IW*(10.0)
      S3 = (-1.0, 0.0)
      NF = 2.196123
      WRITE (6, 162) C1, RS
162   FORMAT ( / , 4X, ` LOAD CAPACITANCE = ', F9.1,  `fF'/
$             4X, ` SOURCE RESISTANCE = ', F9.1,
$                       `ohms',/ )
      WRITE (*, 162) C1, RS
      WRITE (6, 161)
161   FORMAT ( / , 4X, `IW', 9X, `IL', 9X, `Number of
$             terms', 4X, `t(ps)',12X, `V(t)')
      WRITE (*, 161)
      DO 7100 P = 1,P1,P2
      V = 0.0
      T1 = P* (10.0 ** (-12))
      SIGMA = 0.5*T1
      DW = 0.05 / T1
      VT = (0.0, 0.0)
      DO 7000 N = 1,M1, 1
      S1 = SIGMA
      S2 = N*DW
      S = CMPLX(S1,S2)
      Y1 = S*CR1*CIR1 / (CIR1 + CR1)
      Y2 = S*CR2*CIR2 / (CIR2 + CR2)
      Y3 = S*CL1*CIL1 / (CIL1 + CL1)
      Y4 = S*CL2*CIL2 / (CIL2 + CL2)
      G = CSQRT((Y1 + Y2 + Y3 + Y4 + S*CI)*(RI + S*LI))
      Z0 = CSQRT((RI + S*LI) / (Y1 + Y2 + Y3 + Y4 + S*CI))
      ZL = 1.0 / (S*C)
      A = (Z0 / S) / (RS + Z0- (RS- Z0)*
$    ((ZL- Z0) / (ZL + Z0))*CEXP(-2*G*IL1))
      B = ((ZL- Z0) / (ZL + Z0))*CEXP(-2*G*IL1)*A
      VS = B*CEXP(G*IL1) + A*CEXP(-G*IL1)
      TERM = VS*DW*(COS(S2*T1) + (CSQRT(S3))*SIN(S2*TI))*
$        EXP(SIGMA*T1) / 6.284
      VT = VT + TERM
```

```
7000   CONTINUE
       V = CABS(VT)*NF
C*****WRITING THE RESULTS
       WRITE (6,700) IW,IL,M1,P,V
 700   FORMAT (F6.2,5X,F7.2,5X,I7,12X,I7,5X,F15.3)
       WRITE(*,700) IW,IL,M1,P,V
7100   CONTINUE
       GO TO 10
 999   STOP
       END
C
       SUBROUTINE SCIC(IW,C11,C22,C33,C12,C13,C23)
       INTEGER N1X,N2X,N3X,NY,N1,N2,N3,N,I,J,EN,CNT,CR
       REAL A1,B1,C1,D1,A2,B2,C2,D2,E2,F2,G2,I2,J2,K2,
     $      L2,M2,O2,P2,Q2,S2,G(6,6),GIJ,GIJ1,R1,R2,R3,
     $      R4,R5,R6,R7,R8,R9,C1E,C2E,C3E,C1O,C2O,C3O,
     $      C11,C22,C33,C12,C13,C23,DS1,DS2,DS3,IW,T1,
     $      T2,T3,T4,T5,T6,T7,T8,T9,T10,T11,T12,T13,
     $      T14,T15,T16,X(6),Y(6),Z(6),DX(6),DY,IL,T,
     $      K1,S12,S23,L(10),M(10)
       GIJ = 0.0
       I = 1
       J = 1
       EN = 1
       K1 = 0.859155
       N1X = 1
       N2X = 1
       N3X = 1
       NY = 2
       S12 = IW
       S23 = IW
       IL = 100.0
       T = 200.0
       N1 = N1X*NY
       N2 = N2X*NY
       N3 = N3X*NY
       N = N1 + N2 + N3
       DY = IL / NY
       DO 151 J = 1,N1,1
       DX(J) = IW / N1X
 151   CONTINUE
       DO 152 J = N1 + 1,N1 + N2,1
       DX(J) = IW / N2X
```

```
152   CONTINUE
      DO 153  J = N1 + N2 + 1 , N , 1
      DX(J) = IW / N3X
153   CONTINUE
      DS1 = DX(N1)*DY
      DS2 = DX(N1 + N2)*DY
      DS3 = DX(N)*DY
      CNT = 0.0
      DO 5500  CR = 1 , N1X , 1
      DO 5900  I = CNT + 1 , CNT + NY , 1
      X(I) = (2*CR- 1)*((DX(N1)) / 2)
5900  CONTINUE
      CNT = I
5500  CONTINUE
      CNT = N1
      DO 6500  CR = 1 , N2X , 1
      DO 6900  I = CNT + 1 , CNT + NY , 1
      X(I) = (IW + S12) + (2*CR- 1)*((DX(N1 + N2)) / 2)
6900  CONTINUE
      CNT = I
6500  CONTINUE
      CNT = N1 + N2
      DO 7500  CR = 1 , N3X , 1
      DO 7900  I = CNT + 1 , CNT + NY , 1
      X(I) = (IW + S12 + IW + S23) + (2*CR- 1)*((DX(N)) / 2)
7900  CONTINUE
      CNT = I
7500  CONTINUE
      DO 8000  CR = 1 , NY , 1
      DO 8500  I = CR , N , NY
      Y(I) = (2*CR- 1)*(DY / 2)
8500  CONTINUE
8000  CONTINUE
      DO 9000  I = 1 , N , 1
      Z(I) = T
9000  CONTINUE
      DO 300  I = 1 , N , 1
      DO 310  J = 1 , N , 1
      A1 = X(J) - X(I) - ((DX(J)) / 2)
      B1 = X(J) - X(I) + ((DX(J)) / 2)
      C1 = Y(J) - Y(I) - (DY / 2)
      D1 = Y(J) - Y(I) + (DY / 2)
      GIJ1 = 0.0
      EN = 1
```

```
320   A2 = SQRT(A1**2 + C1**2 + ((2*T- 2*EN*T)**2))
      B2 = SQRT(B1**2 + D1**2 + ((2*T- 2*EN*T)**2))
      C2 = SQRT(A1**2 + D1**2 + ((2*T- 2*EN*T)**2))
      D2 = SQRT(B1**2 + C1**2 + ((2*T- 2*EN*T)**2))
      E2 = SQRT(A1**2 + C1**2 + ((2*EN*T)**2))
      F2 = SQRT(B1**2 + D1**2 + ((2*EN*T)**2))
      G2 = SQRT(A1**2 + D1**2 + ((2*EN*T)**2))
      I2 = SQRT(B1**2 + C1**2 + ((2*EN*T)**2))
      J2 = SQRT(A1**2 + C1**2 + ((2*T + (2*EN- 2)*T)**2))
      K2 = SQRT(B1**2 + D1**2 + ((2*T + (2*EN- 2)*T)**2))
      L2 = SQRT(A1**2 + D1**2 + ((2*T + (2*EN- 2)*T)**2))
      M2 = SQRT(B1**2 + C1**2 + ((2*T + (2*EN- 2)*T)**2))
      S2 = SQRT(A1**2 + C1**2 + ((2*EN- 2)*T)**2)
      O2 = SQRT(B1**2 + D1**2 + ((2*EN- 2)*T)**2)
      P2 = SQRT(A1**2 + D1**2 + ((2*EN- 2)*T)**2)
      Q2 = SQRT(B1**2 + C1**2 + ((2*EN- 2)*T)**2)
      T1 = (X(J)- X(I))*(LOG(C1 + A2) + LOG(D1 + B2) + LOG(D1
     $     +G2) + LOG(C1 + I2)- LOG(D1 + C2)- LOG(C1 + D2)
     $     -LOG(C1 + E2)- LOG(D1 + F2))
      T2 = ((DX(J)) / 2)*(LOG(D1 + B2) + LOG(D1 + C2) + LOG(C1
     $     +E2) + LOG(C1 + I2)- LOG(C1 + D2)- LOG(C1 + A2)
     $     -LOG(D1 + G2)- LOG(D1 + F2))
      T3 = (Y(J)- Y(I))*(LOG(A1 + A2) + LOG(B1 + B2) + LOG(B1
     $     +I2) + LOG(A1 + G2)- LOG(B1 + D2)- LOG(A1 + C2)
     $     -LOG(A1 + E2)- LOG(B1 + F2))
      T4 = (DY / 2)*(LOG(B1 + B2) + LOG(B1 + D2) + LOG(A1 + E2)
     $     +LOG(A1 + G2)- LOG(A1 + C2)- LOG(A1 + A2)
     $     -LOG(B1 + I2)- LOG(B1 + F2))
      IF (EN .EQ. 1) THEN
      T5 = 0.0
      T6 = 0.0
      ELSE
      T5 = (2*T- 2*EN*T)*(ATAN(A1*C1 / ((2*T- 2*EN*T)*A2))
     $     +ATAN(B1*D1 / ((2*T- 2*EN*T)*B2)))
      T6 = (2*T- 2*EN*T)*(ATAN(A1*D1 / ((2*T- 2*EN*T)*C2))
     $     +ATAN(B1*C1 / ((2*T- 2*EN*T)*D2)))
      END IF
      T7 = (2*EN*T)*(ATAN(A1*C1 / (2*EN*T*E2)) + ATAN(B1*
     $     D1 / (2*EN*T*F2)))
      T8 = (2*EN*T)*(ATAN(A1*D1 / (2*EN*T*G2)) + ATAN(B1*
     $     C1 / (2*EN*T*I2)))
      T9 = (X(J)- X(I))*(LOG(D1 + K2) + LOG(C1 + J2) + LOG(D1
     $     +P2) + LOG(C1 + Q2)- LOG(D1 + L2)- LOG(C1 + M2)-
     $     LOG(C1 + S2)- LOG(D1 + O2))
      T10 = (DX(J)) / 2)*(LOG(D1 + K2) + LOG(D1 + L2) + LOG(C1
```

```
$       +S2) + LOG(C1 + Q2) - LOG(C1 + M2) - LOG(C1 + J2) -
$       LOG(D1 + O2) - LOG(D1 + P2))
 T11 = (Y(J) - Y(I)) * (LOG(A1 + J2) + LOG(B1 + K2) + LOG(A1
$       +P2) + LOG(B1 + Q2) - LOG(B1 + M2) - LOG(B1 + O2)
$       -LOG(A1 + L2) - LOG(A1 + S2))
 T12 = (DY / 2) * (LOG(B1 + K2) + LOG(B1 + M2) + LOG(A1 +
$       P2) + LOG(A1 + S2) - LOG(A1 + L2) - LOG(A1 + J2)
$       -LOG(B1 + O2) - LOG(B1 + Q2))
 T13 = (2*T + (2*EN- 2)*T) * (ATAN(A1*C1 / ((2*T + (2*EN-
$       2)*T)*J2)) + ATAN(B1*D1 / ((2*T + (2*EN- 2)*T)
$       *K2)))
 T14 = (2*T + (2*EN- 2)*T) * (ATAN(A1*D1 / ((2*T + (2*EN-
$       2)*T)*L2)) + ATAN(B1*C1 / ((2*T + (2*EN- 2)*T)
$       *M2)))
 T15 = 0.0
 T16 = 0.0
 IF (EN .GT. 1) THEN
 T15 = ((2*EN- 2)*T) * (ATAN(A1*C1 / ((2*EN- 2)*T*S2))
$       +ATAN(B1*D1 / ((2*EN- 2)*T*O2)))
 T16 = ((2*EN- 2)*T) * (ATAN(A1*D1 / ((2*EN- 2)*T*P2))
$       +ATAN(B1*C1 / ((2*EN- 2)*T*Q2)))
 END IF
 GIJ = 0.068 * ((((- 1)**(EN- 1)*(K1**EN)) * (T1 + T2 + T3
$       +T4- T5 + T6 + T7- T8) + (((- 1)**EN)*(K1**(EN-
$       1))) * (T9 + T10 + T11 + T12- T13 + T14 + T15- T16)))
 GIJ1 = GIJ1 + GIJ
 IF (ABS(GIJ).GT.(0.0001)) THEN
 EN = EN + 1
 GO TO 320
 ELSE
 G(I,J) = GIJ1
 END IF
310 CONTINUE
300 CONTINUE
 CALL MINV(G,N,D,L,M)
 R1 = 0.0
 R2 = 0.0
 R3 = 0.0
 R4 = 0.0
 R5 = 0.0
 R6 = 0.0
 R7 = 0.0
 R8 = 0.0
 R9 = 0.0
```

```
      DO 1000 I = 1,N1,1
      DO 1001 J = 1,N1,1
      R1 = R1 + G(I,J)
1001 CONTINUE
      DO 1002 J = N1 + 1,N1 + N2,1
      R2 = R2 + G(I,J)
1002 CONTINUE
      DO 1003 J = N1 + N2 + 1,N,1
      R3 = R3 + G(I,J)
1003 CONTINUE
1000 CONTINUE
      DO 1300 I = N1 + 1,N1 + N2,1
      DO 1301 J = 1,N1,1
      R4 = R4 + G(I,J)
1301 CONTINUE
      DO 1302 J = N1 + 1,N1 + N2,1
      R5 = R5 + G(I,J)
1302 CONTINUE
      DO 1303 J = N1 + N2 + 1,N,1
      R6 = R6 + G(I,J)
1303 CONTINUE
1300 CONTINUE
      DO 1600 I = N1 + N2 + 1,N,1
      DO 1601 J = 1,N1,1
      R7 = R7 + G(I,J)
1601 CONTINUE
      DO 1602 J = N1 + 1,N1 + N2,1
      R8 = R8 + G(I,J)
1602 CONTINUE
      DO 1603 J = N1 + N2 + 1,N,1
      R9 = R9 + G(I,J)
1603 CONTINUE
1600 CONTINUE
      C1E = (R1 + R2 + R3)*DS1
      C2E = (R4 + R5 + R6)*DS2
      C3E = (R7 + R8 + R9)*DS3
      C1O = (R1- R2- R3)*DS1
      C2O = (R5- R4- R6)*DS2
      C3O = (R9- R7- R8)*DS3
C*****INTERCONNECTION CAPACITANCES
      C11 = C1E*1.1
      C22 = C2E*1.1
      C33 = C3E*1.1
      C12 = (C3E- C2E- C1E + C1O + C2O- C3O)*0.3
      C13 = (C2E- C1E- C3E + C1O + C3O- C2O)*0.3
```

```
C23 = (C1E- C2E- C3E- C1O + C2O + C3O)*0.3
RETURN
END
```
C
```
SUBROUTINE MINV
(Same as in Appendix 2.1)
```

APPENDIX 3.2

TPDGM
Transverse Propagation Delays in a GaAs MESFET

DIRECTORY OF TERMS:

CGS: Internal Capacitance Between the Gate and the Source

CGD: Internal Capacitance Between the Gate and the Drain

CDC: Internal Capacitance Due to Dipole Layer

CGSE: Electrode Capacitance Between the Source and Gate Electrodes

CGDE: Electrode Capacitance Between the Drain and Gate Electrodes

CSDE: Electrode Capacitance Between the Drain and Source Electrodes

CDE: Self-Capacitance of the Drain Electrode

CGE: Self-Capacitance of the Gate Electrode

LG: Inductance of the Gate Line

RG: Resistance of the Gate Line

RSC: Contact Resistance of the Source Electrode

RDC: Contact Resistance of the Drain Electrode

VS: Voltage on the Source Electrode

VG: Voltage on the Gate Electrode

VD: Voltage on the Drain Electrode

W: Width of the MESFET

GL: Gate Length

GM: Transconductance of the MESFET

RO: Resistivity of the Gate Metal

T: Time in Picoseconds

T1: Time in seconds

NF: Normalization Factor

S: Complex Frequency

N,M: Counters

SIGMA, DW,S1,S2, Term: Expressions

```
C*****DECLARING THE VARIABLES
      REAL LG,RG,CGS,RGS,CGD,GM,W,RDS,SIGMA,DW,T,S1,
     $     S2,CGSE,CGE,CGDE,CSDE,CDE,CDC,GL,W1,T1,I,
     $     GL1,RSC,RDC,NF,VG,VD,VS,RO
      INTEGER N,M
      COMPLEX S,G,IS,IT,TERM,S3
      WRITE(*,160)
  160 FORMAT( 'INTRINSIC PROPAGATION DELAYS IN GaAs
     $     MESFETs'// 'RESULTS'/ )
C*****INPUT (GL AND W ARE IN MICROMETERS; RO IS IN
C     MICROOHM.CM)
  10  READ(*,100,END = 999)GL,W,RO
  100 FORMAT(F5.2,X,F6.2,X,F6.2)
C*****INTERNAL CAPACITANCES FOR E = 1m AND ELECTRODE
C     VOLTAGES FOR A GaAs MESFET
      VS = 0.0
      VG- 0.0
      VD- 5.0
      CGS = 1.5*GL*(10.0**(-9))
      CGD = 4.5*GL*(10.0**(-11))
C*****TYPICAL VALUES FOR A GaAs MESFET WITH W = 1 M,
C     (GATE THICKNESS:.5uM)
      LG = GL*(10.0**(-6))
      RG = RO*2.0*(10.0**4) / GL
      RGS = 3.3*(10.0**(-3))
      RDS = 0.0
      RSC = 10.0**(-3))
      RDC = 10.0**(-3)
      GM = 100.0
      CDC = 4.0
C*****CALCULATING I(t)
      CALL EPCSSGM(GL,C11,C22,C33,C12,C13,C23)
      WRITE(*,164)
  164 FORMAT( / , 'EPCSSGM USED')
      WRITE(*,166)C11,C22,C12,C13,C23
  166 FORMAT(6F9.3)
      CGSE = C12*(10.0**(-11))
      CGE = C22*(10.0**(-11))
      CGDE = C23*(10.0**(-11))
      CSDE = C13*(10.0**(-11))
      CDE = C33*(10.0**(-11))
      W1 = W*(10.0**(-6))
      S3 = (-1.0,0.0)
      WRITE(*,161)
```

```
  161   FORMAT( / `GATE MATERIAL:A1 '4X, `GL',9X,
      $           `RO1(uohm.cm)',X,t(ps)',8X, `I(t)')
C*****CALCULATION OF THE NORMALIZATION FACTOR
       T = 100.0
       I = 0.0
       T1 = T*(10.0**(-12))
       SIGMA = 0.5*T1
       DW = 0.05 / T1
       IT = (0.0,0.0)
       M = 800
       DO 2003 N = 1,M,1
       S1 = SIGMA
       S2 = N*DW
       S = S1 + (CSQRT(S3))*S2 + S*CGSE + S*(CGD + CGDE)))
       IS = (-GM*(CEXP(G*W1)-CEXP(-G*W1)) / (CEXP(G*W1)
      $    +CEXP(-G*W1))) / (S*G*(1 + S*(RGS + RSC)*CGS))
       TERM = IS*DW*(COS(S2*T1) + (CSQRT(S3))*SIN(S2*T1))
      $       *EXP(SIGMA*T1) / 6.284
       IT = IT + TERM
 2003 CONTINUE
       I = CABS(IT) / (GM*W1)
       NF = 1.0 / I
       DO 2100 T = .1,1.0,.1
       I = 0.0
       T1 = T*(10.0**(-12))
       SIGMA = 0.5*T1
       DW = 0.05 / T1
       IT = (0.0,0.0)
       M = 200
       DO 2000 N = 1,M1
       S1 = SIGMA
       S2 = N*DW
       S = S1 + (CSQRT(S3))*S2
       G = CSQRT((S*LG + RG)*(S*CGS / (1 + S*CGS*(RGS + RSC) +
      $    S*CGSE + S*(CGD + CGDE)))
       IS = (-GM*(CEXP(G*W1)-CEXP(-G*W1)) / (CEXP(G*W1)
      $    +CEXP(-G*W1))) / (S*G*(1 + S*(RGS + RSC)*CGS))
       TERM = IS*DW*(COS(S22*T1) + (CSQRT(S3))*SIN(S2*T1))
      $       *EXP(SIGMA*T1) / 6.284
       TERM1 = REAL(TERM)
       IT = IT + TERM1
 2000 CONTINUE
       I = CABS(IT)*NF / (GM*W1)
```

```
C*****WRITING THE RESULTS
      GL1 = GL*10.0
      WRITE(*,300)GL1,W,RO,T,I
  300 FORMAT(F6.2,5X,F7.2,12X,F4.1,5X,F10.3)
 2100 CONTINUE
      DO 2102 T = 1,10,1
      I = 0.0
      T1 = T*(10.0**(-12))
      SIGMA = 0.5*T1
      DW = 0.05 / T1
      IT = (0.0,0.0)
      M = 300
      DO 2002 N = 1,M,1
      S1 = SIGMA
      S2 = N*DW
      S = S1 + (CSQRT(S3))*S2
      G = CSQRT(S*LG + RG)*(S*CGS / (1 + S*CGS*(RGS + RSC)) +
     $    S*CGSE + S*(CGD + CGDE)))
      IS = (-GM*(CEXP(G*W1) - CEXP(-G*W1))) / (CEXP(G*W1) +
     $     CEXP(-G*W1))) / (S*G*(1 + S*(RGS + RSC)*(CGS)))
      TERM = IS*DW*(COS(S2*T1) + (CSQRT(S3))*SIN(S2*T1))
     $        *EXP(SIGMA*T1) / 6.284
      IT = IT + TERM
 2002 CONTINUE
      I = CABS(IT)*NF / (GM*W1)
C*****WRITING THE RESULTS
      GL1 = GL*10.0
      WRITE(*,302)GL1,W,RO,T,I
  302 FORMAT(F6.2,5X,F7.2,5X,F7.2,12X,F4.1,5X,F10.3)
 2102 CONTINUE
      DO 2101 T = 10,30,2
      I = 0.0
      T1 = T*(10.0**(-12))
      SIGMA = 0.5*T1
      DW = 0.05 / T1
      IT = (0.0,0.0)
      M = 500
      DO 2001 N = 1,M,1
      S1 = SIGMA
      S2 = N*DW
      S = S1 + (CSQRT(S3))*S2
      G = CSQRT((S*LG + RG)*(S*CGS / (1 + S*CGS*(RGS + RSC)) +
     $    S*CGSE + S*(CGD + CGDE)))
      IS = (-GM*(CEXP(G*W1) - CEXP(-G*W1))) / (CEXP(G*W1) +
```

```
     $     CEXP(-G*W1))) / (S*G*(1 + S*(RGS + RSC)*CGS))
      TERM = IS*DW*(COS(S2*T1) + (CSQRT(S3))*SIN(S2*T1))
     $         *EXP(SIGMA*T1) / 6.284
      IT = IT + TERM
 2001 CONTINUE
      I = CABS(IT)*NF / (GM*W1)
C*****WRITING THE RESULTS
      WRITE(*,301)GL1,W,RO,T,I
  301 FORMAT(F6.2,5X,F7.2,12X,F4.1,5X,F10.3)
 2101 CONTINUE
      GO TO 10
  999 STOP
      END
C
      SUBROUTINE EPCSSGM (GL,C11,C22,C33,C12,C23)
      INTEGER N1X,N2X,N3X,NY,N1,N2,N3,N,I,J,EN,CNT,CR
      REAL*4 A1,B1,C1,D1,A2,B2,D2,E2,F2,G2,I2,J2,K2,
     $       L2,M2,O2,P2,Q2,W2,G(6,6),GIJ,GIJ1,R1,R2,R3,
     $       R4,R5,R6,R7,R8,R9,C1EVEN,C2EVEN,DS1,DS2,
     $       DS3,C1ODD,C2ODD,C3ODD,C11,C22,C33,C12,
     $       C13,T12,T13,T14,T15,T16,C23,X(6),Y(6),
     $       Z(6),DX(6),DY,SL,GL,DL,W,H,H1,K1,DSG,
     $       DGD,L(11),M(11),T1,T2,T3,T4,T5,T6,T7,T8,
     $       T9,T10,T11
      GIJ = 0.0
      I = 1
      J = 1
      EN = 1
      K1 = 0.859155
      N1X = 1
      N2X = 1
      N3X = 1
      NY = 2
      SL = 10.0
      DL = 10.0
      DSG = 2.0
      DGD = 2.0
      W = 100.0
      H = 200.0
      H1 = 200.0
      SL = SL / 10
      GL = GL / 10
      DL = DL / 10
      DSG = DSG / 10
      DGD = DGD / 10
```

```
        W = W / 10
        H = H / 10
        H1 = H1 / 10
        N1 = N1X*NY
        N2 = N2X*NY
        N3 = N3X*NY
        N = N1 + N2 + N3
        DY = W / NY
        DO 151 J = 1,N1,1
        DX(J) = SL / N1X
151     CONTINUE
        DO 152 J = N1 + 1,N1 + N2,1
        DX(J) = GL / N2X
152     CONTINUE
        DO 153 J = N1 + N2 + 1,N,1
        DX(J) = DL / N3X
153     CONTINUE
        DS1 = DX(N1)*DY
        DS2 = DX(N1 + N2)*DY
        DS3 = DX(N)*DY
        CNT = 0.0
        DO 5500 CR = 1,N1X,1
        DO 5900 I = CNT + 1,CNT + NY,1
        X(I) = (2*CR- 1)*((DX(N1))/2)
5900    CONTINUE
        CNT = I
5500    CONTINUE
        CNT = N1
        DO 6500 CR = 1,N2X,1
        DO 6900 I = CNT + 1,CNT + NY,1
        X(I) = (SL + DSG) + (2*CR- 1)*((DX(N1 + N2))/2)
6900    CONTINUE
        CNT = I
6500    CONTINUE
        CNT = N1 + N2
        DO 7500 CR = 1,N3X,1
        DO 7900 I = CNT + 1,CNT + NY,1
        X(I) = (SL + DSG + GL + DGD) + (2*CR- 1)*((DX(N))/2)
7900    CONTINUE
        CNT = I
7500    CONTINUE
        DO 8000 CR = 1,NY,1
        DO 8500 I = CR,N,NY
        Y(I) = (2*CR- 1)*(DY/2)
8500    CONTINUE
```

```
8000  CONTINUE
      DO 9000 I = 1,N,1
      Z(I) = T
9000  CONTINUE
      DO 9100 I = N1 + 1,N1 + N2,1
      Z(I) = T- DR
9100  CONTINUE
      DO 300 I = 1,N,1
      DO 310 J = 1,N,1
      A1 = X(J) - X(I) - ((DX(J)) / 2)
      B1 = X(J) - X(I) + ((DX(J)) / 2)
      C1 = Y(J) - Y(I) - (DY / 2)
      D1 = Y(J) - Y(I) + (DY / 2)
      GIJ1 = 0.0
      EN = 1
320   A2 = SQRT(A1**2 + C1**2 + ((2*H- 2*EN*T)**2))
      B2 = SQRT(B1**2 + D1**2 + ((2*H- 2*EN*T)**2))
      C2 = SQRT(A1**2 + D1**2 + ((2*H- 2*EN*T)**2))
      D2 = SQRT(B1**2 + C1**2 + ((2*H- 2*EN*T)**2))
      E2 = SQRT(A1**2 + C1**2 + ((2*EN*T)**2))
      F2 = SQRT(B1**2 + D1**2 + ((2*EN*T)**2))
      G2 = SQRT(A1**2 + D1**2 + ((2*EN*T)**2))
      I2 = SQRT(B1**2 + C1**2 + ((2*EN*T)**2))
      J2 = SQRT(A1**2 + C1**2 + ((2*H + (2*EN- 2)*T)**2))
      K2 = SQRT(B1**2 + D1**2 + ((2*H + (2*EN- 2)*T)**2))
      L2 = sQRT(A1**2 + D1**2 + ((2*H + (2*EN- 2)*T)**2))
      M2 = SQRT(B1**2 + C1**2 + ((2*H + (2*EN- 2)*T)**2))
      S2 = SQRT(A1**2 + C1**2 + ((2*EN- 2)*T)**2)
      O2 = SQRT(B1**2 + D1**2 + ((2*EN- 2)*T)**2)
      P2 = SQRT(A1**2 + D1**2 + ((2*EN- 2)*T)**2)
      Q2 = SQRT(B1**2 + C1**2 + ((2*EN- 2)*T)**2)
      T1 = (X(J) - X(I))*(LOG(C1 + A2) + LOG(D1 + B2) + LOG(D1
     $    +G2) + LOG(C1 + I2) - LOG(D1 + C2) - LOG(C1 + D2) -
     $    LOG(C1 + E2) - LOG(D1 + F2))
      T2 = ((DX(J)) / 2)*(LOG(D1 + B2) + LOG(D1 + C2) + LOG(C1
     $    +E2) + LOG(C1 + I2) - LOG(C1 + D2) - LOG(C1 + A2) -
     $    LOG(D1 + G2) - LOG(D1 + F2))
      T3 = (Y(J) - Y(I))*(LOG(A1 + A2) + LOG(B1 + B2) + LOG(B1
     $    +I2) + LOG(A1 + G2) - LOG(B1 + D2) - LOG(A1 + C2) -
     $    LOG(A1 + E2) - LOG(B1 + F2))
      T4 = (DY / 2)*(LOG(B1 + B2) + LOG(B1 + D2) + LOG(A1 + E2)
     $    +LOG(A1 + G2) - LOG(A1 + C2) - LOG(A1 + A2) -
     $    LOG(B1 + I2) - LOG(B1 + F2))
      IF ((EN .EQ. 1) .AND. (T .EQ. H)) THEN
      T5 = 0.0
      T6 = 0.0
```

```
        ELSE
        T5 = ( 2*H- 2*EN*T) * (ATAN (A1*C1 / ( ( 2*H- 2*EN*T) *A2 ) )
     $      +ATAN ( B1*D1 / ( ( 2*H- 2*EN*T) *B2 ) ) )
        T6 = ( 2*H- 2*EN*T) * (ATAN (A1*D1 / ( ( 2*H- 2*EN*T) *C2 ) )
     $      +ATAN ( B1*C1 / ( ( 2*H- 2*EN*T) *D2 ) ) )
        END IF
        T7 = ( 2*EN*T) * (ATAN (A1*C1 / ( 2*EN*T*E2 ) ) + ATAN ( B1*
     $      D1 / ( 2*EN*T*F2 ) ) )
        T8 = ( 2*EN*T) * (ATAN (A1*D1 / ( 2*EN*T*G2 ) ) + ATAN ( B1*
     $      C1 / ( 2*EN*T*I2 ) ) )
        T9 = ( X ( J) - X ( I ) ) * ( LOG ( D1 + K2 ) + LOG ( C1 + J2 ) + LOG ( D1
     $      +P2 ) + LOG ( C1 + Q2 ) - LOG ( D1 + L2 ) - LOG ( C1 + M2 ) -
     $      LOG ( C1 + S2 ) - LOG ( D1 + O2 ) )
        T10 = ( ( DX ( J ) ) / 2 ) * ( LOG ( D1 + K2 ) + LOG ( D1 + L2 ) + LOG
     $      ( C1 + S2 ) + LOG ( C1 + Q2 ) - LOG ( C1 + M2 ) - LOG ( C1 +
     $      J2 ) - LOG ( D1 + O2 ) - LOG ( D1 + P2 ) )
        T11 = ( Y ( J ) - Y ( I ) ) * ( LOG ( A1 + J2 ) + LOG ( B1 + K2 ) + LOG ( A1
     $      +P2 ) + LOG ( B1 + Q2 ) - LOG ( B1 + M2 ) - LOG ( B1 + O2 ) -
     $      LOG ( A1 + L2 ) - LOG ( A1 + S2 ) )
        T12 = ( DY / 2 ) * ( LOG ( B1 + K2 ) + LOG ( B1 + M2 ) + LOG ( A1 +
     $      P2 ) + LOG ( A1 + S2 ) - LOG ( A1 + L2 ) - LOG ( A1 + J2 ) -
     $      LOG ( B1 + O2 ) - LOG ( B1 + Q2 ) )
        T13 = ( 2*H + ( 2*EN- 2 ) *T) * (ATAN (A1*C1 /
     $      ( ( 2*H + ( 2*EN- 2 ) *T) *J2 ) ) + ATAN ( B1*D1 /
     $      ( ( 2*H + ( 2*EN- 2 ) *T) *K2 ) ) )
        T14 = ( 2*H + ( 2*EN- 2 ) *T) * (ATAN (A1*D1 / ( ( 2*H +
     $      ( 2*EN- 2 ) *T) *L2 ) )
        T15 = 0 . 0
        T16 = 0 . 0
        IF ( EN .GT. 1) THEN
        T15 = ( ( 2*EN- 2 ) *T) * (ATAN (A1*C1 / ( ( 2*EN- 2 ) *T*S2 ) )
     $      +ATAN ( B1*D1 / ( ( 2*EN- 2 ) *T*O2 ) ) )
        T16 = ( ( 2*EN- 2 ) *T) * (ATAN (A1*D1 / ( ( 2*EN- 2 ) *T*P2 ) )
     $      +ATAN ( B1*C1 / ( ( 2*EN- 2 ) *T*Q2 ) ) )
        END IF
        GIJ = 0 . 68* ( ( ( ( - 1) ** ( EN- 1) * ( K1**EN) ) * ( T1 + T2 + T3
     $      +T4 - T5 + T6 + T7 - T8 ) + ( ( ( - 1) **EN) * ( K1** ( EN-
     $      1) ) ) * ( T9 + T10 + T11 + T12 - T13 + T14 + T15 - T16 ) ) )
        GIJ1 = GIJ1 + GIJ
        IF ( ABS ( GIJ) .GT. ( 0 . 0001) ) THEN
        EN = EN + 1
        GO TO 320
        ELSE
        G ( I, J) = GIJ1
        END IF
310     CONTINUE
```

```
 300   CONTINUE
       CALL MINV(G,N,D,L,M)
       R1 = 0.0
       R2 = 0.0
       R3 = 0.0
       R4 = 0.0
       R5 = 0.0
       R6 = 0.0
       R7 = 0.0
       R8 = 0.0
       R9 = 0.0
       DO 1000 I = 1,N1,1
       DO 1001 J = 1,N1,1
       R1 = R1 + G(I,J)
1001   CONTINUE
       DO 1002 J = N1 + 1,N1 + N2,1
       R2 = R2 + G(I,J)
1002   CONTINUE
       DO 1003 J = N1 + N2 + 1,N,1
       R3 = R3 + G(I,J)
1003   CONTINUE
1000   CONTINUE
       DO 1300 I = N1 + 1,N1 + N2,1
       DO 1301 J = 1,N1,1
       R4 = R4 + G(I,J)
1301   CONTINUE
       DO 1302 J = N1 + 1,N1 + N2,1
       R5 = R5 + G(I,J)
1302   CONTINUE
       DO 1303 J = N1 + N2 + 1,N,1
       R6 = R6 + G(I,J)
1303   CONTINUE
1300   CONTINUE
       DO 1600 I = N1 + N2 + 1,N,1
       DO 1601 J = 1,N1,1
       R7 = R7 + G(I,J)
1601   CONTINUE
       DO 1602 J = N1 + 1,N1 + N2,1
       R8 = R8 + G(I,J)
1602   CONTINUE
       DO 1603 J = N1 + N2 + 1,N,1
       R9 = R9 + G(I,J)
1603   CONTINUE
1600   CONTINUE
```

```
C1EVEN = ( R1 + R2 + R3 ) *DS1
C2EVEN = ( R4 + R5 + R6 ) *DS2
C3EVEN = ( R7 + R8 + R9 ) *DS3
C1ODD = ( R1- R2- R3 ) *DS1
C2ODD = ( R5- R4- R6 ) *DS2
C3ODD = ( R9- R7- R8 ) *DS3
C11 = C1EVEN*1.1
C22 = C2EVEN*1.1
C33 = C3EVEN*1.1
C12 = ( C3EVEN- C2EVEN- C1EVEN + C1ODD + C2ODD-
$      C3ODD ) *0.3
C13 = ( C2EVEN- C1EVEN- C3EVEN + C1ODD + C3ODD-
$      C2ODD ) *0.3
C23 = ( C1EVEN- C2EVEN- C3EVEN- C1ODD + C2ODD +
$      C3ODD ) *0.3
RETURN
END
```

APPENDIX 3.3

TPDGAM
Transverse Propagation Delays in a GaAs / AlGaAs MODFET

```
DIRECTORY OF TERMS:
     E:                    Semiconductor permittivity
     ES:                   Relative semiconductive per-
                           mittivity
     U0:                   Low- field carrier mobility
     W:                    Channel width
     LG:                   Gate length
     GO:                   Output conductance
     RSS:                  Source resistance
     RGG:                  Gate series resistance
     C0:                   Gate charging capacitance
     DO:                   The distance between the two-
                           dimensional electron gas and
                           the gate
     VSAT:                 Saturation velocity
     CDG:                  Drain- to- gate feedback capac-
                           itance
     CDS:                  Drain- to- source output capac-
                           itance
     GM:                   Transconductance
     LGG:                  Inductance of the gate line
```

LSS: Inductance of the source line
CG: Effective intrinsic capaci-
                         tance along the gate and the
                         source
RI: Effective intrinsic resis-
                         tance along the gate and the
                         source
COMPLEX FUNCTIONS:
CTANH: Internal complex function in-
                         volved in the calculation of
                         the drain current
D: Internal complex function
                         that represents the ratio of
                         voltage on CG to voltage on
                         RI
G1:   External complex function
                         that represents the admit-
                         tance of series combination
                         of CG and RI
G2:   External complex function
                         that represents the admit-
                         tance of parallel combination
                         of CDS and G0
G3:   External complex function
                         that represents the admit-
                         tance of series combination
                         of RSS and LSS
GC: External complex function
                         that represents the admit-
                         tance of CDG
G6:   External complex function
                         that represents the reflected
                         admittance of GC by using
                         Miller's theorem
Zp: Internal complex function
                         that represents the parallel
                         impedance per unit length
                         along the gate line
Zs: Internal complex function
                         that represents the series
                         impedance per unit length
                         along the gate line
GAMA: Internal complex function
                         that represents the propaga-
                         tion constant for the gate
                         transmission line

Y:	External complex function that represents the trans-conductance
A:	Internal complex function that represents the voltage ratio between V1 and V2
BBB:	Internal complex function involved in the calculation of the transconductance
B,BB:	Internal complex functions involved in the calculation of the voltage ratio of V1 to V2
VT:	External complex function that represents the short-circuit drain current
VTT:	Internal complex function involved in the calculation of the drain output current
REAL FUNCTION:	
COSH:	Internal function involved in the calculation of the RSS
INTERNAL TERMS:	
T:	Starting time
DETTAT:	Time interval
TEND:	Final time
GM:	Internal parameter involved in the calculation of the transconductance
W:	Gate width
V(40):	A matrix that contains the drain current
SETIME(40):	A matrix that contains the time at which the drain current has been calculated
DELAY(10):	A matrix that contains the delay time for different GaAs / AlGaAs dimensions
RISE(10):	A matrix that contains the rise time for different GaAs / AlGaAs dimensions
P:	An internal variable that memorizes the starting time T
TE1,TE2,TE3:	Median variables
DA,DO,DS,DI:	Defines the semiconductor thickness within different

	layers (for details see the schematic plots in the text)
DELG:	Gate difference in the channel
VSAT:	Saturation velocity
CG1,CG2:	Median variables used to calculate Cg
RI1:	Median variable used to calculate RI
TO,BETA,VC,R:	Median variables involved in the calculation of Cg and RI
Z(5):	Z matrix used to find the Laplace transformation inversion
KPRIME(5):	A matrix used to find the Laplace transformation inversion
S:	Variable S in the S plane
MPRIME:	Variable used to determine the maximum volume in KPRIME(MPRIME)
ICP1:	Defines the choice of running in the user friendly part
IES:	Defines the choice of relative semiconductor permittivity
IRHO:	Defines the choice of the resistivity of the gate metal material
RHO:	Gate metal resistivity
JJJJJ,III,IIII:	Continuous loop variables

UNITS:

Capacitance:	F
Current:	A
Voltage:	V
Resistance:	ohms
Time:	second
Mass:	g
Inductance:	H
Conductance:	s (1 / ohm)

```
C*****DECLARING VARIABLES
      REAL T, DETTAT,TEND,GM,W,V(30),SETIME(30),
     $     DELAY(10),RISE(10),p
      REAL GO,CDS,RI,CGS,CDG,RSS,RGG,LGG,LG,TE1,TE2,
     $     TE3,RO,RHO
```

```
      REAL RK,RM,RN,COSH,X,O(90),DA,DO,DS,DI,ES,E,DELG
      REAL LSPACE,P12,RC1,RC2,RS1,RS2,ARFA3,BETA3,
     $     GRMA3,K11
      REAL T0,BETA,VC,R,U0,C0,VSAT,CG1,CG2,RI1,TD,
     $     VTH,ND
      COMPLEX Z(5), KPRIME(5),VT,S,GC,G3,G1,ZS,ZP,G6,
     $         Y,YY,G4,G5
      COMPLEX VTT,G2,D,A,B,BB,BBB,GAMA,TANH
      INTEGER MPRIME,I,IJ
      CTANH(S)=(CEXP(s)-CEXP(-S))/(CEXP(S)+CEXP
     $          (-S))
      D(S)=1./(1.+RI*S*CG)
      G2(S)=GO+CDS*S
      G3(S)=1/RSS
      G1(S)=S*CG/(1.+S*CG*RI)
      GC(S)=S*CDG
      BBB(S)=-CMPLX(0.,AIMAG(S))*T0/3.9
      Y(S)=GM*CEXP(BBB(S)*0.61)/(1.-BBB(S))
      B(S)=Y(S)*D(S)*G3(S)/G1(S)+G2(S)*G3(S)/G1(S)
      G5(S)=B(S)/(1.+(Y(S)*D(S)+G2(S))/G1(S)+G2(S)
     $       /GC(S))
      G4(S)=G3(S)-G5(S)
      G6(S)=G5(S)*G1(S)/(G1(S)+G3(S)-G5(S))
      ZP(S)=1./(G6(S)+G1(S)*G4(S)/(G1(S)+G4(S)))
      ZS(S)=RGG+S*LGG
      GAMA(S)=CSQRT(ZS(S)/ZP(S))
      VTT(S)=G1(S)*G5(S)/(G3(S)-G5(S)+G1(S))
      VT(S)=VTT(S)*CTANH(GAMA(S)*W)/GAMA(S)/S
      COSH(X)=EXP(X)/2.+EXP(-X)/2.
      OPEN(10,FILE='ZMATRI',STATUS='OLD')
      OPEN(33,FILE='ELLIPTIC',STATUS='OLD')
      OPEN(6,FILE='IPDAGMD.OUT',STATUS='NEW')
      READ(10,*) (Z(J),J=1,5),(KPRIME(J),J=1,5),
     $            MPRIME
      READ(33,*) (O(J),J=1,90)
C*****REPEATING FORMATS
 1    FORMAT(/15X'*** WRONG INPUT, TRY AGAIN ***'/)
 2    FORMAT(10X,2('----------------------------')
 902  FORMAT(//)
 903  FORMAT(///)
 904  FORMAT(////)
 905  FORMAT(/////)
 906  FORMAT(//////)
```

```
  907  FORMAT( / / / / / / / )
  908  FORMAT( / / / / / / / / )
  909  FORMAT( / / / / / / / / / )
  910  FORMAT( / / / / / / / / / / )
  920  FORMAT( / / / / / / / / / / / / / / / / / / / / )
C*****WRITING THE PROGRAM TITLE ON THE SCREEN
  4    WRITE( * ,905)
       WRITE( * ,5)
  5    FORMAT(17X, '###############################'/,
       $        17X, '##            TPDGAM            ##'/,
       $        17X, '##                             ##',
       $        17X, '##   A GENERAL- PURPOSE MODFET  ##'/,
       $        17X, '##    TRANSVERSE TIME DELAY     ##'/,
       $        17X, '##    PERFORMANCE SIMULATOR     ##'/,
       $        17X, '###############################'/,
       WRITE( * ,701)
  701  FORMAT( / 20X, 'DO YOU WANT TO CONTINUE WITH
       $              "TPDGAM" ?'/
       $        20X, '(Enter 1 for YES or 999 for
       $              NO)'// )
       READ( * , * ,ERR = 4) ICP1
       IF(ICP1.EQ.1) THEN
       GOTO 101
       ELSE IF(ICP1.EQ.999) THEN
       GOTO 999
       ELSE
       GOTO 4
       END IF
C*****OPENING THE OUTPUT FILE
  101  WRITE( * ,920)
       WRITE(6,6)
  6    FORMAT(17X, '###############################'/,
       $        17X, '##          TPDGAM.OUT         ##'/,
       $        17X, '##   GENERAL- PURPOSE MODFET   ##'/,
       $        17X, '##    TRANSVERSE TIME DELAY    ##'/,
       $        17X, '##    PERFORMANCE SIMULATOR    ##'/,
       $        17X, '##        (OUTPUT FILE)        ##'/,
       $        17X, '###############################'/,
C*****DETERMINING WHAT KIND OF CHARACTERISTICS THE
C     USER WANTS
70202 WRITE( * ,905)
  702  WRITE( * ,2)
       WRITE( * ,703)
```

```
 703   FORMAT(11X, 'A N A L Y S I S')
       WRITE(*,2)
       WRITE(*,70303)
70303 FORMAT (11X, 'CHOOSE ONE OF THE FOLLOWING
      $                  ANALYSES:'/,
      $           11X, '1. Normalized Drain Current in a
      $                  Given Time Range.'/,
      $           11X, '2. Dependence of Delays on a Given
      $                  MODFET Parameter.')
       WRITE(*,2)
       WRITE(*,70304)
70304 FORMAT(11X, 'Enter 1 or 2 or 999 to QUIT')
       WRITE(*,2)
       READ(*,*,ERR=70202) MEM
 705   IF(MEM.EQ.1) THEN
       KEK=1
       MDEP=0
       ELSE IF(MEM.EQ.2) THEN
71515 WRITE(*,905)
       WRITE(*,2)
       WRITE(*,70505)
70505 FORMAT(11X, 'D E P E N D E N C E')
       WRITE(*,2)
       WRITE(*,711)
 711   FORMAT(11X, 'CHOOSE ONE OF THE FOLLOWING
      $                  PARAMETERS TO STUDY THE DEPENDENCE'/
      $           15X, '1.       Gate Length Lg'/
      $           15X, '2.       MODFED Width W'/
      $           15X, '3.       Gate Material RHO'/
      $           15X, '4.       Doping Density in AlGaAs
      $                  Layer Nd'/
      $           15X, '5.       Thickness Do')
       WRITE(*,2)
 715   WRITE(*,713)
 713   FORMAT(11X, 'Enter 1-5 to CHOOSE or 999 to QUIT')
       WRITE(*,2)
       READ(*,*,ERR=71515) MDEP
       IF(MDEP.EQ.999) GOTO 999
       ELSE IF (MEM.EQ.999) THEN
       GOTO 999
       ENDIF
       IF(MEM.EQ.1) GOTO 997
       WRITE(*,2)
70610 WRITE(*,70709)
```

```
70709 FORMAT (11X, 'CHOOSE THE NUMBER OF VALUES OF THE
     $              PARAMETER THAT'/,
     $        11X, 'YOU WANT TO USE TO STUDY THE
     $              DEPENDENCE.'/,25X, '(Limit = 10)')
      WRITE(*,2)
      READ(*,*,ERR = 70610) KEK
      IF(KEK.LT.1) GOTO 70610
      IF(KEK.GT.10.) GOTO 70610
      ES = 14.
      GOTO 998
C*****END OF THE CHOICE
 997  KEK = 1
      ES = 14.0
 998  IF(MDEP.EQ.3) GOTO 919
C*****CHOOSING THE GATE MATERIAL
 220  WRITE(*,905)
      WRITE(*,2)
      WRITE(*,232)
 232  FORMAT(17X, 'G A T E   M A T E R I A L')
      WRITE(*,2)
      WRITE(*,230)
 230  FORMAT(11X, 'CHOOSE ONE OF THESE GATE
     $              MATERIALS:'//,
     $        15X, ' MATERIAL    RESISTIVITY
     $                        (micro- ohm*cm)'/,
     $        15X, ' ---------- --------------------'//,
     $        15X, '1.ALUMINIUM          2.8'/,
     $        15X, '2.COPPER             1.7'/,
     $        15X, '3.SILVER             1.6'/,
     $        15X, '4.SELECTED BY USER   ?')
      WRITE(*,2)
      WRITE(*,740)
 740  FORMAT(11X, 'Enter 1- 4 to CHOOSE the Material or
     $              999 to QUIT')
      WRITE(*,2)
      WRITE(*,*)
      READ(*,*ERR = 220) IRHO
 840  IF(IRHO.EQ.1) THEN
      RHO = 2.8
      ELSE IF (IRHO.EQ.2) THEN
      RHO = 1.7
      ELSE IF (IRHO.EQ.3) THEN
      RHO = 1.6
      ELSE IF (IRHO.EQ.4) THEN
      WRITE(*,2)
```

```
846   WRITE(*,*) `                    ENTER THE RESISTIVITY
      $                               (micro- ohm*cm):'
      READ(*,*,ERR = 842) RHO
      ELSE IF(IRHO.EQ.999) THEN
      GOTO 999
      ELSE
      GOTO 220
      END IF
10005 WRITE(*,905)
      WRITE(*,2)
      WRITE(*,10002)
10002 FORMAT(17X, `G A T E   M A T E R I A L')
      WRITE(*,2)
      WRITE(*,10003) RHO
10003 FORMAT(11X, `CHOOSE ONE OF THESE
      $               MATERIALS:'//,
      $        11X, `MATERIAL       RESISTIVITY
      $                            (micro- ohm*cm)'/,
      $        11X, `--------       ----------------'/,
      $        11X, `1. ALUMINUM             2.8'/,
      $        11X, `2. COPPER               1.7'/,
      $        11X, `3. SILVER               1.6'/,
      $        11X, `4. SELECTED BY USER     ',F4.1)
      WRITE(*,2)
      WRITE(*,10004)
10004 FORMAT(11X, `Enter 1- 4 to CHANGE VALUE or 0 to
      $               CONTINUE or 999 to QUIT')
      WRITE(*,2)
      READ(*,*,ERR = 10005) IRHO
      IF (IRHO.EQ.0) THEN
      GOTO 919
      ELSE IF (IRHO.LT.0) THEN
      GOTO 10005
      ELSE IF (IRHO.GT.4) THEN
      IF (IRHO.EQ.999) THEN
      GOTO 999
      ELSE
      GOTO 10005
      ENDIF
      ELSE
      GOTO 840
      ENDIF
842   WRITE(*,1)
      GOTO 840
919   IF (MDEP.EQ.1) GOTO 923
```

```
C*****CHOOSING THE GATE LENGTH
 71    WRITE(*,905)
       WRITE(*,2)
       WRITE(*,73)
 73    FORMAT(17X, 'G A T E   L E N G T H')
       WRITE(*,2)
       WRITE(*,75)
 75    FORMAT(11X, 'PLEASE CHOOSE THE GATE LENGTH'/,
      $         11X, 'Range of the Gate Length is 0.01 to
      $              1.0 micron.')
       WRITE(*,2)
       WRITE (*,77)
 77    FORMAT(11X, 'Enter the value to CHOOSE the
      $              gate length or 999 to QUIT')
       WRITE(*,2)
       WRITE(*,*)
       READ(*,*,ERR=93) LG
87     IF(LG.LT.0.01) THEN
       GOTO 71
       ELSE IF (LG.GT.1.0) THEN
       IF(LG.EQ.999.) GOTO 999
       GOTO 71
       END IF
10012  WRITE(*,905)
       WRITE(*,2)
       WRITE(*,10007)
10007  FORMAT(17X, 'G A T E    L E N G T H')
       WRITE(*,2)
10010  WRITE(*,8881) LG
 8881  FORMAT(11X, 'The Value of the Gate Length
      $              is',F4.2, 'micron.')
       WRITE(*,2)
       WRITE(*,10009)
10009  FORMAT(11X, 'Enter 1 to CHANGE VALUE or 0 to
      $              CONTINUE or 999 to QUIT')
       WRITE(*,2)
       READ(*,*,ERR=10012) ILG
       IF(ILG.EQ.0) THEN
       LG = LG / 1000000.
       GOTO 923
       ELSE IF(ILG.EQ.1) THEN
       GOTO 71
       ELSE IF(ILG.EQ.999) THEN
       GOTO 999
       ELSE
```

```
        GOTO 10012
        END IF
  93    WRITE(*,1)
        GOTO 71
 923    IF(MDEP.EQ.2) GOTO 925
C*****CHOOSING THE MODFET WIDTH
  97    WRITE(*,905)
        WRITE(*,2)
        WRITE(*,99)
  99    FORMAT(11X 'M O D F E T   W I D T H')
        WRITE(*,2)
        WRITE(*,103)
 103    FORMAT (11X, 'PLEASE CHOOSE THE MODFET WIDTH'/,
     $          11X, 'Range of the MODFET Width is 100
     $                to 1000 micron.')
        WRITE(*,2)
        WRITE(*,107)
 107    FORMAT(11X, 'CHOOSE the MODFET width or enter 999
     $                to QUIT')
        WRITE(*,2)
        WRITE(*,*)
        READ(*,*,ERR=97) W
 109    IF(W.LT.100.) THEN
        GOTO 97
        ELSE IF (W.EQ.999.) THEN
        GOTO 999
        ELSE IF (W.GT.1000.) THEN
        GOTO 97
        END IF
10022 WRITE(*,905)
        WRITE(*,2)
        WRITE(*,10017)
10017 FORMAT(17X, 'M O D F E T   W I D T H')
        WRITE(*,2)
10020 WRITE(*,10111) W
10111 FORMAT(11X, 'The Value of the MODFET Width
     $                is',F5.0, 'micron.')
        WRITE(*,2)
        WRITE(*,10019)
10019 FORMAT(11X, 'Enter 1 to CHANGE VALUE or 0 to
     $                CONTINUE or 999 to QUIT')
        WRITE(*,2)
        READ(*,*,ERR=10022) IW
        IF(IW.EQ.0) THEN
        W = W / 100000.
```

```
        GOTO 121
        ELSE IF(IW.EQ.1) THEN
        GOTO 97
        ELSE IF(IW.EQ.999) THEN
        GOTO 999
        ELSE
        GOTO 10022
        END IF
 119    WRITE(*,1)
        GOTO 97
 121    GOTO 925
 925    IF(MDEP.EQ.4) GOTO 927
C*****CHOOSING THE DOPING DENSITY OF THE AlGaAs LAYER
 929    WRITE(*,905)
        WRITE(*,2)
        WRITE(*,931)
 931    FORMAT(17X, 'D O P I N G   D E N S I T Y')
        WRITE(*,2)
        WRITE(*,933)
 933    FORMAT (11X, 'PLEASE CHOOSE THE DOPING DENSITY IN
        $             THE AlGaAs LAYER.'/,
        $       11X, 'Range of the Doping Density is 0.1
        $             to 10. *10^24 / m^3')
        WRITE(*,2)
        WRITE(*,935)
 935    FORMAT(11X, 'Enter the value to CHOOSE the
        $             density or 999 to QUIT')
        WRITE(*,2)
        READ(*,*,ERR=929) ND
 939    IF(ND.LT.0.1) THEN
        GOTO 929
        ELSE IF(ND.GT.10.) THEN
        IF(ND.EQ.999.) GOTO 999
        GOTO 929
        END IF
10032   WRITE(*,905)
        WRITE(*,2)
        WRITE(*,10027)
10027   FORMAT(11X, 'DOPING DENSITY IN THE n- AlGaAs
        $             LAYER')
        WRITE(*,2)
10030   WRITE(*,10503) ND
10503   FORMAT (11X, 'The Value of the Doping Density in
        $             the n- AlGaAs Layer is '/,
        $       11X,F5.2,  '*10^24 / m^3')
```

```
      WRITE(*,2)
      WRITE(*,10029)
10029 FORMAT(11X, 'Enter 1 to CHANGE VALUE or 0 to
     $              CONTINUE or 999 to QUIT')
      WRITE(*,2)
      READ(*,*,ERR=10032) IND
      IF(IND.EQ.0) THEN
      GOTO 927
      ELSE IF(IND.EQ.1) THEN
      GOTO 929
      ELSE IF(IND.EQ.999) THEN
      GOTO 999
      ELSE
      GOTO 10032
      ENDIF
 937  WRITE(*,1)
      GOTO 929
 927  DO 9999
      III=KEK
      IF(MDEP.EQ.1) THEN
      LG=(0.01+0.99/FLOAT(KEK-1)*FLOAT(III-1))/
     $    1000000.
      ELSE IF(MDEP.EQ.2) THEN
      W=(0.1+0.9/FLOAT(KEK -1)*FLOAT(III-1))/1000.
      ELSE IF(MDEP.EQ.3)) THEN
      RHO=1.+99./FLOAT(KEK-1)*FLOAT(III-1)
      ELSE IF(MDEP.EQ.4) THEN
      ND=0.1+9.9/FLOAT(KEK-1)*FLOAT(III-1)
      ELSE IF(MDEP.EQ.5) THEN
      DA=10.+50./FLOAT(KEK-1)*FLOAT(III-1)
      END IF
      DELG=0.04/1000000.
      T=1.
      TEND=100.
      P=T
      DS=2.
      DI=60./1000000000.
      IF(MDEP.EQ.5) GOTO 957
      LG=LG*1000000.
      DA=120.+500.*(LG-0.1)
      DA=DA/10.
      VTH=0.5355-0.00083*ND*(DA-DS)*(DA-DS)
      LG=LG/1000000.
 957  DA=DA/100000000.
      DS=DS/100000000.
```

```
      DO = DA + DS + DI
      TE10 = (1.-VTH) / (LG + DELG)
      VSAT = 23587.59*EXP(5.88172 / 10000000.*TE10)
      TD = (LG + DELG) / VSAT
      E = 1.1 / 10000000000.
      U0 = 0.8
      C0 = E*ES / DO
      BETA = W*C0*U0 / LG
      VC = LG*VSAT / U0
      R = 1. / SQRT(1.+ 2.*(1.- VTH) / VC)
      T0 = 2./3.*R / (1.- R)*LG / VSAT
      CG1 = 2./3.*R*C0*LG*W
      CG2 = (1.- R)*(LG + DELG)*C0*W
      CG = (CG1 + CG2) / W
      RI1 = 1./5./ (BETA*VC*(1.- R))
      RI = RI1 / (1.+ CG2 / CG1) / (1.+ CG2 / CG1)*W
      GM = BETA*VC*(1- R) / W
      GO = 5.09
      CDG = 12.4 / 10000.*LG
C*****CALCULATION OF THE OUTPUT CAPACITANCE ALONG
C     SOURCE AND DRAIN
      RK = LG / (LG + DELG)
      RM = SQRT(1.- RK*RK)
      RM = ATAN(RK / RM)*180./3.1415926
      IF(RM.GT.90.) GOTO 7001
      RM = O(INT(RM) + 1)
 7001 RK = SQRT(1.- RK*RK)
      RN = SQRT(1.- RK*RK)
      RN = ATAN(RK / RN)*180./3.1415926
      IF(RN.GT.90.) GOTO 8001
      RN = O(INT(RN) + 1)
 8001 CDS = E*ES*RM / RN / 2./10.
C*****CALCULATION of RSS
      LSPACE = 1./1000000.
      P12 = 1.5 / 1000./1000000.
      RC1 = 0.255 / 1000.
      RC2 = 1.2 / 1000.
      RS1 = 216.
      RS2 = 1164.
      ARFA3 = 2.*RS2*(RS1*RC2- RS2*RC1)
      BETA3 = 2.*RS2*RS2*RC1 + (RS1*RS1 + RS2*RS2)*RC2
      GRMA3 = (RS2 + RS1)*RC1*RC2 + (RS1 + RS2)*
     $         (RS1 + RS2)*P12
      K11 = SQRT(RS2 + RS1) / P12)
      RSS = (RS1 + RS2)*COSH(K11*LSPACE)
```

```
      RSS = RSS + (RC1 + RC2)*K11*SINH(K11*LSPACE)
      RSS = 1./RSS
      RM = ARFA3 + BETA3*COSH(K11*LSPACE)
      RN = GRMA3*K11*SINH(K11*LSPACE)
      RSS = RSS*(RM + RN)
      RSS = RSS / (RS2 + RS1)
      RSS = RSS + LSPACE*RS2*RS1 / (RS2 + RS1)
      RSS = RSS / 0.0001*W
      RGG = 500000./RHO
      LGG = 0.38 / 1000000.
10060 WRITE(*,905)
      WRITE(*,2)
      WRITE(*,10040)
10040 FORMAT(11X,`I N T R I N S I C   P A R A M E T E R S')
      WRITE(*,2)
      EE = 1000000000000.
      WRITE(*,10041) GO,CDG*EE,CDS*EE,GM,CG*EE,RI
10041 FORMAT(11X, `PARAMETER                       VALUES '/,
     $        11X, `----------------------------------'/,
     $        11X, `1. OUTPUT CONDUCTANCE    = ',F14.7,
     $             GO                    `(S / m)'/,
     $        11X, `2. DRAIN TO              = ',F14.7,
     $             GATE CAPACITANCE CDG  `(PF / m)'/,
     $        11X, `3. DRAIN TO              = ',F14.7,
     $             SOURCE CAPACITANCE CDS` (PF / m)'/,
     $        11X, `4. TRANSCONDUCTANCE      = ',F14.7,
     $             GM                    ` (S / m)'/,
     $        11X, `5. GATE TO               = ',F14.7,
     $             SOURCE CAPACITANCE CG ` (PF / m)'/,
     $        11X, `6. GATE TO               = ',F14.9,
     $             SOURCE RESISTANCE RI  ` (ohm*m)')
      WRITE(*,2)
      IF(KEK.NE.1) THEN
      IF(III.NE.1) THEN
      WRITE(*,*) `        THIS IS ANOTHER DIMENSION OF
     $                A MODFET'
      WRITE(*,*) `        PLEASE HIT ENTER TO CONTINUE
     $                STUDYING'
      WRITE(*,*) `        THE DEPENDENCE.'
      READ(*,*)
      GOTO 10500
      ELSE
      GOTO 34567
      END IF
      ELSE
```

```
      GOTO 34567
      END IF
34567 WRITE(*,10050)
10050 FORMAT(11X, 'Enter 1- 6 to CHOOSE VALUE or 0 to
     $            CONTINUE or 999 to QUIT')
      WRITE(*,2)
      READ(*,*,ERR = 10060) IITR
10190 IF(IITR.EQ.0) THEN
      GOTO 10200
      ELSE IF(IITR.EQ.1) THEN
11060 WRITE(*,*) '          Enter YOUR OWN VALUE OF GO:'
      READ(*,*,ERR = 11060) GO
      GOTO 10060
      ELSE IF(IITR.EQ.2) THEN
12060 WRITE(*,*) '          Enter YOUR OWN VALUE OF CDG:'
      READ(*,*,ERR = 12060) CDG
      CDG = CDG / 1000000000000.
      GOTO 10060
      ELSE IF(IITR.EQ.3) THEN
13060 WRITE(*,*) '          Enter YOUR OWN VALUE OF CDS:'
      READ(*,*,ERR = 13060) CDS
      CDS = CDS / 1000000000000.
      GOTO 10060
      ELSE IF(IITR.EQ.4) THEN
14060 WRITE(*,*) '          Enter YOUR OWN VALUE OF GM:'
      READ(*,*,ERR = 14060) GM
      GOTO 10060
      ELSE IF(IITR.EQ.5) THEN
15060 WRITE(*,*) '          Enter YOUR OWN VALUE OF CG:'
      READ(*,*,ERR = 15060) CG
      CG = CG / 1000000000000.
      GOTO 10060
      ELSE IF(IITR.EQ.6) THEN
16060 WRITE(*,*) '          Enter YOUR OWN VALUE OF RI:'
      READ(*,*,ERR = 16060) RI
      GOTO 10060
      ELSE IF(IITR.EQ.999) THEN
      GOTO 999
      ELSE
      GOTO 10060
      END IF
C*****DETERMINATION OF THE EXTRINSIC PARAMETERS BY THE
C     USER
10200 EE = 1000000000000.
      WRITE(*,905)
```

```
      WRITE(*,2)
      WRITE(*,10340)
10340 FORMAT(11X, 'E X T R I N S I C  P A R A M E T E R S')
      WRITE(*,2)
      WRITE(*,10341) RSS,RGG,LGG*EE
10341 FORMAT(11X, 'PARAMETER                        VALUES'/,
     $         11X, '---------------------------------- '/,
     $         11X, '1. SOURCE RESISTANCE =   F14.7,'
     $                                       (ohm*m)'/,
     $         11X, '2. GATE RESISTANCE   =   F14.7,'
     $                                       (ohm*m)'/,
     $         11X, '3. GATE INDUCTANCE   =   F14.7,'
     $                                       (pH / m) ')
      WRITE(*,2)
      WRITE(*,10350)
10350 FORMAT(11X, 'Enter 1- 3 to CHOOSE VALUE OR 0 to
     $              CONTINUE or 999 to QUIT')
      WRITE(*,2)
      READ(*,*,ERR = 10200) IEXT
10490 IF(IEXT.EQ.0) THEN
      GOTO 10500
      ELSE IF(IEXT.EQ.1) THEN
17200 WRITE(*,*) '              Enter YOUR OWN VALUE OF
     $                          RSS:'
      READ(*,*,ERR = 17200) RSS
      GOTO 10200
      ELSE IF(IEXT.EQ.2) THEN
18200 WRITE(*,*) '              Enter YOUR OWN VALUE OF
     $                          RGG:'
      READ(*,*,ERR = 18200) RGG
      GOTO 10200
      ELSE IF(IEXT.EQ.3) THEN
19200 WRITE(*,*) '              Enter YOUR OWN VALUE OF
     $                          LGG:'
      READ(*,*ERR = 19200) LGG
      LGG = LGG / EE
      GOTO 10200
      ELSE IF(IEXT.EQ.999) THEN
      GOTO 999
      ELSE
      GOTO 10200
      END IF
10500 GOTO 599
 599  WRITE(*,905)
      WRITE(*,699)
```

```
699    FORMAT(11X, 'Please wait. Have some coffee!'// )
       II = 2
       V(1) = 0.
       SETIME(1) = 0.
105    IF(T.GT.TEND) GOTO 50
       V(II) = 0.0
       DO 201 I = 1,MPRIME
       V(II) = V(II) - REAL(VT(Z(I) / T*1000000000000.)
   $        *KPRIME(I))
201    CONTINUE
       V(II) = V(II) / T*1000000000000.
       SETIME(II) = T
       IF(T.GE.10.) THEN
       DETTAT = 10.
       GOTO 3456
       ELSE
       DETTAT = 1.
       END IF
3456   T = T + DETTAT
       II = II + 1
       GOTO 105
50     II = II - 1
       DO 60 J = 2,II - 1
       V(J) = V(J) / V(II - 1)
60     CONTINUE
       RISE(III) = 0.0
       DELAY(III) = 0.0
       DO 777 J = 2,II - 1
       IF(V(J).LT.0.1) GOTO 777
       IF(RISE(III).NE.0.0) GOTO 778
       RISE(III) = -(0.1 - V(J - 1))*(SETIME(J) - SETIME
   $            (J - 1)) / (V(J) - V(J - 1))
       RISE(III) = RISE(III) - SETIME(J - 1)
778    IF(V(J).LT.0.5) GOTO 777
       IF(DELAY(III).NE.0.0) GOTO 779
       DELAY(III) = (0.5 - V(J - 1))*(SETIME(J) - SETIME
   $            (J - 1)) / (V(J) - V(J - 1))
       DELAY(III) = DELAY(III) + SETIME(J - 1)
779    IF(V(J).LT.0.9) GOTO 777
       TE20 = (0.9 - V(J - 1))*(SETIME(J) - SETIME(J - 1)) /
   $        (V(J) - V(J - 1))
       TE20 = TE20 + SETIME(J - 1)
       RISE(III) = RISE(III) + TE20
       GOTO 888
777    CONTINUE
```

```
 888  T = P
9999  CONTINUE
C*****DISPLAYING THE OUTPUT ON THE SCREEN
      EEE = 100000.
      WRITE( * ,905)
      WRITE( * ,2)
      WRITE( * ,40000)
40000 FORMAT(11X, 'S I M U L A T I O N   R E S U L T S')
      WRITE( * ,2)
      IF(KEK.EQ.1) THEN
      WRITE( * ,40001) LG*EEE,W*EEE,RHO,ND
40001 FORMAT(11X, 'INPUT PARAMETERS'/,
     $         17X, 'Gate Length    =        ',F7.2,
     $                                 'micron'/,
     $         17X, 'MODFET Width   =        ',F7.2,
     $                                 ' micron'/,
     $         17X, 'Gate Resistivity        ',F7.2,
     $                                 ' micro-
     $                                 ohm*cm'/,
     $         17X, 'Doping Density =        ',F7.2,
     $                                 '*10^ 24 / m^3')
      WRITE( * ,2)
      WRITE( * ,40020) DELAY(1),RISE(1)
40020 FORMAT(11X, 'PROPAGATION DELAYS'/,
     $         17X, 'Delay Time ',F5.3, ' (ps)'/,17X,
     $              'Rise Time ',F5.3, ' (ps)')
      GOTO 40003
      ELSE
      IF(MDEP.EQ.1) THEN
      WRITE( * ,40002) W*EEE,RHO,ND
40002 FORMAT(11X, 'FIXED INPUT PARAMETERS'/,
     $         17X, 'MODFET Width =      ',F7.2, ' micron'/,
     $         17X, 'Gate Resistivity = ',F7.2,
     $                              ' micro- ohm*cm'/,
     $         17X, 'Doping Density =    ',F7.2,
     $                              ' *10^24 / mm^3'/,
     $         11X, 'PROPAGATION DELAYS')
      DO 4004 J = 1,KEK
      WRITE( * ,40005) 0.01 + 0.99 / FLOAT(KEK-1)*FLOAT
     $              (J-1),DELAY(J),RISE(J)
40005 FORMAT(17X, 'Gate Length = ',F7.2, ' micron'/,
     $         20X, 'Delay Time ',F5.3, ' (ps)', 'Rise Time
     $         ',F5.3, ' (ps)')
40004 CONTINUE
      GOTO 40003
```

```
      ELSE IF (MDEP.EQ.2) THEN
      WRITE(*,40006) LG*EEE,RHO,ND
40006 FORMAT(11X,`FIXED INPUT PARMETERS'/,
      $         17X, `Gate Length =          ',F7.2,
      $                              ` micron'/,
      $         17X, `Gate Resistivity = ',F7.2,
      $                              'micro-ohm*cm'/,
      $         17X, `Doping Density = ',F7.2,
      $                              ` *10~24 / m~3'/,
      $         11X, `PROPAGATION DELAYS')
      DO 40007 J = 1,KEK
      WRITE(*,40008) 100.+900./FLOAT(KEK-1)*FLOAT
      $              (J-1),DELAY(J),RISE(J)
40008 FORMAT(17X, `MODFET Width = ',F7.2, ` micron'/,
      $         20X, `Delay Time ',F5.3, ` (ps)', `Rise Time
      $         ',F5.3, ` (ps)')
40007 CONTINUE
      GOTO 40003
      ELSE IF (MDEP.EQ.3) THEN
      WRITE(*,40010) LG*EEE,W*EEE,ND
40010 FORMAT(11X,`FIXED INPUT PARAMETERS'/,
      $         17X, `Gate Length =          ',F7.2,
      $                              ` micron'/,
      $         17X, `MODFET Width =          ',F7.2,
      $                              ` micron'/,
      $         17X, `Doping Density = ',F7.2,
      $                              ` *10~24 / m~3'/,
      $         11X, `PROPAGATION DELAYS')
      DO 40011 J = 1,KEK
      WRITE(*,40012) 1.+99./FLOAT(KEK-1)*FLOAT
      $              (J-1),DELAY(J),RISE(J)
40012 FORMAT(17X, `Gate Resistivity =
      $         ',F7.2, ` micro-ohm*cm'/,
      $         20X, `Delay Time ',F6.3, ` (ps)',
      $         `RISE Time ',F6.3, ` (ps)')
40011 CONTINUE
      GOTO 40003
      ELSE IF(MDEP.EQ.4) THEN
      WRITE(*,40013) LG*EEE,W*EEE,RHO
40013 FORMAT(11X,`FIXED INPUT PARAMETERS'/,
      $         17X, `Gate Length =          ',F7.2,
      $                              ` micron'/,
      $         17X, `MODFET Width =          ',F7.2,
      $                              ` micron'/,
```

```
      $            17X, `Gate Resistivity =   ',F7.2,
      $                                     ` micro- ohm*cm'/,
      $            11X, `PROPAGATION DELAYS')
          DO 40014 J = 1, KEK
          WRITE( *,40015) 0.1 + 9.9 / FLOAT(KEK- 1)*FLOAT
      $                 (J- 1),DELAY(J),RISE(J),
40015 FORMAT(17X, `Doping Density = ',F7.2, ` *10 ˆ24 /
      $            m ˆ3'/,
      $            20X, `Delay Time ',F5.3, ` (ps)', `Rise Time
      $            ',F5.3, ` (ps)')
40014 CONTINUE
          GOTO 40003
          ELSE IF(MDEP.EQ.5) THEN
          WRITE( *,40016) LG*EEE,W*EEE,RHO,ND
40016 FORMAT(11X,FIXED INPUT PARAMETERS'/,
      $            17X, `Gate Length =       ',F7.2,
      $                                     ` micron'/,
      $            17X, `MODFET Width =      ',F7.2,
      $                                     ` micron'/,
      $            17X, `Gate Resistivity =  ',F7.2,
      $                                     ` micro- ohm*cm'/,
      $            17X, `Doping Density =    ',F7.2,
      $                                     ` *10 ˆ24 / m ˆ3'/,
      $            11X, `PROPAGATION DELAYS')
          DO 40017 J = 1,KEK
          WRITE( *,40018) 180.+ 580./ FLOAT(KEK- 1)*FLOAT
      $                 (J- 1),DELAY(J),RISE(J)
40018 FORMAT(17X, `Thickness do = ',F7.2, ` A'/,20X,
      $                 `Delay Time',F5.3, ` (ps)',
      $                 `Rise Time ',F5.3, ` (ps)')
40017 CONTINUE
          GOTO 40003
          END IF
          END IF
40003 WRITE( *,2)
          WRITE( *,*) `            Please Hit Enter to
      $                 Continue'
          READ( *,*)
40303 WRITE( *,910)
          WRITE( *,2)
          WRITE( *,50001)
50001 FORMAT (11X, `Do you want to write the simulation
      $            results'/,
      $            11X, `on the output file:
      $                 "TPDGAM.OUT"?')
```

```
      WRITE(*,2)
      WRITE(*,50002)
50002 FORMAT(11X, `Enter 1 for YES or 0 for NO or 999
     $            to QUIT')
      WRITE(*,2)
      READ(*,*,ERR=40303) IPP
      IF(IPP.EQ.999) THEN
      GOTO 999
      ELSE IF(IPP.EQ.0) THEN
      GOTO 50005
      ELSE IF(IPP.EQ.1) THEN
      GOTO 50006
      END IF
C*****WRITING THE OUTPUT ON THE OUTPUT FILE
50006 WRITE(6,2)
      WRITE(6,50007)           `
50007 FORMAT(11X, `S I M U L A T I O N   R E S U L T S')
      WRITE(6,2)
      IF(KEK.EQ.1) THEN
      WRITE(6,90001)
90001 FORMAT(11X, `Normalized Drain Current in a Given
     $            Time Range')
      WRITE(6,2)
      WRITE(6,60001) LG*EEE,W*EEE,RHO,ND
60001 FORMAT(11X, `INPUT PARAMETERS'/,
     $        17X, `Gate Length =        ',F7.2,
     $                             ` micron'/,
     $        17X, `MODFET Width =       ',F7.2,
     $                             ` micron'/,
     $        17X, `Gate Resistivity =   `,F7.2,
     $                             ` micro-ohm*cm'/,
     $        17X, `Doping Density =     ',F7.2,
     $                             ` *10^24 / m^3')
      WRITE(6,2)
      WRITE(6,70002)
70002 FORMAT(11X, `I N T R I N S I C   P A R A M E T E R S')
      WRITE(6,2)
      WRITE(6,70001) GO,CDG*EE,CDS*EE,GM,CG*EE,RI
70001 FORMAT(11X, `PARAMETER VALUES '/,
     $        11X, `--------------------------------'/,
     $        11X, `1. OUTPUT
     $             CONDUCTANCE GO = ',F14.7, ` (S / m)'/,
     $        11X, `2. DRAIN TO
     $             GATE CAPACITANCE CDG = ',F14.7,
     $                      ' (PF / m) `/,
```

```
      $          11X, `3. DRAIN TO
      $                 SOURCE CAPACITANCE CDS = ',F14.7,
      $                              ` (PF / m) '/,
      $          11X, `4. TRANS-
      $                 CONDUCTANCE GM = ',F14.7, ` (S /
      $                     m) '/,
      $          11X, `5. GATE TO
      $                 SOURCE CAPACITANCE CG = ',F14.7,
      $                              ` (PF / m) '/,
      $          11X, `6. GATE TO
      $                 SOURCE RESISTANCE RI = ',F14.9,
      $                              ` (ohm*m) ')
        WRITE(6,2)
        WRITE(6,70003)
70003 FORMAT(11X, `E X T R I N S I C   P A R A M E T E R S')
        WRITE(6,2)
        WRITE(6,7006) RSS,RGG,LGG*EE
70006 FORMAT(11X, `PARAMETER VALUES '/,
      $          11X, `-------------------------------'/,
      $          11X, `1. SOURCE RESISTANCE =   ',F14.7,
      $                 ` (ohm*m) '/,
      $          11X, `2. GATE RESISTANCE =   ',F14.7,
      $                 ` (ohm*m) '/,
      $          11X, `3. GATE INDUCTANCE =   ',F14.7,
      $                 ` (pH / m) ')
        WRITE(6,2)
        WRITE(6,70007)
70007 FORMAT(11X, `D R A I N   C U R R E N T')
        WRITE(6,2)
        WRITE(6,70008)
70008 FORMAT(11X, `Time (ps)             Normalized
      $             Drain Current')
        DO 70010 J = 1,II- 1
        WRITE(6,70108) SETIME(J),V(J)
70108 FORMAT(11X,F5.2,20X,F10.2)
70010 CONTINUE
        WRITE(6,2)
        WRITE(6,70011) DELAY(1),RISE(1)
70011 FORMAT (11X, `PROPAGATION DELAYS'/,
      $          17X, `Delay Time ',F5.3, ` (ps)'/,17X, `Rise
      $             Time ',F5.3, ` (ps)')
        WRITE(6,2)
        GOTO 50005
        ELSE
        IF(MDEP.EQ.1) THEN
        WRITE(6,2)
```

```
      WRITE(6,90002)
90002 FORMAT(11X, 'Dependence of Transverse Propagation
     $            Delays'/,
     $        11X, 'in the MODFET on the Gate Length.')
      WRITE(6,2)
      WRITE(6,80002) W*EEE,RHO,ND
80002 FORMAT (11X, 'FIXED INPUT PARAMETERS'/,
     $         17X, 'MODFET Width =     ',F7.2, ' micron'/,
     $         17X, 'Gate Resistivity = ',F7.2,
     $                                   ' micro-
              t$                         ohm*cm'/,
     $         17X, 'Doping Density =    ',F7.2,
     $                                   '*10^24 / m 3'/,
     $         11X, 'PROPAGATION DELAYS')
      DO 80004 J = 1,KEK
      WRITE(6,80005) 0.01 + 0.99 / FLOAT(KEK- 1)*FLOAT
     $             (J- 1),DELAY(J),RISE(J)
80005 FORMAT(17X, 'Gate Length = ',F7.2, ' micron'/,
     $      20X, 'Delay Time ',F5.3, ' (ps)', 'Rise Time
     $      ',F5.3, ' (ps)')
80004 CONTINUE
      GOTO 50005
      ELSE IF(MDEP.EQ.2) THEN
      WRITE(6,2)
      WRITE(6,90005)
90005 FORMAT (11X, 'Dependence of Transverse
     $            Propagation Delays'/,
     $        11X, 'in the MODFET on the MODFET
     $            Width.')
      WRITE(6,2)
      WRITE(6,80006) LG*EEE,RHO,ND
80006 FORMAT (11X, 'FIXED INPUT PARAMETERS'/,
     $         17X, 'Gate Length =      ',F7.2,
     $                                   ' micron'/,
     $         17X, 'Gate Resistivity = ',F7.2,
     $                                   ' micro-
     $                                   ohm*cm'/,
     $         17X, 'Doping Density =   ',F7.2,
     $                                   ' *10^24 / m^3'/,
     $         11X, 'PROPAGATION DELAYS')
      DO 80007 J = 1,KEK
      WRITE(6,80008) 100.+900./ FLOAT(KEK- 1)*FLOAT
     $             (J- 1),DELAY(J),RISE(J)
80008 FORMAT (17X, 'MODFET Width = ',F7.2, ' micron'/,
     $      20X, 'Delay Time ',F5.3, ' (ps)', 'Rise
     $            Time ',F5.3, ' (ps)')
80007 CONTINUE
      GOTO 50005
```

```
      ELSE IF(MDEP.EQ.3) THEN
      WRITE(6,2)
      WRITE(6,90006)
90006 FORMAT (11X, 'Dependence of Transverse
     $              Propagation Delays'/,
     $         11X, 'in the MODFET on the Gate
     $              Resistivity.')
      WRITE(6,2)
      WRITE(6,80010) LG*EEE,W*EEE,ND
80010 FORMAT (11X, 'FIXED INPUT PARAMETER'/,
     $         17X, 'Gate Length =     ',F7.2, 'micron'/,
     $         17X, 'MODFET Width =    ',F7.2, ' micron'/,
     $         17X, 'Doping Density = ',F7.2,
     $                         ' *10^24 / m^3'/,
     $         11X, 'PROPAGATION DELAYS')
      DO 80011 J=1,KEK
      WRITE(6,80012) 1.+99./FLOAT(KEK-1)*FLOAT
     $              (J-1),DELAY(J),RISE(J),
80012 FORMAT (17X, 'Gate Resistivity = ',F7.2,
     $                         ' micro-ohm*cm'/,
     $         20X, 'Delay Time ',F6.3, ' (ps)', 'Rise
     $              Time ',F6.3, ' (ps)')
80011 CONTINUE
      GOTO 50005
      ELSE IF(MDEP.EQ.4) THEN
      WRITE(6,2)
      WRITE(6,90007)
90007 FORMAT (11X, 'Dependence of Transverse
     $              Propagation Delays'/,
     $         11X, 'on the Doping Density in the
     $              AlGaAs Layer.')
      WRITE(6,2)
      WRITE(6,80013) LG*EEE,W*EEE,RHO
80013 FORMAT (11X, 'FIXED INPUT PARAMETERS'/,
     $         17X, 'Gate Length =     ',F7.2,
     $                         ' micron'/,
     $         17X, 'MODFET Width =    ',F7.2,
     $                         'micron'/,
     $         11X, 'PROPAGATION DELAYS')
      DO 80014 J=1,KEK
      WRITE(6,80015) 0.1+9.9/FLOAT(KEK-1)*FLOAT
     $              (J-1),DELAY(J),RISE(J),
80015 FORMAT (17X, 'Doping Density = ',F7.2,
     $              ' *10^24 / m^3'/,
     $         20X, 'Delay Time ',F5.3, ' (ps)', 'Rise
     $              Time ',F5.3, ' (ps)')
```

```
80014 CONTINUE
      GOTO 5005
      ELSE IF(MDEP.EQ. 5) THEN
      WRITE(6,2)
      WRITE(6,90015)
90015 FORMAT (11X, `Dependence of Transverse
    $             Propagation Delays'/,
    $         11X, `in the MODFET on the Thickness
    $             do.')
      WRITE(6,2)
      WRITE(6,80016) LG*EEE,W*EEE,RHO,ND
80016 FORMAT (11X, `FIXED INPUT PARAMETERS'/,
    $         17X, `Gate Length =      'F7.2, ` micron'/,
    $         17X, `MODFET Width =     ',F7.2, ` micron'/,
    $         17X, `Gate Resistivity = ',F7.2,
    $                             ` micro- ohm*cm'/,
    $         17X, `Doping Density =   ',F7.2,
    $                             ` *10^24 / m^3'/,
    $         11X, `PROPAGATION DELAYS')
      DO 80017 J = 1,KEK
      WRITE(6,80018) 180.+ 580./ FLOAT(KEK- 1)*FLOAT
    $             (J- 1),DELAY(J),RISE(J),
80018 FORMAT (17X, `Thickness do = 'F7.2, ` A'/,
    $         20X, `Delay Time ',F5.3, ` (ps)', `Rise
    $             Time ',F5.3, ` (ps)')
80017 CONTINUE
      GOTO 50005
      END IF
      END IF
      50005 WRITE(6,2)
      GOTO 85000
 999  WRITE(*,910)
      WRITE(*,30000)
30000 FORMAT (19X, `##########################'/
    $         19X, `##                      ##'/
    $         19X, `##    Thank You         ##'/
    $         19X, `##    for Using "TPDGAM" ##'/
    $         19X, `##    Have a Nice Day!   ##'/
    $         19X, `##                      ##'
    $         19X, `##########################'////)
      WRITE(*,*) `     PLEASE HIT "ENTER" TO EXIT'
      READ(*,*)
      STOP
      END
```

CHAPTER FOUR

Crosstalk Analysis

Continuous advancements in the field of very large scale integrated circuits (VLSICs) and very high speed integrated circuits (VHSICs) have resulted in smaller chip sizes, smaller device geometries, and millions of closely spaced interconnections in one or more levels that connect the various components on the chip. There are continuous customer demands for higher speeds in the areas of signal processing, high-speed computation, data links, and the related instrumentation. This has made it necessary to develop VHSICs having propagation delays per gate of less than 100 ps. However, the crosstalk among the interconnections in single- as well as multilevel configurations has become a major problem in the development of next-generation high-speed integrated circuits.

In the literature modeling and analysis of coupled interconnections has received considerable attention. Several authors have used the multiconductor transmission line theory [4.1–4.7], and the analysis of coupled lossy transmission lines has also been reported [4.8–4.10]. Nonlinearity of the source and load networks has been addressed by several workers [4.6, 4.9, 4.11]. A lot of effort has been expended to obtain closed-form expressions for signal waveforms on two or three coupled interconnections. For example, the analytical solutions reported in references [4.10], [4.12], and [4.13] are valid for weak-coupling cases because they ignore second-degree coupling, and formulas for the voltage transfer functions for a two-line system without the weak-coupling assumption are presented in reference [4.14]. Closed-form solutions for a system of N lossless lines using cyclic boundary conditions are developed in reference [4.15], and a general crosstalk analysis technique without the weak-coupling or the cyclic boundary condition assumption is presented in reference [4.16]. Crosstalk analysis of parallel multilevel interconnections on the GaAs-based integrated circuit is presented in references [4.17] and [4.18], and an analysis of bilevel crossing interconnections has been carried out in references [4.19] and [4.20].

In this chapter the crosstalk among neighboring interconnections is studied by using a lumped-capacitance approximation in Section 4.1. Next, in Section 4.2, crosstalk in very high speed VLSICs is analyzed by using a coupled multiconductor metal–insulator–semiconductor microstrip line model for the interconnections. In Section 4.3 single-level interconnections are investigated by the frequency domain modal analysis. A transmission line model of the crosstalk effects in single-, bi-, and trilevel high-density interconnections on GaAs-based VHSICs is presented in Section 4.4. This is followed by an analysis of crossing bilevel interconnections on GaAs-based integrated circuits in Section 4.5. The crosstalk effects in multiconductor buses in high-speed GaAs logic circuits are analyzed in Section 4.6.

4.1   LUMPED-CAPACITANCE APPROXIMATION

The lumped-capacitance model of two interconnections [4.5] coupled by the capacitance C_c is shown in Figure 4.1.1. C denotes the ground capacitance of each interconnection. The first interconnection is driven by the unit voltage source of resistance R_s on the left and terminated by the load capacitance C_L on the right. The second interconnection is terminated by the resistance R_S on the left and by the load capacitance C_L on the right. Crosstalk voltage is defined as the voltage $V_2(t)$ induced across the load C_L on the second interconnection. It can be shown that the amplitude of the crosstalk voltage at time t is given by

$$V_2(t) = \frac{1}{2}\left[\exp\left(-\frac{t}{\tau_1}\right) - \exp\left(-\frac{t}{\tau_2}\right)\right] \qquad (4.1.1)$$

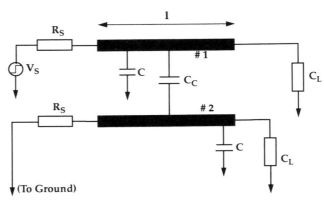

FIGURE 4.1.1   Lumped-capacitance model of two interconnections coupled by the capacitance C_c [4.5]. (© 1984 IEEE)

where

$$\tau_1 = R(C + C_L)$$

and

$$\tau_2 = R(2C_c + C + C_L) \tag{4.1.2}$$

Using calculus, it can be further shown that the maximum value of the crosstalk voltage is given by

$$V_{2,\max} = \frac{1}{2}\left[\exp\left[\left(\frac{n_c - 1}{2n_c}\right)\ln\left(\frac{1 + n_c}{1 - n_c}\right)\right] - \exp\left[\left(-\frac{n_c + 1}{2n_c}\right)\ln\left(\frac{1 + n_c}{1 - n_c}\right)\right]\right]$$

$$(4.1.3)$$

where the capacitance coupling coefficient n_c is given by

$$n_c = \frac{C_c}{C + C_c + C_L} \tag{4.1.4}$$

Based on the lumped-capacitance model, the dependences of the crosstalk voltage V_2 on time in the range 0 to 500 ps for interconnections of widths and separation equal to 2 μm and lengths of 1 and 3 mm are shown in Figure 4.1.2. Figure 4.1.2 also shows the dependence of the maximum crosstalk voltage on the coupling coefficient n_c in the range 0 to 1.

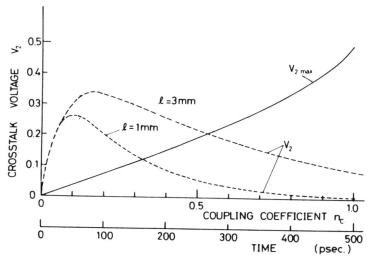

FIGURE 4.1.2 Crosstalk waveform and amplitude derived from the lumped-capacitance approximation [4.5]. (© 1984 IEEE)

It will be shown in the next section that the lumped-capacitance approximation becomes inadequate in high-speed circuits. In fact, it can be shown that this approximation is applicable to interconnections that are at least a few millimeters long with circuit rise times above 200 to 300 ps.

4.2   COUPLED MULTICONDUCTOR MIS MICROSTRIP LINE MODEL OF SINGLE-LEVEL INTERCONNECTIONS

In this section a system of parallel single-level interconnections is modeled as a coupled multiconductor metal–insulator–semiconductor (MIS) microstrip line system having many conductors [4.5]. Interconnections are formed on a surface-passivated semiconductor substrate with a metallized back. This model is particularly suitable for situations where many closely spaced interconnections run parallel for a long time, such as in the case of a semicustom gate array shown in Figure 4.2.1. For simplicity, losses in the semiconductor substrate are ignored, thus making the model especially applicable to interconnections on semi-insulating GaAs or InP or silicon-on-sapphire substrates.

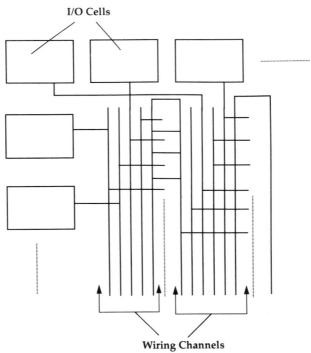

FIGURE 4.2.1   Schematic diagram of a semicustom gate array [4.5]. (© 1984 IEEE)

4.2.1 The Model

The MIS microstrip line model for a system of n strip conductors is shown in Figure 4.2.2a. To incorporate the boundary conditions existing on both sides of the strip line system, a periodic boundary condition is adopted where it is assumed that the same system of n strip line conductors is repeated indefinitely as shown in Figure 4.2.2b. This periodic boundary condition is quite useful for providing a first-order estimate of crosstalk without going into the specific layout design details.

Now, on this n-conductor strip line system, there exist n quasi-TEM modes. Consider a mode, called the θ mode, where the phase angle difference of voltage and current between two adjacent conductors is constant equal to θ. Possible values of θ that satisfy the periodic boundary condition are given by

$$\theta = 0, 2\pi/n, \dots, 2k\pi/n, \dots, 2(n-1)\pi/n \qquad (4.2.1)$$

Then the characteristic impedance $Z_{0\theta}$ and the phase velocity v_{θ} of the θ

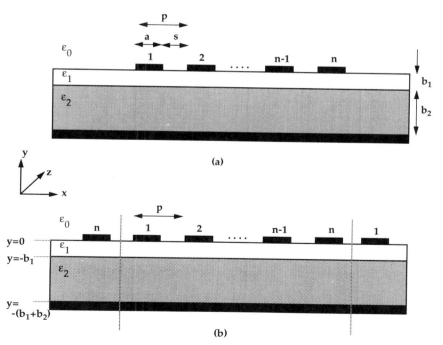

(a)

(b)

FIGURE 4.2.2 (a) Coupled multiconductor MIS microstrip line model having n conductors and (b) periodic boundary condition applied to the model [4.5]. (© 1984 IEEE)

mode are given by

$$Z_{0\theta} = \frac{1}{v_\theta C_\theta} \qquad (4.2.2a)$$

$$v_\theta = c_0 \left(\frac{C_{\theta 0}}{C_\theta} \right)^{1/2} \qquad (4.2.2b)$$

where c_0 is the velocity of light in a vacuum and C_θ and $C_{\theta 0}$ are the static capacitances of the θ mode per conductor per unit length with and without the dielectric loadings, respectively. The static mode capacitances can be found by the Green's function method. The Green's function on the strip plane ($y = 0$ in Figure 4.2.2b) for the θ mode, denoted by $G_\theta(x, x_0)$, is defined as the potential at a point x on the strip plane when a unit charge with a phase factor of $e^{-jm\theta}$ is placed at points $x_0 + mp$, $m = 0, \pm 1$, $\pm 2, \ldots, \pm \infty$, and p is the pitch in Figure 4.2.2b. Yamashita et al. have determined $G_\theta(x, x_0)$ by making a Fourier transformation of the two-dimensional Laplace equation and solving the resultant equation with respect to y, resulting in

$$G_\theta(x, x_0) = \sum_{m=-\infty}^{\infty} \frac{e^{-j\beta_m(x-x_0)}}{p|\beta_m|}$$

$$\times \left[\frac{\varepsilon_1 \coth(b_1\beta_m) + \varepsilon_2 \coth(b_2\beta_m)}{\{\varepsilon_2 \coth(b_2\beta_m)\}\{\varepsilon_0 + \varepsilon_1 \coth(b_1\beta_m)\} + \varepsilon_1\{\varepsilon_1 + \varepsilon_1 \coth(b_1\beta_m)\}} \right]$$

$$(4.2.3)$$

where

$$\beta_m = \frac{2m\pi + \theta}{p}$$

Then the potential on the strip under consideration, denoted by V_0, can be found from the charge density function $\rho_\theta(x)$ for the θ mode at point x on the strip conductor by solving the following equation numerically:

$$V_0 = \int_{-a/2}^{a/2} G_\theta(x, x_0)\rho_\theta(x_0) \, dx_0 \qquad (4.2.4)$$

Then the static capacitance of the θ mode per conductor will be given by

$$C_\theta = \frac{1}{V_0} \int_{-a/2}^{a/2} \rho_\theta(x) \, dx \qquad (4.2.5)$$

The voltage and current on the kth conductor can be expressed in terms of the normal modes, defined previously, by the following equations:

$$V_k(z) = \sum_\theta \left[A_{\theta f} e^{-j(k-1)\theta} e^{j\omega(t-(z/v_\theta))} + A_{\theta r} e^{-j(k-1)\theta} e^{j\omega(t+z/v_\theta)} \right] \quad (4.2.6)$$

$$I_k(z) = \sum_\theta \left[\frac{A_{\theta f}}{Z_{0\theta}} e^{-j(k-1)\theta} e^{j\omega(t-(z/v_\theta))} - \frac{A_{\theta r}}{Z_{0\theta}} e^{-j(k-1)\theta} e^{j\omega(t+z/v_\theta)} \right] \quad (4.2.7)$$

where z denotes the position on the conductor, ω is the angular frequency, and $A_{\theta f}$ and $A_{\theta r}$ are the amplitudes of the forward and backward voltage waves in the θ mode. The mode wave amplitudes $A_{\theta f}$ and $A_{\theta r}$ can be determined by using the known terminal conditions at both ends of each strip conductor. The values of voltage and current in the time domain can be found by an inverse Laplace transformation of the preceding equations.

4.2.2 Numerical Simulations

In the following results [4.5], unless specified otherwise, it is assumed that the interconnections are of width $a = 2$ μm, the substrate is of thickness $b_2 = 200$ μm and relative permittivity $\varepsilon_2 = 12$, and the insulator is of thickness $b_1 = 1$ μm and relative permittivity $\varepsilon_1 = 4$.

First, for the case of $b_1 = 0$ and $b_2 = \infty$, the dependences of the characteristic impedance $Z_{0\theta}$ on the width to pitch ratio (a/p) for various values of θ are shown in Figure 4.2.3. It is interesting to note the high-impedance nature of the interconnection system even for a typical practical case when $a = 2$ μm, $p = 4$ μm, and $b_2 = 200$ μm. This is because of the relatively small value of a/b_2 (which leads to a smaller value of the ground capacitance).

For a system of 10 semi-infinite interconnections with a unit step voltage applied to the input end of the first interconnection and the input ends of other interconnections open circuited, the induced voltage V_i on the ith interconnection is plotted versus i in Figure 4.2.4. It can be seen that the voltage applied to one line tends to have its effect over a long range. This is because of the small shielding effect of the metallized back plane which in turn is due to a small value of the a/b_2 ratio. For a system of five semi-infinite interconnections, the dependence of the induced voltage at an adjacent strip on the interconnection spacing s $(= p - a)$ is shown in Figure 4.2.5. The long-range nature of the induced voltage can be again noted.

For a system of five finite length interconnections with the excitation and loading conditions shown in the inset of Figure 4.2.6, the crosstalk voltage waveform across the load capacitance of interconnection 4 is shown in Figure 4.2.6. The waveform shows an initial time delay (due to the propagation of

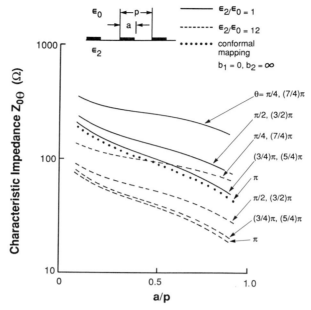

FIGURE 4.2.3   Calculated characteristic impedance $Z_{0\theta}$ of the various modes [4.5]. (© 1984 IEEE)

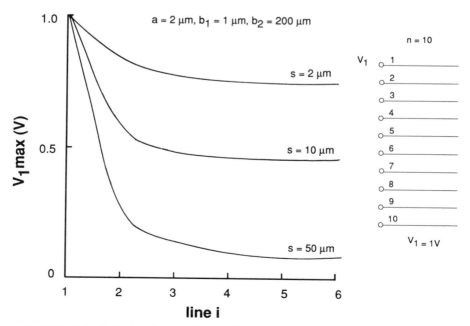

FIGURE 4.2.4   Calculated crosstalk amplitude at the ith interconnection for a system of 10 semi-infinite interconnections [4.5]. (© 1984 IEEE)

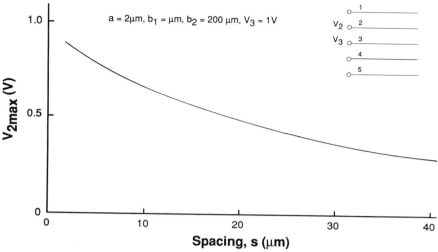

FIGURE 4.2.5 Crosstalk amplitude at the adjacent interconnection versus spacing for a system of five semi-infinite interconnections [4.5]. (© 1984 IEEE)

the wavefront) followed by ringing-type decaying oscillation superposed by ripple-like smaller oscillations. These small oscillations are caused by the velocity mismatches among the various modes involved. For the sake of comparison, the corresponding waveform calculated by the lumped-capacitance approximation (using the network shown in the inset) is also included in Figure 4.2.6, which shows that, as stated earlier, this approximation is not adequate for high-speed circuits. Figure 4.2.7 shows the dependences of the amplitudes of the crosstalk waveforms on the interconnection lengths for the two sets of terminal conditions shown in the insets. This figure shows that the presence of floating interconnections increases the crosstalk amplitude because it effectively increases mutual coupling by reducing the line capacitances.

For a system of five finite length interconnections, the crosstalk voltage waveforms for signal source resistances R_s of 5 kΩ, 700 Ω, and 10 Ω are shown in Figure 4.2.8a. The dependence of the maximum crosstalk voltage on the source resistance in the range 10 to 10,000 Ω is shown in Figure 4.2.8b. These figures show that the oscillations become more dominant and determine the crosstalk amplitude as the signal source resistance is reduced. As R_s is reduced to a few tens of ohms, multiple reflections of the wavefront appear at the initial times and the first negative peak of this transient determines the amplitude of the crosstalk waveform. The result calculated by using the lumped-capacitance approximation is also included in Figure 4.2.8b, which shows that this approximation is valid when R_s is above 2 to 3 kΩ and the response is slow.

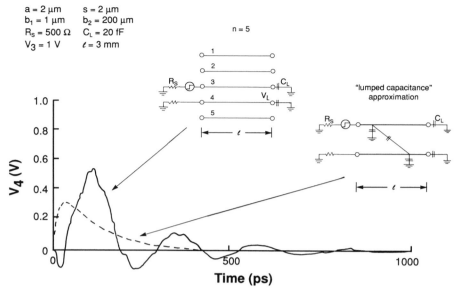

FIGURE 4.2.6 Calculated step response waveforms. The dashed curve is the waveform using the lumped-capacitance approximation [4.5]. (© 1984 IEEE)

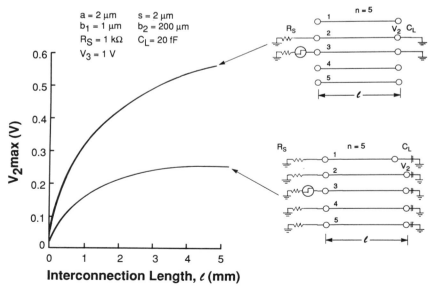

FIGURE 4.2.7 Crosstalk amplitude versus interconnection length for two systems of five interconnections with different terminal conditions [4.5]. (© 1984 IEEE)

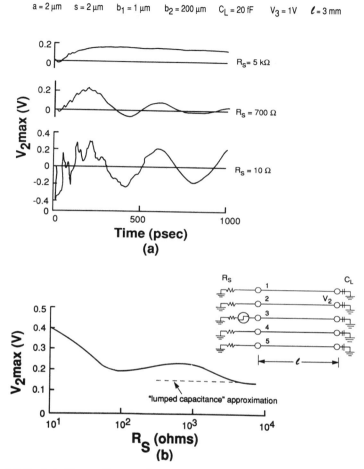

FIGURE 4.2.8 (*a*) Crosstalk waveforms for different signal source resistance R_s values and (*b*) crosstalk amplitude versus R_s [4.5]. (© 1984 IEEE)

4.2.3   Crosstalk Reduction

The preceding results suggest that for reliable operation of very high speed very large scale integrated circuits with sufficient noise margins, it is very important to consider methods of reducing crosstalk. One method of reducing crosstalk is to reduce the substrate thickness in order to provide a solid shielding ground plane in close proximity to the interconnections. However, this method will be effective only if the substrate thickness is reduced below 10 μm. This is clear from Figure 4.2.9 which shows the dependence of the crosstalk coupling coefficient on spacing for several substrate thickness values. Reducing the substrate thickness below 10 μm may not be practically

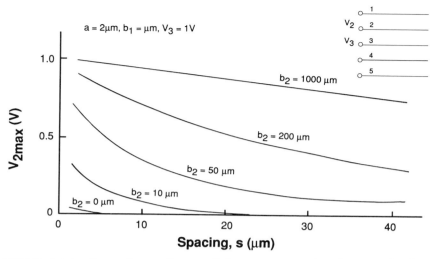

FIGURE 4.2.9 Crosstalk coupling coefficient versus spacing for several substrate thickness values [4.5]. (© 1984 IEEE)

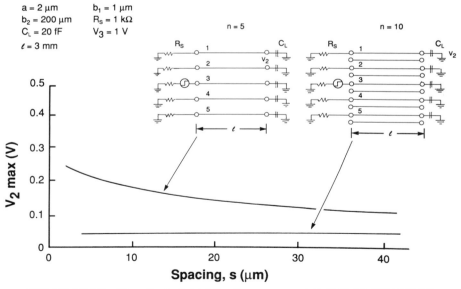

FIGURE 4.2.10 The effect of shielding lines on crosstalk [4.5]. (© 1984 IEEE)

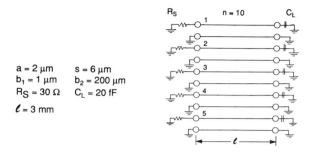

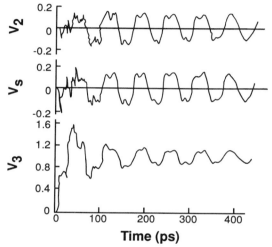

FIGURE 4.2.11   Waveforms at the centers of the adjacent line (V_2), the shielding line (V_S), and the active line (V_3) [4.5]. (© 1984 IEEE)

possible unless a new technology such as semiconductor-on-insulator (SOI) is used.

Crosstalk can also be reduced by providing shielding ground lines adjacent to the active interconnections. This is a very effective method as shown by Figure 4.2.10 which depicts the dependences of the crosstalk voltage on spacing for two systems of five interconnections with and without shielding ground lines between the interconnections. The drawback of this method is that it significantly reduces the wiring channel capacity, particularly when the interconnection capacity is itself a problem in the design of very large scale integrated circuits. It is interesting to note that the potential on a narrow shielding line is not 0 all along the line even if it is grounded on both ends. This is clear from Figure 4.2.11 which shows the waveforms at the centers of the adjacent line, the shielding line, and the active line.

4.3 FREQUENCY DOMAIN MODAL ANALYSIS OF SINGLE-LEVEL INTERCONNECTIONS

In this section a general technique for analyzing crosstalk in coupled single-level lossless interconnections [4.16] is presented. The analysis is carried out without making the weak-coupling or cyclic boundary condition assumptions. First, modal analysis has been done in the frequency domain to obtain closed-form expressions for the voltage and current transfer functions. Then the transfer function is expanded into its Taylor series, and the inverse Fourier transformation is applied to the terms considered significant depending on the accuracy desired in the solution.

4.3.1 The General Technique

Consider a system of N interconnection lines shown in Figure 4.3.1. Let $[C]$, $[L]$, and $[R]$ denote the capacitance, inductance, and resistance matrices of the system. Furthermore, let $E_n(t)$, Z_{Gn}, and Z_{Ln} denote the input signal, the source impedance, and the load impedance for the nth line, where $n = 1, 2, \ldots, N$. Let l be the length of each interconnection line. We define the series impedance matrix $[Z]$ and the parallel admittance matrix $[Y]$ as $[Z] = [R] + j\omega[L]$ and $[Y] = j\omega[C]$.

The N propagation modes that exist in a system of N conductors are defined by N complex modal propagation constants $\gamma_n = \alpha_n + j\omega\beta_n$, where $n = 1, 2, \ldots, N$. Then elements of the voltage eigenvector matrix $[S_v]$ are solutions of the eigenvalue equation

$$\left(\gamma^2[U] + [Z][Y]\right)[S_v] = [0] \tag{4.3.1}$$

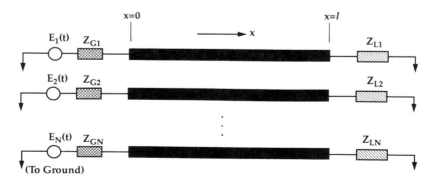

FIGURE 4.3.1 Schematic diagram of a system of N coupled interconnection lines [4.16]. (© 1990 IEEE)

and the current eigenvector matrix $[S_I]$ is given by

$$[S_I] = [Z]^{-1}[S_v][\Gamma]$$ (4.3.2)

where $[U]$ is the identity matrix and $[\Gamma] = \mathrm{diag}\{\gamma_1, \gamma_2, \ldots, \gamma_n\}$. The character-istic impedance matrix $[Z_c]$ is given by $[S_v][S_I]^{-1}$, and the characteristic admittance matrix $[Y_c]$ is equal to $[Z_c]^{-1}$. Then the voltage and current vectors on the interconnection line can be expressed in terms of $[S_v]$ and $[S_I]$ as

$$[V(x)] = [S_v]([W_i(x)] + [W_r(x)])$$ (4.3.3)

$$[I(x)] = [Y_c][S_v]([W_i(x)] - [W_r(x)])$$ (4.3.4)

where

$$[W_i(x)] = [W_{i,n}(0)(e^{-\gamma_n x})]$$

$$[W_r(x)] = [W_{r,n}(0)(e^{\gamma_n x})]$$

and $W_{i,n}$ and $W_{r,n}$ are the amplitudes of the incident and reflected compo-nents of the nth mode. The voltage and current vectors satisfy the following boundary conditions:

$$[V(0)] = [E] - [Z_G][I(0)]$$

$$[V(l)] = [Z_L][I(l)]$$ (4.3.5)

where $[E] = [E_n]$, $[Z_G] = \mathrm{diag}\{Z_{G1}, Z_{G2}, \ldots, Z_{GN}\}$, $[Z_L] = \mathrm{diag}\{Z_{L1}, Z_{L2}, \ldots, Z_{LN}\}$, E_n is the input voltage signal applied to the nth line, Z_{Gn} is the internal impedance of the nth input signal source, and Z_{Ln} is the load impedance of the nth line. Substituting Equations 4.3.3 and 4.3.4 into Equation 4.3.5, we obtain the following linear equations for $[W_i(0)]$ and $[W_r(0)]$:

$$\begin{bmatrix} [S_v] + [Z_G][S_I] & [S_v] - [Z_G][S_I] \\ ([S_v] - [Z_L][S_I])[P] & ([S_v] + [Z_L][S_I])[P]^{-1} \end{bmatrix} \begin{bmatrix} [W_i(0)] \\ [W_r(0)] \end{bmatrix} = \begin{bmatrix} [E] \\ [0] \end{bmatrix}$$ (4.3.6)

where $[P] = \mathrm{diag}\{\exp(-\gamma_n l)\}$. After solving Equation 4.3.6 for $[W_i(0)]$ and $[W_r(0)]$, the voltage and current transfer functions can be determined from the voltage and current spectra obtained from Equations 4.3.3 and 4.3.4.

In general, the voltage and current are first calculated at a finite number of discrete frequencies and then the time domain waveforms are obtained by using the fast Fourier transformation (FFT) technique. If the lines can be considered lossless and are terminated at one or both ends by the line characteristic impedances, then analytical inverse Fourier transformation can be used to obtain closed-form expressions for the time domain waveforms as shown in the following sections for two-, three-, and four-line systems.

4.3.2   Two-Line System

The capacitance and inductance matrices for a two-line system can be written as

$$[C] = \begin{bmatrix} C_{11} & -C_{12} \\ -C_{21} & C_{22} \end{bmatrix}$$

$$[L] = \begin{bmatrix} L_{11} & L_{12} \\ L_{21} & L_{22} \end{bmatrix}$$

(4.3.7)

with $C_{11} = C_{22}$, $C_{12} = C_{21}$, $L_{11} = L_{22}$, and $L_{12} = L_{21}$. Solving Equations 4.3.1 and 4.3.2, the propagation constants $\gamma_n = j\omega\beta_n$ $(n = 1, 2)$ of the two modes are given by

$$\gamma_1 = j\omega\sqrt{(L_{11} + L_{12})(C_{11} - C_{12})}$$

$$\gamma_2 = j\omega\sqrt{(L_{11} - L_{12})(C_{11} + C_{12})}$$

(4.3.8)

Then the voltage and current eigenvector matrices and the characteristic impedance matrix are given by

$$[S_v] = \begin{bmatrix} 1 & 1 \\ 1 & -1 \end{bmatrix}$$

$$[S_I] = \begin{bmatrix} \dfrac{1}{Z_1} & \dfrac{1}{Z_2} \\ \dfrac{1}{Z_1} & -\dfrac{1}{Z_2} \end{bmatrix}$$

(4.3.9)

$$[Z_c] = \left(\frac{1}{2}\right) \begin{bmatrix} Z_1 + Z_2 & Z_1 - Z_2 \\ Z_1 - Z_2 & Z_1 + Z_2 \end{bmatrix}$$

where

$$Z_1 = \left[\frac{L_{11} + L_{12}}{C_{11} - C_{12}} \right]^{1/2}$$

$$Z_2 = \left[\frac{L_{11} - L_{12}}{C_{11} + C_{12}} \right]^{1/2}$$

(4.3.10)

Now, suppose that the load impedances of the two lines are the same, that is, $Z_{L1} = Z_{L2} = Z_L$, the source impedances of the two lines are the same, that is, $Z_{G1} = Z_{G2} = Z_G$, and the signal source $E_1(t)$ is applied to line 1. Then the voltage transfer functions can be written as

$$\frac{V_{1,2}(x,\omega)}{E_1(\omega)} = \frac{1}{2}\left[\frac{1}{P_1}\left(\frac{e^{-\gamma_1 x} + \rho_{L1} e^{-\gamma_1(2l-x)}}{1 - \rho_{L1}\rho_{G1} e^{-2\gamma_1 l}} \right) \pm \frac{1}{P_2}\left(\frac{e^{-\gamma_2 x} + \rho_{L2} e^{-\gamma_2(2l-x)}}{1 - \rho_{L2}\rho_{G2} e^{-2\gamma_2 l}} \right) \right]$$

$$(4.3.11)$$

where

$$\rho_{Ln} = \frac{Z_L - Z_n}{Z_L + Z_n} \qquad n = 1, 2$$

$$\rho_{Gn} = \frac{Z_G - Z_n}{Z_G + Z_n} \qquad n = 1, 2 \qquad\qquad (4.3.12)$$

$$P_n = 1 + \frac{Z_G}{Z_n} \qquad n = 1, 2$$

If the source impedances applied to the two interconnection lines are each equal to Z_{cc} defined as the characteristic impedance of an isolated line, that is, $Z_G \approx Z_{cc}$, then $\rho_{Gn} \approx 0$ ($n = 1, 2$) and Equation 4.3.11 becomes

$$\frac{V_{1,2}(x,\omega)}{E_1(\omega)} = \frac{1}{2}\left[\frac{1}{P_1}\left(e^{-\gamma_1 x} + \rho_{L1} e^{-\gamma_1(2l-x)} \right) \pm \frac{1}{P_2}\left(e^{-\gamma_2 x} + \rho_{L2} e^{-\gamma_2(2l-x)} \right) \right]$$

$$(4.3.13)$$

Furthermore, if the load impedances of the two lines are each equal to Z_{cc}, then Equation 4.3.13 still holds but with $\rho_{Ln} \approx 0$ ($n = 1, 2$).

The closed-form expressions in the time domain can now be determined by the inverse Fourier transformations of the voltage transfer functions given by Equation 4.3.13:

$$V_{1,2}(x,t) = \frac{1}{2}\left[\left\{ \frac{1}{P_1} E_1\left(t - \frac{x}{v_1} \right) \pm \frac{1}{P_2} E_1\left(t - \frac{x}{v_2} \right) \right\} \right.$$

$$\left. + \left\{ \frac{\rho_{L1}}{P_1} E_1\left(t - \frac{2l-x}{v_1} \right) \pm \frac{\rho_{L2}}{P_2} E_1\left(t - \frac{2l-x}{v_2} \right) \right\} \right]$$

$$(4.3.14)$$

where $v_n = j\omega/\gamma_n = 1/\beta_n$ ($n = 1, 2$) are the two propagation velocities.

It is clear from Equation 4.3.14 that one source of crosstalk noise is the mismatch between propagation velocities of different modes. In addition, Equation 4.3.13 indicates that the coupling of the active line with its neighbors degrades the input signal as it travels along the active line.

4.3.3 Three-Line System

Consider a system of three interconnection lines with matched loads having three propagation modes. If the matrix $[A]$ denotes the product of the matrices $[L]$ and $[C]$, that is, $[A] = [L][C]$, then the propagation constants of the three modes will be given by

$$\gamma_1 = j\omega(A_{11} - A_{13})$$

$$\gamma_2 = \frac{1}{\sqrt{2}} j\omega \left[A_{11} + A_{13} + A_{22} + \sqrt{(A_{11} + A_{13} - A_{22})^2 + 8A_{12}A_{21}} \right]^{0.5}$$

$$\gamma_3 = \frac{1}{\sqrt{2}} j\omega \left[A_{11} + A_{13} + A_{22} - \sqrt{(A_{11} + A_{13} - A_{22})^2 + 8A_{12}A_{21}} \right]^{0.5}$$

$$(4.3.15)$$

and the voltage eigenvector matrix is given by

$$[S_v] = \begin{bmatrix} 1 & 1 & 1 \\ 0 & \eta_2 & \eta_3 \\ -1 & 1 & 1 \end{bmatrix} \tag{4.3.16}$$

where

$$\eta_2 = \frac{(A_{22} - A_{11} - A_{13}) + \sqrt{(A_{22} - A_{11} - A_{13})^2 + 8A_{12}A_{21}}}{2A_{12}}$$

and

$$\eta_3 = \frac{(A_{22} - A_{11} - A_{13}) - \sqrt{(A_{22} - A_{11} - A_{13})^2 + 8A_{12}A_{21}}}{2A_{12}} \tag{4.3.17}$$

If the input signal $E_1(t)$ is applied to line 1 (the active line), the source impedances are much smaller as compared to the line characteristic impedances Z_{cc}, that is, $Z_{Gn} = 0$, and if the load impedances are each equal to Z_{cc}, that is, $Z_{Ln} = Z_{cc}$ ($n = 1, 2, 3$), then closed-form expressions for the line voltage waveforms can be determined by following the same steps as for the two-line system:

$$V_1(x,t) = \frac{1}{2}\left[E_1\left(t - \frac{x}{v_1}\right) - \frac{\eta_3}{\eta_2 - \eta_3}E_1\left(t - \frac{x}{v_2}\right) + \frac{\eta_2}{\eta_2 - \eta_3}E_1\left(t - \frac{x}{v_3}\right) \right]$$

$$V_2(x,t) = \frac{1}{2}\left(\frac{\eta_2\eta_3}{\eta_2 - \eta_3}\right)\left[-E_1\left(t - \frac{x}{v_2}\right) + E_1\left(t - \frac{x}{v_3}\right) \right] \qquad (4.3.18)$$

$$V_3(x,t) = \frac{1}{2}\left[-E_1\left(t - \frac{x}{v_1}\right) - \frac{\eta_3}{\eta_2 - \eta_3}E_1\left(t - \frac{x}{v_2}\right) + \frac{\eta_2}{\eta_2 - \eta_3}E_1\left(t - \frac{x}{v_3}\right) \right]$$

4.3.4 Four-Line System

Consider a system of four interconnection lines with matched loads having four propagation modes. If the matrix $[A]$ denotes the product of the matrices $[L]$ and $[C]$, that is, $[A] = [L][C]$, then the propagation constants of the four modes will be given by

$$\gamma_1 = \frac{j\omega}{\sqrt{2}}\left[(A_{11} + A_{14} + A_{22} + A_{23}) \right.$$

$$\left. + \sqrt{(A_{11} + A_{14} - A_{22} - A_{23})^2 + 4(A_{12} + A_{13})(A_{21} + A_{31})} \right]^{0.5}$$

$$\gamma_2 = \frac{j\omega}{\sqrt{2}}\left[(A_{11} + A_{14} + A_{22} + A_{23}) \right.$$

$$\left. - \sqrt{(A_{11} + A_{14} - A_{22} - A_{23})^2 + 4(A_{12} + A_{13})(A_{21} + A_{31})} \right]^{0.5}$$

$$\gamma_3 = \frac{j\omega}{\sqrt{2}}\left[(-A_{11} + A_{14} + A_{22} - A_{23}) \right. \qquad (4.3.19)$$

$$\left. + \sqrt{(A_{11} - A_{14} - A_{22} + A_{23})^2 + 4(A_{12} - A_{13})(A_{21} - A_{31})} \right]^{0.5}$$

$$\gamma_4 = \frac{j\omega}{\sqrt{2}}\left[(-A_{11} + A_{14} + A_{22} - A_{23}) \right.$$

$$\left. - \sqrt{(A_{11} - A_{14} - A_{22} + A_{23})^2 + 4(A_{12} - A_{13})(A_{21} - A_{31})} \right]^{0.5}$$

and the voltage eigenvector is given by

$$
[S_v] = \begin{bmatrix} 1 & 1 & 1 & 1 \\ \eta_1 & \eta_2 & \eta_3 & \eta_4 \\ \eta_1 & \eta_2 & -\eta_3 & -\eta_4 \\ 1 & 1 & -1 & -1 \end{bmatrix}
\tag{4.3.20}
$$

where

$$
\eta_1 = \Big[\big(-A_{11} - A_{14} + A_{22} + A_{23} \big) \\
+ \sqrt{ \big(A_{11} + A_{14} - A_{22} - A_{23} \big)^2 + 4\big(A_{12} + A_{13} \big)\big(A_{21} + A_{31} \big) } \Big] \Big/ \\
\big[2\big(A_{12} + A_{13} \big) \big]
$$

$$
\eta_2 = \Big[\big(-A_{11} - A_{14} + A_{22} + A_{23} \big) \\
- \sqrt{ \big(A_{11} + A_{14} - A_{22} - A_{23} \big)^2 + 4\big(A_{12} + A_{13} \big)\big(A_{21} + A_{31} \big) } \Big] \Big/ \\
\big[2\big(A_{12} + A_{13} \big) \big]
$$

$$
\eta_3 = \Big[\big(-A_{11} + A_{14} + A_{22} - A_{23} \big) \\
+ \sqrt{ \big(A_{11} - A_{14} - A_{22} + A_{23} \big)^2 + 4\big(A_{12} - A_{13} \big)\big(A_{21} - A_{31} \big) } \Big] \Big/ \\
\big[2\big(A_{12} - A_{13} \big) \big]
$$

$$
\eta_4 = \Big[\big(-A_{11} + A_{14} + A_{22} - A_{23} \big) \\
- \sqrt{ \big(A_{11} - A_{14} - A_{22} + A_{23} \big)^2 + 4\big(A_{12} - A_{13} \big)\big(A_{21} - A_{31} \big) } \Big] \Big/ \\
\big[2\big(A_{12} - A_{13} \big) \big]
$$

$$
\tag{4.3.21}
$$

If the input signal $E_1(t)$ is applied to line 1 (the active line), the source impedances are much smaller as compared to the line characteristic impedances Z_{cc}, that is, $Z_{Gn} = 0$, and if the load impedances are each equal to Z_{cc}, that is, $Z_{Ln} = Z_{cc}$ ($n = 1, 2, 3, 4$), then closed-form expressions for the line voltage waveforms can be determined by following the same steps as for the two-line system:

$$V_1(x,t) = \frac{1}{2}\left[-\alpha_2 E_1\left(t - \frac{x}{v_1}\right) + \alpha_1 E_1\left(t - \frac{x}{v_2}\right)\right.$$

$$\left. -\alpha_4 E_1\left(t - \frac{x}{v_3}\right) + \alpha_3 E_1\left(t - \frac{x}{v_4}\right)\right]$$

$$V_2(x,t) = \frac{1}{2}\left[\beta_1\left\{-E_1\left(t - \frac{x}{v_1}\right) + E_1\left(t - \frac{x}{v_2}\right)\right\}\right.$$

$$\left. +\beta_2\left\{-E_1\left(t - \frac{x}{v_3}\right) + E_1\left(t - \frac{x}{v_4}\right)\right\}\right]$$

$$V_3(x,t) = \frac{1}{2}\left[\beta_1\left\{-E_1\left(t - \frac{x}{v_1}\right) + E_1\left(t - \frac{x}{v_2}\right)\right\}\right.$$

$$\left. -\beta_2\left\{-E_1\left(t - \frac{x}{v_3}\right) + E_1\left(t - \frac{x}{v_4}\right)\right\}\right] \qquad (4.3.22)$$

$$V_4(x,t) = \frac{1}{2}\left[-\alpha_2 E_1\left(t - \frac{x}{v_1}\right) + \alpha_1 E_1\left(t - \frac{x}{v_2}\right)\right.$$

$$\left. +\alpha_4 E_1\left(t - \frac{x}{v_3}\right) - \alpha_3 E_1\left(t - \frac{x}{v_4}\right)\right]$$

where

$$v_n = \frac{j\omega}{\gamma_n} \qquad n = 1,2,3,4$$

$$\alpha_1 = \frac{\eta_1}{\eta_1 - \eta_2}$$

$$\alpha_2 = \frac{\eta_2}{\eta_1 - \eta_2}$$

$$\alpha_3 = \frac{\eta_3}{\eta_3 - \eta_4} \qquad (4.3.23)$$

$$\alpha_4 = \frac{\eta_4}{\eta_3 - \eta_4}$$

$$\beta_1 = \alpha_1\eta_2 = \alpha_2\eta_1$$

$$\beta_2 = \alpha_3\eta_4 = \alpha_4\eta_3$$

4.3.5 Simulation Results

A schematic diagram of the coupled interconnections in high-speed circuits and systems is shown in Figure 4.3.1, and the layout of the N uniformly coupled 50-Ω interconnections used in the following simulations [4.16] is shown in Figure 4.3.2. Referring to Figure 4.3.1, we have set $Z_{Gn} = 0$ and $Z_{Ln} = 50\ \Omega$, where $n = 1, 2, \ldots, N$. In Figure 4.3.2, unless otherwise stated, the interconnections are assumed to be of negligible thickness, the substrate is alumina with permittivity $\varepsilon_r = 10$, the width of each interconnection W is equal to the substrate thickness H, the distance between any two adjacent conductors S is $1.5H$, the length of each coupled line is 20 cm, and a ramp signal having an amplitude of 1 V and a rise time of 100 ps is applied to line 1 (the active line).

For a system of two interconnection lines, the time domain voltage waveforms at the load ends of the active line and the neighboring line determined by Equation 4.3.14 are shown in Figure 4.3.3. The capacitance

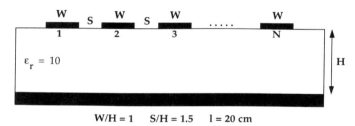

W/H = 1   S/H = 1.5   l = 20 cm

FIGURE 4.3.2 Layout of N uniformly coupled 50-Ω interconnections on an alumina substrate [4.16]. (© 1990 IEEE)

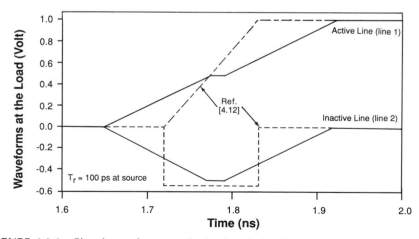

FIGURE 4.3.3 Signal waveforms at the load ends for the two-line system shown in Figure 4.3.2 with $N = 2$ [4.16]. (© 1990 IEEE)

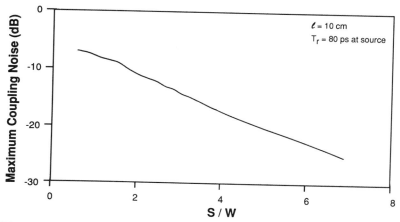

FIGURE 4.3.4 Amplitude of the load end coupling noise as a function of the layout parameter S/W for the two-line system shown in Figure 4.3.2 with $N = 2$ [4.16]. (© 1990 IEEE)

and inductance matrices used in these results, determined by the Green's function method, are

$$[C] = \begin{bmatrix} 1.737 & -0.073 \\ -0.073 & 1.737 \end{bmatrix} \text{pF/cm}$$

$$[L] = \begin{bmatrix} 4.276 & 0.529 \\ 0.529 & 4.276 \end{bmatrix} \text{nH/cm}$$

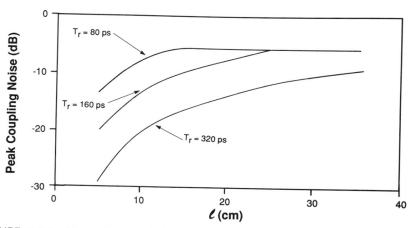

FIGURE 4.3.5 Dependences of the peak coupling noise on the length l of the coupled lines of the two-line system for different rise time T_r values of the signal source [4.16]. (© 1990 IEEE)

For the sake of comparison, Figure 4.3.3 also shows the analysis results from reference [4.12] where weak coupling was assumed. It is clear that the weak-coupling approximation can result in significant errors in crosstalk calculations. For the two-line system, the amplitude of the coupling noise at the load end as a function of the layout parameter S/W is plotted in Figure 4.3.4. Figure 4.3.5 shows the influence of the length of the coupled lines and the rise time of the input signal on the amplitude of the coupling noise.

For a system of three interconnection lines, the time domain voltage waveforms at the load ends of the active line and the neighboring lines

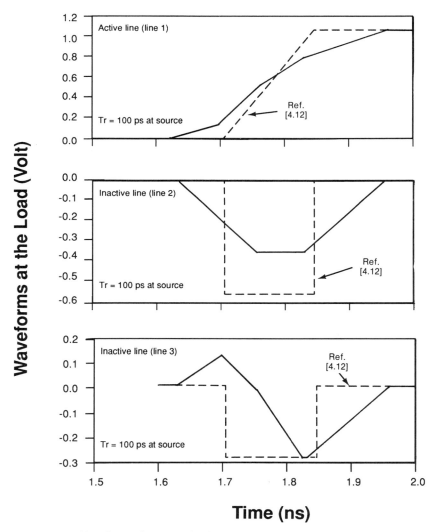

FIGURE 4.3.6   Signal waveforms at the load ends for the three-line system shown in Figure 4.3.2 with $N = 3$ [4.16]. (© 1990 IEEE)

determined by Equation 4.3.18 are shown in Figure 4.3.6. The capacitance and inductance matrices used in these results, determined by the Green's function method, are

$$[C] = \begin{bmatrix} 1.737 & -0.073 & -0.005 \\ -0.073 & 1.741 & -0.073 \\ -0.005 & -0.073 & 1.737 \end{bmatrix} \text{pF/cm}$$

$$[L] = \begin{bmatrix} 4.276 & 0.527 & 0.159 \\ 0.527 & 4.269 & 0.527 \\ 0.159 & 0.527 & 4.276 \end{bmatrix} \text{nH/cm}$$

The results assuming weak coupling from reference [4.12] are also included in Figure 4.3.6 and indicate that this approximation is not satisfactory for typical interconnection configurations.

For a system of four interconnection lines, the time domain voltage waveforms at the load ends of the active line and the disturbed lines determined by Equation 4.3.22 are shown in Figure 4.3.7. The capacitance and inductance matrices used in these results, determined by the Green's function method are

$$[C] = \begin{bmatrix} 1.737 & -0.073 & -0.004 & -0.002 \\ -0.073 & 1.742 & -0.073 & -0.004 \\ -0.004 & -0.073 & 1.742 & -0.073 \\ -0.002 & -0.004 & -0.073 & 1.737 \end{bmatrix} \text{pF/cm}$$

$$[L] = \begin{bmatrix} 4.276 & 0.527 & 0.158 & 0.072 \\ 0.527 & 4.269 & 0.526 & 0.158 \\ 0.158 & 0.526 & 4.269 & 0.527 \\ 0.072 & 0.158 & 0.527 & 4.276 \end{bmatrix} \text{nH/cm}$$

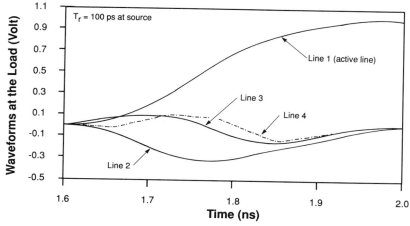

FIGURE 4.3.7 Signal waveforms at the load ends for the four-line system shown in Figure 4.3.2 with $N = 4$ [4.16]. (© 1990 IEEE)

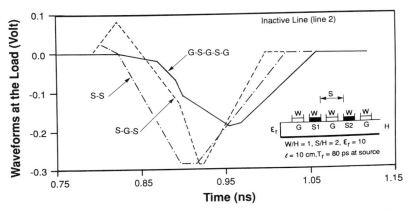

FIGURE 4.3.8 Load waveforms for the signal–signal (S–S), signal–ground–signal (S–G–S), and ground–signal–ground–signal–ground (G–S–G–S–G) configurations [4.16]. (© 1990 IEEE)

The reduction of crosstalk by placing grounded conductors between the signal lines is demonstrated in Figure 4.3.8 which shows the load voltage waveforms on line 2 when a ramp signal having an amplitude of 1 V and a rise time of 80 ps is applied to line 1 for the cases of two signal lines only (S–S), two signal lines with a grounded shield conductor in between (G–G–S), and two signal lines with grounded shield conductors in between as well as on both sides (G–S–G–S–G). It is clear from the simulation results that the grounded conductors should be placed on both sides of each signal line to reduce crosstalk significantly. However, it should be noted that the insertion of ground conductors not only increases the complexity of the circuit but also causes waveform distortion for the signal on the active line.

4.4 TRANSMISSION LINE ANALYSIS OF PARALLEL MULTILEVEL INTERCONNECTIONS

In this section the crosstalk among parallel multilevel interconnections, including single-, bi-, and trilevel configurations, is studied by modeling the interconnections as transmission lines. The model has been utilized to study the dependence of the crosstalk voltage on the interconnection parameters such as their lengths, widths, separations, interlevel distances, driving transistor resistance, and load capacitance.

4.4.1 The Model

As shown in Figure 4.4.1, the interconnection line can be modeled as a transmission line driven by a unit step voltage source having resistance R_s,

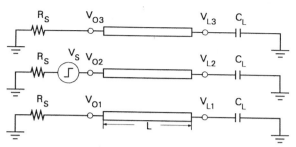

FIGURE 4.4.1 Interconnection driven by a unit step voltage source V_s of resistance R_s and terminated by the load capacitance C_L. The terminal endings on the neighboring interconnections are also shown. Interconnection capacitances as well as the capacitive and inductive couplings between the interconnections are not shown in the figure.

loaded by the capacitance C_L, and coupled to the neighboring interconnection lines by the mutual capacitances and inductances (not shown in the figure). The resistance R_s is determined by the dimensions of the driving transistor, and the capacitance C_L is determined by the parasitic capacitances of the transistor loading the interconnection line. For interconnection lines printed on or embedded in a semi-insulating GaAs substrate, quasi-TEM is the dominant mode of wave propagation, and the transmission line equations are given by

$$\frac{\partial}{\partial x}V(x,t) = -\left[R + L\frac{\partial}{\partial t}\right]I(x,t) \tag{4.4.1}$$

$$\frac{\partial}{\partial x}I(x,t) = -\left[G + C\frac{\partial}{\partial t}\right]V(x,t) \tag{4.4.2}$$

where L and C are the inductance and capacitance matrices per unit length of the interconnections, R is determined by the resistance per unit length of the interconnections, and G is the conductance matrix determined by the conductivity of the substrate. For a semi-insulating GaAs substrate, G can be neglected. The matrices L and C can be determined by the network analog method developed earlier [2.25]. In the s domain, Equations 4.4.1 and 4.4.2 can be written as

$$\frac{d}{dx}V(x,s) = -[R + sL]I(x,s) \tag{4.4.3}$$

$$\frac{d}{dx}I(x,s) = -[G + sC]V(x,s) \tag{4.4.4}$$

Defining

$$Z = R + sL$$

and

$$Y = G + sC$$

Equations 4.4.3 and 4.4.4 can be solved in the s domain, yielding

$$V(x, s) = e^{-\sqrt{ZY}(x)}V_i(s) + e^{-\sqrt{ZY}(L-x)}V_r(s) \qquad (4.4.5)$$

$$I(x, s) = \sqrt{\frac{Y}{Z}} \left[e^{-\sqrt{ZY}(x)}V_i(s) - e^{-\sqrt{ZY}(L-x)}V_r(s) \right] \qquad (4.4.6)$$

In Equations 4.4.5 and 4.4.6, L is the total length of the transmission line, $V_i(s)$ is the voltage vector of the incident wave at $x = 0$, and $V_r(s)$ is the voltage vector of the reflected wave at $x = L$. At the end points, $x = 0$ and $x = L$, Equations 4.4.5 and 4.4.6 yield

$$V(0, s) = V_i(s) + e^{-\sqrt{ZY}L}V_r(s) \qquad (4.4.7)$$

$$I(0, s) = \sqrt{\frac{Y}{Z}} \left[V_i(s) - e^{-\sqrt{ZY}L}V_r(s) \right] \qquad (4.4.8)$$

$$V(L, s) = e^{-\sqrt{ZY}L}V_i(s) + V_r(s) \qquad (4.4.9)$$

$$I(L, s) = \sqrt{\frac{Y}{Z}} \left[e^{-\sqrt{ZY}L}V_i(s) - V_r(s) \right] \qquad (4.4.10)$$

Incorporating the boundary conditions determined by the lumped circuit elements connected to the interconnection line, that is,

$$V(0, s) = V_s(s) - R_s I(0, s) \qquad (4.4.11)$$

and

$$V(L, s) = \frac{1}{sC_L}I(L, s) \qquad (4.4.12)$$

we have

$$V_i(s) + e^{-\sqrt{ZY}L}V_r(s) = (-R_s)\sqrt{\frac{Y}{Z}} \left[V_i(s) - e^{-\sqrt{ZY}L}V_r(s) \right] + V_s(s)$$

$$(4.4.13)$$

and

$$e^{-\sqrt{ZYL}}V_i(s) + V_r(s) = -\left(\frac{1}{sC_L}\right)\sqrt{\frac{Y}{Z}}\left[e^{-\sqrt{ZYL}}V_i(s) - V_r(s)\right] \quad (4.4.14)$$

which can be solved to yield, for $V_i(s)$ and $V_r(s)$,

$$V_r(s) = V_s(s)\left\{-\left[1 + R_s\sqrt{\frac{Y}{Z}}\right]\left[e^{\sqrt{ZYL}}\right]\left[1 - \frac{1}{sC_L}\sqrt{\frac{Y}{Z}}\right]^{-1}\left[1 + \frac{1}{sC_L}\sqrt{\frac{Y}{Z}}\right]\right.$$

$$\left. + \left[1 - R_s\sqrt{\frac{Y}{Z}}\right]\left[\frac{1}{e^{\sqrt{ZYL}}}\right]\right\}^{-1} \quad (4.4.15)$$

$$V_i(s) = -\left[e^{-\sqrt{ZYL}} - \frac{1}{sC_L}\sqrt{\frac{Y}{Z}}e^{-\sqrt{ZYL}}\right]^{-1}\left[1 + \frac{1}{sC_L}e^{-\sqrt{ZYL}}\right]V_r(s)$$

$$(4.4.16)$$

The values for $V_i(s)$ and $V_r(s)$ can be substituted into Equations 4.4.7 to 4.4.10 to obtain expressions for the current and voltage at $x = 0$ and $x = L$ in the s domain. The load voltage is the element of $V(L, s)$ that corresponds to the line on which the voltage source is applied. The other elements of $V(L, s)$ represent crosstalk voltages induced on the neighboring interconnection lines.

In principle, the time domain response can be obtained by the inverse Laplace transformation or by the Fourier transformation. However, the Fourier transformation results in errors due to the finite number of terms included in the summation. Therefore, the inverse Laplace transformation technique is used. If $F(s)$ denotes the Laplace transform of $f(t)$, then

$$F(s) = \int_0^\infty f(t)e^{-st}\,dt \quad (4.4.17)$$

It can be shown [4.21] that, for t on the interval $(0, 2T)$,

$$f(t) = h(t) - E(t) \quad (4.4.18)$$

where $h(t)$ is given by

$$h(t) = \frac{1}{T}\left\{\frac{F(a)}{2} + \sum_{k=1}^\infty \left(\text{Re}\left[F\left(a + \frac{k\pi t}{T}\right)\cos\left(\frac{k\pi t}{T}\right)\right]\right.\right.$$

$$\left.\left. - \text{Im}\left[F\left(a + \frac{k\pi t}{T}\right)\sin\left(\frac{k\pi t}{T}\right)\right]\right)\right\} \quad (4.4.19)$$

and the error $E(t)$ is bounded by

$$E(t) \leq M \left[\frac{e^{\alpha t}}{e^{2T(a-\alpha)} - 1} \right] \qquad (4.4.20)$$

where $1/T$ is the frequency step, M is a constant, and α is related to $f(t)$ such that $f(t)$ is an exponential of order a (i.e., $|f(t)| \leq Ce^{\alpha t}$). When $2T(a - \alpha)$ is large enough and we want our precision to be ε, then a can be chosen to be [4.21]

$$a = \alpha - \frac{\ln(\varepsilon)}{2T} \qquad (4.4.21)$$

Choosing a suitable value of T for the desired accuracy depends on the time range of interest (e.g., 0 to t_{max}) and the computation time. When t is much smaller than $2T$, the approximation of $f(t)$ by Equation 4.4.19 converges very slowly because the frequency step determined by $1/T$ is too small and we need to include many terms for the summation to converge. On the other hand, if t is too close to $2T$, then the error due to the term $E(t)$ in Equation 4.4.18 becomes large as can be seen from Equation 4.4.20. A good choice for T lies in the range $(0.8t_{max}, 1.2t_{max})$.

Numerical computations show that if we apply the inverse Laplace transformation directly, then the summation converges very slowly for small values of t. This is because the frequency step determined by $1/T$ is too small for small t. To solve this problem, we can divide the time range $[0, t_{max}]$ into several time ranges $[0, p^k t_{max}], (p^k t_{max}, p^{k-1} t_{max}], \ldots, (p t_{max}, t_{max}]$ and choose a different value of T for each time range such that T is not too large and the summation in Equation 4.4.19 converges faster. The value of p can be determined by a compromise between the desired accuracy and the computation time and is chosen to be 0.8.

Summation in Equation 4.4.19 usually converges very slowly; it takes more than 5000 terms to achieve an accuracy of four significant digits. To overcome this problem, we can use the Wynn algorithm [4.21, 4.22] to accelerate the summation. The algorithm can be described as follows:

For a summation series S defined as

$$S = \sum_{n=1}^{m} a_n \qquad m = 1, 2, 3, \ldots \qquad (4.4.22)$$

we define a two-dimensional array as

$$\varepsilon_{p+1}^{(m)} = \varepsilon_{p-1}^{(m)} + \frac{1}{\varepsilon_p^{(m)} - \varepsilon_p^{(m-1)}} \qquad p = 1, 2, 3, \ldots \qquad (4.4.23)$$

with

$$\varepsilon_0^{(m)} = 0 \qquad (4.4.24)$$

and

$$\varepsilon_1^{(m)} = S_m \qquad (4.4.25)$$

In principle, $\varepsilon_3^{(m)}, \varepsilon_5^{(m)}, \varepsilon_7^{(m)}, \varepsilon_9^{(m)}, \ldots$ will be better approximations for the summation S_m in Equation 4.4.22. From numerical experiments, it can be found that $\varepsilon_9^{(m)}$ is the best choice for the present problem because higher-order transformations result in rounding errors.

4.4.2 The Program DCMPVI

A listing of the computer program DCMPVI, based on the inverse Laplace transformation technique using the Wynn algorithm and the improved time range selection described previously and written in FORTRAN, is presented in Appendix 4.1. The interconnection capacitances and inductances used in the program are determined by using the network analog method [2.25].

4.4.3 Numerical Simulations Using DCMPVI

The program DCMPVI has been used to study the dependence of crosstalk among the interconnections in the configurations shown in Figures 4.4.2a, b, and c. One of the parameters is varied in a specific range, whereas the others are kept fixed at their typical values. Typical values of the various parameters are as follows: interconnection lengths (L), 1000 μm; interconnection widths (W), 1 μm; interconnection separations (S), 1 μm; interconnection metal resistivity (ρ), 3 $\mu\Omega \cdot$ cm; interlevel distances $(T_{12}$ and $T_{23})$, 2 μm; thickness of the GaAs substrate (T), 200 μm; driving transistor output resistance or source resistance (R_s), 100 Ω; and loading transistor input capacitance or load capacitance (C_L), 100 fF. The thickness of each of the interconnection lines is kept at $0.5W$. In the following discussion, the single-level interconnection configuration shown in Figure 4.4.2a is assumed unless specified otherwise, and the source is applied to one end of the second interconnection on the first level.

Magnitudes of the crosstalk voltages at the load on the first or the third interconnection as functions of time in the range 0 to 200 ps for several interconnection length values are shown in Figure 4.4.3. Figure 4.4.4 shows the dependence of the maximum crosstalk voltage on the interconnection length in the range 20 to 1000 μm. This figure shows that crosstalk increases almost linearly with length in the range 20 to 1000 μm. This is because the capacitance coupling the interconnections increases almost linearly with length. For several interconnection widths, the variations of the crosstalk

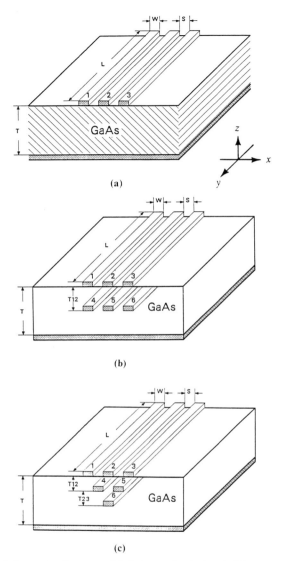

FIGURE 4.4.2   Schematic diagram of (a) three single-level, (b) six bilevel, and (c) six trilevel interconnection configurations.

voltages with time in the range 0 to 200 ps are shown in Figure 4.4.5, and Figure 4.4.6 shows that the maximum crosstalk voltage is almost a logarithmic function of the interconnection width in the range 0.5 to 5 μm. As functions of time in the range 0 to 200 ps, the crosstalk voltages for several interconnection separations are shown in Figure 4.4.7, and Figure 4.4.8 shows the dependence of the maximum crosstalk voltage on the interconnection separa-

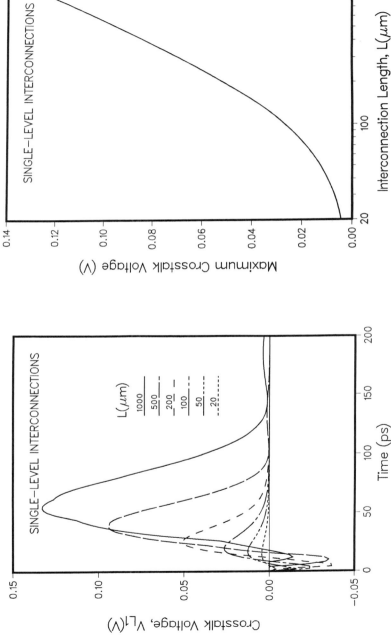

FIGURE 4.4.3 Crosstalk voltage waveforms in the range 0 to 200 ps for several interconnection lengths for the single-level interconnections shown in Figure 4.4.2a.

FIGURE 4.4.4 Dependence of the maximum crosstalk voltage on the interconnection length for the single-level interconnections shown in Figure 4.4.2a.

365

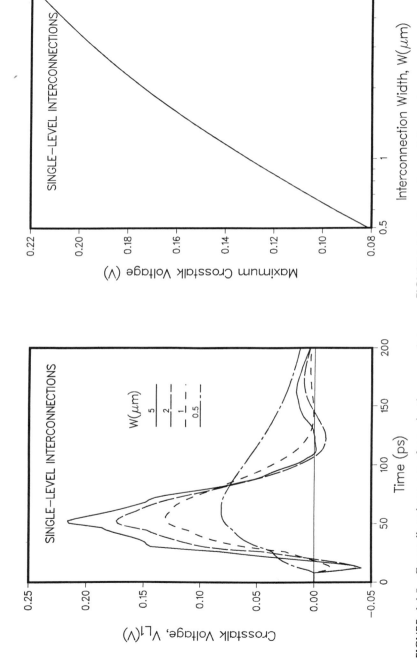

FIGURE 4.4.5 Crosstalk voltage waveforms in the range 0 to 200 ps for several interconnection widths for the single-level interconnections shown in Figure 4.4.2a.

FIGURE 4.4.6 Dependence of the maximum crosstalk voltage on the interconnection width for the single-level interconnections shown in Figure 4.4.2a.

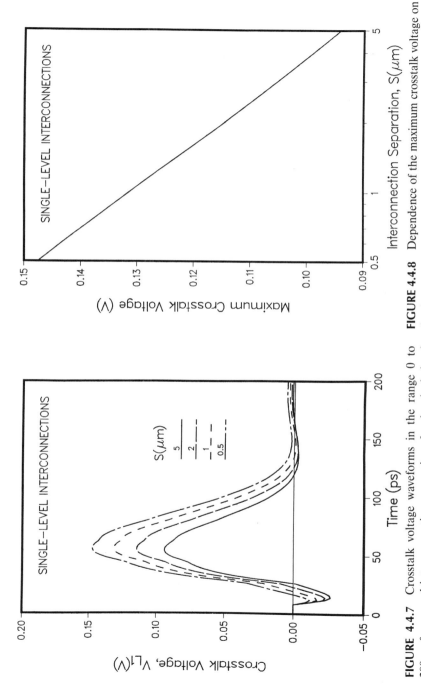

FIGURE 4.4.7 Crosstalk voltage waveforms in the range 0 to 200 ps for several interconnection separations for the single-level interconnections shown in Figure 4.4.2a.

FIGURE 4.4.8 Dependence of the maximum crosstalk voltage on the interconnection separation for the single-level interconnections shown in Figure 4.4.2a.

tion in the range 0.5 to 5 μm. This figure shows that for a separation of 0.5 μm and for typical values of the other parameters, the maximum crosstalk voltage is nearly 15 percent of the input signal, which may be too large to allow error-free operation of some integrated circuits.

Crosstalk voltages as functions of time in the range 0 to 200 ps for several values of the thickness of the GaAs substrate are shown in Figure 4.4.9, and the dependence of the maximum crosstalk voltage on the substrate thickness in the range 5 to 200 μm is shown in Figure 4.4.10. Crosstalk decreases somewhat with the decrease in substrate thickness because of the increased shielding of the coupling field lines by the ground plane. For various interconnection metal resistivity values, the variations of the crosstalk voltage on time in the range 0 to 500 ps are shown in Figure 4.4.11, and the dependence of the maximum crosstalk voltage on the resistivity in the range 0.1 to 200 $\mu\Omega \cdot$ cm is shown in Figure 4.4.12. This figure shows that the crosstalk decreases when the interconnection metal resistivity is increased. This is perhaps because increasing the interconnection resistance filters the high-frequency components from the input signal and their effect on the neighboring lines is reduced.

For several source resistance values, for example, the output resistance of the driving transistor, the crosstalk voltages in the time range 0 to 200 ps are shown in Figure 4.4.13, and Figure 4.4.14 shows the dependence of the maximum crosstalk voltage on the source resistance in the range 0.1 to 1000 Ω. The effect of increasing the source resistance on the crosstalk can be understood in the same way as that of the interconnection resistivity; that is, the RC filtering effect on the input signal increases, thereby reducing the crosstalk voltage. Variations of the crosstalk voltage with time in the range 0 to 200 ps for several load capacitance values, for example, the input capacitance of the loading transistor, are shown in Figure 4.4.15, and Figure 4.4.16 shows the dependence of the maximum crosstalk voltage on the load capacitance in the range 5 to 1000 fF. Figure 4.4.16 shows that the crosstalk decreases rapidly with the increase in load capacitance. This is again due to increased filtering of the high-frequency components on the source line, resulting in reduced induced voltages on the neighboring lines.

When the number of interconnection lines in the single-level configuration of Figure 4.4.2a is increased from 3 to 5, Figure 4.4.17 shows that the crosstalk voltage at the load end of the first-neighbor interconnections is reduced somewhat. This is due to the shielding effect of the second-neighbor lines. Crosstalk voltages induced at the load ends of the first- and second-neighbor interconnections in the time range 0 to 200 ps are shown in Figure 4.4.18. This figure shows that the crosstalk on the second-neighbor interconnections is much less than that on the first-neighbor interconnections. This is because the coupling capacitance between the source line and the second-neighbor interconnection line is less than that for the first-neighbor interconnection.

The crosstalk can also be calculated for the bilevel interconnection configuration shown in Figure 4.4.2b. The crosstalk voltages induced at the load

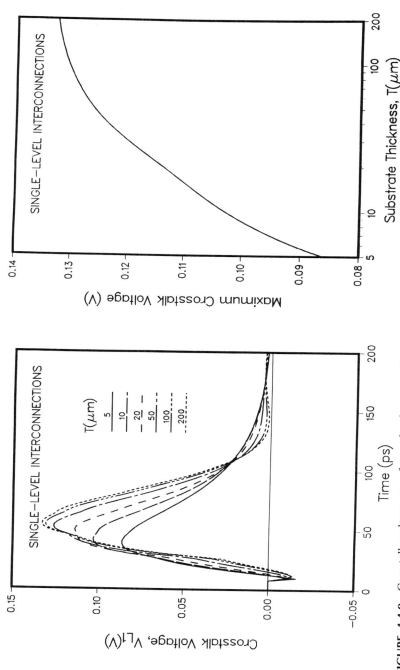

FIGURE 4.4.9 Crosstalk voltage waveforms in the range 0 to 200 ps for several substrate thicknesses for the single-level interconnections shown in Figure 4.4.2a.

FIGURE 4.4.10 Dependence of the maximum crosstalk voltage on the substrate thickness for the single-level interconnections shown in Figure 4.4.2a.

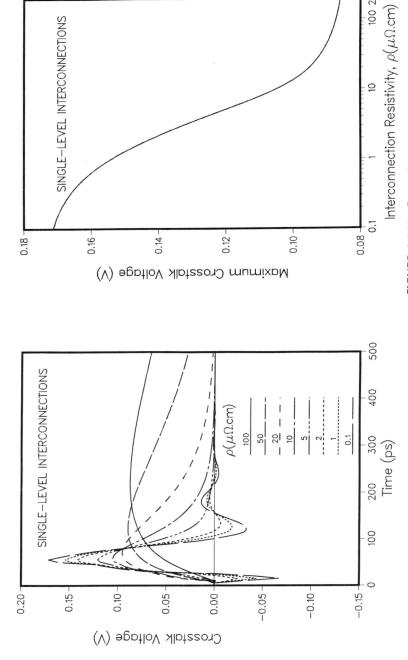

FIGURE 4.4.11 Crosstalk voltage waveforms in the range 0 to 500 ps for several interconnection metal resistivities for the single-level interconnections shown in Figure 4.4.2a.

FIGURE 4.4.12 Dependence of the maximum crosstalk voltage on the interconnection metal resistivity for the single-level interconnections shown in Figure 4.4.2a.

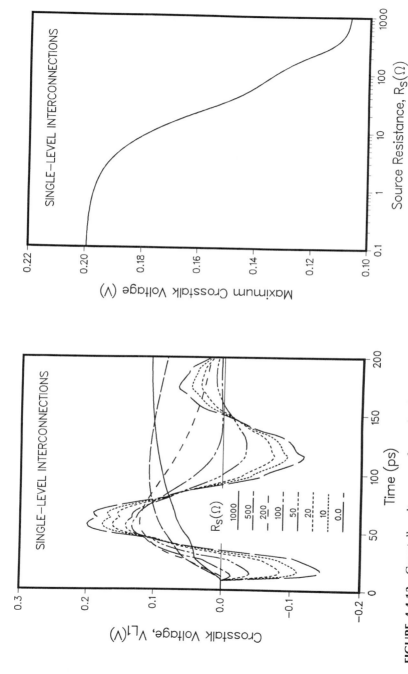

FIGURE 4.4.13 Crosstalk voltage waveforms in the range 0 to 200 ps for several source resistances for the single-level interconnections shown in Figure 4.4.2a.

FIGURE 4.4.14 Dependence of the maximum crosstalk voltage on the source resistance for the single-level interconnections shown in Figure 4.4.2a.

371

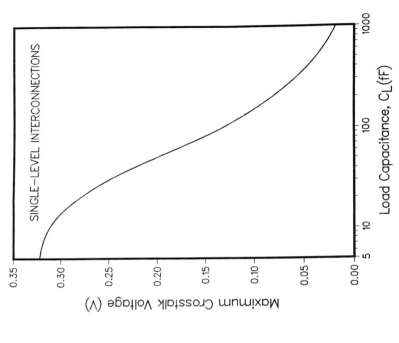

FIGURE 4.4.15 Crosstalk voltage waveforms in the range 0 to 200 ps for several load capacitances for the single-level interconnections shown in Figure 4.4.2*a*.

FIGURE 4.4.16 Dependence of the maximum crosstalk voltage on the load capacitance for the single-level interconnections shown in Figure 4.4.2*a*.

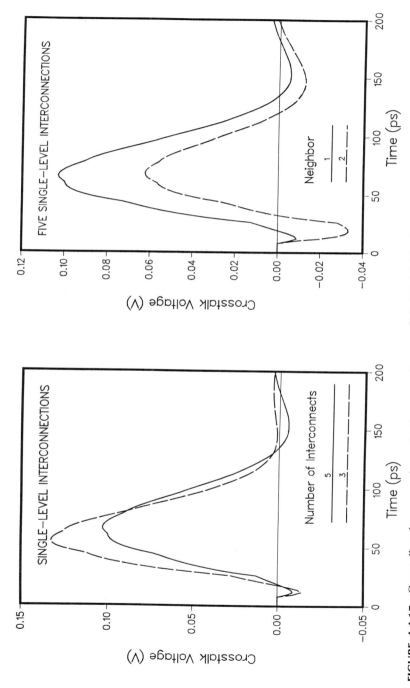

FIGURE 4.4.17 Crosstalk voltage waveforms in the range 0 to 200 ps for three and five interconnections in the single-level configuration shown in Figure 4.4.2a.

FIGURE 4.4.18 Crosstalk voltage waveforms in the range 0 to 200 ps at the load ends of the first- and second-neighbor lines for the five single-level interconnections.

373

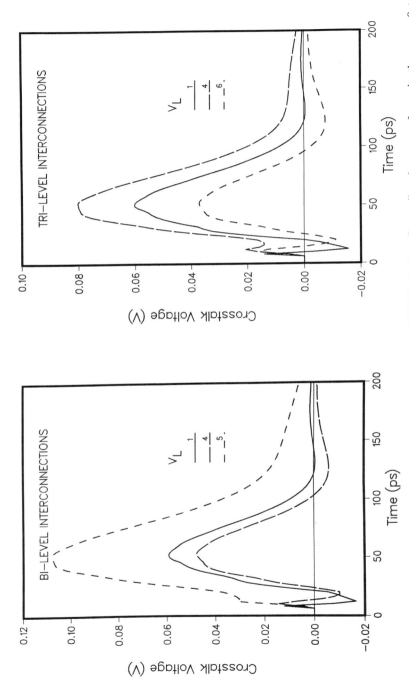

FIGURE 4.4.19 Crosstalk voltage waveforms in the range 0 to 200 ps for the first, fourth, and fifth lines in the bilevel interconnection configuration shown in Figure 4.4.2b.

FIGURE 4.4.20 Crosstalk voltage waveforms in the range 0 to 200 ps for the first, fourth, and sixth lines in the trilevel interconnection configuration shown in Figure 4.4.2c.

ends of the first, fourth, and fifth interconnections in the time range 0 to 200 ps are shown in Figure 4.4.19. It can be seen that the crosstalk on the fifth interconnection is the largest, whereas that on the fourth interconnection is the smallest. This is because the fifth interconnection line is located just below the source interconnection which results in the coupling capacitance being the largest, whereas the coupling capacitance between the source interconnection and the fourth interconnection is the smallest due to the shielding effects of the first and fifth interconnections. Comparison of these results with those for single-level interconnections shows that the crosstalk voltages induced on first-neighbor interconnections in the bilevel configuration are almost half of those in the single-level configuration. For the trilevel interconnection configuration, the crosstalk results are shown in Figure 4.4.20 and can be understood in the same way as those for the bilevel interconnection.

4.5   ANALYSIS OF CROSSING INTERCONNECTIONS

In this section, the crosstalk signal induced in each of the crossing lines embedded in the substrate due to the signal source applied to the main (driven) line printed on the top plane will be studied. Only the capacitive couplings will be considered in this analysis.

4.5.1   Mathematical Analysis

A schematic diagram of the crossing interconnections analyzed in this section is shown in Figure 4.5.1. A driving source is applied only to the main line on the top plane, and the crossing lines in the second plane are not energized. As in the previous chapter, one way of analyzing this interconnection configuration is to divide it into three sections—the source section, the crossing

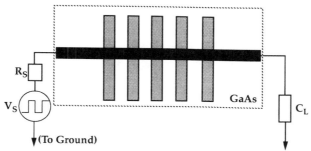

FIGURE 4.5.1 Schematic diagram of the bilevel crossing interconnections analyzed in this section. Each of the crossing interconnections is also terminated by source resistance R_s on one side and load capacitance C_L on the other side (not shown in the figure).

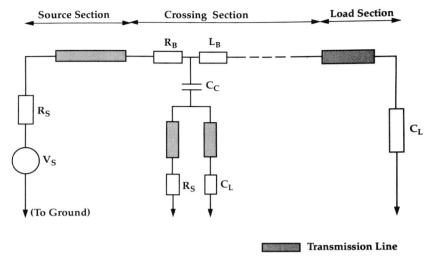

FIGURE 4.5.2   Equivalent circuit of the bilevel crossing interconnections, including capacitive couplings. Inductive couplings are not included.

section, and the load section—with the difference that each of the two sections of every crossing line on either side of the point of coupling with the main line should be modeled as a transmission line. The equivalent circuit used for studying the crosstalk in the crossing interconnections is shown in Figure 4.5.2. The various elements are defined as follows:

V_s = voltage source

R_s = source resistance

L_B = self-inductance of the portion of the driven line between two consecutive crossing lines

R_B = resistance of the portion of the driven line between two consecutive crossing lines

C_c = coupling capacitance between the main line and a crossing line

R_{cl} = line resistance of a crossing line on the left side of the main line

R_{cr} = line resistance of a crossing line on the right side of the main line

L_{cl} = self-inductance of a crossing line on the left side of the main line

L_{cr} = self-inductance of a crossing line on the right side of the main line

C_L = load capacitance

R_r = resistance of the portion of the main line after the crossing lines (the load section portion)

L_r = self-inductance of the portion of the main line after the crossing lines (the load section portion)

C_r = ground capacitance of the portion of the main line after the crossing lines (the load section portion)

Other symbols are defined as they appear. Following the same steps as in Section 3.4.1, the voltage and current in the s domain at the end of the transmission line section, that is, at $x = l$, are given by

$$V(l, s) = e^{-\sqrt{ZY}l}V_i(s) + V_r(s)$$

$$I(l, s) = \sqrt{\frac{Y}{Z}}\left[e^{-\sqrt{ZY}l}V_i(s) - V_r(s)\right]$$

where

$$V_r(s) = \cfrac{V_s(s)e^{-\sqrt{ZY}l}\left[1 - Z_{TX}\sqrt{\dfrac{Y}{Z}}\right]}{\left[1 - R_s\sqrt{\dfrac{Y}{Z}}\right]\left[1 - Z_{TX}\sqrt{\dfrac{Y}{Z}}\right]e^{-2\sqrt{ZY}l} - \left[1 + R_s\sqrt{\dfrac{Y}{Z}}\right]\left[1 + Z_{TX}\sqrt{\dfrac{Y}{Z}}\right]}$$

$$V_i(s) = -\cfrac{1 + Z_{TX}e^{-\sqrt{ZY}l}}{\left[1 - Z_{TX}\sqrt{\dfrac{Y}{Z}}\right]e^{-\sqrt{ZY}l}}V_r(s)$$

with

$$Z_{TX} = Z_{p1}\|Z_X + R_B$$

$$V_s(s) = \frac{1}{s}; \text{ for a unit step input source}$$

$$V_s(s) = \frac{(1 - e^{-sT})}{s}; \text{ for an input pulse train of period } T.$$

Z_x is the impedance of the crossing line as seen by the current flowing in the driven line given by

$$Z_x = \frac{1}{sC_c} + (R_{cl} + sL_{cl} + R_s)\|\left(R_{cr} + sL_{cr} + \frac{1}{sC_L}\right)$$

and the partial load Z_{p1} is given by

$$Z_{p1} = Z_{p2}\|Z_x + Z_B$$

where

$$Z_B = R_B + sL_B$$

$$Z_{p2} = Z_{p3}\|Z_x + Z_B$$

and so on, until

$$Z_{p(n-2)} = Z_{p(n-1)} \| Z_x + Z_B$$

$$Z_{p(n-1)} = Z_{pn} \| Z_x + Z_B$$

and

$$Z_{pn} = R_r + \frac{1}{sC_r} \left\| \left(sL_r + \frac{1}{sC_L} \right) + sL_B \right.$$

The current $I(l, s)$ is the s-domain input current for the crossing section.

In the crossing section the driven line on the top plane and the second-level interconnections embedded in the substrate cross each other. This section is driven by the output of the transmission line section, and the output of this section drives the next section, that is, the load section. The driven line is coupled to the crossing lines by the coupling capacitances which depend on the crossing area (which in turn depends on the line widths and the crossing angle), the interlevel separation, and the substrate dielectric constant. It is assumed that all the interconnection lines are of the same width, thickness, and material. The algorithm can be easily modified for different situations.

After some manipulation it can be shown that the crosstalk voltage on the jth crossing line, that is, the voltage across the load capacitance on the jth crossing line, is given by the expression

$$V_{\text{cross}, j}(s) = \sqrt{\frac{Y}{Z}} \left[e^{(-\sqrt{ZY})l'} V_i'(s) - V_r'(s) \right] \frac{1}{sC_L}$$

where l' is the length of the jth crossing line from the point of its coupling with the main line to its load C_L,

$$Z = R + sL$$
$$Y = G + sC$$

$$V_r'(s) = \frac{V_{s,j}(s) e^{-\sqrt{ZY}l'} \left[1 - \frac{1}{sC_L} \sqrt{\frac{Y}{Z}} \right]}{\left[1 - \frac{1}{sC_L} \sqrt{\frac{Y}{Z}} \right] e^{-2\sqrt{ZY}l'} - \left[1 + \frac{1}{sC_L} \sqrt{\frac{Y}{Z}} \right]}$$

$$V_i'(s) = -\frac{1 + \frac{1}{sC_L} e^{-\sqrt{ZY}l'}}{\left[1 - \frac{1}{sC_L} \sqrt{\frac{Y}{Z}} \right] e^{-\sqrt{ZY}l'}} V_r'(s)$$

and the equivalent of the source voltage for the jth crossing line is given by

$$V_{s,j}(s) = (I_j - I_{j-1})\left(Z_x - \frac{1}{sC_c}\right)$$

where I_j is the current flowing in the driven line after "seeing" the jth crossing line. The currents I_j $(j = 1, 2, \ldots, n)$ are given by

$$I_1 = I_{TX}\frac{Z_x}{Z_x + Z_{p1}}$$

$$I_2 = I_1\frac{Z_x}{Z_x + Z_{p2}}$$

and so on, until

$$I_n = I_{n-1}\frac{Z_x}{Z_x + Z_L'}$$

where $I_{TX}(= I(l, s))$ is the current entering the crossing section and $Z_L'(= Z_{pn})$ is the total impedance of the load section. I_n represents the current flowing into the load section.

4.5.2   Simulation Results

As mentioned earlier, the crosstalk effect can be studied by analyzing the plot of crosstalk voltage for a given set of interconnection parameters in a specific time range and by plotting the maximum crosstalk voltage as a function of the interconnection parameter under investigation. To simulate the crosstalk effects in the embedded crossing interconnections due to a driven interconnection printed on top of the GaAs substrate, a computer program called SPBIGV is presented in Appendix 4.2. It incorporates the steps outlined previously to find $V_{cross}(s)$ and then uses the Padé approximation [1.52] to carry out the inverse Laplace transformation. In the following results one of the parameters is varied in a specific range, whereas the other parameters are kept fixed at their typical values which are as follows: interconnection lengths, 1000 μm each; interconnection widths, 1.0 μm each; interconnection thicknesses, 0.5 μm each; interconnection separations, 1.0 μm each; interconnection material resistivity, 3.0 $\mu\Omega \cdot$ cm; interlevel distance, 2.0 μm; substrate thickness, 200.0 μm; driving source resistance, 100 Ω; and load capacitance, 10 fF. In addition, the number of crossing lines is equal to 25, and the crosstalk plots are those for the 13th crossing interconnection. The frequency of the input square-wave train is 1 GHz.

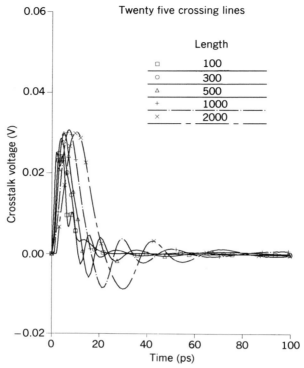

FIGURE 4.5.3 Crosstalk voltage waveforms for several interconnection lengths in the range 0 to 100 ps.

The crosstalk voltage waveforms for several interconnection length values in the time range 0 to 100 ps are shown in Figure 4.5.3, and the dependence of the maximum crosstalk voltage on the interconnection lengths in the range 100 to 2000 μm is shown in Figure 4.5.4. For various interconnection width values, the crosstalk voltage waveforms in the time range 0 to 100 ps are shown in Figure 4.5.5, whereas the dependence of the maximum crosstalk voltage on the interconnection widths in the range 0.2 to 2.0 μm is shown in Figure 4.5.6. For several interconnection material resistivity values, the crosstalk voltage waveforms in the time range 0 to 100 ps are shown in Figure 4.5.7, and the dependence of the maximum crosstalk voltage on the resistivity in the range 1 to 100 $\mu\Omega \cdot$ cm is shown in Figure 4.5.8.

The crosstalk voltage waveforms for several load capacitance values in the time range 0 to 100 ps are shown in Figure 4.5.9, and the dependence of the maximum crosstalk voltage on the load capacitance in the range 5 to 200 fF is shown in Figure 4.5.10. For various driving source resistance values, the crosstalk voltage waveforms in the time range 0 to 100 ps are shown in Figure

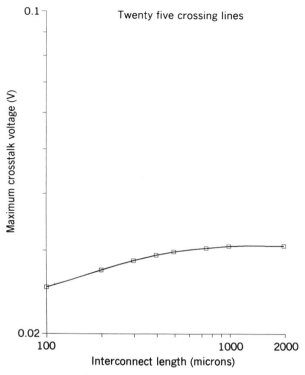

FIGURE 4.5.4   Dependence of the maximum crosstalk voltage on the interconnection length in the range 100 to 2000 μm.

4.5.11, whereas the dependence of the maximum crosstalk voltage on the source resistance in the range 10 to 300 Ω is shown in Figure 4.5.12.

The crosstalk voltage waveforms for several interlevel distance values in the time range 0 to 100 ps are shown in Figure 4.5.13, and the dependence of the maximum crosstalk voltage on the interlevel distance in the range 1 to 5 μm is shown in Figure 4.5.14. For various crossing angle values, the crosstalk voltage waveforms in the time range 0 to 100 ps are shown in Figure 4.5.15, whereas the dependence of the maximum crosstalk voltage on the crossing angle in the range 20° to 100° is shown in Figure 4.5.16. For several values of the number of crossing lines, the crosstalk voltage waveforms for the middle interconnection in the time range 0 to 100 ps are shown in Figure 4.5.17, and the dependence of the maximum crosstalk voltage on the number of crossing lines in the range 8 to 70 is shown in Figure 4.5.18. For several signal frequency values, the crosstalk voltage waveforms in the time range 0 to 100 ps are shown in Figure 4.5.19.

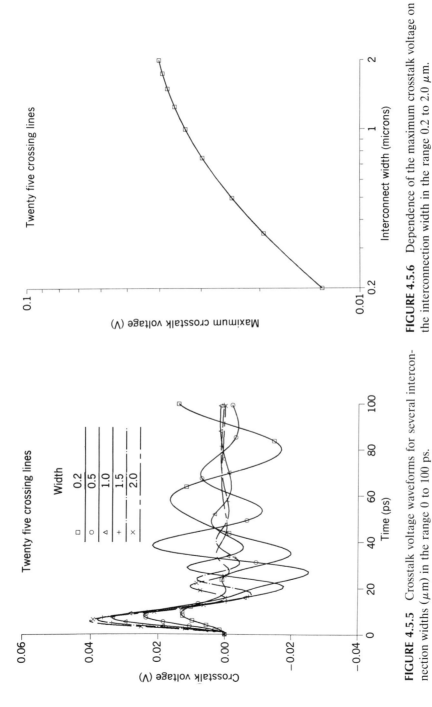

FIGURE 4.5.5 Crosstalk voltage waveforms for several interconnection widths (μm) in the range 0 to 100 ps.

FIGURE 4.5.6 Dependence of the maximum crosstalk voltage on the interconnection width in the range 0.2 to 2.0 μm.

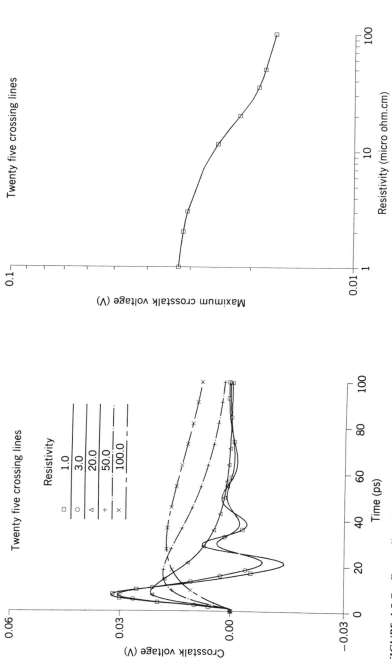

FIGURE 4.5.7 Crosstalk voltage waveforms for several interconnection material resistivities ($\mu\Omega \cdot$ cm) in the range 0 to 100 ps.

FIGURE 4.5.8 Dependence of the maximum crosstalk voltage on the interconnection material resistivity in the range 1 to 100 $\mu\Omega \cdot$ cm.

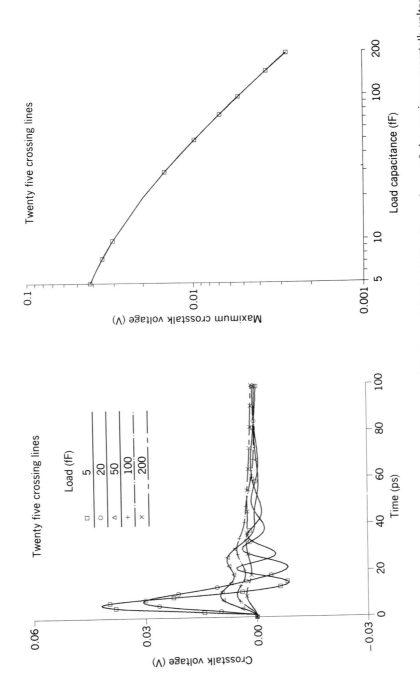

FIGURE 4.5.9 Crosstalk voltage waveforms for several load capacitances in the range 0 to 100 ps.

FIGURE 4.5.10 Dependence of the maximum crosstalk voltage on the load capacitance in the range 5 to 200 fF.

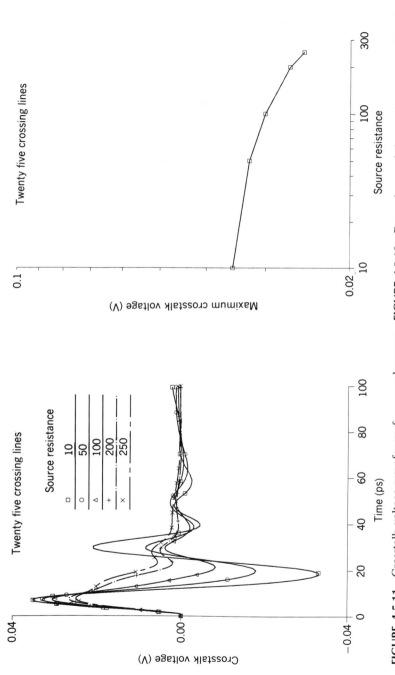

FIGURE 4.5.11 Crosstalk voltage waveforms for several source resistances (Ω) in the range 0 to 100 ps.

FIGURE 4.5.12 Dependence of the maximum crosstalk voltage on the source resistance in the range 10 to 300 Ω.

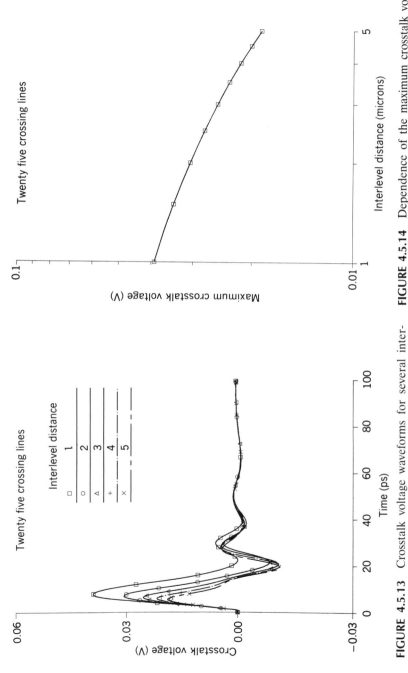

FIGURE 4.5.13 Crosstalk voltage waveforms for several interlevel distances (μm) in the range 0 to 100 ps.

FIGURE 4.5.14 Dependence of the maximum crosstalk voltage on the interlevel distance in the range 1 to 5 μm.

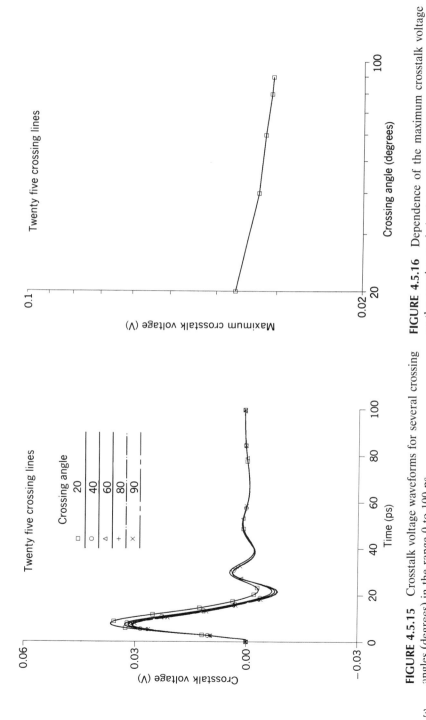

FIGURE 4.5.15 Crosstalk voltage waveforms for several crossing angles (degrees) in the range 0 to 100 ps.

FIGURE 4.5.16 Dependence of the maximum crosstalk voltage on the crossing angle in the range 20° to 90°.

387

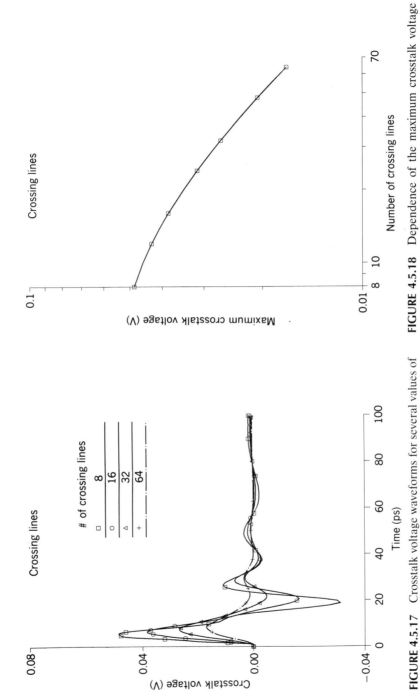

FIGURE 4.5.17 Crosstalk voltage waveforms for several values of the number of crossing interconnections in the range 0 to 100 ps.

FIGURE 4.5.18 Dependence of the maximum crosstalk voltage on the number of crossing interconnections in the range 8 to 70.

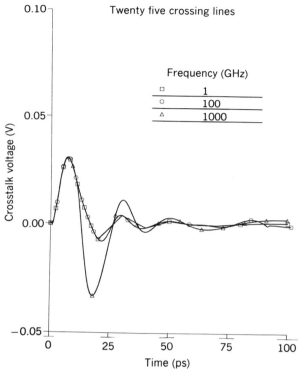

FIGURE 4.5.19 Crosstalk voltage waveforms for several values of the frequency of the input source in the range 0 to 100 ps.

4.6   MULTICONDUCTOR BUSES IN GaAs HIGH-SPEED LOGIC CIRCUITS

The propagation delays, crosstalk, and pulse distortion associated with multiconductor interconnecting buses are critical issues in the design of large scale and very large scale high-speed logic integrated circuits on conventional or GaAs substrates. Modeling of these buses has received considerable attention in the literature, and it is widely accepted that lumped models are inadequate for high-speed integrated circuits. The validity of transmission line models has also been questioned [4.23] because these do not include either surface wave excitation or free-space line or load radiations. Nevertheless, it can be shown that quasi-TEM models are satisfactory if they take into account coupling effects within a multiconductor bus (MBUS) rather than between distant MBUSes. In this section a lossy quasi-TEM model of crosstalk for MBUSes on a semi-insulating GaAs substrate [4.15] is presented.

4.6.1   The Model

A schematic diagram of a high-speed VLSI bus made of N (common values of N are powers of 2, e.g., 8, 16, 32, etc.) parallel equispaced metallic strips deposited either on a semi-insulating substrate (GaAs ICs) or on a thin oxide layer placed on a semiconducting substrate (Si ICs) along with the lower conducting ground plane is shown in Figure 4.6.1. Typical values of the widths, thicknesses, and spacings of the conducting strips usually fall into the ranges: $w = 1$ to 10 μm, $t = 0.5$ to 2 μm, and $s = 1$ to 10 μm, respectively.

Because we are interested in crosstalk between conductors within the same bus and not between distant buses (which are affected by surface wave excitations), we can describe the structure of Figure 4.6.1 by a quasi-TEM model, that is, as a multiconductor transmission line characterized by the capacitance matrix $[C]$, inductance matrix $[L]$, resistance matrix $[R]$, and conductance matrix $[G]$ whose elements are defined per unit length and, in principle, can depend on frequency. Because the GaAs substrate is almost lossless and the Si substrate can be considered lossless as long as the frequency is such that the onset of slow waves can be avoided, the conductance matrix can be neglected. Then the signal propagation on the bus can be described by the well-known generalizations of the Kirchhoff equations [4.24]:

$$\frac{\partial}{\partial z}\mathbf{v}(z,t) = -\left([R] + [L]\frac{\partial}{\partial t}\right)\mathbf{i}(z,t)$$

$$\frac{\partial}{\partial z}\mathbf{i}(z,t) = -[C]\frac{\partial}{\partial t}\mathbf{v}(z,t)$$

(4.6.1)

where $\mathbf{v}(z,t)$ and $\mathbf{i}(z,t)$ are the N-component voltage and current vectors. As shown in Figure 4.6.2, the input signals are fed into the bus by voltage generators having finite internal impedances (simulating the output of the driving stage), and the bus is loaded on the right side by the input impedances of the next logic stage.

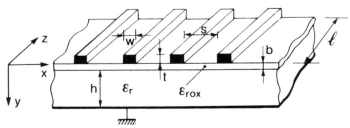

FIGURE 4.6.1   Schematic diagram of the structure of the MBUS [4.15]. (© 1989 IEEE)

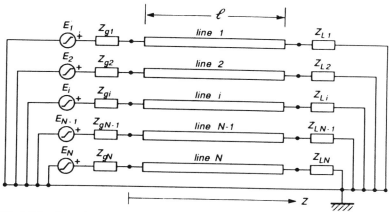

FIGURE 4.6.2 Termination network for the MBUS analyzed in this section [4.15]. (© 1989 IEEE)

For low-speed signals, the MBUS behaves as RC lines, resulting in mainly diffusive transients and strong signal distortion. Above a critical frequency which depends on the propagation mode considered, the bus behaves as lossy LC lines and propagation dominates. Therefore, for a wide range of input signal frequencies, simulation of the transient behavior of the bus can be performed by solving Equations 4.6.1 through standard spectral domain techniques, that is, Fourier analysis and back transformation.

First, the frequency domain response of the N lines is determined. Using standard multiconductor line analysis [4.24], we define the series impedance matrix as

$$[Z_s] = [R] + j\omega[L]$$

and the parallel admittance matrix as

$$[Y_p] = j\omega[C]$$

Now, a symmetrical grounded N-conductor line supports N propagation modes which are called even or odd, depending on whether their potential distribution is even or odd with respect to the center of the line. The N complex modal propagation constants k_i will be a solution of the eigenvalue problem

$$\left(k^2[U] + [Z_s][Y_p]\right)[M_v] = 0$$

where $[M_v]$ is the voltage eigenvector matrix and $[U]$ is the identity matrix.

The current eigenvector matrix $[M_i]$ is then given by

$$[M_i] = \omega[C][M_v]\,\mathrm{diag}\{1/k_i\}$$

and the characteristic admittance matrix is given by

$$[Y_c] = [M_i][M_v]^{-1}$$

The characteristic impedance matrix $[Z_c]$ is the inverse of $[Y_c]$, and the modal impedances are given by the eigenvalues of $[Z_c]$. The voltage and current vectors on the lines are then given by

$$\begin{aligned}
\mathbf{V}(z) &= [M_v][\mathbf{W}^+(z) + \mathbf{W}^-(z)] \\
\mathbf{I}(z) &= [Y_c][M_v][\mathbf{W}^+(z) - \mathbf{W}^-(z)]
\end{aligned} \tag{4.6.2}$$

where

$$\begin{aligned}
\mathbf{W}^\pm &= \{W_i^\pm(z)\} \\
W_i^\pm(z) &= W_i^\pm(0)e^{\mp jk_i z}
\end{aligned} \tag{4.6.3}$$

W_i^+ and W_i^- are the amplitudes of the progressive and regressive components of the ith mode and k_i is the propagation constant of the ith mode. The presence of generators and loads on the bus leads to the following boundary conditions:

$$\begin{aligned}
\mathbf{V}(0) &= \mathbf{E} - \left[\bar{Z}_g\right]\mathbf{I}(0) \\
\mathbf{V}(l) &= [Z_L]\mathbf{I}(l)
\end{aligned} \tag{4.6.4}$$

where $\mathbf{E} = \{E_i(\omega)\}$, $[Z_g] = \mathrm{diag}\{Z_{gi}\}$, $[Z_L] = \mathrm{diag}\{Z_{Li}\}$, E_i is the voltage spectrum of the generator at the input of the ith strip, Z_{gi} is the internal impedance of the ith generator, and Z_{Li} is the load impedance on the ith strip. Substituting Equations 4.6.2 and 4.6.3 into Equation 4.6.4 leads to the following linear system for $\mathbf{W}^\pm(l)$:

$$\begin{bmatrix}
([Y_L] - [Y_c])[M_v] & ([Y_L] + [Y_c])[M_v] \\
([U] + [Z_g][Y_c])[M_v][P]^{-1} & ([U] - [Z_g][Y_c])[M_v][P]
\end{bmatrix}
\begin{bmatrix}
\mathbf{W}^+(l) \\
\mathbf{W}^-(l)
\end{bmatrix} =
\begin{bmatrix}
\mathbf{0} \\
\mathbf{E}
\end{bmatrix} \tag{4.6.5}$$

where

$$[P] = \mathrm{diag}\{e^{-jk_i l}\}$$

After solving Equation 4.6.5, the voltage and current spectra can be obtained from Equation 4.6.2. The time domain response can then be obtained by inverse Fourier transformation.

4.6.2   Lossless MBUS with Cyclic Boundary Conditions

The transient behavior of the MBUS can be analyzed by considering an idealized case of a lossless MBUS with cyclic boundary conditions which can be solved explicitly. If all load and generator impedances are equal and the signal is applied to the kth line only, that is, $Z_{Li} = Z_L$, $Z_{gi} = Z_g$, and $E_i = E\delta_{ik}$, then the solution of Equation 4.6.5 is

$$V_i(\omega) = \left\{ \frac{1}{N} \sum_{n=0}^{N-1} \left[\exp\left(j\frac{2\pi}{N}n(i-k) \right) \right] g_n(\omega) \right\} E(\omega) \qquad (4.6.6)$$

where

$$g_n(\omega) = \frac{(1 - \rho_n)[1 + \Gamma_n(\omega)]e^{-jk_n l}}{2[1 - \rho_n\Gamma_n(\omega)e^{-2jk_n l}]}$$

where ρ_n and Γ_n are the reflection coefficients of Z_g and Z_L with respect to the characteristic impedance Z_n of the nth mode. Equation 4.6.6 represents the output voltage spectra as superpositions of N modal line contributions. The time domain output waveforms can be obtained by the inverse Fourier transformation

$$v_i(t) = \frac{1}{N} \left\{ \sum_{n=0}^{N-1} \left[\exp\left(j\frac{2\pi}{N}n(i-k) \right) \right] h_n(t) \right\} \qquad (4.6.7a)$$

where $h_n(t)$ is the inverse Fourier transform of $[g_n(\omega)E(\omega)]$.

In the practically important case where the load is capacitive (C_{load}), the generator impedance is resistive (R_{gen}), and the driving voltage is a unit step $u(t)$, the modal line contribution $h_n(t)$ is given by

$$h_n(t) = (1 - \rho_n) \sum_{m=0}^{\infty} \rho_n^m [1 - \Phi_m^{(n)}(\tau_m^{(n)})] u(\tau_m^{(n)}) \qquad (4.6.7b)$$

where

$$\tau_m^{(n)} = t - (2m+1)T_n$$

$$T_n = \frac{l}{v_n}$$

$$a_n = \frac{1}{Z_n C_{load}}$$

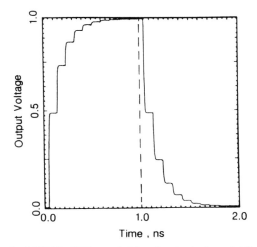

FIGURE 4.6.3 For the MBUS of Figure 4.6.5*a*, the typical modal line contribution of the 0th mode (solid line) in response to a 1-ns unit square pulse (dashed curve) [4.15]. (© 1989 IEEE)

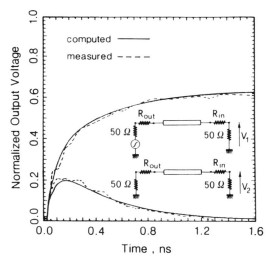

FIGURE 4.6.4 Comparison of the computed results with the experimentally measured results for two coupled lines. The experimental results have been obtained from references [4.25] and [4.26]. The excitation is a tapered unit step with $t_{\text{rise}} = 40$ ps and the other parameters are: $w = 1.5$ μm, $s = 2$ μm, $t = 0.5$ μm, $h = 400$ μm, $b = 0$, $l = 3$ mm, $R_{\text{in}} = 2100$ Ω, $R_{\text{out}} = 380$ Ω, $\varepsilon_r = 12.8$, and the strip conductivity $\gamma = 2.1 \times 10^6$ S/m [4.15]. (© 1989 IEEE)

and

$$\Phi_m^{(n)}(\tau) = e^{-a_n\tau} \sum_{k=0}^{m} \binom{m}{k}(-1)^{m-k}2^k \sum_{i=0}^{k} \frac{(a_n\tau)^i}{i!}$$

Due to the superposition of echoes, the function $h_n(t)$ exhibits a staircase shape as shown in Figure 4.6.3.

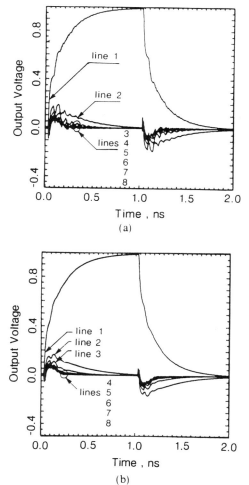

(a)

(b)

FIGURE 4.6.5 Time domain voltage responses of an eight-conductor MBUS to a unit 1-ns voltage pulse applied to line 4, assuming (*a*) lossless strips and (*b*) lossy strips of conductivity $\gamma = 4 \times 10^7$ S/m. The values of the other parameters are: $w = 3$ μm, $s = 4$ μm, $t = 0.5$ μm, $h = 400$ μm, $b = 0$, $l = 5$ mm, $R_g = 2100$ Ω, $C_{load} = 20$ fF, and $\varepsilon_r = 12.9$ [4.15]. (© 1989 IEEE)

4.6.3   Simulation Results

First, the quasi-TEM model can be validated by comparison of the computed results with the experimentally measured results. Such a comparison for two coupled lines is shown in Figure 4.6.4. The experimental results have been obtained from references [4.25] and [4.26]. For these results the excitation is a tapered unit step with t_{rise} = 40 ps and the other parameters are: w =

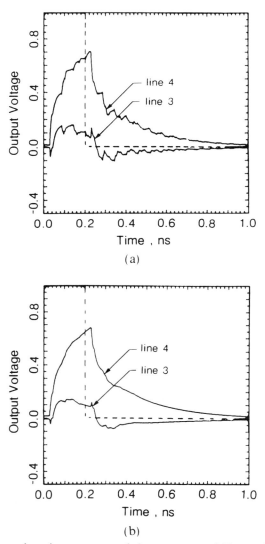

FIGURE 4.6.6   Time domain responses of the structure of Figure 4.6.5 to a typical high-speed digital signal represented by a 0.2-ns square pulse applied to line 4 [4.15]. (© 1989 IEEE)

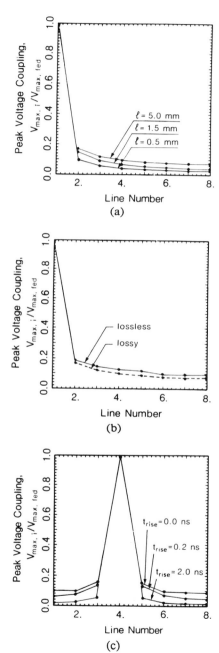

FIGURE 4.6.7 Peak voltage couplings for the MBUS structure of Figure 4.6.5: (*a*) the effect of interconnection length for lossless strips, (*b*) the effect of lossy lines for $l = 5$ mm, and (*c*) the effect of input signal rise time for lossy lines [4.15]. (© 1989 IEEE)

1.5 μm, $s = 2$ μm, $t = 0.5$ μm, $h = 400$ μm, $b = 0$, $l = 3$ mm, $R_{in} = 2100$ Ω, $R_{out} = 380$ Ω, $\varepsilon_r = 12.8$, and the strip conductivity $\gamma = 2.1 \times 10^6$ S/m. The time domain voltage responses of an eight-conductor MBUS to a unit 1-ns voltage pulse applied to line 4 assuming lossless strips, are shown in Figure 4.6.5a (p. 395), and Figure 4.6.5b shows these responses for lossy strips of conductivity $\gamma = 4 \times 10^7$ S/m. The values of the other parameters are: $w = 3$ μm, $s = 4$ μm, $t = 0.5$ μm, $h = 400$ μm, $b = 0$, $l = 5$ mm, $R_g = 2100$ Ω, $C_{load} = 20$ fF, and $\varepsilon_r = 12.9$. The time domain responses of the same structure as in Figure 4.6.5 to a typical high-speed digital signal represented by a 0.2-ns square pulse applied to line 4 are shown in Figure 4.6.6. For the MBUS structure of Figure 4.6.5, the peak voltage couplings are plotted in Figure 4.6.7. Figure 4.6.7a shows the effect of interconnection length for lossless strips, Figure 4.6.7b shows the effect of lossy lines for $l = 5$ mm, and the effect of input signal rise time for lossy lines is shown in Figure 4.6.7c.

EXERCISES

E4.1 Referring to the lumped-capacitance model of Figure 4.1.1, show that the amplitude of the crosstalk voltage at time t is given by

$$V_2(t) = \frac{1}{2}\left[\exp\left(-\frac{t}{\tau_1}\right) - \exp\left(-\frac{t}{\tau_2}\right)\right]$$

where $\tau_1 = R(C + C_L)$ and $\tau_2 = R(2C_c + C + C_L)$. Furthermore, prove that the maximum value of the crosstalk voltage is given by

$$V_{2,\,max} = \frac{1}{2}\left[\exp\left[\left(\frac{n_c - 1}{2n_c}\right)\ln\left(\frac{1 + n_c}{1 - n_c}\right)\right] - \exp\left[\left(-\frac{n_c + 1}{2n_c}\right)\ln\left(\frac{1 + n_c}{1 - n_c}\right)\right]\right]$$

where

$$n_c = \frac{C_c}{C + C_c + C_L}$$

E4.2 Referring to Figure 4.2.2, show that the voltage and current on the kth conductor can be expressed in terms of the normal modes by the equations

$$V_k(z) = \sum_\theta \left[A_{\theta f}e^{-j(k-1)\theta}e^{j\omega(t-(z/v_\theta))} + A_{\theta r}e^{-j(k-1)\theta}e^{j\omega(t+z/v_\theta)}\right]$$

$$I_k(z) = \sum_\theta \left[\frac{A_{\theta f}}{Z_{0\theta}}e^{-j(k-1)\theta}e^{j\omega(t-(z/v_\theta))} - \frac{A_{\theta r}}{Z_{0\theta}}e^{-j(k-1)\theta}e^{j\omega(t+z/v_\theta)}\right]$$

EXERCISES

where z denotes the position on the conductor, ω is the angular frequency, and $A_{\theta f}$ and $A_{\theta r}$ are the amplitudes of the forward and backward voltage waves in the θ mode.

E4.3 The mode wave amplitudes $A_{\theta f}$ and $A_{\theta r}$ in Exercise E4.2 can be determined by using the known terminal conditions at both ends of each strip conductor. Assuming a variety of terminal conditions, find these amplitudes.

E4.4 Using the modifications suggested in Section 3.4.2, extend Section 4.5 to carry out a comprehensive analysis of crosstalk in the crossing interconnections shown in Figure 3.4.7. Comment on the validity of the assumptions and approximations used in your analysis.

E4.5 A few methods of reducing crosstalk are discussed in this chapter. Can you think of other methods? Discuss the merits and drawbacks of each method that you propose.

E4.6 In this chapter crosstalk in the interconnections is modeled using various numerical techniques. Comment on the computer efficiency of these techniques.

E4.7 List and discuss the desirable characteristics of a numerical model that make it more suitable for inclusion in a CAD tool. Review the various techniques presented in this chapter from the point of view of their suitability for inclusion in a CAD tool.

APPENDIX 4.1

DCMPVI
Delay and Crosstalk Analysis of Multilevel Parallel VLSI Interconnections

```
DIRECTORY OF VARIABLES USED:
     RL:     THE PUL INDUCTANCE MATRIX
     RC:     THE CAPACITANCE MATRIX
     AL:     THE LENGTH OF THE INTERCONNECTIONS
     AR:     THE PUL RESISTANCE OF THE
             INTERCONNECTIONS
     AR0:    THE INPUT SOURCE RESISTANCE
     AC0:    THE OUTPUT LOAD CAPACITANCE
     ATMAX:  THE RANGE OF THE TIME INTERVAL TO BE
             ANALYZED
     NT:     THE SAMPLING POINTS IN THE TIME INTERVAL
     RV0:    THE OUTPUT VOLTAGE AT X = 0
     RVD:    THE OUTPUT VOLTAGE AT X = D
     NSOU:   THE POSITION OF THE SOURCE APPLIED
```

```
C*****INPUT DATA FROM THE DATA FILE
      IMPLICIT REAL*16(A-B,O-X)
      COMMON /A / AL,AR,AR0,AC0
      REAL*8 V0(10,0:1000),VD(10,0:1000)
      DIMENSION RL(3,3),RC(3,3)
      OPEN(2,FILE = 'VLITA',STATUS = 'OLD')
      AW = 1.0
      CALL REDIN(IDISK)
      CALL REDIN(NO)
      CALL REDMC(RC,NO)
      CALL REDMA(RL,NO)
      CALL REDRE(AL)
      CALL REDRE(ATM)
      CALL REDIN(NT)
      CALL REDWR(AX)
      CALL REDWR(AR0)
      CALL REDWR(AC0)
      CALL REDWI(NSOU)
      CALL REDIN(NV)
      IDISK = IDISK- 1
 3000 IDISK = IDISK + 1
      IF(NV.EQ.1) THEN
      CALL REDCR(AX,IDISK)
      IF(AX.EQ.9999) GOTO 2000
      END IF
      IF(NV.EQ.2) THEN
      CALL REDCR(AR0,IDISK)
      IF(AR0.EQ.9999) GOTO 2000
      END IF
      IF(NV.EQ.3) THEN
      CALL REDCR(AC0,IDISK)
      IF(AC0.EQ.9999) GOTO 2000
      END IF
      IF(NV.EQ.4) THEN
      CALL REDCI(NSOU,IDISK)
      IF(NSOU.EQ.9999) GOTO 2000
      END IF
      IF(NV.EQ.5) THEN
      CALL REDCR(AS,IDISK)
      IF(AW.EQ.9999) GOTO 2000
      CALL REDMC(RC,NO)
      CALL REDMA(RL,NO)
      END IF
      IF(NV.EQ.6) THEN
      CALL REDCR(AW,IDISK)
```

```fortran
      IF(AW.EQ.9999) GOTO 2000
      CALL REDMC(RC,NO)
      CALL REDMA(RL,NO)
      END IF
      IF(NV.EQ.7) THEN
      CALL REDCR(AL,IDISK)
      IF(AL.EQ.9999) GOTO 2000
      CALL REDMC(RC,NO)
      CALL REDMA(RL,NO)
      END IF
      IF(NV.EQ.0) THEN
      CALL REDWI(NA)
      IF(NA.EQ.9999) GOTO 2000
      END IF
      AR = AX / AW / AW*1.0E4 / 0.5
      CC = 0.80
      NT1 = -1
      KI = INT(ALOG(0.10) / ALOG(CC))
      ATMAX = ATM
      DO 1000 II = KI,0,-1
      NC = NT1
      CI = REAL(II)
      NT1 = INT(NT*CC**II)
      IF(NT1.LE.NC) GOTO 1000
      ATT = NT1*ATMAX / NT
      CALL PA(RL,RC,NSOU,NO,ATT,NT1,NC,V0,VD)
1000  CONTINUE
      NC = NT1
      ATT = ATMAX
      CALL PA(RL,RC,NSOU,NO,ATT,NT,NC,V0,VD)
      DO 10 I = 1,NO
      WRITE(IDISK,5)I
5     FORMAT(1X, `"V0(',I2, `)" ')
      DO 10 J = 0,NT
      WRITE(IDISK,100)ATMAX / NT*J*1.0E12,V0(I,J)
10    CONTINUE
      DO 20 I = 1,NO
      WRITE(IDISK,15)I
15    FORMAT(1X, `"VL(',I2, `)" ')
      DO 20 J = 0,NT
      WRITE(IDISK,100)ATMAX / NT*J*1.0E12,VD(I,J)
20    CONTINUE
100   FORMAT(1X,E12.6,F12.8)
      CLOSE(UNIT = IDISK)
      GOTO 3000
```

```
2000  CLOSE(UNIT = 2 )
      END
      SUBROUTINE PA(RL,RC,NSOU,NO,ATMAX,NT,NC,V0,VD)
      IMPLICIT REAL*16(A- B,O- X)
      IMPLICIT COMPLEX*32(C- F,Y)
      COMMON /A / AL,AR,AR0,AC0
      REAL*8 EP
      COMPLEX*32 CV0(10,0:500),CVD(10,0:500)
      REAL*8 AP(10,0:500),DC,DX,SUM,V0(10,0:1000),
             VD(10,0:1000)
      DIMENSION RL(3,3),RC(3,3)
      DIMENSION CVS(10)
C*****CHOOSE TT, A CONSTANTS
      AC = 1.0
      PI = QARSIN(AC)*2.00000
      NN = 100
      CI = (0.0E0,1.0E0)
      TT = ATMAX*1.1
      ALPHA = 0.00
      AE = 1D- 7
      AE = QLOG(AE)
      AA = -AE / 2.0 / TT + ALPHA
C*****FIND THE FREQUENCY DOMAIN RESULTS
      K = 0
  11  IF(K.GE.NN) GOTO 10
      CX = QCMPLX(AA) + CI*QCMPLX(K*PI / TT)
      CVS(NSOU) = (1.0E0,0.0E0) / CX
      IER = 0
      CALL FS(RL,RC,CX,CV0,CVD,CVS,K,NO,IER)
      K = K + 1
      IF(IER.EQ.0) GOTO 11
      WRITE(*,*)K
  10  NN = K- 1
C*****FIND THE TIME DOMAIN RESPONSES AT BOUNDARY 0
      DO 100 II = 1,NO
      IF(NC.GT.0) GOTO 50
  50  DO 150 KK = NC + 1,NT
      T = KK*ATMAX / NT
      SUM = REAL(CV0(II,0)) / (2.0,0.0)
      DC = SUM
      K = 0
  70  K = K + 1
      IF(K.GT.NN) GOTO 200
      Y = CV0(II,K)
```

```
         DX = (REAL(Y)*DCOS(DBLEQ(K*PI*T / TT))-QIMAG(Y)
     $       *DSIN(DBLEQ(K*PI*T / TT)))
         DC = DC + DX
         DO 20 I = 1,K- 2
20       AP(1,I) = AP(2,I)
         DO 30 I = 1,K- 1
30       AP(2,I) = AP(3,I)
         AP(3,1) = DC
         KI = K
         IF(KI.GT.10) KI = 10
         DO 40 I = 2,KI
         EP = AP(3,I- 1)- AP(2,I- 1)
         AP(3,I) = AP(2,I- 2) + 1.0 / EP
40       CONTINUE
         GOTO 70
C        WRITE(*,*)DX
200      AT = AP(3,7)
         IF(KK.LE.NC) GOTO 150
         V0(II,KK) = AP(3,9)*DEXP(DBLEQ(AA*T)) / TT
         WRITE(*,3)T,V0(II,KK)
  3      FORMAT(1X,D14.5,4F12.7)
150      CONTINUE
100      CONTINUE
C*****FIND THE TIME DOMAIN RESPONSES ON BOUNDARY D
         DO 105 II = 1,NO
 4       FORMAT(1X, '"VD(',I2, ')"  ')
55       DO 155 KK = NC + 1,NT
         T = KK*ATMAX / NT
         SUM = REAL(CVD(II,0)) / (2.0,0.0)
         DC = SUM
         K = 0
75       K = K + 1
         IF(K.GT.NN) GOTO 205
         Y = CVD(II,K)
         DX = (REAL(Y)*DCOS(DBLEQ(K*PI*T / TT))-QIMAG(Y)
     $       *DSIN(DBLEQ(K*PI*T / TT)))
         DC = DC + DX
         DO 25 I = 1,K- 2
25       AP(1,I) = AP(2,I)
         DO 35 I = 1,K- 1
35       AP(2,I) = AP(3,I)
         AP(3,1) = DC
         KI = K
         IF(KI.GT.10) KI = 10
         DO 45 I = 2,KI
```

```
        EP = AP(3,I-1)-AP(2,I-1)
  C     IF(DABS(EP).LE.1E-40) EP=EP*1E20
  C     WRITE(*,*)EP
        AP(3,I) = AP(2,I-2)+1.0/EP
  45    CONTINUE
        GOTO 75
  C     WRITE(*,*)DX
  205   AT = AP(3,7)
        IF(KK.LE.NC) GOTO 155
        VD(II,KK) = AP(3,9)*DEXP(DBLEQ(AA*T))/TT
        WRITE(*,*)VD(II,KK)
  155   CONTINUE
  105   CONTINUE
        RETURN
        END
C*****FIND THE FUNCTION F(S)
        SUBROUTINE FS(RL,RC,CX,CV0,CVD,CVS,K,NO,IER)
        IMPLICIT REAL*16(A-B,O-Z)
        IMPLICIT COMPLEX*32(C-F)
        IMPLICIT INTEGER (I-N)
        COMMON /A/ AL,AR,AR0,AC0
        DIMENSION RL(3,3),RC(3,3),CZ(3,3),CY(3,3),
     $            CW(3,3),CT(3,3)
        DIMENSION CA(3,3),CB(3,3),CE(3,3),CU(3,3),
     $            CV(3,3),CF(3,3)
        DIMENSION CVR(10),CVI(10),CVX(10),
     $            CVU(10),CVS(10)
        COMPLEX*32 CV0(10,0:500),CVD(10,0:500)
        COMPLEX*32 ONE
        COMPLEX SA(3,3),SVX(10),SU(3,3)
        REAL WK(100)
        DATA ONE /(1.0E0,0.0E0)/
        CC = CX*(1.0E-7,0.0)
        CALL MAS(NO,CC,RL,CW)
        CALL PLI(NO,CW,AR,CZ)
        CC = CX /QCMPLX(AL)*(1.0E-15,0.0)
        CALL MAS(NO,CC,RC,CY)
        CALL MAT(NO,CZ,CY,CA)
C*****FIND THE EIGENVALUES
        DO 210 I = 1,NO
        DO 210 J = 1,NO
```

```
210   SA(I,J) = CA(I,J)
      CALL EIGCC(SA,NO,NO,2,SVX,SU,NO,WK,IER)
      DO 220 I = 1,NO
220   CVX(I) = SVX(I)
      DO 230 I = 1,NO
      DO 230 J = 1,NO
230   CU(I,J) = SU(I,J)
      CALL COMP(NO,CVX,CU,CV)
      CALL CSQR(NO,CVX,CVU)
      CALL COMP(NO,CVU,CU,CV)
      CALL INV(NO,CZ,CW)
      CALL MAT(NO,CW,CV,CB)
      CALL CTEXP(NO,CVU,CVX,AL)
      CALL CON(NO,CVX,IER)
      CALL COMP(NO,CVX,CU,CE)
      CALL CTEXP(NO,CVU,CVX,-AL)
      CALL COMP(NO,CVX,CU,CF)
      CALL MAT(NO,CE,CF,CW)
      CC = ONE / CX / QCMPLX(AC0)
      CALL MAC(NO,CC,CB,CV)
      CALL PLI(NO,CV,-1.0,CU)
      CALL INV(NO,CU,CV)
      CC = ONE / CX / QCMPLX(AC0)
      CALL MAC(NO,CC,CB,CW)
      CALL PLI(NO,CW,1.0,CU)
      CALL MAT(NO,CV,CU,CW)
      CALL MAT(NO,CF,CW,CT)
      CC = QCMPLX(AR0)
      CALL MAC(NO,CC,CB,CW)
      CALL PLI(NO,CW,1.0,CU)
      CALL MAT(NO,CU,CT,CV)
      CC = QCMPLX(-AR0)
      CALL MAC(NO,CC,CB,CU)
      CALL PLI(NO,CU,1.0,CW)
      CALL MAT(NO,CW,CE,CU)
      CALL MPL(NO,CU,CV,CW)
      CALL MAT(NO,CE,CW,CU)
      CALL INV(NO,CU,CW)
      CALL MAT(NO,CW,CE,CV)
      CALL MUV(NO,CV,CVS,CVR)
      CALL MUV(NO,CT,CVR,CVI)
      CALL MUV(NO,CE,CVR,CVX)
      DO 40 II = 1,NO
      CV0(II,K) = CVI(II) + CVX(II)
```

```
 40     CONTINUE
 C      WRITE(*,3)CVI(1),CVX(1)
 C      WRITE(*,3)CV0(1,K),1 / CX
  3     FORMAT(1X,6D15.8)
        CALL MUV(NO,CE,CVI,CVX)
        DO 50 I = 1,NO
        CVD(I,K) = CVX(I) + CVR(I)
 50     CONTINUE
        RETURN
        END
C*****READ CAPACITANCE MATRIX
        SUBROUTINE REDMC(A,N)
        REAL*16 A,X
        DIMENSION A(3,3)
        CHARACTER*20 CH
        READ(2,*)CH
        DO 20 I = 1,N
        DO 20 J = I,N
        READ(2,*)N1,N2,A(I,J)
        A(J,I) = A(I,J)
 20     CONTINUE
        DO 30 I = 1,N
        DO 40 J = 1,N
 40     A(I,J) = -A(I,J)
        X = 0.000
        DO 50 J = 1,N
 50     X = X- A(I,J)
        A(I,I) = X
 30     CONTINUE
        RETURN
        END
C*****READ A REAL*16MATRIX
        SUBROUTINE REDMA(A,N)
        REAL*16 A
        DIMENSION A(3,3)
        CHARACTER*20 CH
        READ(2,*)CH
        DO 20 I = 1,N
        DO 20 J = 1,N
 20     READ(2,*)N1,N2,A(I,J)
        RETURN
        END
C*****READ A REAL NUMBER
        SUBROUTINE REDWR(X)
        REAL*16 X
```

```
      CHARACTER*35 CH
      READ(2,*)CH
      READ(2,*)X
      WRITE(*,10)CH,X
      WRITE(1,10)CH,X
 10   FORMAT(1X, ' " ',A35, '= ',D12.5, ' " ')
      RETURN
      END
C*****READ A REAL NUMBER
      SUBROUTINE REDCR(X,I)
      REAL*16 X
      CHARACTER*35 CH
      READ(2,*)CH
      READ(2,*)X
      WRITE(*,10)CH,X
      WRITE(I,10)CH,X
 10   FORMAT(1X, ' " ',A35, '= ',D12.5, ' " ')
      RETURN
      END
C*****READ A REAL*16NUMBER
      SUBROUTINE REDRE(X)
      REAL*16 X
      CHARACTER*20 CH
      READ(2,*)CH
      READ(2,*)X
      WRITE(*,10)CH,X
C     WRITE(1,10)CH,X
 10   FORMAT(1X,A20, '= ',F12.5)
      RETURN
      END
C*****READ AN INTEGER
      SUBROUTINE REDWI(K)
      CHARACTER*35 CH
      READ(2,*)CH
      READ(2,*)K
      WRITE(*,10)CH,K
      WRITE(1,10)CH,K
 10   FORMAT(1X, ' " ',A35, '= ',I2, ' " ')
      RETURN
      END
C*****READ AN INTEGER
      SUBROUTINE REDCI(K,I)
      CHARACTER*35 CH
      READ(2,*)CH
      READ(2,*)K
```

```
      WRITE(*,10)CH,K
      WRITE(I,10)CH,K
 10   FORMAT(1X, ` " ',A35, `= ',I2, ` " ')
      RETURN
      END
C*****READ AN INTEGER
      SUBROUTINE REDIN(K)
      CHARACTER*20 CH
      READ(2,*)CH
      READ(2,*)K
      WRITE(*,10)CH,K
C     WRITE(1,10)CH,K
 10   FORMAT(1X,A20, `= ',I4)
      RETURN
      END
C
      SUBROUTINE MAC(N,CS,CA,CB)
      COMPLEX*32  CS,CA(3,3),CB(3,3)
      DO 10 I=1,N
      DO 10 J=1,N
      CB(I,J)=CS*CA(I,J)
 10   CONTINUE
      RETURN
      END
C
      SUBROUTINE MAS(N,CS,RA,CA)
      REAL*16 RA(3,3)
      COMPLEX*32  CS,CA(3,3)
      DO 20 I=1,N
      DO 20 J=1,N
      CA(I,J)=CS*QCMPLX(RA(I,J))
 20   CONTINUE
      RETURN
      END
C
      SUBROUTINE PLI(N,CW,AR,CZ)
      REAL*16 AR
      COMPLEX*32  CW(3,3),CZ(3,3)
      DO 10 I=1,N
      DO 20 J=1,N
 20   CZ(I,J)=CW(I,J)
      CZ(I,I)=QCMPLX(AR)+CW(I,I)
 10   CONTINUE
      RETURN
      END
```

```
C
      SUBROUTINE MPL(N,CU,CV,CW)
      COMPLEX*32  CU(3,3),CV(3,3),CW(3,3)
      DO 10 I = 1,N
      DO 10 J = 1,N
      CW(I,J) = CU(I,J) + CV(I,J)
  10  CONTINUE
      RETURN
      END
C
      SUBROUTINE MAT(N,CZ,CY,CA)
      COMPLEX*32  CZ(3,3),CY(3,3),CA(3,3)
      DO 10 I = 1,N
      DO 10 J = 1,N
      CA(I,J) = (0.0,0.0)
      DO 20 K = 1,N
  20  CA(I,J) = CA(I,J) + CZ(I,K)*CY(K,J)
  10  CONTINUE
      RETURN
      END
C
      SUBROUTINE MUV(N,CA,CX,CY)
      COMPLEX*32  CA(3,3),CX(10),CY(10)
      DO 10 I = 1,N
      CY(I) = (0.0,0.0)
      DO 20 K = 1,N
  20  CY(I) = CY(I) + CA(I,K)*CX(K)
  10  CONTINUE
      RETURN
      END
C
      SUBROUTINE CSQR(N,CVX,CVU)
      COMPLEX*32  CVX(10),CVU(10)
      DO 10 I = 1,N
  10  CVU(I) = CQSQRT(CVX(I))
      RETURN
      END
C
      SUBROUTINE CTEXP(N,CVX,CVU,R)
      REAL*16 R
      COMPLEX*32  CVX(10),CVU(10)
      DO 10 I = 1,N
  10  CVU(I) = CQEXP(CVX(I)*QCMPLX(-R))
      RETURN
      END
```

```
C
      SUBROUTINE CON(N,CVX,IER)
      COMPLEX*32  CVX(10)
      REAL*16 AMX,AMI
      AMX = 1E- 29
      AMI = 1E29
      DO 10 I = 1,N
      IF(AMX.LT.CQABS(CVX(I))) AMX = CQABS(CVX(I))
      IF(AMI.GT.CQABS(CVX(I))) AMI = CQABS(CVX(I))
  10  CONTINUE
      IF(AMX / AMI.GT.1E14)   IER = 1
      RETURN
      END
C
      SUBROUTINE COMP(N,CVU,CU,CB)
      COMPLEX*32  CVU(10),CU(3,3),CW(3,3),CB(3,3)
      CALL INV(N,CU,CW)
      DO 10 I = 1,N
      DO 10 J = 1,N
  10  CU(I,J) = CU(I,J)*CVU(J)
      CALL MAT(N,CU,CW,CB)
      RETURN
      END
C*****LU FACTORIZATION FOR LINEAR EQUATIONS  B = INV(A)
      SUBROUTINE INV(N,F,A)
      IMPLICIT COMPLEX*32(A- F,O- Z)
      DIMENSION A(3,3),B(3,3),F(3,3)
      DO 60 I = 1,N
      DO 60 J = 1,N
  60  A(I,J) = F(I,J)
      DO 5 I = 1,N
      DO 6 J = 1,N
  6   B(I,J) = (0.0,0.0)
      B(I,I) = (1.0,0.0)
  5   CONTINUE
      DO 10 I = 1,N
      DO 20 J = 1,N
      IF(I.EQ.J) GOTO 20
      C = A(J,I) / A(I,I)
      DO 30 K = 1,N
C     IF(K.EQ.I) GOTO 30
      A(J,K) = A(J,K) - C*A(I,K)
      B(J,K) = B(J,K) - C*B(I,K)
  30  CONTINUE
  20  CONTINUE
```

```
 10     CONTINUE
        DO 40 I = 1,N
        DO 40 L = 1,N
        B(I,L) = B(I,L) / A(I,I)
 40     CONTINUE
        DO 50 I = 1,N
        DO 50 L = 1,N
        A(I,L) = B(I,L)
 50     CONTINUE
        RETURN
        END
C
        SUBROUTINE PRN(N,CHA,A)
        IMPLICIT COMPLEX*32(A- H,O- Z)
        DIMENSION A(3,3)
        CHARACTER*2 CHA
        WRITE(*,10) CHA,N
 10     FORMAT(1X, `MATRIX',A4,1X, `N = ',I4,1X, `IS:',/ )
        CALL PRI(N,N,A)
        RETURN
        END
C
        SUBROUTINE PRI(N,M,Y)
        IMPLICIT COMPLEX*32(A- H,O- Z)
        DIMENSION Y(3,3)
        DO 10 I = 1,N
        WRITE(7,20)   (Y(I,J),J = 1,M)
        WRITE(*,20)   (Y(I,J),J = 1,M)
 20     FORMAT(1X,6D12.6)
 10     CONTINUE
        RETURN
        END
```

APPENDIX 4.2

SPBIGV
Signal Propagation Analysis of Bilevel Crossing Interconnections on GaAs-Based VLSI

```
        INTEGER CHOICE
        OPEN(1,FILE = `CHOICE.DAT',STATUS = `OLD')
        READ(1,*)CHOICE
        IF(CHOICE.EQ.1) THEN
        CALL COMPUTE1()
        ELSEIF(CHOICE.EQ.2) THEN
```

```
      CALL COMPUTE2()
      ELSEIF(CHOICE.EQ.3) THEN
      CALL COMPUTE3
      ENDIF
      END
C*****FOR SINGLE INTERCONNECTION
      SUBROUTINE COMPUTE1()
      COMPLEX*16 ZI(5),KPRIME(5),S,ZY
      COMPLEX*16 V,VS,ZO,ZL,Y,VI,VR,GAMMA,Z
      REAL TP,DELTATP,TENDP,T,DELTAT,VT,PARAM(6)
      REAL C11,C22,C12,C13,BEGT,ENDT,FF
      REAL L11,L22,L12,L13
      REAL IW,IL,R,L,CL,RHO,RS,RISET,DELAYT
      REAL AREA,THICK,PERIOD,LEVDIST,SEP,SUBTHICK
      INTEGER DELAY,BEG,END,I,VARY,NUMBER,CROSSNUM
      OPEN(1,FILE = 'GVOUT.DAT',STATUS = 'UNKNOWN')
      OPEN(2,FILE = 'GRISE',STATUS = 'UNKNOWN')
      OPEN(3,FILE = 'GDELAY',STATUS = 'UNKNOWN')
      OPEN(4,FILE = 'ZMATRI',STATUS = 'OLD')
      READ(4,*) (ZI(J),J = 1,5),(KPRIME(J),
     $           J = 1,5),MPRIME
C*****READING THE INPUT FILE
      OPEN(5,FILE = 'INPUT.DAT',STATUS = 'OLD')
      READ(5,*)IW,IL,THICK,RHO,RS,CL,SEP,LEVDIST,
     $           SUBTHICK,CROSSNUM
C*****READING THE PARAMETER TO BE VARIED
      READ(5,*)VARY
C*****NUMBER OF VALUES TO BE VARIED
      READ(5,*)NUMBER
C*****READING THE PARAMETER VALUES AND STORING IN
C     IN AN ARRAY
      READ(5,*)PARAM(1)
      IF(NUMBER.GE.2) THEN
      DO 25 I = 2,NUMBER
      READ(5,*)PARAM(I)
 25   CONTINUE
      ENDIF
      PERIOD = 1.0D- 09
      CL = CL*1.0D- 15
      CALL CAPACIT(2,IW,C11,C22,C12,C13)
      CALL SCIL(IW,L11,L22,L12,L13)
      M11 = L11*1.0D- 13
      M22 = L22*1.0D- 13
      M12 = L12*1.0D- 13
      M13 = L13*1.0D- 13
```

```
C*****READING THE START, END, AND STEP TIMES
      READ(5,*)TP,TENDP,DELTATP
      OPEN(8,FILE = 'VOUT.DAT',STATUS = 'UNKNOWN')
C*****ARRANGING THE VALUES IN ASCENDING ORDER
      DO 50 I = 1,NUMBER
      DO 60 J = 1,NUMBER- 1
      IF(PARAM(J).GT.PARAM(J + 1)) THEN
      TEMP = PARAM(J)
      PARAM(J) = PARAM(J + 1)
      PARAM(J + 1) = TEMP
      ENDIF
 60   CONTINUE
 50   CONTINUE
      RHO = RHO / 100
      DO 111 I = 1,NUMBER
      T = TP*1.0D- 12
      DELTAT = DELTATP*1.0D- 12
      TEND = TENDP*1.0D- 12
      IF(VARY.EQ.1) THEN
      IL = PARAM(I)
      WRITE(8,333) 'IL = ',IL
      CALL CAPACIT(VARY,IL,C11,C22,C12,C13)
      ENDIF
      IF(VARY.EQ.2) THEN
      IW = PARAM(I)
      WRITE(8,333) 'IW= ',IW
      CALL CAPACIT(VARY,IW,C11,C22,C12,C13)
      ENDIF
      IF(VARY.EQ.3) THEN
      THICK = PARAM(I)
      WRITE(8,333) 'THICKNESS = ',THICK
      ENDIF
      IF(VARY.EQ.4) THEN
      RS = PARAM(I)
      WRITE(8,333) 'RS = ',RS
      ENDIF
      IF(VARY.EQ.5) THEN
      CL = PARAM(I)
      WRITE(8,333) 'CL = ',CL
      CL = CL*1.0D- 15
      ENDIF
      IF(VARY.EQ.6) THEN
      RHO = PARAM(I)
      WRITE(8,333) 'RHO = ',RHO
      RHO = RHO / 100
```

```
      ENDIF
      IF(VARY.EQ.7) THEN
      SUBTHICK = PARAM(I)
      WRITE(8,333) `SUBSTRATE THICK = ',SUBTHICK
      CALL CAPACIT(VARY,SUBTHICK,C11,C22,C12,C13)
      CALL INDUCT(SUBTHICK,L11,L22,L12,L13)
      ENDIF
 333  FORMAT( / ,A,F7.2)
C     TO CONVERT INTO MICRONS
C*****INITIALIZATIONS
      DELAY = 0
      BEG = 0
      END = 0
      DELAYT = 0.0
      RISET = 0.0
      CALL SKNDEPTH(IW,THICK,AREA,PERIOD)
      R = RHO / AREA
      L = 1.0D- 12*IW
      NFLAG = 1
 10   IF(T.GT.TEND) GOTO 121
      IF (NFLAG.EQ.1) THEN
      T = 1.0D- 6
      ENDIF
      VT = 0.0
      DO 30 K = 1,MPRIME
      S = ZI(K) / T
      VS = 1.0 / S
      C = C22*1.0D- 18
      Z = R + S*L
      Y = S*C
      GAMMA = CDSQRT(Z*Y)
      ZL = 1.0 / (S*CL)
      ZY = CDEXP(- 1.0*GAMMA*IL)
      ZO = CDSQRT(Z / Y)
      VR = ((1.+ (RS / ZO)) / ZY)*(1.+ (ZL / ZO)) /
     $    (1- (ZL / ZO))
      VR = VS / ((1.- (RS / ZO))*ZY- VR)
      VI = -((1.+ (ZL / ZO)) / (ZY*(1.- (ZL / ZO))))*VR
      V = (ZY*VI- VR) / ZO*ZL
 30   VT = VT- DREAL(V*KPRIME(K))
      CONTINUE
      IF(NFLAG.EQ.1) THEN
      FF = VT / T
      NFLAG = 2
      T = TP*1.0D- 12
```

```
        GOTO 10
        ELSE
        VT = (VT / T) / FF
        WRITE(1,14)(T*1.0D + 12),VT
        IF((VT.GT.0.5).AND.(DELAY.EQ.0)) THEN
        DELAYT = T*1.0D + 12
        DELAY = 1
        ENDIF
        IF((VT.GT.0.1).AND.(BEG.EQ.0)) THEN
        BEGT = T*1.0D + 12
        BEG = 1
        ENDIF
        IF((VT.GT.0.9).AND.(END.EQ.0)) THEN
        ENDT = T*1.0D + 12
        END = 1
        RISET = (ENDT- BEGT)
        ENDIF
        ENDIF
        T = T + DELTAT
        GOTO 10
121     IF((RISET.NE.0.0).AND.(RISET.LE.TENDP)) THEN
        IF(VARY.EQ.6) THEN
        WRITE(2,5) 100*PARAM(I),RISET
        ELSE
        WRITE(2,5) PARAM(I),RISET
        WRITE(8,*) 'RISE TIME = ', RISET
        ENDIF
        ENDIF
        IF(VARY.EQ.6) THEN
        WRITE(3,5) 100*PARAM(I),DELAYT
        ELSE
        WRITE(3,5) PARAM(I),DELAYT
        WRITE(8,*) 'DELAY TIME = ',DELAYT
        ENDIF
14      FORMAT(5X,F6.2,5X,F8.3)
5       FORMAT(5X,F8.2,3X,F8.2)
        WRITE(1,*) '-1       -1'
111     CONTINUE
        CLOSE(1)
        CLOSE(2)
        CLOSE(3)
        CLOSE(4)
        CLOSE(5)
        RETURN
        END
```

```
C*****FOR PARALLEL INTERCONNECTIONS
      SUBROUTINE COMPUTE2()
      COMPLEX*16 ZI(5),KPRIME(5),S,ZY,ZA,CURRENT
      COMPLEX*16 V,VS,ZO,ZL,Y,VI,VR,GAMMA,Z,ZB
      COMPLEX*16 Y1,Y2,Y3,Y4,ZS,PARALL,VR1,VR2
      REAL CI,CR1,CR2,CL1,CL2,CIL1,CIL2,CIR1,CIR2
      REAL TP,DELTATP,TENDP,T,DELTAT,VT,PARAM(6)
      REAL C11,C22,C12,C13,BEGT,ENDT,R1CRMAX,R2CRMAX
      REAL L11,L22,L12,L13,VCR1,VCR2,R1CRMIN,R2CRMIN
      REAL M11,M22,M12,M13
      REAL NF,IW,IL,R,L,CL,RHO,RS,RISET,DELAYT
      REAL AREA,THICK,PERIOD,LEVDIST,SEP,SUBTHICK
      INTEGER DELAY,BEG,END,I,VARY,NUMBER,CROSSNUM
      OPEN(1,FILE = 'GVOUT.DAT',STATUS = 'UNKNOWN')
      OPEN(2,FILE = 'GRISE',STATUS = 'UNKNOWN')
      OPEN(3,FILE = 'GDELAY',STATUS = 'UNKNOWN')
      OPEN(4,FILE = 'GVCR1.DAT',STATUS = 'UNKNOWN')
      OPEN(5,FILE = 'GVCR2.DAT',STATUS = 'UNKNOWN')
      OPEN(7,FILE = 'GR1CRMAX',STATUS = 'UNKNOWN')
      OPEN(10,FILE = 'GR2CRMAX',STATUS = 'UNKNOWN')
      OPEN(8,FILE = 'ZMATRI',STATUS = 'OLD')
      READ(8,*) (ZI(J),J = 1,5),(KPRIME(J),
     $J = 1,5),MPRIME
C*****READING THE INPUT FILE
      OPEN(9,FILE = 'INPUT.DAT',STATUS = 'OLD')
      READ(9,*)IW,IL,THICK,RHO,RS,CL,SEP,LEVDIST,
     $        SUBTHICK
      READ(9,*)CROSSNUM
C*****READING THE PARAMETER TO BE VARIED
      READ(9,*)VARY
C*****NUMBER OF VALUES TO BE VARIED
      READ(9,*)NUMBER
C*****READING THE PARAMETER VALUES AND STORING
C     IN AN ARRAY
      READ(9,*)PARAM(1)
      IF(NUMBER.GE.2) THEN
      DO 25 I = 2,NUMBER
      READ(9,*)PARAM(I)
  25  CONTINUE
      ENDIF
      PERIOD = 1.0D- 09
      CL = CL*1.0D- 15
      CALL CAPACIT(2,IW,C11,C22,C12,C13)
      CALL SCIL(IW,L11,L22,L12,L13)
      M11 = L11*1.0D- 13
```

```
      M22 = L22*1.0D- 13
      M12 = L12*1.0D- 13
      M13 = L13*1.0D- 13
      CI = C22*1.0D- 18
C*****READING THE START, END, AND STEP TIMES
      READ(9,*)TP,TENDP,DELTATP
      OPEN(12,FILE = 'VOUT.DAT',STATUS = 'UNKNOWN')
      OPEN(13,FILE = 'VCROSS.DAT',STATUS = 'UNKNOWN')
C*****ARRANGING THE VALUES IN ASCENDING ORDER
      DO 50 I = 1,NUMBER
      DO 60 J = 1,NUMBER- 1
      IF(PARAM(J).GT.PARAM(J + 1)) THEN
      TEMP = PARAM(J)
      PARAM(J) = PARAM(J + 1)
      PARAM(J + 1) = TEMP
      ENDIF
 60   CONTINUE
 50   CONTINUE
C*****ALL THE VALUES HAVE TO BE IN MICRONS
      RHO = RHO / 100
      CI = 3*CI
C*****START ITERATIONS
      DO 111 I = 1,NUMBER
      T = TP*1.0D- 12
      DELTAT = DELTATP*1.0D- 12
      TEND = TENDP*1.0D- 12
      IF(VARY.EQ.1) THEN
      IL = PARAM(I)
      WRITE(12,333) 'IL = ',IL
      WRITE(13,333) 'IL = ',IL
      CALL CAPACIT(VARY,IL,C11,C22,C12,C13)
      ENDIF
      IF(VARY.EQ.2) THEN
      IW = PARAM(I)
      WRITE(12,333) 'IW = ',IW
      WRITE(13,333) 'IW = ',IW
      CALL CAPACIT(VARY,IW,C11,C22,C12,C13)
      ENDIF
      IF(VARY.EQ.3) THEN
      THICK = PARAM(I)
      WRITE(12,333) 'THICKNESS = ',THICK
      WRITE(13,333) 'THICKNESS = ',THICK
      ENDIF
      IF(VARY.EQ.8) THEN
      SEP = PARAM(I)
```

```
      WRITE(12,333) `SEPARATION = ',SEP
      WRITE(13,333) `SEPARATION = ',SEP
      CALL CAPACIT(VARY,SEP,C11,C22,C12,C13)
      ENDIF
      IF(VARY.EQ.4) THEN
      RS = PARAM(I)
      WRITE(12,333) `RS = ',RS
      WRITE(13,333) `RS = ',RS
      ENDIF
      IF(VARY.EQ.5) THEN
      CL = PARAM(I)
      WRITE(12,333) `CL = ',CL
      WRITE(13,333) `CL = ',CL
      CL = CL*1.0D- 15
      ENDIF
      IF(VARY.EQ.6) THEN
      RHO = PARAM(I)
      WRITE(12,333) `RHO = ',RHO
      WRITE(13,333) `RHO = ',RHO
      RHO = RHO / 100
      ENDIF
      IF(VARY.EQ.7) THEN
      SUBTHICK = PARAM(I)
      WRITE(12,333) `SUBTHICK = ',SUBTHICK
      WRITE(13,333) `SUBTHICK = ',SUBTHICK
      CALL CAPACIT(VARY,SUBTHICK,C11,C22,C12,C13)
      CALL INDUCT(SUBTHICK,L11,L22,L12,L13)
      M11 = L11D- 13
      M22 = L22D- 13
      M12 = L12D- 13
      M13 = L13D- 13
      ENDIF
 333  FORMAT( / ,A,F7.2)
C*****INITIALIZATIONS
      DELAY = 0
      BEG = 0
      END = 0
      DELAYT = 0.0
      RISET = 0.0
      CALL SKNDEPTH(IW,THICK,AREA,PERIOD)
      R = RHO / AREA
      L = M22
      NFLAG = 1
 10   IF(T.GT.TEND) GOTO 121
      IF (NFLAG.EQ.1) THEN
      T = 1.0D- 6
```

```
ENDIF
VT = 0.0
VCR1 = 0.0
VCR2 = 0.0
VR2 = (0.0,0.0)
VR1 = (0.0,0.0)
R1CRMAX = 0.0
R2CRMAX = 0.0
R1CRMIN = 100.0
R2CRMIN = 100.0
DO 30  K = 1,MPRIME
S = ZI(K) / T
VS = 1.0 / S
CIL1 = C12*1.0D- 18
CIR1 = CIL1
CIL2 = C13*1.0D- 18
CIR2 = CIL2
CR1 = CI
CR2 = CR1
CL1 = CR1
CL2 = CL1
Y1 = S*CR1*CIR1 / (CIR1 + CR1)
Y2 = S*CR2*CIR2 / (CIR2 + CR2)
Y3 = S*CL1*CIL1 / (CIL1 + CL1)
Y4 = S*CL2*CIL2 / (CIL2 + CL2)
Y = Y1 + Y2 + Y3 + Y4 + S*CI
ZS = RS + R*IL + S*L*IL + PARALL(1.0 / (S*CL),1.0 /
$(S*CI*IL))
 Z = R + S*L- S*S*(2*M12*M12 + 2*M13*M13) / ZS
 Z = R + S*L
 GAMMA = CDSQRT(Z*Y)
 ZL = 1.0 / (S*CL)
 ZY = CDEXP(- 1.0*GAMMA*IL)
 ZO = CDSQRT(Z / Y)
 VR = ((1.+ (RS / ZO)) / ZY)*(1.+ (ZL / ZO)) / (1- (ZL /
$ZO))
 VR = VS / ((1.- (RS / ZO))*ZY- VR)
 VI = - ((1.+ (ZL / ZO)) / (ZY*(1.- (ZL /
$    ZO))))*VR
 CURRENT = (ZY*VI- VR) / ZO
 V = CURRENT*ZL
 VT = VT- DREAL(V*KPRIME(K))
 ZA = RS + R*IL + S*L*IL
 ZB = PARALL(ZL,(1 / S*CI*IL))
 VR1 = (ZB / (ZA + ZB))*(ZA*(CIL1)*IL*S*V-
$CURRENT*M12*S*IL)
```

```
      VR2 = ( ZB / ( ZA + ZB ) ) * ( ZA * ( CIL2 ) * IL*S*V-
$       CURRENT*S*M13*IL)
      VCR2 = VCR2 - DREAL ( VR2 * KPRIME ( K ) )
      VCR1 = VCR1 - DREAL ( VR1 * KPRIME ( K ) )
30    CONTINUE
      IF ( NFLAG.EQ.1 ) THEN
      NF = VT / T
      NFLAG = 2
      T = TP * 1.0D - 12
      GOTO 10
      ELSE
      VT = ( VT / T ) / NF
      VCR1 = ( VCR1 / T )
      VCR2 = ( VCR2 / T )
      WRITE ( 1 , 14 ) ( T * 1.0D + 12 ) , VT
      IF ( VARY.EQ.4 ) THEN
      IF ( VCR1.GT. - 80D - 03 ) THEN
      WRITE ( 4 , 15 ) ( T * 1.0D + 12 ) , VCR1
      ELSE
      IF ( VCR1.GT. - 25D - 03 ) THEN
      WRITE ( 4 , 15 ) ( T * 1.0D + 12 ) , VCR2
      ENDIF
      ENDIF
      ENDIF
      IF ( VCR2.GT. - 25D - 03 ) THEN
      WRITE ( 5 , 15 ) ( T * 1.0D + 12 ) , VCR2
      ENDIF
      IF ( VCR1.GT.R1CRMAX ) R1CRMAX = VCR1
      IF ( VCR1.LT.R1CRMIN ) R1CRMIN = VCR1
      IF ( VCR2.GT.R2CRMAX ) R2CRMAX = VCR2
      IF ( VCR2.LT.R2CRMIN ) R2CRMIN = VCR2
      IF ( DUMMY.EQ. 'Y' ) THEN
      WRITE ( 12 , * ) '     TIME            VOUT'
      WRITE ( 13 , * ) '     TIME            VCROSS'
      WRITE ( 12 , 14 ) ( T * 1.0D + 12 ) , VT
      WRITE ( 13 , 15 ) ( T * 1.0D + 12 ) , VCR1
      WRITE ( 13 , 15 ) ( T * 1.0D + 12 ) , VCR2
      ENDIF
      IF ( ( VT.GT.0.5 ) .AND. ( DELAY.EQ.0 ) ) THEN
      DELAYT = T * 1.0D + 12
      DELAY = 1
      ENDIF
      IF ( ( VT.GT.0.1 ) .AND. ( BEG.EQ.0 ) ) THEN
      BEGT = T * 1.0D + 12
```

```
        BEG = 1
        ENDIF
        IF((VT.GT.0.9).AND.(END.EQ.0)) THEN
        ENDT = T*1.0D + 12
        END = 1
        RISET = (ENDT- BEGT)
        ENDIF
        ENDIF
        T = T + DELTAT
        GOTO 10
121     IF((RISET.NE.0.0).AND.(RISET.LT.TENDP)) THEN
        IF(VARY.EQ.6) THEN
        WRITE(2,5) 100*PARAM(I),RISET
        ELSE
        WRITE(2,5) PARAM(I),RISET
        ENDIF
        ENDIF
        IF(VARY.EQ.6) THEN
        WRITE(3,6) 100*PARAM(I),DELAYT
        ELSE
        WRITE(3,6) PARAM(I),DELAYT
        ENDIF
        IF(VARY.EQ.6) THEN
        WRITE(7,6) 100*PARAM(I),R1CRMAX*1000
        ELSE
        WRITE(7,6) PARAM(I),R1CRMAX*1000
        ENDIF
        IF(VARY.EQ.6) THEN
        WRITE(10,6) 100*PARAM(I),R2CRMAX*1000
        ELSE
        WRITE(10,6) PARAM(I),R2CRMAX*1000
        ENDIF
14      FORMAT(5X,F6.2,5X,F8.3)
15      FORMAT(5X,F6.2,5X,E10.3)
5       FORMAT(5X,F8.2,3X,F8.2)
6       FORMAT(5X,F8.2,3X,E9.3)
        WRITE(1,*) `-1     -1'
        WRITE(4,*) `-1     -1'
        WRITE(5,*) `-1     -1'
111     CONTINUE
        CLOSE(1)
        CLOSE(2)
        CLOSE(3)
        CLOSE(4)
        CLOSE(5)
```

```
      CLOSE(10)
      CLOSE(7)
      CLOSE(8)
      RETURN
      END
C*****FOR PARALLEL AND CROSSING INTERCONNECTIONS
      SUBROUTINE COMPUTE3()
      COMPLEX*16 S,VS,ZCC,ZCL,ZRIGHT,ZLEFT,ZCLOAD
      COMPLEX*16 TXLOAD,LMLOAD,ZY,ZO,VR,VI,
                 CURRENT,CUR
      COMPLEX*16 VOUTPUT,VCRSTALK,PARALL,ZA
      COMPLEX*16 XCUREN,PRLOAD,ZS,VR1,VR2,V1,I1
      COMPLEX*16 KPRIME(5),ZX(5),ZCOUP,Z,Y,ZB
      COMPLEX*16 Y1,Y2,Y3,Y4,RIGHT1,RIGHT2,GAMMA
      REAL C11,C22,C12,C13,D11,D12,D22,D13
      REAL M12,M22,M11,M13,VCR1,VCR2,SPACE
      REAL CIL1,CIL2,CIR1,CIR2,CR1,CR2,CL1,CL2
      REAL CC,INLEN,LOADLEN,CL,LLEFT,LRIGHT,
     $     LLOAD,CLOAD
      REAL RHO,R,RLOAD,RLEFT,RRIGHT,RISE,DELAY,
     $     XMAXCR,R1CRMAX,R2CRMAX
      REAL LHALF,T,DELTAT,PARAM(10),LEN,AREA,IW
      REAL STRATE,CCOUPL,CCOUPF,PERIOD,C,L,RS,SEP
      REAL VOUT,VCROSS,NF,THICK,LDIS,RSPACE,LSPACE
      INTEGER TOPLEV,BOTMLEV,CROSNUM,NFLAG,VARY,
     $ NUMBER
      INTEGER MPRIME,BFLAG,DFLAG,EFLAG
      COMMON / BOTH / ZO,GAMMA,ZCL
      COMMON / VCROSS / XCUREN,ZRIGHT,ZLEFT
      COMMON / VOUT / CURRENT,LMLOAD
      COMMON / CAPS / C11,C22,C12,C13,M11,M22,M12,M13
      OPEN(UNIT = 1,FILE = 'GVOUT.DAT',STATUS =
     $     'UNKNOWN')
      OPEN(UNIT = 2,FILE = 'GVCROSS.DAT',STATUS =
     $      'UNKNOWN')
      OPEN(UNIT = 3,FILE = 'GVCR1.DAT',STATUS
     $     = 'UNKNOWN')
      OPEN(UNIT = 4,FILE = 'GVCR2.DAT',STATUS
     $     = 'UNKNOWN')
      OPEN(5,FILE = 'INPUT.DAT',STATUS = 'UNKNOWN')
      OPEN(12,FILE = 'GRISE',STATUS = 'UNKNOWN')
      OPEN(7,FILE = 'GDELAY',STATUS = 'UNKNOWN')
      OPEN(8,FILE = 'GMAXCR',STATUS = 'UNKNOWN')
      OPEN(9,FILE = 'GR1CRMAX',STATUS = 'UNKNOWN')
      OPEN(10,FILE = 'GR2CRMAX',STATUS = 'UNKNOWN')
      OPEN(11,FILE = 'ZMATRI',STATUS = 'OLD')
```

```
      READ(11,*) (ZX(J),J=1,5),(KPRIME(J),
     $           J=1,5),MPRIME
      CLOSE(11)
      READ(5,*)IW,LEN,THICK,RHO,RS,CL,SEP,LDIS,
     $           STRATE,CROSNUM
      CL = CL*1.0D- 15
      PERIOD = 1.E- 09
      SPACE = 1.0
      CALL SCIC(IW,C11,C22,C12,C13)
      CALL SCIL(IW,M11,M22,M12,M13)
      M12 = M12*1.0D- 13
      M13 = M13*1.0D- 13
      M11 = M11*1.0D- 13
      M22 = M22*1.0D- 13
      CALL CAPACIT(9,LDIS,D11,D22,D12,D13)
C*****READING THE PARAMETER TO BE VARIED
      READ(5,*)VARY
C*****NUMBER OF VALUES TO BE VARIED
      READ(5,*)NUMBER
C*****READING THE PARAMETER VALUES AND STORING IN
C     AN ARRAY
      READ(5,*)PARAM(1)
      IF(NUMBER.GE.2) THEN
      DO 25 I = 2,NUMBER
      READ(5,*)PARAM(I)
 25   CONTINUE
      ENDIF
C*****READING THE START, END, AND STEP TIMES
      READ(5,*)TP,TENDP,DELTATP
      TOPLEV = 5
      BOTMLEV = 16
      CROSNUM = 8
C*****ARRANGING THE VALUES IN ASCENDING ORDER
      DO 50 I = 1,NUMBER
      DO 60 J = 1,NUMBER- 1
      IF(PARAM(J).GT.PARAM(J + 1)) THEN
      TEMP = PARAM(J)
      PARAM(J) = PARAM(J + 1)
      PARAM(J + 1) = TEMP
      ENDIF
 60   CONTINUE
 50   CONTINUE
      CLOSE(5)
      OPEN(13,FILE = 'VOUT.DAT',STATUS = 'UNKNOWN')
      OPEN(14,FILE = 'VCROSS.DAT',STATUS = 'UNKNOWN')
```

```
      OPEN(15,FILE = `VCROSS1.DAT',STATUS = `UNKNOWN')
      OPEN(16,FILE = `VCROSS2.DAT',STATUS = `UNKNOWN')
      WRITE(13,*) `      TIME (PS)    VCROSS'
      WRITE(14,*) `      TIME (PS)    VCROSS'
      WRITE(15,*) `      TIME (PS)    VCROSS'
      WRITE(16,*) `      TIME (PS)    VCROSS'
C*****CONVERT EVERYTHING TO MICRONS
      RHO = RHO / 100
C*****LOOP WHERE ALL THE CALCULATIONS ARE MADE
      DO 600 I = 1,NUMBER
      NFLAG = 1
      DFLAG = 0
      BFLAG = 0
      EFLAG = 0
      DELAY = 0.0
      RISE = 0.0
      T = TP*1.0D- 12
      TEND = TENDP*1.0D- 12
      DELTAT = DELTATP*1.0D- 12
      CCOUPL = .049*IW**2
      CCOUPF = 1.651*IW
      CC = (CCOUPL + CCOUPF)*2.E- 15 / LDIS
      IF(VARY.EQ.1) THEN
      LEN = PARAM(I)
      WRITE(13,333) `IL = ',LEN
      WRITE(14,333) `IL = ',LEN
      WRITE(15,333) `IL = ',LEN
      WRITE(16,333) `IL = ',LEN
      CALL CAPACIT(VARY,LEN,C11,C22,C12,C13)
      ENDIF
      IF(VARY.EQ.2) THEN
      IW = PARAM(I)
      WRITE(13,333) `IW = ',IW
      WRITE(14,333) `IW = ',IW
      WRITE(15,333) `IW = ',IW
      WRITE(16,333) `IW = ',IW
      CALL CAPACIT(VARY,IW,C11,C22,C12,C13)
      ENDIF
      IF(VARY.EQ.3) THEN
      THICK = PARAM(I)
      WRITE(13,333) `THICKNESS = ',THICK
      WRITE(14,333) `THICKNESS = ',THICK
      WRITE(15,333) `THICKNESS = ',THICK
      WRITE(16,333) `THICKNESS = ',THICK
      ENDIF
```

```
IF(VARY.EQ.8) THEN
SEP = PARAM(I)
WRITE(13,333) 'SEPARATION = ',SEP
WRITE(14,333) 'SEPARATION = ',SEP
WRITE(15,333) 'SEPARATION = ',SEP
WRITE(16,333) 'SEPARATION = ',SEP
CALL CAPACIT(VARY,SEP,C11,C22,C12,C13)
ENDIF
IF(VARY.EQ.9) THEN
LDIS = PARAM(I)
WRITE(13,333) 'LEVEL DISTANCE = ',LDIS
WRITE(14,333) 'LEVEL DISTANCE = ',LDIS
WRITE(15,333) 'LEVEL DISTANCE = ',LDIS
WRITE(16,333) 'LEVEL DISTANCE = ',LDIS
CALL CAPACIT(VARY,LDIS,D11,D22,D12,D13)
CC = D12*1.0D- 17
ENDIF
IF(VARY.EQ.4) THEN
RS = PARAM(I)
WRITE(13,333) 'RS = ',RS
WRITE(14,333) 'RS = ',RS
WRITE(15,333) 'RS = ',RS
WRITE(16,333) 'RS = ',RS
ENDIF
IF(VARY.EQ.5) THEN
CL = PARAM(I)
WRITE(13,333) 'CL = ',CL
WRITE(14,333) 'CL = ',CL
WRITE(15,333) 'CL = ',CL
WRITE(16,333) 'CL = ',CL
CL = CL*1.0D- 15
ENDIF
IF(VARY.EQ.6) THEN
RHO = PARAM(I)
WRITE(13,333) 'RHO = ',RHO
WRITE(14,333) 'RHO = ',RHO
WRITE(15,333) 'RHO = ',RHO
WRITE(16,333) 'RHO = ',RHO
RHO = RHO / 100
ENDIF
IF(VARY.EQ.7) THEN
STRATE = PARAM(I)
WRITE(13,333) 'SUBSTRATE THICK = ',STRATE
WRITE(14,333) 'SUBSTRATE THICK = ',STRATE
WRITE(15,333) 'SUBSTRATE THICK = ',STRATE
```

```
      WRITE(16,333) 'SUBSTRATE THICK = ',STRATE
      CALL CAPACIT(VARY,STRATE,C11,C22,C12,C13)
      CALL INDUCT(STRATE,M11,M22,M12,M13)
      M11 = M11*1.0D- 13
      M22 = M22*1.0D- 13
      M12 = M12*1.0D- 13
      M13 = M13*1.0D- 13
      ENDIF
      IF(VARY.EQ.10) THEN
      BOTMLEV = PARAM(I)
      WRITE(13,334) 'CROSS NO = ',BOTMLEV
      WRITE(14,334) 'CROSS NO = ',BOTMLEV
      WRITE(15,334) 'CROSS NO = ',BOTMLEV
      WRITE(16,334) 'CROSS NO = ',BOTMLEV
      ENDIF
  333 FORMAT( / ,A,F7.2)
  334 FORMAT( / ,A,I4)
      L = M22
      C = C22*1.0D- 18
C*****C IN F / MICRONS AND L IN H / MICRONS
      CALL SKNDEPTH(IW,THICK,AREA,PERIOD)
      R = RHO / AREA
C*****CALCULATION OF THE CIRCUIT MODEL VALUES
      LHALF = LEN / 2.0
      INLEN = (LEN- (BOTMLEV- 1)*SEP + BOTMLEV*IW) / 2.0
      LOADLEN = INLEN
      RRIGHT = R*LHALF
      RLEFT = RRIGHT
      LLEFT = L*LHALF
      LRIGHT = LLEFT
      LLOAD = L*LOADLEN
      CLOAD = C*LOADLEN
      RLOAD = R*LOADLEN
      LSPACE = L*SEP
      RSPACE = R*SEP
      CSPACE = C*SEP
C*****BEGINNING OF LOOP TO CALCULATE THE OUTPUT AND
C     CROSSTALK VOLTAGES
C*****CALCULATE THE STEADY- STATE VALUE AT 10,000
C     PS FOR FIRST LOOP, AND
C*****PROCEED WITH CALCULATIONS AFTER THAT FOR
C     GIVEN TIME PERIOD
      XMAXCR = 0.0
      R1CRMAX = 0.0
      R2CRMAX = 0.0
```

```
500    IF(T.GT.TEND) GOTO 111
       IF(NFLAG.EQ.1) THEN
       T = 1.0D- 6
       ENDIF
       VOUT = 0.
       VCROSS = 0.
       VCR1 = 0.0
       VCR2 = 0.0
       RIGHT2 = (0.,0.)
       RIGHT1 = (0.,0.)
       VOUTPUT = (0.,0.)
       VCRSTALK = (0.,0.)
C*****CALCULATE THE IMPEDANCE VALUES IN LAPLACE
C      DOMAIN
       DO 450 II = 1,5
       S = ZX(II) / T
       VS = 1.0 / S
       ZCC = 1.0 / (S*CC)
       ZCL = 1.0 / (S*CL)
       ZCLOAD = 1.0 / (S*CLOAD)
       ZSPACE = RSPACE + S*LSPACE
       CI = C22*1.0D- 18
       CIR1 = C12*1.0D- 18
       CIR2 = C13*1.0D- 18
       CIL1 = CIR1
       CIL2 = CIR2
       CR1 = CI
       CR2 = CR1
       CL1 = CR2
       CL2 = CL1
       Y1 = S*CR1*CIR1 / (CIR1 + CR1)
       Y2 = S*CR2*CIR2 / (CIR2 + CR2)
       Y3 = S*CL1*CIL1 / (CIL1 + CL1)
       Y4 = S*CL2*CIL2 / (CIL2 + CL2)
       Y = Y1 + Y2 + Y3 + Y4 + S*CI
       ZS = RS + R*LEN + S*M22*LEN + PARALL(1.0 / (S*CL),
      $     1.0 / (S*C*LEN))
       Z = R + S*M22- (S*S)*(2*M12*M12 + 2*M13*M13) / ZS
       GAMMA = CDSQRT(Z*Y)
       ZY = CDEXP(- 1.0*GAMMA*INLEN)
       ZO = CDSQRT(Z / Y)
       TXLOAD = RLOAD + S*LLOAD + PARALL(ZCL,1 / (S*CLOAD))
       LMLOAD = TXLOAD
       ZRIGHT = S*LRIGHT + RRIGHT + PARALL(ZCL,1 /
      $          (S*CI*LHALF))
```

```
      ZLEFT = PARALL((S*LLEFT + RLEFT + RS),(1 /
     $       (S*CI*LHALF)))
      ZCOUP = PARALL(ZRIGHT,ZLEFT) + ZCC
      TXLOAD = PARALL(TXLOAD,ZCOUP)
C*****CALCULATE EQUIVALENT TRANSMISSION LINE
C     IMPEDANCE
      DO 440 K = 1,BOTMLEV- 1
      TXLOAD = Z + PARALL(TXLOAD,(1 / Y))
      TXLOAD = PARALL(TXLOAD,ZCOUP)
  440 CONTINUE
C*****CALCULATE REFLECTED AND INCIDENT VOLTAGES
      VR = ((1.+ (RS / ZO)) / ZY)*(1.+ (TXLOAD / ZO)) /
     $    (1- (TXLOAD / ZO))
      VR = VS / ((1.- (RS / ZO))*ZY- VR)
      VI = -((1.+ (TXLOAD / ZO)) / (ZY*(1.- (TXLOAD /
     $      ZO))))*VR
C*****CALCULATE PARALLEL LOAD AND CURRENTS FOR
C     SUBROUTINE CALCULATIONS
      CURRENT = (ZY*VI- VR) / ZO
      I1 = CURRENT
      V1 = CURRENT*TXLOAD
      ZA = RS + R*LEN + S*L*LEN
      ZB = PARALL(ZCL,1 / (S*CI*LEN))
      VR1 = (ZB / (ZA + ZB))*(ZA*(CIL1)*LEN*S*V1-
     $      M12*S*LEN*I1)
      VR2 = (ZB / (ZA + ZB))*(ZA*(CIL2)*LEN*S*V1-
     $      M13*S*LEN*I1)
      VCR2 = VCR2- DREAL(VR2*KPRIME(II))
      VCR1 = VCR1- DREAL(VR1*KPRIME(II))
      DO 445 KK = 1,BOTMLEV- 1
      PRLOAD = LMLOAD
      DO 443 III = KK,BOTMLEV- 1
      PRLOAD = PARALL(PRLOAD,(1 / Y)) + Z
      PRLOAD = PARALL(PRLOAD,ZCOUP)
  443 CONTINUE
      CUR = CURRENT
      CURRENT = CURRENT*ZCOUP / (ZCOUP + PRLOAD)
      IF(KK.EQ.CROSNUM) XCUREN = CUR- CURRENT
  445 CONTINUE
      CUR = CURRENT
      CURRENT = CURRENT*ZCOUP / (ZCOUP + LMLOAD)
      IF(BOTMLEV.EQ.CROSNUM)XCUREN = CUR- CURRENT
      CALL CRSTALK(VCRSTALK,LHALF)
      VCROSS = VCROSS- DREAL(VCRSTALK*KPRIME(II))
      CALL OUTPUT(VOUTPUT,LOADLEN)
```

```
      VOUT = VOUT- DREAL(VOUTPUT*KPRIME(II))
  450   CONTINUE
C*****CALCULATE NORMALIZING FACTOR
      IF(NFLAG.EQ.1) THEN
      NF = VOUT / T
      NFLAG = 2
      T = TP*1.0D- 12
      GOTO 500
      ELSE
      VCROSS = VCROSS / T
      IF(VCROSS.GT.XMAXCR) XMAXCR = VCROSS
      WRITE(2,300)T*1.0D + 12,VCROSS*1000
      VCR1 = (VCR1 / T)
      VCR2 = (VCR2 / T)
      IF(VCR1.LT.- 50.0D- 03) VCR1 = VCR1 / 2
      WRITE(3,300)T*1.0D + 12,VCR1*1000
      IF(VCR1.GT.R1CRMAX) R1CRMAX = VCR1
      IF(VCR2.LT.- 40.0D- 03) VCR2 = VCR2 / 2
      WRITE(4,300)T*1.0D + 12,VCR2*1000
      IF(VCR2.GT.R2CRMAX) R2CRMAX = VCR2
      VOUT = (VOUT / T) / NF
      WRITE(1,200)T*1.0D + 12,VOUT
      ENDIF
      IF((VOUT.GT.0.5).AND.(DFLAG.EQ.0)) THEN
      DELAY = T*1.0D + 12
      DFLAG = 1
      ENDIF
      IF((VOUT.GT.0.1).AND.(BFLAG.EQ.0)) THEN
      BEG = T*1.0D + 12
      BFLAG = 1
      ENDIF
      IF((VOUT.GT.0.9).AND.(EFLAG.EQ.0)) THEN
      END = T*1.0D + 12
      EFLAG = 1
      RISE = (END- BEG)
      ENDIF
      T = T + DELTAT
      GOTO 500
  111   IF((RISE.NE.0.0).AND.(RISE.LT.(TEND*1.0D +
     $    12))) THEN
      IF(VARY.EQ.6) THEN
      WRITE(12,5) 100*PARAM(I),RISE
      ELSE
      WRITE(12,5) PARAM(I),RISE
      ENDIF
```

```
      ENDIF
      IF(VARY.EQ.6) THEN
      WRITE(7,5) 100*PARAM(I),DELAY
      ELSE
      WRITE(7,5) PARAM(I),DELAY
      ENDIF
      IF(VARY.EQ.6) THEN
      WRITE(9,9) 100*PARAM(I),R1CRMAX*1000
      ELSE
      WRITE(9,9) PARAM(I),R1CRMAX*1000
      ENDIF
      IF(VARY.EQ.6) THEN
      WRITE(10,9) 100*PARAM(I),R2CRMAX*1000
      ELSE
      WRITE(10,9) PARAM(I),R2CRMAX*1000
      ENDIF
      IF(VARY.EQ.6) THEN
      WRITE(8,9) 100*PARAM(I),XMAXCR*1000
      ELSE
      WRITE(8,9) PARAM(I),XMAXCR*1000
      ENDIF
14    FORMAT(5X,I3,5X,F7.3)
5     FORMAT(5X,F8.2,3X,F7.3)
9     FORMAT(5X,F8.2,3X,E20.6)
      WRITE(1,*) `-1    -1'
      WRITE(2,*) `-1    -1'
      WRITE(3,*) `-1    -1'
      WRITE(4,*) `-1    -1'
600   CONTINUE
200   FORMAT(5X,F5.1,10X,F8.5)
300   FORMAT(5X,F5.1,10X,E20.8)
      CLOSE(1)
      CLOSE(2)
      CLOSE(3)
      CLOSE(4)
      CLOSE(8)
      CLOSE(9)
      CLOSE(10)
      CLOSE(12)
      CLOSE(7)
      RETURN
      END
C*****SUBROUTINE TO CALCULATE THE CROSSTALK VOLTAGE
      SUBROUTINE CRSTALK(VCRSTALK,LEN)
```

```
         COMPLEX*16  XCUREN,VCROSS,VR,VI,VCRSTALK,
                     ZO,ZY,ZCL
         COMPLEX*16  ZRIGHT,ZLEFT,GAMMA
         REAL LEN
         COMMON / BOTH / ZO,GAMMA,ZCL
         COMMON / VCROSS / XCUREN,ZRIGHT,ZLEFT
         ZY = CDEXP(-1.0*GAMMA*LEN)
         XCUREN = XCUREN*ZLEFT / (ZLEFT + ZRIGHT)
         VCROSS = XCUREN*ZRIGHT
         VR = (1.0 / ZY)*(1.0 + (ZCL / ZO)) / (1.0- (ZCL / ZO))
         VR = VCROSS / (ZY- VR)
         VI = -((1.+ (ZCL / ZO)) / (ZY*(1.- (ZCL / ZO))))*VR
         VCRSTALK = (ZY*VI- VR)*ZCL / ZO
         RETURN
         END
C*****SUBROUTINE  TO  CALCULATE  THE  OUTPUT  VOLTAGE
         SUBROUTINE  OUTPUT(VOUTPUT,LEN)
         COMPLEX*16  VLOAD,CURRENT,LMLOAD,VR,VI,
        $            ZO,ZY,ZCL,VOUTPUT
         COMPLEX*16  GAMMA
         REAL LEN
         COMMON / BOTH / ZO,GAMMA,ZCL
         COMMON / VOUT / CURRENT,LMLOAD
         ZY = CDEXP(-1.0*GAMMA*LEN)
         VLOAD = CURRENT*LMLOAD
         VR = (1./ ZY)*(1.+ (ZCL / ZO)) / (1- (ZCL / ZO))
         VR = VLOAD / (ZY- VR)
         VI = -((1.+ (ZCL / ZO)) / (ZY*(1.- (ZCL / ZO))))*VR
         VOUTPUT = (ZY*VI- VR)*ZCL / ZO
         RETURN
         END
C*****FUNCTION  TO  COMPUTE  PARALLEL  COMBINATIONS
         COMPLEX*16  FUNCTION  PARALL(Z1,Z2)
         COMPLEX*16  Z1,Z2
         PARALL = Z1*Z2 / (Z1 + Z2)
         RETURN
         END
C*****THE  FOLLOWING  CODE  TAKES  CARE  OF  THE  AREA
C      CHANGE  DUE  TO  SKIN  DEPTH
         SUBROUTINE  SKNDEPTH(IW,THICK,AREA,PERIOD)
         REAL AREA,THICK,SKDEPTH,IW,PERIOD
         SKDEPTH = 0.085E + 06*SQRT(PERIOD)
         AREA = 2.*SKDEPTH*(IW + THICK- 2.*SKDEPTH)
         IF(SKDEPTH.GT.(IW / 2.))  AREA = IW*THICK
         RETURN
         END
```

```
C
      SUBROUTINE SCIC(IW,C11,C22,C12,C13)
      REAL C1(100),C2(100),C3(100),C4(100)
      REAL C6(100),C5(100)
      REAL C11,C22,C12,C13,IW,IS
      INTEGER NIS
      NIS = IW*10
      IF(((IW*10)-NIS).GE.0.5) THEN
      NIS = NIS + 1
      ENDIF
      OPEN(18,FILE = 'CAPACITANCE.DAT',STATUS = 'OLD')
      READ(18,*)
      DO 10 I = 1,NIS
      READ(18,*)IS,C1(I),C2(I),C3(I),C4(I),
             C5(I),C6(I)
   10 CONTINUE
      C11 = C1(NIS)
      C22 = C2(NIS)
      C12 = C4(NIS)
      C13 = C6(NIS)
      CLOSE(18)
      RETURN
      END
C
      SUBROUTINE CAPACIT(VARY,PARAMVAL,C11,C22,
     $                   C12,C13)
      INTEGER VARY,N
      REAL C11,C22,C12,C13,C25,C44,PARAMVAL,TEMP,OLD
      OLD = PARAMVAL
      IF(VARY.EQ.1) THEN
      OPEN(19,FILE = "LENGTH.DAT",STATUS = "OLD")
      IF(PARAMVAL.LT.100.0) PARAMVAL = 100.0
      IF(PARAMVAL.GT.1000.0) PARAMVAL = 1000.0
      N = PARAMVAL / 10
      IF(N.GT.10) THEN
      N = N- 10
      DO 10 I = 1,N
      READ(19,*)
   10 CONTINUE
      ENDIF
      ENDIF
      IF(VARY.EQ.2) THEN
      OPEN(19,FILE = "WIDTH.DAT",STATUS = "OLD")
      IF(PARAMVAL.LT.0.5) PARAMVAL = 0.5
      IF(PARAMVAL.GT.10.0) PARAMVAL = 10.0
```

```
        N = PARAMVAL*10
        IF(N.GT.5) THEN
        N = N- 5
        DO 11 I = 1,N
        READ(19,*)
11      CONTINUE
        ENDIF
        ENDIF
        IF(VARY.EQ.8) THEN
        OPEN(19,FILE = "SEPARATION.DAT",STATUS = "OLD")
        IF(PARAMVAL.LT.0.1) PARAMVAL = 0.1
        IF(PARAMVAL.GT.10.0) PARAMVAL = 10.0
        N = PARAMVAL*10
        IF(N.GT.1) THEN
        DO 12 I = 1,N- 1
        READ(19,*)
12      CONTINUE
        ENDIF
        ENDIF
        IF(VARY.EQ.9) THEN
        OPEN(19,FILE = "LEVDIST.DAT",STATUS = "OLD")
        IF(PARAMVAL.LT.0.1) PARAMVAL = 0.1
        IF(PARAMVAL.GT.20.0) PARAMVAL = 20.0
        N = PARAMVAL*10
        DO 13 I = 1,N- 1
        READ(19,*)
13      CONTINUE
        ENDIF
        IF(VARY.EQ.7) THEN
        OPEN(19,FILE = "THICK.DAT",STATUS = "OLD")
        IF(PARAMVAL.LT.10) PARAMVAL = 10.0
        IF(PARAMVAL.GT.500.0) PARAMVAL = 500.0
        N = PARAMVAL / 10
        IF(N.GT.1) THEN
        DO 14 I = 1,N- 1
        READ(19,*)
14      CONTINUE
        ENDIF
        ENDIF
        READ(19,*)
        READ(19,*)
        IF(VARY.EQ.9) THEN
        READ(19,*)TEMP,C11,C22,C25,C13,C12,C44,C55
        ELSE
```

```
      READ(19,*)TEMP,C11,C22,C12,C13
      IF(VARY.EQ.8) THEN
      C11 = C11*10
      C13 = C13*10
      C12 = C12*10
      C22 = C22*10
      ENDIF
      ENDIF
      CLOSE(19)
      PARAMVAL = OLD
      RETURN
      END
C

      SUBROUTINE SCIL(IW,L11,L22,L12,L13)
      REAL L11,L22,L12,L13,IW
      INTEGER NIS
      OPEN(20,FILE = "INIW.DAT",STATUS = `OLD')
      READ(20,*)
      READ(20,*)
      IF(IW.LT.0.1) IW = 0.1
      IF(IW.GT.10.0) IW = 10.0
      NIS = IW*10
      IF(NIS.EQ.1) THEN
      READ(20,*)L11,L22,L12,L13
      ELSE
      DO 10 I = 1,NIS- 1
      READ(20,*)
10    CONTINUE
      ENDIF
      READ(20,*)L11,L22,L12,L13
      CLOSE(20)
      RETURN
      END
C

      SUBROUTINE INDUCT(THICK,L11,L22,L12,L13)
      REAL L11,L22,L12,L13,THICK
      INTEGER NIS
      OPEN(31,FILE = "INTHICK.DAT",STATUS = `OLD')
      READ(31,*)
      READ(31,*)
      IF(THICK.LT.10) THICK = 10.0
      IF(THICK.GT.1000.0) THICK = 1000.0
      NIS = THICK / 10.0
      IF(NIS.EQ.1) THEN
```

```
      READ(31,*)L11,L22,L12,L13
      GOTO 20
      ELSE
      DO 10 I=1,NIS-1
      READ(31,*)
 10   CONTINUE
      ENDIF
      READ(31,*)L11,L22,L12,L13
 20   CLOSE(31)
      RETURN
      END
```

FILE: ZMATRI

```
      (11.83009373916819D0,1.593753005885813D0),
      (11.22085377939519D0,4.792864167565669D0),
      (9.933383722175002D0,8.033106634266296D0),
      (7.781146264464616D0,11.36889164904993D0),
      (4.234522494797000D0,14.95704378128156D0),
      (16286.62368050479D0,-139074.7115516051D0),
      (-28178.11171305162D0,74357.58237274176D0),
      (14629.74025233142D0,-19181.80818501836D0),
      (-2870.418161032078D0,1674.109484084304D0),
      (132.1659412474876D0,17.47674798877164D0),
      5
```

FILE: INIW.DAT (Inductances for Single-Level Interconnections)

Width	L11	L22	L12	L13
0.10	21.9157	22.4731	14.6051	10.9911
0.20	19.4419	19.6655	12.7633	10.1383
0.30	17.8134	17.9000	11.6595	9.5412
0.40	16.6600	16.6864	10.9244	9.0998
0.50	15.8000	15.8000	10.4000	8.7600
0.60	15.1339	15.1237	10.0075	8.4902
0.70	14.6025	14.5902	9.7030	8.2705
0.80	14.1684	14.1582	9.4604	8.0879
0.90	13.8066	13.8008	9.2631	7.9332
1.00	13.5000	13.5000	9.1000	7.8000
1.10	13.2359	13.2430	8.9637	7.6829
1.20	13.0046	13.0205	8.8488	7.5770
1.30	12.7975	12.8258	8.7516	7.4750
1.40	12.6043	12.6536	8.6693	7.3512
1.50	12.4000	12.5000	8.6000	7.0000

Width	L11	L22	L12	L13
1.60	11.9191	12.3616	8.5421	7.4098
1.70	12.5073	12.2357	8.4943	7.3072
1.80	12.2463	12.1196	8.4556	7.2410
1.90	12.1086	12.0101	8.4247	7.1870
2.00	12.0000	11.9000	8.4000	7.1400
2.10	11.9065	11.7455	8.3796	7.0979
2.20	11.8233	11.9629	8.3614	7.0595
2.30	11.7482	11.7521	8.3431	7.0243
2.40	11.6798	11.6611	8.3229	6.9916
2.50	11.6174	11.5872	8.2998	6.9610
2.60	11.5605	11.5212	8.2735	6.9320
2.70	11.5087	11.4604	8.2445	6.9041
2.80	11.4627	11.4037	8.2136	6.8761
2.90	11.4241	11.3504	8.1818	6.8456
3.00	11.4000	11.3000	8.1500	6.8000
3.10	11.4427	11.2521	8.1188	4.2610
3.20	10.9941	11.2065	8.0887	6.8634
3.30	11.1558	11.1629	8.0600	6.8198
3.40	11.1496	11.1211	8.0328	6.7946
3.50	11.1277	11.0810	8.0071	6.7746
3.60	11.1022	11.0423	7.9829	6.7572
3.70	11.0759	11.0050	7.9602	6.7413
3.80	11.0499	10.9689	7.9389	6.7267
3.90	11.0246	10.9339	7.9188	6.7129
4.00	11.0000	10.9000	7.9000	6.7000
4.10	10.9763	10.8670	7.8823	6.6878
4.20	10.9535	10.8348	7.8655	6.6761
4.30	10.9316	10.8034	7.8498	6.6651
4.40	10.9105	10.7727	7.8348	6.6545
4.50	10.8903	10.7426	7.8207	6.6444
4.60	10.8708	10.7132	7.8073	6.6348
4.70	10.8521	10.6842	7.7946	6.6256
4.80	10.8341	10.6557	7.7825	6.6167
4.90	10.8167	10.6277	7.7710	6.6082
5.00	10.8000	10.6000	7.7600	6.6000
5.10	10.7839	10.5727	7.7495	6.5921
5.20	10.7684	10.5456	7.7395	6.5845
5.30	10.7534	10.5189	7.7299	6.5772
5.40	10.7389	10.4923	7.7207	6.5702
5.50	10.7249	10.4660	7.7120	6.5634
5.60	10.7114	10.4398	7.7035	6.5568
5.70	10.6983	10.4138	7.6954	6.5505
5.80	10.6857	10.3878	7.6876	6.5444
5.90	10.6734	10.3619	7.6801	6.5384

Width	L11	L22	L12	L13
6.00	10.6616	10.3361	7.6729	6.5327
6.10	10.6501	10.3102	7.6659	6.5271
6.20	10.6390	10.2844	7.6592	6.5217
6.30	10.6282	10.2585	7.6527	6.5165
6.40	10.6177	10.2326	7.6464	6.5114
6.50	10.6075	10.2065	7.6404	6.5065
6.60	10.5977	10.1804	7.6345	6.5017
6.70	10.5881	10.1540	7.6289	6.4971
6.80	10.5787	10.1276	7.6234	6.4926
6.90	10.5697	10.1009	7.6181	6.4882
7.00	10.5608	10.0740	7.6129	6.4839
7.10	10.5523	10.0469	7.6079	6.4798
7.20	10.5439	10.0195	7.6031	6.4757
7.30	10.5358	9.9918	7.5984	6.4718
7.40	10.5279	9.9637	7.5938	6.4680
7.50	10.5201	9.9353	7.5894	6.4642
7.60	10.5126	9.9065	7.5851	6.4606
7.70	10.5053	9.8773	7.5809	6.4570
7.80	10.4981	9.8477	7.5768	6.4536
7.90	10.4911	9.8176	7.5728	6.4502
8.00	10.4843	9.7870	7.5689	6.4469
8.10	10.4777	9.7558	7.5652	6.4437
8.20	10.4712	9.7241	7.5615	6.4406
8.30	10.4648	9.6917	7.5579	6.4375
8.40	10.4586	9.6587	7.5544	6.4345
8.50	10.4526	9.6250	7.5510	6.4316
8.60	10.4467	9.5906	7.5477	6.4287
8.70	10.4409	9.5554	7.5444	6.4259
8.80	10.4352	9.5194	7.5413	6.4232
8.90	10.4297	9.4825	7.5382	6.4205
9.00	10.4243	9.4447	7.5352	6.4179
9.10	10.4190	9.4059	7.5322	6.4153
9.20	10.4138	9.3661	7.5293	6.4128
9.30	10.4087	9.3251	7.5265	6.4103
9.40	10.4037	9.2830	7.5237	6.4079
9.50	10.3988	9.2397	7.5210	6.4056
9.60	10.3940	9.1951	7.5184	6.4032
9.70	10.3894	9.1491	7.5158	6.4010
9.80	10.3848	9.1016	7.5133	6.3987
9.90	10.3803	9.0526	7.5108	6.3966
10.00	10.3758	9.0019	7.5084	6.3944

FILE: INTHICK.DAT (Inductances for Single-Level Inter connections)

Thickness	L11	L22	L12	L13
10.00	8.7500	8.7000	4.3750	3.1250
20.00	10.1000	10.0500	5.7500	4.3750
30.00	10.9000	10.8500	6.5700	5.2050
40.00	11.2218	11.3856	7.1141	5.7487
50.00	11.8200	11.7700	7.5000	6.1250
60.00	12.1101	12.0598	7.7854	6.3888
70.00	12.3376	12.2868	7.9993	6.5449
80.00	12.5223	12.4707	8.1459	6.1294
90.00	12.6813	12.6277	7.9638	7.2777
100.00	12.9200	12.8700	8.6250	7.2500
110.00	12.8498	12.8094	8.6572	7.3112
120.00	12.9600	12.9140	8.7270	7.3791
130.00	13.0438	12.9963	8.7954	7.4431
140.00	13.1149	13.0666	8.8581	7.5014
150.00	13.1769	13.1281	8.9146	7.5539
160.00	13.2317	13.1825	8.9654	7.6013
170.00	13.2805	13.2311	9.0113	7.6440
180.00	13.3244	13.2747	9.0529	7.6827
190.00	13.3640	13.3142	9.0906	7.7179
200.00	13.4000	13.3500	9.1250	7.7500
210.00	13.4329	13.3827	9.1565	7.7794
220.00	13.4630	13.4127	9.1854	7.8063
230.00	13.4907	13.4403	9.2121	7.8312
240.00	13.5162	13.4657	9.2367	7.8541
250.00	13.5399	13.4893	9.2595	7.8754
260.00	13.5619	13.5112	9.2807	7.8952
270.00	13.5823	13.5316	9.3005	7.9136
280.00	13.6014	13.5506	9.3190	7.9308
290.00	13.6193	13.5684	9.3363	7.9469
300.00	13.6360	13.5851	9.3525	7.9620
310.00	13.6518	13.6007	9.3677	7.9762
320.00	13.6666	13.6155	9.3820	7.9896
330.00	13.6806	13.6294	9.3956	8.0022
340.00	13.6937	13.6425	9.4084	8.0141
350.00	13.7062	13.6550	9.4204	8.0253
360.00	13.7181	13.6667	9.4319	8.0360
370.00	13.7293	13.6779	9.4428	8.0461
380.00	13.7399	13.6885	9.4531	8.0557
390.00	13.7501	13.6986	9.4630	8.0649
400.00	13.7597	13.7082	9.4723	8.0736
410.00	13.7689	13.7174	9.4812	8.0819
420.00	13.7777	13.7262	9.4898	8.0898
430.00	13.7861	13.7345	9.4979	8.0974

Thickness	L11	L22	L12	L13
440.00	13.7941	13.7425	9.5057	8.1046
450.00	13.8018	13.7502	9.5132	8.1116
460.00	13.8092	13.7575	9.5203	8.1182
470.00	13.8163	13.7646	9.5272	8.1246
480.00	13.8231	13.7713	9.5338	8.1307
490.00	13.8296	13.7778	9.5401	8.1366
500.00	13.8359	13.7841	9.5462	8.1423

FILE: LENGTH.DAT (Capacitances for Single-Level Inter connections)

Length	C11 = C33	C22	C12 = C23	C13
10.00	1.935	1.998	0.370	0.139
20.00	2.963	2.584	0.851	0.290
30.00	3.640	3.067	1.339	0.435
40.00	4.248	3.487	1.858	0.590
50.00	4.812	3.869	2.400	0.753
60.00	5.346	4.227	2.957	0.924
70.00	5.856	4.566	3.528	1.101
80.00	6.347	4.892	4.109	1.285
90.00	6.823	5.207	4.699	1.474
100.00	7.286	5.513	5.295	1.667
110.00	7.737	5.812	5.898	1.865
120.00	8.178	6.104	6.505	2.068
130.00	8.611	6.392	7.116	2.275
140.00	9.037	6.676	7.731	2.485
150.00	9.457	6.956	8.348	2.699
160.00	9.870	7.233	8.968	2.917
170.00	10.277	7.507	9.590	3.137
180.00	10.680	7.778	10.213	3.361
190.00	11.077	8.047	10.839	3.587
200.00	11.471	8.314	11.466	3.816
210.00	11.860	8.578	12.094	4.046
220.00	12.246	8.841	12.723	4.280
230.00	12.629	9.101	13.354	4.514
240.00	13.010	9.362	13.985	4.751
250.00	13.386	9.619	14.618	4.991
260.00	13.759	9.875	15.251	5.231
270.00	14.130	10.130	15.885	5.474
280.00	14.498	10.383	16.520	5.718
290.00	14.864	10.635	17.156	5.964
300.00	15.227	10.885	17.791	6.210
310.00	15.588	11.135	18.428	6.459
320.00	15.948	11.383	19.065	6.708
330.00	16.305	11.630	19.704	6.959

Length	C11 = C33	C22	C12 = C23	C13
340.00	16.660	11.876	20.342	7.210
350.00	17.014	12.121	20.980	7.463
360.00	17.366	12.365	21.619	7.717
370.00	17.717	12.609	22.259	7.972
380.00	18.065	12.851	22.899	8.227
390.00	18.412	13.092	23.539	8.483
400.00	18.757	13.332	24.181	8.740
410.00	19.101	13.571	24.824	9.000
420.00	19.443	13.810	25.464	9.258
430.00	19.785	14.048	26.107	9.517
440.00	20.125	14.285	26.750	9.777
450.00	20.465	14.521	27.394	10.038
460.00	20.803	14.757	28.036	10.300
470.00	21.140	14.992	28.681	10.561
480.00	21.476	15.227	29.321	10.824
490.00	21.811	15.461	29.967	11.088
500.00	22.144	15.695	30.611	11.352
510.00	22.478	15.927	31.257	11.616
520.00	22.810	16.159	31.898	11.880
530.00	23.140	16.390	32.544	12.145
540.00	23.471	16.622	33.188	12.412
550.00	23.799	16.852	33.832	12.678
560.00	24.128	17.083	34.476	12.944
570.00	24.455	17.312	35.120	13.212
580.00	24.782	17.541	35.770	13.480
590.00	25.108	17.768	36.416	13.746
600.00	25.434	17.996	37.066	14.014
610.00	25.757	18.225	37.706	14.285
620.00	26.082	18.450	38.363	14.552
630.00	26.404	18.677	39.002	14.820
640.00	26.728	18.902	39.657	15.091
650.00	27.048	19.129	40.300	15.362
660.00	27.373	19.353	40.958	15.629
670.00	27.694	19.579	41.598	15.899
680.00	28.013	19.806	42.238	16.172
690.00	28.333	20.030	42.888	16.443
700.00	28.651	20.254	43.537	16.716
710.00	28.969	20.477	44.182	16.988
720.00	29.288	20.699	44.838	17.260
730.00	29.603	20.922	45.481	17.531
740.00	29.920	21.145	46.129	17.805
750.00	30.237	21.366	46.787	18.079
760.00	30.552	21.587	47.433	18.349
770.00	30.867	21.809	48.077	18.623

Length	C11 = C33	C22	C12 = C23	C13
780.00	31.181	22.030	48.728	18.896
790.00	31.495	22.250	49.380	19.171
800.00	31.809	22.471	50.027	19.446
810.00	32.121	22.689	50.676	19.718
820.00	32.433	22.910	51.333	19.994
830.00	32.745	23.129	51.977	20.268
840.00	33.057	23.349	52.627	20.545
850.00	33.368	23.568	53.279	20.822
860.00	33.679	23.785	53.930	21.095
870.00	33.990	24.002	54.581	21.367
880.00	34.299	24.221	55.223	21.644
890.00	34.607	24.439	55.868	21.919
900.00	34.920	24.658	56.535	22.202
910.00	35.227	24.873	57.179	22.472
920.00	35.534	25.090	57.823	22.748
930.00	35.844	25.307	58.490	23.030
940.00	36.150	25.524	59.120	23.301
950.00	36.459	25.739	59.789	23.581
960.00	36.766	25.955	60.454	23.862
970.00	37.071	26.172	61.078	24.135
980.00	37.379	26.385	61.749	24.413
990.00	37.688	26.599	62.415	24.691
1000.00	37.987	26.813	63.040	24.959

FILE: LEVDIST.DAT (Capacitances for Bilevel Interconnections)

Lev. Dist.	C11	C22	C12	C13	C25	C44	C55
0.10	4.1041	5.2706	0.6197	1.2910	399.2693	24.3093	26.2795
0.20	5.1228	5.0061	0.6635	1.2389	346.7396	16.9497	25.1653
0.30	5.8567	4.7617	2.0302	1.1954	303.5253	223.8980	24.2348
0.40	6.4120	4.5367	3.4618	1.1605	267.6671	43.6525	23.4507
0.50	6.8479	4.3300	4.9410	1.1342	237.6600	37.6719	22.7847
0.60	7.2001	4.1409	6.4521	1.1164	212.3455	35.6018	22.2155
0.70	7.4914	3.9683	7.9806	1.1073	190.8259	34.5589	21.7263
0.80	7.7369	3.8115	9.5141	1.1066	172.4004	33.9354	21.3042
0.90	7.9472	3.6696	11.0414	1.1144	156.5178	33.5240	20.9388
1.00	8.1297	3.5418	12.5534	1.1305	142.7411	33.2346	20.6215
1.10	8.2901	3.4272	14.0422	1.1548	130.7209	33.0220	20.3455
1.20	8.4324	3.3251	15.5016	1.1873	120.1760	32.8607	20.1052
1.30	8.5599	3.2347	16.9263	1.2277	110.8782	32.7355	19.8959
1.40	8.6750	3.1554	18.3125	1.2759	102.6409	32.6366	19.7136
1.50	8.7796	3.0863	19.6573	1.3318	95.3108	32.5574	19.5549
1.60	8.8755	3.0269	20.9587	1.3951	88.7608	32.4936	19.4171
1.70	8.9637	2.9765	22.2152	1.4656	82.8851	32.4417	19.2978
1.80	9.0453	2.9345	23.4262	1.5432	77.5950	32.3995	19.1948
1.90	9.1212	2.9004	24.5915	1.6277	72.8158	32.3652	19.1063

Lev. Dist.	C11	C22	C12	C13	C25	C44	C55
2.00	9.1922	2.8736	25.7114	1.7187	68.4842	32.3373	19.0309
2.10	9.2588	2.8536	26.7865	1.8161	64.5464	32.3148	18.9671
2.20	9.3214	2.8400	27.8175	1.9196	60.9562	32.2969	18.9138
2.30	9.3807	2.8323	28.8057	2.0291	57.6742	32.2829	18.8699
2.40	9.4368	2.8300	29.7521	2.1441	54.6661	32.2723	18.8345
2.50	9.4902	2.8328	30.6582	2.2645	51.9025	32.2645	18.8067
2.60	9.5411	2.8403	31.5253	2.3901	49.3576	32.2593	18.7859
2.70	9.5898	2.8521	32.3550	2.5205	47.0089	32.2563	18.7714
2.80	9.6364	2.8679	33.1487	2.6555	44.8369	32.2553	18.7626
2.90	9.6812	2.8875	33.9079	2.7948	42.8243	32.2561	18.7590
3.00	9.7243	2.9104	34.6341	2.9382	40.9559	32.2583	18.7601
3.10	9.7659	2.9365	35.3288	3.0855	39.2182	32.2620	18.7656
3.20	9.8061	2.9654	35.9934	3.2363	37.5993	32.2670	18.7750
3.30	9.8450	2.9971	36.6292	3.3904	36.0886	32.2731	18.7880
3.40	9.8827	3.0311	37.2378	3.5476	34.6767	32.2802	18.8042
3.50	9.9193	3.0674	37.8203	3.7076	33.3552	32.2883	18.8235
3.60	9.9549	3.1057	38.3780	3.8702	32.1165	32.2972	18.8455
3.70	9.9895	3.1458	38.9121	4.0352	30.9538	32.3070	18.8701
3.80	10.0233	3.1876	39.4237	4.2023	29.8609	32.3175	18.8969
3.90	10.0563	3.2310	39.9141	4.3713	28.8325	32.3286	18.9259
4.00	10.0885	3.2757	40.3841	4.5420	27.8635	32.3404	18.9568
4.10	10.1201	3.3216	40.8348	4.7141	26.9494	32.3528	18.9894
4.20	10.1510	3.3687	41.2671	4.8876	26.0861	32.3657	19.0237
4.30	10.1812	3.4168	41.6820	5.0622	25.2700	32.3791	19.0595
4.40	10.2110	3.4658	42.0803	5.2377	24.4976	32.3930	19.0966
4.50	10.2401	3.5155	42.4628	5.4139	23.7659	32.4074	19.1350
4.60	10.2688	3.5660	42.8302	5.5907	23.0720	32.4221	19.1745
4.70	10.2970	3.6170	43.1833	5.7678	22.4133	32.4373	19.2150
4.80	10.3248	3.6686	43.5229	5.9452	21.7876	32.4529	19.2565
4.90	10.3521	3.7206	43.8494	6.1227	21.1926	32.4688	19.2989
5.00	10.3791	3.7730	44.1636	6.3002	20.6264	32.4850	19.3420
5.10	10.4057	3.8257	44.4660	6.4775	20.0871	32.5016	19.3858
5.20	10.4319	3.8787	44.7573	6.6544	19.5730	32.5184	19.4303
5.30	10.4578	3.9318	45.0378	6.8310	19.0826	32.5356	19.4754
5.40	10.4834	3.9851	45.3081	7.0069	18.6144	32.5530	19.5210
5.50	10.5088	4.0385	45.5688	7.1823	18.1671	32.5707	19.5670
5.60	10.5338	4.0920	45.8201	7.3569	17.7395	32.5887	19.6135
5.70	10.5585	4.1454	46.0626	7.5306	17.3304	32.6069	19.6604
5.80	10.5831	4.1989	46.2966	7.7034	16.9387	32.6253	19.7076
5.90	10.6073	4.2522	46.5226	7.8752	16.5635	32.6440	19.7551
6.00	10.6314	4.3055	46.7408	8.0459	16.2039	32.6629	19.8028
6.10	10.6552	4.3586	46.9517	8.2154	15.8590	32.6820	19.8508
6.20	10.6789	4.4116	47.1555	8.3837	15.5280	32.7013	19.8989
6.30	10.7023	4.4645	47.3526	8.5507	15.2102	32.7208	19.9472
6.40	10.7256	4.5171	47.5431	8.7164	14.9048	32.7405	19.9957
6.50	10.7487	4.5695	47.7275	8.8807	14.6113	32.7604	20.0442
6.60	10.7716	4.6217	47.9060	9.0435	14.3289	32.7805	20.0928
6.70	10.7943	4.6736	48.0788	9.2048	14.0572	32.8007	20.1415
6.80	10.8169	4.7252	48.2462	9.3646	13.7957	32.8211	20.1902
6.90	10.8394	4.7765	48.4083	9.5229	13.5437	32.8417	20.2390
7.00	10.8617	4.8276	48.5654	9.6796	13.3009	32.8625	20.2877

Lev. Dist.	C11	C22	C12	C13	C25	C44	C55
7.10	10.8839	4.8783	48.7178	9.8347	13.0667	32.8834	20.3364
7.20	10.9060	4.9287	48.8655	9.9881	12.8409	32.9044	20.3851
7.30	10.9279	4.9788	49.0088	10.1398	12.6230	32.9257	20.4338
7.40	10.9498	5.0285	49.1478	10.2899	12.4125	32.9470	20.4823
7.50	10.9715	5.0779	49.2828	10.4383	12.2093	32.9686	20.5308
7.60	10.9931	5.1269	49.4138	10.5850	12.0129	32.9902	20.5793
7.70	11.0146	5.1756	49.5411	10.7300	11.8231	33.0120	20.6276
7.80	11.0360	5.2238	49.6647	10.8733	11.6396	33.0340	20.6758
7.90	11.0574	5.2718	49.7849	11.0148	11.4620	33.0561	20.7239
8.00	11.0786	5.3193	49.9017	11.1547	11.2901	33.0783	20.7718
8.10	11.0998	5.3664	50.0152	11.2927	11.1237	33.1006	20.8196
8.20	11.1209	5.4132	50.1256	11.4291	10.9626	33.1231	20.8673
8.30	11.1419	5.4596	50.2331	11.5637	10.8065	33.1457	20.9148
8.40	11.1628	5.5056	50.3376	11.6966	10.6552	33.1685	20.9622
8.50	11.1837	5.5512	50.4393	11.8278	10.5085	33.1914	21.0094
8.60	11.2045	5.5964	50.5384	11.9573	10.3663	33.2144	21.0564
8.70	11.2252	5.6412	50.6348	12.0851	10.2283	33.2375	21.1032
8.80	11.2459	5.6857	50.7288	12.2112	10.0944	33.2608	21.1499
8.90	11.2665	5.7297	50.8203	12.3356	9.9644	33.2841	21.1964
9.00	11.2870	5.7734	50.9095	12.4583	9.8381	33.3076	21.2427
9.10	11.3075	5.8166	50.9964	12.5794	9.7155	33.3312	21.2888
9.20	11.3280	5.8595	51.0812	12.6988	9.5964	33.3550	21.3347
9.30	11.3484	5.9020	51.1638	12.8166	9.4806	33.3788	21.3804
9.40	11.3687	5.9441	51.2445	12.9328	9.3681	33.4028	21.4259
9.50	11.3891	5.9858	51.3231	13.0474	9.2586	33.4269	21.4712
9.60	11.4093	6.0272	51.3999	13.1603	9.1522	33.4511	21.5162
9.70	11.4295	6.0681	51.4748	13.2717	9.0486	33.4754	21.5611
9.80	11.4497	6.1087	51.5479	13.3816	8.9478	33.4998	21.6057
9.90	11.4699	6.1489	51.6194	13.4899	8.8496	33.5243	21.6502
10.00	11.4900	6.1887	51.6891	13.5967	8.7541	33.5490	21.6944
10.10	11.5101	6.2282	51.7572	13.7020	8.6610	33.5738	21.7384
10.20	11.5301	6.2672	51.8238	13.8058	8.5704	33.5986	21.7822
10.30	11.5501	6.3060	51.8888	13.9081	8.4821	33.6236	21.8257
10.40	11.5701	6.3443	51.9524	14.0090	8.3960	33.6487	21.8691
10.50	11.5901	6.3823	52.0146	14.1084	8.3120	33.6740	21.9122
10.60	11.6100	6.4199	52.0753	14.2065	8.2302	33.6993	21.9551
10.70	11.6299	6.4572	52.1348	14.3031	8.1504	33.7247	21.9977
10.80	11.6498	6.4941	52.1929	14.3984	8.0725	33.7503	22.0402
10.90	11.6697	6.5307	52.2498	14.4923	7.9965	33.7759	22.0824
11.00	11.6895	6.5670	52.3054	14.5848	7.9224	33.8017	22.1244
11.10	11.7093	6.6029	52.3599	14.6761	7.8500	33.8276	22.1661
11.20	11.7291	6.6384	52.4132	14.7660	7.7794	33.8535	22.2077
11.30	11.7489	6.6736	52.4654	14.8547	7.7104	33.8796	22.2490
11.40	11.7687	6.7085	52.5165	14.9420	7.6430	33.9058	22.2901
11.50	11.7884	6.7431	52.5665	15.0282	7.5771	33.9321	22.3309
11.60	11.8082	6.7773	52.6156	15.1131	7.5128	33.9586	22.3716
11.70	11.8279	6.8112	52.6636	15.1968	7.4499	33.9851	22.4120
11.80	11.8476	6.8448	52.7106	15.2793	7.3885	34.0117	22.4522
11.90	11.8673	6.8781	52.7567	15.3606	7.3284	34.0385	22.4921
12.00	11.8870	6.9110	52.8019	15.4408	7.2696	34.0653	22.5319
12.10	11.9066	6.9437	52.8462	15.5198	7.2122	34.0923	22.5714

Lev. Dist.	C11	C22	C12	C13	C25	C44	C55
12.20	11.9263	6.9760	52.8896	15.5977	7.1560	34.1194	22.6107
12.30	11.9459	7.0081	52.9322	15.6745	7.1010	34.1465	22.6498
12.40	11.9656	7.0398	52.9740	15.7502	7.0472	34.1738	22.6886
12.50	11.9852	7.0713	53.0149	15.8249	6.9945	34.2012	22.7273
12.60	12.0048	7.1024	53.0551	15.8985	6.9430	34.2287	22.7657
12.70	12.0244	7.1333	53.0945	15.9710	6.8925	34.2563	22.8039
12.80	12.0441	7.1639	53.1332	16.0425	6.8431	34.2841	22.8419
12.90	12.0637	7.1942	53.1712	16.1131	6.7948	34.3119	22.8796
13.00	12.0833	7.2242	53.2084	16.1826	6.7474	34.3398	22.9172
13.10	12.1029	7.2539	53.2450	16.2512	6.7010	34.3679	22.9545
13.20	12.1225	7.2834	53.2809	16.3188	6.6555	34.3961	22.9916
13.30	12.1421	7.3126	53.3161	16.3854	6.6109	34.4243	23.0285
13.40	12.1616	7.3415	53.3508	16.4511	6.5673	34.4527	23.0652
13.50	12.1812	7.3702	53.3848	16.5160	6.5244	34.4812	23.1017
13.60	12.2008	7.3986	53.4182	16.5799	6.4825	34.5098	23.1380
13.70	12.2204	7.4267	53.4510	16.6429	6.4413	34.5386	23.1741
13.80	12.2400	7.4546	53.4832	16.7051	6.4010	34.5674	23.2100
13.90	12.2596	7.4822	53.5149	16.7664	6.3614	34.5963	23.2456
14.00	12.2792	7.5096	53.5460	16.8269	6.3226	34.6254	23.2811
14.10	12.2988	7.5367	53.5766	16.8865	6.2846	34.6545	23.3163
14.20	12.3184	7.5636	53.6067	16.9454	6.2472	34.6838	23.3514
14.30	12.3380	7.5903	53.6362	17.0034	6.2106	34.7132	23.3862
14.40	12.3575	7.6167	53.6653	17.0606	6.1746	34.7427	23.4209
14.50	12.3771	7.6428	53.6939	17.1171	6.1393	34.7723	23.4553
14.60	12.3967	7.6688	53.7220	17.1727	6.1046	34.8021	23.4896
14.70	12.4164	7.6945	53.7496	17.2277	6.0706	34.8319	23.5237
14.80	12.4360	7.7200	53.7768	17.2819	6.0372	34.8619	23.5575
14.90	12.4556	7.7452	53.8036	17.3354	6.0044	34.8919	23.5912
15.00	12.4752	7.7703	53.8299	17.3881	5.9722	34.9221	23.6247
15.10	12.4948	7.7951	53.8558	17.4402	5.9406	34.9524	23.6580
15.20	12.5145	7.8197	53.8813	17.4916	5.9095	34.9829	23.6911
15.30	12.5341	7.8441	53.9063	17.5423	5.8790	35.0134	23.7240
15.40	12.5538	7.8682	53.9310	17.5923	5.8490	35.0441	23.7567
15.50	12.5734	7.8922	53.9553	17.6417	5.8195	35.0748	23.7892
15.60	12.5931	7.9160	53.9792	17.6904	5.7905	35.1057	23.8216
15.70	12.6127	7.9395	54.0028	17.7385	5.7620	35.1367	23.8537
15.80	12.6324	7.9629	54.0260	17.7859	5.7341	35.1679	23.8857
15.90	12.6521	7.9860	54.0488	17.8327	5.7065	35.1991	23.9175
16.00	12.6718	8.0090	54.0713	17.8790	5.6795	35.2305	23.9491
16.10	12.6915	8.0317	54.0934	17.9246	5.6529	35.2620	23.9806
16.20	12.7112	8.0543	54.1152	17.9696	5.6267	35.2936	24.0118
16.30	12.7309	8.0766	54.1367	18.0141	5.6010	35.3253	24.0429
16.40	12.7506	8.0988	54.1579	18.0580	5.5757	35.3572	24.0738
16.50	12.7704	8.1208	54.1787	18.1013	5.5508	35.3891	24.1046
16.60	12.7901	8.1426	54.1993	18.1441	5.5263	35.4212	24.1352
16.70	12.8099	8.1642	54.2195	18.1863	5.5023	35.4534	24.1656
16.80	12.8297	8.1857	54.2395	18.2281	5.4786	35.4858	24.1958
16.90	12.8494	8.2069	54.2592	18.2692	5.4552	35.5182	24.2258
17.00	12.8692	8.2280	54.2785	18.3099	5.4323	35.5508	24.2557
17.10	12.8890	8.2489	54.2977	18.3501	5.4097	35.5835	24.2854
17.20	12.9089	8.2697	54.3165	18.3897	5.3875	35.6164	24.3150
17.30	12.9287	8.2903	54.3351	18.4289	5.3656	35.6494	24.3444

Lev. Dist.	C11	C22	C12	C13	C25	C44	C55
17.40	12.9485	8.3107	54.3534	18.4675	5.3440	35.6825	24.3736
17.50	12.9684	8.3309	54.3714	18.5057	5.3228	35.7157	24.4027
17.60	12.9882	8.3510	54.3893	18.5435	5.3019	35.7490	24.4316
17.70	13.0081	8.3709	54.4068	18.5807	5.2813	35.7825	24.4603
17.80	13.0280	8.3906	54.4241	18.6176	5.2611	35.8161	24.4889
17.90	13.0479	8.4102	54.4412	18.6539	5.2411	35.8498	24.5173
18.00	13.0678	8.4296	54.4581	18.6898	5.2214	35.8837	24.5456
18.10	13.0878	8.4489	54.4747	18.7253	5.2021	35.9177	24.5737
18.20	13.1077	8.4680	54.4911	18.7604	5.1830	35.9518	24.6017
18.30	13.1277	8.4870	54.5073	18.7950	5.1642	35.9861	24.6295
18.40	13.1476	8.5058	54.5233	18.8292	5.1457	36.0205	24.6571
18.50	13.1676	8.5245	54.5391	18.8631	5.1274	36.0550	24.6846
18.60	13.1876	8.5430	54.5546	18.8965	5.1095	36.0897	24.7120
18.70	13.2076	8.5614	54.5700	18.9295	5.0917	36.1245	24.7392
18.80	13.2277	8.5796	54.5851	18.9621	5.0743	36.1594	24.7663
18.90	13.2477	8.5977	54.6001	18.9944	5.0570	36.1945	24.7932
19.00	13.2678	8.6156	54.6149	19.0262	5.0401	36.2297	24.8199
19.10	13.2879	8.6335	54.6294	19.0577	5.0233	36.2650	24.8466
19.20	13.3080	8.6511	54.6438	19.0889	5.0068	36.3005	24.8730
19.30	13.3281	8.6687	54.6580	19.1196	4.9906	36.3361	24.8994
19.40	13.3482	8.6861	54.6721	19.1500	4.9745	36.3719	24.9256
19.50	13.3683	8.7033	54.6859	19.1801	4.9587	36.4078	24.9516
19.60	13.3885	8.7205	54.6996	19.2098	4.9431	36.4438	24.9775
19.70	13.4087	8.7375	54.7131	19.2392	4.9277	36.4800	25.0033
19.80	13.4289	8.7543	54.7265	19.2682	4.9125	36.5163	25.0289
19.90	13.4491	8.7711	54.7397	19.2969	4.8976	36.5528	25.0544
20.00	13.4693	8.7877	54.7527	19.3253	4.8828	36.5894	25.0798

FILE: SEPARATION.DAT (Capacitances for Single-Level Interconnections)

Separation	C11	C22	C12	C13
0.10	36.258	21.357	95.627	28.398
0.20	36.401	22.286	89.162	28.241
0.30	36.566	23.091	83.880	27.959
0.40	36.759	23.780	79.523	27.553
0.50	36.959	24.407	75.783	27.140
0.60	37.160	24.969	72.572	26.698
0.70	37.370	25.486	69.748	26.256
0.80	37.574	25.960	67.264	25.814
0.90	37.783	26.405	65.026	25.390
1.00	37.987	26.813	63.040	24.959
1.10	38.190	27.207	61.213	24.564
1.20	38.390	27.574	59.559	24.169
1.30	38.587	27.925	58.033	23.794
1.40	38.782	28.258	56.632	23.425
1.50	38.974	28.576	55.335	23.076
1.60	39.161	28.879	54.135	22.731

Separation	C11	C22	C12	C13
1.70	39.346	29.176	52.996	22.411
1.80	39.529	29.459	51.942	22.095
1.90	39.708	29.730	50.953	21.790
2.00	39.884	29.992	50.024	21.492
2.10	40.059	30.249	49.139	21.212
2.20	40.227	30.497	48.307	20.942
2.30	40.396	30.737	47.518	20.674
2.40	40.561	30.971	46.767	20.419
2.50	40.726	31.199	46.049	20.168
2.60	40.885	31.420	45.371	19.927
2.70	41.041	31.635	44.725	19.693
2.80	41.201	31.848	44.093	19.470
2.90	41.352	32.055	43.497	19.250
3.00	41.503	32.258	42.924	19.036
3.10	41.652	32.455	42.376	18.827
3.20	41.800	32.646	41.852	18.622
3.30	41.944	32.839	41.338	18.429
3.40	42.089	33.023	40.849	18.235
3.50	42.230	33.206	40.375	18.047
3.60	42.369	33.384	39.922	17.864
3.70	42.505	33.564	39.473	17.693
3.80	42.643	33.735	39.048	17.517
3.90	42.777	33.907	38.631	17.348
4.00	42.907	34.072	38.236	17.185
4.10	43.041	34.237	37.844	17.020
4.20	43.168	34.401	37.467	16.866
4.30	43.297	34.558	37.105	16.707
4.40	43.422	34.716	36.747	16.558
4.50	43.549	34.873	36.396	16.412
4.60	43.671	35.026	36.060	16.271
4.70	43.794	35.175	35.734	16.127
4.80	43.914	35.324	35.415	15.988
4.90	44.034	35.470	35.105	15.851
5.00	44.149	35.619	34.797	15.726
5.10	44.267	35.758	34.506	15.591
5.20	44.381	35.903	34.213	15.468
5.30	44.500	36.042	33.927	15.341
5.40	44.611	36.177	33.658	15.216
5.50	44.723	36.312	33.390	15.093
5.60	44.835	36.449	33.123	14.976
5.70	44.946	36.584	32.860	14.867
5.80	45.051	36.713	32.615	14.748

Separation	C11	C22	C12	C13
5.90	45.160	36.844	32.366	14.635
6.00	45.266	36.975	32.121	14.528
6.10	45.373	37.101	31.885	14.418
6.20	45.478	37.227	31.653	14.312
6.30	45.578	37.349	31.432	14.208
6.40	45.683	37.476	31.204	14.106
6.50	45.787	37.595	30.987	14.002
6.60	45.887	37.718	30.770	13.906
6.70	45.986	37.841	30.555	13.812
6.80	46.087	37.957	30.352	13.710
6.90	46.186	38.077	30.144	13.617
7.00	46.283	38.192	29.946	13.524
7.10	46.379	38.309	29.748	13.434
7.20	46.474	38.423	29.558	13.342
7.30	46.568	38.536	29.369	13.254
7.40	46.662	38.650	29.181	13.168
7.50	46.756	38.762	28.996	13.081
7.60	46.850	38.871	28.817	12.996
7.70	46.940	38.980	28.641	12.911
7.80	47.033	39.089	28.465	12.827
7.90	47.121	39.199	28.293	12.748
8.00	47.212	39.306	28.122	12.669
8.10	47.301	39.413	27.955	12.590
8.20	47.389	39.516	27.793	12.508
8.30	47.476	39.621	27.631	12.435
8.40	47.561	39.723	27.475	12.358
8.50	47.649	39.827	27.315	12.282
8.60	47.736	39.928	27.161	12.207
8.70	47.819	40.030	27.009	12.135
8.80	47.903	40.131	26.858	12.062
8.90	47.989	40.230	26.708	11.991
9.00	48.070	40.326	26.568	11.918
9.10	48.152	40.427	26.421	11.852
9.20	48.234	40.526	26.275	11.785
9.30	48.313	40.621	26.141	11.714
9.40	48.395	40.717	25.999	11.649
9.50	48.475	40.813	25.862	11.584
9.60	48.556	40.910	25.723	11.520
9.70	48.634	41.004	25.592	11.453
9.80	48.712	41.096	25.462	11.389
9.90	48.792	41.188	25.331	11.326
10.00	48.870	41.282	25.201	11.264

FILE: THICK.DAT (Capacitances for Single-Level Interconnections)

Substrate Thickness	C11	C22	C12	C13
10.00	63.471	45.299	55.635	15.454
20.00	51.095	36.150	59.275	19.834
30.00	46.496	32.851	60.602	21.592
40.00	44.051	31.110	61.297	22.548
50.00	42.553	30.047	61.725	23.140
60.00	41.537	29.324	62.018	23.540
70.00	40.801	28.805	62.228	23.837
80.00	40.252	28.418	62.379	24.056
90.00	39.834	28.118	62.501	24.218
100.00	39.494	27.880	62.600	24.358
110.00	39.217	27.685	62.680	24.471
120.00	38.986	27.522	62.745	24.565
130.00	38.789	27.380	62.806	24.634
140.00	38.622	27.264	62.849	24.708
150.00	38.481	27.163	62.892	24.766
160.00	38.355	27.075	62.924	24.816
170.00	38.245	26.998	62.950	24.860
180.00	38.148	26.931	62.976	24.902
190.00	38.062	26.866	63.019	24.929
200.00	37.987	26.813	63.040	24.959
210.00	37.918	26.767	63.046	24.994
220.00	37.854	26.720	63.067	25.012
230.00	37.795	26.681	63.085	25.043
240.00	37.742	26.642	63.100	25.063
250.00	37.693	26.607	63.117	25.081
260.00	37.648	26.576	63.128	25.100
270.00	37.605	26.547	63.138	25.119
280.00	37.566	26.521	63.148	25.139
290.00	37.532	26.492	63.167	25.147
300.00	37.492	26.471	63.168	25.167
310.00	37.464	26.445	63.177	25.172
320.00	37.432	26.424	63.186	25.186
330.00	37.405	26.405	63.197	25.200
340.00	37.378	26.387	63.201	25.208
350.00	37.355	26.370	63.207	25.219
360.00	37.332	26.354	63.215	25.230
370.00	37.312	26.339	63.217	25.238
380.00	37.289	26.325	63.225	25.247
390.00	37.273	26.309	63.238	25.249
400.00	37.252	26.297	63.236	25.261

Substrate Thickness	C11	C22	C12	C13
410.00	37.237	26.283	63.248	25.264
420.00	37.218	26.271	63.249	25.268
430.00	37.202	26.261	63.253	25.280
440.00	37.187	26.251	63.257	25.286
450.00	37.174	26.240	63.265	25.291
460.00	37.159	26.232	63.265	25.302
470.00	37.146	26.223	63.268	25.305
480.00	37.135	26.211	63.277	25.303
490.00	37.123	26.203	63.279	25.306
500.00	37.113	26.195	63.290	25.311
510.00	37.101	26.191	63.278	25.321
520.00	37.091	26.183	63.284	25.325
530.00	37.082	26.176	63.289	25.331
540.00	37.069	26.169	63.286	25.336
550.00	37.062	26.162	63.291	25.337
560.00	37.051	26.156	63.290	25.343
570.00	37.042	26.150	63.293	25.347
580.00	37.035	26.141	63.303	25.344
590.00	37.025	26.136	63.306	25.351
600.00	37.017	26.132	63.302	25.358
610.00	37.008	26.128	63.299	25.361
620.00	37.004	26.118	63.313	25.356
630.00	36.995	26.114	63.311	25.361
640.00	36.988	26.111	63.311	25.370
650.00	36.981	26.104	63.323	25.370
660.00	36.973	26.101	63.318	25.374
670.00	36.970	26.095	63.321	25.372
680.00	36.961	26.091	63.319	25.375
690.00	36.954	26.088	63.320	25.379
700.00	36.950	26.082	63.331	25.380
710.00	36.943	26.078	63.330	25.384
720.00	36.939	26.075	63.329	25.387
730.00	36.932	26.073	63.327	25.394
740.00	36.926	26.069	63.331	25.396
750.00	36.922	26.066	63.324	25.398
760.00	36.918	26.060	63.334	25.396
770.00	36.913	26.057	63.329	25.395
780.00	36.906	26.053	63.342	25.401
790.00	36.903	26.049	63.342	25.399
800.00	36.898	26.048	63.339	25.406
810.00	36.894	26.043	63.338	25.402
820.00	36.887	26.042	63.340	25.409
830.00	36.886	26.039	63.338	25.411

Substrate Thickness	C11	C22	C12	C13
840.00	36.880	26.035	63.347	25.411
850.00	36.878	26.028	63.353	25.404
860.00	36.874	26.028	63.353	25.415
870.00	36.867	26.027	63.344	25.420
880.00	36.864	26.020	63.357	25.411
890.00	36.858	26.021	63.346	25.421
900.00	36.855	26.018	63.350	25.423
910.00	36.851	26.015	63.351	25.420
920.00	36.849	26.010	63.356	25.417
930.00	36.846	26.009	63.355	25.425
940.00	36.844	26.006	63.361	25.424
950.00	36.838	26.005	63.356	25.426
960.00	36.834	26.004	63.356	25.430
970.00	36.832	26.001	63.352	25.429
980.00	36.828	25.998	63.358	25.428
990.00	36.825	25.997	63.358	25.434
1000.00	36.825	25.994	63.363	25.431

FILE: WIDTH.DAT (Capacitances for Single-Level Interconnections)

Width	C11	C22	C12	C13
0.50	34.021	25.408	51.647	23.805
0.60	34.902	25.790	54.721	24.181
0.70	35.750	26.074	57.155	24.502
0.80	36.541	26.330	59.368	24.727
0.90	37.285	26.575	61.311	24.871
1.00	37.987	26.813	63.040	24.959
1.10	38.662	27.044	64.640	25.023
1.20	39.301	27.275	66.019	25.036
1.30	39.924	27.498	67.328	25.028
1.40	40.522	27.719	68.511	25.000
1.50	41.105	27.933	69.619	24.949
1.60	41.667	28.149	70.606	24.880
1.70	42.211	28.363	71.528	24.812
1.80	42.745	28.570	72.400	24.727
1.90	43.260	28.777	73.187	24.636
2.00	43.768	28.983	73.941	24.543
2.10	44.261	29.185	74.632	24.438
2.20	44.747	29.385	75.284	24.332
2.30	45.217	29.586	75.888	24.226
2.40	45.681	29.786	76.453	24.120
2.50	46.137	29.982	76.995	24.006

Width	C11	C22	C12	C13
2.60	46.585	30.178	77.502	23.892
2.70	47.025	30.374	77.970	23.777
2.80	47.459	30.569	78.415	23.663
2.90	47.886	30.761	78.846	23.546
3.00	48.307	30.953	79.247	23.430
3.10	48.722	31.145	79.622	23.314
3.20	49.129	31.338	79.976	23.201
3.30	49.534	31.527	80.321	23.086
3.40	49.931	31.717	80.640	22.973
3.50	50.324	31.905	80.947	22.859
3.60	50.712	32.093	81.238	22.747
3.70	51.094	32.278	81.513	22.633
3.80	51.473	32.467	81.772	22.526
3.90	51.848	32.651	82.026	22.413
4.00	52.219	32.836	82.263	22.305
4.10	52.585	33.021	82.491	22.198
4.20	52.948	33.205	82.708	22.091
4.30	53.307	33.389	82.907	21.988
4.40	53.662	33.572	83.104	21.885
4.50	54.013	33.753	83.299	21.780
4.60	54.361	33.935	83.471	21.679
4.70	54.708	34.116	83.643	21.577
4.80	55.051	34.298	83.807	21.478
4.90	55.390	34.479	83.963	21.380
5.00	55.728	34.659	84.113	21.282
5.10	56.061	34.839	84.253	21.187
5.20	56.394	35.019	84.388	21.092
5.30	56.722	35.198	84.519	20.998
5.40	57.049	35.377	84.645	20.904
5.50	57.373	35.556	84.762	20.813
5.60	57.695	35.734	84.876	20.724
5.70	58.014	35.913	84.984	20.635
5.80	58.331	36.090	85.089	20.546
5.90	58.647	36.267	85.189	20.460
6.00	58.959	36.445	85.283	20.375
6.10	59.271	36.623	85.372	20.290
6.20	59.582	36.797	85.466	20.201
6.30	59.887	36.975	85.542	20.121
6.40	60.193	37.152	85.623	20.041
6.50	60.496	37.327	85.698	19.960
6.60	60.797	37.503	85.770	19.880
6.70	61.096	37.679	85.839	19.803
6.80	61.394	37.855	85.905	19.725
6.90	61.690	38.029	85.968	19.649

Width	C11	C22	C12	C13
7.00	61.984	38.204	86.028	19.573
7.10	62.277	38.378	86.087	19.497
7.20	62.568	38.553	86.143	19.424
7.30	62.858	38.727	86.193	19.351
7.40	63.145	38.901	86.244	19.279
7.50	63.432	39.075	86.291	19.209
7.60	63.717	39.249	86.335	19.139
7.70	64.000	39.422	86.379	19.070
7.80	64.283	39.595	86.420	19.002
7.90	64.564	39.768	86.458	18.934
8.00	64.844	39.941	86.496	18.867
8.10	65.121	40.115	86.529	18.802
8.20	65.399	40.287	86.563	18.737
8.30	65.675	40.457	86.601	18.669
8.40	65.947	40.630	86.626	18.608
8.50	66.220	40.802	86.655	18.545
8.60	66.492	40.975	86.679	18.484
8.70	66.763	41.147	86.703	18.423
8.80	67.032	41.318	86.727	18.363
8.90	67.301	41.490	86.750	18.303
9.00	67.568	41.662	86.770	18.244
9.10	67.835	41.833	86.789	18.186
9.20	68.100	42.004	86.809	18.128
9.30	68.364	42.175	86.827	18.070
9.40	68.627	42.346	86.840	18.014
9.50	68.890	42.516	86.856	17.958
9.60	69.151	42.688	86.867	17.904
9.70	69.412	42.858	86.879	13.849
9.80	69.671	43.029	86.890	17.795
9.90	69.929	43.199	86.900	17.742
10.00	70.186	43.369	86.910	17.689

Electromigration-Induced Failure Analysis

The term *electromigration* refers to mass transport in metals under high stress conditions, especially under high current densities and high temperatures. This phenomenon has been studied in different metallizations during the last several years [5.1–5.64] and presents a key problem in VLSI circuits because it causes open-circuit and short-circuit failures in the VLSI interconnections. Nowadays, there is a trend to fabricate VLSI circuits on small chip areas to save space and to reduce propagation delays. According to the scaling theory for both bipolar and FET circuits, if the chip area is decreased by a factor k, the current density increases by at least the same factor in both cases, and this becomes one of the primary reasons for the circuit failure.

In this chapter several factors related to electromigration in VLSI interconnections are reviewed in Section 5.1. In this section the basic problems that cause electromigration are outlined, the mechanisms and dependence of electromigration on several factors are discussed, testing and monitoring techniques and guidelines are presented, and the methods of reducing electromigration in VLSI interconnections are briefly discussed. The various models of integrated circuit reliability, including the series model of failure mechanisms in VLSI interconnections, are presented in Section 5.2. In Section 5.3 a model of electromigration due to repetitive pulsed currents is developed. In Section 5.4 the series model is used to analyze electromigration-induced failure in several VLSI interconnection components, including multisection interconnections. Several computer programs that analyze electromigration in VLSI interconnections are discussed briefly in Section 5.5.

5.1 ELECTROMIGRATION IN VLSI INTERCONNECTION METALLIZATIONS: AN OVERVIEW

5.1.1 Problems Caused by Electromigration

As mentioned earlier, smaller chip areas are desirable because device miniaturization has become a continuing trend in VLSI. To obtain a better

TABLE 5.1.1   Scaling of Device Parameters

Device Parameters	FET [5.69]	Bipolar [5.70]
Device dimension	$1/k$	$1/k$
Voltage	$1/k$	~ 1
Current	$1/k$	$1/k$
Delay time/circuit	$1/k$	$1/k$
Power density	1	$\sim k$
Line resistance	k	k
Line current density	k	$\sim k^2$

understanding of the problems associated with electromigration, dimensional scaling and its effects on current density should be considered. Because different devices have different operational principles, scaling theories and problems may differ. For example, when the dimension of an FET device is reduced by a factor k, the time delay per circuit decreases by a factor k, whereas the power dissipation remains constant and the current density increases by a factor k. In bipolar devices the scaling structure is nonlinear. Therefore, it is difficult to get a generalized picture of how scaling affects the current density. The basic scaling theories for both FET and bipolar devices are summarized in Table 5.1.1. Despite this problem, it is possible to classify the problems caused by electromigration into two categories: geometry-related problems and material-related problems [5.65–5.71].

5.1.1.1   Geometry-Related Problems   Geometry-related problems arise as a result of the reduction of the interconnection dimensions to the micron or submicron range. In metal films, with a grain size about the same or even larger than the film thickness, the flux generated is confined mainly along the grain boundaries. As a consequence, the small number of grains across the line increases the importance of each individual inhomogeneous site of the grain structure and its effect on the overall mass flow pattern. This makes each individual divergent site potentially more damaging because a line can fail without requiring a statistical linkage of several divergent sites. Another problem concerns the device contacts and step coverages. As the dimensions of the device contacts decrease, they become comparable to those of the interconnection lines, thus subjecting them to about the same amount of current densities as the conductor lines. In some cases the stress generated by the abrupt structural variations in contacts and steps can play an important role in causing their failure.

5.1.1.2   Material-Related Problems   Material-related problems are basically caused by high current densities. Three associated problems in electromigration are referred to as joule heating, current crowding, and material reactions.

Joule Heating   As the chip size decreases, heat distribution becomes a serious problem. This is especially true in the case of bipolar VLSI interconnections because the power density increases by a factor k when the dimensions decrease by the same factor, based on the assumption of constant voltage. For a metal wire that can afford a certain current density rate of about 10^5 A/m^2-s before melting, joule heat generated by current density in the interconnection line exceeding half of this limit must be completely removed through the substrate and/or some passivation layer. The cooling rate has to be faster than the heating rate due to the current density, say, above 10^6 A/cm^2, any imperfection of the substrate may result in thermal runaway and destroy the line because of inadequate space for heat dissipation. This also raises the strip temperature which accelerates the diffusion process, thus reducing the mean time to failure (MTF).

Current Crowding   Current crowding refers to uneven distribution of currents along the metallization lines. It occurs especially in metallizations with structural inhomogeneities. It can alter the local electromigration driving force, thus affecting the mass transport pattern. It can also cause the atoms in the metallization lines to migrate with different velocities, resulting in the formation of voids that cause open-circuit failure.

Material Reactions   Material reactions are part of the effects caused by electromigration. As significant mass accumulation and depletion occur, the amount of mass transport is significant enough to generate enough stress to induce extrusion in the passive layer. It can also change the electrical properties of the junction contacts [5.71]. Furthermore, the joule heat can suppress or promote any unwanted interfacial material reactions. These problems can alter the device and interconnection characteristics and degrade the VLSI reliability [5.68].

5.1.2   Electromigration Mechanism and Factors

A lot of research has been carried out to study the electromigration pattern as well as the factors that affect electromigration [5.1–5.64, 5.72–5.135]. In this section the basic mechanisms and the associated factors affecting electromigration are discussed.

5.1.2.1   Mechanism   In general, a metallization line consists of an aggregate of metallic ions. These ions are held together by a binding force and opposed by a repulsive electrostatic force. At any given temperature, some of these ions may have sufficient energy to escape from the potential well that binds them in the lattice. When they reach the saddle point of the potential well, they are free from the lattice and become *activated*. The energy needed to achieve this is known as the *activation energy*. Because a metallization line also contains a certain concentration of vacancies, these ions can diffuse out

of the lattice into an adjacent vacancy. This process is known as *self diffusion*. In the absence of an electric current, the self-diffusion process is more or less isentropic; that is, the probability of each nearest ion around the vacancy exchanging with the vacancy is equal. Under no concentration gradient or chemical potential [5.104, 5.105], a random rearrangement of individual ions takes place, resulting in no mass transportation. Once the current is applied, the situation changes. Now there are two external forces exerted on the metallization, namely, the frictional force and the electrostatic force. The frictional force is due to the momentum exchange with the crystal, and its magnitude is proportional to the current density. The electrostatic force is due to the interactions between the electric fields created by the electrons and the positively charged metallic ions. The electric field due to the electrons will attract the positively charged metallic ions toward the cathode against the electron wind, and its magnitude, denoted by E, is given by

$$E = \rho J \tag{5.1.1}$$

where ρ is the density of ions and J is the current density. Because of the presence of *shielding electrons*, the frictional force is always greater than the electrostatic force.

Consider a metal strip as shown in Figure 5.1.1. The frictional force and the electrostatic force are denoted by $\mathbf{F}_1$ and $\mathbf{F}_2$, respectively. The frictional force is acting in the direction of the current flow, and the electrostatic force is acting against the current flow. The electric field $\mathbf{E}$ also acts against the current flow. Because $\mathbf{F}_1$ is much greater than $\mathbf{F}_2$, the net force, denoted by $\mathbf{F}$, will be in the direction of the current flow. Defining the direction of the net force as being positive, we have

$$\mathbf{F} = \mathbf{F}_1 - \mathbf{F}_2 = (Z^*e)\mathbf{E} \tag{5.1.2}$$

where (Z^*e) is the effective charge assigned to the migrated ion with Z^*

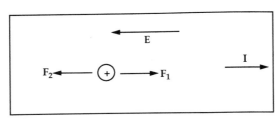

FIGURE 5.1.1   Frictional and electrostatic forces ($\mathbf{F}_1$ and $\mathbf{F}_2$, respectively) inside a current-carrying metal strip.

given by [5.22]

$$Z^* = Z\left(\frac{\rho_d Nm}{2\rho N_d m} - 1 \right)$$ (5.1.3)

where

  Z = electron-to-atom ratio
  ρ_d = defect resistivity
  N_d = density of defects
  ρ = resistivity of metal
  N = density of metal
  m^* = effective electron mass
  m = free electron mass

The first and second terms in Equation 5.1.3 correspond to the forces $\mathbf{F}_1$ and $\mathbf{F}_2$, respectively. According to the Nernst–Einstein equation, the average drift velocity $\mathbf{v}$ is given by

$$\mathbf{v} = \mu \mathbf{F}$$ (5.1.4)

where

  μ = mobility = D/fkT
  D = self-diffusion coefficient = $D_0 \exp(-E_a/kT)$
  f = correlation factor depending on the lattice structure; in most cases
     $f = 1$
  k = Boltzmann's constant
  E_a = activation energy
  T = absolute temperature

The induced flux due to the creation of this frictional force is now given by [5.94]

$$\psi_A = N\mathbf{v}$$ (5.1.5)

Combining Equations 5.1.1, 5.1.2, 5.1.4, and 5.1.5, we get

$$\psi_A = \frac{ND\rho J}{fkT}(Z^*e)$$ (5.1.6)

or

$$\psi_A = \left(\frac{ND_0 \rho J}{fkT} \right)(Z^*e) \exp\left(-\frac{E_a}{kT} \right)$$ (5.1.7)

In general, ψ_A may not be the same throughout the metallization because of structural inhomogeneities. Such a divergence of flux in the metallization is more likely to occur under high-current-density conditions. If the divergence becomes significant, the original isentropic self-diffusion is perturbed and the ions moving along the current flow have a higher probability of exchanging positions with the vacancies. As a result, the original random process changes to a directional process in which the metallic ions move opposite to the electron wind direction, whereas the vacancies move in the opposite direction. The metallic ions condense to form whiskers, whereas the vacancies condense to form voids [5.105–5.108]. This process results in a change in the density of the metal ions with respect to time. The rate of this change, dN/dt, can be expressed as [5.33]

$$\frac{dN}{dt} = -V \operatorname{div}(\psi_A) \tag{5.1.8}$$

where V is the volume and

$$\operatorname{div}(\psi_A) = \frac{d\psi_A}{dx} + \frac{d\psi_A}{dy} + \frac{d\psi_A}{dz}$$

The formation of voids causes some of the metallization lines to fail, forcing the current to go through the rest of the lines, resulting in an increase in the current density and the joule heat. The production of joule heat can increase the local temperature and cause more lines to fail [5.91]. Furthermore, as whiskers and hillocks form, a concentration gradient is produced which may create a stress-related force, enhancing the mass transport process and causing more lines to fail [5.109–5.111]. All these processes continue as a loop as shown in Figure 5.1.2 until the circuit fails to work. The mean time to failure, MTF or t_{50}, is defined as the time taken for 50 percent of the lines to fail and is given by

$$\text{MTF} = A'J^{-n} \exp\left(\frac{E_a}{kT}\right) \tag{5.1.9}$$

where

E_a = activation energy
J = current density
T = temperature in degrees kelvin
A' = constant depending on geometry and material properties
k = Boltzmann's constant
n = constant ranging from 1 to 7

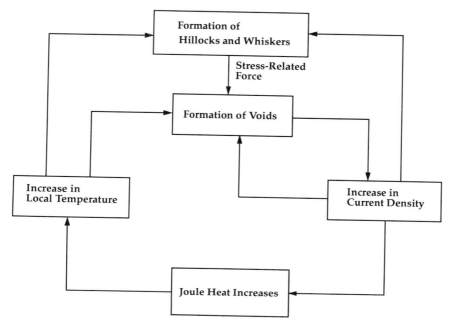

FIGURE 5.1.2   Schematic diagram of the various factors that contribute to electromigration in VLSI interconnection metallizations (modified from [5.91].)

The value of n is stated last because of its variance found in different reference texts and research works [5.112]. Some of the n values reported in different works are listed in Table 5.1.2. The deviation of n values has been explained as due to the overestimation of joule heating, resulting in low values of n, and the underestimation of joule heating, resulting in an

TABLE 5.1.2   Values of the Exponent n Found in the Literature

Source [Reference]	Current Density	n
Huntington and Grone [5.21]	$< 0.5\ \mathrm{MA/cm^2}$	1
Attardo [5.114]	$0.5–1\ \mathrm{MA/cm^2}$	1.5
Black [5.83]	$0.45–2.88\ \mathrm{MA/cm^2}$	$2+$
Blair et al. [5.54]	$1–2\ \mathrm{MA/cm^2}$	6–7
Chabra and Ainslie [5.85]	—	1–3
Venable and Lye [5.90]	—	1
Sigsbee [5.88, 5.89]	$\approx 1\ \mathrm{MA/cm^2}$	1
Vaidya et al. [5.62]	—	2
Danso and Tullos [5.51]	$0.168–0.704\ \mathrm{MA/cm^2}$	1.7
Chern et al. [5.41]	—	2.5 ± 0.5

apparent very large current density dependence and hence high values of n. In general, the correct value of n should lie between 1 and 2 [5.124]. If the cross-sectional area A is also taken into account [5.83], then Equation 5.1.9 is modified as

$$\text{MTF} = AJ^{-n} \exp\left(\frac{E_a}{kT}\right) \qquad (5.1.10)$$

It is also interesting to study the speed of the metallic ions and its relationship to the MTF. According to Gimpelson [5.115], the migration velocity v_m can be expressed as

$$\mathbf{v}_m = GJ \exp\left(-\frac{E_a}{kT}\right) \qquad (5.1.11)$$

where G is a proportionality constant. Combining Equations 5.1.10 and 5.1.11, the MTF can be expressed as

$$\text{MTF} = G^n \frac{A}{(v_m)^n} \exp\left(-\frac{(n-1)E_a}{kT}\right) \qquad (5.1.12)$$

5.1.1.2 Factors Some of the several known factors that induce electromigration can be classified as follows:

Current Density Current density is the key factor that contributes to the frictional forces as well as to the flux divergence. At a high current density, the momentum exchange between the current carriers and the metallic ions becomes significantly large, resulting in a very large frictional force and flux divergence along the metallization lines which results in mass transport which leads to the line failure. It is obvious from Table 5.1.3 that the MTF decreases as the current density increases. This result has been verified by the research [5.1–5.61, 5.72–5.103, 5.116, 5.117].

Thermal Effects Thermal gradients and the line temperature are two other important factors that cause electromigration. It has been reported that electromigration proceeds from a high temperature to a low temperature and that thermal gradients are very important in the electromigration process because they can induce a thermal force that enhances further mass transport in the metallization lines [5.33, 5.94, 5.118, 5.119]. Thermal gradients are dependent on the metallization structure as well as on the processing techniques.

Line temperature is also an important factor in the electromigration process [5.12, 5.14, 5.120–5.124]. According to Equation 5.1.9, the MTF decreases with an increase in the line temperature. This conclusion can also be drawn from Table 5.1.4. In general, if the VLSI system is operating at room

TABLE 5.1.3   Dependence of the Mean Time to Failure on the Current Density for Three Kinds of Aluminum Film Conductors Having a Cross-Sectional Area of 10^{-7} cm^2 and at a Temperature of 160°C (Derived from the Data in Reference [5.83])

Current Density (MA/cm^2)	Mean Time to Failure (h)		
	Small Crystallite	Large Crystallite	Glassed Large Crystallite
0.1	15,500	120,000	—
0.2	4,000	30,000	—
0.4	960	7,800	65,000
0.6	450	3,300	29,000
0.8	250	1,900	15,000
1.0	155	1,250	11,000
2.0	40	300	2,700
4.0	10	75	700
6.0	—	33	370
8.0	—	18	—

temperature under normal conditions, thermal effects can be considered insignificant.

Line Length and Line Width   Table 5.1.5 shows the relationship between the MTF and the line length. As mentioned earlier, voids, hillocks, and whiskers are formed along the interconnection line during electromigration, creating a

TABLE 5.1.4   Dependence of the Mean Time to Failure on Temperature for Three Kinds of Aluminum Film Conductors Having a Cross-Sectional Area of 10^{-7} cm^2 and Carrying Current Density of 1 MA / cm^2 (Derived from the Data in Reference [5.83])

Temperature (°C)	Mean Time to Failure (h)		
	Small Crystallite	Large Crystallite	Glassed Large Crystallite
40	23,000	—	—
60	7,700	—	—
80	3,000	—	—
100	1,280	47,000	—
120	580	12,500	—
140	300	3,800	50,000
160	155	1,250	11,000
180	90	450	2,800
200	52	180	800
220	32	80	255
240	21	37	90
260	14	18	34

TABLE 5.1.5   Dependence of the Median Time to Failure on the Length of the Interconnection Line with a Width of 2 μm and a Median Grain Size of 1.25 μm (Derived from the Data in Reference [5.93])

Length (μm)	Median time to Failure (h)
10	530
20	380
30	325
40	315

stress-related force that enhances further electromigration. The magnitude of this force is proportional to the concentration gradient. If the lines are long, the concentration gradient will be much larger, resulting in a shorter electromigration lifetime as compared to shorter lines [5.125].

A lot of work has been done to study the effects of line width on the electromigration lifetime as well [5.126–5.129]. It has been found that the electromigration lifetime is inversely proportional to the line width. This is because, for small line widths, the cross-sectional area will also be small, resulting in a higher current density that may degrade the electromigration lifetime. The experimental data on this relationship are shown in Table 5.1.6.

Activation Energy and Material Structure   The activation energy of a metallization line depends on its material structure, and, therefore, different metallization lines may have different activation energy values. For VLSI interconnections, metallizations having high activation energy are desirable because they lead to enhanced stability. Material structure also affects the electromigration lifetime in many ways. Known aspects include grain orientation, grain size, and grain boundaries. Research has shown that electromigration is related to structural inhomogeneity [5.33, 5.35, 5.36, 5.124]. An ideal

TABLE 5.1.6   Dependence of the Median Time to Failure on the Width of the Interconnection Line with a Length of 25 μm and a Median Grain Size of 0.75 μm (Derived from the Data in Reference [5.93])

Width (μm)	Median Time to Failure (h)
0.5	165
1.0	220
1.5	270
2.0	305
2.5	335

TABLE 5.1.7 Dependence of the Median Time to Failure on the Median Grain Size for an Interconnection Line with a Width of 1 μm and a Length of 20 μm (Derived from the Data in Reference [5.93].)

Median Grain Size (μm)	Median Time to Failure (h)
1.0	245
1.5	330
2.0	405
2.5	460
3.0	515

metallization line is the one with uniform grain size and regular grain orientation. Unfortunately, this is not possible as there is always some degree of inhomogeneity that induces flux divergence [5.131, 5.134, 5.135]. As the metallization line becomes more inhomogeneous in structure, this flux becomes more divergent, resulting in a smaller MTF. Based on previous studies, it is known that electromigration is confined mainly in the grain boundaries [5.6, 5.33, 5.35, 5.79, 5.84]. Smaller grain size means that more grain boundaries are available for electromigration. Table 5.1.7 shows the experimental relationship between grain size and MTF. The fact that a smaller grain size degrades the electromigration lifetime has been verified by many researchers [5.39, 5.79, 5.93]. If the grain size is large enough to be comparable to the strip width, then the single grain can act as a barrier to the migrating atoms [5.35, 5.130, 5.133, 5.135].

5.1.3 Electromigration Under Pulsed-DC and AC Conditions

So far, electromigration under steady-state DC conditions has been discussed. However, it is important to understand electromigration under pulsed-DC and AC conditions. Based on recent research, it can be stated that under pulsed-DC conditions, the MTF is inversely proportional to the duty cycle [5.89, 5.136–5.142]. This can be explained as follows: Equation 5.1.9 shows that the MTF is a function of the average value of the steady-state current density. For a periodic current pulse with frequency f, pulse height J, and duty cycle D, the average value of the pulse is given by DJ. Therefore, if D is closer to 1, then the pulse will have a higher average value, resulting in a lower MTF. Under pulsed-DC conditions, the mean time to failure can be written as

$$\text{MTF} = A(DJ)^{-n}\exp\left(\frac{E_a}{kT}\right) \qquad (5.1.13)$$

Under AC conditions, at a frequency below the kilohertz range, electromigration is not detected [5.46]. Using a similar approach as before, a possible explanation for this is that the average value of the current density under AC conditions is 0. Therefore, electromigration may not be easily detected. However, the actual explanation is still not well known and further investigation is required. Research is also required under high-frequency AC conditions, especially in the gigahertz range, to find out their impact on the electromigration mechanism.

5.1.4   Testing and Monitoring of Electromigration

Many methods can be used for testing and monitoring electromigration [5.143–5.151]. Two techniques used frequently employ resistance measurement and noise measurement although the latter is rather difficult in practice.

5.1.4.1 Resistance Measurement   In general, when an open-circuit failure occurs, the resistance goes up, whereas when a short-circuit failure occurs, the resistance goes down. Therefore, by measuring the resistance one can check whether electromigration has taken place. The MTF can be determined by finding the time during which the ratio of the change of resistance to the original resistance reaches a certain value. Rodbell and Shatynski used the ratio of 0.5 because this value corresponds to the transition from predominantly electromigration to predominantly thermomigration [5.144]. A standard method of evaluation for VLSI interconnections using this approach is called *accelerated testing* in which high current density and high temperature are applied to the metallization lines [5.144]. This technique results in the reduction of complicated testing and is widely used in studying electromigration.

5.1.4.2 Noise Measurement   Metal thin films generate thermal noise and current noise. The noise voltage spectra $S(f)$ is given by

$$S(f) = 4kTR + \frac{k'V^\beta}{f^\alpha} \qquad (5.1.14)$$

where

$$k = \text{Boltzmann's constant}$$
$$T = \text{temperature of the film in degrees kelvin}$$
$$R = \text{resistance of the film in ohms}$$
$$V = IR = \text{DC voltage applied across the film}$$
$$f = \text{frequency}$$
$$k', \alpha, \beta = \text{constants characterizing the current noise spectrum}$$

The first term corresponds to thermal noise, and the second term corresponds to current noise. In most cases the first term is negligible because the current noise dominates. In aluminum films the current noise is relatively small. Therefore, the measurement of current noise may require special attention. In general, the current noise spectral density of continuous metal thin films at room temperature follows Hooge's equation

$$S_c(f) = \frac{\gamma V^\beta}{N_c f^\alpha} = \frac{\gamma (IR)^\beta}{N_c f^\alpha} \qquad (5.1.15)$$

where N_c is the total number of free charge carriers in the film. For a uniform cross section, N_c is proportional to the volume of the film. Therefore, $S_c(f)$ is detectable only in small films. For nonuniform cross sections, the current density distribution should also be taken into account because the current crowding effect will cause the noise to increase.

Electromigration results in the formation of voids and hillocks, and this also leads to a change in the noise level. Using a normal line denoted by a as a reference and the line under test denoted by b, the respective noise voltage spectra can be expressed as

$$S_a(f) = K_a \frac{(IR_a)^\beta}{f^\alpha} \qquad (5.1.16)$$

and

$$S_b(f) = K_b \frac{(IR_b)^\beta}{f^\alpha} \qquad (5.1.17)$$

Therefore, the ratio $S_b(f)/S_a(f)$ becomes

$$\frac{S_b(f)}{S_a(f)} = \left[\frac{K_b}{K_a}\right]\left[\frac{R_b}{R_a}\right]^\beta \qquad (5.1.18)$$

If this ratio is much larger or smaller than 1, then this implies that electromigration may take place [5.151].

5.1.5 General Guidelines for Testing Electromigration

It has been suggested in the literature [5.92] that the following guidelines should be followed for the testing procedure.

5.1.5.1   Dimensions of the Test Line

1. The test line should have the minimum interconnection width used for that set of the IC family.
2. The length of the test line must be greater than 1 mm to obtain accurate results.

5.1.5.2   Test Line Preparation

1. The current to the test line should be fed by a wider lead (between two to five times the width), and leads must be greater than 0.125 mm on both sides to reach the bond pads. Long bond pads greater than 1 mm should be avoided because they do not represent typical IC interconnections.
2. The test line fabrication process should simulate the interconnection process for the IC family. For example, the test line should share the same parameters and thickness, go through an identical processing as the other lines in the IC family, and be packaged in a standard IC package very similar to that used for the IC family.

5.1.5.3   Testing Conditions

1. The thickness data (after film deposition and/or lead patterning) coupled with the width of the line should be used to calculate the current density. If a multilayer metal such as a barrier layer/conductor is used, then the cross section of the primary conductor system should be used for the current density calculation.
2. A current density between 0.8 and 1 MA/cm^2, depending on the structure of the line, is recommended.
3. High temperature is not recommended because the microstructure properties of the film may change at high temperature, leading to erroneous results. In addition, thermomigration may also take place. An ambient temperature between 125 and 215°C is recommended.
4. The test temperature should be reported. If the resistance of the leads and the temperature coefficient of resistance are accurately determined, the line temperature may be reported as the test temperature.
5. For the sake of accuracy, sample sizes of 15 to 20 should be used for testing electromigration at a chosen test temperature.

5.1.5.4   Calculations and Plots

1. Lognormal probability plots are recommended to determine the mean time to failure and standard deviation.

2. An Arrhenius plot of the MTF versus $1/T$ ($°K$) with at least three or four data points should be used to determine the activation energy.

3. Because electromigration-induced failures are caused by divergences of atomic fluxes and the atomic flux is directly proportional to the current density, use $n = 1$ in Equation 5.1.10 for the MTF at low current densities and use $n = 2$ for optimistic estimates of the MTF at operating temperatures and at current densities less than 1 MA/cm^2. Use $n = 1.5$ when electromigration test data are collected at 1 MA/cm^2 and have to be extrapolated to current densities in the range 0.1 to 0.6 MA/cm^2. Three current densities in the range 0.6 to 1.2 MA/cm^2 may be used to determine the value of the exponent n.

4. Failure times are assumed to obey a lognormal distribution

$$f(t) = \frac{1}{\sigma t}\exp\left[-\frac{1}{2}\left(\frac{\ln(t) - \ln(t_{50})}{\sigma}\right)^2\right] \qquad (5.1.19)$$

The instantaneous failure, by definition, corresponds to the decrease in the number of surviving samples at time t and is given by

$$\lambda(t) = \frac{f(t)}{1 - F(t)} \qquad (5.1.20)$$

where the cumulative failure density function

$$F(t) = \int_0^t f(t)\, dt \qquad (5.1.21)$$

corresponds to the probability of failure in total time t. From the preceding equations, it is obvious that the failure rate increases with time and reflects the true wear-out mechanism of the interconnection due to electromigration-induced damage.

5. If the conductor crosses an oxide step, a thinning step for the film thickness should be determined, and a minimum cross section of the conductor at the oxide side should be used to calculate the maximum current density.

6. If a pulsed current is used for testing, then the peak current or the maximum current pulse height in a lead should be used for the current density calculation and to find the MTF. If a transient is present, similar corrections are recommended.

7. Because reliability of the film interconnections is determined by their microstructure and alloy composition, detailed test procedures should be established to characterize the as-deposited and annealed films. Routine process control procedures should be followed to verify that the film properties are reproduced.

5.1.6 Reduction of Electromigration

A lot of effort has gone into reducing electromigration in VLSI interconnections [5.152–5.170]. The most common solutions can be summarized as follows.

5.1.6.1 Substrate Overcoating

The basic reason for overcoating the substrate is to prevent the formation of vacancies needed for diffusion and to presumably fill up the broken bonds on the surface of the metallization [5.73, 5.79, 5.116, 5.152–5.159, 5.170]. This is also called *passivation*. With the addition of a passivation layer, the joule heat can be dissipated more easily. In order to form a passivation layer, the substrate is basically sealed hermetically by the overcoating layer. The materials mostly used are oxides such as SiO and anodic oxides as well as dielectric layers such as Al_2O_3–SiO_2 and P_2O_5–SiO_2. This technique has proven to be effective in improving electromigration lifetimes [5.12, 5.87]. It has been further shown that the increase in thickness of these layers increases the electromigration lifetime as long as the thickness does not exceed 6000 Å [5.154, 5.160–5.162].

5.1.6.2 Alloying of Metallization

The addition of alloys of the correct type and concentration has also been shown to improve the electromigration lifetime [5.163, 5.164, 5.166, 5.170]. For example, it has been shown that the addition of Ti–Si to Al increases the electromigration lifetime by more than an order of magnitude, whereas the addition of Cr–Si does not lead to any noticeable improvement [5.47]. Other reports have shown that the addition of 0.4% Cu to Al with or without the addition of Si results in better electromigration lifetimes than pure Al [5.38, 5.156, 5.158, 5.159]. The reason for this is that by adding the proper concentration of correct impurities into the original metallization line, the structure of the line changes substantially, resulting in improvement of the electromigration lifetimes [5.156–5.159]. However, one of the major problems is the increase in resistance after alloying. This has been demonstrated by adding manganese into the aluminum and Al–Cu metallizations [5.156]. In short, alloying with Cu (typical levels of 0.5%, 1%, 2%, and 4% have been widely used and reported) has been the industry standard for many years. However, Cu is very hard to etch dry for VLSI applications. This has resulted in an interest in Al/Ti and Al/Si/Ti alloys as alternatives.

5.1.6.3 Encapsulated Multilayer Interconnections

Encapsulation has the effect of preventing the formation of hillocks. It can be done by using refractory metals and spacer technology. The refractory metal is deposited by biased sputtering and by anisotropic etching of the material. Several layers of the refractory metal are deposited to ensure reliability. Another way to achieve encapsulation is to form a native oxide layer on the interconnection [5.160]. In order to be effective, the native oxide has to be thicker than the film to ensure the removal of hillocks. This approach has also been shown to improve the electromigration lifetimes [5.161, 5.162].

5.1.6.4 Gold Metallization   It has been shown that a gold-based intercon-nection system has a much better MTF than aluminum films [5.163]. The key reason for this is that gold has a very high activation energy. In particular, at high current densities and high-temperature operations, gold interconnec-tions have been shown to perform better. In general, gold can be deposited by vacuum evaporation techniques. However, because of its inert nature, adhesion of gold to the insulating layer by chemical bonding is extremely difficult. Therefore, gold has to be used in a multilayer system where more than one layer of metallization is used to adhere to the insulator as well as to the gold.

5.1.6.5 Deposition Techniques   It has been shown that the MTF of a VLSI system has a close relationship with the deposition technique employed [5.164, 5.167, 5.168]. For example, it is found that the MTF is smaller for the sputtered film technique than for the *e*-beam technique [5.165]. One possible explanation may be that different deposition techniques may change the defect structure of a metallization and that may change the electromigration pattern.

5.2 MODELS OF IC RELIABILITY

The reliability of an integrated circuit is a measure of the promise that it will carry out its function correctly during a given time period. In general,

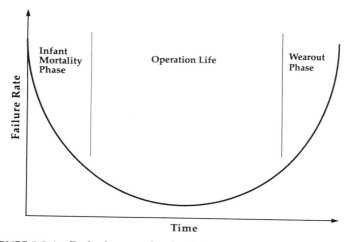

FIGURE 5.2.1   Bathtub curve showing failure rate as a function of time.

reliability is expressed graphically by a bath-tub curve as shown in Figure 5.2.1. The portion of the curve depicting high failure rates at small times is called the infant mortality phase and accounts for the major built-in flaws in the components. The portion of the curve depicting high failure rates at large times is called the wear-out phase and accounts for the actual wear-out of the components. The rest of the curve defines the operating life of the integrated circuit. In general, the reliability of an integrated circuit can be enhanced by using better design techniques for its components, employing better manufacturing methods, using more stringent screening procedures, and providing redundancy within the integrated circuit so that it will perform its assigned function even if some of its components actually fail. Several mathematical models to predict the reliability of an integrated circuit or the components thereof have been proposed in the literature.

5.2.1 Arrhenius Model

Several physical mechanisms that result in device failure can be modeled by the Arrhenius relationship expressed as

$$\lambda(T) = \lambda(T_0) \exp\left[\frac{E_a}{k}\left(\frac{1}{T_0} - \frac{1}{T}\right)\right] \qquad (5.2.1)$$

where

T = temperature in degrees kelvin
T_0 = reference temperature in degrees kelvin
$\lambda(T)$ = failure rate at temperature T
E_a = activation energy for the failure mechanism in electron-volts
k = Boltzmann's constant in electron-volts per degree kelvin

Relationship (5.2.1) indicates that a physical mechanism having a lower activation energy results in a higher failure rate. The same is true for systems at higher operating temperatures.

5.2.2 Mil-Hdbk-217D Model

This is a semiempirical model based on the measured lifetimes of a large number of devices after screening. It states that the failure rate λ in units of failures/10^6 h can be predicted by the expression [5.171]

$$\lambda = \Pi_Q[C_1\Pi_T\Pi_V + (C_2 + C_3)\Pi_E]\Pi_L \qquad (5.2.2)$$

where Π_Q is a quality factor dependent on the burn-in procedure used to remove devices suffering from built-in problems, Π_T is an acceleration factor dependent on the operating temperature, Π_V is a stress factor dependent on the operating voltage, Π_E is a factor dependent on the environment, Π_L is a learning factor, and C_1, C_2, and C_3 are failure rates dependent on the complexity of the system expressed by the number of equivalent gates, number of pins, package type, and so on. The values of C_1, C_2, and C_3 depend on the devices and their technologies and have been tabulated for several cases in reference [5.171]. The Mil-Hdbk-217D model is a widely used model, and the data for this model have been constantly under revision to include new devices and technologies.

5.2.3 Series Model

A series model for calculating the reliability of an integrated circuit due to wear-out has been presented by Frost and Poole [5.172]. It is based on the assumptions that an integrated circuit consists of several basic elements that are not necessarily identically distributed, the states of the various elements with respect to their being functional or failed are mutually statistically independent, the failure distribution of each element is known a priori, and the failure of any one element of the series system causes the IC to fail.

The failure rate λ_s of a system of n elements having failure rates λ_i ($i = 1, 2, 3, \ldots, n$) can be found by adding the failure rates of the elements; that is,

$$\lambda_s(t) = \sum_{i=1}^{n} \lambda_i(t) \qquad (5.2.3)$$

If the n elements are identical, that is,

$$\lambda_1(t) = \lambda_2(t) = \cdots = \lambda_n(t) = \lambda(t)$$

then Equation 5.2.3 reduces to

$$\lambda_s(t) = n\lambda(t) \qquad (5.2.4)$$

The probability of failure function $F_s(t)$ of a series system can be determined by using the formula

$$F_s(t) = 1 - \prod_{i=1}^{n} [1 - F_i(t)] \qquad (5.2.5)$$

where $F_i(t)$ is the probability of failure function for the ith element.

The series model can be used to predict the reliability of a system with respect to any of the physical processes which cause wear-out. These include interconnection metallization failure due to electromigration or corrosion, oxide shorts, threshold voltage shifts in metal-oxide-semiconductor (MOS) devices, and alpha-particle-induced soft errors. A physical process can cause two types of defects which result in the failure of the system: structural defects and performance defects. A structural defect represents an abrupt change in the circuit topology such as the one caused by open circuiting of a conductor. A performance defect represents a continuous degradation of the system until its operation performance falls below an acceptable level. The series model treats these two defects in the same way.

5.2.4   Series – Parallel Model

As shown in Section 5.4, an interconnection or a component thereof can be modeled as a series–parallel combination of several straight segments. Then the probability of failure as a function of time, that is, $F_{sp}(t)$, can be determined by

$$F_{sp}(t) = \left[1 - \{1 - F_{11}(t)\}^{N_{11s}}\{1 - F_{12}(t)\}^{N_{12s}} \dots \{1 - F_{1n}(t)\}^{N_{1ns}}\right]^{N_{1p}}$$

$$\times \left[1 - \{1 - F_{21}(t)\}^{N_{21s}}\{1 - F_{22}(t)\}^{N_{22s}} \dots \{1 - F_{2n}(t)\}^{N_{2ns}}\right]^{N_{2p}} \dots$$

$$\times \left[1 - \{1 - F_{m1}(t)\}^{N_{m1s}}\{1 - F_{m2}(t)\}^{N_{m2s}} \dots \{1 - F_{mn}(t)\}^{N_{mns}}\right]^{N_{mp}}$$

$$(5.2.6)$$

where the total number of parallel units is equal to $N_{1p} + N_{2p} + \cdots + N_{mp}$, N_{mp} is the number of identical parallel units in the mth set, and the total number of identical series units in the mth set of parallel units is equal to $N_{m1s} + N_{m2s} + \cdots + N_{mns}$. The function $F_{mn}(t)$ in Equation 5.2.6 is the probability of failure function for the nth unit of the mth set. For a series system of N_s identical units, Equation 5.2.6 reduces to

$$F_s(t) = 1 - [1 - F(t)]^{N_s} \qquad (5.2.7)$$

in agreement with Equation 5.2.5. For a parallel system of N_p identical units, it becomes

$$F_p(t) = [F(t)]^{N_p} \qquad (5.2.8)$$

5.3   MODELING OF ELECTROMIGRATION DUE TO REPETITIVE PULSED CURRENTS

In the past, most of the work on electromigration effects in VLSI interconnections was limited to steady (DC) currents, and the chip design rules were based on these DC models. However, most VLSI devices are now digital and use unipolar or bipolar pulsed currents throughout the chip. In a few modeling efforts [5.138, 5.142] and experimental studies [5.136–5.140] concerned with pulsed or alternating currents, the pulsed current guidelines have been developed from the DC design rules by substituting the average current density of the pulsed current for the DC current density. In other words, if r denotes the duty factor of the pulsed current of density J_p (assumed constant), then the corresponding DC current density J_{DC} is given by

$$J_{DC} = rJ_p \qquad (5.3.1)$$

In principle, according to Equation 5.3.1, the current density J_p can be increased in direct proportion as the duty factor r is decreased with no effect on the design rules. This is simply not true in all cases. In this section a simulation model for the major physical processes that influence electromigration-induced damage in interconnections due to pulsed electric currents [5.173] is presented. It should be noted that experimental verification of the model is required before its predictions can be used in design guidelines.

5.3.1   Modeling of Physical Processes

An expression that adequately describes the mass flow rate due to an electrical current density is

$$J_a = \left(\frac{ND}{kT} \right)(Z^*e)E \qquad (5.3.2)$$

where

J_a = atomic flux in atoms per square centimeter per second
N = number of metallic ions per cubic centimeter
D = diffusion coefficient in square centimeters per second
k = Boltzmann's constant in joules per degree kelvin
T = temperature in degrees kelvin
Z^* = effective mobile ion charge number
e = electronic charge = 1.6×10^{-19} C
E = electric field strength in volts per centimeter

In Equation 5.3.2 the divergence of metallic ion flux due to geometric conditions, microstructural conditions, thermal conditions, or any combination thereof can be expressed in terms of the mass continuity equation

$$\frac{\partial N}{\partial t} + \nabla \cdot J_a = 0 \qquad (5.3.3)$$

Furthermore, the effect of local heating on the movement of metal atoms can be included in terms of the temperature dependence of the diffusion coefficient D in Equation 5.3.2 given by

$$D = D_0 \exp\left(-\frac{E_a}{kT}\right) \qquad (5.3.4)$$

where D_0 is a numerical factor independent of temperature and E_a is the activation energy whose value depends on the predominant manner of diffusion. It should be noted that the rate of electromigration-induced degradation of the interconnection line is also influenced by the mechanical stress generated by the difference in thermal expansion coefficients and mechanical properties such as elastic moduli of the line and its surrounding material.

To account for the several physical factors present in a complex system consisting of the interconnection line, its dielectric overcoating, its dielectric undercoating, and the substrate, Equation 5.3.2 should be modified to

$$J_a = \left(\frac{ND}{kT}\right)(-\nabla U) \qquad (5.3.5)$$

where U is the electrochemical potential which, as a first approximation, should be taken as

$$U = Z^*eV + kT \ln\left(\frac{N}{N_0}\right) + \Omega S_{nm} + \mu_0 \qquad (5.3.6)$$

where

V = electric potential in volts
N_0 = equilibrium metal ion concentration at reference condition in number per cubic meter
Ω = atomic volume in cubic meters
S_{nm} = mechanical stress in newtons per square meter
μ_0 = reference chemical potential in joules

Substituting Equation 5.3.6 into Equation 5.3.5, we get

$$J_a = \left(\frac{ND}{kT}\right)\left[Z^*eE - \left(\frac{kT}{N}\right)(\nabla N) - \Omega\nabla(S_{nm})\right] \qquad (5.3.7)$$

Equation 5.3.7 states that the electric force caused by the exchange of momentum between the electrons and the metallic ions is opposed by the diffusion force caused by the nonequilibrium ion concentration differences and the mechanical force caused by the longitudinal pressure differences.

Now, as done previously [5.90], we can define a term P, called the porosity, as the local incremental change in metal ion concentration given by the expression

$$\frac{\partial P}{\partial t} = -\left(\frac{1}{N}\right)\frac{\partial N}{\partial t} \qquad (5.3.8)$$

Combining Equations 5.3.3 and 5.3.5, dividing the resulting equation on both sides by N, and substituting into Equation 5.3.8, we obtain

$$\frac{\partial P}{\partial t} = -\left(\frac{1}{N}\right)\nabla \cdot \left[\left(\frac{ND}{kT}\right)(\nabla U)\right] \qquad (5.3.9)$$

5.3.2 First-Order Model Development

First, we assume that the grain sizes in the interconnection line follow a lognormal distribution characterized by a median value D_{50} and standard deviation s. Next, for an interconnection line of length L, we divide it into N_l segments of equal length D_{50}; that is, $N_l = L/D_{50}$, where N_l is taken as the nearest integer value. Furthermore, if W is the width of the interconnection line, we partition it into N_w parallel strips of width D_{50}, each with some remaining strip of width less than D_{50} such that $N_w = W/D_{50}$, where N_w is taken as the larger nearest integer. For a line of width less than D_{50}, $N_w = 1$. Thus, each interconnection segment of length D_{50} has N_w locations or nodes where mass flux divergence is possible. The mass flux divergence factor D_f at each node defined by the indices k and l with $1 \leq k \leq N_l$ and $1 \leq l \leq N_w$ can now be calculated from the relationship

$$D_f(k,l) = \sum_i \sin\left(\frac{\theta_i}{2}\right)\cos(\phi_i) - \sum_j \sin\left(\frac{\theta_j}{2}\right)\cos(\phi_j) \qquad (5.3.10)$$

where ϕ is the random grain boundary angle with respect to the longitudinal centerline of the metallization line for each grain boundary on either side of each node and θ is another random angle selected for each grain boundary on either side of the node used to calculate a mobility factor for mass transfer along the grain boundary [5.135].

The divergence of the metal ion flux at the node (k,l) can now be calculated from

$$\nabla \cdot J_a(k,l) = \left[\frac{ND}{D_{50}kT}D_f(k,l)\right](-\nabla U) \qquad (5.3.11)$$

where, as a first-order approximation, it is assumed that the electric field, mobile metallic ion concentration gradient, and longitudinal pressure gradient are appropriately averaged macroscopic quantities, and, therefore, the forcing function terms in the factor $-\nabla U$ can be regarded as constants with respect to the divergence operation. The rate of porosity development at the node (k, l) is then given by

$$\frac{\partial P}{\partial t} = \left[\frac{D_0}{D_{50}kT} D_f(k, l) \right] \left[\exp\left(-\frac{E_a}{kT} \right) \right] (-\nabla U) \qquad (5.3.12)$$

and the increment of porosity ΔP developed at node (k, l) over an increment of time Δt can be obtained from

$$\Delta P(k, l) = \left[\frac{\partial P}{\partial t} \right] \Delta t \qquad (5.3.13)$$

The calculation of ΔP in Equation 5.3.13 needs an evaluation of every force term in $-\nabla U$.

The first force term in $-\nabla U$ is due to the electric field E and is equal to Z^*eE. Including the effect of local current crowding due to the development of porosity [5.2] at node (k, l), the local value of the electric field E is given in terms of the local current density J by the expression

$$E = J \cdot \rho = \left[\frac{J_0}{1 - P(k, l)} \right] \cdot \rho_0 [1 + \alpha\{T(k) - T_a\}] \qquad (5.3.14)$$

where

J_0 = initial current density uniform throughout the undamaged interconnection line in amperes per square centimeter

ρ_0 = initial electrical resistivity of the interconnection metal at temperature T_a in ohm centimeters

α = temperature coefficient of resistivity

$T(k)$ = local temperature at the boundary of kth segment

T_a = ambient temperature

It should be noted that the porosity factor $1/[1 - P(k, l)]$ in Equation 5.3.14 is used only for $P(k, l) > 0$. Furthermore, for a continuous train of unipolar current pulses applied to the interconnection line resulting in local current density pulses of amplitude J_p for a duration of δ seconds with a repetition period of Γ seconds, the duty factor r of these pulses is given by

$$r = \frac{\delta}{\Gamma} \tag{5.3.15}$$

resulting in a local power dissipation of $r\rho(J_p)^2$. This heat flows away from the interconnection line longitudinally by thermal conduction and transversely through a dielectric layer (such as silicon dioxide) to the substrate (such as silicon) acting as a heat sink assumed to be at the constant ambient temperature T_a. This heat flow is given in terms of the local temperature $T(k)$ by the equation

$$r\rho(J_p)^2 = \frac{K_m}{(D_{50})^2}[T(k) - T(k - l)] + \frac{K_0}{d_0 d_m}[T(k) - T_a]$$
$$+ \frac{K_m}{(D_{50})^2}[T(k) - T(k + l)] \tag{5.3.16}$$

where

K_m = thermal conductivity of the interconnection metal in watts per centimeter degrees kelvin

K_0 = thermal conductivity of the dielectric layer in watts per centimeter degrees kelvin

d_0 = thickness of the dielectric layer in centimeters

d_m = thickness of the interconnection metal in centimeters

The next force term in $-\nabla U$ is due to diffusion and can be considered as equivalent to the force exerted by a threshold electric field E_{th}; that is,

$$Z^*eE_{th} = \left(\frac{kT}{L}\right)\ln\left[\frac{1 - F_g}{1 - F_l}\right] \tag{5.3.17}$$

where

L = length of the interconnection line in centimeters

F_g = average fractional mass gain along the line (corresponding to negative porosity)

F_l = average fractional mass loss along the line (corresponding to positive porosity)

The last force term in $-\nabla U$ is due to a pressure gradient along the length of the line and is caused by the transfer of mass by the electromigration and the tendency to accumulate mass at various places along the line. It can be approximated by

$$\Omega \frac{dS_{nm}}{dx} = \left(\frac{\Delta V_0}{\Delta N_0} \right) \left(\frac{1}{L} \right) \left(\frac{1}{\beta} \right) \left(\frac{\Delta N}{N_0} \right) \tag{5.3.18}$$

which has been obtained by putting the approximate expression for the bulk compressibility

$$\beta = \left(\frac{1}{V_0} \right) \frac{dV}{dS} \tag{5.3.19}$$

into its incremental form

$$\Delta S = \left(\frac{1}{\beta} \right) \left(\frac{\Delta V}{V_0} \right) \tag{5.3.20}$$

and combining it with the relationship between volume increase and mass increase

$$\frac{\Delta V}{V_0} = \frac{\Delta N}{N_0} \tag{5.3.21}$$

In terms of the average fractional mass gain F_g, Equation 5.3.18 can be rewritten as

$$\Omega \frac{dS_{nm}}{dx} = \left(\frac{\Delta V_0}{\Delta N_0} \right) \left(-\frac{F_g}{\beta L} \right) \tag{5.3.22}$$

Substituting the force terms given by Equations 5.3.14, 5.3.17, and 5.3.22 into Equations 5.3.12 and 5.3.13, the increment of porosity ΔP developed over an increment of time Δt can be obtained from

$$\Delta P(k,l) = \left[\frac{D_0 D_f(k,l)}{D_{50} kT(k)} \right] \left[\exp\left(-\frac{E_a}{kT(k)} \right) \right]$$

$$\times \left[Z^* e j_0 \rho_0 \{1 + \alpha[T(k) - T_a]\} \left[\frac{r}{1 - P(k,l)} \right] \right.$$

$$\left. - \left[\frac{kT(k)}{L} \right] \ln\left[\frac{1 - F_g}{1 - F_l} \right] - \left(\frac{\Delta V_0}{\Delta N_0} \right) \left(-\frac{F_g}{\beta L} \right) \right] \tag{5.3.23}$$

It should be noted that a factor r has been inserted in the electric force term because this force is applied for a fraction of the time only, whereas the diffusion and pressure gradient force terms are present at all times. Furthermore, the time increment Δt can be larger than or equal to one pulse repetition period Γ.

In general, the failure criterion for the interconnection line can be stated in terms of the attainment of the maximum tolerable fractional increase in the line resistance, the elevation of the temperature at a node to the melting point of the interconnection metal, or the attainment of the pressure level at any point along the line that exceeds the strength of the covering layer, if present. In this section the results are calculated using the fractional change in the line resistance R/R_0 as an indicator of the progress of electromigration-induced damage:

$$\frac{R}{R_0} = \left(\frac{1}{N_l}\right)\left[\sum_k \frac{1}{\sum_l \left(\frac{N_w}{1 - P(k,l)}\right)}\right] \qquad (5.3.24)$$

where only a loss of mass is considered to affect the line resistance; that is, $P(k,l)$ is taken to be 0 for those nodes where there is an accumulation of mass.

5.3.3 Modeling Results for DC Currents

In order to validate the physical factors included in the preceding simulation model, the simulation results obtained using the model can be compared with the experimental observations of various workers. In the following results the values of the various parameters used in the model are taken as follows: constant factor in the diffusion coefficient (D_0), 10^{-4} cm^2/s; effective charge on the metal ion (Z^*), -1; activation energy for diffusion (E_a), 0.67 eV (typical of Al–Cu alloys); bulk compressibility (β), 1.33×10^{-11} m^2/N (for Al); and thermal conductivity of the oxide layer, 0.0096 W/cm · °C. In addition, the Wiedemann–Franz law is used for the thermal conductivity of the interconnection metal, and the temperature dependence for the metal resistivity is given by

$$\rho = 2.42 \times 10^{-6}[1 + 0.00475(T - 273)]\,\Omega \cdot \text{cm} \qquad (5.3.25)$$

The effect of an oxide coating in reducing the rate of electromigration in an interconnection line of length (L) = 50 μm, width (W) = 2 μm with D_{50} = 2 μm, s = 0.5 carrying a DC current of density (J) = 1 MA/cm^2 at temperature (T) = 200°C is shown in Figure 5.3.1. This figure shows that the time at which the line resistance begins to rise very rapidly increases nearly six times for the coated line (shown by circles) than with the uncoated line (shown by squares). Such a significant rise in the time to failure for coated lines has been observed experimentally by many workers.

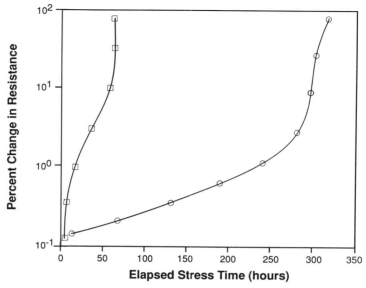

FIGURE 5.3.1   Simulation results showing the effect of oxide coating on the rate of development of electromigration-induced line failure [5.173]. (© 1988 IEEE)

Using a failure criterion of 10 percent resistance change, the effect of line length on the failure time is shown in Figure 5.3.2. The line parameters are: $W = 2$ μm, $D_{50} = 2$ μm, $s = 0.5$ subjected to a DC current of $J = 1$ MA/cm^2 at $T = 200°$C. The squares indicate results based on the present model and the circles indicate results calculated from the statistical model presented in [5.125]. This figure shows that the lifetime increases rapidly as the line gets shorter, which is in agreement with experimental observations.

The simulation results showing the dependences of the median failure time on the normalized width (W/D_{50}) for 20 lines with $L = 50$ μm subjected to a DC current of $J = 1$ MA/cm^2 at $T = 200°$C are shown in Figure 5.3.3. For the upper curve (with squares), $D_{50} = 3$ μm and $s = 0.5$; for the middle curve (with circles), $D_{50} = 2$ μm and $s = 0.5$; and for the lower curve (with triangles), $D_{50} = 1$ μm and $s = 0.5$. All curves indicate a minimum of about $W/D_{50} = 1$, which is in agreement with the observations of Kinsbron [5.126].

The effect of the DC current density on the failure time is shown in Figure 5.3.4. The upper curve (with squares) is for a line of length 50 μm and an activation energy of 0.67 eV (characteristic of Al–Cu alloys) with both ends kept at the ambient test temperature of 200°C and an oxide thickness of 1 μm with the substrate held at the ambient temperature. The medium curve (with circles) shows the effect of allowing the ends of the line to float, that is, adiabatic end conditions. The lower curve (with triangles) is for a 200-μm

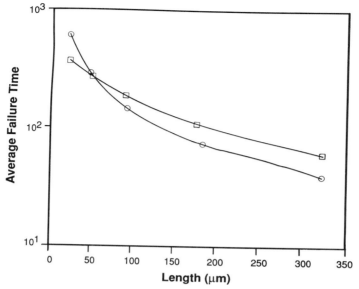

FIGURE 5.3.2   Simulation results showing the effect of line length on failure time [5.173]. (© 1988 IEEE)

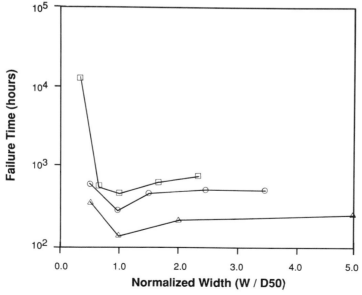

FIGURE 5.3.3   Simulation results showing the effect of line width on failure time [5.173]. (© 1988 IEEE)

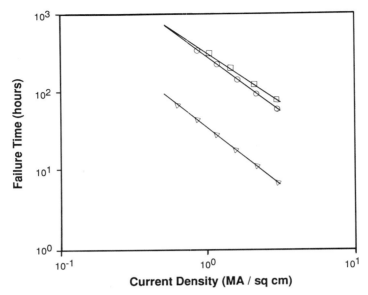

FIGURE 5.3.4   Simulation results showing the effect of DC current density on failure time [5.173]. (© 1988 IEEE)

line having an activation energy of 0.55 eV (characteristic of Al–Si lines) with adiabatic end conditions. The upper, middle, and lower curves correspond to -1.2, -1.5, and -1.5 power dependences on the DC current densities, respectively. These values agree very well with experiments.

5.3.4   Modeling Results for Pulsed Currents

For pulsed current following the relationship $J_p = J_{DC}/r$ with $J_{DC} = 1$ MA/cm^2 (typical of accelerated testing of electromigration), the percentage changes in the line resistance as functions of the elapsed stress time for r values of 0.03125, 0.0625, 0.125, 0.25, 0.5, and 1.0 are shown in Figure 5.3.5. The value of $r = 1.0$ corresponds to the DC case. For these results both ends of the lines are kept at the ambient temperature of 200°C and the values of the line and other parameters are: $L = 50$ μm, $W = 2$ μm, $D_{50} = 2$ μm, $s = 0.5$, and $T = 200$°C. Figure 5.3.5 shows that, for very short duty cycles, there is a significant decrease in the time at which the line resistance begins to increase rapidly.

Assuming a more general relationship between the DC current density and the peak current density given by

$$J_p = \frac{J_{DC}}{(r)^m} \qquad (5.3.26)$$

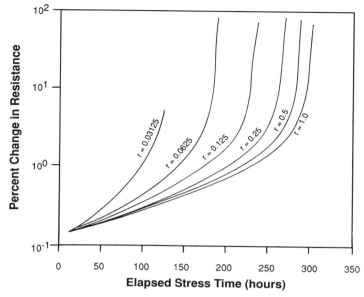

FIGURE 5.3.5 Simulation results showing the effect of peak current density on failure time for various values of r [5.173]. (© 1988 IEEE)

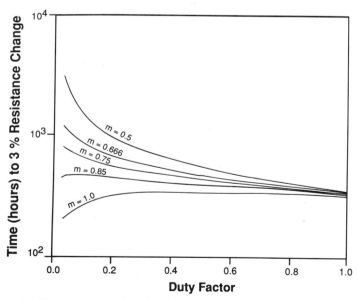

FIGURE 5.3.6 Simulation results showing the effect of duty factor exponent on failure time [5.173]. (© 1988 IEEE)

where m is a constant in the range 0 to 1, the dependences of the times required to reach a 3 percent change in the line resistance on the duty factor r for values of $m = 0.5, 0.666, 0.75, 0.85,$ and 1.0 (for curves from top to bottom) are shown in Figure 5.3.6. These results assume a 1-μm-thick oxide layer with the surface below the oxide and the ends held at the ambient temperature. It should be noted that, for J_p given by Equation 5.3.26, the local power dissipation is given by

$$ r\rho(J_p)^2 = r\rho\left(\frac{J_{DC}}{r^m}\right)^2 = \frac{\rho(J_{DC})^2}{r^{2m-1}} \qquad (5.3.27) $$

which shows that, at a 5 percent duty cycle ($r = 0.05$), there is 20 times as much power dissipation as in the DC case ($m = 1.0$) but only about 11 times as much power dissipation when $m = 0.9$.

5.4   FAILURE ANALYSIS OF VLSI INTERCONNECTION COMPONENTS

In general, an interconnection line on an IC chip consists of several components such as straight segments, bends, steps, plugs, and vias. In addition, there are power and ground buses serving several logic gates on the chip. For submicron-width interconnection lines, there can be sections along the line length suffering from material overflows. In a recent report [5.174], a multi-section interconnection has been introduced which can be designed in three possible configurations: horizontal, vertical, and mixed. A multisection intersection differs from a typical interconnection in that a driver and its load are connected by more than one interconnection line, thus providing more than one path for the current or voltage signal to flow.

    In this section an analysis of electromigration-induced failure in each of the interconnection components listed previously is presented. First, using the effects of the average flux density on the grain boundary migration in the interconnections, expressions for the effective lengths, widths, and thicknesses of the straight segments equivalent to each of the components are derived. Then the series model of failure mechanisms in the interconnections [5.172] is used to determine the series or series–parallel combinations of straight segments equivalent to each interconnection component. Then the development of a program called EMVIC for studying electromigration effects in the components is described. Finally, EMVIC is used to study the dependence of the electromigration-induced MTF on the various parameters of each component. The standard deviation of the corresponding lognormal failure distribution (σ) for a straight segment is also studied.

5.4.1   Reduction of Components into Straight Segments

First, a straight interconnection segment, shown in Figure 5.4.1a, of length L, width W, and thickness T carrying a current I at a given temperature has been analyzed. Then, by considering the effects of the average flux density on the grain boundary migration in each interconnection component, it has been reduced to a series–parallel combination of equivalent straight interconnection segments. The average flux density in a component has been determined by using the interconnection current I and the average cross-sectional area throughout the component.

It can be shown that the additional area in an interconnection bend of angle θ_B, shown shaded in Figure 5.4.1b, is equivalent to a straight segment of length L_B and width W_B given by the expressions

$$L_B = \frac{\pi W |(180 - \theta_B)|}{360}$$

$$W_B = \frac{W^2\left(1 + \sqrt{\tan\left(\frac{\theta_B}{2}\right)}\right)}{W + L_B} \tag{5.4.1}$$

For a bend angle of $90°$, expressions (5.4.1) yield values in agreement with those derived by Frost and Poole [5.172].

An interconnection line of length L, width W, and thickness T having a single step of height H and angle θ_S, shown in Figure 5.4.1c, is equivalent to three straight segments each of width W, lengths L_{S1}, L_{S2}, and L_{S3}, and thicknesses T_{S1}, T_{S2}, and T_{S3}, respectively, given by the expressions

$$L_{S1} = L + \frac{H}{\tan\theta_S}$$

$$T_{S1} = T$$

$$L_{S2} = T\cos\theta_S + \frac{H}{\sin\theta_S}$$

$$T_{S2} = T\cos\theta_S \tag{5.4.2}$$

$$L_{S3} = \frac{\pi T(180 - \theta_S)(1 - \cos\theta_S)}{720}$$

$$T_{S3} = \frac{T^2(1 + \cos\theta_S(\cos\theta_S - \sin\theta_S))}{2L_{S3} + T(1 - \cos\theta_S)}$$

Two straight sections of an interconnection line of total length L, width W, and thickness T joined by a single plug of length H and square dimension W_P, shown in Figure 5.4.1d, is equivalent to three straight segments of

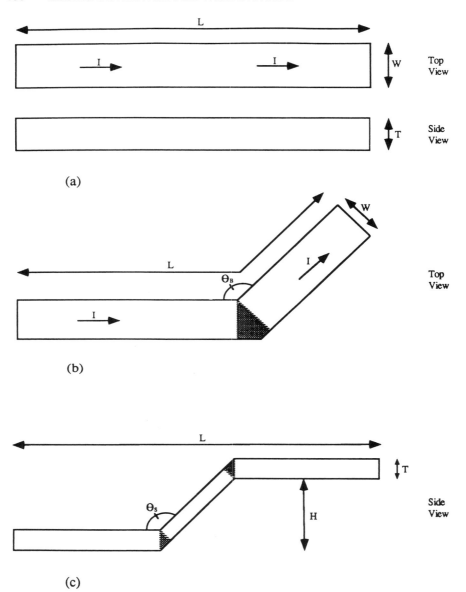

FIGURE 5.4.1 Schematic diagrams of the various interconnection components: (*a*) straight segment, (*b*) bend, (*c*) step, (*d*) plug, (*e*) overflow, (*f*) via, (*g*) horizontal multisection interconnection, (*h*) vertical multisection interconnection, and (*i*) power and ground buses. .

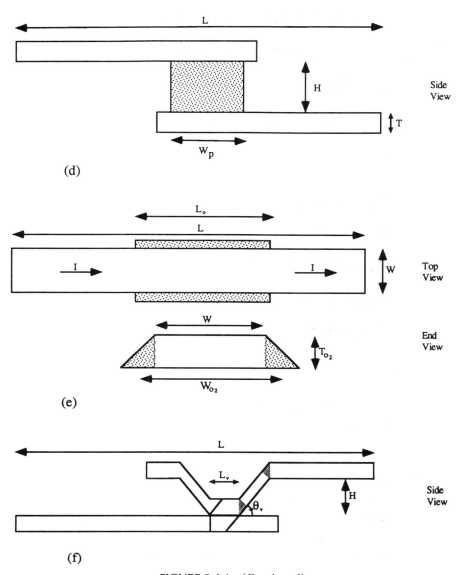

FIGURE 5.4.1   (Continued)

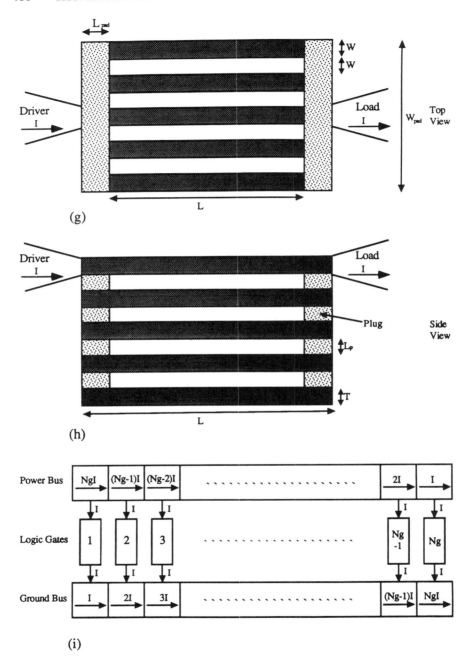

(g)

(h)

(i)

FIGURE 5.4.1 (Continued)

lengths L_{P1}, L_{P2}, and L_{P3}, widths W_{P1}, W_{P2}, and W_{P3}, and thicknesses T_{P1}, T_{P2} and T_{P3}, respectively, given by the expressions

$$L_{P1} = L - W_P$$

$$W_{P1} = W$$

$$T_{P1} = T$$

$$L_{P2} = H$$

$$W_{P2} = W_P$$

$$T_{P2} = W_P \qquad (5.4.3)$$

$$L_{P3} = \frac{\pi}{8}(T + W_P)$$

$$W_{P3} = W$$

$$T_{P3} = \frac{T(W + L_P)}{L_{P3}}$$

An interconnection line of length L, width W, and thickness T having a length L_O suffering from overflow (top and end views are shown schematically in Figure 5.4.1e) is equivalent to two straight segments of lengths L_{O1} and L_{O2}, widths W_{O1} and W_{O2}, and thicknesses T_{O1} and T_{O2} given by the expressions

$$L_{O1} = L - L_O$$

$$T_{O1} = T$$

$$W_{O1} = W$$

$$L_{O2} = L_O$$

$$T_{O2} = \frac{-W + \sqrt{W^2 + 4WT}}{2} \qquad (5.4.4)$$

$$W_{O2} = \frac{WT}{T_{O2}}$$

Two straight sections of an interconnection line of total length L, width W, and thickness T joined by a via of height H, width W_V, and angle θ_V, shown in Figure 5.4.1f, is equivalent to four straight segments, each of width W, lengths L_{V1}, L_{V2}, L_{V3}, and L_{V4}, and thicknesses T_{V1}, T_{V2}, T_{V3}, and T_{V4}, respectively, given by the expressions

$$L_{V1} = \frac{\theta_V \pi T (1 + \cos \theta_V)}{720}$$

$$T_{V1} = \frac{T^2 [1 + \cos \theta_V (\cos \theta_V + \sin \theta_V)]}{2 L_{V1} + T (1 + \cos \theta_V)}$$

$$L_{V2} = \frac{H}{\sin \theta_V} - T \sin \theta_V$$

$$T_{V2} = T \cos \theta_V$$

$$L_{V3} = \frac{T}{2 \sin \left[\arctan \left(\dfrac{T}{W_V} \right) \right]}$$
(5.4.5)

$$T_{V3} = \frac{\dfrac{T^2}{2 \tan \theta_V} + T \left[W_V - \dfrac{T}{\tan \theta_V} \right]}{L_{V3}}$$

$$L_{V4} = L - W_V - \frac{H}{\tan \theta_V}$$

$$T_{V4} = T$$

A horizontal multisection interconnection of length L consists of a parallel combinations of N interconnections, each of length L, width W, and thickness T, placed between two rectangular pads, each of length L_{pad} and width W_{pad}, where

$$W_{\text{pad}} = (2N - 1)W$$
(5.4.6)

on each side which are in turn connected to the interconnection driver and its load. A schematic diagram of the top view of a horizontal multisection interconnection is shown in Figure 5.4.1g.

A vertical multisection interconnection of length L consists of a parallel combination of N interconnections, one of which is printed on top of the substrate, whereas the others are embedded in the substrate exactly below the top section. Each section is of length L, width W, and thickness T. The sections are connected to each other at the ends by conducting plugs each of length L_p. A schematic diagram of the side view of a vertical multisection interconnection is shown in Figure 5.4.1h. A mixed multisection interconnection is formed by mixing the horizontal and vertical multisection interconnections; that is, it has a few sections printed on top of the substrate in addition to a few sections embedded in the substrate.

As shown in Figure 5.4.1i, a power or ground bus serving N_g gates on the integrated circuit chip can be modeled as a series combination of N straight segments carrying currents equal to $I, 2I, 3I, \ldots, N_g I$, where I is the current in each gate.

5.4.2 Calculation of MTF and Lognormal Standard Deviation

First, for a basic conductor element of length 10 μm, the median time to failure can be found by using the expression [5.172]

$$\text{MTF} = 1523.0 \left(\frac{WT}{I \times 10^5} \right)^n \left(W - 3.07 + \frac{11.63}{W^{1.7}} \right) \exp \left(\frac{10,740.74 E_a}{T_K} \right) \quad (5.4.7)$$

where I is the interconnection current in milliamperes, n is the current density exponent, E_a is the activation energy of the interconnection material in electron-volts, T_K is the temperature in degrees kelvin, W is the interconnection width in micrometers, and T is the interconnection thickness in micrometers. Then, as a first approximation, the MTF of a series combination of N elements (MTF_s) can be found by using the expression

$$\frac{1}{\text{MTF}_s} = \frac{1}{\text{MTF}_1} + \frac{1}{\text{MTF}_2} + \cdots + \frac{1}{\text{MTF}_N} \quad (5.4.8)$$

whereas that of a parallel combination of N elements (MTF_p) can be found by using the expression

$$\text{MTF}_p = \text{MTF}_1 + \text{MTF}_2 + \cdots + \text{MTF}_N \quad (5.4.9)$$

The lognormal standard deviation σ of a basic conductor element of width W (in micrometers) is given by [5.172]

$$\sigma(W) = \frac{2.192}{W^{2.625}} + 0.787 \quad (5.4.10)$$

Then, for a straight segment of length L, it can be calculated by using the expression

$$\sigma_n = \sigma n^{-0.304} \quad (5.4.11)$$

where

$$n = \frac{L \, (\mu\text{m})}{10} \quad (5.4.12)$$

5.4.3   The Program EMVIC

A listing of the program EMVIC is presented in Appendix 5.1. This program is interactive and extremely user-friendly and is written in FORTRAN-77. The program EMVIC can be used to determine the MTF and lognormal standard deviation of a straight interconnection segment as well as the MTF values of the interconnection bend, interconnection step, interconnection plug, interconnection via, interconnection overflow, horizontal multisection interconnection, vertical multisection interconnection, mixed multisection interconnection, and power/ground bus. First, the user can utilize the default values or choose his or her own values for the several parameters of any component listed previously. After the user defines the component, EMVIC calculates the MTF and σ (for a straight segment only) and displays the results on the screen. The user can choose to write the simulation results on an output file called EMVIC.OUT. A flowchart of the program EMVIC is shown in Figure 5.4.2.

For a straight segment, the parameters include its length, width, thickness, temperature, current, current density exponent, and material activation energy. In addition to these parameters, the other components are defined by the following additional parameters:

Interconnection bend: Bend angle

Interconnection step: Step height, step angle

Interconnection plug: Plug length, square plug dimension, plug material activation energy, lower-level material activation energy

Interconnection via: Via height, via width, via angle, lower-level material activation energy

Interconnection overflow: Overflow length

Horizontal multisection interconnection: Number of horizontal sections, source/sink pad lengths

Vertical multisection interconnection: Number of vertical sections, vertical plug lengths, plug material activation energy

Mixed multisection interconnection: Number of horizontal sections, number of embedded vertical sections, vertical plug lengths, source/sink pad lengths, plug material activation energy

Power or ground bus: Number of gates served by the bus, current in each gate

5.4.4   Simulation Results Using EMVIC

The program EMVIC has been used to study the dependence of the MTF on the various parameters of each interconnection component. In the following results, the current density exponent is set at 1.0.

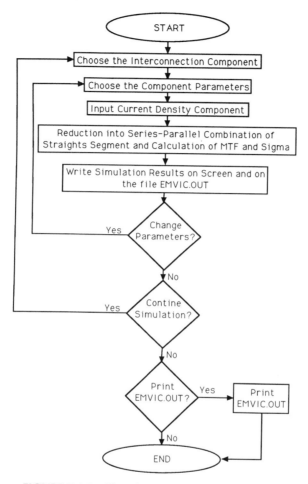

FIGURE 5.4.2   Flowchart of the program EMVIC.

First, for a straight interconnection segment, the dependences of the MTF and $\log(\sigma)$ on the segment width in the range 0.5 to 5 μm are shown in Figure 5.4.3, and the dependence of the MTF on the segment length in the range 10 to 100 μm is shown in Figure 5.4.4. The relatively sharp increase in the MTF and σ for widths less than nearly 2 μm is due to the so-called bamboo effect. The dependence of the MTF on the interconnection current for a 20-μm-long, 2-μm-wide, 0.5-μm-thick straight segment in the range 2 to 20 mA at 100° C is shown in Figure 5.4.5, and the dependence of the MTF on the temperature of a straight segment in the range 20 to 200° C is shown in Figure 5.4.6. For an interconnection bend, the dependence of the MTF on the bend angle in the range 10° to 150° is shown in Figure 5.4.7. This figure

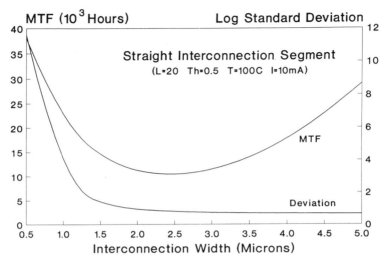

FIGURE 5.4.3   MTF and $\log(\sigma)$ as a function of interconnection width for a straight interconnection segment.

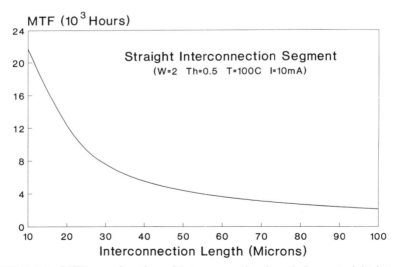

FIGURE 5.4.4   MTF as a function of interconnection length for a straight interconnection segment.

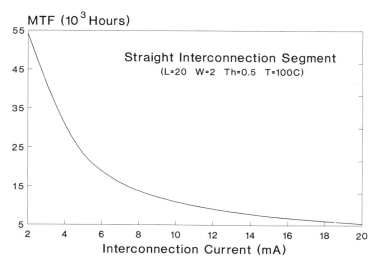

FIGURE 5.4.5   MTF as a function of interconnection current for a straight interconnection segment.

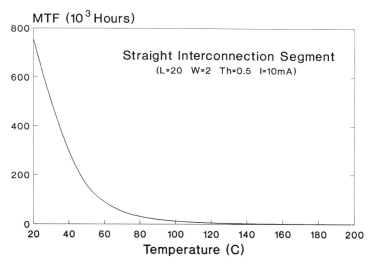

FIGURE 5.4.6   MTF as a function of interconnection temperature for a straight interconnection segment.

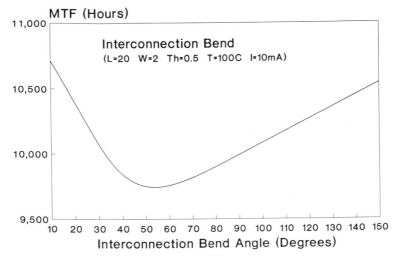

FIGURE 5.4.7 MTF as a function of bend angle for an interconnection bend.

shows that a bend angle of nearly 50° results in the lowest MTF value. For an interconnection step, the dependence of the MTF on the step angle in the range 90.1° to 160° is shown in Figure 5.4.8 and that on the step height in the range 1 to 10 μm is shown in Figure 5.4.9. Figure 5.4.8 shows that the MTF decreases rapidly as the step angle approaches 90°. This is because of the gradual thinning of the material at the step. For an interconnection plug,

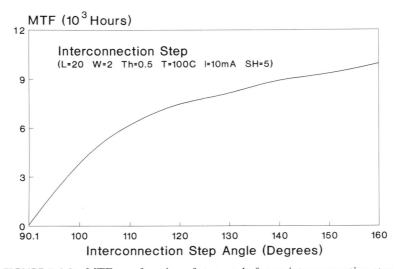

FIGURE 5.4.8 MTF as a function of step angle for an interconnection step.

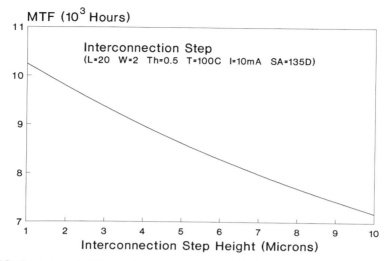

FIGURE 5.4.9   MTF as a function of step height for an interconnection step.

the dependence of the MTF on the plug length in the range 1 to 10 μm is shown in Figure 5.4.10 and that on the dimension of its square side in the range 0.5 to 2.0 μm is shown in Figure 5.4.11. The dependence of the MTF on the via height for an interconnection via is shown in Figure 5.4.12, that on the via angle is shown in Figure 5.4.13, and that on the via width is shown in Figure 5.4.14. For an interconnection of length 20 μm, the dependence of

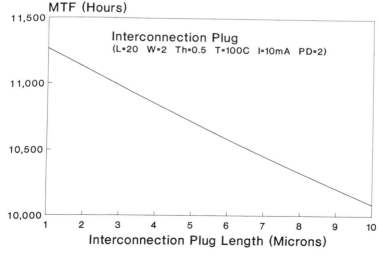

FIGURE 5.4.10   MTF as a function of plug length for an interconnection plug.

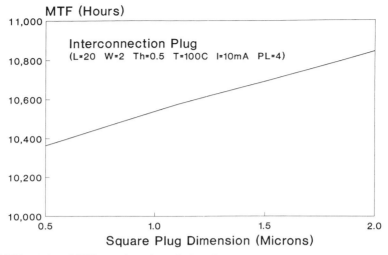

FIGURE 5.4.11   MTF as a function of plug dimension for an interconnection plug.

the MTF on the length of the section of the interconnection suffering from overflow in the range 2 to 20 μm is shown in Figure 5.4.15.

For a horizontal multisection interconnection, the dependence of the MTF on the number of horizontal sections in the range 1 to 5 is shown in Figure 5.4.16. This figure shows that the MTF varies nearly as n^2, where n is the number of sections. This is because the current density in each section is

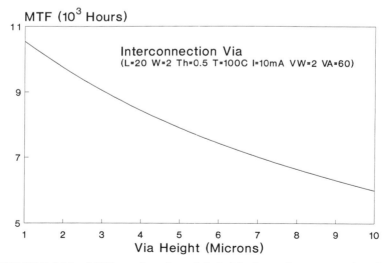

FIGURE 5.4.12   MTF as a function of via height for an interconnection via.

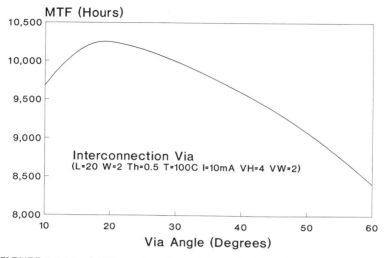

FIGURE 5.4.13   MTF as a function of via angle for an interconnection via.

nearly $1/n$ of that in the original single-section interconnection and further because all sections must fail before the interconnection fails completely. A similar dependence on the number of vertical sections for a vertical multisection interconnection is shown in Figure 5.4.17. However, compared to the horizontal configuration, the vertical multisection interconnection offers the advantage that it does not require any additional space on the chip. For a

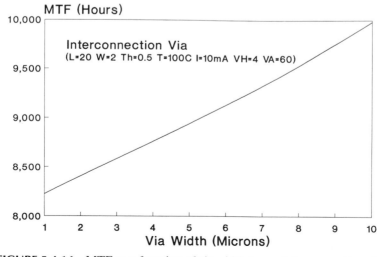

FIGURE 5.4.14   MTF as a function of via width for an interconnection via.

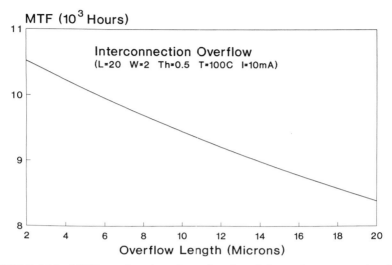

FIGURE 5.4.15 MTF as a function of overflow length for an interconnection flow.

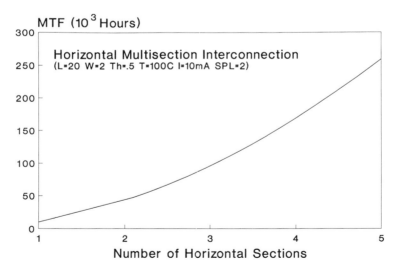

FIGURE 5.4.16 MTF as a function of number of sections for a horizontal multisection interconnection.

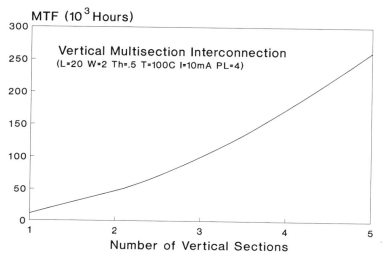

FIGURE 5.4.17 MTF as a function of number of sections for a vertical multisection interconnection.

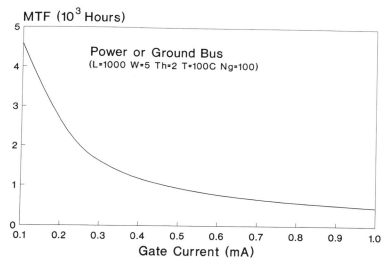

FIGURE 5.4.18 MTF as a function of current in each gate for a power or ground bus.

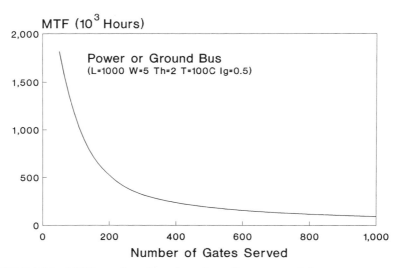

FIGURE 5.4.19   MTF as a function of number of gates served for a power or ground bus.

1000-μm-long power or ground bus serving 100 identical gates, the dependence of the MTF on the current in each gate in the range 0.1 to 1 mA is shown in Figure 5.4.18. This figures shows that increasing the gate currents results in lower MTF values for the bus, as expected. Finally, the dependence of the MTF on the number of gates served by the bus is shown in Figure 5.4.19.

5.5   COMPUTER-AIDED FAILURE ANALYSIS

Rapid developments in VLSI over the last decade have resulted in integrated circuit chips consisting of millions of devices and interconnections. In addition, the reductions of device and other dimensions has led to ever-increasing complexity of these chips. With the scaling of the device and interconnection dimensions, several factors need to be considered which have an important bearing on the reliability of a chip. These include the small geometry effects in MOSFETs and MESFETs such as hot-carrier effects, dielectric breakdown, electromigration effects in the interconnections, and radiation effects.

The reliability performance of a VLSI chip is of major concern to a designer. In the past, because of the lack of CAD tools, VLSI reliability tests were limited to the transistor level. In today's submicron age it is almost impossible to do without CAD tools for designing IC chips and for predicting their reliability under various operating conditions. In fact, over the past few years, several CAD tools have emerged which address different aspects of the reliability if an IC chip.

5.5.1 RELIANT for Reliability of VLSI Interconnections

RELIANT is a CAD tool developed by researchers at Clemson University [5.175] for the purpose of predicting the reliability of interconnections because of wear-out due to electromigration. RELIANT predicts the instantaneous failure rate of the interconnection pattern as a function of time. The algorithm used in RELIANT is based on the principle of fracturing the interconnection pattern into a number of interconnection components, including straight segments, bonding pads, contact windows, vias between two metal layers, and steps resulting from discontinuities in the wafer surface. These components are assumed to be statistically independent which is valid as long as the time of analysis is much smaller than the median time to failure and when the current density is low enough so that any thermal interactions among the components can be considered negligibly small. This latter requirement is usually satisfied if the current density is less than $10^6 \, \text{A}/\text{cm}^2$.

A simplified flow chart of RELIANT is shown in Figure 5.5.1. It shows that RELIANT consists of three main modules called EXTREM, COMBINE, and SIRPRICE. The function of EXTREM is to fracture the interconnection patterns contained in a Caltech Intermediate Format (CIF) file into the various components and to produce a database file called DB1 containing the physical description of each component in terms of its type and physical dimensions. EXTREM also identifies the active devices and produces a SPICE-compatible netlist of the RC equivalent network including all parasitic interconnection resistances and capacitances of each branch of the interconnection pattern. The function of COMBINE is to read a file called SPC containing the user-defined device models, analysis parameters, and external components such as voltage sources and load resistors and then to add this information to the extracted netlist to produce a file called SPR. The function of SIRPRICE is to read the file SPR and to call a modified version of SPICE 2G.6 to perform a transient simulation of the extracted circuit and to produce files containing current-time data $j(t)$ for each resistor corresponding to each branch of the interconnection pattern. The cross-sectional area of each component is determined from the physical information contained in the file DB1, and an effective current density in the component is computed by using the expression

$$ J_{\text{eff}} = \frac{1}{\Gamma t} \int_0^{t_{\text{final}}} \sinh[\Gamma j(t)] \, dt \qquad (5.5.1) $$

where Γ is a constant [5.175]. The median time to failure (t_{50}) is then

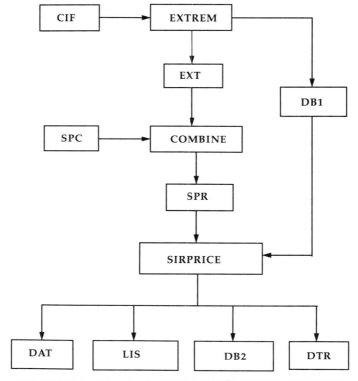

FIGURE 5.5.1 Flowchart of RELIANT [5.175]. (© 1988 IEEE)

calculated by using the equation

$$ t_{50} = \left(\frac{G}{J_{\text{eff}}} \right) \exp\left(\frac{E_a}{kT} \right) \tag{5.5.2} $$

where k is Boltzmann's constant, T is the absolute temperature, E_a is the activation energy, and G depends on the physical dimensions of the component contained in the file DB1. The standard deviation σ of the lognormal failure distribution of each component is also calculated from the physical information in the file DB1. The instantaneous failure rate of the interconnection pattern is then calculated using a suitable failure distribution such as the most commonly and experimentally tested lognormal distribution. SIRPRICE produces several data files called DAT, LIS, DB2, and DTR containing the failure rates for each ccmponent and the entire circuit, the reliability data, and other data used for interfacing to other program modules.

5.5.2   SPIDER for Checking Current Density and Voltage Drop in Interconnection Metallizations

As is well known, high current densities in interconnection metallizations lead to electromigration of metal atoms and voltage drop and should be properly accounted for in order to avoid any serious reliability problems. SPIDER is a CAD tool developed by researchers at Texas Instruments, Inc. [5.176] for the purpose of checking current density and voltage drop in VLSI interconnections. In fact, it is a system of programs employing a simplified hierarchical approach developed to aid VLSI designers to ensure adequate current-carrying capacity in the metallization patterns on an integrated circuit chip. SPIDER includes both the detection and correction algorithms for current density and voltage drop and can be used in the initial design phase as well as for layout verification.

SPIDER uses a hierarchical approach and can be used at any level of circuit design. the lowest-level subcircuits can be analyzed for current waveforms using SPICE which can then be used for the design and analysis at the

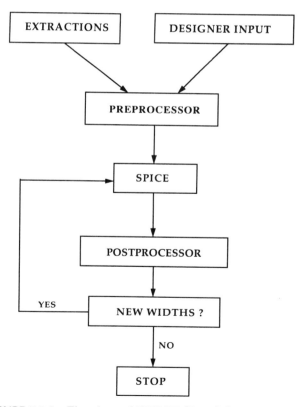

FIGURE 5.5.2   Flowchart of SPIDER [5.176]. (© 19886 IEEE)

next higher circuit level. An abbreviated form of the flowchart of SPIDER is shown in Figure 5.5.2. The various steps can be summarized as follows.

1. First, the various metallization patterns which could be power supply lines, ground lines, clock lines, or other signal lines are represented in terms of equivalent resistive and capacitive elements which are determined by using a parasitic element extraction program. This results in an *RC* network suitable for analysis by SPICE. The designer also identifies the nodes at which the current enters or leaves the conductor.

2. Next, transient current waveforms at each identified node are determined by the designer by analysis of the individual subcircuit.

3. Next, SPICE is used to determine the current waveform flowing through each resistance.

4. Next, the continuous DC current densities equivalent to the current waveforms of step 3 are calculated by using the procedure derived by McPherson and Ghate [5.177]. These current densities are then compared with the desired values specified by the designer. If, in a given region, the calculated current density exceeds the specified value, then the width of the metallization is increased; otherwise, no change in the width is made if it is below the specified value.

5. Steps 3 and 4 are then repeated for the revised values of the widths, and the process is carried out until the final set of line widths is found.

EXERCISES

E5.1   According to Equation 5.3.16, the local power dissipation from the interconnection line is given by

$$r\rho(J_p)^2 = \frac{K_m}{(D_{50})^2}[T(k) - T(k-l)] + \frac{K_0}{d_0 d_m}[T(k) - T_a]$$

$$+ \frac{K_m}{(D_{50})^2}[T(k) - T(k+l)]$$

This equation does not account for the details of heat transfer from the substrate to the ambient environment. Comment on the significance of this missing factor and modify the equation to include this process.

E5.2   Equation 5.3.16 is time independent. This is valid as long as the pulse repetition rate is of the order of megahertz because the thermal time constant for a typical metal line/dielectric layer combination is usually one or more microseconds. Modify the equation so that it is also valid for lower pulse repetition rates.

E5.3 By considering the effects of the average flux density on the grain boundary migration in an interconnection bend of angle θ_B, show that the additional area (shown shaded in Figure 5.4.1b) is equivalent to a straight segment of length L_B and width W_B given by the expressions

$$L_B = \frac{\pi W |(180 - \theta_B)|}{360}$$

$$W_B = \frac{W^2\left(1 + \sqrt{\tan\left(\frac{\theta_B}{2}\right)}\right)}{W + L_B}$$

E5.4 Show that an interconnection line of length L, width W, and thickness T having a single step of height H and angle θ_S, shown in Figure 5.4.1c, is equivalent to three straight segments, each of width W, lengths L_{S1}, L_{S2}, and L_{S3}, ad thicknesses T_{S1}, T_{S2}, and T_{S3}, respectively, given by the expressions

$$L_{S1} = L + \frac{H}{\tan \theta_S}$$

$$T_{S1} = T$$

$$L_{S2} = T \cos \theta_S + \frac{H}{\sin \theta_S}$$

$$T_{S2} = T \cos \theta_S$$

$$L_{S3} = \frac{\pi T (180 - \theta_S)(1 - \cos \theta_S)}{720}$$

$$T_{S3} = \frac{T^2(1 + \cos \theta_S(\cos \theta_S - \sin \theta_S))}{2L_{S3} + T(1 - \cos \theta_S)}$$

E5.5 Show that the two straight sections of an interconnection line of total length L, width W, and thickness T joined by a single plug of length H and square dimension W_P, shown in Figure 5.4.1d, is equivalent to three straight segments of lengths L_{P1}, L_{P2}, and L_{P3}, widths W_{P1}, W_{P2}, and W_{P3}, and thicknesses T_{P1}, T_{P2}, and T_{P3}, respectively, given by the expressions

$$L_{P1} = L - W_P$$

$$W_{P1} = W$$

$$T_{P1} = T$$

$$L_{P2} = H$$

$$W_{P2} = W_P$$

$$T_{P2} = W_P$$

$$L_{P3} = \frac{\pi}{8}(T + W_P)$$

$$W_{P3} = W$$

$$T_{P3} = \frac{T(W + L_P)}{L_{P3}}$$

E5.6   Show that an interconnection line of length L, width W, and thickness T having a length L_O suffering from overflow (top and end views are shown schematically in Figure 5.4.1e) is equivalent to two straight segments of lengths L_{O1} and L_{O2}, widths W_{O1} and W_{O2}, and thicknesses T_{O1} and T_{O2} given by the expressions

$$L_{O1} = L - L_O$$

$$T_{O1} = T$$

$$W_{O1} = W$$

$$L_{O2} = L_O$$

$$T_{O2} = \frac{-W + \sqrt{W^2 + 4WT}}{2}$$

$$W_{O2} = \frac{WT}{T_{O2}}$$

E5.7   Show that the two straight sections of an interconnection line of total length L, width W, and thickness T joined by a via of height H, width W_V, and angle θ_V, shown in Figure 5.4.1f, are equivalent to four straight segments, each of width W, lengths L_{V1}, L_{V2}, L_{V3}, and L_{V4}, and thicknesses T_{V1}, T_{V2}, T_{V3}, and T_{V4}, respectively, given by

$$L_{V1} = \frac{\theta_V \pi T (1 + \cos \theta_V)}{720}$$

$$T_{V1} = \frac{T^2 [1 + \cos \theta_V (\cos \theta_V + \sin \theta_V)]}{2 L_{V1} + T(1 + \cos \theta_V)}$$

$$L_{V2} = \frac{H}{\sin \theta_V} - T \sin \theta_V$$

$$T_{V2} = T \cos \theta_V$$

$$L_{V3} = \frac{T}{2 \sin \left[\arctan \left(\dfrac{T}{W_V} \right) \right]}$$

$$T_{V3} = \frac{\dfrac{T^2}{2 \tan \theta_V} + T \left[W_V - \dfrac{T}{\tan \theta_V} \right]}{L_{V3}}$$

$$L_{V4} = L - W_V - \frac{H}{\tan \theta_V}$$

$$T_{V4} = T$$

E5.8 The simulation results using EMVIC presented in Section 5.4.4 are based on the approximate equations (5.4.8) and (5.4.9). More accurate results can be obtained by using the probability of failure equations (5.2.6) to (5.2.8). Determine the MTF by first plotting the probability of failure as a function of time for each interconnection component described in Section 5.4.

APPENDIX 5.1

EMVIC
Electromigration-Induced Failure Analysis of
VLSI Interconnection Components

```
DIRECTORY OF TERMS:
        AE:         Activation Energy of Interconnection
                    Material in eV
        BANGLE:     Interconnection Bend Angle in Degrees
        BAE:        Activation Energy of the Bus Material
                    in eV
```

BL:	Total Bus Length in Microns
BT:	Bus Thickness in Microns
BW:	Bus Width in Microns
CLEAR:	C-Routine used to Clear Screen
CURRENT:	Interconnection Current in mA
GC:	Current in Each Gate Served by the Bus in mA
IL:	Interconnection Length in Microns
IPL:	Interconnection Plug Length in Microns
IT:	Interconnection Thickness in Microns
IW:	Interconnection Width in Microns
JE:	Value of the Current Density Exponent
LAE:	Activation Energy of Lower Level Material in eV
MANGLE:	Maximum Allowed Interconnection Step Angle in Degrees
MTF:	Median Time to Failure in Hours
NBVS:	Number of Embedded (Buried) Vertical Sections for MMSI
NGB:	Number of Gates Served by the Bus (Assumed Identical)
NHS:	Number of Horizontal Sections
NVS:	Number of Vertical Sections
OL:	Overflow Length in Microns
PAE:	Activation Energy of Plug Material in eV
PL:	Source/Sink Pad Lengths for HMSI in Microns
PRINT:	C-Routine used to Print emvim.out
SANGLE:	Interconnection Step Angle in Degrees
SHEIGHT:	Interconnection Step Height in Microns
SIGMA:	Lognormal Standard Deviation
SPD:	Square Interconnection Plug Dimension in Microns
TEMPC:	Interconnection Temperature in C
TEMP:	Interconnection Temperature in K
VANGLE:	Interconnection Via Angle in Degrees
MVANGLE:	Minimum Via Angle in Degrees
VH:	Via Height in Microns
VPAE:	Plug Activation Energy in eV for the VMSI and MMSI

```
      VPL:        Plug Length in Microns for the
                  VMSI and MMSI
      VW:         Via Width in Microns
SUBROUTINES:
      BEND:       For Interconnection Bends
      EMVICOUT1 to EMVICOUT11: For Writing on the
                  Output File
      HMSI:       For Horizontal Multisection
                  Interconnections
      MMSI:       For Mixed Multisection
                  Interconnections
      OVERFLOW:   For Interconnection Overflows
      PGBUS:      For Power and Ground Buses
      PLUG:       For Interconnection Plugs
      STEP:       For Interconnection Steps
      STRAIGHT:   For Straight Interconnection Segments
      VIA:        For Interconnection Vias
      VMSI:       For Vertical Multisection
                  Interconnections
C*****DECLARING VARIABLES*****
      REAL*8   IL, IW, IT, TEMP, CURRENT, BANGLE, MTF,
      $        SIGMA, MANGLE, CLEAR, I, TEMPC, SANGLE,
      $        SHEIGHT, FRATE(100), MVANGLE, PRINT, OL,
      $        IPL, SPD, TIME(100), MAXTIME, TIMESTEP,
      $        AE, PAE, PL, VH, VW, VANGLE, LAE, BL,
      $        BW, BT, GC, BAE, VPL, VPAE, JE
      INTEGER NP, NHS, NVS, NGB, NBVS
      CHARACTER*1 CCP1, IGP, SSIP, CCP2, WRP, CP3, CDEP
  900 FORMAT (10X,2( '-----------------------------'))
  902 FORMAT ( / / )
  903 FORMAT ( / / / )
  904 FORMAT ( / / / / )
  905 FORMAT ( / / / / / )
  906 FORMAT ( / / / / / / )
  919 FORMAT (11X 'One or More Parameters have
      $        MEANINGLESS Values...'/
      $        11X 'Press RETURN to Choose New
      $        Value(s)...')
C*****The First Screen*****
   10 I = CLEAR()
      WRITE (*,903)
      WRITE (*,20)
```

```
 20    FORMAT (15X, `################################'/
       $      15X, `##                               ##'/
       $      15X, `##          WELCOME TO           ##'/
       $      15X, `##                               ##'/
       $      15X, `##          E  M  V  I  C         ##'/
       $      15X, `##        ELECTROMIGRATION        ##'/
       $      15X, `##          IN THE VLSI           ##'/
       $      15X, `## INTERCONNECTION COMPONENTS     ##'/
       $      15X, `##                               ##'/
       $      15X, `################################'/
       $      15X, `Enter P to PROCEED or Q to QUIT ')
       READ (*,*, ERR = 10) CCP1
       IF (CCP1 .EQ. "P" .OR. CCP1 .EQ. "p") THEN
       GO TO 25
       ELSE IF (CCP1 .EQ. "Q" .OR. CCP1 .EQ. "q") THEN
       GO TO 1000
       ELSE
       GO TO 10
       END IF
C*****Opening the Output File*****
 25    OPEN (8, FILE = "emvic.out")
       WRITE (8,28)
 28    FORMAT (15X, `################################'/
       $      15X, `##                               ##'/
       $      15X, `##        E M V I C . O U T       ##'/
       $      15X, `##                               ##'/
       $      15X, `##        ELECTROMIGRATION        ##'/
       $      15X, `##          IN THE VLSI           ##'/
       $      15X, `## INTERCONNECTION COMPONENTS     ##'/
       $      15X, `##         (OUTPUT FILE)          ##'/
       $      15X, `##                               ##'/
       $      15X, `################################'//)
C*****Initial Values of Component Parameters*****
       IL = 100.0
       IW = 2.0
       IT = 0.5
       TEMPC = 100.0
       TEMP = TEMPC + 273.0
       CURRENT = 10.0
       AE = 0.54
       JE = 1.0
       BANGLE = 90.0
       SANGLE = 135.0
```

```
          SHEIGHT = 5.0
          MANGLE = 90.0 + (180.0 / 3.142)*ATAN(IL / SHEIGHT)
          PAE = 0.6
          LAE = 0.54
          IPL = 4.0
          SPD = 2.0
          LAE = 0.54
          VANGLE = 60.0
          VH = 4.0
          VW = 2.0
          MVANGLE = 90.0- (180.0 / 3.142)*ATAN((IL- VW) / VH)
          OL = 5.0
          NHS = 5
          PL = 2.0
          NVS = 5
          VPL = 4.0
          VPAE = 0.6
          NHS = 5
          PL = 2.0
          NBVS = 4
          VPL = 4.0
          VPAE = 0.6
          BL = 10000.0
          BW = 10.0
          BT = 5.0
          BAE = 0.54
          NGB = 100
          GC = 0.5
C*****The Interconnection Components*****
  30      I = CLEAR( )
          WRITE (*,903)
          WRITE (*,900)
          WRITE (*,40)
  40      FORMAT (11X, 'I N T E R C O N N E C T I O N
     $                 C O M P O N E N T')
          WRITE (*,900)
          WRITE (*,50)
  50      FORMAT (11X, 'Choose ONE of the Following
     $                 Components:'/
     $            11X, ' A. Straight Interconnection
     $                    Segment'/
     $            11X, ' B. Interconnection Bend'/
     $            11X, ' C. Interconnection Step'/
```

```
    $          11X, ` D. Interconnection Plug'/
    $          11X, ` E. Interconnection Via'/
    $          11X, ` F. Interconnection Overflow'/
    $          11X, ` G. Horizontal Multisection
    $                  Interconnection'/
    $          11X, ` H. Vertical Multisection
    $                  Interconnection'/
    $          11X, ` I. Mixed Multisection
    $                  Interconnection'/
    $          11X,' J. Power or Ground Bus')
     WRITE (*,900)
     WRITE (*,*) `ENTER A- J TO CHOOSE or Q to QUIT'
     WRITE (*,900)
     READ (*,*, ERR = 30) IGP
     IF (IGP .EQ. "A" .OR. IGP .EQ. "a") THEN
     GO TO 60
     ELSE IF (IGP .EQ. "B" .OR. IGP .EQ. "b") THEN
     GO TO 70
     ELSE IF (IGP .EQ. "C" .OR. IGP .EQ. "c") THEN
     GO TO 80
     ELSE IF (IGP .EQ. "D" .OR. IGP .EQ. "d") THEN
     GO TO 240
     ELSE IF (IGP .EQ. "E" .OR. IGP .EQ. "e") THEN
     GO TO 90
     ELSE IF (IGP .EQ. "F" .OR. IGP .EQ. "f") THEN
     GO TO 100
     ELSE IF (IGP .EQ. "G" .OR. IGP .EQ. "g") THEN
     GO TO 110
     ELSE IF (IGP .EQ. "H" .OR. IGP .EQ. "h") THEN
     GO TO 120
     ELSE IF (IGP .EQ. "I" .OR. IGP .EQ. "i") THEN
     GO TO 130
     ELSE IF (IGP .EQ. "J" .OR. IGP .EQ. "j") THEN
     GO TO 140
     ELSE IF (IGP .EQ. "Q" .OR. IGP .EQ. "q") THEN
     GO TO 999
     ELSE
     GO TO 30
     END IF
C*****Parameters for a Straight Interconnection
C     Segment
 60   I = CLEAR()
     WRITE (*,903)
     WRITE (*,*)
```

```
      WRITE (*,900)
      WRITE (*,62)
62    FORMAT (11X, 'S T R A I G H T
     $            I N T E R C O N N E C T I O N')
      WRITE (*,900)
      WRITE (*,64) IL, IW, IT, TEMPC, CURRENT, AE
64    FORMAT (11X, 'Following Are the Current Values of
     $            Parameters:'/
     $       11X, ' A. Interconnection Length (Micron)
     $               = ',F10.2 /
     $       11X, ' B. Interconnection Width (Micron)
     $               = ',F10.2 /
     $       11X,' C. Interconnection Thickness
     $               (Micron) = ',F10.2 /
     $       11X, ' D. Interconnection Temperature (C)
     $               = ',F10.2 /
     $       11X, ' E. Interconnection Current (mA)
     $               = ',F10.2 /
     $       11X, ' F. Material Activation Energy (eV)
     $               = ',F10.2)
      WRITE (*,900)
      WRITE (*,66)
66    FORMAT (11X, 'ENTER A- F to CHANGE VALUE or P to
     $            PROCEED or Q to QUIT')
      WRITE (*,900)
      READ (*,*,ERR = 60) SSIP
      IF (SSIP .EQ. "A" .OR. SSIP .EQ. "a") THEN
      WRITE (*,*) 'Enter the Interconnection Length
     $            (Micron):'
      READ (*,*,ERR = 60) IL
      GO TO 60
      ELSE IF (SSIP .EQ. "B" .OR. SSIP .EQ. "b") THEN
      WRITE (*,*) 'Enter the Interconnection Width
     $            (Micron):'
      READ (*,*,ERR = 60) IW
      GO TO 60
      ELSE IF (SSIP .EQ. "C" .OR. SSIP .EQ. "c") THEN
      WRITE (*,*) 'Enter the Interconnection Thickness
     $            (Micron):'
      READ (*,*,ERR = 60) IT
      GO TO 60
      ELSE IF (SSIP .EQ. "D" .OR. SSIP .EQ. "d") THEN
      WRITE (*,*) 'Enter the Interconnection
     $            Temperature (C):'
```

```
      READ (*,*,ERR=60) TEMP        TEMP=TEMPC+273.0
      GO TO 60
      ELSE IF (SSIP .EQ. "E" .OR. SSIP .EQ. "e") THEN
      WRITE (*,*) 'Enter the Interconnection Current
     $           (mA):'
      READ (*,*,ERR=60) CURRENT
      GO TO 60
      ELSE IF (SSIP .EQ. "F" .OR. SSIP .EQ. "f") THEN
      WRITE (*,*) 'Enter the Activation Energy (eV):'
      READ (*,*,ERR=60) AE
      GO TO 60
      ELSE IF (SSIP .EQ. "P" .OR. SSIP .EQ. "p") THEN
      IF (IL .LE. 0 .OR. IW .LE. 0 .OR. IT .LE. 0 .OR.
     $    CURRENT .LE. 0 .OR. AE .LE. 0 .OR. TEMP
     $    .LE. 0) THEN
      WRITE (*,919)
      READ (*,*)
      GO TO 60
      END IF
      GO TO 280
      ELSE IF (SSIP .EQ. "Q" .OR. SSIP .EQ. "q") THEN
      GO TO 999
      ELSE
      GO TO 60
      END IF
C*****Parameters for an Interconnection Bend*****
  70  I=CLEAR()
      WRITE (*,904)
      WRITE (*,900)
      WRITE (*,72)
  72  FORMAT (11X,'I N T E R C O N N E C T I O N  B E N D')
      WRITE (*,900)
      WRITE (*,74) IL, IW, IT, TEMPC, CURRENT, AE,
     $            BANGLE
  74  FORMAT (11X, 'Following Are the Current Values of
     $            Parameters:'/
     $        11X, ' A. Interconnection Length (Micron)
     $               = ',F10.2 /
     $        11X, ' B. Interconnection Width (Micron)
     $               = ',F10.2 /
```

```
   $          11X, ` C. Interconnection Thickness
   $                  (Micron) = ',F10.2 /
   $          11X, ` D. Interconnection Temperature (C)
   $                  = ',F10.2 /
   $          11X, ` E. Interconnection Current (mA)
   $                  = ',F10.2 /
   $          11X, ` F. Material Activation Energy (eV)
   $                  = ',F10.2 /
   $          11X, ` G. Interconnection Bend Angle
   $                  (Degree) = ',F10.2)
     WRITE (*,900)
     WRITE (*,76)
76   FORMAT (11X, `ENTER A- G to CHANGE VALUE or P to
   $              PROCEED or Q to QUIT')
     WRITE (*,900)
     READ (*,*,ERR = 70) SSIP
     IF (SSIP .EQ. "A" .OR. SSIP .EQ. "a") THEN
     WRITE (*,*) `Enter the Interconnection Length
   $              (Micron):'
     READ (*,*,ERR = 70) IL
     GO TO 70
     ELSE IF (SSIP .EQ. "B" .OR. SSIP .EQ. "b") THEN
     WRITE (*,*) `Enter the Interconnection Width
   $              (Micron):'
     READ (*,*,ERR = 70) IW
     GO TO 70
     ELSE IF (SSIP .EQ. "C" .OR. SSIP .EQ. "c") THEN
     WRITE (*,*) `Enter the Interconnection Thickness
   $              (Micron):'
     READ (*,*,ERR = 70) IT
     GO TO 70
     ELSE IF (SSIP .EQ. "D" .OR. SSIP .EQ. "d") THEN
     WRITE (*,*) `Enter the Interconnection
   $              Temperature (C):'
     READ (*,*,ERR = 70) TEMP        TEMP = TEMPC + 273.0
     GO TO 70
     ELSE IF (SSIP .EQ. "E" .OR. SSIP .EQ. "e") THEN
     WRITE (*,*) `Enter the Interconnection Current
   $              (mA):'
     READ (*,*,ERR = 70) CURRENT
     GO TO 70
     ELSE IF (SSIP .EQ. "F" .OR. SSIP .EQ. "f") THEN
     WRITE (*,*) `Enter the Activation Energy (eV):'
```

```
      READ (*,*,ERR=70) AE
      GO TO 70
      ELSE IF (SSIP .EQ. "G" .OR. SSIP .EQ. "g") THEN
      WRITE (*,*) `Enter the Bend Angle (Degree):'
      READ (*,*,ERR=70) BANGLE
      GO TO 70
      ELSE IF (SSIP .EQ. "P" .OR. SSIP .EQ. "p") THEN
      IF (IL .LT. 0 .OR. IW .LE. 0 .OR. IT .LE. 0 .OR.
     $    CURRENT .LE. 0
     $    .OR. AE .LE. 0 .OR. TEMP .LE. 0 .OR. BANGLE
     $    .LE. 0 .OR.
     $    BANGLE .GT. 180.0) THEN
      WRITE (*,919)
      READ (*,*)
      GO TO 70
      END IF
      GO TO 280
      ELSE IF (SSIP .EQ. "Q" .OR. SSIP .EQ. "q") THEN
      GO TO 999
      ELSE
      GO TO 70
      END IF
C*****Parameters for an Interconnection Step*****
  80  I = CLEAR()
      WRITE (*,903)
      WRITE (*,900)
      WRITE (*,82)
  82  FORMAT (11X,`I N T E R C O N N E C T I O N   S T E P')
      WRITE (*,900)
      WRITE (*,84) IL, IW, IT, TEMPC, CURRENT, AE,
     $         SHEIGHT, SANGLE, MANGLE
  84  FORMAT (11X, `Following Are the Current Values of
     $             Parameters:'/
     $         11X, ` A. Interconnection Length (Micron)
     $                = ',F10.2 /
     $         11X, ` B. Interconnection Width (Micron)
     $                = ',F10.2 /
     $         11X, ` C. Interconnection Thickness
     $                (Micron) = ',F10.2 /
     $         11X, ` D. Interconnection Temperature (C)
     $                = ',F10.2 /
     $         11X, ` E. Interconnection Current (mA)
     $                = ',F10.2 /
```

```
$          11X, ` F. Material Activation Energy (eV)
$                     = ',F10.2 /
$          11X, ` G. Step Height (Micron)
$                     = ',F10.2 /
$          11X, ` H. Step Angle (Degree)
$                     = ',F10.2 /
$          11X, `     Range: >90 and <',F5.1)
    WRITE (*,900)
    WRITE (*,86)
86  FORMAT (11X, `ENTER A- H to CHANGE VALUE or P to
$               PROCEED or Q to QUIT')
    WRITE (*,900)
    READ (*,*,ERR = 80) SSIP
    IF (SSIP .EQ. "A" .OR. SSIP .EQ. "a") THEN
    WRITE (*,*) `Enter the Interconnection Length
$               (Micron):'
    READ (*,*,ERR = 80) IL
    MANGLE = 90.0 + (180.0 / 3.142)*ATAN( IL / SHEIGHT)
    GO TO 80
    ELSE IF (SSIP .EQ. "B" .OR. SSIP .EQ. "b") THEN
    WRITE (*,*) `Enter the Interconnection Width
$               (Micron):'
    READ (*,*,ERR = 80) IW
    GO TO 80
    ELSE IF (SSIP .EQ. "C" .OR. SSIP .EQ. "c") THEN
    WRITE (*,*) `Enter the Interconnection Thickness
$               (Micron):'
    READ (*,*,ERR = 80) IT
    GO TO 80
    ELSE IF (SSIP .EQ. "D" .OR. SSIP .EQ. "d") THEN
    WRITE (*,*) `Enter the Interconnection
$               Temperature (C):'
    READ (*,*,ERR = 80) TEMP       TEMP = TEMPC + 273.0
    GO TO 80
    ELSE IF (SSIP .EQ. "E" .OR. SSIP .EQ. "e") THEN
    WRITE (*,*) `Enter the Interconnection Current
$               (mA):'
    READ (*,*,ERR = 80) CURRENT
    GO TO 80
    ELSE IF (SSIP .EQ. "F" .OR. SSIP .EQ. "f") THEN
    WRITE (*,*) `Enter the Activation Energy (eV):'
    READ (*,*,ERR = 80) AE
    GO TO 80
```

```
      ELSE IF (SSIP .EQ. "G" .OR. SSIP .EQ. "g") THEN
      WRITE (*,*) `Enter the Step Height (Micron):'
      READ (*,*,ERR = 80) SHEIGHT
      MANGLE = 90.0 + (180.0 / 3.142)*ATAN(IL / SHEIGHT)
      GO TO 80
      ELSE IF (SSIP .EQ. "H" .OR. SSIP .EQ. "h") THEN
      WRITE (*,*) `Enter the Step Angle (Degree):'
      READ (*,*,ERR = 80) SANGLE
      GO TO 80
      ELSE IF (SSIP .EQ. "P" .OR. SSIP .EQ. "p") THEN
      IF (IL .LE. 0 .OR. IW .LE. 0 .OR. IT .LE. 0 .OR.
     $    CURRENT .LE. 0
     $    .OR. AE .LE. 0 .OR. TEMP .LE. 0 .OR. SHEIGHT
     $    .LE. 0) THEN
      WRITE (*,919)
      READ (*,*)
      GO TO 80
      END IF
      IF (SANGLE .LE. 90 .OR. SANGLE .GE. MANGLE) THEN
      WRITE (*,81)
   81 FORMAT (11X, `STEP ANGLE IS OUT OF RANGE!...
     $              CHOOSE IT AGAIN:')
      READ (*,*,ERR = 80) SANGLE
      GO TO 80
      END IF
      GO TO 280
      ELSE IF (SSIP .EQ. "Q" .OR. SSIP .EQ. "q") THEN
      GO TO 999
      ELSE
      GO TO 80
      END IF
C*****Parameters for an Interconnection Plug*****
      I = CLEAR( )
      WRITE (*,902)
      WRITE (*,900)
      WRITE (*,241)
  241 FORMAT (11X, `I N T E R C O N N E C T I O N  P L U G')
      WRITE (*,900)
      WRITE (*,242) IL, IW, IT, TEMPC, CURRENT, AE,
     $              PAE, LAE, IPL, SPD
  242 FORMAT (11X, `Following Are the Current Values of
     $              Parameters:'/
     $        11X, ` A. Interconnection Length (Micron)
     $                 = ',F10.2 /
```

```
$              11X, ` B. Interconnection Width (W)
$                     (Micron) = ',F10.2 /
$              11X, ` C. Interconnection Thickness
$                     (Micron) = ',F10.2 /
$              11X, ` D. Interconnection Temperature (C)
$                        = ',F10.2 /
$              11X, ` E. Interconnection Current (mA)
$                        = ',F10.2 /
$              11X, ` F. Int. Material Activation Energy
$                     (eV) = ',F10.2 /
$              11X, ` G. Plug Material Activations
$                     Energy (eV) = ',F10.2 /
$              11X, ` H. Lower-Level Activation Energy
$                     (eV) = ',F10.2 /
$              11X, ` I. Plug Length (Micron)
$                        = ',F10.2 /
$              11X, ` J. Square Plug Dimension (Micron)
$                     (<W) = ',F10.2)
      WRITE (*,900)
      WRITE (*,243)
243   FORMAT (11X, `ENTER A-J to CHANGE VALUE or P to
$                 PROCEED or Q to QUIT')
      WRITE (*,900)
      READ (*,*,ERR = 240) SSIP
      IF (SSIP .EQ. "A" .OR. SSIP .EQ. "a") THEN
      WRITE (*,*) `Enter the Interconnection Length
$                 (Micron):'
      READ (*,*,ERR = 240) IL
      GO TO 240
      ELSE IF (SSIP .EQ. "B" .OR. SSIP .EQ. "b") THEN
      WRITE (*,*) `Enter the Interconnection Width
$                 (Micron):'
      READ (*,*,ERR = 240) IW
      GO TO 240
      ELSE IF (SSIP .EQ. "C" .OR. SSIP .EQ. "c") then
      WRITE (*,*) `Enter the Interconnection Thickness
$                 (Micron):'
      READ (*,*,ERR = 240) IT
      GO TO 240
      ELSE IF (SSIP .EQ. "D" .OR. SSIP .EQ. "d") THEN
      WRITE (*,*) `Enter the Interconnection
$                 Temperature (C):'
```

```
      READ (*,*,ERR=240) TEMP      TEMP=TEMPC+273.0
      GO TO 240
      ELSE IF (SSIP .EQ. "E" .OR. SSIP .EQ. "e") THEN
      WRITE (*,*) 'Enter the Interconnection current
     $            (mA):'
      READ (*,*,ERR=240) CURRENT
      GO TO 240
      ELSE IF (SSIP .EQ. "F" .OR. SSIP .EQ. "f") THEN
      WRITE (*,*) 'Enter the Interconnection
     $            Activation Energy (eV):'
      READ (*,*,ERR=240) AE
      GO TO 240
      ELSE IF (SSIP .EQ. "G" .OR. SSIP .EQ. "g") THEN
      WRITE (*,*) 'Enter the Plug Activation Energy
     $            (eV):'
      READ (*,*,ERR=240) PAE
      GO TO 240
      ELSE IF (SSIP .EQ. "H" .OR. SSIP .EQ. "h") THEN
      WRITE (*,*) 'Enter the LL Activation Energy
     $            (eV):'
      READ (*,*,ERR=240) LAE
      GO TO 240
      ELSE IF (SSIP .EQ. "I" .OR. SSIP .EQ. "i") THEN
      WRITE (*,*) 'Enter the Plug Length (Micron):'
      READ (*,*,ERR=240) IPL
      GO TO 240
      ELSE IF (SSIP .EQ. "J" .OR. SSIP .EQ. "j") THEN
      WRITE (*,*) 'Enter the Plug Dimension (Micron):'
      READ (*,*,ERR=240) SPD
      GO TO 240
      ELSE IF (SSIP .EQ. "P" .OR. SSIP .EQ. "p") THEN
      IF (IL .LE. 0 .OR. IW .LE. 0 .OR. IT .LE. 0 .OR.
     $    CURRENT .LE. 0
     $    .OR. AE .LE. 0 .OR. TEMP .LE. 0 .OR. IPL
     $    .LE. 0 .OR. SPD
     $    .LE. 0 .OR. PAE .LE. 0 .OR. LAE .LE. 0) THEN
      WRITE (*,919)
      READ (*,*)
      GO TO 240
      END IF
      IF (SPD .GT. IW) THEN
      WRITE (*,244)
```

```
 244    FORMAT (11X, 'PLUG DIMENSION IS OUT OF RANGE!...
     $               CHOOSE IT AGAIN:')
        READ (*,*,ERR = 240) SPD
        GO TO 240
        END IF
        GO TO 280
        ELSE IF (SSIP .EQ. "Q" .OR. SSIP .EQ. "q") THEN
        GO TO 999
        ELSE
        GO TO 240
        END IF
C*****Parameters for an Interconnection Via*****
  90    I = CLEAR()
        WRITE (*,902)
        WRITE (*,900)
        WRITE (*,92)
  92    FORMAT (11X, 'I N T E R C O N N E C T I O N  V I A')
        WRITE (*,900)
        WRITE (*,94) IL, IW, IT, TEMPC, CURRENT, AE,
     $               LAE, VH, VW, VANGLE, MVANGLE
  94    FORMAT (11X, 'Following Are the Current Values of
     $               Parameters:'/
     $          11X, ' A. Interconnection Length (Micron)
     $               = ',F10.2 /
     $          11X, ' B. Interconnection Width (Micron)
     $               = ',F10.2 /
     $          11X, ' C. Interconnection Thickness
     $               (Micron) = ',F10.2 /
     $          11X, ' D. Interconnection Temperature (C)
     $               = ',F10.2 /
     $          11X, ' E. Interconnection Current (mA)
     $               = ',F10.2 /
     $          11X, ' F. Int. Material Activation Energy
     $               (eV) = ',F10.2 /
     $          11X, ' G. Lower-Level Activation Energy
     $               (eV) = ',F10.2 /
     $          11X, ' H. Via Height (Micron)
     $               = ',F10.2 /
     $          11X, ' I. Via Width (Micron)
     $               = ',F10.2 /
     $          11X, ' J. Via Angle (Degree)
     $               = ',F10.2 /
     $          11X, '    Range: <90 and >',F4.1)
        WRITE (*,900)
```

```
      WRITE (*,96)
96    FORMAT (11X, `ENTER A-J to CHANGE VALUE or P to
      $               PROCEED or Q to QUIT')
      WRITE (*,900)
      READ (*,*,ERR=90) SSIP
      IF (SSIP .EQ. "A" .OR. SSIP .EQ. "a") THEN
      WRITE (*,*) `Enter the Interconnection Length
      $               (Micron):'
      READ (*,*,ERR=90) IL
      MVANGLE = 90.0- (180.0 / 3.142)*ATAN((IL-VW) / VH)
      GO TO 90
      ELSE IF (SSIP .EQ. "B" .OR. SSIP .EQ. "b") THEN
      WRITE (*,*) `Enter the Interconnection Width
      $               (Micron):'
      READ (*,*,ERR=90) IW
      GO TO 90
      ELSE IF (SSIP .EQ. "C" .OR. SSIP .EQ. "c") THEN
      WRITE (*,*) `Enter the Interconnection Thickness
      $               (Micron):'
      READ (*,*,ERR=90) IT
      GO TO 90
      ELSE IF (SSIP .EQ. "D" .OR. SSIP .EQ. "d") THEN
      WRITE (*,*) `Enter the Interconnection
      $               Temperature (C):'
      READ (*,*,ERR=90) TEMP      TEMP = TEMPC + 273.0
      GO TO 90
      ELSE IF (SSIP .EQ. "E" .OR. SSIP .EQ. "e") THEN
      WRITE (*,*) `Enter the Interconnection Current
      $               (mA):'
      READ (*,*,ERR=90) CURRENT
      GO TO 90
      ELSE IF (SSIP .EQ. "F" .OR. SSIP .EQ. "f") THEN
      WRITE (*,*) `Enter the Interconnection
      $               Activation Energy (eV):'
      READ (*,*,ERR=90) AE
      GO TO 90
      ELSE IF (SSIP .EQ. "G" .OR. SSIP .EQ. "g") THEN
      WRITE (*,*) `Enter the LL Activation Energy
      $               (eV):'
      READ (*,*,ERR=90) LAE
      GO TO 90
      ELSE IF (SSIP .EQ. "H" .OR. SSIP .EQ. "h") THEN
      WRITE (*,*) `Enter the Via Height (Micron):'
```

```fortran
      READ (*,*,ERR=90) VH
      MVANGLE = 90.0- (180.0 / 3.142)*ATAN((IL- VW) / VH)
      GO TO 90
      ELSE IF (SSIP .EQ. "I" .OR. SSIP. .EQ. "i") THEN
      WRITE (*,*) 'Enter the Via Width (Micron):'
      READ (*,*,ERR=90) VW
      MVANGLE = 90.0- (180.0 / 3.142)*ATAN((IL- VW) / VH)
      GO TO 90
      ELSE IF (SSIP .EQ. "J" .OR. SSIP .EQ. "j") THEN
      WRITE (*,*) 'Enter the Via Angle (Degree):'
      READ (*,*,ERR=90) VANGLE
      GO TO 90
      ELSE IF (SSIP .EQ. "P" .OR. SSIP .EQ. "p") THEN
      IF (IL .LE. 0 .OR. IW .LE. 0 .OR. IT .LE. 0 .OR.
     $    CURRENT .LE. 0
     $    .OR. AE .LE. 0 .OR. TEMP .LE. 0 .OR. VH .LE.
     $    0 .OR. VW
     $    .LE. 0 .OR. LAE .LE. 0) THEN
      WRITE (*,919)
      READ (*,*)
      GO TO 90
      END IF
      IF (VANGLE .GE. 90 .OR. VANGLE .LE. MVANGLE)
     $    THEN
      WRITE (*,91)
   91 FORMAT (11X, 'VIA ANGLE IS OUT OF RANGE!...
     $               CHOOSE IT AGAIN:')
      READ (*,*,ERR=90) VANGLE
      GO TO 90
      END IF
      GO TO 280
      ELSE IF (SSIP .EQ. "Q" .OR. SSIP .EQ. "q") THEN
      GO TO 999
      ELSE
      GO TO 90
      END IF
C*****Parameters for an Interconnection Overflow*****
  100 I = CLEAR()
      WRITE (*,904)
      WRITE (*,900)
      WRITE (*,102)
```

```
102  FORMAT (11X, `I N T E R C O N N E C T I O N
    $             O V E R F L O W')
     WRITE (*,900)
     WRITE (*,104) IL, IW, IT, TEMPC, CURRENT, AE, OL
104  FORMAT (11X, `Following Are the Current Values of
    $             Parameters:'/
    $        11X, ` A. Interconnection Length (L)
    $              (Micron) = ',F10.2 /
    $        11X, ` B. Interconnection Width (Micron)
    $              = ',F10.2 /
    $        11X, ` C. Interconnection Thickness
    $              (Micron) = ',F10.2 /
    $        11X, ` D. Interconnection Temperature (C)
    $              = ',F10.2 /
    $        11X, ` E. Interconnection Current (mA)
    $              = ',F10.2 /
    $        11X, ` F. Material Activation Energy (eV)
    $              = ',F10.2 /
    $        11X, ` G. Overflow Length (Micron) (<L)
    $              = ',F10.2)
     WRITE (*,900)
     WRITE (*,106)
106  FORMAT (11X, `ENTER A- G to CHANGE VALUE or P to
    $             PROCEED or Q to QUIT')
     WRITE (*,900)
     READ (*,*,ERR = 100) SSIP
     IF (SSIP .EQ. "A" .OR. SSIP .EQ. "a") THEN
     WRITE (*,*) `Enter the Interconnection Length
    $             (Micron):'
     READ (*,*,ERR = 100) IL
     GO TO 100
     ELSE IF (SSIP .EQ. "B" .OR. SSIP .EQ. "b") THEN
     WRITE (*,*) `Enter the Interconnection Width
    $             (Micron):'
     READ (*,*,ERR = 100) IW
     GO TO 100
     ELSE IF (SSIP .EQ. "C" .OR. SSIP .EQ. "c") THEN
     WRITE (*,*) `Enter the Interconnection Thickness
    $             (Micron):'
     READ (*,*,ERR = 100) IT
     GO TO 100
     ELSE IF (SSIP. EQ. "D" .OR. SSIP .EQ. "d") THEN
     WRITE (*,*) `Enter the Interconnection
    $             Temperature (C):'
     READ (*,*,ERR = 100) TEMPC
```

```
     TEMP = TEMPC + 273.0
     GO TO 100
     ELSE IF (SSIP .EQ. "E" .OR. SSIP .EQ. "e") THEN
     WRITE (*,*) `Enter the Interconnection Current
   $             (mA):'
     READ (*,*,ERR = 100) CURRENT
     GO TO 100
     ELSE IF (SSIP .EQ. "F" .OR. SSIP .EQ. "f") THEN
     WRITE (*,*) `Enter the Activation Energy (eV):'
     READ (*,*,ERR = 100) AE
     GO TO 100
     ELSE IF (SSIP .EQ. "G" .OR. SSIP .EQ. "g") THEN
     WRITE (*,*) `Enter the Overflow Length
   $             (Micron):'
     READ (*,*,ERR = 100) OL
     GO TO 100
     ELSE IF (SSIP .EQ. "P" .OR. SSIP .EQ. "p") THEN
     IF (IL .LE. 0 .OR. IW .LE. 0 .OR. IT .LE. 0 .OR.
   $    CURRENT .LE. 0 .OR. AE .LE. 0 .OR. TEMP
   $    .LE. 0) THEN
     WRITE (*,919)
     READ (*,*)
     GO TO 90
     END IF
     IF (OL .GT. IL) THEN
     WRITE (*,108)
 108 FORMAT (11X, `OVERFLOW LENGTH IS OUT OF RANGE!
   $             ...CHOOSE IT AGAIN:')
     READ (*,*,ERR = 100) OL
     GO TO 100
     END IF
     GO TO 280
     ELSE IF (SSIP .EQ. "Q" .OR. SSIP .EQ. "q") THEN
     GO TO 999
     ELSE
     GO TO 100
     END IF
C*****Parameters for a Horizontal Multisection
C    Interconnection
 110 I = CLEAR()
     WRITE (*,903)
     WRITE (*,900)
     WRITE (*,112)
```

```
112  FORMAT (11X, `H O R I Z O N T A L
     $               M U L T I S E C T I O N'/
     $         11X, `I N T E R C O N N E C T I O N')
      WRITE (*,900)
      WRITE (*,114) IL, IW, IT, TEMPC, CURRENT, AE,
     $              NHS, PL
114  FORMAT (11X, `Following Are the Current Values of
     $               Parameters:'/
     $         11X, ` A. Interconnection Length (Micron)
     $               = ',F10.2 /
     $         11X, ` B. Interconnection Width (Micron)
     $               = ',F10.2 /
     $         11X, ` C. Interconnection Thickness
     $               (Micron) = ',F10.2 /
     $         11X, ` D. Interconnection Temperature (C)
     $               = ',F10.2 /
     $         11X, ` E. Interconnection Current (mA)
     $               = ',F10.2 /
     $         11X, ` F. Material Activation Energy (eV)
     $               = ',F10.2 /
     $         11X, ` G. Number of Horizontal Sections
     $               = ',I7 /
     $         11X, ` H. Source / Sink Pad Lengths
     $               (Micron) = ',F10.2)
      WRITE (*,900)
      WRITE (*,116)
116  FORMAT (11X, `ENTER A- H to CHANGE VALUE or P to
     $               PROCEED or Q to QUIT')
      WRITE (*,900)
      READ (*,*,ERR = 110) SSIP
      IF (SSIP .EQ. "A" .OR. SSIP .EQ. "a") THEN
      WRITE (*,*) `Enter the Interconnection Length
     $               (Micron):'
      READ (*,*,ERR = 110) IL
      GO TO 110
      ELSE IF (SSIP .EQ. "B" .OR. SSIP .EQ. "b") THEN
      WRITE (*,*) `Enter the Interconnection Width
     $               (Micron):'
      READ (*,*,ERR = 110) IW
      GO TO 110
      ELSE IF (SSIP .EQ. "C" .OR. SSIP .EQ. "c") THEN
      WRITE (*,*) `Enter the Interconnection Thickness
     $               (Micron):'
      READ (*,*,ERR = 110) IT
      GO TO 110
```

```fortran
      ELSE IF (SSIP .EQ. "D" .OR. SSIP .EQ. "d") THEN
      WRITE (*,*) 'Enter the Interconnection
     $           Temperature (C):'
      READ (*,*,ERR = 110) TEMPC
      TEMP = TEMPC + 273.0
      GO TO 110
      ELSE IF (SSIP .EQ. "E" .OR. SSIP .EQ. "e") THEN
      WRITE (*,*) 'Enter the Interconnection Current
     $           (mA):'
      READ (*,*,ERR = 110) CURRENT
      GO TO 110
      ELSE IF (SSIP .EQ. "F" .OR. SSIP .EQ. "f") THEN
      WRITE (*,*) 'Enter the Activation Energy (eV):'
      READ (*,*,ERR = 110) AE
      GO TO 110
      ELSE IF (SSIP .EQ. "G" .OR. SSIP .EQ. "g") THEN
      WRITE (*,*) 'Enter the Number of Sections:'
      READ (*,*,ERR = 110) NHS
      GO TO 110
      ELSE IF (SSIP .EQ. "H" .OR. SSIP .EQ. "h") THEN
      WRITE (*,*) 'Enter the Pad Lengths (Micron):'
      READ (*,*,ERR = 110) PL
      GO TO 110
      ELSE IF (SSIP .EQ. "P" .OR. SSIP .EQ. "p") THEN
      IF (IL .LE. 0 .OR. IW .LE. 0 .OR. IT .LE. 0 .OR.
     $    CURRENT .LE. 0 .OR. AE .LE. 0 .OR. TEMP .LE.
     $    0 .OR. PL .LE. 0 .OR. NHS .LT. 1) THEN
      WRITE (*,919)
      READ (*,*)
      GO TO 110
      END IF
      GO TO 280
      ELSE IF (SSIP .EQ. "Q" .OR. SSIP .EQ. "q") THEN
      GO TO 999
      ELSE
      GO TO 110
      END IF
C*****Parameters for a Vertical Multisection
C     Interconnection
  120 I = CLEAR()
      WRITE (*,902)
      WRITE (*,900)
```

```
        WRITE (*,122)
  122   FORMAT (11X, `V E R T I C A L
     $            M U L T I S E C T I O N`/
     $         11X, `I N T E R C O N N E C T I O N`)
        WRITE (*,900)
        WRITE (*,124) IL, IW, IT, TEMPC, CURRENT, AE,
                      VPAE, VPL, NVS
  124   FORMAT (11X, `Following Are the Current Values of
                  Parameters:`/
     $         11X, ` A. Interconnection Length (Micron)
     $                = `,F10.2 /
     $         11X, ` B. Interconnection Width (Micron)
     $                = `,F10.2 /
     $         11X, ` C. Interconnection Thickness
     $                (Micron) = `,F10.2 /
     $         11X, ` D. Interconnection Temperature (C)
     $                = `,F10.2 /
     $         11X, ` E. Interconnection Current (mA)
     $                = `,F10.2 /
     $         11X, ` F. Int. Material Activation Energy
     $                (eV) = `,F10.2 /
     $         11X, ` G. Plug Material Activation Energy
     $                (eV) = `,F10.2 /
     $         11X, ` H. Length of Each Plug (Micron)
     $                = `,F10.2 /
     $         11X, ` I. Number of Vertical Sections
     $                = `,I7)
        WRITE (*,900)
        WRITE (*,126)
  126   FORMAT (11X, `ENTER A- I to CHANGE VALUE or P to
     $            PROCEED or Q to QUIT`)
        WRITE (*,900)
        READ (*,*,ERR = 120) SSIP
        IF (SSIP .EQ. "A" .OR. SSIP .EQ. "a") THEN
        WRITE (*,*) `Enter the Interconnection Length
     $            (Micron):`
        READ (*,*,ERR = 120) IL
        GO TO 120
        ELSE IF (SSIP .EQ. "B" .OR. SSIP .EQ. "b") THEN
        WRITE (*,*) `Enter the Interconnection Width
     $            (Micron):`
        READ (*,*,ERR = 120) IW
        GO TO 120
```

```
  ELSE IF (SSIP .EQ. "C" .OR. SSIP .EQ. "c") THEN
  WRITE (*,*) `Enter the Interconnection Thickness
$            (Micron):'
  READ (*,*,ERR=120) IT
  GO TO 120
  ELSE IF (SSIP .EQ. "D" .OR. SSIP .EQ. "d") THEN
  WRITE (*,*) `Enter the Interconnection
$            Temperature (C):'
  READ (*,*,ERR=120) TEMPC
  TEMP = TEMPC + 273.0
  GO TO 120
  ELSE IF (SSIP .EQ. "E" .OR. SSIP .EQ. "e") THEN
  WRITE (*,*) `Enter the Interconnection Current
$            (mA):'
  READ (*,*,ERR=120) CURRENT
  GO TO 120
  ELSE IF (SSIP .EQ. "F" .OR. SSIP .EQ. "f") THEN
  WRITE (*,*) `Enter the Interconnection
$            Activation Energy (eV):'
  READ (*,*,ERR=120) AE
  GO TO 120
  ELSE IF (SSIP .EQ. "G" .OR. SSIP .EQ. "g") THEN
  WRITE (*,*) `Enter the Plug Activation Energy
$            (eV):'
  READ (*,*,ERR=120) VPAE
  GO TO 120
  ELSE IF (SSIP .EQ. "H" .OR. SSIP .EQ. "h") THEN
  WRITE (*,*) `Enter the Length of Each Plug
$            (Micron):'
  READ (*,*,ERR=120) VPL
  GO TO 120
  ELSE IF (SSIP .EQ. "I" .OR. SSIP .EQ. "i") THEN
  WRITE (*,*) `Enter the Number of Vertical
$            Sections:'
  READ (*,*,ERR=120) NVS
  NBVS = NVS- 1
  GO TO 120
  ELSE IF (SSIP .EQ. "P" .OR. SSIP .EQ. "p") THEN
  IF (IL 0 .OR. IW .LE. 0 .OR. IT .LE. 0 .OR.
$    CURRENT .LE. 0 .OR. AE .LE. 0 .OR.
$    TEMP .LE. 0 .OR. VPL .LE. 0 .OR.
$    NVS .LT. 1 .OR. VPAE .LE. 0) THEN
  WRITE (*,919)
  READ (*,*)
  GO TO 120
```

```
      END IF
      GO TO 280
      ELSE IF (SSIP .EQ. "Q" .OR. SSIP .EQ. "q") THEN
      GO TO 999
      ELSE
      GO TO 120
      END IF
C*****Parameters for a Mixed Multisection
C     Interconnection
 130  I = CLEAR( )
      WRITE (*,*)
      WRITE (*,900)
      WRITE (*,132)
 132  FORMAT (11X, 'M I X E D  M U L T I S E C T I O N'/
     $         11X, 'I N T E R C O N N E C T I O N')
      WRITE (*,900)
      WRITE (*,134) IL, IW, IT ,TEMPC, CURRENT ,AE,
     $              NHS, PL, NBVS, VPL, VPAE
 134  FORMAT (11X 'Following Are the Current Values of
     $              Parameters:'/
     $         11X, ' A. Interconnection Length (Micron)
     $              = ',F10.2 /
     $         11X, ' B. Interconnection Width (Micron)
     $              = ',F10.2 /
     $         11X, ' C. Interconnection Thickness
     $              (Micron) = ',F10.2 /
     $         11X, ' D. Interconnection Temperature (C)
     $              = ',F10.2 /
     $         11X, ' E. Interconnection Current (mA)
     $              = ',F10.2 /
     $         11X, ' F. Int. Material Activation Energy
     $              (eV) = ',F10.2 /
     $         11X, ' G. Number of Horizontal Sections
     $              = ',I7 /
     $         11X, ' H. Source / Sink Pad Lengths
     $              (Micron) = ',10.2 /
     $         11X, ' I. Number of Embedded Vertical
     $              Sections = ',I7 /
     $         11X, ' J. Length of Each Plug (Micron)
     $              = ',F10.2 /
     $         11X, ' K. Plug Material Activation
     $              Energy(eV) = ',F10.2)
      WRITE (*,900)
      WRITE (*,136)
```

```
136   FORMAT (11X, 'ENTER A- K to CHANGE VALUE or P to
      $              PROCEED or Q to QUIT')
      WRITE (*,900)
      READ (*,*,ERR = 130) SSIP
      IF (SSIP .EQ. "A" .OR. SSIP .EQ. "a") THEN
      WRITE (*,*) 'Enter the Interconnection Length
      $            (Micron):'
      READ (*,*,ERR = 130) IL
      GO TO 130
      ELSE IF (SSIP .EQ. "B" .OR. SSIP .EQ. "b") THEN
      WRITE (*,*) 'Enter the Interconnection Width
      $            (Micron):'
      READ (*,*,ERR = 130) IW
      GO TO 130
      ELSE IF (SSIP .EQ. "C" .OR. SSIP .EQ. "c") THEN
      WRITE (*,*) 'Enter the Interconnection Thickness
      $            (Micron):'
      READ (*,*,ERR = 130) IT
      GO TO 130
      ELSE IF (SSIP .EQ. "D" .OR. SSIP .EQ. "d") THEN
      WRITE (*,*) 'Enter the Interconnection
      $            Temperature (C):'
      READ (*,*,ERR = 130) TEMPC
      TEMP = TEMPC + 273.0
      GO TO 130
      ELSE IF (SSIP .EQ. "E" .OR. SSIP .EQ. "e") THEN
      WRITE (*,*) 'Enter the Interconnection Current
      $            (mA):'
      READ (*,*,ERR = 130) CURRENT
      GO TO 130
      ELSE IF (SSIP .EQ. "F" .OR. SSIP .EQ. "f") THEN
      WRITE (*,*) 'Enter the Activation Energy (eV):'
      READ (*,*,ERR = 130) AE
      GO TO 130
      ELSE IF (SSIP .EQ. "G" .OR. SSIP .EQ. "g") THEN
      WRITE (*,*) 'Enter the Number of Horizontal
      $            Sections:'
      READ (*,*,ERR = 130) NHS
      GO TO 130
      ELSE IF (SSIP .EQ. "H" .OR. SSIP .EQ. "h") THEN
      WRITE (*,*) 'Enter the Pad Lengths (Micron):'
      READ (*,*,ERR = 130) PL
      GO TO 130
```

```
      ELSE IF (SSIP .EQ. "I" .OR. SSIP .EQ. "i") THEN
      WRITE (*,*) `Enter Number of Embedded Vertical
     $           Sections:'
      READ (*,*,ERR=130) NBVS
      GO TO 130
      ELSE IF (SSIP .EQ. "J" .OR. SSIP .EQ. "j") THEN
      WRITE (*,*) `Enter the Length of Each Plug
     $           (Micron):'
      READ (*,*,ERR=130) VPL
      GO TO 130
      ELSE IF (SSIP .EQ. "K" .OR. SSIP .EQ. "k") THEN
      WRITE (*,*) `Enter the Plug Activation Energy
     $           (eV):'
      READ (*,*,ERR=130) VPAE
      GO TO 130
      ELSE IF (SSIP .EQ. "P" .OR. SSIP .EQ. "p") THEN
      IF (IL .LE. 0 .OR. IW .LE. 0 .OR. IT .LE. 0 .OR.
     $    CURRENT .LE. 0.OR. AE .LE. 0 .OR. TEMP .LE.
     $    0 .OR. VPL
     $    .LE. 0 .OR. NHS .LT. 1 .OR. NBVS .LT. 0 .OR.
     $    VPAE .LE. 0 .OR. PL .LE. 0)
     $    THEN
      WRITE (*,919)
      READ (*,*)
      GO TO 130
      END IF
      GO TO 280
      ELSE IF (SSIP .EQ. "Q" .OR. SSIP .EQ. "q") THEN
      GO TO 999
      ELSE
      GO TO 130
      END IF
C*****Parameters for a Power and Ground Bus*****
  140 I = CLEAR()
      WRITE (*,904)
      WRITE (*,900)
      WRITE (*,142)
  142 FORMAT (11X, `P O W E R  O R  G R O U N D  B U S')
      WRITE (*,900)
      WRITE (*,144) BL, BW, BT, TEMPC, BAE, NGB, G
  144 FORMAT (11X, `Following Are the Current Values of
     $           Parameters:'/
     $        11X, ` A. Total Bus Length (Micron)
     $             = ',F10.2 /
```

```
$           11X, ` B. Bus Width (Micron)
$                 = ',F10.2 /
$           11X, ` C. Bus Material Thickness (Micron)
$                 = ',F10.2 /
$           11X, ` D. Bus Temperature (C)
$                 = ',F10.2 /
$           11X, ` E. Bus Material Activation Energy
$                 (eV) = ',F10.2 /
$           11X, ` F. Number of Gates Served by the
$                 Bus = ',I7 /
$           11X, ` G. Current in Each Gate (mA)
$                 = ',F10.2)
      WRITE (*,900)
      WRITE (*,146)
146   FORMAT (11X, `ENTER A- G to CHANGE VALUE or P to
$                 PROCEED or Q to QUIT')
      WRITE (*,900)
      READ (*,*,ERR = 140) SSIP
      IF (SSIP .EQ. "A" .OR. SSIP .EQ. "a") THEN
      WRITE (*,*) `Enter the Bus Length (Micron):'
      READ (*,*,ERR = 140) BL
      GO TO 140
      ELSE IF (SSIP .EQ. "B" .OR. SSIP .EQ. "b") THEN
      WRITE (*,*) `Enter the Bus Width (Micron): '
      READ (*,*,ERR = 140) BW
      GO TO 140
      ELSE IF (SSIP .EQ. "C" .OR. SSIP .EQ. "c") THEN
      WRITE (*,*) `Enter the Bus Thickness (Micron):'
      READ (*,*,ERR = 140) BT
      GO TO 140
      ELSE IF (SSIP .EQ. "D" .OR. SSIP .EQ. "d") THEN
      WRITE (*,*) `Enter the Bus Temperature (C):'
      READ (*,*,ERR = 140) TEMPC
      TEMP = TEMPC + 273.0
      GO TO 140
      ELSE IF (SSIP .EQ. "E" .OR. SSIP .EQ. "e") THEN
      WRITE (*,*) `Enter the Activation Energy (eV):'
      READ (*,*,ERR = 140) BAE
      GO TO 140
      ELSE IF (SSIP .EQ. "F" .OR. SSIP .EQ. "f") THEN
      WRITE (*,*) `Enter the Number of Gates Served:'
      READ (*,*,ERR = 140) NGB
      GO TO 140
```

```
      ELSE IF (SSIP .EQ. "G" .OR. SSIP .EQ. "g") THEN
      WRITE (*,*) `Enter the Current in Each Gate
     $              (mA):'
      READ (*,*,ERR = 140) G     GO TO 140
      ELSE IF (SSIP .EQ. "P" .OR. SSIP .EQ. "p") THEN
      IF (BL .LE. 0 .OR. BW .LE. 0 .OR. BT .LE. 0 .OR.
     $    BAE .LE. 0 .OR. NGB .LT. 1 .OR. TEMP .LE. 0
          .OR. GC .LE. 0) THEN
      WRITE (*,919)
      READ (*,*)
      GO TO 140
      END IF
      GO TO 280
      ELSE IF (SSIP .EQ. "Q" .OR. SSIP .EQ. "q") THEN
      GO TO 999
      ELSE
      GO TO 140
      END IF
C*****The Current Density Exponent*****
  280  I = CLEAR()
      WRITE (*,906)
      WRITE (*,900)
      WRITE (*,282)
  282  FORMAT (11X, `C U R R E N T   D E N S I T Y
     $              E X P O N E N T')
      WRITE (*,900)
      WRITE (*,284) JE
  284  FORMAT (11X,/,11X, `Value of Current Density
     $              Exponent = ',F6.2,/ )
      WRITE (*,900)
      WRITE (*,286)
  286  FORMAT (11X, `ENTER C to CHANGE VALUE or P to
     $              PROCEED')
      WRITE (*,900)
      READ (*,*,ERR = 280) CDEP
      IF (CEEP .EQ. "C" .OR. CDEP .EQ. "c") THEN
      WRITE (*,*) `Enter the Current Density
     $              Exponent:'
      READ (*,*,ERR = 280) JE
      GO TO 280
      ELSE IF (CDEP .EQ. "P" .OR. CDEP .EQ. "p") THEN
      IF (JE .LT. 1.0) THEN
      WRITE (*,287)
```

```
287  FORMAT (11X, 'Value of the Exponent Appears to be
     $            WRONG...'/
     $            11X, 'Enter the CORRECT VALUE...')
     READ (*,*) JE
     GO TO 280
     END IF
     GO TO 288
     ELSE
     GO TO 280
     END IF
288  IF (IGP .EQ. "A" .OR. IGP .EQ. "a") THEN
     GO TO 150
     ELSE IF (IGP .EQ. "B" .OR. IGP .EQ. "b") THEN
     GO TO 160
     ELSE IF (IGP .EQ. "C" .OR. IGP .EQ. "c") THEN
     GO TO 170
     ELSE IF (IGP .EQ. "D" .OR. IGP .EQ. "d") THEN
     GO TO 245
     ELSE IF (IGP .EQ. "E" .OR. IGP .EQ. "e") THEN
     GO TO 180
     ELSE IF (IGP .EQ. "F" .OR. IGP .EQ. "f") THEN
     GO TO 190
     ELSE IF (IGP .EQ. "G" .OR. IGP .EQ. "g") THEN
     GO TO 200
     ELSE IF (IGP .EQ. "H" .OR. IGP .EQ. "h") THEN
     GO TO 210
     ELSE IF (IGP .EQ. "I" .OR. IGP .EQ. "i") THEN
     GO TO 220
     ELSE IF (IGP .EQ. "J" .OR. IGP .EQ. "j") THEN
     GO TO 230
     END IF
C*****Calculations*****
150  CALL STRAIGHT (IL,IW,IT,CURRENT,TEMP,AE,JE,MTF,
     $               SIGMA)
     GO TO 250
160  CALL BEND (IL,IW,IT,CURRENT,TEMP,AE,BANGLE,
     $           JE,MTF,SIGMA)
     GO TO 250
170  CALL STEP (IL,IW,IT,CURRENT,TEMP,AE,SANGLE,
     $           SHEIGHT,JE,MTF,SIGMA)
     GO TO 250
```

```
245  CALL PLUG (IL,IW,IT,CURRENT,TEMP,AE,PAE,LAE,IPL,
     $          SPD,JE,MTF,SIGMA)
     GO TO 250
180  CALL VIA (IL,IW,IT,CURRENT,TEMP,AE,LAE,VH,
     $          VW,VANGLE,JE,MTF,SIGMA)
     GO TO 250
190  CALL OVERFLOW (IL,IW,IT,CURRENT,TEMP,AE,OL,JE,
     $              MTF,SIGMA)
     GO TO 250
200  CALL HMSI (IL,IW,IT,CURRENT,TEMP,AE,NHS,PL,
     $          JE,MTF,SIGMA)
     GO TO 250
210  CALL VMSI (IL,IW,IT,CURRENT,TEMP,AE,VPL,VPAE,
     $          NVS,JE,MTF,SIGMA)
     GO TO 250
220  CALL MMSI (IL,IW,IT,CURRENT,TEMP,AE,NHS,
     $          PL,NBVS,VPL,VPAE,JE,MTF,SIGMA)
     GO TO 250
230  CALL PGBUS (BL,BW,BT,TEMP,BAE,NGB,GC,JE,
     $           MTF,SIGMA)
     GO TO 250
C*****Simulation Results*****
250  I = CLEAR()
     WRITE (*,*)
     WRITE (*,900)
     WRITE (*,260)
260  FORMAT (11X,'S I M U L A T I O N  R E S U L T S')
     WRITE (*,900)
     IF (IGP .EQ. "A" .OR. IGP .EQ. "a") THEN
     WRITE (*,312)
312  FORMAT (11X,'COMPONENT: STRAIGHT INTERCONNECTION
     $            SEGMENT')
     WRITE (*,314) IL, IW, IT, TEMPC, CURRENT, JE, AE
314  FORMAT (11X,'    Interconnection Length (Micron)
     $                = ',F12.2 /
     $        11X,'    Interconnection Width (Micron)
     $                = ',F12.2 /
     $        11X,'    Interconenction Thickness
     $                (Micron) = ',F12.2 /
     $        11X'    Interconnection Temperature (C)
     $                = ',F12.2 /
```

```
    $         11X `     Interconnection Current (mA)
    $                   = ',F12.2 /
    $         11X `     Current Density Exponent
    $                   = ',F12.2 /
    $         11X `     Material Activation Energy (eV)
    $                   = ',F12.2)
      ELSE IF (IGP .EQ. "B" .OR. IGP .EQ. "b") THEN
      WRITE (*,316)
316   FORMAT (11X, `COMPONENT: INTERCONNECTION BEND')
      WRITE (*,318) IL, IW, TEMPC, CURRENT, JE, AE,
    $         BANGLE
318   FORMAT (11X, `     Interconnection Length (Micron)
    $                   = ',F12.2 /
    $         11X, `    Interconnection Width (Micron)
    $                   = ',F12.2 /
    $         11X, `    Interconnection Thickness
    $                   (Micron) = ',F12.2 /
    $         11X, `    Interconnection Temperature (C)
    $                   = ',F12.2 /
    $         11X, `    Interconnection Current (mA)
    $                   = ',F12.2 /
    $         11X, `    Current Density Exponent
    $                   = ',F12.2 /
    $         11X, `    Material Activation Energy (eV)
    $                   = ',F12.2 /
    $         11X, `    Interconnection Bend (Degree)
    $                   = ',F12.2)
      ELSE IF (IGP .EQ. "C" .OR. IGP .EQ. "c") THEN
      WRITE (*,320)
320   FORMAT (11X, `COMPONENT: INTERCONNECTION STEP')
      WRITE (*,322) IL, IW, IT, TEMPC, CURRENT, JE,
    $             AE, SHEIGHT, SANGLE
322   FORMAT (11X, `     Interconnection Length (Micron)
    $                   = ',F12.2 /
    $         11X, `    Interconnection Width (Micron)
    $                   = ',F12.2 /
    $         11X, `    Interconnection Thickness
    $                   (Micron) = ',F12.2 /
    $         11X, `    Interconnection Temperature (C)
    $                   = ',F12.2 /
    $         11X, `    Interconnection Current (mA)
    $                   = ',F12.2 /
    $         11X, `    Current Density Exponent
    $                   = ',F12.2 /
```

```
      $          11X, `   Material Activation Energy (eV)
      $                  = ',F12.2 /
      $          11X, `   Step Height (Micron)
      $                  = ',F12.2 /
      $          11X, `   Step Angle (Degree)
      $                  = ',F12.2)
        ELSE IF (IGP .EQ. "D" .OR. IGP .EQ. "d") THEN
        WRITE (*,324)
  324   FORMAT (11X, `COMPONENT: INTERCONNECTION PLUG')
        WRITE (*,326) IL, IW, IT, TEMPC, CURRENT, JE,
      $                AE, PAE, LAE, IPL, SPD
  326   FORMAT (11X, `   Interconnection Length (Micron)
      $                  = ',F12.2 /
      $          11X, `   Interconnection Width (Micron)
      $                  = ',F12.2 /
      $          11X, `   Interconnection Thickness
      $                  (Micron) = ',F12.2 /
      $          11X, `   Interconnection Temperature (C)
      $                  = ',F12.2 /
      $          11X, `   Interconnection Current (mA)
      $                  = ',F12.2 /
      $          11X, `   Current Density Exponent
      $                  = ',F12.2 /
      $          11X, `   Int. Material Activation Energy
      $                  (eV) = ',F12.2 /
      $          11X, `   Plug Material Activation Energy
      $                  (eV) = ',F12.2 /
      $          11X, `   Lower Level Activation Energy
      $                  (eV) = ',F12.2 /
      $          11X, `   Plug Length (Micron)
      $                  = ',F12.2 /
      $          11X, `   Square Plug Dimension (Micron)
      $                  = ',F12.2)
        ELSE IF (IGP .EQ. "E" .OR. IGP .EQ. "e") THEN
        WRITE (*,328)
  328   FORMAT (11X, `COMPONENT: INTERCONNECTION VIA')
        WRITE (*,330) IL, IW, IT, TEMPC, CURRENT, JE,
      $                AE, LAE, VH, VW, VANGLE
  330   FORMAT (11X, `   Interconnection Length (Micron)
      $                  = ',F12.2 /
      $          11X, `   Interconnection Width (Micron)
      $                  = ',F12.2 /
      $          11X, `   Interconnection Thickness
      $                  (Micron) = ',F12.2 /
```

```
      $         11X, `   Interconnection Temperature (C)
      $                  = ',F12.2 /
      $         11X, `   Interconnection Current (mA)
      $                  = ',F12.2 /
      $         11X, `   Current Density Exponent
      $                  = ',F12.2 /
      $         11X, `   Int. Material Activation Energy
      $                  (eV) = ',F12.2 /
      $         11X, `   Lower-Level Activation Energy
      $                  (eV) = ',F12.2 /
      $         11X, `   Via Height (Micron)
      $                  = ',F12.2 /
      $         11X, `   Via Width (Micron)
      $                  = ',F12.2 /
      $         11X, `   Via Angle (Degree)
      $                  = ',F12.2)
        ELSE IF (IGP .EQ. "F" .OR. IGP .EQ. "f") THEN
        WRITE (*,332)
  332   FORMAT (11X, `COMPONENT: INTERCONNECTION
      $              OVERFLOW')
        WRITE (*,334) IL, IW, IT, TEMPC, CURRENT, JE,
      $         AE, OL
  334   FORMAT (11X, `   Interconnection Length (Micron)
      $                  = ',F12.2 /
      $         11X, `   Interconnection Width (Micron)
      $                  = ',F12.2 /
      $         11X, `   Interconnection Thickness
      $                  (Micron) = ',F12.2 /
      $         11X, `   Interconnection Temperature (C)
      $                  = ',F12.2 /
      $         11X, `   Interconnection Current (mA)
      $                  = ',F12.2 /
      $         11X, `   Current Density Exponent
      $                  = ',F12.2 /
      $         11X, `   Material Activation Energy (eV)
      $                  = ',F12.2 /
      $         11X, `   Overflow Length (Micron)
      $                  = ',F12.2)
        ELSE IF (IGP .EQ. "G" .OR. IGP .EQ. "g") THEN
        WRITE (*,336)
  336   FORMAT (11X, `COMPONENT: HORIZONTAL MULTISECTION
      $              INTERCONNECTION')
        WRITE (*,338) IL, IW, IT, TEMPC, CURRENT, JE,
      $         AE, PL, NHS
```

```
338  FORMAT (11X, `   Interconnection Length (Micron)
     $                   = ',F12.2 /
     $           11X, `   Interconnection Width (Micron)
     $                   = ',F12.2 /
     $           11X, `   Interconnection Thickness
     $                   (Micron) = ',F12.2 /
     $           11X, `   Interconnection Temperature (C)
     $                   = ',F12.2 /
     $           11X, `   Interconnection Current (mA)
     $                   = ',F12.2 /
     $           11X, `   Current Density Exponent
     $                   = ',F12.2 /
     $           11X, `   Material Activation Energy (eV)
     $                   = ',F12.2 /
     $           11X, `   Source / Sink Pad Lengths
     $                   (Micron) = ',F12.2 /
     $           11X, `   Number of Horizontal Sections
     $                   = ',I9)
       ELSE IF (IGP .EQ. "H" .OR. IGP "h") THEN
       WRITE (*,340)
340  FORMAT (11X, `COMPONENT: VERTICAL MULTISECTION
     $              INTERCONNECTION')
       WRITE (*,342) IL, IW, IT, TEMPC, CURRENT, JE,
     $              AE, VPAE, VPL, NVS
342  FORMAT (11X, `   Interconnection Length (Micron)
     $                   = ',F12.2 /
     $           11X, `   Interconnection Width (Micron)
     $                   = ',F12.2 /
     $           11X, `   Interconnection Thickness
     $                   (Micron) = ',F12.2 /
     $           11X, `   Interconnection Temperature (C)
     $                   = ',F12.2 /
     $           11X, `   Interconnection Current (mA)
     $                   = ',F12.2 /
     $           11X, `   Current Density Exponent
     $                   = ',F12.2 /
     $           11X, `   Int. Material Activation Energy
     $                   (eV) = ',F12.2 /
     $           11X, `   Plug Material Activation Energy
     $                   (eV) = ',F12.2 /
     $           11X, `   Length of Each Plug (Micron)
     $                   = ',F12.2 /
     $           11X, `   Number of Vertical Sections
     $                   = ',I9)
```

```
      ELSE IF (IGP .EQ. "I" .OR. IGP .EQ. "i") THEN
      WRITE (*,344)
344   FORMAT (11X, `COMPONENT: MIXED MULTISECTION
   $               INTERCONNECTION')
      WRITE (*,346) IL, IW, IT, TEMPC, CURRENT, JE,
   $          AE, NHS, PL, NBVS, VPL, VPAE
246   FORMAT (11X, `    Interconnection Length (Micron)
   $                   = ',F12.2 /
   $          11X, `   Interconnection Width (Micron)
   $                   = ',F12.2 /
   $          11X, `   Interconnection Thickness
   $                  (Micron) = ',F12.2 /
   $          11X, `   Interconnection Temperature (C)
   $                   = ',F12.2 /
   $          11X, `   Interconnection Current (mA)
   $                   = ',F12.2 /
   $          11X, `   Current Density Exponent
   $                   = ',F12.2 /
   $          11X, `   Int. Material Activation Energy
   $                  (eV) = ',F12.2 /
   $          11X, `   Number of Horizontal Sections
   $                   = ',I9 /
   $          11X, `   Source / Sink Pad Lengths
   $                  (Micron) = ',F12.2 /
   $          11X, `   Number of Embedded Vertical
   $                  Sections = ',I9 /
   $          11X, `   Length of Each Plug (Micron)
   $                   = ',F12.2 /
   $          11X, `   Plug Material Activation Energy
   $                  (eV) = ',F12.2)
      ELSE IF (IGP .EQ. "J" .OR. IGP .EQ. "j") THEN
      WRITE (*,348)
348   FORMAT (11X, `COMPONENT: POWER OR GROUND BUS')
      WRITE (*,350) BL, BW, BT, TEMPC, BAE, JE, NGB, G
350   FORMAT (11X, `    Total Bus Length (Micron)
   $                   = ',F12.2 /
   $          11X, `   Bus Width (Micron)
   $                   = ',F12.2 /
   $          11X, `   Bus Material Thickness (Micron)
   $                   = ',F12.2 /
   $          11X, `   Bus Temperature (C)
   $                   = ',F12.2 /
   $          11X, `   Bus Material Activation Energy
   $                  (eV) = ',F12.2 /
   $          11X, `   Current Density Exponent
```

```
     $                               = ',F12.2 /
     $           11X, '    Number of Gates Served by the
     $                     Bus = ',I9 /
     $           11X, '    Current in Each Gate (mA)
     $                          = ',F12.2)
      END IF
      IF (MTF .LT. 0.017) THEN
      MTF = MTF*3600.0
      WRITE (*,278) MTF, SIGMA
 278  FORMAT (11X, 'SIMULATION RESULTS:'/
     $           11X, '    Median Time to Failure
     $                     (Seconds) = ',F12.2 /
     $           11X, '    Lognormal Standard Deviation
     $                          = ',F12.2)
      MTF = MTF / 3600.0
      ELSE IF (MTF .LT. 1.0) THEN
      MTF = MTF*60.0
      WRITE (*,277) MTF, SIGMA
 277  FORMAT (11X, 'SIMULATION RESULTS:'/
     $           11X, '    Median Time to Failure
     $                     (Minutes) = ',F12.2 /
     $           11X, '    Lognormal Standard Deviation
     $                          = ',F12.2)
      MTF = MTF / 60.0
      ELSE IF (MTF .LE. 100000.0) THEN
      WRITE (*,271) MTF, SIGMA
 271  FORMAT (11x, 'SIMULATION RESULTS:'/
     $           11X, '    Median Time to Failure (Hours)
     $                          = ',F12.2 /
     $           11X, '    Lognormal Standard Deviation
     $                          = ',F12.2)
      ELSE IF (MTF .LE. 100000000.0) THEN
      MTF = MTF / 1000.0
      WRITE (*,272) MTF, SIGMA
 272  FORMAT (11X, 'SIMULATION RESULTS:'/
     $           11X, '    Median Time to Failure
     $                     (10^3 Hours) = ',F12.2 /
     $           11X, '    Lognormal Standard Deviation
     $                          = ',F12.2)
      MTF = MTF*1000.0
      ELSE IF (MTF .LE. 100000000000.0) THEN
      MTF = MTF / 1000000.0
      WRITE (*,273) MTF, SIGMA
 273  FORMAT (11X, 'SIMULATION RESULTS:'/
     $           11X, '    Median Time to Failure
```

```
     $                    (10^6 Hours) = ',F12.2 /
     $          11X, `    Lognormal Standard Deviation
     $                      = ',F12.2)
       MTF = MTF*1000000.0
       ELSE IF (MTF .LE. 100000000000000.0) THEN
       MTF = MTF / 1000000000.0
       WRITE (*,274) MTF, SIGMA
 274   FORMAT (11X, `SIMULATION RESULTS:'/
     $          11X, `    Median Time to Failure
     $                    (10^9 Hours) = ',F12.2 /
     $          11X, `    Lognormal Standard Deviation
     $                      = ',F12.2)
       MTF = MTF*1000000000.0
       ELSE IF (MTF .LE. 100000000000000000.0) THEN
       MTF = MTF / 1000000000000.0
       WRITE (*,275) MTF, SIGMA
 275   FORMAT (11x, `SIMULATION RESULTS:'/
     $          11X, `    Median Time to Failure
     $                    (10^12 Hours) = ',F12.2 /
     $          11X, `    Lognormal Standard Deviation
     $                      = ',F12.2)
       MTF = MTF*1000000000000.0
       ELSE
       WRITE (*,276) MTF, SIGMA
 276   FORMAT (11x, `SIMULATION RESULTS:'/
     $          11X, `    Median Time to Failure (Hours)
     $                      = ',F12.2 /
     $          11X, `    Lognormal Standard Deviation
     $                      = ',F12.2)
       END IF
       WRITE (*,900)
       WRITE (*,264)
 264   FORMAT (11X, `Do You Want to Write These Results
     $                on EMVIC.OUT?'/
     $          11X, `(Enter Y for YES or N for NO or Q
     $                to QUIT EMVIC)')
       WRITE (*,900)
       READ (*,*,ERR = 250) WRP
       IF (WRP .EQ. "Y" .OR. WRP .EQ. "y") THEN
       IF (IGP .EQ. "A" .OR. IGP .EQ. "a") THEN
       CALL EMVICOUT1 (IL,IW,IT,TEMPC,CURRENT,AE,
     $                JE,MTF,SIGMA)
       ELSE IF (IGP .EQ. "B" .OR. IGP .EQ. "b") THEN
       CALL EMVICOUT2 (IL,IW,IT,TEMPC,CURRENT,AE,
     $                BANGLE,JE,MTF,SIGMA)
```

```
      ELSE IF (IGP .EQ. "C" .OR. IGP .EQ. "c") THEN
      CALL EMVICOUT3 (IL,IW,IT,TEMPC,CURRENT,AE,
     $                SANGLE,SHEIGHT,JE,MTF,SIGMA)
      ELSE IF (IGP .EQ. "D" .OR. IGP .EQ. "d") THEN
      CALL EMVICOUT4 (IL,IW,IT,TEMPC,CURRENT,AE,
     $                PAE,LAE,IPL,SPD,JE,MTF,SIGMA)
      ELSE IF (IGP .EQ. "E" .OR. IGP .EQ. "e") THEN
      CALL EMVICOUT5 (IL,IW,IT,TEMPC,CURRENT,AE,
     $                LAE,VH,VW,VANGLE,JE,MTF,SIGMA)
      ELSE IF (IGP .EQ. "F" .OR. IGP .EQ. "f") THEN
      CALL EMVICOUT6 (IL,IW,IT,TEMPC,CURRENT,AE,
     $                OL,JE,MTF,SIGMA)
      ELSE IF (IGP .EQ. "G" .OR. IGP .EQ. "g") THEN
      CALL EMVICOUT7 (IL,IW,IT,TEMPC,CURRENT,AE,
     $                NHS,PL,JE,MTF,SIGMA)
      ELSE IF (IGP .EQ. "H" .OR. IGP .EQ. "h") THEN
      CALL EMVICOUT8 (IL,IW,IT,TEMPC,CURRENT,AE,
     $                VPAE,VPL,NVS,JE,MTF,SIGMA)
      ELSE IF (IGP .EQ. "I" .OR. IGP .EQ. "i") THEN
      CALL EMVICOUT9 (IL,IW,IT,TEMPC,CURRENT,AE,
     $                NHS,PL,NBVS,VPL,VPAE,JE,MTF,
     $                SIGMA)
      ELSE IF (IGP .EQ. "J" .OR. IGP .EQ. "j") THEN
      CALL EMVICOUT10 (BL,BW,BT,TEMPC,BAE,NGB,GC,
     $                 JE,MTF,SIGMA)
      END IF
      ELSE IF (WRP .EQ. "N" .OR. WRP .EQ. "n") THEN
      GO TO 300
      ELSE IF (WRP .EQ. "Q" .OR. WRP .EQ. "q") THEN
      GO TO 999
      ELSE
      GO TO 250
      END IF
C*****Continue Analysis of the Previous Component*****
  300 I = CLEAR()
      WRITE (*,906)
      WRITE (*,900)
      WRITE (*,302)
  302 FORMAT (11X, `C O N T I N U E   S I M U L A T I O N ?')
      WRITE (*,900)
      WRITE (*,304)
  304 FORMAT ( / ,12X, `DO YOU WANT TO FURTHER ANALYZE
     $                THE PREVIOUS'/
     $            12X, `INTERCONNECTION COMPONENT ?'/ )
```

```
      WRITE (*,900)
      WRITE (*,306)
 306  FORMAT (11X, 'Enter Y for YES or N for NO')
      WRITE (*,900)
      READ (*,*,ERR = 300) CCP2
      IF (CCP2 .EQ. "Y" .OR. CCP2 .EQ. "y") THEN
      IF (IGP .EQ. "A" .OR. IGP .EQ. "a") THEN
      GO TO 60
      ELSE IF (IGP .EQ. "B" .OR. IGP .EQ. "b") THEN
      GO TO 70
      ELSE IF (IGP .EQ. "C" .OR. IGP .EQ. "c") THEN
      GO TO 80
      ELSE IF (IGP .EQ. "D" .OR. IGP .EQ. "d") THEN
      GO TO 240
      ELSE IF (IGP .EQ. "E" .OR. IGP .EQ. "e") THEN
      GO TO 90
      ELSE IF (IGP .EQ. "F" .OR. IGP .EQ. "f") THEN
      GO TO 100
      ELSE IF (IGP .EQ. "G" .OR. IGP .EQ. "g") THEN
      GO TO 110
      ELSE IF (IGP .EQ. "H" .OR. IGP .EQ. "h") THEN
      GO TO 120
      ELSE IF (IGP .EQ. "I" .OR. IGP .EQ. "i") THEN
      GO TO 130
      ELSE IF (IGP .EQ. "J" .OR. IGP .EQ. "j") THEN
      GO TO 140
      END IF
      ELSE IF (CCP2 .EQ. "N" .OR. CCP2 .EQ. "n") THEN
      GO TO 400
      ELSE
      GO TO 300
      END IF
C*****Analysis of Other Components*****
 400  I = CLEAR()
      WRITE (*,906)
      WRITE (*,900)
      WRITE (*,402)
 402  FORMAT (11X, 'S I M U L A T E   O T H E R
     $             C O M P O N E N T S ?')
      WRITE (*,900)
      WRITE (*,404)
 404  FORMAT ( / ,12X, 'DO YOU WANT TO ANALYZE OTHER
     $             INTERCONNECTION COMPONENTS ?'/ )
      WRITE (*,900)
      WRITE (*,406)
```

```
 406   FORMAT (11X, 'Enter Y for YES or N for NO AND
       $                 QUIT EMVIC')
       WRITE (*,900)
       READ (*,*,ERR = 400) CCP2
       IF (CCP2 .EQ. "Y" .OR. CCP2 .EQ. "y") THEN
       GO TO 30
       ELSE IF (CCP2 .EQ. "N" .OR. CCP2 .EQ. "n") THEN
       GO TO 999
       ELSE
       GO TO 400
       END IF
C*****Printing the Output File*****
 999   I = CLEAR()
       WRITE (*,906)
       WRITE (*,*)
       WRITE (*,997)
 997   FORMAT (17X, 'PPPPPPPPPPPPPPPPPPPPPPPPPPPPPPPPP'
       $          17X, 'P                                P'/
       $          17X, 'P       DO YOU WANT TO PRINT      P'/
       $          17X, 'P            EMVIC.OUT?           P'/
       $          17X, 'P                                P'/
       $          17X, 'PPPPPPPPPPPPPPPPPPPPPPPPPPPPPPPPP'/
       $          17X, 'P   Enter Y for YES or N for NO   P'/
       $          17X, 'PPPPPPPPPPPPPPPPPPPPPPPPPPPPPPPPP')
       WRITE (*,904)
       READ (*,*,ERR = 999) CP3
       IF (CP3 .EQ. "Y" .OR. CP3 .EQ. "y") THEN
       I = PRINT()
       GO TO 1000
       ELSE IF (CP3 .EQ. "N" .OR. CP3 .EQ. "n") THEN
       GO TO 1000
       ELSE
       GO TO 999
       END IF
1000   I = CLEAR()
       WRITE (*,905)
       WRITE (*,902)
       WRITE (*,998)
 998   FORMAT (17X, '*********************************'/
       $          17X, '**                             **'/
       $          17X, '** THANK YOU FOR USING E M V I C **'/
       $          17X, '**          HAVE A NICE DAY!     **'/
       $          17X, '**                             **'/
       $          17X, '*********************************'//)
```

```
      WRITE (*,904)
      READ (*,*)
      I = CLEAR()
      STOP
      END
C*****Subroutine STRAIGHT for Straight Interconnection
C     Segments
      SUBROUTINE STRAIGHT (IL,IW,IT,CURRENT,TEMP,AE,
     $                     JE,MTF,SIGMA)
      REAL*8 IL, IW, IT, CURRENT, TEMP, MTF, SIGMA,
     $       NE, AE, SIGMA1, MTF1, JE
      MTF1 = (1523.0)*((IW*IT / (CURRENT*10**5))**JE)*
     $       (IW- 3.07 + 11.63 / (IW**1.7))*EXP(10740.74*AE
     $       /TEMP)
      SIGMA1 = 2.192 / (IW**2.625) + 0.787
      NE = IL / 10.0
      SIGMA = SIGMA1 / (NE**0.304)
      MTF = MTF1 / NE
      RETURN
      END
C*****Subroutine BEND for Interconnection Bends*****
      SUBROUTINE BEND (IL,IW,IT,CURRENT,TEMP,AE,
     $                 BANGLE,JE,MTF,SIGMA)
      REAL*8 IL, IW, IT, CURRENT, TEMP, BANGLE, MTF,
     $       SIGMA, MTF1, MTF2, MTF3, SIGMA1, SIGMA2,
     $       SIGMA3, MTFI, LEFF, WEFF, ABEND, IL1,
     $       IL2, NE, MTF4, NEEFF, AE, JE
      LEFF = 3.142*IW*(180.0- BANGLE) / 360.0
      ABEND = (IW**2) / (TAN(3.142*0.5*BANGLE / 180.0))
      WEFF = (ABEND + IW**2.0) / (LEFF + IW)
      IL1 = IL / 2.0
      IL2 = IL / 2.0
      CALL STRAIGHT(IL1,IW,IT,CURRENT,TEMP,AE,JE,
     $              MTF1,SIGMA1)
      CALL STRAIGHT(IL2,IW,IT,CURRENT,TEMP,AE,JE,
     $              MTF2,SIGMA2)
      CALL STRAIGHT(LEFF,WEFF,IT,CURRENT,TEMP,AE,
     $              JE,MTF3,SIGMA3)
      CALL STRAIGHT(IL,IW,IT,CURRENT,TEMP,AE,JE,
     $              MTF4,SIGMA)
      MTFI = (1.0 / MTF1) + (1.0 / MTF2) + (1.0 / MTF3)
      MTF = 1.0 / MTFI
      SIGMA1 = 2.192 / (IW**2.625) + 0.787
      NE = IL / 10.0
      NEEFF = NE*(MTF4 / MTF)
```

```
      SIGMA = SIGMA1 / (NEEFF**0.304)
      RETURN
      END
C*****Subroutine STEP for Interconnection Steps*****
      SUBROUTINE STEP (IL,IW,IT,CURRENT,TEMP,AE,
     $                 SANGLE,SHEIGHT,JE,MTF,SIGMA)
      REAL*8 IL, IW, IT, CURRENT, TEMP, SANGLE,
     $       SHEIGHT, MTF, SIGMA, MTF1, MTF2, MTF3,
     $       MTFI, MTF4, IL1, IL2, IL3, SANGLE1,
     $       IT2, IT3, SIGMA1, NE, NEEFF, AE, JE
      SANGLE1 = 3.142*(180.0- SANGLE) / 180.0
      IL1 = IL- SHEIGHT / (TAN(SANGLE1))
      CALL STRAIGHT(IL1,IW,IT,CURRENT,TEMP,AE,JE,
     $              MTF1,SIGMA)
      IL2 = SHEIGHT / (SIN(SANGLE1))- IT*SIN(SANGLE1)
      IT2 = IT*COS(SANGLE1)
      CALL STRAIGHT(IL2,IW,IT2,CURRENT,TEMP,AE,JE,
     $              MTF2,SIGMA)
      IL3 = (3.142*IT*(180.0- SANGLE)*(1.0 +
     $       COS(SANGLE1))) / 360.0
      IT3 = ((IT**2.0)*(1.0 + COS(SANGLE1)*(SIN(SANGLE1)
     $       +COS(SANGLE1)))) / (2.0*IL3*IT*(1.0 + COS
     $       (SANGLE1)))
      CALL STRAIGHT(IL3,IW,IT3,CURRENT,TEMP,AE,
     $              JE,MTF3,SIGMA)
      MTFI = (1.0 / MTF1) + (1.0 / MTF2) + (1.0 / MTF3)
      MTF = 1.0 / MTFI
      CALL STRAIGHT(IL,IW,IT,CURRENT,TEMP,AE,
     $              JE,MTF4,SIGMA)
      SIGMA1 = 2.192 / (IW**2.625) + 0.787
      NE = IL / 10.0
      NEEFF = NE*(MTF4 / MTF)
      SIGMA = SIGMA1 / (NEEFF**0.304)
      RETURN
      END
C*****Subroutine PLUG for Interconnection Vias*****
      SUBROUTINE PLUG (IL,IW,IT,CURRENT,TEMP,AE,
     $                 PAE,LAE,IPL,SPD,JE,MTF,SIGMA)
      REAL*8  IL, IW, IT, CURRENT, TEMP, IPL, SPD,
     $        MTF, SIGMA, IL3, IT3, MTF1, MTF2, MTF3,
     $        MTF4, NEEFF, NE, IL1, MTFI, SIGMA1, AE,
     $        PAE, LAE, MTF5, MTF6, JE
      IL1 = (IL- PD) / 2.0
      CALL STRAIGHT(IL1,IW,IT,CURRENT,TEMP,AE,JE,
     $              MTF1,SIGMA)
```

```
      CALL STRAIGHT(IL1,IW,IT,CURRENT,TEMP,LAE,JE,
     $             MTF5,SIGMA)
      CALL STRAIGHT(IPL,SPD,SPD,CURRENT,TEMP,PAE,
     $             JE,MTF2,SIGMA)
      IL3 = 3.142*(IT+SPD)/8.0
      IT3 = IT*(IW+SPD)/(2.0*IL3)
      CALL STRAIGHT(IL3,IW,IT3,CURRENT,TEMP,AE,JE,
     $             MTF3,SIGMA)
      CALL STRAIGHT(IL3,IW,IT3,CURRENT,TEMP,LAE,
     $             JE,MTF4,SIGMA)
      MTFI = (1.0/MTF1)+(1.0/MTF2)+(1.0/MTF3)+
     $       (1.0/MTF4)+(1.0/MTF5)
      MTF = 1.0/MTFI
      CALL STRAIGHT(IL,IW,IT,CURRENT,TEMP,AE,JE,
     $             MTF6,SIGMA)
      SIGMA1 = 2.192/(IW**2.625)+0.787
      NE = IL/10.0
      NEEFF = NE*(MTF6/MTF)
      SIGMA = SIGMA1/(NEEFF**0.304)
      RETURN
      END
C*****Subroutine VIA for Interconnection Vias*****
      SUBROUTINE VIA (IL,IW,IT,CURRENT,TEMP,AE,
     $               LAE,VH,VW,VANGLE,JE,MTF,SIGMA)
      REAL*8  IL, IW, IT, CURRENT, TEMP, VH, VW, MTF,
     $        SIGMA, IL3, IT3, MTF1, MTF2, MTF3, MTF4,
     $        NEEFF, NE, MTFI, SIGMA1, AE, LAE,
     $        VANGLE, MTF5, IL1, IT1, IL2, IT2,
     $        VANGLE1, MTF6, MTF7, MTF8, MTF9, IL5,
     $        IL6, IL7, IL8, MTFI2, JE
      VANGLE1 = 3.142*VANGLE/180.0
      IL6 = (IL-VW-VH/(TAN(VANGLE1)))/2.0
      CALL STRAIGHT(IL6,IW,IT,CURRENT,TEMP,AE,JE,
     $             MTF6,SIGMA)
      IL5 = (IL-VW-VH/(TAN(VANGLE1)))/2.0
      CALL STRAIGHT(IL5,IW,IT,CURRENT,TEMP,LAE,JE,
     $             MTF5,SIGMA)
      IL2 = VH/(SIN(VANGLE1))-IT*SIN(VANGLE1)
      IT2 = IT*COS(VANGLE1)
      CALL STRAIGHT(IL2,IW,IT2,CURRENT,TEMP,AE,JE,
     $             MTF2,SIGMA)
      IL1 = (3.142*IT*VANGLE*(1.0+COS(VANGLE1)))/
     $      360.0
      IT1 = ((IT**2.0)*(1.0+COS(VANGLE1)*(SIN(VANGLE1)
     $      +COS(VANGLE1))))
```

```
$          / ( 2.0*IL1*IT*( 1.0 + COS ( VANGLE1 ) ) )
 CALL STRAIGHT( IL1, IW, IT1, CURRENT, TEMP, AE, JE,
$               MTF1, SIGMA )
 IL3 = IT / ( 2.0*SIN( ATAN( IT / VW ) ) )
 IT3 = ( ( IT**2 ) / ( 2.0*TAN( VANGLE1 ) ) + IT*( VW- IT /
$        TAN( VANGLE ) ) ) / IL3
 CALL STRAIGHT( IL3, IW, IT3, CURRENT, TEMP, AE, JE,
$               MTF3, SIGMA )
 CALL STRAIGHT( IL3, IW, IT3, CURRENT, TEMP, LAE, JE,
$               MTF4, SIGMA )
 MTFI = ( 1.0 / MTF1 ) + ( 1.0 / MTF2 ) + ( 1.0 / MTF3 ) +
$        ( 1.0 / MTF4 ) + ( 1.0 / MTF5 ) + ( 1.0 / MTF6 )
 MTF = 1.0 / MTFI
 IL7 = IL / 2.0
 CALL STRAIGHT( IL7, IW, IT, CURRENT, TEMP, AE, JE,
$               MTF7, SIGMA )
 IL8 = IL / 2.0
 CALL STRAIGHT( IL8, IW, IT, CURRENT, TEMP, AE, JE,
$               MTF8, SIGMA )
 MTFI2 = ( 1.0 / MTF7 ) + ( 1.0 / MTF8 )
 MTF9 = 1.0 / MTFI2
 SIGMA1 = 2.192 / ( IW**2.625 ) + 0.787
 NE = IL / 10.0
 NEEFF = NE*( MTF9 / MTF )
 SIGMA = SIGMA1 / ( NEEFF**0.304 )
 RETURN
 END
C*****Subroutine OVERFLOW for Interconnection
C     Overflows
 SUBROUTINE OVERFLOW ( IL, IW, IT, CURRENT, TEMP,
$                      AE, OL, JE, MTF, SIGMA )
 REAL*8  IL, IW, IT, CURRENT, TEMP, OL, MTF,
$         SIGMA, IL1, JE, IW2, IT2, MTF1, MTF2,
$         MTF4, NE, NEEFF, MTFI, AE
 IL1 = IL- OL
 CALL STRAIGHT( IL1, IW, IT, CURRENT, TEMP, AE, JE,
$               MTF1, SIGMA )
 IT2 = 0.5*( 0.0- IW + ( IW*IW + 4.0*IW*IT )**0.5 )
 IW2 = IW*IT / IT2
 CALL STRAIGHT( OL, IW2, IT2, CURRENT, TEMP, AE, JE,
$               MTF2, SIGMA )
 MTFI = ( 1.0 / MTF1 ) + ( 1.0 / MTF2 )
 MTF = 1.0 / MTFI
 CALL STRAIGHT( IL, IW, IT, CURRENT, TEMP, AE, JE,
$               MTF4, SIGMA )
```

```fortran
      SIGMA1 = 2.192 / (IW**2.625) + 0.787
      NE = IL / 10.0
      NEEFF = NE*(MTF4 / MTF)
      SIGMA = SIGMA1 / (NEEFF**0.304)
      RETURN
      END
C*****Subroutine HMSI for Horizontal Multisection
C     Interconnections
      SUBROUTINE HMSI (IL,IW,IT,CURRENT,TEMP,AE,
     $                 NHS,PL,JE,MTF,SIGMA)
      REAL*8  IL, IW, IT, CURRENT, TEMP, MTF, SIGMA,
     $        SIGMA1, JE, CURRENTS, MTFS1, ILP, MTFP,
     $        MTFS, MTF4, NE, NEEFF, AE, IWP,
     $        MTFI, PL, ILS
      INTEGER NHS
      ILS = IL
      CURRENTS = CURRENT / NHS
      CALL STRAIGHT(ILS,IW,IT,CURRENTS,TEMP,AE,JE,
     $              MTFS1,SIGMA)
      MTFS = NHS*MTFS1
      ILP = PL
      IWP = (2*NHS-1)*IW
      CALL STRAIGHT(ILP,IWP,IT,CURRENT,TEMP,AE,JE,
     $              MTFP,SIGMA)
      MTFI = (1.0 / MTFS) + (1.0 / MTFP)
      MTF = 1.0 / MTFI
      CALL STRAIGHT(IL,IW,IT,CURRENT,TEMP,AE,JE,
     $              MTF4,SIGMA)
      SIGMA1 = 2.192 / (IW**2.625) + 0.787
      NE = IL / 10.0
      NEEFF = NE*(MTF4 / MTF)
      SIGMA = SIGMA1 / (NEEFF**0.304)
      RETURN
      END
C*****Subroutine VMSI for Vertical Multisection
C     Interconnections
      SUBROUTINE VMSI(IL,IW,IT,CURRENT,TEMP,AE,
     $        VPL,VPAE,NVS,JE,MTF,SIGMA)
      REAL*8  IL, IW, IT, CURRENT, TEMP, AE, VPL,
     $        VPAE, MTF, SIGMA, MTFS, MTF4, SIGMA1,
     $        NE, NEEFF, MTFS1, MTFP1, JE, ILP, IWP,
     $        ITP, CURRENTS, CURRENTP, MTFSI
      INTEGER I, NVS, NVS1
      CURRENTS = CURRENT / NVS
```

```
      CALL STRAIGHT(IL,IW,IT,CURRENTS,TEMP,AE,JE,
     $             MTFS1,SIGMA)
      MTF = MTFS1
      ILP = 2.0*VPL
      IWP = IW
      ITP = IW
      NVS1 = NVS- 1
      DO 10 I = 1,NVS1,1
      CURRENTP = CURRENT*(1.0- FLOAT(I) / FLOAT(NVS))
      CALL STRAIGHT(ILP,IWP,ITP,CURRENTP,TEMP,
     $             VPAE,JE,MTFP1,SIGMA)
      MTFSI = (1.0 / MTFS1) + (1.0 / MTFP1)
      MTFS = 1.0 / MTFSI
      MTF = MTF + MTFS
  10  CONTINUE
      CALL STRAIGHT(IL,IW,IT,CURRENT,TEMP,AE,JE,
     $             MTF4,SIGMA)
      SIGMA1 = 2.192 / (IW**2.625) + 0.787
      NE = IL / 10.0
      NEEFF = NE* (MTF4 / MTF)
      SIGMA = SIGMA1 / (NEEFF**0.304)
      RETURN
      END
C*****Subroutine MMSI for Mixed Multisection
C     Interconnections
      SUBROUTINE MMSI (IL,IW,IT,CURRENT,TEMP,AE,
     $                 NHS,PL,NBVS,VPL,VPAE,JE,MTF,
     $                 SIGMA)
      REAL*8  IL, IW, IT, CURRENT, TEMP, AE, PL, VPL,
     $        VPAE, MTF, SIGMA, MTFS, MTFP, ILP,
     $        CURRENTP, MTFI, CURRENTS, MTFS1, IWP,
     $        CURRENTV, MTFP1, MTFSI, SIGMA1, NE,
     $        NEEFF, MTF4, JE
      INTEGER NHS, NBVS, NVS, I
      CURRENTS = CURRENT / (NHS + NBVS)
      CALL STRAIGHT(IL,IW,IT,CURRENTS,TEMP,AE,JE,
     $             MTFS1,SIGMA)
      MTFS = NHS*MTFS1
      IWP = (2*NHS- 1)*IW
      CALL STRAIGHT(PL,IWP,IT,CURRENT,TEMP,AE,JE,
     $             MTFP,SIGMA)
      MTFI = (1.0 / MTFS) + (1.0 / MTFP)
      MTF = 1.0 / MTFI
      CURRENTV = CURRENT- NHS*CURRENTS
      ILP = 2.0*VPL
```

```
      NVS = NBVS + 1
      DO 10 I = 1,NBVS,1
      CURRENTP = CURRENTV*(1.0- FLOAT(I) / FLOAT(NVS))
      CALL STRAIGHT(ILP,IW,IW,CURRENTP,TEMP,VPAE,
     $              JE,MTFP1,SIGMA)
      MTFS1 = (1.0 / MTFS1) + (1.0 / MTFP1)
      MTFS = 1.0 / MTFSI
      MTF = MTF + MTFS
  10  CONTINUE
      CALL STRAIGHT(IL,IW,IT,CURRENT,TEMP,AE,JE,
     $              MTF4,SIGMA)
      SIGMA1 = 2.192 / (IW**2.625) + 0.787
      NE = IL / 10.0
      NEEFF = NE* (MTF4 / MTF)
      SIGMA = SIGMA1 / (NEEFF**0.304)
      RETURN
      END
C*****Subroutine PGBUS for Power and Ground Buses*****
      SUBROUTINE PGBUS (BL,BW,BT,TEMP,BAE,NGB,GC,
     $                  JE,MTF,SIGMA)
      REAL*8  BL, BW, BT, TEMP, BAE, GC, MTF, SIGMA,
     $        BSL, MTFS, MTFI, SIGMA1, NE, NEEFF,
     $        MTF4, CURRENT, JE
      INTEGER NGB, I
      BSL = BL / NGB
      MTFI = 0.0
      DO 10 I = 1,NGB,1
      CURRENT = GC*I
      CALL STRAIGHT(BSL,BW,BT,CURRENT,TEMP,BAE,JE,
     $              MTFS,SIGMA)
      MTFI = MTFI + (1.0 / MTFS)
  10  CONTINUE
      MTF = 1.0 / MTFI
      CURRENT = NGB*GC / 2.0
      CALL STRAIGHT(BL,BW,BT,CURRENT,TEMP,BAE,JE,
     $              MTF4,SIGMA)
      SIGMA1 = 2.192 / (BW**2.625) + 0.787
      NE = BL / 10.0
      NEEFF = NE*(MTF4 / MTF)
      SIGMA = SIGMA1 / (NEEFF**0.304)
      RETURN
      END
C*****Subroutine EMVICOUT1 for Writing the Output File
C     for STRAIGHT
```

```
      SUBROUTINE EMVICOUT1 (IL,IW,IT,TEMPC,
     $                      CURRENT,AE,JE,MTF,SIGMA)
      REAL*8 IL, IW, IT, TEMPC, CURRENT, MTF, SIGMA,
     $       AE, JE
  900 FORMAT (10X,2( `------------------------------'))
      WRITE (8,900)
      WRITE (8.62)
   62 FORMAT (11X, `COMPONENT: STRAIGHT INTERCONNECTION
     $            SEGMENT')
      WRITE (8,64) IL, IW, IT, TEMPC, CURRENT, JE, AE
   64 FORMAT (11X,/
     $         11X, `    Interconnection Length (Micron)
     $              = ',F10.2 /
     $         11X, `    Interconnection Width (Micron)
     $              = ',F10.2 /
     $         11X, `    Interconnection Thickness
     $              (Micron) = ',F10.2 /
     $         11X, `    Interconnection Temperature (C)
     $              = ',F10.2 /
     $         11X, `    Interconnection Current (mA)
     $              = ',F10.2 /
     $         11X, `    Current Density Exponent
     $              = ',F10.2 /
     $         11X, `    Material Activation Energy (eV)
     $              = ',F10.2)
      CALL EMVICOUT11 (MTF, SIGMA)
      WRITE (8,900)
      RETURN
      END
C*****Subroutine EMVICOUT2 for Writing the Output File
C     for BEND
      SUBROUTINE EMVICOUT2 (IL,IW,IT,TEMPC,CURRENT,
     $                      AE,BANBLE,JE,MTF,SIGMA)
      REAL*8 IL, IW, IT, TEMPC, CURRENT, BANGLE, MTF,
     $       SIGMA, AE, JE
  900 FORMAT (10X,2( `------------------------------'))
      WRITE (8,900)
      WRITE (8,62)
   62 FORMAT (11X, `COMPONENT: INTERCONNECTION BEND')
      WRITE (8,64) IL, IW, IT, TEMPC, CURRENT, JE, AE,
     $             BANGLE
   64 FORMAT (11X,/
     $         11X, `    Interconnection Length (Micron)
     $              = ',F10.2 /
     $         11X, `    Interconnection Width (Micron)
     $              = ',F10.2 /
```

```
      $           11X, `   Interconnection Thickness
      $                    (Micron) = ',F10.2 /
      $           11X, `   Interconnection Temperature (C)
      $                       = ',F10.2 /
      $           11X, `   Interconnection Current (mA)
      $                       = ',F10.2 /
      $           11X, `   Current Density Exponent
      $                       = ',F10.2 /
      $           11X, `   Material Activation Energy (eV)
      $                       = ',F10.2 /
      $           11X, `   Interconnection Bend (Degree)
      $                       = ',F10.2)
       CALL EMVICOUT11 (MTF,SIGMA)
       WRITE (8,900)
       RETURN
       END
C*****Subroutine EMVICOUT3 for Writing the Output File
C     for STEP
       SUBROUTINE EMVICOUT3 (IL,IW,IT,TEMPC,CURRENT,
      $                    AE,SANGLE,SHEIGHT,JE,MTF,SIGMA)
       REAL*8  IL, IW, IT, TEMPC, CURRENT, SANGLE,
      $        SHEIGHT, MTF, SIGMA, AE, JE
  900  FORMAT (10X,2( `----------------------------'))
       WRITE (8,900)
       WRITE (8,62)
   62  FORMAT (11X, `COMPONENT: INTERCONNECTION STEP')
       WRITE (8,64) IL, IW, IT, TEMPC, CURRENT, JE, AE,
      $             SHEIGHT, SANGLE
   64  FORMAT (11X,/
      $           11X, `   Interconnection Length (Micron)
      $                   = ',F10.2 /
      $           11X, `   Interconnection Width (Micron)
      $                   = ',F10.2 /
      $           11X, `   Interconnection Thickness
      $                    (Micron) = ',F10.2 /
      $           11X, `   Interconnection Temperature (C)
      $                   = ',F10.2 /
      $           11X, `   Interconnection Current (mA)
      $                   = ',F10.2 /
      $           11X, `   Current Density Exponent
      $                   = ',F10.2 /
      $           11X, `   Material Activation Energy (eV)
      $                   = ',F10.2 /
      $           11X, `   Step Height (Micron)
      $                   = ',F10.2 /
      $           11X, `   Step Angle (Degree)
```

```
      $                              = ',F10.2)
       CALL EMVICOUT11 (MTF,SIGMA)
       WRITE (8,900)
       RETURN
       END
C*****Subroutine EMVICOUT4 for Writing the Output File
C     for PLUG
       SUBROUTINE EMVICOUT4 (IL,IW,IT,TEMPC,CURRENT,
      $                      AE,PAE,LAE,IPL,SPD,JE,MTF,
      $                      SIGMA)
       REAL*8 IL, IW, IT, TEMPC, CURRENT, MTF, SIGMA,
      $       IPL, SPD, AE, PAE, LAE, JE
 900   FORMAT (10X,2( '----------------------------'))
       WRITE (8,900)
       WRITE (8,62)
  62   FORMAT (11X, 'COMPONENT: INTERCONNECTION PLUG')
       WRITE (8,64) IL, IW, IT, TEMPC, CURRENT, JE, AE,
      $             PAE, LAE, IPL, SPD
  64   FORMAT (11X, '   Interconnection Length (Micron)
      $                 = ',F10.2 /
      $        11X, '   Interconnection Width (Micron)
      $                 = ',F10.2 /
      $        11X, '   Interconnection Thickness
      $                 (Micron) = ',F10.2 /
      $        11X, '   Interconnection Temperature (C)
      $                 = ',F10.2 /
      $        11X, '   Interconnection Current (mA)
      $                 = ',F10.2 /
      $        11X, '   Current Density Exponent
      $                 = ',F10.2 /
      $        11X, '   Int. Material Activation Energy
      $                 (eV) = ',F10.2 /
      $        11X, '   Plug Material Activation Energy
      $                 (eV) = ',F10.2 /
      $        11X, '   Lower-Level Activation Energy
      $                 (eV) = ',F10.2 /
      $        11X, '   Plug Length (Micron)
      $                 = ',F10.2 /
      $        11X, '   Square Plug Dimension (Micron)
      $                 = ',F10.2)
       CALL EMVICOUT11 (MTF,SIGMA)
       WRITE (8,900)
       RETURN
       END
```

```
C*****Subroutine EMVICOUT5 for Writing the Output File
C     for VIA
      SUBROUTINE EMVICOUT5 (IL,IW,IT,TEMPC,CURRENT,
     $                      AE,LAE,VH,VW,VANGLE,JE,
     $                      MTF,SIGMA)
      REAL*8 IL, IW, IT, TEMPC, CURRENT, MTF, SIGMA,
     $       AE, LAE, VH, VW, VANGLE, JE
 900  FORMAT (10X,2( `----------------------------'))
      WRITE (8,900)
      WRITE (8,62)
 62   FORMAT (11X, `COMPONENT: INTERCONNECTION VIA')
      WRITE (8,64) IL, IW, IT, TEMPC, CURRENT, JE, AE,
     $             LAE, VH, VW, VANGLE
 64   FORMAT (11X, `     Interconnection Length (Micron)
     $                 = ',F10.2 /
     $         11X, `    Interconnection Width (Micron)
     $                 = ',F10.2 /
     $         11X, `    Interconnection Thickness
     $                (Micron) = ',F10.2 /
     $         11X, `    Interconnection Temperature (C)
     $                 = ',F10.2 /
     $         11X, `    Interconnection Current (mA)
     $                 = ',F10.2 /
     $         11X, `    Current Density Exponent
     $                 = ',F10.2 /
     $         11X, `    Int. Material Activation Energy
     $                (eV) = ',F10.2 /
     $         11X, `    Lower-Level Activation Energy
     $                (eV) = ',F10.2 /
     $         11X, `    Via Height (Micron)
     $                 = ',F10.2 /
     $         11X, `    Via Width (Micron)
     $                 = ',F10.2 /
     $         11X, `    Via Angle (Degree)
     $                 = ',F10.2)
      CALL EMVICOUT11 (MTF,SIGMA)
      WRITE (8,900)
      RETURN
      END
C*****Subroutine EMVICOUT6 for Writing the Output File
C     for OVERFLOW
      SUBROUTINE EMVICOUT6 (IL,IW,IT,TEMPC,CURRENT,
     $                      AE,OL,JE,MTF,SIGMA)
      REAL*8 IL, IW, IT, TEMPC, CURRENT, MTF, SIGMA,
     $       OL, AE, JE
```

```
 900    FORMAT (10X,2( `------------------------------'))
        WRITE (8,900)
        WRITE (8,62)
 62     FORMAT (11X, `COMPONENT: INTERCONNECTION
       $                OVERFLOW')
        WRITE (8,64) IL, IW, IT, TEMPC, CURRENT, JE, AE,
       $                OL
 64     FORMAT (11x,/
       $           11X, `    Interconnection Length (Micron)
       $                  = ',F10.2 /
       $           11X, `    Interconnection Width (Micron)
       $                  = ',F10.2 /
       $           11X, `    Interconnection Thickness
       $                  (Micron) = ',F10.2 /
       $           11X, `    Interconnection Temperature (C)
       $                  = ',F10.2 /
       $           11X, `    Interconnection Current (mA)
       $                  = ',F10.2 /
       $           11X, `    Current Density Exponent
       $                  = ',F10.2 /
       $           11X, `    Material Activation Energy (eV)
       $                  = ',F10.2 /
       $           11X, `    Overflow Length (Micron)
       $                  = ',F10.2)
        CALL EMVICOUT11 (MTF,SIGMA)
        WRITE (8,900)
        RETURN
        END
C*****Subroutine EMVICOUT7 for Writing the Output File
C     for HMS
        SUBROUTINE EMVICOUT7 (IL,IW,IT,TEMPC,CURRENT,
       $                AE,NHS,PL,JE,MTF,SIGMA)
        REAL*8 IL, IW, IT, TEMPC, CURRENT, MTF, SIGMA,
       $        AE, PL, JE
        INTEGER NHS
 900    FORMAT (10X,2( `----------------------------'))
        WRITE (8,900)
        WRITE (8,62)
 62     FORMAT (11X, `COMPONENT: HORIZONTAL MULTISECTION
       $                INTERCONNECTION')
        WRITE (8,64) IL, IW, IT, TEMPC, CURRENT, JE, AE,
       $                PL, NHS
 64     FORMAT (11X,/
       $           11X, `    Interconnection Length (Micron)
       $                  = ',F10.2 /
```

```
      $           11X, `    Interconnection Width (Micron)
      $                       = ',F10.2 /
      $           11X, `    Interconnection Thickness
      $                     (Micron) = ',F10.2 /
      $           11X, `    Interconnection Temperature (C)
      $                       = ',F10.2 /
      $           11X, `    Interconnection Current (mA)
      $                       = ',F10.2 /
      $           11X, `    Current Density Exponent
      $                       = ',F10.2 /
      $           11X, `    Material Activation Energy (eV)
      $                       = ',F10.2 /
      $           11X, `    Source / Sink Pad Lengths
      $                     (Micron) = ',F10.2 /
      $           11X, `    Number of Horizontal Sections
      $                       = ',I7)
        CALL EMVICOUT11 (MTF,SIGMA)
        WRITE (8,900)
        RETURN
        END
C*****Subroutine EMVICOUT8 for Writing the Output File
C     for VMS
        SUBROUTINE EMVICOUT8 (IL,IW,IT,TEMPC,CURRENT,
      $                       AE,VPAE,VPL,NVS,JE,MTF,
      $                       SIGMA)
        REAL*8  IL, IW, IT, TEMPC, CURRENT, MTF, SIGMA,
      $         AE, VPAE, VPL, JE
        INTEGER NVS
  900   FORMAT (10X,2( `-----------------------------'))
        WRITE (8,900)
        WRITE (8,62)
   62   FORMAT (11X, `COMPONENT: VERTICAL MULTISECTION
      $                INTERCONNECTION')
        WRITE (8,64) IL, IW, IT, TEMPC, CURRENT, JE, AE,
      $                VPAE, VPL, NVS
   64   FORMAT (11X,/
      $           11X, `    Interconnection Length (Micron)
      $                       = ',F10.2 /
      $           11X, `    Interconnection Width (Micron)
      $                       = ',F10.2 /
      $           11X, `    Interconnection Thickness
      $                     (Micron) = ',F10.2 /
      $           11X, `    Interconnection Temperature (C)
      $                       = ',F10.2 /
```

```
      $          11X, `    Interconnection Current (mA)
      $                      = ',F10.2 /
      $          11X, `    Current Density Exponent
      $                      = ',F10.2 /
      $          11X, `    Int. Material Activation Energy
      $                    (eV) = ',F10.2 /
      $          11X, `    Plug Material Activation Energy
      $                    (eV) = ',F10.2 /
      $          11X, `    Length of Each Plug (Micron)
      $                      = ',F10.2 /
      $          11X, `    Number of Vertical Sections
      $                      = ',I7)
        CALL EMVICOUT11 (MTF,SIGMA)
        WRITE (8,900)
        RETURN
        END
C*****Subroutine EMVICOUT9 for Writing the Output File
C     for MMI
        SUBROUTINE EMVICOUT9 (IL,IW,IT,TEMPC,CURRENT,
      $                       AE,NHS,PL,NBVS,VPL,VPAE,
      $                       JE,MTF,SIGMA)
        REAL*8  IL, IW, IT, TEMPC, CURRENT, MTF, SIGMA,
      $         AE, PL, VPL, VPAE, JE
        INTEGER NHS, NBVS
  900   FORMAT (10X,2( `-----------------------------'))
        WRITE (8,900)
        WRITE (8,62)
   62   FORMAT (11X, `COMPONENT: MIXED MULTISECTION
      $            INTERCONNECTION')
        WRITE (8,64) IL, IW, IT, TEMPC, CURRENT, JE, AE,
      $            NHS, PL, NBVS, VPL, VPAE
   64   FORMAT (11X,/
      $          11X, `    Interconnection Length (Micron)
      $                      = ',F10.2 /
      $          11X, `    Interconnection Width (Micron)
      $                      = ',F10.2 /
      $          11X, `    Interconnection Thickness
      $                    (Micron) = ',F10.2 /
      $          11X, `    Interconnection Temperature (C)
      $                      = ',F10.2 /
      $          11X, `    Interconnection Current (mA)
      $                      = ',F10.2 /
      $          11X, `    Current Density Exponent
      $                      = ',F10.2 /
```

```
     $            11X, `     Int. Material Activation Energy
     $                      (eV) = ',F10.2 /
     $            11X, `     Number of Horizontal Sections
     $                         = ',I7 /
     $            11X, `     Source / Sink Pad Lengths
     $                      (Micron) = ',F10.2 /
     $            11X, `     Number of Embedded Vertical
     $                      Sections = ',I7 /
     $            11X, `     Length of Each Plug (Micron)
     $                         = ',F10.2 /
     $            11X, `     Plug Material Activation Energy
     $                      (eV) = ',F10.2)
       CALL EMVICOUT11 (MTF,SIGMA)
       WRITE (8,900)
       RETURN
       END
C*****Subroutine EMVICOUT10 for Writing the Output
C     File for PGBUS
       SUBROUTINE EMVICOUT10 (BL,BW,BT,TEMPC,BAE,NGB,
     $                        GC,JE,MTF,SIGMA)
       REAL*8 BL, BW, BT, TEMPC, BAE, GC, MTF, SIGMA,
     $        JE
       INTEGER NGB
 900   FORMAT (10X,2('-------------------------------'))
       WRITE (8,900)
       WRITE (8,62)
 62    FORMAT (11X, `COMPONENT: POWER OR GROUND BUS')
       WRITE (8,64) BL, BW, BT, TEMPC, BAE, JE, NGB, GC
 64    FORMAT (11X,/
     $            11X, `     Total Bus Length (Micron)
     $                         = ',F10.2 /
     $            11X, `     Bus Width (Micron)
     $                         = ',F10.2 /
     $            11X, `     Bus Material Thickness
     $                      (Micron) = ',F10.2 /
     $            11X, `     Bus Temperature (C)
     $                         = ',F10.2 /
     $            11X, `     Bus Material Activation Energy
     $                      (eV) = ',F10.2 /
     $            11X, `     Current Density Exponent
     $                         = ',F10.2 /
     $            11X, `     Number of Gates Served by the
     $                      Bus = ',I7 /
     $            11X, `     Current in Each Gate (mA)
     $                         = ',F10.2)
```

```
      CALL EMVICOUT11 (MTF,SIGMA)
      WRITE (8,900)
      RETURN
      END
C*****Subroutine EMVICOUT11 for Writing MTF and SIGMA
C     on the Output File
      SUBROUTINE EMVICOUT11 (MTF,SIGMA)
      REAL*8 MTF, SIGMA
      IF (MTF .LT. 0.017) THEN
      MTF = MTF*3600.0
      WRITE (8,278) MTF, SIGMA
 278  FORMAT ( / ,11X, `SIMULATION RESULTS:'/
     $          11X, ` Median Time to Failure
     $                  (Seconds) = ',F12.2 /
     $          11X, ` Lognormal Standard Deviation
     $                  = ',F12.2)
      MTF = MTF / 3600.0
      ELSE IF (MTF .LT. 1.0) THEN
      MTF = MTF*60.0
      WRITE (8,277) MTF, SIGMA
 277  FORMAT ( / ,11X, `SIMULATION RESULTS:'/
     $          11X, ` Median Time to Failure
     $                  (Minutes) = ',F12.2 /
     $          11X, ` Lognormal Standard Deviation
     $                  = ',F12.2)
      MTF = MTF / 60.0
      ELSE IF (MTF .LE. 100000.0) THEN
      WRITE (8,271) MTF, SIGMA
 271  FORMAT ( / ,11X, `SIMULATION RESULTS:'/
     $          11X, ` Median Time to Failure
     $                  (Hours) = ',F10.2 /
     $          11X, ` Lognormal Standard Deviation
     $                  = ',F10.2)
      ELSE IF (MTF .LE. 100000000.0) THEN
      MTF = MTF / 1000.0
      WRITE (8,272) MTF, SIGMA
 272  FORMAT ( / ,11X, `SIMULATION RESULTS:'/
     $          11X, ` Median Time to Failure
     $                  (10^3 Hours) = ',F10.2 /
     $          11X, ` Lognormal Standard Deviation
     $                  = ',F10.2)
      MTF = MTF*1000.0
      ELSE IF (MTF .LE. 100000000000.0) THEN
      MTF = MTF / 1000000.0
      WRITE (8,273) MTF, SIGMA
```

```
273   FORMAT ( / ,11X, `SIMULATION RESULTS:'/
    $            11X, ` Median Time to Failure
    $                   (10^6 Hours) = ',F10.2 /
    $            11X, ` Lognormal Standard Deviation
    $                   = ',F10.2)
      MTF = MTF*1000000.0
      ELSE IF (MTF .LE. 100000000000000.0) THEN
      MTF = MTF / 1000000000.0
      WRITE (8,274) MTF, SIGMA
274   FORMAT ( / ,11X, `SIMULATION RESULTS:'/
    $            11X, ` Median Time to Failure
    $                   (10^9 Hours) = ',F10.2 /
    $            11X, ` Lognormal Standard Deviation
    $                   = ',F10.2)
      MTF = MTF*1000000000.0
      ELSE IF (MTF .LE. 100000000000000000.0) THEN
      MTF = MTF / 1000000000000.0
      WRITE (8,275) MTF, SIGMA
275   FORMAT ( / ,11X, `SIMULATION RESULTS:'/
    $            11X, ` Median Time to Failure
    $                   (10^12 Hours) = ',F10.2 /
    $            11X, ` Lognormal Standard Deviation
    $                   = ',F10.2)
      MTF = MTF*1000000000000.0
      ELSE
      WRITE (8,276) MTF, SIGMA
276   FORMAT ( / ,11X, `SIMULATION RESULTS:'/
    $            11X, ` Median Time to Failure
    $                   (Hours)',F10.2 /
    $            11X, ` Lognormal Standard Deviation
    $                   = ',F10.2)
      END IF
      RETURN
      END
```

CHAPTER SIX

Future Interconnection Technologies

In this chapter three interconnection technologies that seem promising for future high-speed integrated circuits are discussed. First, active interconnections driven by several mechanisms are analyzed in Section 6.1. Next, in Section 6.2, the advantages, issues, and challenges associated with optical interconnections are discussed. The propagation characteristics of superconducting interconnections as well as a comparison of superconducting interconnections with normal metal interconnections are presented in Section 6.3.

6.1 ACTIVE INTERCONNECTIONS

It has been known for some time that transistors can be scaled down in size in such a way that the device propagation delay decreases in direct proportion to the device dimensions. However, if the interconnections are scaled down, it results in RC delays that begin to dominate the integrated circuit chip performance at submicron dimensions. In other words, for high-density high-speed submicron-geometry chips, it is mostly the interconnection rather than the device performance that determines the chip performance. So far, interconnection delays have been reduced by using higher-conductivity gate materials and multilayer interconnections and by keeping the interconnection thickness almost constant irrespective of the scaling of the devices, and so on. In fact, in scaling from the 10-μm to the 1-μm design rules, the interconnection thicknesses have been reduced by a factor of 2 or less. Now, because of the limitations of the optical lithography systems, it is essential that other approaches be developed to lower the interconnection delays. One way of solving this problem is to replace the passive interconnections on a chip by the active interconnections, that is, by inserting inverters or "repeaters" at appropriate spacings depending on the preferred driving mechanism.

Several methods for reducing transit delays in an interconnection have been discussed in the literature [6.1, 6.2]. These include driving the interconnection using minimum size inverters, optimum size inverters, and cascaded inverters. An analysis of these driving methods for silicon-based integrated circuits is presented in reference [6.1]. In this section these methods have been examined for GaAs-based integrated circuits [6.2]. Propagation times (defined as the time taken by the output signal to go from 0 to 90 percent of its steady-state value) have been calculated for each of these three methods for several interconnection dimensions and have been compared among each other and with the case when the interconnection is driven by a single typical GaAs MESFET. Results are given for two interconnection materials: aluminum with resistivity $\rho = 3 \ \mu\Omega \cdot$ cm and WSi_2 with $\rho = 30 \ \mu\Omega \cdot$ cm.

6.1.1   Interconnection Delay Model

An interconnection having a total resistance R_i and a capacitance C_i driven by a transistor of resistance R_s and driving a load capacitance C_L is shown in Figure 6.1.1. Assuming a unit step voltage source, the propagation times in distributed and lumped RC networks can be approximated as $1.0RC$ and $2.3RC$, respectively [6.3]. Therefore, an approximate expression for the total delay in the interconnection shown in Figure 6.1.1 will be

$$T_{90\%} = 1.0R_iC_i + 2.3(R_sC_L + R_sC_i + R_iC_L) \qquad (6.1.1)$$

Ignoring the terms containing the load capacitance C_L, we have

$$T_{90\%} \approx R_iC_i + 2.3R_sC_i \qquad (6.1.2)$$

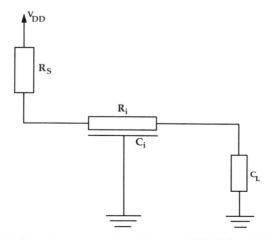

FIGURE 6.1.1   Interconnection delay model [6.1]. (© 1985 IEEE)

This expression is in agreement with that derived by Sakurai [6.4]. Because both the interconnection resistance and capacitance increase linearly with the length, the propagation time expressed by Equation 6.1.2 will increase nearly as the square of the interconnection length. It can be shown that this dependence can be made linear if the entire interconnection length is divided into smaller sections and each section is driven by a repeater.

6.1.2   Active Interconnection Driven by Minimum Size Inverters

A schematic diagram of an active interconnection driven by minimum size inverters as repeaters is shown in Figure 6.1.2. As shown in this figure, the use of inverters divides the interconnection into smaller subsections. The various symbols used in the figure are:

R_i = total resistance of the interconnection line
C_i = total capacitance of the interconnection line
R_r = output resistance of the minimum size inverter
C_r = input capacitance of the minimum size inverter
R_s = resistance of the GaAs MESFET
C_L = load capacitance
n = number of inverters

To achieve the shortest total propagation time using minimum size inverters, the optimum number of inverters can be found using calculus to be [6.1]

$$n = \sqrt{\frac{R_i C_i}{2.3 R_r C_r}} \qquad (6.1.3)$$

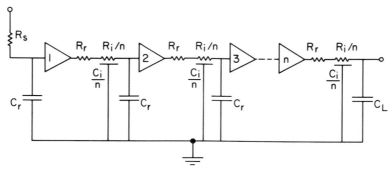

FIGURE 6.1.2   Schematic diagram of an interconnection driven by minimum size inverters [6.1]. (© 1985 IEEE)

TABLE 6.1.1   Comparison of the Propagation Times for the Four Methods of Driving an Interconnection and for Several Lengths of the Intercorrection

Interconnection Material: Aluminum ($\rho = 3 \, \mu\Omega \cdot cm$)

(Interconnection Width = Interconnection Separation = 1 μm; Load = 100 fF; Source Resistance = 700 Ω)

Propagation Times for the Four Driving Methods
(All Times Are in Nanoseconds)

Interconnection Length	GaAs MESFET	Minimum Size Repeaters	Optimum Size Repeaters	Cascaded Drivers
1 mm	0.05	a	a	0.24
2 mm	0.08	a	a	0.27
5 mm	0.17	2.31	0.11	0.34
1 cm	0.33	4.16	0.20	0.46
2 cm	0.80	7.87	0.29	0.76
5 cm	3.5	18.98	0.54	2.79
10 cm	15.1	37.51	0.97	11.49

a For interconnection lengths below 2 mm, the method was found unsuitable because the number of repeaters as given by the equation for n was less than 1.

The propagation time for each of the subsections driven by minimum size inverters can be determined by using the algorithm presented in Section 3.2, whereas the additional delay caused by the first stage can be found by the approximate expression for lumped RC networks given by Wilnai [6.3] to be $2.3 R_s C_r$. A listing of the computer program IPDMSR for determining the propagation time in an active interconnection driven by minimum size repeaters is presented in Appendix 6.1. The results using aluminum as the interconnection material are listed in Tables 6.1.1 and 6.1.2, whereas the results using WSi$_2$ as the interconnection material are listed in Tables 6.1.3 and 6.1.4.

6.1.3   Active Interconnection Driven by Optimum Size Inverters

Propagation times can be improved by increasing the size of the inverters by a factor of k, where k is given by [6.1]

$$k = \sqrt{\frac{R_r C_i}{R_i C_r}} \qquad (6.1.4)$$

This is because the current driving capability of the inverter is directly

TABLE 6.1.2   Comparison of the Propagation Times for the Four Methods of Driving an Interconnection and for Several Interconnection Widths

Interconnection Material: Aluminum ($\rho = 3\ \mu\Omega \cdot$ cm)

(Interconnection Length $= 1$ cm; Load $= 100$ fF; Source Resistance $= 700\ \Omega$)

Propagation Times for the Four Driving Methods
(All Times Are in Nanoseconds)

Interconnection Width	GaAs MESFET	Minimum Size Repeaters	Optimum Size Repeaters	Cascaded Drivers
0.1 μm	0.98	3.01	0.04	0.85
0.2 μm	0.50	3.10	0.08	0.52
0.5 μm	0.39	3.56	0.15	0.38
1.0 μm	0.33	4.03	0.20	0.46
2.0 μm	0.31	4.5	0.35	0.70
5.0 μm	0.25	a	a	1.38
10.0 μm	0.27	a	a	2.39

^{a}For interconnection widths above 5.0 μm, the method was found unsuitable because the number of repeaters as given by the equation for n was less than 1.

TABLE 6.1.3   Comparison of the Propagation Times for the Four Methods of Driving an Interconnection and for Several Lengths of the Interconnection

Interconnection Material: WSi$_2$ ($\rho = 30\ \mu\Omega \cdot$ cm)

(Interconnection Width $=$ Interconnection Separation $= 1\ \mu$m; Load $= 100$ fF; Source Resistance $= 700\ \Omega$)

Propagation Times for the Four Driving Methods
(All Times Are in Nanoseconds)

Interconnection Length	GaAs MESFET	Minimum Size Repeaters	Optimum Size Repeaters	Cascaded Drivers
1 mm	0.07	a	a	0.27
2 mm	0.14	1.11	0.13	0.34
5 mm	0.41	2.14	0.23	0.62
1 cm	1.35	3.85	0.39	1.42
2 cm	4.62	7.28	0.71	4.49
5 cm	9.6	17.55	1.67	22.3
10 cm	19.98	34.69	3.26	80.28

^{a}For interconnection lengths below 2 mm, the method was found unsuitable because the number of repeaters as given by the equation for n was less than 1.

TABLE 6.1.4   Comparison of the Propagation Times for the Four Methods of Driving an Interconnection and for Several Interconnection Widths

Interconnection Material: WSi$_2$ (ρ = 30 $\mu\Omega \cdot$ cm)

(Interconnection Width = Interconnection Separation = 1 μm; Load = 100 fF; Source Resistance = 700 Ω)

Propagation Times for the Four Driving Methods
(All Times Are in Nanoseconds)

Interconnection Width	GaAs MESFET	Minimum Size Repeaters	Optimum Size Repeaters	Cascaded Drivers
0.1 μm	8.9	2.79	0.05	10.6
0.2 μm	5.0	2.99	0.09	5.85
0.5 μm	2.21	3.5	0.38	2.18
1.0 μm	1.35	3.82	0.39	1.42
2.0 μm	0.8	4.34	0.42	1.19
5.0 μm	0.52	5.23	0.56	1.59
10.0 μm	0.36	6.34[a]	0.82[a]	2.48

[a]For interconnection widths above 10 μm, the method was found unsuitable because the number of repeaters as given by the equation for n was less than 1.

proportional to its width/length ratio. When this ratio is increased by a factor of k, the output resistance of the inverter becomes R_r/k and the input capacitance of the inverter becomes kC_r. A schematic diagram of an active interconnection driven by optimum size inverters is shown in Figure 6.1.3. In this case the additional delay caused by the first stage will be approximately $2.3kR_sC_r$. A listing of the computer program IPDOSR for determining the propagation time in an active interconnection driven by

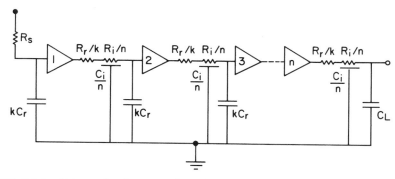

FIGURE 6.1.3   Schematic diagram of an interconnection driven by optimum size inverters [6.1]. (© 1985 IEEE)

optimum size repeaters is given in Appendix 6.2. The total propagation times for this case are also listed in Tables 6.1.1 to 6.1.4.

6.1.4   Active Interconnection Driven by Cascaded Inverters

A schematic diagram of an active interconnection driven by cascaded inverters is shown in Figure 6.1.4. In this case, instead of a single driver, a chain of inverters is used that increase in size until the last inverter is large enough to drive the interconnection. The optimal delay is obtained by using a sequence of n inverters that increase gradually in size (each by a factor of 2.71828 over the previous one). The optimum value of n is given by [6.1]

$$n = \ln\left[\frac{C_i}{C_r}\right] \qquad (6.1.5)$$

In this case the additional delay caused by the first stage and the first $n - 1$ inverters is given approximately by

$$2.3R_sC_r + 2.3(2.71828)(n - 1)R_rC_r \qquad (6.1.6)$$

and the propagation time in the interconnection driven by the last inverter can be found by using the algorithm presented in Section 3.2. A listing of the program IPDCR for determining the propagation time in an active interconnection driven by cascaded repeaters is presented in Appendix 6.3. The results for this case are listed in Tables 6.1.1 to 6.1.4.

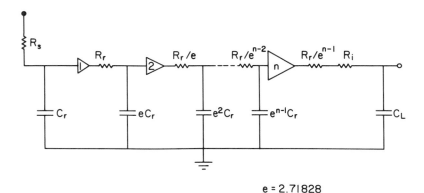

$$e = 2.71828$$

FIGURE 6.1.4   Schematic diagram of an interconnection driven by cascaded drivers [6.1]. (© 1985 IEEE)

6.1.5 Dependence of Propagation Time on Interconnection Driving Mechanism

A comparison of the propagation times for each of the four methods of driving an interconnection, that is, using a single GaAs MESFET, using minimum size inverters, using optimum size inverters, and using cascaded inverters, for several interconnection length values in the range 1 mm to 10 cm is shown in Table 6.1.1. For these results the interconnection material is taken to be aluminum and the other parameters are shown in the table. This table shows that minimum size and optimum size inverters cannot be used to drive interconnections of lengths of 2 mm and below. Otherwise, among the four methods, the method of using optimum size inverters yields the lowest propagation times. For interconnection lengths of 1 and 2 mm, using a single GaAs MESFET results in lower propagation times than the method of using cascaded inverters. Table 6.1.2 shows the propagation times for each of the four methods for several interconnection widths in the range 0.1 to 10.0 μm. This table shows that the methods of using minimum size and optimum size inverters are not suitable for interconnection widths of 5 μm and above. Otherwise, for interconnection widths below about 1 μm, the method of using optimum size inverters results in the lowest propagation times among the four methods. For interconnection widths between 2 and 10 μm, using a single GaAs MESFET yields the lowest propagation times.

When the interconnection material is changed to WSi_2, the propagation times for the four methods of driving an interconnection for several interconnection length and interconnection width values are shown in the Tables 6.1.3 and 6.1.4, respectively. These tables show that, in this case, minimum size and optimum size inverters cannot be used for interconnection lengths of 1 mm and below and for interconnection widths above 10 μm. The method of using optimum size inverters is found to result in the lowest propagation times for all interconnection length values (see Table 6.1.3) and for interconnection widths below 5 μm (see Table 6.1.4). For interconnection widths above 5 μm, driving the interconnection with a single GaAs MESFET results in the lowest propagation times.

6.2 OPTICAL INTERCONNECTIONS

As integrated circuits become larger in size and faster in speed, a large fraction of the available chip area and bandwidth is used by the interconnection system. Pinout and pin capacitance limitations place severe restrictions on the size and speed realizable by the integrated circuit. Furthermore, a large amount of power is used in driving the communication lines only. For example, on a typical current steering Shottky logic chip, 80 percent of its power is consumed in driving its communication lines [6.5]. Thus, conventional interconnections are becoming a major problem in the development of next-generation VLSI systems.

Optical interconnection technology is emerging rapidly to provide relief from the problems associated with conventional interconnections [6.6]. Techniques have been developed to integrate optical devices and materials with electronic circuits. It is now possible to integrate optoelectronic devices such as photodiodes, LEDs, and laser diodes with high-density silicon-based electronic circuits by depositing GaAs or other heterostructure layers on top of a processed silicon wafer and building the optical devices in the layers [6.7]. Techniques for constructing optical waveguides and mirrors on a silicon substrate have also been developed [6.8–6.10]. In this section the advantages, challenges, and other issues associated with optical interconnections are addressed [6.6].

6.2.1 Advantages of Optical Interconnections

On-chip as well as chip-to-chip optical interconnections offer several advantages over conventional interconnections in that they do not suffer from the drawbacks of the latter. As stated previously, the drawbacks of conventional interconnections become more pronounced when the integrated circuit becomes more complex either by scaling down the transistor size or by scaling up the chip size [6.11].

The first drawback of conventional interconnections results from their capacitive loading effects which increase as the chip size increases. In fact, in present-day chips, interconnection delays dominate the device delays and the chip speed is limited primarily by the delays associated with the interconnection capacitances. On the other hand, optical interconnections are free from any capacitive loading effects. The speed of propagation of a signal using an optical interconnection is determined by the speed of light and the refractive index of the optical transmission medium only. Even if the times taken to convert from an electrical signal to an optical signal and back are taken into consideration, optical interconnections turn out to be as fast as conventional interconnections for distances as small as a millimeter; for longer distances, an optical interconnection is much faster than a conventional metallic interconnection.

The second drawback of conventional interconnections is the crosstalk among the nearby electrical paths which is also caused by the stray and other coupling capacitances among the interconnections. This crosstalk increases as the interconnections are brought closer and as the bandwidth of the signals is increased. Furthermore, as the signal frequency goes up, the self-inductances and mutual inductances of the metallic interconnections go up, resulting in higher crosstalk. In contrast, optical interconnections do not suffer from the problem of crosstalk.

The next drawback of conventional interconnections is the limitation on the number of pinouts available for chip-to-chip connections on a chip.

According to a well-known empirical relationship, called Rent's rule, which applies to random logic circuitry, the number of pins required for chip-to-chip interconnections increases approximately as the 0.61th power of the number of devices and other components on the chip, whereas the perimeter available for fabricating these pins increases only as the 0.5th power of the number of devices on the chip. (In general, fewer pins are required for memories and more are required for telecommunications circuitry.) This problem can be alleviated with chip-to-chip optical interconnections because they operate at much higher speeds than conventional input/output (I/O) pins, allowing the multiplexing of a large number of I/O signals in a single I/O fiber. Furthermore, optical chip-to-chip interconnections can be anchored directly to the interior of a chip rather than to a pin on its perimeter.

The next problem faced by conventional metallic interconnections is their failure caused by electromigration. Electromigration-induced failure becomes more pronounced as the interconnections become smaller. Optical interconnections do not suffer from electromigration. However, it is interesting to note that optical interconnections can break down due to optical damage which occurs only in certain materials at rather high optical power densities. For example, for the optical medium $LiNbO_3$, the threshold for optical damage is of the order of tens of kilowatts per square centimeter and that for other optical dielectric materials such as glass and oxides is an order of magnitude higher.

It should be noted that when the limitations of conventional VLSI systems are alleviated by using optical interconnection technologies, several new computing architectures become available, allowing much quicker handling of complex problems such as matrix operations, digital filtering, distributed symbolic connections, and other interconnection-intensive algorithms. Furthermore, optical chip-to-chip interconnections offer the promise of significantly enhancing the performance of high-throughput performance systems such as supercomputers, and fifth-generation computing systems [6.12].

6.2.2   Systems Issues and Challenges

In order to develop large systems with optical interconnections, several researchers have chosen to employ thin-film waveguides rather than free-space, holographic, or optical fiber interconnections. This is primarily because the planarity of substrates with thin-film waveguides on them allows the use of conventional processing techniques, whereas the use of optical fibers for intrachip communication may require specialized equipment. In addition, holographic techniques are less mature than thin-film techniques. However, it should be noted that the use of thin-film waveguides poses alignment and coupling problems which can be resolved by careful process control.

The material chosen for the development of systems with optical interconnections depends on several factors. For constructing optical devices, many researchers have used epitaxial deposition on a silicon substrate because silicon offers a stable base for electronic circuitry and because long-wavelength optics requires epitaxial techniques on silicon or gallium arsenide. An additional advantage of silicon-based processing is that by developing an epitaxial technique for silicon that can yield three-dimensional structures, one can still incorporate a layer of GaAs circuitry where extremely high speed, available only with GaAs, is required. For example, GaAs circuitry may be used to provide multiplexors to achieve speed matching between the electronic circuitry and the optical interconnections.

Fault tolerance is a crucial issue in the development of large systems with optical interconnections. We have seen that the greatest advantage of optical interconnections lies in larger systems employing chip-to-chip, wafer-to-wafer, or board-to-board connections rather than in smaller systems employing on-chip connections. In addition, large systems have the greatest need for fault tolerance.

6.2.3 Material Processing Issues and Challenges

The development of optical interconnection systems requires specialized material processing techniques. One of the processing techniques that has shown great promise in this field is called molecular beam epitaxy (MBE). Currently, MBE is used primarily as a research tool, and it is important to make it widely available as a manufacturing process. MBE can be used to build the three-dimensional structures needed to build optoelectronic systems. For example, it can be used to deposit layers of compound semiconductors such as GaAs, GaInAlAsP, InAlAsP, and so forth to construct superlattices. The techniques to build optoelectronic components such as photodiodes, LEDs, and laser diodes using MBE need to be refined.

It is also important to refine the etching and material deposition techniques for constructing optical waveguides, mirrors, and so on. Techniques for anchoring optical fibers onto any part of a substrate with great accuracy need to be developed. Reliable connections between the Si and GaAs layers are required. It will be extremely helpful to integrate the processes for Si and GaAs which, at present, are very different [6.13]. Last but not least, it is obvious that optical interconnection technology will require many more processing steps than electronic circuit technologies, and it may be necessary to develop techniques to decrease the number of steps required to achieve an acceptable yield.

6.2.4 Design Issues and Challenges

Integrating on-chip and chip-to-chip optical interconnections with the electronic circuitry requires careful designing of the various optical structures such as optical waveguides, detectors, sources, and so forth. A few well-known materials for constructing optical waveguides are glass, zinc oxide, and silicon nitride. Material selection for the optical waveguide depends on several factors such as the refractive index of the material, attenuation at the wavelength of operation, ease of patterning, and ease of deposition. Channels with very smooth sidewalls are formed in the substrate such as silicon by an etching mechanism so that the light beam does not suffer significant loss due to scattering. The channels are tapered down in size to the size of the optical detector such that the transition from the waveguide to the detector is very gradual and does not cause any serious loss of signal.

The material in which the optical detector is fabricated depends on the wavelength of the optical signal. In future applications it is expected that the optical signal will be in the near infrared and the optical detectors will be fabricated on the silicon wafer itself because silicon is the best-known detector material at these wavelengths. However, silicon cuts off at 1.1 μm and, therefore, for optical signals of wavelength greater than 1.1 μm, the detectors and the sources will have to be fabricated in an InP-type compound semiconductor.

For fabricating an optical source, silicon is not a suitable substrate because it is an indirect bandgap material. On the other hand, GaAs is an excellent material for fabricating an extremely efficient and reliable light source. The best way of utilizing the silicon-based electronic circuitry with the GaAs source depends on successful heteroepitaxial techniques of depositing GaAs on silicon. This is done by first depositing a layer of germanium (Ge) on silicon because Ge and GaAs have closely matching lattice constants. The bandwidth of the structure will depend on the ability of the light source to modulate at high frequencies. Furthermore, the power from the source should be high enough for long-distance communication.

6.3   SUPERCONDUCTING INTERCONNECTIONS

6.3.1   Advantages of Superconducting Interconnections

The signal propagation characteristics, including transit delays, of chip-to-chip interconnection lines have a major effect on the total performance of an electronic system. An attempt to reduce the interconnection delays by scaling down their dimensions results in increased signal losses in the interconnection [6.14]. This is due to the increased series resistance and higher dispersion of the interconnection. This adverse effect can be almost eliminated by replacing normal metallic interconnections by superconducting interconnections which have very low series resistance at frequencies up to the energy gap frequency of the material [6.15, 6.16]. In fact, in recent years, the advent of high-critical-temperature superconductors [6.17–6.19] has opened up the possibility of realizing high-density and very fast interconnections on silicon as well as GaAs-based high-performance integrated circuits.

The major advantages of superconducting interconnections over normal metallic interconnections can be summarized as follows:

1. The signal propagation time on a superconducting interconnection will be much smaller than the signal propagation time on a normal metallic interconnection.
2. The packing density of the integrated circuit can be increased without incurring the high losses associated with high-density normal metallic interconnections.
3. There is virtually no signal dispersion on superconducting interconnections for frequencies up to several tens of gigahertz.

6.3.2 Propagation Characteristics of Superconducting Interconnections

In this subsection an analysis of the propagation characteristics [6.20] on a superconducting microstrip line with dielectric thickness t_d, strip line thickness t_c, ground plane thickness t_g, and penetration depth λ_L, shown in Figure 6.3.1, is presented. In the structure shown in Figure 6.3.1, material 1 is air with $\varepsilon_r = 1.0$; material 2 is Ba–Y–Cu–O with critical temperature $(T_c) = 92.5$ K, normal state resistivity $(\rho_n) = 200\ \mu\Omega \cdot$ cm, $\lambda_L(0) = 1400$ Å; material 3 is SiO$_2$ with $\varepsilon_r = 3.9$; material 4 is Ba–Y–Cu–O with $T_c = 92.5$ K, $\rho_n = 200\ \mu\Omega \cdot$ cm, $\lambda_L(0) = 1400$ Å; and material 5 is SiO$_2$ with $\varepsilon_r = 3.9$. It is assumed that the permeability of each medium is that of the free space μ_0, the loss tangent of dielectrics is negligible, the fringing field effects at the edges of the line can be neglected, and high T_c superconductors have standard superconducting behavior below J_c, H_{c1}, T_c, and the energy gap

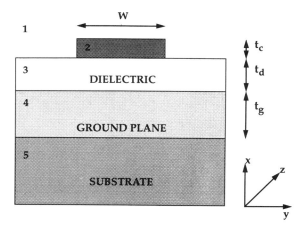

FIGURE 6.3.1   Schematic diagram of the superconducting microstrip structure analyzed in this section [6.20]. (© 1987 IEEE)

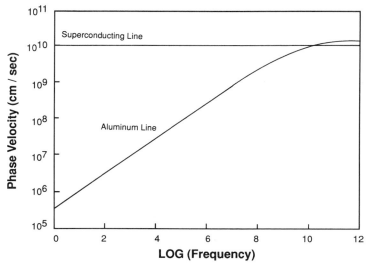

FIGURE 6.3.2   Comparison of the phase velocities at 77 K for superconducting and normal aluminum lines [6.20]. (© 1987 IEEE)

frequency. It can be further assumed that the only nonzero component of the magnetic field is H_y and that all fields are independent of y. In other words, in addition to the time dependence given by $e^{j\omega t}$, the nonzero field components in rectangular coordinates are $H_y(x)e^{-\gamma z}$, $E_x(x)e^{-\gamma z}$, and $E_z(x)e^{-\gamma z}$.

Using the two-fluid model [6.21, 6.22], the total current J_T in a superconductor consists of normal current J_n and a supercurrent J_s; that is,

$$\mathbf{J}_T = \mathbf{J}_n + \mathbf{J}_s \tag{6.3.1}$$

where the supercurrent component obeys London's equations

$$\begin{aligned} \mathbf{E} &= j\omega\mu_0\lambda_L^2\mathbf{J}_s \\ \mathbf{H} &= -\lambda_L^2\nabla \times \mathbf{J}_s \end{aligned} \tag{6.3.2}$$

where λ_L is the penetration depth of the superconductor. The boundary value problem presented in Figure 6.3.1 can be solved by using Equations 6.3.1 and 6.3.2 and Maxwell's equations to obtain the propagation constant γ which is valid for frequencies up to several gigahertz (note that the normal current component is negligible for these frequencies). The propagation constant γ is given by

$$\gamma^2 = -\mu_0\varepsilon_3\omega^2\left[1 + \frac{\lambda_{L,2}}{t_d}\coth\left(\frac{t_c}{\lambda_{L,2}}\right) + \frac{\lambda_{L,4}}{t_d}\coth\left(\frac{t_g}{\lambda_{L,4}}\right)\right] \tag{6.3.3}$$

According to Equation 6.3.3, γ is purely imaginary, indicating that the propagation characteristics of a superconducting microstrip line are lossless and dispersionless.

The phase velocity of propagation for the superconducting microstrip is given by

$$v_p = \frac{\omega}{\text{Im}(\gamma)} = \frac{1}{\sqrt{\mu_0 \varepsilon_3 \left[1 + \dfrac{\lambda_{L,2}}{t_d} \coth\left(\dfrac{t_c}{\lambda_{L,2}} \right) + \dfrac{\lambda_{L,4}}{t_d} \coth\left(\dfrac{t_g}{\lambda_{L,4}} \right) \right]}} \quad (6.3.4)$$

Equation 6.3.4 indicates that the phase velocity depends strongly on the superconducting layer thickness, the penetration depth of the superconducting layers, and the dielectric constants of the dielectric layers. Because the penetration depth is a function of the temperature given by

$$\lambda_L(T) = \frac{\lambda_L(0)}{\sqrt{1 - \left(\dfrac{T}{T_c} \right)^4}} \quad (6.3.5)$$

the phase velocity also depends on the temperature, particularly for temperatures near the critical temperature T_c. It can also be seen from Equation 6.3.4 that the phase velocity is a function of the dielectric constant only when the dielectric thickness and the superconducting layer thickness are much larger than the penetration depth.

Using the two-fluid model, the conductivity of a superconductor is given by [6.22]

$$\sigma = \sigma_{\text{normal}} \left(\frac{T}{T_c} \right)^4 - j \frac{1}{\mu_0 \omega [\lambda_{L,2}(0)]^2} \left[1 - \left(\frac{T}{T_c} \right)^4 \right] \quad (6.3.6)$$

where σ_{normal} is the normal state conductivity of the superconductor at a temperature just above T_c.

6.3.3 Comparison with Normal Metallic Interconnections

In this subsection a comparison of the propagation characteristics of superconducting and normal aluminum interconnections at 77 K [6.20] is presented. The interconnection dimensions and other transmission line parameters for the aluminum line are as follows:

Width of the microstrip line $(W) = 2~\mu m$

Thickness of the microstrip $(t_c) = 0.5~\mu m$

Interdielectric thickness $(t_d) = 1~\mu m$

Ground plane thickness $(t_g) = 1~\mu m$

Relative dielectric constant for the interdielectric = 3.9

Relative dielectric constant for the substrate = 3.9

Conductivity of 0.5-μm-thick aluminum at 77 K = 1.5×10^6 S/cm

Capacitance of the line = 1.54 pF/cm

Inductance of the line for frequencies up to 10 GHz = 2.95 nH/cm (decreasing to 2.25 nH/cm for frequencies above 100 GHz, due to skin effect)

Series resistance of the line for frequencies up to 10 GHz = 77.6 Ω/cm (increases as the frequency increases above 10 GHz, due to skin effect)

A comparison of the phase velocities at 77 K for the superconducting line and the aluminum line for frequencies up to 10^{12} Hz is shown in Figure 6.3.2 (p. 579), and a comparison of the attenuation for the two lines in the frequency range 10^6 to 10^{12} Hz is shown in Figure 6.3.3. First, for the normal aluminum interconnection line, it can be seen that its phase velocity is much

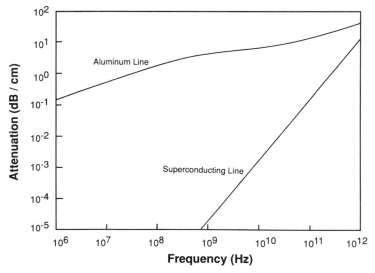

FIGURE 6.3.3 Comparison of the attenuations at 77 K for superconducting and normal aluminum lines [6.20]. (© 1987 IEEE)

less than that of the superconducting line for frequencies up to 100 MHz. Furthermore, its phase velocity depends very strongly on the frequency, indicating that the line is very dispersive. Figure 6.3.3 indicates that, for the normal aluminum line, its maximum useful length (attenuation < 3 dB) is limited by attenuation to be 2 cm at 100 MHz and only 2 mm at 10 GHz.

For the superconducting interconnection line, it can be seen from Figure 6.3.2 that its phase velocity is nearly constant at frequencies up to 1 THz at 77 K; that is, the line is virtually nondispersive. However, as shown in Figure 6.3.3, the attenuation of the superconducting line is a function of frequency and temperature; it is very small for frequencies up to 10 GHz and increases with increasing frequency. Therefore, superconducting interconnections can operate with negligible dispersion and low loss at frequencies of several gigahertz for lengths exceeding several meters.

EXERCISES

E6.1 Show that for the shortest total propagation time using minimum size inverters, the optimum number of inverters is given by the following expression (symbols are defined in Section 6.1.2):

$$n = \sqrt{\frac{R_i C_i}{2.3 R_r C_r}}$$

E6.2 Show that the value of k for optimum size inverters is given by the following expression (symbols are defined in Section 6.1.2):

$$k = \sqrt{\frac{R_r C_i}{R_i C_r}}$$

E6.3 Show that the optimal delay is obtained by using a sequence of n inverters that increase gradually in size (each by a factor of 2.71828 over the previous one), where n is given by the following expression (symbols are defined in Section 6.1.2):

$$n = \ln\left[\frac{C_i}{C_r}\right]$$

E6.4 Think about the various research problems that need to be solved before optical interconnections can be used for on-chip and chip-to-chip communications.

E6.5 Think about the various research problems that need to be solved
before superconducting interconnections can be used for on-chip and
chip-to-chip communications.

APPENDIX 6.1

IPDMSR
Propagation Delays in an Active Interconnection Driven by Minimum Size Repeaters

```
C*****DECLARING THE VARIABLES
      REAL IW,IL,SIGMA,DW,T,S1,S2,LI,RI,RS,AD,K,
     $     T1,V,CI,CL1,CL2,CR1,CR2,CIL1,CIR1,CIL2,
     $     CIR2,NF,TERM1,RO,IL1,C,C1,IW1,RR,CR,RINT,
     $     CINT
      INTEGER N,M
      COMPLEX*8 S,G,VS,VT,TERM,S3,Y1,Y2,Y3,Y4,ZL,Z0,
     $           A,B
      WRITE (*,160)
  160 FORMAT ( 'PROPAGATION DELAYS IN PARALLEL
     $          INTERCONNECTIONS'/,
     $          'RESULTS FOR LOSSY LINES'/ 'LOAD:C'/
     $          'SOURCE RESISTANCE = RS'/
     $          'USING MINIMUM SIZE REPEATERS:'/
     $          'COUPLING INCLUDED: FIRST AND SECOND
     $          NEIGHBORS'// )
   10 READ (*,100,END = 999) IW,IL,RO,C1,RS
  100 FORMAT (F6.2,X,F6.2,X,F6.2,X,F6.0,X,F6.0)
      LI = IW * (10.0 ** (-7))
      RI = RO*2.0 * (10.0 ** 4) / IW
C*****TYPICAL VALUES FOR MINIMUM SIZE REPEATERS
      RR = 10000.0
      CR = IW*1.17*(10.0 ** (-15))
C*****CALCULATING V(t) AFTER INCLUDING THE NEIGHBOR
C     COUPLINGS
      CALL SCIC (IW,C11,C22,C33,C12,C13,C23)
      CI   = C22*(10.0 ** (-11))
      CIR1 = C23*(10.0 ** (-11))
      CIR2 = C13*(10.0 ** (-11))
      CIL1 = C12*(10.0 ** (-11))
      CIL2 = C13*(10.0 ** (-11))
      CR1  = C22*(10.0 ** (-11))
      CR2  = C22*(10.0 ** (-11))
      CL1  = C22*(10.0 ** (-11))
```

```
      CL2  = C22*(10.0 ** (-11))
      C    = C1*(10.0 ** (-15))
      IL1  = IL*(10.0 ** (-6))
      IW1  = IW*(10.0)
      S3   = (-1.0,0.0)
      CINT = CI * IL1
      RINT = RI * IL1
      K    = SQRT((RINT*CINT) / (2.3*RR*CR))
      IL1  = IL1 / K
      AD   = 2.3 * RS * CR * (10.0 ** 12)
      WRITE (*,165) AD,K
  165 FORMAT ( 'ADDITIONAL DELAY = ',F15.9, 'ps'/
     $          'NUMBER OF REPEATERS = ', F10.4,/,
     $          'FOR THE FIRST K-1 SECTIONS:'/ )
C*****FOR THE FIRST K-1 SECTIONS
C*****CALCULATION OF THE NORMALIZATION FACTOR
      T    = 100.0
      V    = 0.0
      T1   = T*(10.0 ** (-9))
      SIGMA = 0.5*T1
      DW   = 0.05 / T1
      VT   = (0.0,0.0)
      M    = 1000
      DO 2003 N = 1,M,1
      S1   = SIGMA
      S2   = N*DW
      S    = CMPLX(S1,S2)
      Y1   = S*CR1*CIR1 / (CIR1 + CR1)
      Y2   = S*CR2*CIR2 / (CIR2 + CR2)
      Y3   = S*CL1*CIL1 / (CIL1 + CL1)
      Y4   = S*CL2*CIL2 / (CIL2 + CL2)
      G    = CSQRT((Y1 + Y2 + Y3 + Y4 + S*CI)*(RI + S*LI))
      Z0   = CSQRT((RI + S*LI) / (Y1 + Y2 + Y3 + Y4 + S*CI))
      ZL   = 1.0 / (S*CR)
      A    = (Z0 / S) / (RR + Z0- (RR- Z0)*((ZL- Z0) /
     $       (ZL + Z0))*CEXP(-2*G*IL1))
      B    = ((ZL- Z0) / (ZL + Z0))*CEXP(-2*G*IL1)*A
      VS   = B*CEXP(G*IL1) + A*CEXP(-G*IL1)
      TERM = VS*DW*(COS(S2*T1) + (CSQRT(S3))
     $       *SIN(S2*T1))*EXP(SIGMA*T1) / 6.284
      TERM1 = REAL(TERM)
      VT   = VT + TERM1
 2003 CONTINUE
      V    = CABS(VT)
      NF   = 1.0 / V
```

```
      WRITE (*,161)
 161  FORMAT ( / ,4X, 'IW',9X, 'IL',9X,
     $           'RO(microohm.cm)',4X, 't(ps)',9X, 'V(t)')
      DO 2100 T = 10.0,100.0,10.0
      V     = 0.0
      T1    = T*(10.0 ** (-12))
      SIGMA = 0.5*T1
      DW    = 0.05 / T1
      VT    = (0.0,0.0)
      M     = 600
      DO 2000 N = 1,M,1
      S1    = SIGMA
      S2    = N*DW
      S     = CMPLX(S1,S2)
      Y1    = S*CR1*CIR1 / (CIR1 + CR1)
      Y2    = S*CR2*CIR2 / (CIR2 + CR2)
      Y3    = S*CL1*CIL1 / (CIL1 + CL1)
      Y4    = S*CL2*CIL2 / (CIL2 + CL2)
      G     = CSQRT((Y1 + Y2 + Y3 + Y4 + S*CI)*(RI + S*LI))
      Z0    = CSQRT((RI + S*LI) / (Y1 + Y2 + Y3 + Y4 + S*CI))
      ZL    = 1.0 / (S*CR)
      A     = (Z0 / S) / (RR + Z0- (RR- Z0)*((ZL- Z0) /
     $        (ZL + Z0))*CEXP(- 2*G*IL1))
      B     = ((ZL- Z0) / (ZL + Z0))*CEXP(- 2*G*IL1)*A
      VS    = B*CEXP(G*IL1) + A*CEXP(- G*IL1)
      TERM  = VS*DW*(COS(S2*T1) + (CSQRT(S3))
     $        *SIN(S2*T1))*EXP(SIGMA*T1) / 6.284
      TERM1 = REAL(TERM)
      VT    = VT + TERM1
 2000 CONTINUE
      V     = CABS(VT)*NF
      WRITE (*,300) IW1,IL,RO,T,V
 300  FORMAT (F6.2,5X,F7.2,5X,F7.2,12X,F7.3,5X,F15.3)
 2100 CONTINUE
C*****FOR THE LAST SECTION
      WRITE (*,465)
 465  FORMAT ( 'FOR THE LAST SECTION'/ )
C*****CALCULATION OF THE NORMALIZATION FACTOR
      T     = 100.0
      V     = 0.0
      T1    = T*(10.0 ** (-9))
      SIGMA = 0.5*T1
      DW    = 0.05 / T1
      VT    = (0.0,0.0)
      M     = 1000
```

```
      DO 4003 N = 1,M,1
      S1    = SIGMA
      S2    = N*DW
      S     = CMPLX(S1,S2)
      Y1    = S*CR1*CIR1 / (CIR1 + CR1)
      Y2    = S*CR2*CIR2 / (CIR2 + CR2)
      Y3    = S*CL1*CIL1 / (CIL1 + CL1)
      Y4    = S*CL2*CIL2 / (CIL2 + CL2)
      G     = CSQRT((Y1 + Y2 + Y3 + Y4 + S*CI)*(RI + S*LI))
      Z0    = CSQRT((RI + S*LI) / (Y1 + Y2 + Y3 + Y4 + S*CI))
      ZL    = 1.0 / (S*C)
      A     = (Z0 / S) / (RR + Z0- (RR- Z0)*((ZL- Z0) / (ZL +
     $        Z0))*CEXP(- 2*G*IL1))
      B     = ((ZL- Z0) / (ZL + Z0))*CEXP(- 2*G*IL1)*A
      VS    = B*CEXP(G*IL1) + A*CEXP(- G*IL1)
      TERM  = VS*DW*(COS(S2*T1) + (CSQRT(S3))*SIN(S2*
     $        T1))*EXP(SIGMA*T1) / 6.284
      TERM1 = REAL(TERM)
      VT    = VT + TERM1
 4003 CONTINUE
      V     = CABS(VT)
      NF    = 1.0 / V
      WRITE (*,461)
  461 FORMAT ( / ,4X, `IW',9X, `IL',9X, `RO(microohm.cm)',
     $        4X, `t(ns)',9X, `V(t)')
      DO 4100 T = 10.0,100.0,10.0
      V     = 0.0
      T1    = T*(10.0 ** (- 12))
      SIGMA = 0.5*T1
      DW    = 0.05 / T1
      VT    = (0.0,0.0)
      M     = 600
      DO 4000 N = 1,M,1
      S1    = SIGMA
      S2    = N*DW
      S     = CMPLX(S1,S2)
      Y1    = S*CR1*CIR1 / (CIR1 + CR1)
      Y2    = S*CR2*CIR2 / (CIR2 + CR2)
      Y3    = S*CL1*CIL1 / (CIL1 + CL1)
      Y4    = S*CL2*CIL2 / (CIL2 + CL2)
      G     = CSQRT((Y1 + Y2 + Y3 + Y4 + S*CI)*(RI + S*LI))
      Z0    = CSQRT((RI + S*LI) / (Y1 + Y2 + Y3 + Y4 + S*CI))
      ZL    = 1.0 / (S*C)
      A     = (Z0 / S) / (RR + Z0- (RR- Z0)*((ZL- Z0) / (ZL +
     $        Z0))*CEXP(- 2*G*IL1))
```

```
      B        = ((ZL-Z0)/(ZL+Z0))*CEXP(-2*G*IL1)*A
      VS       = B*CEXP(G*IL1)+A*CEXP(-G*IL1)
      TERM     = VS*DW*(COS(S2*T1)+(CSQRT(S3))*SIN(S2
     $           *T1))*EXP(SIGMA*T1)/6.284
      TERM1    = REAL(TERM)
      VT       = VT+TERM1
 4000 CONTINUE
      V        = CABS(VT)*NF
      WRITE (*,500) IW1,IL,RO,T,V
  500 FORMAT (F6.2,5X,F7.2,5X,F7.2,12X,F7.3,5X,F15.3)
 4100 CONTINUE
      GO TO 10
  999 STOP
      END

      SUBROUTINE SCIC
      (Same as in Appendix 3.1)
```

APPENDIX 6.2

IPDOSR
Propagation Delays in an Active Interconnection Driven by Optimum Size Repeaters

```
C*****DECLARING THE VARIABLES
      REAL IW,IL,SIGMA,DW,T,S1,S2,LI,RI,RS,AD,K,
     $     T1,V,CI,CL1,CL2,CR1,CR2,CIL1,CIR1,CIL2,
     $     CIR2,NF,TERM1,RO,IL1,C,C1,IW1,RR,CR,RINT,
     $     CINT,H
      INTEGER N,M
      COMPLEX*8 S,G,VS,VT,TERM,S3,Y1,Y2,Y3,Y4,ZL,Z0,
     $          A,B
      WRITE (*,160)
  160 FORMAT ( `PROPAGATION DELAYS IN PARALLEL
     $          INTERCONNECTIONS'/,
     $          `RESULTS FOR LOSSY LINES'/ `LOAD:C'/
     $          `SOURCE RESISTANCE=RS'/
     $          `USING OPTIMUM SIZE REPEATERS:'/
     $          `COUPLING INCLUDED: FIRST AND SECOND
     $          NEIGHBORS'// )
C*****INPUT (IW AND IL ARE IN MICROMETERS; RO IS IN
C            MICROOHM.CM )
   10 READ (*,100,END=999) IW,IL,RO,C1,RS
  100 FORMAT (F6.2,X,F6.2,X,F6.2,X,F6.0,X,F6.0)
```

```
      LI = IW * (10.0 ** (-7))
      RI = RO*2.0 * (10.0 ** 4) / IW
C*****TYPICAL VALUES FOR MINIMUM SIZE REPEATERS
      RR = 10000.0
      CR = IW*1.17*(10.0 ** (-15))
C*****CALCULATING V(t) AFTER INCLUDING THE NEIGHBOR
C     COUPLINGS:
      CALL SCIC (IW,C11,C22,C33,C12,C13,C23)
      CI   = C22*(10.0 ** (-11))
      CIR1 = C23*(10.0 ** (-11))
      CIR2 = C13*(10.0 ** (-11))
      CIL1 = C12*(10.0 ** (-11))
      CIL2 = C13*(10.0 ** (-11))
      CR1  = C22*(10.0 ** (-11))
      CR2  = C22*(10.0 ** (-11))
      CL1  = C22*(10.0 ** (-11))
      CL2  = C22*(10.0 ** (-11))
      C    = C1*(10.0 ** (-15))
      IL1  = IL*(10.0 ** (-6))
      IW1  = IW*(10.0)
      S3   = (-1.0,0.0)
      CINT = CI * IL1
      RINT = RI * IL1
      K    = SQRT((RINT*CINT) / (2.3*RR*CR))
      H    = SQRT((RR*CINT) / (RINT*CR))
      IL1  = IL1 / K
      AD   = 2.3 * RS * CR * H * (10.0 ** 12)
      WRITE (*,165) AD,K
  165 FORMAT ( `ADDITIONAL DELAY = ',F15.9, `ps',/,
     $          `NUMBER OF REPEATERS = ', F10.4,/,
     $          `FOR THE FIRST K-1 SECTIONS:',/ )
C*****FOR THE FIRST K-1 SECTIONS
      RR   = RR / H
      CR   = CR*H
C*****CALCULATION OF THE NORMALIZATION FACTOR
      T    = 100.0
      V    = 0.0
      T1   = T*(10.0 ** (-9))
      SIGMA= 0.5*T1
      DW   = 0.05 / T1
      VT   = (0.0,0.0)
      M    = 1000
      DO 2003 N=1,M,1
      S1   = SIGMA
      S2   = N*DW
      S    = CMPLX(S1,S2)
```

```
     Y1    = S*CR1*CIR1 / (CIR1 + CR1)
     Y2    = S*CR2*CIR2 / (CIR2 + CR2)
     Y3    = S*CL1*CIL1 / (CIL1 + CL1)
     Y4    = S*CL2*CIL2 / (CIL2 + CL2)
     G     = CSQRT((Y1 + Y2 + Y3 + Y4 + S*CI)*(RI + S*LI))
     Z0    = CSQRT((RI + S*LI) / (Y1 + Y2 + Y3 + Y4 + S*CI))
     ZL    = 1.0 / (S*CR)
     A     = (Z0 / S) / (RR + Z0- (RR- Z0)*((ZL- Z0) / (ZL +
    $        Z0))*CEXP(- 2*G*IL1))
     B     = ((ZL- Z0) / (ZL + Z0))*CEXP(- 2*G*IL1)*A
     VS    = B*CEXP(G*IL1) + A*CEXP(- G*IL1)
     TERM  = VS*DW*(COS(S2*T1) + (CSQRT(S3))*SIN(S2*T1))
    $        *EXP(SIGMA*T1) / 6.284
     TERM1= REAL(TERM)
     VT    = VT + TERM1
2003 CONTINUE
     V     = CABS(VT)
     NF    = 1.0 / V
     WRITE (*,161)
161  FORMAT ( / ,4X, `IW',9X, `IL',9X, `RO(microohm.cm)
    $          ',4X, `t(ps)',9X, `V(t)')
     DO 2100 T = 10.0,100.0,10.0
     V     = 0.0
     T1    = T*(10.0 ** (-12))
     SIGMA= 0.5*T1
     DW    = 0.05 / T1
     VT    = (0.0,0.0)
     M     = 600
     DO 2000 N = 1,M,1
     S1    = SIGMA
     S2    = N*DW
     S     = CMPLX(S1,S2)
     Y1    = S*CR1*CIR1 / (CIR1 + CR1)
     Y2    = S*CR2*CIR2 / (CIR2 + CR2)
     Y3    = S*CL1*CIL1 / (CIL1 + CL1)
     Y4    = S*CL2*CIL2 / (CIL2 + CL2)
     G     = CSQRT((Y1 + Y2 + Y3 + Y4 + S*CI)*(RI + S*LI))
     Z0    = CSQRT((RI + S*LI) / (Y1 + Y2 + Y3 + Y4 + S*CI))
     ZL    = 1.0 / (S*CR)
     A     = (Z0 / S) / (RR + Z0- (RR- Z0)*((ZL- Z0) / (ZL +
    $        Z0))*CEXP(- 2*G*IL1))
     B     = ((ZL- Z0) / (ZL + Z0))*CEXP(- 2*G*IL1)*A
     VS    = B*CEXP(G*IL1) + A*CEXP(- G*IL1)
     TERM  = VS*DW*(COS(S2*T1) + (CSQRT(S3))*SIN(S2*T1))
    $        *EXP(SIGMA*T1) / 6.284
     TERM1= REAL(TERM)
```

```
      VT   = VT + TERM1
 2000 CONTINUE
      V    = CABS(VT)*NF
C*****WRITING THE RESULTS
      WRITE (*,300) IW1,IL,RO,T,V
  300 FORMAT (F6.2,5X,F7.2,5X,F7.2,12X,F7.3,5X,F15.3)
 2100 CONTINUE
C*****FOR THE LAST SECTION
      WRITE (*,465)
  465 FORMAT ( 'FOR THE LAST SECTION'/ )
C*****CALCULATION OF THE NORMALIZATION FACTOR
      T    = 100.0
      V    = 0.0
      T1   = T*(10.0 ** (-9))
      SIGMA= 0.5*T1
      DW   = 0.05 / T1
      VT   = (0.0,0.0)
      M    = 1000
      DO 4003 N = 1,M,1
      S1   = SIGMA
      S2   = N*DW
      S    = CMPLX(S1,S2)
      Y1   = S*CR1*CIR1 / (CIR1 + CR1)
      Y2   = S*CR2*CIR2 / (CIR2 + CR2)
      Y3   = S*CL1*CIL1 / (CIL1 + CL1)
      Y4   = S*CL2*CIL2 / (CIL2 + CL2)
      G    = CSQRT((Y1 + Y2 + Y3 + Y4 + S*CI)*(RI + S*LI))
      Z0   = CSQRT((RI + S*LI) / (Y1 + Y2 + Y3 + Y4 + S*CI))
      ZL   = 1.0 / (S*C)
      A    = (Z0 / S) / (RR + Z0- (RR- Z0)*((ZL- Z0) / (ZL
     $       +Z0))*CEXP(- 2*G*IL1))
      B    = ((ZL- Z0) / (ZL + Z0)*CEXP(- 2*G*IL1)*A
      VS   = B*CEXP(G*IL1) + A*CEXP(- G*IL1)
      TERM = VS*DW*(COS(S2*T1) + (CSQRT(S3))*SIN(S2*T1)
     $       *EXP(SIGMA*T1) / 6.284
      TERM1= REAL(TERM)
      VT   = VT + TERM1
 4003 CONTINUE
      V    = CABS(VT)
      NF   = 1.0 / V
      WRITE (*,461)
  461 FORMAT ( / ,4X, 'IW',9X, 'IL',9X, 'RO(microohm.cm)',
     $          4X, 't(ns)',9X, 'V(t)')
      DO 4100 T = 10.0,100.0,10.0
      V    = 0.0
      T1   = T*(10.0 ** (-12))
```

```
       SIGMA= 0.5*T1
       DW    = 0.05 / T1
       VT    = (0.0,0.0)
       M     = 600
       DO 4000 N = 1,M,1
       S1    = SIGMA
       S2    = N*DW
       S     = CMPLX(S1,S2)
       Y1    = S*CR1*CIR1 / (CIR1 + CR1)
       Y2    = S*CR2*CIR2 / (CIR2 + CR2)
       Y3    = S*CL1*CIL1 / )CIL1 + CL1)
       Y4    = S*CL2*CIL2 / (CIL2 + CL2)
       G     = CSQRT((Y1 + Y2 + Y3 + Y4 + S*CI)*(RI + S*LI))
       Z0    = CSQRT((RI + S*LI) / (Y1 + Y2 + Y3 + Y4 + S*CI))
       ZL    = 1.0 / (S*C)
       A     = (Z0 / S) / (RR + Z0 - (RR - Z0)*((ZL - Z0) / (ZL +
      $        Z0))*CEXP(-2*G*IL1))
       B     = ((ZL - Z0) / (ZL + Z0))*CEXP(-2*G*IL1)*A
       VS    = B*CEXP(G*IL1) + A*CEXP(-G*IL1)
       TERM  = VS*DW*(COS(S2*T1) + (CSQRT(S3))*SIN(S2*T1))
      $        *EXP(SIGMA*T1) / 6.284
       TERM1= REAL(TERM)
       VT    = VT + TERM1
 4000 CONTINUE
       V     = CABS(VT)*NF
       WRITE (*,500) IW1,IL,RO,T,V
 500   FORMAT (F6.2,5X,F7.2,5X,F7.2,12X,F7.3,5X,F15.3)
 4100 CONTINUE
       GO TO 10
 999   STOP
       END

       SUBROUTINE SCIC
       (Same as in Appendix 3.1)
```

APPENDIX 6.3

IPDCR
Propagation Delays in an Active Interconnection Driven by Cascaded Repeaters

```
C*****DECLARING THE VARIABLES
       REAL IW,IL,SIGMA,DW,T,S1,S2,LI,RI,RS,AD,K,
      $     T1,V,CI,CL1,CL2,CR1,CR2,CIL1,CIR1,CIL2,
      $     CIR2,NF,TERM1,RO,IL1,C,C1,IW1,RR,CR,RINT,
```

```
      $     CINT
       INTEGER N,M
       COMPLEX*8 S,G,VS,VT,TERM,S3,Y1,Y2,Y3,Y4,ZL,Z0,
      $         A,B
       WRITE (*,160)
 160   FORMAT ( `PROPAGATION DELAYS IN PARALLEL
      $          INTERCONNECTIONS'/,
      $          'RESULTS FOR LOSSY LINES'/ `LOAD:C'/
      $          'SOURCE RESISTANCE = RS'/
      $          'USING CASCADED DRIVERS:'/
      $          'COUPLING INCLUDED: FIRST AND SECOND
      $          NEIGHBORS'// )
C*****INPUT ( IW AND IL ARE IN MICROMETERS; RO IS IN
C          MICROOHM.CM )
 10    READ (*,100,END=999) IW,IL,RO,C1,RS
 100   FORMAT (F6.2,X,F6.2,X,F6.2,X,F6.0,X,F6.0)
       LI = IW * (10.0 ** (-7))
       RI = RO*2.0 * (10.0 ** 4) / IW
       RR = 10000.0
       CR = IW*1.17*(10.0 ** (-15))
C*****CALCULATING V(t) AFTER INCLUDING THE NEIGHBOR
C      COUPLINGS:
       CALL SCIC (IW,C11,C22,C33,C12,C13,C23)
       CI   = C22*(10.0 ** (-11))
       CIR1 = C23*(10.0 ** (-11))
       CIR2 = C13*(10.0 ** (-11))
       CIL1 = C12*(10.0 ** (-11))
       CIL2 = C13*(10.0 ** (-11))
       CR1  = C22*(10.0 ** (-11))
       CR2  = C22*(10.0 ** (-11))
       CL1  = C22*(10.0 ** (-11))
       CL2  = C22*(10.0 ** (-11))
       C    = C1*(10.0 ** (-15))
       IL1  = IL*(10.0 ** (-6))
       IW1  = IW*(10.0)
       S3   = (-1.0,0.0)
       CINT = CI * IL1
       RINT = RI * IL1
       K    = LOG(CINT / CR)
       AD   = (2.3*RS*CR+2.3*2.7183*RR*CR*(K
      $      -1))*(10.0**12)
       WRITE (*,165) AD,K
 165   FORMAT ( `ADDITIONAL DELAY = ',F14.9, `ps',/,
      $         NUMBER OF DRIVERS = 5 ', F10.4,/ )
```

```
C*****FOR THE LAST SECTION
      WRITE (*,465)
  465 FORMAT ('FOR THE LAST SECTION'/)
      RR = RR / (2.7183 ** (K- 1))
C*****CALCULATION OF THE NORMALIZATION FACTOR
      T     = 1000.0
      V     = 0.0
      T1    = T*(10.0 ** (- 9))
      SIGMA= 0.5*T1
      DW    = 0.05 / T1
      VT    = (0.0,0.0)
      M     = 1000
      DO 4003 N = 1,M,1
      S1    = SIGMA
      S2    = N*DW
      S     = CMPLX(S1,S2)
      Y1    = S*CR1*CIR1 / (CIR1 + CR1)
      Y2    = S*CR2*CIR2 / (CIR2 + CR2)
      Y3    = S*CL1*CIL1 / (CIL1 + CL1)
      Y4    = S*CL2*CIL2 / (CIL2 + CL2)
      G     = CSQRT((Y1 + Y2 + Y3 + Y4 + S*CI)*(RI + S*LI))
      Z0    = CSQRT((RI + S*LI) / (Y1 + Y2 + Y3 + Y4 + S*CI))
      ZL    = 1.0 / (S*C)
      A     = (Z0 / S) / (RR + Z0- (RR- Z0)*((ZL- Z0) / (ZL +
     $        Z0))*CEXP(- 2*G*IL1))
      B     = ((ZL- Z0) / (ZL + Z0))*CEXP(- 2*G*IL1)*A
      VS    = B*CEXP(G*IL1) + A*CEXP(- G*IL1)
      TERM = VS*DW*(COS(S2*T1) + (CSQRT(S3))*SIN(S2*
     $        T1))*EXP(SIGMA*T1) / 6.284
      TERM1= REAL(TERM)
      VT    = VT + TERM1
 4003 CONTINUE
      V     = CABS(VT)
      NF    = 1.0 / V
      WRITE (*,461)
  461 FORMAT ( / ,4X, 'IW',9X, 'IL',9X, 'RO(microohm.cm)
     $          ',4X, 't(ps)',9X, 'V(t)')
      DO 4101 T = 10,100.0,10.0
      V     = 0.0
      T1    = T*(10.0 ** (- 12))
      SIGMA= 0.5*T1
      DW    = 0.05 / T1
      VT    = (0.0,0.0)
      M     = 600
      DO 4001 N = 1,M,1
```

```
      S1    = SIGMA
      S2    = N*DW
      S     = CMPLX(S1,S2)
      Y1    = S*CR1*CIR1 / (CIR1 + CR1)
      Y2    = S*CR2*CIR2 / (CIR2 + CR2)
      Y3    = S*CL1*CIL1 / (CIL1 + CL1)
      Y4    = S*CL2*CIL2 / (CIL2 + CL2)
      G     = CSQRT((Y1 + Y2 + Y3 + Y4 + S*CI)*(RI + S*LI))
      Z0    = CSQRT((RI + S*LI) / (Y1 + Y2 + Y3 + Y4 + S*CI))
      ZL    = 1.0 / (S*C)
      A     = (Z0 / S) / (RR + Z0 - (RR- Z0)*((ZL- Z0) / (ZL
     $        +Z0))*CEXP(- 2*G*IL1))
      B     = ((ZL- Z0) / (ZL + Z0))*CEXP(- 2*G*IL1)*A
      VS    = B*CEXP(G*IL1) + A*CEXP(- G*IL1)
      TERM = VS*DW*(COS(S2*T1) + (CSQRT(S3))*SIN(S2
     $        *T1))*EXP(SIGMA*T1) / 6.284
      TERM1= REAL(TERM)
      VT    = VT + TERM1
 4001 CONTINUE
      V     = CABS(VT)*NF
C*****WRITING THE RESULTS
      WRITE (*,401) IW1,IL,RO,T,V
  401 FORMAT (F6.2,5X,F9.1,5X,F7.2,12X,F7.1,5X,F15.3)
 4101 CONTINUE
      GO TO 10
  999 STOP
      END

      SUBROUTINE SCIC
      (Same as in Appendix 3.1)
```

References

Chapter 1 — Preliminary Concepts and More

[1.1] R. M. Lum and J. K. Klingert, "Improvements in the Heteroepitaxy of GaAs on Si," *Appl. Phys. Lett.*, **51**, July 1987.

[1.2] J. Varrio, H. Asonen, A. Salokatve, and M. Pessa, "New Approach to Growth of High Quality GaAs Layers on Si Substrates," *Appl. Phys. Lett.*, **51**(22), Nov. 1987.

[1.3] P. C. Zalm, C. W. T. Bulle-Lieuwma, and P. M. J. Maree, "Silicon Molecular Beam Epitaxy on GaP and GaAs," *Philips Tech. Rev.*, **43**, May 1987.

[1.4] N. Yokoyama, T. Ohnishi, H. Onodera, T. Shinoki, A. Shibatomi, and H. Ishikawa, "A GaAs 1K Static RAM Using Tungsten Silicide Gate Self-Aligned Technology," *IEEE J. Solid State Circuits*, Oct. 1983.

[1.5] H. K. Choi, G. W. Turner, T. H. Windhorn, and B. Y. Tsaur, "Monolithic Integration of GaAs/AlGaAs Double-Heterostructure LED's and Si MOS-FET's," *IEEE Electron. Device Lett.*, Sept. 1986.

[1.6] M. I. Aksun, H. Morkoc, L. F. Lester, K. H. G. Duh, P. M. Smith, P. C. Chao, M. Longerbone, and L. P. Erickson, "Performance of Quarter-Micron GaAs MOSFETs on Si Substrates," *Appl. Phys. Lett.*, **49**, Dec. 1986.

[1.7] T. C. Chong and C. G. Fonstad, "Low-Threshold Operation of AlGaAs/GaAs Multiple Quantum Lasers Grown on Si Substrates by Molecular Beam Epitaxy," *Appl. Phys. Lett.*, **27**, July 1987.

[1.8] W. Dobbelaere, D. Huang, M. S. Unlu, and H. Morkoc, "AlGaAs/GaAs Multiple Quantum Well Reflection Modulators Grown on Si Substrates," *Appl. Phys. Lett.*, July 1988.

[1.9] W. T. Masselink, T. Henderson, J. Klem, R. Fischer, P. Pearah, H. Morkoc, M. Hafich, P. D. Wang, and G. Y. Robinson, "Optical Properties of GaAs on (100) Si Using Molecular Beam Epitaxy," *Appl. Phys. Lett.*, **45**(12), Dec. 1984.

[1.10] J. B. Posthill, J. C. L. Tran, K. Das, T. P. Humphreys, and N. R. Parikh, "Observation of Antiphase Domains Boundaries in GaAs on Silicon by Transmission Electron Microscopy," *Appl. Phys. Lett.*, Sept. 1988.

[1.11] R. Fischer, H. Morkoc, D. A. Neuman, H. Zabel, C. Choi, N. Otsuka, M. Longerbone, and L. P. Erickson, "Material Properties of High-Quality GaAs Epitaxial Layers Grown on Si Substrates," *J. Appl. Phys.*, **60**(5), Sept. 1986.

[1.12]   L. T. Tran, J. W. Lee, H. Schichijo, and H. T. Yuan,"GaAs/AlGaAs Heterojunction Emitter-Down Bipolar Transistors Fabricated on GaAs-on-Si Substrate," *IEEE Electron. Device Lett.*, **EDL-8**(2), Feb. 1987.

[1.13]   N. El-masry, J. C. Tarn, T. P. Humphreys, N. Hamaguchi, N. H. Karam, and S. M. Bedair, "Effectiveness of Strained-Layer Superlattices in Reducing Defects in GaAs Epilayers Grown on Silicon Substrates," *Appl. Phys. Lett.*, **51**(20), Nov. 1987.

[1.14]   J. H. Kim, A. Nouhi, G. Radhakrishnan, J. K. Liu, R. J. Lang, and J. Katz, "High-Peak-Power Low-Threshold AlGaAs/GaAs Stripe Laser Diodes on Si Substrate Grown by Migration-Enhanced Molecular Beam Epitaxy," *Appl. Phys. Lett.*, Oct. 1988.

[1.15]   S. Sakai, S. S. Chang, R. V. Ramaswamy, J. H. Kim, G. Radhakrishnan, J. K. Liu, and J. Katz, "GaAs/AlGaAs Light-Emitting Diodes on GaAs-Coated Si Substrates Grown by Liquid Phase Epitaxy," *Appl. Phys. Lett.*, Sept. 26, 1988.

[1.16]   D. S. Gardner et al., "Layered and Homogeneous Films of Aluminum and Aluminum/Silicon with Titanium and Tungsten for Multilevel Interconnects," *IEEE Trans. Electron. Devices*, **ED-32**(2), 174–183, Feb. 1985.

[1.17]   K. C. Saraswat and F. Mohammadi, "Effect of Scaling of Interconnections on the Time Delay of VLSI Circuits," *IEEE Trans. Electron. Devices*, **ED-29**(4), 645, April 1982.

[1.18]   M. H. Woods, "The Implications of Scaling on VLSI Reliability," *Seminar Notes from 22nd Int. Reliability Phys. Seminar*.

[1.19]   E. Philofsky and E. L. Hall, "A Review of the Limitations of Aluminum Thin Films on Semiconductor Devices," *Trans. Parts, Hybrids, and Packaging*, **PHP-11**(4), 281, Dec. 1975.

[1.20]   R. A. Levy and M. L. Green, "Characterization of LPCVD Aluminum for VLSI Processing," *Proc. 1984 Symp. on VLSI Technology*, Japan Society of Applied Physics and IEEE Electron Devices Society, p. 32, Sept. 1984.

[1.21]   K. C. Saraswat, S. Swirhun, and J. P. McVittie, "Selective CVD of Tungsten for VLSI Technology," *Proc. Symp. on VLSI Science and Technology*, Electrochemical Society, May 1984.

[1.22]   J. P. Roland, N. E. Handrickson, D. D. Kessler, D. E. Novy, Jr., and D. W. Quint, "Two-Layer Refractory Metal IC Process," *Hewlett-Packard J.*, **34**(8), 30–32, Aug. 1983.

[1.23]   D. L. Brors, K. A. Monnig, J. A. Fair, W. Coney, and K. Saraswat, "CVD Tungsten—A Solution for the Poor Step Coverage and High Contact Resistance of Aluminum," *Solid State Tech.*, **27**(4), 313, April 1984.

[1.24]   F. M. d'Heurle, "The Effect of Copper Additions on Electromigration in Aluminum Thin Films," *Metallurgical Trans.*, **2** 689–693, March 1971.

[1.25]   R. Rosenberg, M. J. Sullivan, and J. K. Howard, "Effect of Thin Film Interactions on Silicon Device Technology," *Thin Films Interdiffusion and Reactions*, J. M. Poeate, K. N. Tu, and J. W. Mayer, Eds, Electrochemical Society, Wiley, New York, pp. 48–54, 1978.

[1.26]   J. McBrayer, "Diffusion of Metals in Silicon Dioxide," Ph.D. Dissertation, Stanford University, Dec. 1983.

[1.27]   J. K. Howard, J. H White, and P. S. Ho, "Intermetallic Compounds of Al and Transition Metals: Effect of Electromigration in 1–2 mm Wide Lines," *J. Appl. Phys.*, **49**(7), 4083, July 1978.

[1.28]   S. S. Iyer and C. Y. Ting, "Electromigration Study of the Al–Cu/Ti/Al–Cu Systems," *Proc. 1984 Int. Reliability Phys. Symp.*, April 1984.

[1.29]   J. P. Tardy and K. N. Tu, "Interdiffusion and Marker Analysis in Aluminum Titanium Thin Film Bilayers," *Proc. 1984 Electronic Materials Conf.*, T. C. Harman, Ed., Metallurgical Society of AIME, p. 12, June 1984.

[1.30]   K. Hinode, S. Iwata, and M. Ogirima, "Electromigration Capacity and Microstructure of Layered Al/Ta Film Conductor," *Extended Abstracts, Electrochemical Society*, **83-1**, 678, May 1983.

[1.31]   F. M. d'Heurle, A. Gangulee, C. F. Aliotta, and V. A. Ranieri, "Electromigration of Ni in Al Thin-Film Conductors," *J. Appl. Phys.*, **46**(11), 4845, Nov. 1975.

[1.32]   F. M. d'Heurle and A. Gangulee, " Solute Effects on Grain Boundary Electromigration and Diffusion," *The Nature and Behavior of Grain Boundaries*, H. Hu, Ed., Plenum, New York, p. 339, 1972.

[1.33]   F. M. d'Heurle, A. Gangulee, C. F. Aliotta, and V. A. Ranieri, " Effects of Mg Additions on the Electromigration Behavior of Al Thin Film Conductors," *J. Electron. Mat.*, **4**(3), 497, 1975.

[1.34]   F. Fischer and F. Neppl, "Sputtered Ti-Doped Al–Si for Enhanced Interconnect Reliability," *Proc. 1984 Int. Reliability Phys. Symp.*, IEEE Electron Devices and Reliability Societies, 1984.

[1.35]   C. J. Santoro, "Thermal Cycling and Surface Reconstruction in Aluminum Thin Films," *J. Electrochem. Soc.*, **116**(3), 361, March 1969.

[1.36]   K. C. Cadien and D. L. Losee, "A Method for Eliminating Hillocks in Integrated-Circuit Metallizations," *J. Vac. Sci. Tech.*, 82–83, Jan.–Mar. 1984.

[1.37]   A. Rev, P. Noel, and P. Jeuch, "Influence of Temperature and Cu Doping on Hillock Formation in Thin Aluminum Film Deposited on Ti:W," *Proc. First Int. IEEE VLSI Multilevel Interconnection Conf.*, IEEE Electron Devices Society and Components, Hybrids, and Manufacturing Society, p. 139, June 1984.

[1.38]   P. B. Ghate and J. C. Blair, "Electromigration Testing of Ti:W/Al and Ti:W/Al–Cu Film Conductors," *Thin Solid Films*, **55**, 113, Nov. 1978.

[1.39]   T. W. Barbee, Jr., "Synthesis of Metastable Materials by Sputter Deposition Techniques," *Synthesis and Properties of Metastable Phases*, E. S. Machlin and T. J. Rowland, Eds., Metallurgical Society of AIME, p. 93, Oct. 1980.

[1.40]   T. W. Barbee, Jr., "Synthesis of Multilayer Structures by Physical Vapor Deposition Techniques," *Multilayer Structures*, Chang and Giessen, Eds., Academic, New York, 1984.

[1.41]   T. W. Barbee, Jr., "Multilayers for X-Ray Optical Applications," *Springer Series in Optical Sciences, Vol. 43: X-Ray Microscopy*, G. Schmahl and D. Rudolph, Eds., Springer, Heidelberg, p. 144, 1984.

[1.42]   D. S. Gardner, T. L. Michalka, T. W. Barbee, Jr., K. C. Saraswat, J. P. McVittie, and J. D. Meindl, "Aluminum Alloys with Titanium, Tungsten, and Copper for Multilayer Interconnections," *Proc. 42nd Annual Device Res. Conf.*, IEEE Electron Devices Society, p. IIB-3, June 1984.

598 REFERENCES

[1.43] D. S. Gardner, T. L. Michalka, T. W. Barbee, Jr., K. C. Saraswat, J. P. McVittie, and J. D. Meindl," Aluminum Alloys with Titanium, Tungsten, and Copper for Multilayer Interconnections, " *1984 Proc. First Int. IEEE VLSI Multilevel Interconnection Conf.*, IEEE Electron Devices Society and Components, Hybrids, and Manufacturing Society, p. 68, June 1984.

[1.44] D. S. Gardner, R. B. Beyers, T. L. Michalka, K. C. Saraswat, T. W. Barbee, Jr., and J. D. Meindl, "Layered and Homogeneous Films of Aluminum and Aluminum/Silicon with Titanium, Zirconium, and Tungsten for Multilevel Interconnects," *IEDM Tech. Dig.*, Dec. 1984.

[1.45] J. W. Goodman, F. I. Leonberger, S. Y. Kung, and R. A. Athale, "Optical Interconnections for VLSI Systems," *Proc. IEEE*, **72**(7), 850–866, July 1984.

[1.46] L. D. Hutcheson, P. Haugen, and A. Hussain, "Optical Interconnects Replace Hardwire," *IEEE Spectrum*, 30–35, March 1987.

[1.47] J. W. Goodman, R. K. Kostuk, and B. Clymer, "Optical Interconnects: An Overview," *Proc. IEEE VLSI Multilevel Interconnection Conf.*, Santa Clara, CA, pp. 219–224, June 1985.

[1.48] T. Bell, "Optical Computing: A Field in Flux," *IEEE Spectrum*, Aug. 1986.

[1.49] Special Issue on Optical Interconnections, *Optical Engineering*, Oct. 1986.

[1.50] R. F. Harrington, "Matrix Methods for Field Problems," *Proc. IEEE*, **55**(2), 136–149, Feb. 1967.

[1.51] L. V. Kantorovich and V. I. Krylov, *Approximate Methods of Higher Analysis*, 4th ed., translated by C. D. Benster, Wiley, New York, Chapter 4, 1959.

[1.52] J. Vlach and K. Singhal. *Computer Methods for Circuit Analysis and Design*, Van Nostrand Reinhold, New York, Chapter 10, 1983.

[1.53] K. Singhal and J. Vlach, "Computation of Time Domain Response by Numerical Inversion of the Laplace Transform," *J. Franklin Institute*, **299**(2), 109–126, Feb. 1975.

[1.54] R. J. Antinone and G. W. Brown, "The Modeling of Resistive Interconnects for Integrated Circuits," *IEEE J. Solid State Circuits*, **SC-18**(2), 200–203, April 1983.

[1.55] G. D. Mey, "A Comment on 'The Modeling of Resistive Interconnects for Integrated Circuits,' " *IEEE J. Solid State Circuits*, **SC-19**(4), 542–543, Aug. 1984.

[1.56] L. N. Dworsky, *Modern Transmission Line Theory and Applications*, Wiley, New York, 1979.

[1.57] A. E. Ruehli and P. A. Brennan, "Accurate Metallization Capacitances for Integrated Circuits and Packages," *IEEE J. Solid State Circuits*, **SC-8**, 289–290, Aug. 1973.

[1.58] I. Gradshteyn and I, Ryzhik, *Tables of Integrals, Series and Products*, Academic, New York, p. 36, 1980.

[1.59] Y. R. Kwon, V. M. Hietala, and K. S . Champlin, "Quasi-TEM Analysis of 'Slow-Wave' Mode Propagation on Coplanar Microstructure MIS Transmission Lines," *IEEE Trans. Microwave Theory Tech.*, **MTT-35**(6), 545–551, June 1987.

[1.60] K. C. Gupta, R. Garg, and I. J. Bahl, *Microstrip Lines and Slotlines*, Artech House, Dedham, MA, 1979.

[1.61] J. R. Brews, "Transmission Line Models for Lossy Waveguide Interconnections in VLSI," *IEEE Trans. Electron. Devices*, **ED-33**(9), 1356–1365, Sept. 1986.

[1.62] H. E. Kallman and R. E. Spencer, "Transient Response," *Proc. IRE*, **33**, 169–195, 1945.

Chapter 2 — Parasitic Capacitances and Inductances

[2.1] K. J. Binns and P. J. Lawrenson, *Analysis and Computation of Electric and Magnetic Field Problems*, Macmillan, New York, 1963.

[2.2] Y. Rahmat-Samii, T. Itoh, and R. Mittra, "A Spectral Domain Technique for Solving Coupled Microstrip Line Problems," *Archiv für Electronick und Ubertragungstechnik*, **27**, 69–71, 1973.

[2.3] N. G. Alexopoulos, J. A. Maupin, and P. T. Greiling, "Determination of the Electrode Capacitance Matrix for GaAs FETs," *IEEE Trans. Microwave Theory Tech.*, **MTT-28**(5), 459–466, 1980.

[2.4] K. H. Huebner, *The Finite Element Method for Engineers*, Wiley, New York, 1975.

[2.5] J. W. Duncan, "The Accuracy of Finite-Difference Solutions of Laplace's Equations," *IEEE Trans. Microwave Theory Tech.*, **MTT-15**, 575–582, Oct. 1967.

[2.6] G. Liebmann, "Solutions of Partial Differential Equations with a Resistance Network Analogue," *Brit. J. Appl. Phys.*, **1**, 92–103, April 1950.

[2.7] B. L. Lennartson, "A Network Analog Method for Computing the TEM Characteristics of Planar Transmission Lines," *IEEE Trans. Microwave Theory Tech.*, **MTT-20**, 586–591, Sept. 1972.

[2.8] C. L. Chao, "A Network Reduction Technique for computing the Characteristics of Microstrip Lines," *Proc. IEEE Symp. Circuits Syst.*, 537–541, 1977.

[2.9] C. L. Chao, "A Network Reduction Technique for Microstrip Three Dimensional Problems," *IEEE MTT-S Int. Symp. Dig.*, 73–75, 1978.

[2.10] V. K. Tripathi and R. J. Bucolo, "A Simple Network Analog Approach for the Quasi-Static Characteristics of General Lossy Anisotropic Layered Structures," *IEEE Trans. Microwave Theory Tech.*, MTT-33, 1458–1464, Dec. 1985.

[2.11] V. K. Tripathi and R. J. Bucolo, "Analysis and Modelling of Multilevel Parallel and Crossing Interconnection Lines," *IEEE Trans. Microwave Theory Tech.*, **MTT-34**(3), 650–658, March 1987.

[2.12] C. L. Chao, "Characteristics of Unsymmetical Broadside-Coupled Strips in an Inhomogenous Dielectric Medium," *IEEE Int. Microwave Symp. Dig.*, 119–121, May 1975.

[2.13] C. P. Wen, "Co-planar-Waveguide Directional Couplers," *IEEE Trans. Microwave Theory Tech.*, **MTT-18**, 318–322, June 1970.

[2.14] T. Hatsuda, "Computation of Coplanar-Type Strip-Line Characteristics by Relaxation Method and Its Application to Microwave Circuits," *IEEE Trans. Microwave Theory Tech.*, **MTT-23**, 795–802, Oct. 1975.

[2.15] A. E. Ruehli and P. A Brennan, "Efficient Capacitance Calculations for Three-Dimensional Multiconductor Systems," *IEEE Trans Microwave Theory Tech.*, **MTT-21**, 2, Feb. 1973.

[2.16]   A. E. Ruehli and P. A. Brennan, "Capacitance Models for Integrated Circuit Metallization Wires," *IEEE J. Solid State Circuits*, **SC-10**, 530–536, Dec. 1975.

[2.17]   A. E. Ruehli and P. A. Brennan, "Accurate Metallization Capacitances for Integrated Circuits and Packages," *IEEE J. Solid State Circuits*, **SC-8**, 288–290, Aug. 1973.

[2.18]   C. D. Taylor, G. N. Elkhouri, and T. E. Wade, "On the Parasitic Capacitances of Multilevel Parallel Metallization Lines," *IEEE Trans. Electron. Devices*, **ED-32**(11), Nov. 1985.

[2.19]   W. H. Dierking and J. D. Bastian, "VLSI Parasitic Capacitance Determination by Flux Tubes," *IEEE Circuits Syst. Mag.*, 11–18, March 1982.

[2.20]   N. G. Alexopoulos and N. K. Uzunoglu, "A Simple Analysis of Thick Microstrip on Anisotropic Substrates," *IEEE Trans. Microwave Theory Tech.*, **MTT-26**, 455–456, June 1978.

[2.21]   A. Farrar and A. T. Adams, "Computation of Lumped Microstrip Capacities by Matrix Methods—Rectangular Sections and End Effects," *IEEE Trans. Microwave Theory Tech.*, **MTT-19**, 495–497, May 1971.

[2.22]   P. D. Patel, "Calculation of Capacitance Coefficients for a System of Irregular Finite Conductors on a Discrete Sheet," *IEEE Trans. Microwave Theory Tech.*, **MTT-19**(11), 862–869, Nov. 1971.

[2.23]   T. Sakurai and K. Tamaru, "Simple Formulas for Two- and Three-Dimensional Capacitances," *IEEE Trans. Electron. Devices*, **ED-30**, 183–185, Feb. 1983.

[2.24]   Z. Ning, P. M. Dewilde, and F. L. Neerhoff, "Capacitance Coefficients for VLSI Multilevel Metallization Lines," *IEEE Trans. Electron. Devices*, **ED-34**(3), 644–649, March 1987.

[2.25]   A. K. Goel and Y. R. Huang, "Parasitic Capacitances and Inductances for Multilevel Interconnections on GaAs-Based Integrated Circuits," *J. Electromag. Waves Appl.*, **5**(4/5), 477–502, 1991.

[2.26]   H. T. Youn, Y. Lin, S. Y. Chiang, "Properties of Interconnection on Silicon, Sapphire and Semiinsulating Gallium Arsenide Substrates," *IEEE Trans. Electron. Devices*, **ED-29**, 439–444, April 1982.

[2.27]   A. K. Goel, "Electrode Parasitic Capacitances in Self-Aligned and Deep-Recessed GaAs MESFETs," *Solid State Electronics*, **31**(10), 1471–1476, 1988.

[2.28]   R. F. Harrington, *Field Computation by Moment Methods*, Macmillan, New York, 1968.

[2.29]   J. A. Maupin, "Self- and Mutual-Capacitance of Printed or Embedded Patch Conductors," M.S. Thesis, University of California, Los Angeles, 1979.

[2.30]   E. Weber, *Electromagnetic Fields Theory and Applications*, Wiley, New York, 1957.

[2.31]   I. Stakgold, *Boundary Value Problems of Mathematical Physics*, vol. 2, Macmillan, New York, 1968.

[2.32]   C. A. Liechti, *IEEE Trans. Microwave Theory Tech.*, **MTT-24**(6), 279–300, June 1976.

[2.33]   T. Chen and M. S. Shur, *IEEE Trans. Electron. Devices*, **ED-12**(5), 883–891, May 1985.

Chapter 3 — Propagation Delays

[3.1] N. C. Cirillo, Jr., and J. K. Abrokwah, "8.5 Picosecond Ring Oscillator Gate Delay with Self-Aligned Gate Modulation-Doped $n + (Al, Ga)/As/GaAs$ FET's," *IEEE Trans. Electron. Devices*, **ED-32**, 2530, Nov. 1985.

[3.2] N. J. Shah, S. S. Pei, C. W. Tu, and R. C. Tiberio, "Gate-Length Dependence of the Speed of SSI Circuits Using Submicrometer Selectively-Doped Heterostructure Transistor Technology," *IEEE Trans. Electron. Devices*, **ED-33**, 543–547, May 1986.

[3.3] R. K. Jain, "Electro-Optic Sampling of High-Speed III–V Devices and ICs," *IEEE/Cornell Conf. on High Speed Semiconductor Devices and Circuits*, IEEE Cat. No. 87CH2526-2, pp. 22–25, 1987.

[3.4] C. W. Ho, "Theory and Computer Aided Anaylsis of Lossless Transmission Lines," *IBM J. Res. Devlop.*, 17, 249–255, 1973.

[3.5] A. E. Ruehli, "Survey of Computer-Aided Electrical Analysis of Integrated Circuit Interconnection," *IBM J. Res. Develop.*, 22, 526–539, Nov. 1979.

[3.6] A. J. Gruodis and C. S. Chang, "Coupled Lossy Transmission Line Characterization and Simulation," *IBM J. Res. Develop.*, 25, 25–41, Jan. 1981.

[3.7] H. T. Youn et al., "Properties of Interconnections on Silicon, Sapphire and Semiinsulating Gallium Arsenide Substrates," *IEEE Trans. Electron. Devices*, **ED-29**, 439–444, April 1982.

[3.8] I. Chilo and T. Arnaud, "Coupling Effects in the Time Domain for an Interconnecting Bus in High Speed GaAs Logic Circuits," *IEEE Trans. Electron. Devices*, **ED-31**, 347–352, March 1984.

[3.9] V. K. Tripathi et al., "Accurate Computer Aided Analysis of Crosstalk in Single and Multilayered Interconnections for High Speed Digital Circuits," *Proc. 34th Electronic Components Conf.*, New Orleans, May 1984.

[3.10] S. Seki and H. Hasegawa, "Analysis of Crosstalk in Very High-Speed LSI/VLSIs Using a Coupled Multi-Conductor Stripline Model," *IEEE Trans. Microwave Theory Tech.*, **MTT-32**, 1715–1720, Dec. 1984.

[3.11] H. Hasegawa and S. Seki, "Analysis of Interconnection Delay on Very High-Speed LSI/VLSI Chips Using a MIS Microstrip Line Model," *IEEE Trans. Electron. Devices*, **ED-31**, 1954–1960, Dec. 1984.

[3.12] F. Fukuoka et al., "Analysis of Multilayer Interconnection Lines for a High Speed Digital Integrated Circuit," *IEEE Trans. Microwave Theory Tech.*, **MTT-33**, 527–532, June 1985.

[3.13] V. K. Tripathi and J. B. Rettig, "A SPICE Model for Multiple Coupled Microstrips and Other Transmission Lines," *IEEE Trans. Microwave Theory Tech.*, **MTT-33**(12), 1513–1518, Dec. 1985.

[3.14] V. K. Tripathi and R. J. Bucuolo, "Analysis and Modelling of Multilevel Parallel and Crossing Interconnection Lines," *IEEE Trans. Microwave Theory Tech.*, **MTT-34**(3), March 1987.

[3.15] A. R. Djordevic, T. K. Sarkar, and R. F. Harrington, "Analysis of Lossy Transmission Lines with Arbitrary Nonlinear Terminal Networks," *IEEE Trans. Microwave Theory Tech.*, **MTT-34**, 660–666, June 1986.

[3.16] A. K. Goel, "Transit Times in the High-Density Interconnections on GaAs-Based VHSIC," *IEE Proc*, **135**(5), 129–135, Oct. 1988.

[3.17] A. K. Goel and Y. R. Huang, "Efficient Characterization of Multilevel Interconnections on the GaAs-Based VLSIC's," *Microwave Opt. Tech. Lett.*, **1**(7), 252–257, 1988.

[3.18] K. W. Goossen and R. B. Hammond, "Modeling of Picosecond Pulse Propagation in Microstrip Interconnections on Integrated Circuits," *IEEE Trans. Microwave Theory Tech.*, **37**(3), 469–478, March 1989.

[3.19] A. K. Goel and C. R. Li, "Microcomputer Simulation of Single-Level High-Density VLSI Interconnection Capacitances," *Proc. SCS Multiconf. on Modelling and Simulation on Microcomputers*, San Diego, CA, pp. 132–137, 1988.

[3.20] H. E. Kallman and R. E. Spencer, "Transient Response," *Proc. IRE*, **33**, 169–195, 1945.

[3.21] K. S. Crump, "Numerical Inversion of Laplace Transforms Using a Fourier Series Approximation," *J. ACM*, **23**, 89–96, Jan. !976.

[3.22] R. M. Simon, M. T. Stroot, and G. H. Weiss, "Numerical Inversion of Laplace Transforms with Application to Percentage Labeled Mitoses Experiments," *Computer Biomedical Res.*, **5**, 596–607, 1972.

[3.23] C. W. Ho, "Theory and Computer Aided Analysis of Lossless Transmission Lines," *IBM J. Res. Develop.*, **17**, 249, 1973.

[3.24] F. Y. Chang, "Transient Analysis of Lossless Coupled Transmission Lines in a Nonhomogenous Dielectric Medium," *IEEE Trans. Microwave Theory Tech.*, **MTT-18**, 616–626, Sept. 1970.

[3.25] A. J. Gruodis and C. S. Chang, "Coupled Lossy Transmission Line Characterization and Simulation," *IBM J. Res. Develop.*, **25**, 25–41, Jan. 1981.

[3.26] J. E. Carroll and P. R. Rigg, "Matrix Theory for *n*-Line Microwave Coupler Design," *Proc. Inst. Elec. Eng.*, **127**, pt. H, 309–314, Dec. 1980.

[3.27] H. Lee, "Computational Methods for Quasi TEM Parameters of MIC Planar Structures," Ph.D. Thesis, Oregon State University, 1983.

[3.28] V. K. Tripathi et al., "Accurate Computer Aided Analysis of Crosstalk in Single and Multilayered Interconnections for High Speed Digital Circuits," *Proc. 34th Electronic Component Conf.*, New Orleans, May 1984.

[3.29] P. L. Kuznetsov and R. L. Stratonovich, *The Propagation of Electromagnetic Waves in Multiconductor Transmission Lines*, Pergamon, Elmsford, NY, 1984.

[3.30] H. Uchida, *Fundamentals of Coupled Lines and Multiwire Antennas*, Sesaki Publishing, Sendai, 1967.

[3.31] V. K. Tripathi, "Asymmetric Coupled Transmission Lines in an Inhomogenous Medium," *IEEE Trans. Microwave Theory Tech*, **MTT-23**, 734–739, Sept. 1975.

[3.32] Y. K. Chin, "Analysis and Applications of Multiple Coupled Line Structures in an Inhomogeneous Medium," Ph.D. Thesis, Oregon State University, 1982.

[3.33] V. K. Tripathi, "On the Analysis of Symmetrical Three Line Microstrip Lines," *IEEE Trans. Microwave Theory Tech.*, **MTT-25**, 726–729, Sept. 1977.

[3.34] K. W. Goossen and R. B. Hammond, "Modeling of Picosecond Pulse Propagation in Microstrip Interconnections on Integrated Circuits," *IEEE Trans. Microwave Theory Tech.*, 37(3), 469–478, March 1989.

[3.35] D. G. Corr and J. B. Davies, "Computer Analysis of Fundamental and Higher Order Modes in Single and Coupled Microstrip," *IEEE Trans. Microwave Theory Tech.*, **MTT-20**, 669–678, 1972.

[3.36] M. V. Schneider, "Microstrip Lines for Microwave Integrated Circuits," *Bell Syst. Tech.*, **48**, 1421, 1969.

[3.37] K. C. Gupta, R. Garg, and R. Chadha, *Computer-Aided Design of Microwave Circuits*, Artech House, Dedham, MA, p. 62, 1981.

[3.38] E. Yamashita, K. Atsuki, and T. Ueda, "An Approximate Dispersion Formula of Microstrip Lines for Computer-Aided Design of Microwave Integrated Circuits," *IEEE Trans. Microwave Theory Tech.*, **MTT-27**, 1036, 1979.

[3.39] R. A. Pucel, D. J. Masse, and C. P. Hartwig, "Losses in Microstrip," *IEEE Trans. Microwave Theory Tech.*, **MTT-16**, 342, 1968.

[3.40] J. D. Welch and H. J. Pratt, "Losses in Microstrip Transmission Systems for Integrated Microwave Circuits," *NEREM Rec.*, **8**, 100, 1966.

[3.41] A. Wilnai, "Open-Ended *RC* Line Model Predicts MOSFET IC Response," *EDN*, 53–54, Dec. 1971.

[3.42] P. H. Ladbrooke, "Some Effects of Wave Propagation in the Gate of a Microwave MESFET," *Electron. Lett.*, **14**, 21–22, Jan. 1978.

[3.43] Y. A. Ren and H. L. Hartnagel, "Wave Propagation Studies on MESFET Electrodes," *Int. J. Electron.*, **51**, 663–668, Nov. 1981.

[3.44] R. L. Kuvas, "Equivalent Circuit Model of FET Including Distributed Gate Effects," *IEEE Trans. Electron. Devices*, **ED-27**, 1193–1195, June 1980.

[3.45] R. LaRue, C. Yuen, and G. Zdasiuk, "Distributed GaAs FET Circuit Model for Broadband and Millimeter Wave Applications," *IEEE MTT-S Dig.*, 164–166, 1984.

[3.46] R. Dawson, "Equivalent Circuit of the Schottky-Barrier Field-Effect Transistor at Microwave Frequencies," *IEEE Trans. Microwave Theory Tech.*, **MTT-23**, 499–501, June 1975.

[3.47] G. Vendelin and M. Omori, "Circuit Model for the GaAs MESFET Valid to 12 GHz," *Electron. Lett.*, **11**, 60–61, Feb. 1975.

[3.48] See, for example, J. Millman, *Microelectrics*, McGraw-Hill, New York, 1960.

[3.49] A. K. Goel and C. R. Westgate, "Electrode Parasitic Capacitances in Single-Gate GaAs MESFET's," *Proc. 1985 Int. Symp. Microelectronics*, Anaheim, CA, Nov. 11–14, pp. 287–292.

[3.50] A. K. Goel and C. R. Westgate, "Modeling of the Transverse Delays in GaAs MESFETs," *IEEE Trans. Microwave Theory Tech.*, 36(10), 1411–1417, Oct. 1988.

[3.51] J. W. Nilsson, *Electric Circuits*, 2nd ed., Addison-Wesley, Reading, MA, 1987.

[3.52] M. B. Das, "Millimeter-Wave Performance of Ultrasubmicrometer-Gate Field-Effect Transistors: A Comparison of MODFET, MESFET and PBT Structures," *IEEE Trans. Electron. Devices*, **ED-34**(7), 1429–1440, July 1987.

[3.53]   P. Roblin, "Nonlinear Parasitics in MODFETs and MODFET I–V Characteristics," *IEEE Trans. Electron. Devices*, **35**(8), 1207–1213, Aug. 1988.

[3.54]   S. Kawamura et al., "Three-Dimensional CMOS IC's Fabricated by Using Beam Recrystallization," *IEEE Electron. Devices Lett.*, **EDL-4**, 366, 1983.

[3.55]   S. Akiyama et al., "Multilayer CMOS Device Fabricated on Laser Recrystallized Silicon Islands," *IEDM Tech. Dig.*, 352, 1983.

[3.56]   Y. Akasaka et al., "Integrated MOS Devices in Double Active Layers," *Proc. Symp. VLSI Technol.*, 90, 1984.

[3.57]   M. Nakano, "3-D SOI/CMOS," *IEDM Tech. Dig.*, 792, 1984.

[3.58]   S. Kataoka, "An Attempt Towards an Artificial Retina: 3-D Technology for an Intelligent Image Sensor," *Proc. Int. Conf. Solid State Sensors and Actuators*, 440, 1985.

[3.59]   K. Sugahara et al., "SOI/SOI/Bulk-Si Triple-Level Structure for Three-Dimensional Devices," *IEEE Electron. Device Lett.*, **EDL-7**, 193, 1986.

[3.60]   D. A. Antoniadis, "Three-Dimensional Integrated Circuit Technology," *Proc. Materials Res. Soc. Meeting*, Nov. 1983.

[3.61]   A. L. Robinson, L. A. Glasser, and D. A. Antoniadis, "A Simple Interconnect Delay Model for Multilayer Integrated Circuits," *Proc. IEEE VLSI Multilevel Interconnection Conf.*, 267–273, 1986.

[3.62]   K. Sarawat and F. Mohammadi, "Effect of Scaling of Interconnections on Time Delay of VLSI Circuits," *IEEE Trans. Electron. Devices*, **ED-29**, 645, 1982.

[3.63]   T. P. Chow and A. Steckl, "A Review of Refractory Gates for MOS VLSI," *IEDM Tech. Dig.*, 513, 1983.

Chapter 4 — Crosstalk Analysis

[4.1]   J. Chilo and T. Arnaud , "Coupling Effects in the Time Domain for an Interconnecting Bus in High-Speed GaAs Logic Circuits," *IEEE Trans. Electron. Devices*, **ED-31**, 347–352, March 1984.

[4.2]   M. Riddle, S. Ardalan, and J. Suh, "Derivation of the Voltage and Current Transfer Functions for Multiconductor Transmission Lines," *Proc. IEEE Int. Symp. on Circuits and Systems*, Portland, OR, pp. 2219–2222, May 8–11, 1989.

[4.3]   A. R. Djordjevic and T. K. Sarkar, "Analysis of Time Response of Lossy Multiconductor Transmission Line Networks," *IEEE Trans. Microwave Theory Tech.*, **MTT-35**, 898–908, Oct. 1987.

[4.4]   F. Romeo and M. Santomauro, "Time Domain Simulation of n Coupled Transmission Lines," *IEEE Trans. Microwave Theory Tech.*, **MTT-35**, 131–137, Feb. 1987.

[4.5]   S. Seki and H. Hasegawa, "Analysis of Crosstalk in Very High-Speed LSI/VLSI Using a Coupled Multiconductor Stripline Model," *IEEE Trans. Microwave Theory Tech.*, **MTT-32**, 1715–1720, Dec. 1984.

[4.6]   A. R. Djordevic, T. K. Sarkar, and R. F. Harrington, "Time Domain Response of Multiconductor Transmission Lines," *Proc. IEEE*, **75**, 743–764, June 1987.

[4.7] S. Frankel, *Multiconductor Transmission Line Analysis*, Artech House, Norwood, MA, 1977.

[4.8] A. J. Gruodis and C. S. Chang, "Coupled Lossy Transmission Line Characterization and Simulation," *IBM Res. Develop.*, **25**, 25–41, Jan. 1981.

[4.9] A. R. Djordevic, T. K. Sarkar, and R. F. Harrington, "Analysis of Lossy Transmission Lines with Arbitrary Nonlinear Terminal Networks," *IEEE Trans. Microwave Theory Tech.*, **MTT-34**, 660–666, June 1986.

[4.10] J. Kim and J. F. McDonald, "Transient and Crosstalk Analysis of Slightly Lossy Interconnection Lines for Wafer Scale Integration and Wafer Scale Hybrid Packaging–Weak Coupling Case," *IEEE Trans. Circuits and Systems*, **CAS-35**, 1369–1382, Nov. 1988.

[4.11] S. P. Castillo, C. H. Chan, and R. Mittra, "Analysis of *N*-Conductor Transmission Line Systems with Non-Linear Loads with Applications to CAD Design of Digital Circuits," *Proc. Int. Symp. Electromagn. Compat.*, San Diego, CA, pp. 174–175, Sept. 16–18, 1986.

[4.12] C. S. Chang, G. Crowder, and M. F. McAllister, "Crosstalk in Multilayer Ceramic Packaging," *Proc. IEEE Int. Symp. Circuits and Systems*, Chicago, pp. 6–11, April 1981.

[4.13] H. R. Kaupp, "Pulse Crosstalk Between Microstrip Transmission Lines," *Proc. 7th Int. Electronic Packaging Symp.*, Los Angeles, pp. 1–12, Aug. 22–23, 1966.

[4.14] J. C. Isaacs, Jr. and N. A. Strakhov, "Crosstalk in Uniformly Coupled Lossy Transmission Lines," *Bell Syst. Tech. J.*, **52**, 101–115, Jan. 1973.

[4.15] G. Ghione, I. Maio, and G. Vecchi, "Modeling of Multiconductor Buses and Analysis of Crosstalk, Propagation Delay and Pulse Distortion in High-Speed GaAs Logic Circuits," *IEEE Trans. Microwave Theory Tech.*, **MTT-37**, 445–456, March 1989.

[4.16] H. You and M. Soma, "Crosstalk Analysis of Interconnection Lines and Packaging in High-Speed Integrated Circuits," *IEEE Trans. Circuits and Systems*, **37**(8), 1019–1026, Aug. 1990.

[4.17] A. K. Goel and Y. R. Huang, "Modelling of Crosstalk Among the GaAs-Based VLSI Interconnections," *IEE Proc.*, **136**(6), 361–368, Dec. 1989.

[4.18] Y. R. Huang, "Characterization of Multilevel Interconnections on GaAs-Based VLSI," M.S. Thesis, Michigan Technological University, 1988.

[4.19] P. J. Prabhakaran, "Analysis of Crossing Interconnections on GaAs-Based VLSICs," M.S. Thesis, Michigan Technological University, 1989.

[4.20] M. K. Mathur, "Workstation and Microcomputer Analyses of Crossing VLSI Interconnections," M.S. Thesis, Michigan Technological University, 1991.

[4.21] K. S. Crump, "Numerical Inversion of Laplace Transforms Using a Fourier Series Approximation," *J. ACM*, **23**, 89–96, Jan. 1976.

[4.22] R. M. Simon, M. T. Stroot, and G. H. Weiss, "Numerical Inversion of Laplace Transforms with Application to Percentage Labeled Mitoses Experiments," *Computer and Biomedical Res.*, **5**, 596–607, 1972.

[4.23] T. K. Sarkar and J. R. Mosig, "Comparison of Quasi-Static and Exact Electromagnetic Fields from a Horizontal Electric Dipole Above a Lossy Dielectric Backed by an Imperfect Ground Plane," *IEEE Trans. Microwave Theory Tech.*, **MTT-34**, 379–387, April 1986.

[4.24] J. Siegl, V. Tulaja, and R. Hoffman, "General Analysis of Interdigitated Microstrip Couplers," *Siemens Forsch.-u. Entwickl.-Ber.*, **10**(4), 228–236, 1981.

[4.25] N. Moisan, "Etude Theorique et Experimentale Des Effets De Propagation dans les Circuits Logiques Rapides," Doctorate Thesis, Institut National des Sciences Appliquees de Rennes, France, Oct. 1986.

[4.26] N. Moisan, J. M. Flóch, and J. Citerne, "Efficient Modelling Technique of Lossy Microstrip Line Sections in Digital GaAs Circuits," *Proc. 16th European Microwave Conf.*, 698–704, 1986.

Chapter 5 — Electromigration-Induced Failure Analysis

[5.1] N. V. Doan and G, Boebec, "Migration Sous L'effect Dun' Champ Electrique de Ag^{110} et de Sb^{124} Dans l'argent," *J. Phys. Chem. Solids*, **31**, 475–484, 1970.

[5.2] D. F. Kalinovich, I. I. Kovenskii, M. O. Smolin, and V. M. Statsenko, "Electrotransport of Molybdenum in Ni-18 at % Mo Alloy," *Fiz. Tverd. Tela (USSR)*, **12**, 3042–3044, 1970.

[5.3] J. C. Peacock and A. D. Wilson, "Electrotransport of Tungsten and Life of a Filament," *J. Appl. Phys.*, **39**, 6037–6041, 1968.

[5.4] D. L. Kennedy, "Electrotransport in Thin Indium Films," *J. Appl. Phys.*, 6102–6104, 1968.

[5.5] R. M. Valleta and H. S. Lehman, "AL–Cu for Semiconductor Metallurgy," *Extended Abstracts, Electrochemical Society Meeting*, Atlantic City, NJ, p. 474, Oct. 1970.

[5.6] L. Berenbaum and R. Rosenberg, "Electromigration Damage in Al–Cu Thin Films," *IRPS*, 1971.

[5.7] E. Nagapawa and H. Okabayaski, "Electromigration of Sputtered Al–Si Alloy Films," *IRPS*, 64–70, 1979.

[5.8] T. Mori, M. Meshii, and J. W. Kaufman, "Quenching Rate and Quenched-in Lattice in Gold," *J. Appl. Phys.*, **33**, 2776–2780, 1962.

[5.9] D. O. Boyle, "Observations on Electromigration and the Soret Effect in Tungsten," *J. Appl. Phys.*, **36**, 2849–2853, 1965.

[5.10] L. Berenbaum and B. Patnaik, "Study of Failure Mechanisms in Al–Cu Films by High Voltage Microscopy," *Appl. Phys. Lett.*, **18**, 284–286, 1971.

[5.11] P. B. Ghate, "Some Observations on the Electromigration in Aluminium Films," *Appl. Phys. Lett.*, **11**, 14–16, 1967.

[5.12] I. A. Blech, "Electromigration in Thin Aluminum Films on Titanium Nitride," *J. Appl. Phys.*, **47**, 1203–1208, April 1976.

[5.13] J. K. Howard and R. F. Ross, "Electromigration Effects in Aluminum on Silicon Substrates," *Appl. Phys. Lett.*, **11**, 85–87, 1967.

[5.14] R. C. Pitelli, "Electromigration of TiPdAu Conductors," *IRPS*, 171–174, 1972.

[5.15] A. Ladding, "Current-Induced Motion of Lattice Defects in Indium Metal," *J. Phys. Chem. Solids*, **26**, 143–151, 1965.

[5.16]   P. S. Ho and H. B. Huntington, "Electromigration and Void Observation in Silver," *J. Phys. Chem. Solids*, **27**, 1319–1329, 1966.

[5.17]   P. S. Ho, "Electromigration and Soret Effect in Cobalt," *J. Phys. Chem. Solids*, **27**, 1331–1338, 1966.

[5.18]   J. F. D'Amico and H. B. Huntington, "Electromigration and Thermomigration in Gamma-Uranium," Report Department of Physics, Rensselaer Polytechnic Institute, Troy, NY, pp. 1044–1048.

[5.19]   R. V. Penny, "Current-Induced Mass Transport in Aluminum," *J. Phys. Chem. Solids*, **25**, 335–345, 1964.

[5.20]   A. R. Grone, "Current-Induced Marker Motion in Copper," *J. Phys. Chem. Solids*, **20**, 88–98, 1961.

[5.21]   H. B. Huntington and A. R. Grone, "Current-Induced Marker Motion in Gold Wires," *J. Phys. Chem. Solids*, **20**, 76–87, 1961.

[5.22]   J. R. Black, "Aluminium Conductor Failure by Mass Transport," *Proc. 3rd Int. Congress on Microelectronics*, Munich, Germany, pp. 141–162, Nov. 1968.

[5.23]   G. M. Newmann, "On Thermotransport in Tungsten," *Z. Naturforsch A*, **22**, 393–395, 1967.

[5.24]   D. Campbell and H. Huntington, "Thermomigration and Electromigration in Zirconium," *Phys. Rev.*, **179**, 601–612, 1969.

[5.25]   D. Campbell and H. Huntington, "Electron Transfer of Silver and Copper Between Crystallites," *Phys. Metals Metallogr. (USSR)*, **16**(4), 1964.

[5.26]   H. Dubler and H. Wever, "Thermo- and Electrotransport in *b*-Titanium and *b*-Zirkonium," *Phys. Status Solidi*, **25**, 109–118, 1968.

[5.27]   S. C. Ho, T. Hehenkamp, and H. B. Huntington, "Thermal Diffusion in Platinum," *J. Phys. Chem. Solids*, **26**, 251–258, 1965.

[5.28]   T. Thernquist and A. Lodding, "Electro- and Thermotransport in Lithium," *Proc. Int. Conf. Vacancies and Interstitials in Metals*, Kernsfor Schungsanlage Julich, pp. 55–68, Sept. 1968.

[5.29]   T. Hehenkamp, "Diffusion und Elektrotransport von Kohlenstoff in Kobalt," *Acta Met.*, **14**, 887–893, 1966.

[5.30]   H. Hering and H. Wever, "Electro- and Thermotransport in Nickel," *J. Phys. Chem.*, **1**, 310–325, 1967.

[5.31]   G. M. Newmann and W. Hirschwald, "Electrotransport in Tungsten," *Z. Naturforsch A*, **22**, 388–392, 1967.

[5.32]   H. J. Stepper and H. Wever, "Electrodiffusion in Dilute Copper Alloys," *J. Phys. Chem. Solids*, **28**, 1103–1108, 1967.

[5.33]   I. A. Blech and E. S. Meieran, "Direct Transmission Electron Microscope Observations of Electrotransport in Aluminum Films," *Appl. Phys. Lett.*, **11**, 263–266, 1967.

[5.34]   K. R. Kodbell and S. R. Shatynski, "Electromigration in Sputtered Al–Cu Thin Films," *Thin Solid Films*, **116**, 95–102, 1984,

[5.35]   M. J. Attardo and R. Rosenberg, "Electromigration Damage in Aluminium Film Conductors," *J. Appl. Phys.*, **41**, 2381–2386, 1970.

[5.36]   F. d'Heurle and I. Ames, "Electromigration in Single Crystal Aluminium Films," *Appl. Phys. Lett.*, **16**, 80–81, 1970.

[5.37] T. E. Hartman and J. C. Blair, "Electromigration in Thin Gold Films," *IEEE Trans. Electron. Devices*, **ED-16**(4), 407–410, 1969.

[5.38] P. B. Ghate, "Electromigration Testing of Al-Alloy Films," *IRPS*, 243–251, 1981.

[5.39] S. S. Iyer and C. Ting, "Electromigration Lifetime Studies of Submicrometer Linewidth Al–Cu Conductors," *IEEE Trans. Electron. Devices*, **ED-31**(10), 1468–1471, Oct. 1984.

[5.40] J. Chern, W. G. Oldham, and N. Cheung, "Contact Electromigration Induced Leakage Failure in Aluminium–Silicon to Silicon Contacts," *IEEE Trans. Electron. Devices*, **ED-32**(4), 1341–1346, July 1985.

[5.41] J. Chern, W. G. Oldham, and N. Cheung, "Electromigration in Al–Si Contacts—Induced Open-Circuit Failure," *IEEE Trans. Electron Devices*, **ED-31**(9), 1256–1261, Sept. 1986.

[5.42] S. D. Steenwyk and E. F. Kankowski, "Electromigration in Aluminium to Tantalum Silicide Contacts," *IRPS*, 30–37, 1986.

[5.43] G. D. Giacomo, "Electromigration Depletion in Pb–Sn Films," *IRPS*, 72–76, 1979.

[5.44] S. S. Iyer and C. Ting, "Electromigration Study on the Al–Cu/Ti/Al–Cu Systems," *IRPS*, 273–274, 1981.

[5.45] E. Levine and J. Kitchen, "Electromigration-Induced Damage and Structural Change in Cr–Al/Cu and Al/Cu Interconnection Lines," *IRPS*, 242–248, 1984.

[5.46] W. Hasse, J. Schulte, and J. Grawl, "Electromigration of Silicon and Phosphorous in Tantalum Polycide Interconnections," *IEEE Trans. Electron. Devices*, **ED-34**(3), 659–663, 1987.

[5.47] D. K. Sadana, J. M. Towner, M. H. Norcott, and R. C. Ellwanger, "Some TEM Observations on Electromigrated Al and Al-Alloy Interconnects," *IRPS*, 38–43, 1986.

[5.48] B. Grabe and H. U. Screiber, "Lifetime and Drift Velocity Analysis for Electromigration in Sputtered Al Films, Multilayers and Alloys," *Solid State Electronics*, **26**, 1023–1032, 1983.

[5.49] J. P. Tardy and K. N. Tu, "Interdiffusion and Marker Analysis for Electromigration in Aluminium Titanium Thin Film Bilayers," *Electron. Mat. Conf.*, 12, June 1984.

[5.50] C. F. Dunn, F. R. Brotzen, and J. W. McPherson, "Electromigration and Microstructural Properties of Al–Si/Ti/Al–Si VLSI Metallization," *J. Electron. Mat.*, **15**(8), 273–277, Sept. 1986.

[5.51] K. A. Danso and T. Tullos, "Thin Film Metallization Studies and Device Lifetime Prediction Using Al–Si, Al–Cu–Si Conductor Test Bars," *Microelectronics and Reliability*, **21**, 513–527, 1981.

[5.52] I. A. Blech and E. Kinsborn, "Electromigration in Thin Gold Films on Molybdenum Surfaces," *Thin Solid Films*, **55**, 113–123, 1978.

[5.53] P. B. Ghate and J. C. Blair, "Electromigration Testing of TiW/Al and TiW/Al–Cu Film Conductors," *Thin Solid Films*, **25**, 327–334, 1971.

[5.54] J. C. Blair, P. B. Ghate, and C. T. Haywood, "Electromigration-Induced Failure in Aluminium Film Conductors," *Appl. Phys. Lett.*, **17**, 281–283, 1970.

[5.55] S, Vaidya and A. K. Sinha, "Electromigration-Induced Leakage at Shallow Junction Contacts Metallized with Aluminium/Polysilicon," *IRPS*, 50–54, 1982.

[5.56] S. Vaidya, A. K. Sinha, and J. M. Andrews, "Contact-Electromigration-Induced Failure Shallow Junction Leakage with Al/Poly Si Metallization," *J. Electrochem. Soc.*, **132**(2), 496–501, Feb. 1983.

[5.57] G. S. Prokop and R. R. Joseph, "Electromigration Failure at Aluminium–Silicon Contacts," *J. Appl. Phys.*, **43**(6), 2595–2602, 1972.

[5.58] I. A. Blech and H. Sello, "The Failure of Thin Aluminum Current Carrying Strips on Oxidized Silicon," *Phys. Failure in Electronics*, **5**, 496–505, June 1967.

[5.59] J. Howard and R. F. Ross, "Electromigration Effects in Aluminium on Silicon Substrates," *Appl. Phys. Lett.*, **11**(3), 85–87, Aug. 1967.

[5.60] G. J. VanGurp, "Electromigration in Aluminum Films Containing Si," *Appl. Phys. Lett.*, **19**, 476–479, 1971.

[5.61] A. J. Learn, "Electromigration Effects in Aluminium Alloy Metallization," *J. Electron. Mat.*, **3**(2), 531–552, 1974.

[5.62] S. Vaidya, D. B. Fraser, and W. S. Lindenberger, "Electromigration in Fine-line Sputtered Gun Al," *J. Appl. Phys.*, **51**, 4475–4482, 1980.

[5.63] J. R. Black, "Electromigration of Al–Si Alloy Films," *IRPS*, 233–240, 1978.

[5.64] J. R. Lloyd, M. J. Sullivan, G. S. Hopper, J. T. Coffin, E. T. Severn, and J. L. Jozwiak, "Electromigration Failure in Thin Film Silicides and Polysilicon/Silicide (Polycide)," *IRPS*, 198–202, 1983.

[5.65] P. S. Ho, "Basic Problems for Electromigration in VLSI Applications," *IRPS*, 288–290, 1982.

[5.66] P. S. Ho, F. M. d'Heurle, and A. Gangulee, *Electro- and Thermotransport in Metals and Alloys*, R. E. Hummel and H. B. Huntington, Eds., AIME, New York, pp. 108–159, 1977.

[5.67] P. S. Ho, "Motion of Inclusion Induced by a Direct Current and a Temperature Gradient," *J. Appl. Phys.*, **41**, 64–68, 1970.

[5.68] J. R. Lloyd, P. M. Smith, and G. S. Prokop, "The Role of Metal and Passivation Defects in Electromigration-Induced Damage in Thin Film Conductors," *Thin Solid Films*, **93**, 385–396, 1982.

[5.69] R. H. Dennard, F. H. Gaensslen, H. N. Yu, V. L. Rideout, E. Bassous, and A. R. LeBlanc, "Design of Ion-Implanted MOSFET's with Very Small Physical Dimensions," *IEEE J. Solid State Circuits*, **SC-9**, 256, 1974.

[5.70] D. D. Tang and P. M. Solomon, "Bipolar Transistor Design for Optimized Power-Delay Logic Circuits," *IEEE J. Solid State Circuits*, **SC-14**, 679–684, 1979.

[5.71] J. R. Lloyd, "Electromigration-Induced Extrusions in Multi-Level Technologies," *IRPS*, 208–209, 1983.

[5.72] J. Verhoenen, "Electrotransport in Metals," *Metallurgical Rev.*, **8**, 311–368, 1963.

[5.73] J. R. Black, "Metallization Failures in Integrated Circuits," RADC Tech. Rep., TR-68-243, Oct. 1968.

[5.74] K. E. Schwartz, *Electrolytische Wonderung in Flussizen und Festern Metallen*, Leipzig, 1940.

[5.75] J. Verhoeven, "Electrotransport as a Means of Purifying Metals," *J. Metals*, **18**, 26–31, 1966.

[5.76] H. B. Huntington and S. C. Ho, "Electromigration in Metals," *J. Phys. Soc. Japan*, **18**, Suppl. II, 202–208, 1963.

[5.77] C. Bosvieux and J. Friedel, "Sur l'electrolyte Des Alliages Metallignes," *J. Phys. Chem. Solids*, **23**, 123–136, 1962.

[5.78] S. M. Klostman, A. N. Timoferv, and I. S. Trakhtenberg, "On the Mechanism of Lattice Electromigration in metals," *Phys. Status Solidi*, **18**, 847–852, 1966.

[5.79] F. M. d'Heurle, "Electromigration and Failure in Electronics: An Introduction," *Proc. IEEE*, **59**(10), 1409–1418, 1971.

[5.80] N. V. Doan, "Effect de Valence en Electromigration Dans L'argent," *J. Phys. Chem. Solids*, **31**, 2079–2085, 1970.

[5.81] D. Chabra, N. Ainslie, and D. Jepsen, "Theory of Failure in Thin Film Conductors," Presented at Electrochemical Society Meeting, Dallas, May 1967.

[5.82] W. Mutter, "Electromigration in Metal Film Conductors," *Abstracts, Electrochemical Society Spring Meeting*, Dallas, pp. 96–98, May 1967.

[5.83] J. R. Black, "Electromigration—A Brief Survey and Some Recent Results," *IEEE Trans. Electron. Devices*, **ED-16**, 338–347, April 1967.

[5.84] J. R. Devaney, "Investigation of Current-Induced Mass Transport in Thin metal Conducting Stripes," *Proc. 3rd Scanning Electron Microscope Symp.*, O. Johaii, Ed., Chicago, pp. 417–424, April 1970.

[5.85] D. S. Chabra and N. G. Ainslie, "Open Circuit Failures in Thin Film Conductors," Tech. Report 22.419, IBM Components Div., E. Fishkill Facility, New York, July 1967.

[5.86] F. M. d'Heurle and R. Rosenberg, "Electromigration in Thin Films," *Physics of Thin Films*, Vol. 7, Haas, Francombe, and Hoffman, Eds., Academic, New York, 1972.

[5.87] F. M. d'Heurle and P. S. Ho, "Electromigration in Thin Films," *Thin Films Interdiffusion and Reactions*, Poate, Tu, and Mayer, Eds., Wiley, New York, pp. 243–304, 1978.

[5.88] R. A. Sigbee, "Failure Model for Electromigration," *IRPS*, 301–305, 1973.

[5.89] R. A. Sigbee, "Electromigration and Metalization Lifetime," *J. Appl. Phys.*, **44**, 2533–2540, 1973.

[5.90] J. D. Venable and R. G. Lye, "A Statistical Model for Electromigration Induced Failure in Thin Film Conductors," *IRPS*, 159–164, 1972.

[5.91] K. Nikawa, "Monte Carlo Calculations Based on the Generalized Electromigration Failure Model," *IRPS*, 175–181, 1981.

[5.92] P. B. Ghate, "Electromigration-Induced Failures in VLSI Interconnects," *IRPS*, 292–299, 1982.

[5.93] J. M. Scheon, "Monte Carlo Calculations of Structure-Induced Electromigration Failure," *J. Appl. Phys.*, **51**, 513–517, 1980.

[5.94]   J. R. Black, "Physics of Electromigration," *IRPS*, 142–145, 1972.

[5.95]   C. B. Oliver and D. E. Bowers, "Theory of the Failure of Semiconductor Contacts by Electromigration," *IRPS*, 116–120, 1970.

[5.96]   R. W. Thomas and D. W. Calabrese, "Phenomenological Observations on Electromigration," *IRPS*, 1–4, 1983.

[5.97]   S. Luby, "Electromigration Defect Formation in Thin Films," *Thin Solid Films*, **116**, 97, 1984.

[5.98]   P. B. Ghate, "Failure Mechanism Studies in Multilevel Metallization Systems," Final Tech. Report, RADC TR-71-186, Rome Air Development Center, Air Force System Command, Griffiss Air Force Base, NY, Sept. 1971.

[5.99]   H. B. Huntington, "Electromigration in Metals," *Diffusion in Solids—Recent Developments*, A. S. Norwick and J. J. Burton, Eds., Academic, New York, p. 303, 1975.

[5.100] E. J. Goldberg and T. W. Adolphson, "A Failure Mechanism of Semiconductor Devices and Its Analysis," *IRPS*, 144–147, 1967.

[5.101] S. K. Ghandi, *VLSI Fabrication Principles*, Wiley, New York, 1982.

[5.102] P. P. Metchant, "Electromigration: An Overview," *Hewlett-Packard J.*, 28, Aug. 1982.

[5.103] V. B. Fiks, "On the Mechanism of the Mobility of Ions in Metals," *Solid State Phys. (USSR)*, **1**, 2959, 14–27, 1959.

[5.104] P. G. Shewmon, *Diffusion in Solids*, McGraw-Hill, New York, 1963.

[5.105] Y. Adda and J. Phillibert, *La Diffusion dans les Solides*, Presses Universitaites de France, Paris, 1966.

[5.106] S. C. Ho and H. B. Huntington, "Electromigration and Void Observation in Silver," *J. Phys. Chem. Solids*, **27**, 1319–1329, 1966.

[5.107] R. R. Patil and H. B. Huntington, "Electromigration and Associated Void Formation in Silver," *J. Phys. Chem. Solids*, **31**, 463–474, 1970.

[5.108] R. W. Berry, G. M. Bonton, W. C. Ellis, and D. E. Engling, "Growth of Whisker Crystals and Related Morphologies by Electrotransport," *Appl. Phys. Lett.*, **9**, 263–265, 1966.

[5.109] R. Vanselow, R. Masters, and R. Welnes, "Crystal Forms of Hillocks and Voids Formed by Electromigration on Ultrapure Gold and Silver Wires," *Appl. Phys.*, **12**, 341–345, 1975.

[5.110] B. Selikson, "Void Formation Failure Mechanisms in Integrated Circuits," *Proc. IEEE*, **57**(9), 1594–1598, 1969.

[5.111] I. A. Blech and C. Herring, "Stress Generation by Electromigration," *Appl. Phys. Lett.*, **29**(3), 131–133, 1976.

[5.112] I. A. Blech and K. L. Tai, "Measurement of Stress Gradients Generated by Electromigration," *Appl. Phys. Lett.*, **30**(8), 387–389, 1977.

[5.113] J. Partridge and G. Littlefield, "Aluminium Electromigration Parameters," *IRPS*, 119–125, 1985.

[5.114] M. J. Attardo, IBM, Private Communication (refer to [5.90]).

[5.115] G. E. Gimpelson, "An Elementary Relationship Between the Electromigration Mean-Time to Failure and the Migration Velocity," *VLSI Multilevel Interconnection Conf.*, 84–89, 1984.

[5.116] R. G. Shepheard and R. P. Sopher, "Effects of Current Density and Temperature on Lifetime of Aluminium Thin Film Conductors," *Abstracts, Electrochemical Society Spring Meeting*, Dallas, May 1967.

[5.117] H. C. Schafft, "Thermal Analysis of Electromigration and the Current Density Dependence," *IRPS*, 93–99, 1985.

[5.118] H. A. Schafft, "Thermal Analysis of Electromigration Test Structures," *IEEE Trans. Electron. Devices*, **ED-34**(3), 664–672, March 1987.

[5.119] A. D. LeClaire, "Some Predicted Effects of Temperature Gradients on Diffusion in Crystals," *Phys. Rev.*, **93**, 344, 1954.

[5.120] H. B. Huntington, "Driving Forces for Thermal Mass Transport," *J. Phys. Chem. Solids*, **29**, 1641–1651, 1968.

[5.121] R. A. Oriani, "Thermomigration in Solid Metals," *J. Phys. Chem. Solids*, **30**, 339–351, 1969.

[5.122] G. M. Newmann, "On Thermotransport in Tungsten," *Z. Naturforsch A*, **22**, 393–395, 1967.

[5.123] S. C. Ho, T. Hehenkamp, and H. B. Huntington, "Thermal Diffusion in Platinum," *J. Phys. Chem. Solids*, **26**, 251–258, 1965.

[5.124] J. M. Towner, "Electromigration-Induced Short-Circuit Failure," *IRPS*, 81–86, 1985.

[5.125] B. Agrawala, M. Attardo, and A. P. Indraham, "The Dependence of Electro-migration-Induced Failure Time on the Length and Width of Thin Film Conductors," *J. Appl. Phys.*, **41**, 3954–3960, 1970.

[5.126] E. Kinsbrun, "A Model for the Width Dependence of Electromigration Lifetimes in Aluminium Thin Film Stripes," *Appl. Phys. Lett.*, **36**, 968–970, 1980.

[5.127] S. Vaidya, T. T. Sheng, and A. K. Sinha, "Linewidth Dependence of Electromigration in Evaporated Al–.5% Cu," *Appl. Phys. Lett.*, **36**, 464–466, 1980.

[5.128] J. Arzigian, "Aluminium Electromigration Lifetime Variations with Linewidth: The Effects of Changing Stress Conditions," *IRPS*, 32–34, 1983.

[5.129] G. A. Scogan, B. N. Agrawala, P. P. Peressini, and A. Brouillard, "Width Dependence of Electromigration Life in Al–Cu, Al–Cu–Si, and Ag Conductors," *IRPS*, 151–155, 1975.

[5.130] M. Saito and S. Mirota, "Investigation of Grain Boundary and Lifetime in Aluminium Interconnections," *Elec. Comm. Lab. Tech. J.*, **22**, 1375–1398, 1973.

[5.131] D. Turnball and R. Z. Hoffman, "The Effect of Relative Crystal and Boundary Orientation on Grain Boundary Diffusion Rates," *Acta Metallurgica*, **2**, 419–426, 1954.

[5.132] N. G. Einspruch and G. B. Larrabee, Eds., *VLSI Electronics, Microstructure Science*, Vol. 6, Academic, New York, 1983.

[5.133] R. Rosenbert and L. Berenbaum, "Atomic Transport in Solids and Liquids," *Valag der Zeitschrift fur Naturformschung*, Ladding and Lagerwall, Eds., Tubingen, p. 113, 1971.

[5.134] J. K. Howard and R. F. Ross, "The Effect of Preferred Orientation on the Rate of Electromigration and Its Implication to the Cracked-Stripe Failure Mode," IBM Technical Rep. 22.601, March 1968.

[5.135] M. J. Attardo, R. Rutledge, and R. C. Jack, "Statistical Metallurgical Model for Electromigration Failure in Aluminium Thin-Film Conductors," *J. Appl. Phys.*, **42** 4343–4349, 1971.

[5.136] E. Kinsbron, C. M. Melliar Smith, and A. T. English, "Failure of Small Thin-Film Conductors Due to High Current-Density Pulses," *IEEE Trans. Electron. Devices*, **ED-26**(1), 22–26, 1979.

[5.137] R. J. Miller, "Electromigration Failure Under Pulsed-Current Conditions," *IRPS*, **16**, 241–247, 1978.

[5.138] J. R. Davis, "Electromigration in Aluminium Thin Films Under Pulse-Current Conditions," *Proc. IEE*, 1209–1212, 1976.

[5.139] A. T. English, K. L. Tai, and P. A. Turner, " Electromigration in Conductor Stripes Under Pulsed DC Powering." *Appl. Phys. Lett.*, **21**, 397–398, Oct. 1982.

[5.140] J. Towner and E. Van de Ven, "Aluminium Electromigration Under Pulsed DC Conditions," *IRPS*, 36–39, 1983.

[5.141] A. T. English and E. Kinsbron, "Electromigration Transport Mobility Associated with Pulsed Direct Current in Fine-Grained Al–0.5% Cu Thin Films," *J. Appl. Phys.*, **54**, (1), 275–280, 1983.

[5.142] J. M. Schoen, " A Model of Electromigration Failure Under Pulsed Condition," *J. Appl. Phys.*, **51**, (1), 508–512, Jan. 1980.

[5.143] K. P. Rodbell and R. Shatynski, "A New Method for Detecting Electromigration Failure in VLSI Metallization," *IEEE Trans. Electron. Devices*, **ED-31**, (2), 232–233, 1984.

[5.144] T. A. Burkett and R. L. Miller, "Electromigration Evaluation—MTF Modeling and Accelerated Testing," *IRPS*, 264–272, 1984.

[5.145] R. Rosenberg and L. Berenbaum, "Resistance Monitoring and Effects of Nonadhesion During Electromigration in Aluminium Films," *Appl. Phys. Lett.*, **12**(5), 201–204, 1968.

[5.146] R. E. Hummel, R. T. Deltoff, and H. J. Geier, "Activation Energy for Electrotransport in Thin Aluminium Film by Resistance Measurements," *J. Phys. Chem. Solids*, **37**, 73–80, 1976.

[5.147] Y. Z. Lu and Y. C. Cheng, "Measurement Techniques of Electromigration," *Microelectric and Reliability*, **23**(6), 1103–1108, 1983.

[5.148] R. W. Pasco and J. A. Schwartz, "Temperature-Ramp Resistance Analysis to Characterize Electromigration," *Solid State Electronics*, **26**(5), 445–452, 1983.

[5.149] P. M. Austin and A.F. Mayadas, "Correlation Between Resistance Ratios and Electromigration Failure in Thin Films," (submitted to *J. Vac. Sci. Tech.*).

[5.150] D. J. LaCombe and E. Parks, "A Study of Resistance During Electromigration," *IRPS*, 74–80, 1985.

[5.151] T. M. Chen, T. P. Djen, and R. D. Moore, "Electromigration and $1/f$ Noise of Aluminium Thin Films," *IRPS*, 87–92, 1985.

[5.152] H. Kroemer, Fairchild Semiconductor Technical Memorandum 275, Nov. 1966.

[5.153] I. A. Blech and E. S. Meiein, "Electromigration in Integrated Circuits," *IRPS*, 243–247, 1970.

[5.154] S. M. Spitzer and S. Shwartz, "The Effects of Dielectric Overcoating on Electromigration," *IEEE Trans. Electron. Devices*, **ED-16**(4), 348–350, 1969.

[5.155] D. Whitcomb, "Advanced Technology of Interconnections in Micro-electronics," Report prepared by Motorola Inc. for NASA/ERC under contract NAS-132, Jan. 1968.

[5.156] G. Schnable, Philco-Ford Corp., Blue Bell, PA, Private Communication, March 1968.

[5.157] K. G. Kemp and K. F. Poole, "A Study of Electromigration in Double Level Metal Systems Using Oxide and Polymer Dielectrics," *IRPS*, 54–57, 1987.

[5.158] T. Wada, H. Higuchi, and T. Ajiki, "New Phenomena of Electromigration in Double-Layer Metallization," *IRPS*, 203–207, 1983.

[5.159] H. A. Schafft, C. P. Youngkins, T. C. Grant, C. Y. Kao, and A. N. Saxena, "Effect of Passivation and Passivation Defects on Electromigration Failure in Aluminium Metallization," *IRPS*, 250–255, 1984.

[5.160] L. Yau, C. Hong, and D. Crook, "Passivation Material and Thickness Effects on the MTTF of Al–Si Metallization," *IRPS*, 115–118, 1985.

[5.161] J. R. Lloyd and P. M. Smith, "The Effects of Passivation Thickness on the Electromigration Lifetime of Al/Cu Thin Conductor," *J. Vac. Sci. Tech.*, **A1**(3), 455–458, April–June 1985.

[5.162] L. E. Felton, D. H. Norbury, J. A. Schwartz, and R. W. Pasco, "Composition Grain Size and Passiviation Thickness Effects on Electromigration of Al-Alloy Films," *ECS Presentation*, New Orleans, Oct. 1984.

[5.163] F. M. d'Heurle and A. Gangulee, "Effects of Complex Alloy Additions on Electromigration in Aluminium Thin Films," *IRPS*, 165–169, 1972.

[5.164] A. Gangulee and F. M. d'Heurle, "Effect of Alloying Additions on Electromigration Failure in Thin Aluminum Films," *Appl. Phys. Lett.*, **19**, 76–77, 1971.

[5.165] I. Ames, F. M. d'Heurle, and R. E. Horstmann, "Reduction of Electromigration in Aluminium Films by Copper Doping," *IBM J. Res. Develop.*, **14**, 461–463, 1970.

[5.166] M. C. Shine and F. M. d'Heurle, "Activation Energy for Electromigration in Aluminium Films Alloyed with Copper," *IBM J. Res. Develop.*, 378–383, Sept. 1971.

[5.167] H. Harada, S. Harada, Y. Hirate, T. Naguchi, and H. Mochizuki, "Perfect Hillockless Metallization (PHM) Process for VLSI," *IDEM Tech. Dig.*, 46–49, Dec. 1986.

[5.168] H. J. Bhatt, "Superior Aluminium for Interconnection of Monolitic Integrated Circuits," *IDEM Tech. Dig.*, 48–50, Oct. 1970.

[5.169] C. J. Delloca and A. J. Learn, "Anodization of Aluminium to Inhibit Hillock Growth and High Temperature Processing," *Thin Solid Films*, **8**, R47–R50, 1971.

[5.170] L. E. Terry and R. W. Wilson, "Metallization Systems for Silicon Integrated Circuits," *Proc. IEEE*, **57**, 1580–1586, 1969.

[5.171] Mil-Hdbk-217D, *Reliability Prediction of Electronic Equipment*, Reliability Analysis Center, RADC, 1982.

[5.172] D. F. Frost and K. F Poole, "A Method for Predicting VLSI-Device Reliability Using Series Models for Failure Mechanisms," *IEEE Trans. Reliability*, **R-36**(2), 234–242, 1987.

[5.173] J. W. Harrison, Jr., "A Simulation Model for Electromigration in Fine-Line Metallization of Integrated Circuits Due to Repetitive Pulsed Currents," *IEEE Trans. Electron. Devices*, **35**(12), 2170–2179, Dec. 1988.

[5.174] A. K. Goel and M. M. Leipnitz, "Analysis of the Electromigration Induced Failure in the VSLI Interconnection Components and the Multi-section Interconnections," Final Report Submitted to the USAF-RDL Faculty Summer Research Program Sponsored by the Air Force Office of Scientific Research, July 1991.

[5.175] D. F. Frost, K. F. Poole, and D. A. Haeussler, "RELIANT: A Reliability Analysis Tool for VSLI Interconnects," *Proc. IEEE Custom Integrated Circuits Conf.*, 27.8.1–27.8.4, 1988.

[5.176] J. E. Hall, D. E. Hocevar, P. Yang, and M. J. McGraw, "SPIDER—A CAD System for Checking Current Density and Voltage Drop in VLSI Metallization Patterns," *Proc. Int. Conf. Comp. Aided Design*, 278–281, 1986.

[5.177] J. W. McPherson and P. B. Ghate, "A Methodology for the Calculation of Continuous DC Electromigration Equivalents from Transient Current Waveforms," *Proc. Symp. Electromigration of Metals*, Published in *J. Electrochem. Soc.*, **85-6**, 64, 1985.

Chapter 6 — Future Interconnection Technologies

[6.1] H. B. Bokaglu and J. D. Meindl, "Optimal Interconnection Circuits for VLSI," *IEEE Trans. Electron. Devices*, **ED-32**(5), 903–909, May 1985.

[6.2] A. K. Goel, "Dependence of Interconnection Delays on Driving Mechanism for GaAs-Based VLSI," *Electron. Lett.*, **23**(20), 1066–1067, Sept. 1987.

[6.3] A. Wilnai, "Open-Ended *RC* Line Model Predicts MOSFET IC Response," *EDN*, 53–54, Dec. 1971.

[6.4] T. Sakurai, "Approximation of Wiring Delay in MOSFET LSI," *IEEE J. Solid State Circuits*, **SC-18**, 418–426, Aug. 1983.

[6.5] R. W. Keyes, "Fundamental Limits in Digital Information Processing," *Proc. IEEE*. **69**(2), Feb. 1981.

[6.6] J. Fried and S. Sriram, "Optical Interconnect for Wafer-Scale Silicon Systems," *Proc. 1984 V-MIC Conf.*, 159–166, 1984.

[6.7] Y. Omachi, Y. Shinoda, and T. Nishioka, "GaAs LEDs Fabricated on SiO_2-Coated Si Wafers," *IEDM Tech. Dig.*, 315–318, 1983.

[6.8] J. T. Boyd and D. A. Ramey, "Optical Channel Waveguide Arrays Coupled to Integrated Charge-Coupled Devices and Their Applications," *SPIE Guided Wave Optical Systems and Devices*, **176**, 141–147, 1979.

[6.9]   S. Sriram, "Fiber-Coupled Multichannel Waveguide Arrays with an Integrated Distributed Feedback Dye Laser Source," Ph.D. Dissertation, University of Cincinnati, 1980.

[6.10]   J. W. Goodman, "Optical Interconnection in Electronics," *SPIE Tech. Symp.*, Los Angeles, Jan. 1984.

[6.11]   K. C. Saraswat and F. Mohammadi, "Effect of Scaling of Interconnections on the Time Delay of VLSI Circuits," *IEEE Trans. Electron. Devices*, **ED-29**, 645–650, 1982.

[6.12]   A. Hussain, "Optical Interconnect on Digital Integrated Circuits and Systems," *SPIE Optical Interfaces for Digital Circuits and Systems*, **466**, 10–20, 1984.

[6.13]   C. E. Weitzel and J. M. Fray, "A Comparison of GaAs and Si Processing Technology," *Semiconductor International*, 73–89, June 1982.

[6.14]   O. K. Kwon and R. F. W. Pease, "Closely-Packed Microstrip Lines as Very High-Speed Chip-to-Chip Interconnects," *Proc. IEEE Int. Electron. Manufacturing Tech. Symp.*, 34–39, Sept. 1986.

[6.15]   R. W. Keyes, E. P. Harris, and K. L. Konnerth, "The Role of Low Temperature in the Operation of Logic Circuitry," *Proc. IEEE*, **58**(12), 1914–1932, 1970.

[6.16]   R. L. Kautz, "Miniaturization of Normal-State and Superconducting Striplines," *J. Res. Nat. Bur. Stand*, **84**(3), 247–259, 1979.

[6.17]   M. K. Wu et al., "Superconductivity at 93 K in a New Mixed-Phase Y–Ba–Cu–O Compound System at Ambient Pressure," *Phys. Rev. Lett.*, **58**(9), 908–910, 1987.

[6.18]   J. Z. Sun et al., "Superconductivity and Magnetism in the High-T_c Superconductor Y–Ba–Cu–O," *Phys. Rev. Lett.*, **58**(15), 1574–1576, 1987.

[6.19]   R. J. Cava et al., "Bulk Superconductivity at 91 K in Single Phase Oxygen-Deficient Perovskite $Ba_2YCu_3O_{9-\delta}$," *Phys. Rev. Lett.*, **58**(16), 1676–1679, 1987.

[6.20]   O. K. Kwon, B. W. Langley, R. F. W. Pease, and M. R. Beasely, "Superconductors as Very High-Speed System Level Interconnects," *IEEE Electron. Device Lett.*, **EDL-8**(12), 582–585, Dec. 1987.

[6.21]   P. London, *Superfluids*, **1**, Wiley, New York, 1950.

[6.22]   M. Tinkham, *Superconductivity*, Gordon and Breach, New York, 1965.

Index